A GUIDE to COLLEGE PROGRAMS in TEACHER PREPARATION

A GUIDE to
COLLEGE
PROGRAMS in
TEACHER
PREPARATION

NATIONAL COUNCIL for ACCREDITATION of TEACHER EDUCATION

Jossey-Bass Publishers
San Francisco

Jossey-Bass books and products are available through most bookstores. To contact Jossey-Bass directly, call (888) 378-2537, fax to (800) 605-2665, or visit our website at www.josseybass.com.

Substantial discounts on bulk quantities of Jossey-Bass books are available to corporations, professional associations, and other organizations. For details and discount information, contact the special sales department at Jossey-Bass.

Manufactured in the United States of America.

Library of Congress Cataloging-in-Publication Data

A guide to college programs in teacher preparation / National Council for Accreditation of Teacher Education. — 1st ed.
    p. cm.
  Rev. ed. of: Teacher preparation. 1996.
  ISBN 0-7879-4693-1 (alk. paper)
   1. Teachers colleges—Accreditation—United States Directories.
  2. Teachers colleges—United States Directories. I. National
Council for Accreditation of Teacher Education. II. Teacher
preparation.
  LB2165.G75   1999
  370'.71'102573—dc21   99-11026

FIRST EDITION
PB Printing   10 9 8 7 6 5 4 3 2 1

Contents

As you begin to explore the field of teaching, there is no better place to start than this *Guide*. There are more than 1,000 institutions with programs to prepare teachers in the U.S. today. Of these, 500 have received the profession's seal of approval. They have met the national professional standards of the National Council for Accreditation of Teacher Education (NCATE). The *Guide* describes the programs of study leading to initial teacher licensure offered at the 500 NCATE accredited institutions. In addition, the *Guide* provides a state-by-state list of programs at accredited institutions that meet subject matter standards of professional associations affiliated with NCATE. Programs that meet subject matter standards of these associations provide the highest level of quality assurance to the consumer. Meeting the subject matter standards demonstrates that the programs are developed using the latest research and practice in particular fields of teaching, and that they are up-to-date.

What sets NCATE accredited institutions apart? NCATE is the teaching profession's accrediting body—its mechanism to help ensure high quality teacher preparation. Institutions that have gained NCATE accreditation have met national standards in areas such as design of curriculum, assessment of candidate performance, faculty qualifications, supervision of clinical experiences, and adequate and up-to-date resources.

Americans are demanding high standards of their teachers so that student achievement can truly be world class. This revolution in education can only accomplished by providing each child with teachers who have received thorough preparation for their profession. Graduation from an NCATE-accredited school equips teachers with the tools they need to meet the challenges of today's classrooms.

Obviously, high school students and adults making career choices must consider a variety of factors when choosing a teacher preparation program. Location, reputation, program options, tuition, and other factors will all play a part in your decision. But by using this *Guide*, you can be confident that the institution you select will provide you with the kind of education you need to become a qualified teacher.

Sincerely,

Al Wise

Arthur E. Wise

President, National Council for Accreditation of Teacher Education

Introduction

Teacher preparation and teacher performance are at the top of the national agenda today. Forecasters project that we will need to hire two million new teachers over the next decade. How should teachers be prepared? What kinds of programs develop effective teachers? How do prospective teachers find these programs?

This *Guide* has been prepared to help prospective teachers, career advisors, recruiters, and employers gain information about teacher preparation programs that have met national standards. The accredited schools of education listed in this *Guide*—approximately 500 of them—have demonstrated their commitment to high quality teacher preparation.

This introduction provides an overview of the current trends and issues in education that affect teacher preparation today, and discusses the role that accreditation has played in moving the field forward into the twenty-first century.

Teaching Today

Today's preschool through twelfth grade classrooms present new challenges for our nation's teachers. The profession of teaching is undergoing dramatic changes. Many reforms are taking place. First, the way teachers are prepared for their roles is different today than it was twenty years ago. Public officials are emphasizing the importance of effective teacher performance. The focus on performance is leading to a greater emphasis on clinical preparation. New clinical school sites and more extensive field preparation make today's teacher preparation more challenging—and more effective. Second, public officials want to ensure that teachers know what they are teaching. Many states now require a subject matter major. Third, the nature of the students in the classrooms is vastly different as a result of shifting immigration patterns. Fourth, teaching methods are changing as a result of a growing body of knowledge about teaching. Fifth, technology is rapidly making its mark in classrooms today. Last but not least, teaching is beginning to attain true professional status. Teachers today are expected to have and use a growing body of knowledge about teaching and learning, and to continue their professional development throughout their careers. New opportunities are opening up for teachers who attain advanced certification.

Reform in Clinical Practice

One of the common complaints about teacher preparation in the past was that it did not adequately prepare teachers for "real life" in the classroom. There was a gap between theory learned in college courses and practice in the P-12 classroom, and most candidates were left to themselves to make the connections. In addition, most colleges worked with P-12 schools in a one-sided, arms-length relationship. P-12 teachers who supervised student teachers were needed, but not necessarily connected to the college program. Student teachers usually worked with just one supervising teacher in one placement, and had little opportunity for feedback from anyone other than the supervising teacher. University supervisors rarely appeared in the student teachers' classrooms.

A dramatic shift has taken place in clinical education at accredited colleges and universities that prepare teachers. Accredited schools of education are expected to work in a collegial partnership with P-12 schools. Mentoring teachers are expected to work closely with the college and should receive training for their roles. In addition, the mentoring teachers should be a part of a team that monitors the clinical work of the candidates. In the best situations, these teachers play an integral role in developing the vision of the kind of teacher the college will produce.

Many schools of education now operate special sites for clinical education called professional development schools, or PDSs (also known in some institutions as "partner schools"). There may be as many as 1,000 PDS sites operating today. Professional development schools are structured partnerships between one or more P-12 schools or a school district and a college or university. The PDS is located at a P-12 school site. The goals of PDSs are improving the education of future teachers, improving P-12 student learning, supporting continuous teacher development, and jointly conducting research on best practices in teaching. Many accredited schools of education now operate professional development schools.

In a PDS, the university or college maximizes the opportunities to integrate theory and practice in teaching. University professors often teach courses on-site at the PDS. P-12 teachers may be visiting or adjunct professors within the school of education. At some sites, future teachers teach a portion of the day and then review their teaching in a methods class on-site. The PDS functions as a "learning community" where student teachers/interns have the opportunity to observe several master teachers and to gain their feedback. Student teachers/interns are usually placed in cohort groups with their peers. They are given opportunities to observe each other in the classroom and to provide peer feedback. They are also expected to be a part of the life of the school in which they practice their teaching, often from the first day of school.

Institutions that do not have a PDS *per se* should have clinical education sites with many of the same features of a PDS. The bottom line is that future teachers need plenty of opportunities to interact with and learn from several master teachers. Peers, teachers, and university/college supervisors should provide feedback throughout the clinical practice experiences—not just at two or three pre-planned evaluations. The program should provide continuous assessment by mentor teachers and university supervisors.

Reform in Subject Matter Expectations

Public officials want to ensure that teachers know the subjects they are teaching. Some states have passed laws that require teachers to gain a degree in a subject matter area. Many colleges and universities have developed post-baccalaureate programs leading directly to a license, fifth-year master's degree programs, or five-year combined bachelors/master's programs that lead a license. These programs help to ensure that the candidate has a thorough knowledge of subject matter gained in a four-year program; the fifth year or post-baccalaureate program accommodates the important professional and clinical portions of a future teacher's education.

State and federal policymakers have renewed their interest in tests of subject matter knowledge. Many states now use tests to determine whether new teachers have mastered the subject they will teach. The most common test is PRAXIS, developed by the Educational Testing Service (ETS). A few states have created their own tests. It is likely that teacher candidates in most states will be required to take a subject matter exam and pass it with a score that the state deems acceptable in order to gain an initial teaching license. Some states require tests of professional and pedagogical knowledge as well. These are paper and pencil tests. However, the teaching field is developing other types of performance-oriented assessments to help evaluate the future teacher's ability in the classroom.

The best way for a future teacher to prepare for these exams is to gain a solid preparation (1) in the liberal arts, (2) in the area she or he plans to teach, and (3) in how to teach the specific subject area. Analyze how many credit hours are required in the subject matter area. The hours should be equivalent to that of a major, if the institution does not require a major. Elementary education candidates as well as secondary education and middle school candidates should choose a school of education that places emphasis on integrating subject matter and how to teach it (called content-specific pedagogy). Accredited schools of education are expected to collaborate with the arts and sciences in developing the curriculum to ensure that content and best practice are integrated—for example, that teachers have a deep understanding of the mathematical concept (i.e. fractions) and how to best teach the concept

National Council for Accreditation of Teacher Education

for student understanding. In some states, elementary education majors gain a subject matter degree first and enter a fifth year master's program.

Change in Student Population

The student population in public schools has changed dramatically in recent years. Instead of a homogenous classroom consisting primarily of one or two ethnic groups with a Judeo-Christian background, a teacher is faced with students who do not speak English, but a variety of other languages; special education students, many of whom are mainstreamed into classrooms; and a diverse group of students in terms of socioeconomic, cultural, religious, and ethnic background. Classrooms of today thus hold greater challenges for teachers and for students. Accredited schools of education help prepare future teachers for the realities of today's classroom. Teachers are prepared to help all children learn, and candidates gain clinical experiences in a variety of diverse settings.

The Growing Use of Information Technology

Technology in the classroom used to mean overhead projectors. Now teachers need to be prepared to use the Internet as a teaching and research tool, and to teach their students how to use it. Teachers also need to be familiar with and learn to use a variety of software programs that enhance instruction. Information technology in instruction is a revolution that has just begun. Technology will not replace the teacher, but teachers must be able to use it effectively as a teaching and learning tool.

The Professionalization of Teaching

As Americans compete in the global marketplace, the demands for improved American P-12 student achievement have increased. Teacher quality is the number one school-based factor in enhancing student achievement. Thus, the attention of public officials has shifted to improving teacher preparation and performance. A number of new initiatives and organizations are changing the way teachers are licensed and the requirements for continuing professional development. In addition, a new organization, the National Board for Professional Teaching Standards, now offers teachers advanced certification in specific subject areas and developmental levels. The certification recognizes excellence in teaching, and states as well as school districts are now offering incentives to teachers who are board certified.

Teacher Preparation

Teacher preparation has changed dramatically from the old stereotype of weak "Mickey Mouse" course offerings. The field has a body of knowledge about teaching and learning that did not exist twenty-five years ago, and research is ongoing in each subject matter area to help determine how children learn best. Teachers at NCATE accredited institutions are expected to acquire this body of knowledge and be able to apply it in the classroom. Some states are in the process of revising their criteria for entry to schools of education, setting more rigorous criteria (for example, Massachusetts and Pennsylvania). They are also setting more rigorous standards for entry to teaching (see below).

Likewise, NCATE updates accreditation standards for teacher preparation programs every five years to ensure that current thinking and best practice is incorporated. The field develops a consensus through NCATE about what is important in teacher preparation, and then ensures that accredited schools meet these expectations. States respect NCATE as the profession's accrediting body, and use NCATE standards in a variety of ways. The states are in active partnership with NCATE to join together state and national professional expectations in the preparation of teachers. NCATE is the profession's seal of approval; it signifies a level of quality and a commitment to improve teacher preparation at the institution.

Licensing and Continuing Professional Development

Many states have increased requirements for a teacher license in the past decade, and are likely to continue this trend for the foreseeable future. As mentioned previously, some states require teachers to have a bachelor's degree in a discipline. In some cases, teachers enter a fifth year program and attain a master's degree and initial teacher licensure. They may also enter a post-baccalaureate program leading to initial licensure, and the credits earned may be counted toward a master's degree at a future time. States now usually require some form of testing for initial licensure (see discussion under previous section, "Reform in Subject Matter Expectation").

Licensure expectations vary by state. Many states are working together to create some common expectations. A task force with members from 33 states has joined together to create model state licensing standards. Exams are now being developed using these standards. State exams in the future will more than likely include a paper and pencil component to test subject matter knowledge and professional knowledge, and a performance component to determine a teacher's effectiveness in the classroom.

Many states have reciprocity, which means that they accept other states' requirements when teachers apply for a license. Graduates of NCATE accredited institutions will generally find it easier to apply for a license if they move from one state to another, because many states have reciprocity agreements that recognize graduation from NCATE-accredited schools.

To gain more information about licensure requirements, contact the state authority for teacher licensing. **A complete list of state contacts for teacher licensure, including web site addresses, can be found in the back of this *Guide*.**

States have also changed requirements for continuing professional development. Most states now require teachers to take courses within a five-year period to maintain the teaching license.

National Board Certification

The National Board for Professional Teaching Standards (NBPTS), started in 1987 with funding from Congress and private foundations, now offers advanced certification for experienced teachers. The National Board certificate is a demonstration of excellence in teaching. The certification process currently costs $2,000 and takes about one academic year to complete. The teacher completes the assessment tasks in conjunction with daily teaching responsibilities. Many states and school districts pay the cost of the assessment or reimburse the teacher. In some cases, the teacher must pass the assessments and become National Board certified in order to be reimbursed. Many states are now offering financial incentives to National Board certified teachers. Some states provide a yearly cash award for the ten-year life of the certificate.

The certificate is prestigious. National Board certified teachers are already in demand as speakers, trainers, mentors, and supervisors. Many school districts are creating new staffing patterns so that National Board certified teachers can provide technical assistance to other teachers in a school or district. These National Board certified teachers may teach part-time and conduct supervision part-time, or may be selected to provide professional development to the school or district. The certificate provides new career alternatives for teachers who remain in the classroom while providing help to other teachers. Check the National Board web site at www.nbpts.org for specific information.

What to Look for in a Teacher Preparation Program Today

Teacher preparation has changed dramatically in the past decade at many colleges and universities—chief among them NCATE-accredited schools of education. Research on teaching and learning has led to new teaching methods, new ways of organizing classrooms, and new roles for the teacher. Here are some key questions to ask as you are selecting a program. When you look at accredited schools listed in this *Guide*, you'll know that these questions have already been answered. An on-site team of educators has evaluated the schools to determine whether they meet NCATE's professional standards.

Admission

What are the admissions standards to the college or university? What are the admissions standards to the school of education? In most colleges, students are admitted to the school of education at the end of the sophomore year. High standards for entry to the school of education (a grade point average usually above a 2.5 in general courses taken the first year or two of college), satisfactory performance on an entry test if required, interviews with faculty, and other requirements are signs that the institution has made a commitment to high quality teacher preparation.

Degree

What type of degrees are offered? Are you able to gain a degree in a subject matter area and become eligible for a license within a four-year program? Would the bachelor's degree be in the field of education? This *Guide* will provide many of the answers to these questions for you.

Financial Aid

What are the sources for financial aid? See the back of this *Guide* for more information. In addition, many of the institutional listings in this *Guide* provide specific information about scholarships.

Curriculum

- Does the curriculum require that prospective teachers gain a broad base of liberal arts knowledge? A solid foundation in the liberal arts and general college study of history, English, language, mathematics, and sciences is key to a well-rounded, knowledgeable teacher. Accredited schools of education require candidates to gain a solid background in the arts and sciences.
- As the old saying goes, you can't teach what you don't know. How does the college or university ensure that the teacher knows the content he or she has chosen to teach? Is the candidate required to gain a sufficient number of credit hours in a subject matter area? Does the college require a major or the equivalent of a major in a candidate's chosen subject matter area if the candidate will be teaching in middle or secondary school?
- If the candidate plans to teach elementary school, will the candidate gain sufficient mastery of professional and content knowledge—how to teach mathematics, reading, science, social studies, and other subjects to young children? Recently some states have raised the number of credit hours required for the teaching of reading.
- Are the programs of study designed using the subject matter standards developed by professional associations? Ask to see the standards of the National Council of Teachers of Mathematics, the National Council for the Social Studies, the National Council of Teachers of English, and so on. Is the faculty aware of the standards and do they integrate them into their courses? NCATE requires accredited schools of education to use these standards in designing their programs.
- Does the program of study in the school of education attend to diversity in the curriculum and provide

multicultural and global perspectives? Children of all ethnic backgrounds are in today's classrooms. Does the program prepare teachers to help all children learn? NCATE requires accredited schools of education to ensure that candidates are able to teach children from diverse backgrounds.

- Does the program provide opportunities for candidates to gain knowledge of methods for teaching exceptional learners? Children with special needs are being mainstreamed into classrooms. What type of knowledge of special education is required of all candidates? Accredited schools are required to provide opportunities for candidates to gain knowledge and skill in working with special needs children.

- Does the program have adequate resources to support the candidates? Is information technology integrated into the program of study? How is this done? Are candidates prepared to use technology as a teaching tool by the end of their program of study? Are they given opportunities to practice doing so throughout the program? Accredited schools are integrating technology into their curricula. Some are more advanced than others, but accredited schools recognize the growing importance of information technology.

Clinical Education

- Is there a commitment by the college or university to provide superior clinical education to the candidate? Are student teaching/internship sites carefully chosen and monitored by a faculty member responsible for this function? Does the institution limit the number of candidates per student teaching supervisor? Accredited schools limit the student teacher-faculty ratio to eighteen to one, or less.

- How many opportunities do candidates have to interact with children in P-12 classrooms throughout the program of study? Accredited programs take candidates to school sites their freshman year. This early opportunity to observe and reflect provides an individual with more data to determine if a teaching career is the right direction. After candidates are admitted to a program, they observe, tutor, teach mini-lessons, work with small groups, and reflect on teaching and learning. These early opportunities should build on each other, with the responsibilities of the candidates increasing each semester. No candidate should reach student teaching only to realize that teaching is not for him or her.

- How long is the student teaching/internship experience? How much of the experience is observation vs. teaching responsibility? In a high quality program, candidates should be well-prepared to assume full responsibility for teaching during most of the student teaching/internship experience. Progressive clinical experiences during the semesters prior to student teaching should have paved the way for a full-time student teaching experience over the course of at least a semester.

- Is the student teaching/internship experience using the old "apprenticeship" model in which the candidate works with only one cooperating teacher? Or are candidates exposed to a variety of master teachers, and do candidates have the opportunity to work with them and gain feedback from them on improving classroom performance? Are candidates encouraged to think critically about classroom practices?

- What opportunities are there for the prospective teacher to receive feedback from other classmates, mentor teachers and university professors? Some internship programs are now structured so that candidates teach for half a day and then take a seminar in which they reflect on their performance in the classroom. This immediate feedback loop provides the candidate with excellent learning opportunities. Many accredited schools are providing such opportunities.

- Video has proven to be a useful teaching tool that helps teachers reflect on their practice. Are candidates given the opportunity to see themselves on videotape? How often?

National Council for Accreditation of Teacher Education

Evaluation of Candidate Performance

The college should provide assessments of teacher candidate performance throughout the preparation program. Courses should build in a variety of assessments of the candidate's knowledge and performance. Key points where assessment results help candidates move from one phase of the program to another include program entry, entry to student teaching or internship, and program exit/recommendation for a license. What type of evaluation of actual classroom performance takes place? How frequently does the university supervisor observe and provide feedback? Does the university supervisor coordinate with and talk on a regular basis to the student teaching/internship supervisor at the school site about the candidate's performance?

Faculty

- Is the mentor teacher at the school site where student teaching/internship takes place provided with training by the college or university? Are there any mentor teachers from the P-12 school site that serve as adjunct professors at the university and teach or co-teach courses that the candidates take?
- Are faculty qualified to hold their positions? How many have doctorates? How many have current or recent (past five years) P-12 school experience? Do the faculty who are involved in clinical education and methods courses have current or recent P-12 teaching experience?

Flexibility

Are evening classes offered? Can part of the program be completed part-time? These are important questions for those in the workforce who are making a career change.

Program Type and Length

There are now an increasing variety of program options for individuals interested in a teaching career. Traditionally, candidates entered a four-year undergraduate program and graduated with a bachelor's degree in education or a subject matter degree. Many states have passed legislation in the past ten years requiring candidates to attain a degree in a subject area, along with the preparation necessary to attain a license to teach. This development is initiating changes in the structure of teacher preparation programs on many campuses. Instead of the traditional four-year undergraduate program, many colleges and universities now offer 5th year programs of study which are designed for individuals with bachelor's degrees. These candidates will gain a master's degree and a teaching license. Fifth year programs are usually one full year or more in length, using one or both summers in addition to the academic year of study. Student teaching/internship is included in these programs.

Too, as the need for teachers has increased in the past several years, and will continue to increase in the foreseeable future, colleges and universities have developed programs for the non-traditional teacher candidate—the adult who already has a college degree but who wants to change careers and gain a teaching license. The military "Troops to Teachers" program (see "Additional Resources" section on page 535 of this *Guide*) is a prime example of this movement. Many colleges and universities have now developed post-baccalaureate programs that accept adults who already have bachelors' degrees and who are now ready to focus on teaching as a career.

Thus there are many good options for candidates looking for high quality teaching programs. This *Guide* lists programs in the following categories:

Four Year Programs

These are traditional programs of study for those at the undergraduate level. The individual who chooses to teach at the elementary level will usually gain a degree in Elementary Education. The person who will teach middle school or high school may gain a degree in education or alternatively major in a subject field and gain preparation for licensing. At accredited institutions, the individual should gain the equivalent of a subject matter major if middle school or high school teaching is the goal. A few schools note that their programs of study are 4 ½ years. In other cases, candidates may want to find out how long it takes the "typical" student to complete the program.

Post-Baccalaureate Programs

These programs are geared to individuals who already have a bachelor's degree and who want to gain initial teacher licensure. These programs are designed as high quality alternative route programs. All require a student teaching/ internship experience and the acquisition of professional and pedagogical knowledge. Upon completion of the program, the successful candidate will be eligible for initial teacher licensure, but will not gain a master's degree. Courses can generally lead to a master's degree if the individual decides to pursue further study.

Five Year Programs

These programs are usually combined bachelor's/master's degree programs. Typically, upon successful completion, the individual will have a master's degree and be eligible for an initial teaching license. In some cases, the five-year program will only provide the graduate with a bachelor's degree and graduate credit, and eligibility for an initial teaching license. At a few schools, five-year programs are composed of two bachelor's degrees—one in a content area and one in education.

Fifth Year Programs

These programs are geared to individuals who already have a bachelor's degree. Upon successful completion, the candidate will have a master's degree and be eligible for an initial teaching license.

All of the programs listed in this *Guide* are offered at professionally accredited schools of education. Candidates can be assured that teachers, teacher educators, and state policymakers have reviewed the schools of education to determine that they deserve the NCATE seal of approval.

What if I don't see a particular school in this *Guide*?

Professional accreditation in the field of teacher preparation has been voluntary in most states. Unaccredited institutions may have good reputations, but they may or may not focus on preparing teachers. For example, some schools are research institutions and are renowned for their scholarship, but may or may not provide high quality resources for teacher preparation. Many states are currently reviewing their policies toward professional accreditation in the teaching field. Three states that have recently passed legislation requiring accreditation for schools of education are New York, Maryland, and Alaska. More of these schools, and others, will be included in the next edition of this *Guide*.

Some unaccredited programs are of good quality; many others are of poor quality. Having the NCATE seal of approval provides the candidate with the knowledge that these are programs that have met national professional standards. These programs have been scrutinized by professionals in the field, and have been judged to merit professional accreditation. This scrutiny provides the consumer with a level of confidence from which a search for the right program can proceed.

About NCATE

NCATE is committed to accountability and improvement in teacher preparation. NCATE holds teacher education programs accountable for the following essential elements of teacher preparation:

- Ensuring that teacher candidates know the subject matter they plan to teach and how to teach it effectively for improved P-12 student learning.
- Evaluating what candidates know and are able to do using a variety of assessment measures.
- Ensuring that candidates work from a solid base of research and best practice.
- Ensuring that candidates are reflective, critical thinkers who can use the base of knowledge they have acquired, analyze their practice, and change what does not work.
- Ensuring that colleges and universities reach out to P-12 schools to create collegial partnerships focused on candidate and student learning. NCATE realizes that the days of the "ivory tower" in teacher preparation are over.
- Ensuring that schools of education help candidates learn to integrate technology into their teaching practice effectively.
- Ensuring that candidates are prepared to help all children learn.

What NCATE Accreditation Means to Future Teachers

- *Preparation for the Classrooms of Today*. NCATE accredited institutions prepare teachers for teaching in diverse environments with all types of students. NCATE institutions prepare real teachers for real classrooms. Institutions and P-12 schools work together closely to support new teacher preparation and development.
- *Preparation for Initial Licensure*. Teacher candidates who graduate from NCATE-accredited schools will be better prepared for initial licensing and advanced board certification. NCATE is working with states that wish to establish common licensing expectations and to align accreditation standards with licensing standards.
- *Preparation for National Board certification*. NCATE is working with the National Board for Professional Teaching Standards to help institutions develop programs of study for experienced teachers that focus on effective teaching, and that help prepare teachers for the kinds of assessments contained in the NBPTS certification examinations.
- *Reciprocity*. Graduates of NCATE accredited schools will generally find it easier to apply for a license when moving from state to state, as many states have reciprocity agreements based on graduation from NCATE institutions.

What NCATE Accreditation Means to the Public

The NCATE stamp of approval assures the public

- that new teacher graduates know their subject matter and the most effective ways to teach it,
- that candidate performance is thoroughly assessed throughout the program and before candidates are recommended for a license,
- that the school of education has undergone rigorous external review by professionals in the field, including classroom teachers, and
- that the school of education meets standards set by the teaching profession.

How to Use This *Guide*

NCATE accredited institutions are listed alphabetically by state in the "Institutional Listings" section of this *Guide*. Each listing contains the following information:

- A **"Just the Facts" section** with school address, telephone, website address, tuition (in most cases, 1999 information), and whether the institution has off-campus locations; a brief profile that tells whether the school is in an urban, suburban, or rural area, whether the school is small (under 3,000 students), medium (3,000 to 10,000 students) or large (over 10,000 students), and whether the school is coed or single sex.
- **An introduction to the teacher education program** at the college or university that includes a statement about the type of teacher the school is trying to produce.
- **A section called "Clinical Experiences"** that provides details about the clinical opportunities offered (for example, some offer international placements).
- **A section entitled "Noteworthy"** that lists highlights about the school, including recognition/awards received, scholarships offered, and unique features of the school.
- **Teacher Preparation Program Information.** This section provides a list of teacher preparation programs for beginning teachers. Many of these schools of education have advanced master's degree, specialist degree, and doctoral degree programs for experienced teachers in such fields as administration, curriculum and instruction, education leadership, education policy, school psychology, school library media specialist, and other specializations. They may also offer programs leading to a license for speech pathologists, school counselors, and school nurses. **However, this *Guide* lists only initial *teacher* preparation programs. For advanced programs, check the institution's website for further information.**

Program Type and Length

This *Guide* lists the following types of programs:

Four-Year Programs

These are undergraduate programs. Individuals will graduate with a degree in education or a subject matter major and be eligible for initial teacher licensure.

Post-Baccalaureate Programs

These programs are designed for individuals who already have a bachelor's degree and who want to gain an initial teaching license. These programs are high quality alternate route programs. All require student teaching/internship and the acquisition of professional and pedagogical knowledge. Some colleges have formal post-baccalaureate programs; at other institutions, candidates take the courses they need to become eligible for initial teacher licensure. The successful candidate will become eligible for an initial teacher license but will not gain a master's degree. Courses taken may count toward a master's degree if the individual pursues further study.

Five-Year Programs

These programs are usually combined bachelor's/master's degree programs. Typically, upon successful completion, the individual will have a master's degree and be eligible for an initial teaching license. In some cases, the five-year program will only provide the graduate with a bachelor's degree and graduate credit, and eligibility for an initial

National Council for Accreditation of Teacher Education

teaching license. At a few schools, five-year programs are composed of two bachelor's degrees—one in a content area and one in education. These programs are noted in the narrative section of the institution's page in this *Guide*.

Fifth Year Programs

These programs are geared to individuals who already have a bachelor's degree. Upon successful completion, the candidate will have a master's degree and be eligible for an initial teaching license.

Accuracy of Information

The information included in this *Guide* was provided by the institutions, and was correct at the time of publication. However, program and tuition information may change at any time. Please contact the institutions for the latest information about their programs. Phone numbers and Website addresses are noted in the "Just the Facts" section of each institution's page in this *Guide*.

Accreditation Decisions

NCATE makes accreditation decisions in the fall and spring each year. You may wish to check the NCATE Website (**www.ncate.org**) for the most recent list of NCATE-accredited schools of education.

The following schools of education were accredited for the first time, or for the first time under NCATE's new system developed in 1987, as this *Guide* went to publication in March 1999. Please check the institution Websites for more information.

Chowan College (NC)—www.chowan.edu
Coastal Carolina University (SC)—www.coastal.edu
New Mexico Highlands University—www.nmhu.edu
Northeastern Illinois University—www.neiu.edu
Southwest Missouri State University—www.smsu.edu
University of Delaware—www.udel.edu
University of Maryland Baltimore County—www.umbc.edu
Virginia Union University—www.vuu.edu

Accredited institutions are reviewed every five years. The majority of these institutions are granted continuing accreditation. However, some institutions may have their accreditation revoked, or may be put on probation. Several of the institutions in this *Guide* are currently accredited with probation. This accreditation decision indicates that the school of education has serious and significant weaknesses related to the NCATE standards. As a result of the continuing accreditation review, NCATE has determined that weaknesses with respect to standards will place an institution's accreditation in jeopardy if left uncorrected.

Institutions whose accreditation is continued with probation must schedule an accreditation visit to take place within two years of the semester in which a probationary decision was rendered. The school of education will remain accredited at least until this accreditation visit. Following the review, NCATE may decide to continue accreditation, continue accreditation with stipulations, or revoke accreditation.

Institutions on Probation

At the time of publication, the following institutions were accredited with probation. Please check the NCATE Website for the latest accreditation information on these or any other institutions.

Andrews University (MI)
Augustana College (SD)
Philander Smith College (AR)
California State University--Dominguez Hills
The Citadel (SC)
College of St. Benedict and St. John's University (MN)
Freed-Hardeman University (TN)
Indiana University Northwest
Kentucky State University
Lewis-Clark State College (ID)
Mars Hill College (NC)
Minot State University (ND)
North Georgia College and State University (At the advanced level only. This *Guide* only lists initial programs)
Roosevelt University (IL)
Spring Arbor College (MI)
Western Oregon University (At the advanced level only. This *Guide* only lists initial programs)
Western Washington University

Alabama A & M University

The School of Education at Alabama A & M University helps committed candidates become great teachers. Teacher training programs are available in early childhood, elementary, middle, secondary, and special education. Admission to the university does not automatically qualify potential candidates for entry into the teacher education program; faculty members consult with aspiring teachers during their first two years of study to help them decide whether a career in teaching is right for them. Candidates work in a learning environment designed to enhance understanding and confidence while developing professional skills.

Just the facts...

Alabama A & M University
School of Education
P.O. Box 262
Normal, AL 35762
(256) 851-5500
Website: www.asnaam.aamu.edu
Profile: Suburban, Medium, Co-Ed
UG Tuition: $1,166.00/sem. in-state; $2,132.00/sem. out-of-state
G Tuition: $1,166.00/sem. in-state; $2,132.00/sem. out-of-state
Off Campus Programs: No

Clinical Experiences

Candidates are provided with four phases of opportunities to participate in experiences in public schools. The first phase is classroom observation in a variety of settings. The second phase involves observation in classrooms in the candidate's major area of concentration. The third phase allows candidates to develop and refine their teaching skills and techniques in the classroom. The final phase is a full-time twelve-week student teaching experience in which candidates assume total responsibility for instruction and classroom management under the supervision of master's level teachers in the candidate's area of specialization.

Noteworthy

Alabama A & M University is especially proud of its School of Education and the high-caliber graduates of its many programs. The employment rate of its graduates is also noteworthy—more than 90 percent of all graduates are employed in their major area of specialization within one year of graduation.

Teacher Preparation Program Information

The following programs are 4 year programs:
Early Childhood Education (P-3), Elementary Education (K-6), P-12 Education (Art, Music, Physical Education), Secondary Education (Agriscience Technology, Biology, Business, Chemistry, English/Language Arts, Family & Consumer Sciences, Foreign Languages, General Science, Mathematics, Physics, Social Sciences, Technical, Technology), Special Education (Collaborative Teacher K-6, Collaborative Teacher 6-12, Early Childhood)

The following programs are post-baccalaureate programs:
Early Childhood Education (P-3), Elementary Education (K-6), P-12 Education (Art, Music, Physical Education), Secondary Education (Agriscience Technology, Biology, Business, Chemistry, English/Language Arts, Family & Consumer Sciences, Foreign Languages, General Science, Mathematics, Physics, Social Sciences, Technical, Technology), Special Education (Collaborative Teacher K-6, Collaborative Teacher 6-12, Early Childhood)

The following programs are 5th year programs:
Early Childhood Education (P-3), Elementary Education (K-6), P-12 Education (Art, Music, Physical Education), Secondary Education (Agriscience Technology, Biology, Business, Chemistry, English/Language Arts, Family & Consumer Sciences, Foreign Languages, General Science, Mathematics, Physics, Social Sciences, Technical, Technology), Special Education (Collaborative Teacher K-6, Collaborative Teacher 6-12)

Alabama State University

Alabama State University has played an important role in the education and preparation of African American teachers since 1886. The College of Education provides opportunities for all candidates to succeed as educators. The faculty believe that the educator is a decision maker who makes a full range of decisions in planning, implementing, and evaluating instruction. All programs combine content knowledge, professional knowledge, and practical skills application. The College of Education awards the Bachelor of Science, the Master of Education and the Educational Specialist degree in programs that lead to licensure in teaching as well as leadership positions.

Just the facts...

Alabama State University
College of Education
915 South Jackson Street
Montgomery, AL 36101-0301
(334) 229-4250
Website: http://asu.alasu.edu/academic/COE/
Profile: Urban, Medium, Co-Ed
UG Tuition: $900.00/sem. in-state; $1,800.00/sem. out-of-state
G Tuition: $85.00/cr. hr. in-state; $170.00/cr. hr. out-of-state
Off Campus Programs: Yes

Clinical Experiences

Clinical experiences at Alabama State University include pre-internship clinical placements that range from observation to hands-on participation. The internship consists of twelve weeks of progressive clinical experiences, and ends with the candidate assuming full responsibility for his or her class. ASU has a professional development school relationship with Southlawn Middle School. Faculty from ASU and Southlawn work together to investigate and collaborate on issues at the middle school; they focus on curriculum review, program development, and action research.

Noteworthy

Scholarships are designated for candidates in the university's education programs. The DeWitt Wallace program provides opportunities for individuals who have worked as teacher aides or in other school staff positions to become fully licensed teachers with a baccalaureate degree. ASU, a historically black university, also provides minority scholarships for non-African American candidates. ASU's Alternative Fifth-Year Programs lead to the Master of Education degree and licensure eligibility for those who did not complete a teacher education program as undergraduates. The college houses the university's psychology program, facilitating excellent collaboration between the disciplines of education and psychology.

Teacher Preparation Program Information

The following programs are 4 year bachelor degree programs:
Early Childhood Education, Elementary Education (Elementary Education K-6), K-12 Education (Art, Music, Physical Education), Secondary Education (Biology, Business, Chemistry, English/Language Arts, General Science, Health, History, Mathematics, Social Science), Special Education (Collaborative Teacher 6-12, Elementary Collaborative Teacher)

The following programs are post-baccalaureate programs:
Early Childhood Education, Elementary Education (Elementary Education K-6), K-12 Education (Art, Music, Physical Education), Secondary Education (Biology, Business, Chemistry, English/Language Arts, General Science, Health, History, Mathematics, Social Science), Special Education (Collaborative Teacher 6-12, Elementary Collaborative Teacher)

The following programs are 5th year programs:
Early Childhood Education, K-12 Education (Music, Physical Education), Secondary Education (Biology, English/Language Arts, Health, History, Mathematics, Social Science), Special Education (Collaborative Teacher 6-12, Elementary Collaborative Teacher)

Athens State University

Athens State University believes that the teacher of tomorrow will be able to meet the challenges of a changing and increasingly diverse society. ASU believes teachers can impart to students the ability to think rather than to memorize, to create rather than copy. The teacher education program prepares teachers who develop performance-based instruction, think reflectively, and solve problems. Candidates become effective communicators, knowledgeable scholars, positive professionals, resourceful curriculum planners, skilled facilitators of developmental growth, capable classroom managers, competent evaluators, and reflective lifelong learners.

Just the facts...

Athens State University
School of Education
300 North Beaty Street
Athens, AL 35611
(256) 233-8187
Website: www.athens.edu
Profile: Urban, Small, Co-Ed
UG Tuition: $69.00/cr. hr. in-state; $138.00/cr. hr. out-of-state
Off Campus Programs: No

Clinical Experiences

Candidates participate in diverse clinical experiences in P-12 schools beginning with time spent in a rural school and a city school with a 30 percent or greater minority population. Subsequent experiences include the CAPS program (Candidate Assisted Practice Sites). Two elementary courses are taught in several elementary schools; a secondary methods course places candidates in a school over a period of time with the same middle school and high school students. A sequence of experiences in other courses moves candidates from assisting to teaching in P-12 schools.

Noteworthy

ASU has built a reputation for providing personal attention to each student. Courses are scheduled so that students are on campus two days a week, allowing time for field site work and substitute teaching. Most courses are offered in the evening. Faculty members collaborate with P-12 teachers on joint research projects in reading, writing, math, young adult literature, and physical education. A Reading/Math Clinic operated by ASU provides the tutorial assistance of education majors for 230 students in grades 1-6 each year. About half of ASU's teacher education students receive financial assistance through loans, grants, scholarships, or work-study.

Teacher Preparation Program Information

The following programs are 4 year programs:

Elementary Education, Physical Education, Secondary Education (Biology, Career Technical Education, Chemistry, Comprehensive Science, History, Language Arts, Mathematics, Social Science), Special Education (Collaborative Teacher K-6, Collaborative Teacher 6-12)

Auburn University

The primary mission of the College of Education is to provide programs for the preservice and advanced education of teachers and instructional support personnel who will provide leadership and service in their fields. Candidates are prepared to have respect for their professional role; reflect on their professional activities and their effects on others; develop personal philosophies that embrace understanding of and appreciation for cultural and ethnic diversity; and build upon empirical and experiential knowledge within their profession.

Just the facts...

Auburn University
College of Education
3084 Haley Center
Auburn, AL 36849-5219
(334) 884-4446
Website: www.auburn.edu
Profile: Suburban, Large, Co-Ed
UG Tuition: $920.00/quart. in-state; $2,760/quart. out-of-state
G Tuition: $920.00/quart. in-state; $2,760/quart. out-of-state
Off Campus Programs: No

Clinical Experiences

Experiences in education settings comprise an integral part of every preparation program in the College of Education. While local school systems provide an array of clinical experiences for students in programs at all levels, there also are programs that provide such experiences as internships at the Disney Celebration School, or through the Consortium of Overseas Student Teaching. The full-quarter internship of 50 days (300 hours) provides candidates the opportunity to teach in area schools or other school sites.

Noteworthy

Three initiatives in the college have developed around professional development school (PDS) concepts: the Alabama Power Learning Coalition, the Auburn City Schools Professional Development System, and direct PDS activities with Lee County (AL) schools. The Learning Coalition was cited in the Holmes Group publication *Tomorrow's Schools of Education* as an example of the type of coalition that future colleges and schools of education should be developing. The College has participated with several universities in developing the Celebration School Teaching Academy, sponsored by the Disney Development Corporation.

Teacher Preparation Program Information

The following programs are 4 year programs:

Early Childhood Education, Elementary Education, K-12 Education (Music, Physical Education), Middle School Education (Language Arts, Science, Social Studies), Secondary Education (Biology, Chemistry, English/Language Arts, French, General Science, Geography, German, Mathematics, Physics, Political Science, Social Studies, Spanish, Vocational Agriculture, Vocational Business Office, Vocational Marketing, Vocational Trade & Industrial), Special Education (Early Childhood, Mild Learning/Behavioral Disability)

The following programs are 5 year programs:

Special Education (Learning Disability)

The following programs are 5th year programs:

K-12 Education (Adult Education, Music, Physical Education), Secondary Education (Biology, Chemistry, English/Language Arts, French, General Science, Mathematics, Physics, Spanish, Vocational Agriculture, Vocational Business Office, Vocational Marketing, Vocational Trade & Industrial), Special Education (Early Childhood, Emotional Conflict, Mental Retardation)

Auburn University—Montgomery

Professional study in the School of Education is based on a model that recognizes and prepares teachers as decision makers. In addition to teacher preparation, the School of Education offers programs that prepare candidates for administrative, counseling, and other education-related positions in schools and human service agencies. The School of Education is committed to providing challenging opportunities for a diverse learning community in a nurturing environment.

Just the facts...

Auburn University—Montgomery
School of Education
P.O. Box 244023
Montgomery, AL 36124-4023
(334) 244-3413
Website: www.aum.edu
Profile: Urban, Medium, Co-Ed
UG Tuition: $728.00/quart. in-state; $2,184.00/quart. out-of-state
G Tuition: $800.00/quart. in-state; $2,400.00/quart. out-of-state
Off Campus Programs: No

Clinical Experiences

The School of Education programs combine classroom and real world experiences. Teacher candidates profit from firsthand experiences in school or community agency settings starting in the freshman year. The School of Education has established special arrangements with several secondary and elementary partnership schools. Candidates have opportunities for clinical experiences in fourteen surrounding school districts, thus ensuring diverse field involvement.

Noteworthy

The School of Education, through its Teacher-In-Residence and Professor-In-Residence programs, ensures that its teacher preparation programs are relevant to real world classroom practice. Two exceptional public school teachers are awarded full-time teaching positions in the School of Education for a two-year period, and three university professors are awarded Professor-In-Residence positions at area schools. The university professors work in K-12 classrooms on a weekly basis. The School of Education administers a DeWitt-Wallace Pathways to Teaching Program in which teacher aides and substitute teachers are granted scholarships to complete the teacher education program.

Teacher Preparation Program Information

The following programs are 4 year programs:
Early Childhood Education, Elementary Education, K-12 Education (Art, Physical Education), Secondary Education (Biology, English/Language Arts, General Science, History, Mathematics, Social Studies), Special Education (Collaborative K-6, Collaborative Teacher 6-12, Early Childhood)

The following programs are 5th year programs:
Early Childhood Education, Elementary Education, K-12 Education (Art, Physical Education), Secondary Education (Biology, English/Language Arts, History, Mathematics, Physical Education, Social Studies), Special Education (Collaborative K-6, Collaborative Teacher 6-12, Early Childhood)

Birmingham-Southern College

Birmingham-Southern's Division of Education programs combine a strong liberal arts foundation with individualized teaching and advising to prepare candidates to become fully licensed teachers. Faculty members are committed to setting examples for candidates to follow, as faculty participate in collaborative teaching and continuous involvement in schools in the immediate community. The Division of Education has an active follow-up program of support for graduates who are in their first two years of teaching.

Just the facts...

Birmingham Southern College
Division of Education
900 Arkadelphia Road
Birmingham, AL 35254
(205) 226-4810
Website: www.bsc.edu
Profile: Urban, Small, Co-Ed
UG Tuition: $6,875.00/semester
Off Campus Programs: No

Clinical Experiences

Birmingham-Southern's unique 4-1-4 calendar facilitates intense involvement in field experiences during candidates' first two years in college. Early mandatory field experiences in two different settings helps candidates make better choices about teaching as a career. All education courses during the senior year have required field experiences that culminate in a twelve-week internship split between two different settings. The senior interim term in January may be spent in an internship in local schools.

Noteworthy

Birmingham-Southern College is one of the few undergraduate institutions in the United States that provides dual licensure eligibility in special education and elementary education in grades K-6. This Collaborative/Elementary Program integrates knowledge and strategies for teaching those in regular classrooms and special needs children throughout the four-year program. The collaborative links that have been established with local public schools in the Birmingham area are a key feature of the program.

Teacher Preparation Program Information

The following programs are 4 year programs:

Early Childhood Education, Elementary Education, K-12 Education (Art, Music), Secondary Education (Art, Biology, Chemistry, French, German, History, Language Arts, Mathematics, Physics, Political Science, Social Studies, Spanish), Special Education (Collaborative K-6)

The following programs are post-baccalaureate programs:

Early Childhood Education, Elementary Education, K-12 Education (Art, Music), Secondary Education (Art, Biology, Chemistry, French, German, History, Language Arts, Mathematics, Physics, Political Science, Social Studies, Spanish), Special Education (Collaborative K-6)

Jacksonville State University

Jacksonville State University is located in a unique part of Alabama, at the foothills of the Appalachians about one and one-half hours northeast of Birmingham and two hours west of Atlanta. The College of Education and Professional Studies is the largest teacher preparation institution in the state of Alabama, and works to meet the needs of the region, state, and nation through its wide-ranging service and research activities. The faculty are committed to developing professionals who are creative decision makers who effectively solve problems using the concepts and practices appropriate to their disciplines.

Just the facts...

Jacksonville State University
College of Education and Professional Studies
700 Pelham Road North
Jacksonville, AL 36265
(256) 782-5445
Website: www.jsu.edu
Profile: Urban, Medium, Co-Ed
UG Tuition: $1,120.00/sem. in-state; $2,240.00/sem. out-of-state
G Tuition: $1,120.00/sem. in-state; $2,240.00/sem. out-of-state
Off Campus Programs: No

Clinical Experiences

The College of Education and Professional Studies offers five levels of clinical experiences: college classroom, teaching/learning center and nursery school practica, block practica experiences in local schools, student teaching in schools, and the first year teaching support team. This comprehensive and sequential system for clinical experiences ensures that the teacher candidate experiences a wide variety of settings for both observation and practice. Practica range anywhere from 85 hours to over 200 hours. The student teaching experience is fifteen weeks long, and the candidate is observed by both a qualified cooperating teacher and a university supervisor.

Noteworthy

The College of Education and Professional Studies is a partner in a professional development school (PDS). Candidates may be involved in activities at the PDS through the Special Friends Program, which focuses on improving the academic and social skills of at-risk children in grades K-3, and Arts in the Integrated Curriculum, which gives candidates in elementary and early childhood education the opportunity to prepare activities that integrate the arts into the academic curriculum. The College maintains a multimedia laboratory to support instructional technology courses for both undergraduate and graduate students.

Teacher Preparation Program Information

The following programs are 4 year programs:
Early Childhood Education, Elementary Education, P-12 Education (French, Music, Physical Education, Spanish), Secondary Education (Biology, Consumer & Family Science/Home Economics, English/Language Arts, General Science, Health, Mathematics, Social Studies, Technology), Special Education (Collaborative Teacher, Hearing Impaired)

The following programs are post-baccalaureate programs:
Early Childhood Education, Elementary Education, P-12 Education (French, Music, Physical Education, Spanish), Middle School Education (English/Language Arts, Mathematics, Science, Social Studies), Secondary Education (Biology, Family & Consumer Science/Home Economics, English/Language Arts, General Science, Health, Mathematics, Social Studies), Special Education (Early Childhood, Collaborative Teacher)

The following programs are 5th year programs:
Early Childhood Education, Elementary Education, P-12 Education (Music, Physical Education), Secondary Education (Biology, English/Language Arts, General Science, Mathematics, Social Studies), Special Education (Collaborative Teacher, Early Childhood)

Oakwood College

Oakwood College, founded in 1896, is a historically black, liberal arts, Seventh-day Adventist institution. Oakwood's mission is to offer mental, physical, and spiritual education to students from diverse backgrounds. Candidates are prepared with a strong foundation in general, professional, and specialty studies. Teacher candidates are taught the skills needed for success in both parochial and public classrooms. The department teaches candidates to integrate biblical truths in all curricular and extra-curricular experiences as they practice in church-operated schools. Within public schools, candidates are taught to model for their students positive values, a healthy lifestyle, respect for each person, and a commitment to global service.

Just the facts...

Oakwood College
Department of Education
7000 Adventist Boulevard
Knight Hall
Huntsville, AL 35896
(256) 726-7157
Website: www.oakwood.edu
Profile: Urban, Small, Co-Ed
UG Tuition: $4,040.00/semester
Off Campus Programs: No

Clinical Experiences

All field experiences are coordinated within the context of a required series of preparatory education courses. Freshmen observe classrooms in local schools. Sophomores practice their teaching skills in an on-campus simulated classroom setting. This campus teaching is followed in the junior year by a ten-day practicum that exposes candidates to real-life classrooms under supervised conditions. During the final internship, seniors engage in twelve weeks of full-time classroom activities in their specialty areas.

Noteworthy

Oakwood takes pride in its on-campus K-12 school that serves as a laboratory (particularly in multigrade experiences) for teacher candidates. The education building houses a curriculum materials and technology lab that provides candidates with access to teaching materials and multimedia equipment. Candidates can join an education club that focuses on leadership training, pre-professional activities, community service, and a projected model technologies classroom for the 21st century. The department recently received a grant from the American Honda Foundation in order to conduct a summer computer camp for disadvantaged children ages 7-11 living in the city of Huntsville, Alabama.

Teacher Preparation Program Information

The following programs are 4 year programs:

Elementary Education (Elementary Education K-6), K-12 Education (Music, Physical Education), Secondary Education (Biology, Business, Chemistry, English/Language Arts, Family & Consumer Science, Mathematics, Social Science)

Samford University

Samford University's School of Education and Professional Studies nurtures future teachers' natural leadership skills and helps them prepare for successful professional careers and an active life of community service. The faculty is committed to a continuous process of inquiry and reflection focused on learning opportunities that enable candidates to achieve personal and professional success. The school prepares teachers to be facilitators who are able to provide resources, guidance, and instruction to learners as they develop knowledge and problem-solving skills.

Just the facts...

Samford University
School of Education and Professional Studies
800 Lakeshore Drive
Birmingham, AL 35229
(205) 870-2559
Website: www.samford.edu
Profile: Suburban, Medium, Co-Ed
UG Tuition: $4,952.00/semester
G Tuition: $344.00/credit hour
Off Campus Programs: No

Clinical Experiences

All education courses at Samford University require observation in the local schools as part of the required coursework. Intensive field experiences in urban, rural and suburban educational settings are available to candidates. Candidates must successfully complete fourteen full weeks of student teaching. During this time, each candidate attends seminars designed to be supportive of student teachers and to provide them an outlet for analysis and reflection upon the classroom experiences, challenges, and problems encountered in the internship experience. Each student teacher is required to prepare a professional portfolio during the internship.

Noteworthy

The Media Resource Center provides education students with a laboratory for the School of Education's Technology Consortium and a distance learning laboratory for teacher education students. The Curriculum Materials Center houses a wide variety of textbooks, videotapes, CDs, and other teaching materials. Faculty members use student, graduate and employer input to develop new and better programs and processes. Many scholarships are available to candidates in the School of Education. These include the Duren Scholarship (for candidates who wish to teach science or mathematics), a number of minority scholarships, and a scholarship for entering freshmen who exhibit promise as future teachers.

Teacher Preparation Program Information

The following programs are 4 year programs:
Early Childhood Education, Elementary Education, P-12 Education (French, German, Music, Physical Education, Spanish), Secondary Education (Biology, English/Language Arts, French, General Science, German, History, Mathematics, Social Studies, Spanish), Special Education (Early Childhood, Elementary Collaborative Teacher)

The following programs are post-baccalaureate programs:
Early Childhood Education, Elementary Education, P-12 Education (French, German, Music, Physical Education, Spanish), Secondary Education (Biology, English/Language Arts, French, General Science, German, History, Mathematics, Social Studies, Spanish), Special Education (Early Childhood, Elementary Collaborative Teacher)

The following programs are 5th year programs:
Early Childhood Education, Elementary Education

Troy State University

Troy State University prides itself on its tradition of excellence in academics, administration, student activities, and athletics since its founding 112 years ago. The purpose of the College of Education is to provide undergraduate students with opportunities that will enable them to become contributing members of society, and to experience success in their workplaces, homes, and communities. Through coursework, research and independent assignments, laboratory and field experiences, and involvement with professional associations and organizations, the College of Education strives to promote knowledge, openmindedness, and communication, computational, technological, and problem-solving skills in its students.

Just the facts...

Troy State University
College of Education
206 McCartha Hall
Troy, AL 36082
(334) 670-3474
Website: www.troy.edu
Profile: Urban, Medium, Co-Ed
UG Tuition: $1,125.00/sem. in-state; $2,250.00/sem. out-of-state
G Tuition: $102.00/cr. hr. in-state; $210.00/cr. hr. out-of-state
Off Campus Programs: Yes

Clinical Experiences

The College of Education believes that the clinical experiences program is the cornerstone of the teacher education program. Field experiences begin early in the program and provide candidates with a variety of educational experiences. The field experiences are structured so that they are integrated into methods courses. Field experiences include classroom observation/participation, community service, and professional development activities to enhance the skills and knowledge of the prospective teacher. The culminating experience is a twelve-week internship in a public school classroom.

Noteworthy

Money magazine named TSU one of the top 25 Best Buys among public universities and colleges, on the basis of in-state tuition, in 1996. Studies conducted by the University of Delaware in 1996 and 1997 rate TSU as one of the most efficient universities in the nation, and the National Association of College and University Business Officers honored TSU in 1997 with one of only five national awards in recognition of its efforts to improve quality and reduce the cost of educational programs. TSU graduates are highly recruited by school systems nationally. The College of Education offers a variety of distance learning courses to its students.

Teacher Preparation Program Information

The following programs are 4 year programs:

Elementary Education (K-6), K-12 Education (Art, Music-Instrumental, Music-Vocal/Choral, Physical Education), Secondary Education (Biology, Chemistry, Comprehensive General Science, Comprehensive Mathematics, Comprehensive Social Sciences, English/Language Arts, French, Health Education, History, Latin, Mathematics, Physics, Spanish), Special Education (Collaborative Teacher K-6)

The following programs are 5th year programs:

Elementary Education (K-6), K-12 Education (Art, Music-Instrumental, Music-Vocal/Choral, Physical Education), Secondary Education (Biology, Chemistry, Comprehensive General Science, Comprehensive Mathematics, Comprehensive Social Sciences, English/Language Arts, French, Health Education, History, Latin, Mathematics, Physics, Spanish), Special Education (Collaborative Teacher K-6)

Troy State University Dothan

Troy State University Dothan is a commuter university of predominantly non-traditional adult students. TSUD endeavors to develop in its teacher candidates an appreciation of the arts, humanities, and sciences; the desire and ability to reason critically and creatively; an appreciation and respect for the dignity and worth of the individual; the skills necessary to participate effectively in a democratic society; and the skills for continuing to acquire new knowledge. The university emphasizes superior teaching, ongoing professional development, scholarship, applied research, program development, student services, and public service.

Just the facts...

Troy State University Dothan
School of Education
P.O. Box 8368
Dothan, AL 36304-0368
(334) 983-6556
Website: www.tsud.edu
Profile: Suburban, Small, Co-Ed
UG Tuition: $68.00/cr. hr. in-state; $136.00/cr. hr. out-of-state
G Tuition: $68.00/cr. hr. in-state; $140.00/cr. hr. out-of-state
Off Campus Programs: Yes

Clinical Experiences

Field-based experiences provide candidates with opportunities to observe, plan, and teach in a variety of settings, including professional development schools. There are three components to the program: school-based observation that takes place before the candidate is admitted into the teacher education program; experiences where candidates observe, plan, and teach; and an internship where candidates assume full teaching responsibility for a minimum of twelve weeks. All field-based experiences include support from classroom teachers and university faculty.

Noteworthy

The School of Education has formed professional development school (PDS) partnerships with area schools. In participating courses, candidates spend part of their in-class time at a PDS over the course of the term. Candidates have the opportunity to use technology to design and implement special summer programs for children, and may join student education organizations such as Kappa Delta Pi, the Council for Exceptional Children, and the Student Alabama Education Association.

Teacher Preparation Program Information

The following programs are 4 year programs:
Early Childhood Education, Elementary Education, Secondary Education (Biology, General Science, History, Language Arts, Mathematics, Social Studies), Special Education (Learning Disability, Emotional Conflict, Mild Learning/Behavioral Disability)

The following programs are post-baccalaureate programs:
Early Childhood Education, Elementary Education, Middle School Education (English, Mathematics, Science, Social Studies), Secondary Education (Biology, General Science, History, Language Arts, Mathematics, Social Studies), Special Education (Emotional Conflict, Learning Disability, Mild Learning/Behavioral Disability)

The following programs are 5th year programs:
Early Childhood Education, Elementary Education, Secondary Education (Biology, General Science, History, Language Arts, Mathematics, Social Studies)

Tuskegee University

Tuskegee University has prepared teachers since 1881. Undergraduate programs to prepare candidates for professional teacher licensure are offered in early childhood, elementary, general science, mathematics, and physical education. A master's level program is available in general science education. Faculty in the Division of Education are committed to teaching that is student-centered, rather than teacher-dominated. Education programs at Tuskegee University have produced substantial numbers of teachers who serve the profession in every region of the country and abroad. The entire university is dedicated to improving the quality of education in the various communities served by its graduates.

Just the facts...

Tuskegee University
College of Liberal Arts and Education
Moton Hall - 203
Tuskegee, AL 36088
(334) 727-8784
Website: www.acd.tusk.edu
Profile: Rural, Medium, Co-Ed
UG Tuition: $4,331.00/semester
G Tuition: $4,331.00/semester
Off Campus Programs: No

Clinical Experiences

Field-based experiences are integrated into the programs during the second semester of the freshman year, in which candidates must spend twelve hours observing in a public school. During the second semester of the sophomore year, candidates spend another twelve hours assisting teachers with routine classroom activities. After candidates have completed 60 hours of general studies and are admitted to the professional education program, they are required to spend twelve hours per methods course per semester observing and teaching in public schools. The student teaching semester is the culminating experience for students in teacher education.

Noteworthy

Freshman year placement of candidates in public schools helps them decide early in their college experience if teaching is the right career for them. This early experience also helps candidates more quickly develop their own teaching and learning philosophies. Faculty and students are involved in a professional development school partnership. All classrooms in the Division of Education, as well as the computer, curriculum, and media center labs, are wired for Internet access, which helps faculty and candidates enrich and enhance their teaching.

Teacher Preparation Program Information

The following programs are 4 year programs:
Early Childhood Education, Elementary Education, K-12 Education (Physical Education), Secondary Education (General Science, Language Arts, Mathematics)

The following programs are 5 year programs
Secondary Education (General Science)

The following programs are 5th year programs:
Secondary Education (General Science)

University of Alabama

As part of the premier institution of higher education in Alabama, the College of Education provides teaching, research, and service that addresses state and regional needs and national and international concerns. The College of Education offers programs and courses that enable teachers and other education professionals to become reflective decision makers who facilitate student learning. The College of Education encourages an understanding of the links among instruction, assessment, and technology in the context of a global, multicultural, and diverse educational environment.

Just the facts...

The University of Alabama
College of Education
Box 870231
Tuscaloosa, AL 35487-0231
(205) 348-6050
Website: www.ua.edu
Profile: Urban, Large, Co-Ed
UG Tuition: $1,297.00/sem. in-state; $3,404.00/sem. out-of-state
G Tuition: $1,297.00/sem. in-state; $3,404.00/sem. out-of-state
Off Campus Programs: Yes

Clinical Experiences

Candidates enrolled in clinical courses are placed in a wide variety of school-based settings. Most professional education courses have clinical components, requiring from 4 to 90 hours in a school-based practicum. The culminating undergraduate and fifth year clinical experience is a full-time internship requiring up to 600 hours in a classroom setting. The college has several public school partnerships that provide candidates the opportunity to become part of the school through collaborative planning with mentor teachers at the school, and through college courses taught on-site.

Noteworthy

The College of Education recognizes the outstanding academic achievement of its candidates in numerous ways, including three categories of honor at the baccalaureate level during graduation, numerous awards and recognitions during Honors Week each spring, and through merit-based and need-based scholarships. The College of Education is widely recognized as a source of diverse and innovative programs both in teacher licesnsure fields as well as non-licensure fields.

Teacher Preparation Program Information

The following programs are 4 year programs:
Elementary Education, Multiple Abilities, P-12 Education (French, German, Japanese, Latin, Music, Physical Education, Russian, Spanish), Secondary Education (Comprehensive Science, Comprehensive Social Studies, English/Language Arts, French, German, Home Economics, Japanese, Latin, Mathematics, Russian, Spanish), Special Education (Collaborative, Early Childhood)

The following programs are 5th year programs:
Elementary Education, Multiple Abilities, P-12 Education (ESL, French, German, Japanese, Latin, Music, Russian, Spanish), Secondary Education (Comprehensive Science, Comprehensive Social Studies, English/Language Arts, French, German, Home Economics, Japanese, Latin, Mathematics, Russian, Spanish), Special Education (Collaborative, Early Childhood)

University of Alabama at Birmingham

The UAB School of Education is dedicated to the construction, discovery, dissemination, and application of knowledge. The school values and utilizes the strengths of a diverse society for the preparation of teachers and other human service professionals who apply "best practices" in a variety of settings to maximize the development of the whole individual. The School of Education has traditionally emphasized a strong liberal arts base for candidates enrolled in education programs. Faculty members believe that the ultimate outcome of professional teacher preparation is to develop educators who are capable of making decisions that lead to the best teaching and learning situations for all involved.

Just the facts...

University of Alabama at Birmingham
School of Education
901 South 13th Street
Birmingham, AL 35294-1250
(205) 934-5322
Website: www.uab.edu
Profile: Urban, Large, Co-Ed
UG Tuition: $84.00/cr. hr. in-state; $168.00/cr. hr. out-of-state
G Tuition: $96.00/cr. hr. in-state; $192.00/cr. hr. out-of-state
Off Campus Programs: No

Clinical Experiences

Faculty in the School of Education believe programs must prepare professionals through guided practice within applied contexts. The School of Education has designed programs that integrate real-world experiences in classrooms, laboratories, and agencies. Field experiences allow for the application of theory in practical settings, and are designed to be appropriate for the teacher candidate's level of knowledge and stage of professional development. A service learning component is embedded throughout each program.

Noteworthy

The School of Education has a number of scholarships available for both graduate and undergraduate majors with attention given to the recruitment of underrepresented populations. One outstanding program at UAB is the Teacher in Residence Program, intended to strengthen the relationship between local school systems and the School of Education. In collaboration with the Birmingham Bar Association and Bell South, the UAB School of Education and six urban school districts are developing Conflict Resolution and Peer Mediation curricula in fourteen area K-12 schools.

Teacher Preparation Program Information

The following programs are 4 year programs:
Early Childhood Education, Elementary Education, K-12 Education (Art, French, German, Physical Education, Spanish), Secondary Education (Biology, Chemistry, English/Language Arts, General Science, Health, Mathematics, Physics, Political Science, Social Studies), Special Education (Learning Disability)

The following programs are post-baccalaureate programs:
Early Childhood Education, Elementary Education, K-12 Education (Art, Physical Education, Reading), Middle School Education (Language Arts, Mathematics, Science, Social Studies), Secondary Education (Biology, Chemistry, English/Language Arts, General Science, Health, Mathematics, Physics, Political Science, Social Studies), Special Education (Early Childhood, Learning Disability, Mental Retardation, Severe Behavioral Disabilities/Handicaps)

The following programs are 5th year programs:
Early Childhood Education, Elementary Education, K-12 Education (Art, Physical Education), Secondary Education (Biology, Chemistry, English/Language Arts, Health, Mathematics, Physics, Political Science, Social Studies), Special Education (Early Childhood, Learning Disability, Mental Retardation, Severe Behavioral Disabilities/Handicaps)

University of Montevallo

The University of Montevallo, founded in 1896, offers candidates a strong background in liberal studies and professional programs. The College of Education at the University of Montevallo has as its primary goal the preparation of school professionals who have the sound knowledge and practical experience to make wise and informed decisions in the world of educational practice. The education programs at the University of Montevallo are sequentially structured to provide the knowledge and experience necessary for the development of aspiring professionals. Therefore, the central theme of the teacher education program is "Teacher as Developing Professional."

Just the facts...

University of Montevallo
College of Education
Station 6360
Montevallo, AL 35115
(205) 665-6360
Website: www.montevallo.edu
Profile: Suburban, Medium, Co-Ed
UG Tuition: $99.00/cr. hr. in-state; $198.00/cr. hr.out-of-state
G Tuition: $107.00/cr. hr.in-state; $214.00/cr. hr. out-of-state
Off Campus Programs: No

Clinical Experiences

Clinical experiences are provided at various times throughout the candidates' programs. A major component of the initial education course required of all undergraduates is field experience. Early childhood and elementary methods courses are blocked together to allow opportunities for extended observation and participation. The semester prior to internship, candidates seeking secondary licensure observe and participate in the classroom where their internship will occur. All candidates complete a fifteen-week internship at an upper and a lower grade level.

Noteworthy

The College of Education offers a First Year Teacher Quality Assurance Program to all graduates who successfully complete their internships. This program allows first year teachers supervisory assistance and/or remediation from College of Education faculty. Numerous scholarships are available, including the Minority Teachers Scholarship, which encourages minority students to enter the education field. Candidates are required to take two courses in technology, thus enhancing their skills in using technology for teaching and learning. Opportunities for student involvement are provided through the Student Chapter of Alabama Education (SAEA) and Kappa Delta Pi.

Teacher Preparation Program Information

The following programs are 4 year programs:

Early Childhood Education, Elementary Education, K-12 Education (Art, Hearing Impaired, Music, Physical Education), Middle School Education (Biology, Chemistry, English/Language Arts, General Science, History, Mathematics, Social Science), Secondary Education (Biology, Chemistry, Driver Education/Safety, English/Language Arts, Family & Consumer Science, French, General Science, German, History, Mathematics, Social Science, Spanish)

The following programs are post-baccalaureate programs:

Early Childhood Education, Elementary Education, K-12 Education (Art, Music, Physical Education), Secondary Education (Biology, Chemistry, Driver Education/Safety, English/Language Arts, Family & Consumer Science, French, General Science, German, History, Mathematics, Social Science, Spanish)

The following programs are 5th year programs:

Early Childhood Education, Elementary Education, K-12 Education (Art, Music, Physical Education), Secondary Education (Biology, Chemistry, English/Language Arts, Family & Consumer Sciences, General Science, History, Mathematics, Social Science)

University of North Alabama

The University of North Alabama traces its establishment to the opening of LaGrange College, first chartered in 1830. It became the first state-supported teacher training institution south of the Ohio River. The undergraduate program has a strong liberal arts base, with a heavy emphasis on the academic discipline the candidate plans to teach. The preservice program places a major emphasis on novice skills such as basic teaching skills, problem solving, critical thinking, and awareness of and accommodation for student diversity.

Just the facts...

University of North Alabama
College of Education
UNA Box 5031
Florence, AL 35632-0001
(256) 765-0001
Website: www2.una.edu/education
Profile: Urban, Medium, Co-Ed
UG Tuition: $86.00/cr. hr. in-state; $175.00/cr. hr. out-of-state
G Tuition: $98.00/cr. hr. in-state; $199.00/cr. hr. out-of-state
Off Campus Programs: No

Clinical Experiences

Clinical experiences begin early in the program and continue throughout the initial preparation program, culminating with the internship. Experiences include tutoring, small-group teaching, assisting public school practitioners, using computer-assisted instruction, administering diagnostics, interviewing practitioners and administrators, and attending school board meetings. Candidates plan, teach, and practice the skills they have developed in prior courses and experiences. A full-semester internship is required for both elementary and secondary student teachers.

Noteworthy

The College of Education guarantees the success of individuals who complete approved programs of studies in the teacher education program and who are employed in their area of specialization. The college will provide remedial education at no cost to graduates who were recommended for licensure by the college, but who were deemed unsatisfactory based on a performance evaluation within two years of their graduation. Programs emphasize continual self-evaluation regarding philosophy, curriculum, and involvement in the school and community.

Teacher Preparation Program Information

The following programs are 4 year programs:
Elementary Education, K-12 Education (Art, Music, Physical Education), Secondary Education (Biology, Chemistry, English/Language Arts, French, General Science, Geography, German, Mathematics, Mathematics/Computer Science, Physics, Social Science, Spanish, Vocational Business Office, Vocational Home Economics/Human Environmental Science, Vocational Marketing)

The following programs are 5th year programs:
K-12 Education (Music, Physical Education), Secondary Education (Biology, Chemistry, English/Language Arts, General Science, History, Mathematics, Mathematics/Computer Science, Social Studies, Vocational Business Office)

University of South Alabama

The University of South Alabama's College of Education has five major goals: (1) to prepare professional educators to meet the needs of children, youth, and adults; (2) to prepare support personnel to meet the educational needs of schools; (3) to assist schools in improving instructional programs; (4) to prepare students in professional areas other than teaching; and (5) to conduct research to expand, enhance, and evaluate instructional programs. The education programs are based on the knowledge of established and current educational research, and emphasize systematic problem solving.

Just the facts...

University of South Alabama
College of Education-UCOM 3600
75 N. University
Mobile, AL 36688
(334) 380-2738
Website: www.coe.usouthal.edu
Profile: Urban, Large, Co-Ed
UG Tuition: $82.50/cr. hr. in-state; $165.00/cr. hr. out-of-state
G Tuition: $106.50/cr. hr. in-state; $213.00/cr. hr. out-of-state
Off Campus Programs: No

Clinical Experiences

All teacher education programs at the University of South Alabama include early field experiences and a fourteen-week internship. The Department of Curriculum and Instruction has developed a professional development school relationship with several local elementary schools. Candidates in the undergraduate program in special education currently spend approximately 900 hours in a variety of clinical placements. Care is taken to vary the level and type of placements to ensure the most comprehensive experience for every candidate.

Noteworthy

The College of Education has seven computer labs that are fully networked and connected to the Internet. All College of Education students have access to the labs seven days a week. In 1998, a Technology Across the Curriculum program was implemented. A Writing Across the Curriculum program has been offered for several years.

Teacher Preparation Program Information

The following programs are 4 year programs:
Elementary Education (Elementary Education K-6), K-12 Education (Art, Music, Physical Education), Secondary Education (Biology, Chemistry, English/Language Arts, General Science, Geography, Health, History, Mathematics, Physics, Social Studies), Special Education (Collaborative Teaching, Early Childhood)

The following programs are 5th year programs:
Early Childhood Education, Elementary Education (Elementary Education K-6), K-12 Education (Art, French, German, Music, Physical Education, Spanish), Secondary Education (Biology, English/Language Arts, Mathematics, Social Studies), Special Education (Collaborative Teaching, Early Childhood, Gifted/Talented)

University of West Alabama

The Julia Tutwiler College of Education at The University of West Alabama offers a variety of nationally recognized programs for students who are interested in careers as teachers. The College of Education is organized into four departments: Elementary and Early Childhood Education, Secondary Education, Instructional Support, and Physical Education and Athletic Training. Teacher education at UWA is guided by the belief that the best learning occurs when students participate in the discovery of information and are able to use that information in a social context. UWA prepares teachers who employ the skills of collaboration, application, inquiry, and reflection.

Just the facts...

The University of West Alabama
College of Education
Station 8
Livingston, AL 35470
(205) 652-2341
Website: www.westal.edu
Profile: Rural, Small, Co-Ed
UG Tuition: $63.00/quart. in-state; $126.00/quart. out-of-state
G Tuition: $73.00/quart. in-state; $146.00/quart. out-of-state
Off Campus Programs: No

Clinical Experiences

Structured experiences in P-12 classrooms are required prior to admission to the teacher education program. Many professional courses in the College of Education have a field-based component in which candidates work in schools while assisted and monitored by a college-based supervisor. Candidates complete full-time internships that take place over ten weeks or for 300 hours. Interns are placed in schools with teachers who have a master's degree and at least three years of teaching experience. In addition, the college supervisor holds a doctorate and has specialized training and pre-college teaching experience in the candidate's field of study. Most interns are placed in schools within a 60-mile radius of UWA.

Noteworthy

The College of Education has much to offer in its programs, facilities, and faculty. UWA graduates are highly sought after by school systems in Alabama and neighboring states. Some scholarships are set aside for education students, including the Carol Parnell Cunningham, Julia Tutwiler, Ralph and Margaret Lyon, and Aver Rumley scholarships. More than 95 percent of UWA's faculty members hold an earned doctorate and all faculty in the teacher preparation program have pre-college teaching experience. Most classes are small (15-25 students) allowing faculty to get to know students as individuals. Faculty provide hands-on experiences in classes which provide practical applications as well as theoretical knowledge.

Teacher Preparation Program Information

The following programs are 4 year programs:
Early Childhood Education, Elementary Education (Elementary Education K-6), K-12 Education (Physical Education), Middle School Education (General Science, Language Arts, Mathematics, Science, Social Studies), Secondary Education (Biology, Chemistry, English/Language Arts, General Science, History, Mathematics, Physical Education), Special Education (Elementary Collaborative Teacher)

The following programs are 5 year programs:
Early Childhood Education, Elementary Education (Elementary Education K-6)

Arkansas State University

The mission of initial level teacher education at the College of Education is to prepare future educators who manifest commonly held beliefs about schools and society and by demonstrating specific knowledges, performances, and dispositions identified by teaching professionals, the academic community of Arkansas State University, and national and state standards for the profession. The guiding framework of the college is "Learning to Teach, Teaching to Learn."

Just the facts...

Arkansas State University
College of Education
P.O. Box 940
State University, AR 72467-0940
(870) 972-3057
Website: www.astate.edu
Profile: Rural, Large, Co-Ed
UG Tuition: $1,092.00/sem. in-state; $2,796.00/sem. out-of-state
G Tuition: $1,380.00/sem. in-state; $3,468.00/sem. out-of-state
Off Campus Programs: Yes

Clinical Experiences

Clinical experiences begin early in candidates' courses of study at the college, and provide practice with a diverse group of students. Candidates interact with children in a variety of environments through service learning components embedded in their professional studies coursework. Mid-level experiences occur in professional development schools. Candidates eventually take part in a semester-long, multifaceted field experience.

Noteworthy

While preparation at the undergraduate level focuses on initial teacher preparation, graduate initiatives support National Board Teaching Standards through performance-based outcome measures required for state and national licensure. Non-education programs offered by the college include Rehabilitation Counseling, Psychology and Counseling, Exercise Science, Sports Medicine and Training, and Sports Promotion. The college supports twelve scholarships across its undergraduate and graduate programs in addition to ASU university-wide scholarships.

Teacher Preparation Program Information

The following programs are 4 year programs:
Early Childhood Education, Elementary Education, K-12 Education (Art, French, Spanish, Health, Music, Physical Education), Secondary Education (Agriculture, Art, Biology, Business, Chemistry, Earth Science, English/Language Arts, Health, Mathematics, Physics, Psychology, Science, Social Studies, Vocational Agriculture)

The following programs are post-baccalaureate programs:
K-12 Education (Reading), Middle School Education (English, Foreign Languages, Mathematics, Science, Social Studies)

Arkansas Tech University

The School of Education at Arkansas Tech University has developed performance-based programs in early childhood education, middle level education, and secondary education. Program designs and assessments are based on INTASC model state licensing standards and Arkansas performance standards for licensure. Each program area has a different theme upon which its coursework and practical experiences are based. The early childhood education program is based on the idea of the teacher as a lifelong learner; the middle level education program is based on the concept of the teacher as a team player; and the secondary education program is based on the view of the teacher as a decision maker.

Clinical Experiences

Clinical experiences are an integral part of each program, beginning with candidates' second year at Arkansas Tech. Each experience and assessment is designed around performance-based standards. A unique program feature is the cohort school, a partnership between the university and a K-12 school. Selected school faculty are appointed as adjunct faculty at the university. Interns assigned to the school are assigned to a cohort that has the collective responsibility for the induction of the intern into the teaching profession.

Just the facts...

Arkansas Tech University
School of Education
Box 8749
Russellville, AR 72801-2222
(501) 968-0350
Website: www.atu.edu
Profile: Rural, Medium, Co-Ed
UG Tuition: $96.00/cr. hr. in-state; $192.00/cr. hr. out-of-state
G Tuition: $98.00/cr. hr. in-state; $196.00/cr. hr. out-of-state
Off Campus Programs: Yes

Noteworthy

Four scholarships are available yearly for African American teacher candidates. Minority scholarships are available through a state-funded minority grant program that assigns recipients to a minority mentor in the local school system. Recipients work with the mentor in his or her classroom to acquire a better understanding of what is required to become a teacher. The Student Development Center offers support programs to help ensure that scholarship students will be successful in their program of study.

Teacher Preparation Program Information

The following programs are 4 year programs:

Early Childhood Education, Elementary Education (Elementary Education K-6), K-12 Education (Adult Education, Music, Physical Education/Health), Middle Level Education, Secondary Education (Biology, Business, Chemistry, English/Language Arts, French, German, Spanish, General Science, Mathematics, Music, Physical Education, Physical Sciences, Physics, Social Studies, Speech, Science)

Harding University

Harding University is the largest private university in Arkansas. More than 4,300 students from all 50 states and more than 40 foreign countries are enrolled in the liberal arts, Christian university. For 75 years, it has been Harding's mission to provide a quality education that will lead to an understanding and philosophy consistent with Christian ideals. Harding places among the top 100 schools in the nation for National Merit Scholar enrollment, and 30 percent of its student body is from the top 10 percent of their class. The faculty in the School of Education prepares teachers who are scholarly, nurturing, and self-directed facilitators of student learning.

Just the facts...

Harding University
School of Education
Box 12254
Searcy, AR 72149-0001
(501) 279-4242
Website: www.harding.edu
Profile: Rural, Medium, Co-Ed
UG Tuition: $251.00/credit hour
G Tuition: $279.00/credit hour
Off Campus Programs: No

Clinical Experiences

In addition to a number of opportunities for early hands-on clinical experiences, candidates are required to participate in a pre-professional semester immediately prior to their student teaching semester. Throughout the pre-professional semester, while taking classes on campus, candidates work in area schools with experienced P-12 teachers in their academic disciplines. Candidates then have opportunities to share and learn from each other when they meet for class on campus.

Noteworthy

Several campus organizations provide teacher education candidates with professional service opportunities. Teacher candidates are active in Dactylology Club, Kappa Delta Pi, National Association of Teachers of Singing, Pied Pipers children's theater group, Student Council for Exceptional Children, TEACH club, and Ujima African-American culture club. Students serve on the Student Council for Exceptional Children at the local, state, and national levels as well as in the annual state Special Olympics held on campus. Harding students conduct an after school tutoring program for children in public housing and an annual inner-city carnival. Teacher candidates have opportunities to work in the Curriculum Lab.

Teacher Preparation Program Information

The following programs are 4 year programs:
Elementary Education, K-12 Education (Art, French, Music, Physical Education, Spanish), Secondary Education (Art, Biology, Chemistry, English/Language Arts, ESL, Family & Consumer Sciences, General Science, Gifted & Talented, Health, Mathematics, Middle School Emphasis, Physical Sciences, Physics, Social Studies), Special Education (Mildly Disabled)

The following programs are post-baccalaureate programs:
Early Childhood Special Education, Reading, Secondary Education (with content emphasis)

Henderson State University

Henderson State University was founded for the purpose of preparing outstanding teachers. In 1997, *U.S. News and World Report* ranked Henderson State as the southern institution with the third-highest proportion of education majors. Known as Arkansas' "Public Liberal Arts College," the university provides a strong foundation of liberal studies across all fields. Henderson State has a student enrollment of 3,600 students with a minority population of fifteen percent. The School of Education endorses the role of the informed professional educator and creates opportunities for its candidates to engage in best practices of teaching, learning, and technology.

Just the facts...

Henderson State University
School of Education
Arkadelphia, AR 71999-0001
(870) 230-5367 or 1 (800) 228-7333
Website: www.hsu.edu
Profile: Urban, Medium, Co-Ed
UG Tuition: $1,608.00/sem. in-state; $2,136.00/sem. out-of-state
G Tuition: $120.00/cr. hr. in-state; $240.00/cr. hr. out-of-state
Off Campus Programs: No

Clinical Experiences

Clinical experiences are an integral part of the School of Education programs. Alliances and partnerships are actively sought and secured to promote collaboration and interaction with agencies and public schools involved in educational improvement. Relevant placements for candidates provide various degrees of interaction and responsibility at well-established clinical sites. The university has an accredited early childhood laboratory school for three and four year olds located on the HSU campus. The laboratory school provides optimal practica experiences for candidates.

Noteworthy

The School of Education is planning a state-of-the-art education facility to open in 2000. The building will house the teacher media lab, early childhood laboratory school, and multimedia teaching classrooms. Graduates from Henderson's teacher education program are highly recruited by public schools from surrounding states, such as Texas, Louisiana, and Oklahoma. The university is located 35 miles from Hot Springs and five miles from beautiful Lake DeGray on the Ouachita River.

Teacher Preparation Program Information

The following programs are 4 year programs:

Early Childhood Education, Elementary Education (Language Arts, Mathematics, Science, Social Studies), Middle School Education (English, Mathematics, Science, Social Studies), Secondary Education (Art, Biology, Business, Chemistry, Communication/Theatre Arts, English, Family & Consumer Sciences, Foreign Language, Mathematics, Music, Physical Education, Physics, Social Science)

The following programs are post-baccalaureate programs:

Early Childhood Education, Elementary Education (Language Arts, Mathematics, Science, Social Studies), Middle School Education (English, Mathematics, Science, Social Studies), Secondary Education (Art, Biology, Business, Chemistry, Communication/Theatre Arts, English, Family & Consumer Sciences, Foreign Language, Mathematics, Music, Physical Education, Physics, Social Science)

Hendrix College

Hendrix College, established in 1876, is a residential, private, liberal arts institution affiliated with the Methodist Church, serving approximately one thousand students. Instead of two semesters, Hendrix has three terms in each academic year. The college refers to this plan as the "term system." Students take three classes per term for a total of nine classes per year, and typically devote one-third of their coursework to their major, one-third to electives, and one-third to meeting general graduation requirements. Hendrix College is dedicated to the cultivation of whole persons through the transmission of knowledge, the refinement of intellect, the development of character, and the encouragement of a concern for values.

Just the facts...

Hendrix College
Education Department
1600 Washington Avenue
Conway, AR 72032
(501) 450-1379
Website: www.hendrix.edu
Profile: Suburban, Small, Co-Ed
UG Tuition: $10,695.00/year
Off Campus Programs: No

Clinical Experiences

All courses in the education program include activities such as observation, tutoring, and mentoring. Candidates may also intern in various school settings, and participate in professional offerings at the local and state levels. Candidates spend time in culturally diverse schools. They also observe opening school procedures in their hometown. This component helps candidates learn how to establish a positive climate in the classroom during the first week of school. Student teaching involves twelve weeks of teaching in an elementary, middle, or high school in Arkansas.

Noteworthy

The Department of Education offers small class sizes for one-to-one interaction with faculty. It houses a curriculum library and provides a computer center for student use. All dorm rooms are connected by cables to this center, allowing teacher candidates to access the Internet and e-mail from their rooms. Candidates attend state meetings of the Arkansas Education Association and other professional associations such as the International Reading Association and the National Science Teachers Association. Hendrix College is rated as a Best Value by *Money Magazine* and ranked as a national liberal arts college by *U.S. News and World Report*.

Teacher Preparation Program Information

The following programs are 4 year programs:

Liberal arts degree plus licensing: Early Childhood Education (PreK-4), Middle School Education 4-8 (Language Arts/Social Studies, Mathematics/Science), P-8 Education (Art, Music, Physical Education), Secondary Education 7-12 (English, Foreign Language, Life/Earth Science, Mathematics, Physical/Earth Science, Physical Education, Social Studies, Speech/Drama)

John Brown University

John Brown University's mission stresses Christian higher education that contributes to the intellectual, spiritual, and occupational effectiveness of its students. The Division of Teacher Education works to prepare teachers who are reflective professionals and skilled decision makers who exhibit Christlike characteristics. Candidates are prepared to work in public, private, and Christian schools. The faculty is committed to preparing competent teachers who are ready to work in a multicultural society and with exceptional students.

Just the facts...

John Brown University
Division of Teacher Education
2000 W. University
Siloam Springs, AR 72761
(501) 524-7280
Website: www.jbu.edu
Profile: Rural, Small, Co-Ed
UG Tuition: $4,430.00/semester
Off Campus Programs: No

Clinical Experiences

An especially important part of the Division of Education's teacher and counselor preparation programs is its partnership with a professional development school (PDS). The division works with the Siloam Springs Public Schools and community to improve the quality of teacher preparation and the quality of education for schoolchildren. Candidates begin field experiences in their sophomore year by being placed with teams of four classroom teachers. The candidates then continue working with their team for the next three years. Student teaching is a fifteen-week experience during the candidate's senior year.

Noteworthy

The heart of the PDS is the instructional team, which consists of classroom teachers, university faculty, and candidates working as student interns, associate teachers, and assistant teachers in their sophomore, junior, and senior years, with input from the arts and sciences faculty of the university. These team members work cooperatively to guide schoolchildren to reach their maximum potential. The Walton scholarship program is a successful university effort to recruit Central and South American students to increase the diversity of John Brown's student population.

Teacher Preparation Program Information

The following programs are 4 year programs:

Elementary Education, K-12 Education (Mild/Moderate Handicapped, Music, Physical Education), Middle School Education (English, Mathematics, Physical Education, Science, Social Studies), Secondary Education (Biology, Chemistry, Coaching, English/Language Arts, General Science, Health, Mathematics, Physical Sciences, Social Studies), Special Education

The following programs are post-baccalaureate programs:

K-12 Education (Mild/Moderate Handicapped), Middle School Education, (English, Mathematics, Physical Education, Science, Social Studies), Secondary Education (General Science, Health, Physical Sciences), Special Education

Lyon College

At Lyon, prospective teachers complete a major in one of the liberal arts or sciences. In the senior year, they also complete a concentration in elementary, middle school, or secondary education and, simultaneously, serve a year-long internship in one of Lyon's partner school districts. Lyon offers three education concentrations leading to teacher licensure: The Early Childhood Education Concentration (preschool-grade 4); The Middle School Education Concentration (grades 4-8); and The Secondary Education Concentration (grades 7-12).

Just the facts...

Lyon College
Teacher Education
2300 Highland Road
Batesville, AR 72501
(870) 698-4373
Website: www.lyon.edu
Profile: Rural, Small, Co-Ed
UG Tuition: $5,025.00/semester
Off Campus Programs: No

Clinical Experiences

At Lyon, student teachers spend their entire senior year as half-time students/half-time teachers. Interns begin work in the fall semester the day their mentor teachers report to their classrooms in mid-August. Interns help their mentor teachers prepare the classroom for the children. When the fall semester begins at Lyon, interns take college classes while continuing as part-time teachers in public school classrooms during the rest of the academic year. As a result, teacher candidates may learn about a teaching method one day, try it out the next, and discuss it in class the day after. It also means that candidates work with a mentor teacher and a class full of students throughout an entire school year.

Noteworthy

Lyon College combines a liberal arts or science major, a focused curriculum in teaching methods, and a year-long internship in its teacher preparation program. The teacher preparation program has captured a great deal of attention nationwide; the Winthrop Rockefeller Foundation is backing the program with a special grant. In recent years Lyon's education graduates, all of whom have majored in liberal arts and sciences, have averaged well above the 90th percentile on the ETS exam in Education, a national exam designed for education majors.

Teacher Preparation Program Information

The following programs are 4 year programs:
Elementary Education, Middle School Education, Secondary Education (Biology, Chemistry, English, General Science, Mathematics, Social Studies)

The following programs are post-baccalaureate programs:
Elementary Education, Middle School Education, Secondary Education (Biology, Chemistry, English, General Science, Mathematics, Social Studies)

Ouachita Baptist University

Ouachita Baptist University provides the sensitivity and experiences required for prospective teachers to become effective professionals in the classroom. Each major is a carefully designed course of study that includes a wide variety of offerings, including studies in the liberal arts and sciences as well as professional education courses. The teacher education program is a university-wide responsibility coordinated through a Teacher Education Council composed of representatives from all academic disciplines.

Just the facts...

Ouachita Baptist University
Teacher Education
410 Ouachita Street
Arkadelphia, AR 71998
(870) 245-5149
Website: www.obu.edu
Profile: Rural, Small, Co-Ed
UG Tuition: $4,205.00/semester
Off Campus Programs: No

Clinical Experiences

The Teacher Education Program has designed a three-tiered clinical and field experience program for candidates. First, candidates are required to spend a minimum of 20 hours observing in classrooms where the students vary in socioeconomic, racial, and/or cultural backgrounds, as well as with students with exceptionalities and different learning styles. Second, candidates observe and participate in activities and subject matter related to their chosen field. Finally, a twelve-week, full-time student teaching experience provides candidates the opportunity to observe, participate, and teach in a classroom.

Noteworthy

An Education major may also receive an English as a Second Language (ESL) endorsement from Ouachita by completing required courses. The State of Arkansas does not currently offer licensure in ESL, but the required coursework will provide the necessary background for teaching in an ESL program. Ouachita Baptist University participates in the ADHE Minority Student Scholarship Program.

Teacher Preparation Program Information

The following programs are 4 year programs:
Early Childhood Education, K-12 Education (Art, Music, Physical Education), Middle School Education (Language Arts/Social Studies, Mathematics/Science), Secondary Education (Biology, Business, Chemistry, English, Family & Consumer Science, French, General Science, Health, Journalism, Mathematics, Physical Education, Physical Science, Physics, Social Studies, Spanish, Speech)

The following programs are post-baccalaureate programs:
Early Childhood Education, K-12 Education (Art, Music, Physical Education), Middle School Education (Language Arts/Social Studies, Mathematics/Science), Secondary Education (Biology, Business, Chemistry, English, Family & Consumer Science, French, General Science, Health, Journalism, Mathematics, Physical Education, Physical Science, Physics, Social Studies, Spanish, Speech)

Philander Smith College

Philander Smith College is a small, privately supported, historically black liberal arts college that has prepared excellent teachers since 1883. The faculty in the Division of Education is dedicated to providing a high quality educational program for all candidates regardless of race, age, religion, national background, or gender. Education of teacher candidates is a cooperative effort that incorporates the spiritual, physical, social, and intellectual abilities of the candidates and faculty. Candidates are encouraged to explore ideas, develop knowledge, and augment practice through scientific and scholarly endeavors.

Just the facts...

Philander Smith College
Division of Education
812 West 13th Street
Little Rock, AR 72202
(501) 370-5248
Website: www.philander.edu
Profile: Urban, Small, Co-Ed
UG Tuition: $137.00/credit hour
Off Campus Programs: No

Clinical Experiences

Clinical experience at Philander Smith integrates current research and theory with the realities of the classroom and actual teaching. Experiences are divided into three levels during the course of the candidate's college years: level one includes 30 hours of classroom experience, level two includes 10 to 30 hours of classroom experience per methods course, and level three includes daily work in a classroom for a minimum of twelve weeks. A fourth level, consisting of two visits per semester minimum by a faculty member, is provided to graduates at no charge in order to assist them in their graduate studies or in their classroom teaching. Each experience is guided by practicing professionals.

Noteworthy

Philander Smith College participates in the Walton Delta Scholarship Program, which is intended to combat the shortage of minority teachers in the Arkansas Delta. Over a seven year period, 100 Philander Smith teacher candidates are being targeted to focus their teaching efforts in the Arkansas Delta. The Sylvia T. Caruth Endowed Education Scholarship is awarded to junior year teacher candidates. Teacher education students at Philander Smith College enjoy the advantages of small class size, which encourages student participation in classroom discussion and allows individualized attention from faculty.

Teacher Preparation Program Information

The following programs are 4 year programs:
Elementary Education, Middle School Education (English, Mathematics), Secondary Education (Biology, English/Language Arts, Mathematics, Physical Education), Special Education

Southern Arkansas University

Southern Arkansas University's professional education programs are focused on preparing educators as professional members of collaborative teams and leaders in building stronger schools for tomorrow. The undergraduate programs are built upon a strong liberal arts foundation and include content area studies and a professional component that integrates instruction with field experience. The graduate programs build on and extend prior knowledge and experiences and are intended to produce intellectual leaders for the education profession. The teacher education program is based on essential knowledge, research findings, and sound professional practice.

Just the facts...

Southern Arkansas University
School of Education
S.A.U. Box 9408
Magnolia, AR 71753
(870) 235-4057
Website: www.saumag.edu
Profile: Rural, Small, Co-Ed
UG Tuition: $996.00/sem. in-state; $1,524.00/sem. out-of-state
G Tuition: $102.00/cr. hr. in-state; $148.00/cr. hr. out-of-state
Off Campus Programs: No

Clinical Experiences

Education majors participate in a minimum of three field experiences. The first experience is an observation of grades K-12. The second experience involves tutoring and small group instruction. The third experience is microteaching and classroom management followed by twelve weeks of student teaching. Kindergarten specialists engage in an additional six credit hours of practica at local schools. Candidates in the master's program in school counseling participate in practica and internships in area public schools under the supervision of a credentialed site supervisor and a university supervisor.

Noteworthy

SAU ranks in the top two percent nationally of similar-sized public institutions in the amount of scholarship money available to students. Almost 1,200 students (out of 2,712) defrayed their expenses through campus jobs in 1997-98. SAU's tuition—the lowest of all four-year institutions in Arkansas—makes a college education accessible to low-income students. Academic support is available through a free tutoring center as well as through paid student tutors. Modern computer labs and a Curriculum Center Library are of high quality, and are used not only by teacher education students, but also by area teachers. In addition, academic support has expanded to include distance learning options.

Teacher Preparation Program Information

The following programs are 4 year programs:

Elementary Education (Art, Early Childhood, English, French, General Science, Kinesiology, Language Arts, Mathematics, Music, Social Studies, Spanish), K-12 Education (Art, Health, Kinesiology, Music, Recreation), Secondary Education (Agriculture, Art, Biological Science, Business, Computer Technology/Business, Chemistry, English, French, General Science, Journalism, Kinesiology, Mathematics, Physics, Social Studies, Spanish), Special Education (Mild Disabilities)

The following programs are post-baccalaureate programs:

Elementary Education, Secondary Education

The following programs are 5th year programs:

Elementary Education, Secondary Education

University of Arkansas at Fayetteville

The mission of the College of Education and Health Professions is to enhance the quality of life of the citizens of Arkansas, the nation, and the world through the development of scholar-practitioners in education, health, and human services. The expectation of the college is that every educator should access, use, and generate knowledge; plan, implement, and model best practice; understand, respect, and value diversity; communicate, cooperate, and collaborate with others; make decisions based upon professional standards and ethical criteria; and know about learners and learning, teachers and teaching, and schools and schooling.

Just the facts...

University of Arkansas at Fayetteville
College of Education and Health Professions
324 Graduate Education Building
Fayetteville, AR 72701
(501) 575-3208
Website: www.uark.edu
Profile: Urban, Large, Co-Ed
UG Tuition: $93.00/cr. hr. in-state; $253.00/cr. hr. out-of-state
G Tuition: $161.00/cr. hr. in-state; $383.00/cr. hr. out-of-state
Off Campus Programs: Yes

Clinical Experiences

Pre-education core courses are required, each of which has an early clinical experience component ranging from 12 to 30 hours. Specialized field experiences are required components of selected junior and senior level professional education courses. Many of those courses, especially those in elementary and special education, are delivered on-site in a partner school. In their fifth year, when candidates are working toward their Master of Arts in Teaching degree, the entire year is spent on-site in a partner school.

Noteworthy

The University of Arkansas at Fayetteville restructured its teacher preparation programs in 1992 so that teacher candidates in all areas (except art and music) must complete both a bachelor's degree in their content area and a Master of Arts in Teaching. In 1992, the Northwest Arkansas Partnership was established. The Partnership has allowed the University of Arkansas at Fayetteville to move away from traditional models of preparing teachers toward a site-based model dependent on the collaboration of and contributions from all education stakeholders.

Teacher Preparation Program Information

The following programs are 5 year programs:
Elementary Education (Elementary Education K-6), K-12 Education (Art, Music, Physical Education), Secondary Education (Agriculture, Biology, Chemistry, Consumer & Family Science/Home Economics, Earth Science, Economics, English/Language Arts, French, German, Spanish, General Science, Geography, Health, History, Journalism, Mathematics), Special Education (Mildly Mentally Handicapped)

The following programs are 5th year programs
Special Education (Gifted/Talented, Severe Behavioral Disabilities/Handicaps)

University of Arkansas at Little Rock

The University of Arkansas at Little Rock is an interactive metropolitan university, one of a new class of American universities emerging in the past twenty years to meet the challenge of a changing society and work force. UALR is large enough to meet the diverse needs of a dynamic student body, yet small enough to offer personal attention to individual students. The College of Education provides professional coursework for preservice and inservice teachers at the early childhood, middle, secondary and adult levels as well as in special education, gifted and talented education, and reading. The college also offers a master's degree in counseling and master's and doctoral degrees in educational administration and supervision.

Just the facts...

University of Arkansas at Little Rock
College of Education
2801 South University
Little Rock, AR 72204
(501) 569-3113
Website: www.ualr.edu
Profile: Urban, Large, Co-Ed
UG Tuition: $109.00/cr. hr. in-state; $262.00/cr. hr. out-of-state
G Tuition: $149.00/cr. hr. in-state; $304.00/cr. hr. out-of-state
Off Campus Programs: No

Clinical Experiences

Field experiences offer candidates the opportunity to hone their professional skills while under the guidance of professional educators. Field experiences take place in local schools and districts that serve students from diverse races, cultures, economic levels, and with different academic abilities. Candidates enrolled in practica and internships are observed by university faculty and school personnel and are regularly provided feedback through conferences and peer discussion groups. Field placements begin at admission to the program and continue throughout the curriculum, culminating in a full-semester internship.

Noteworthy

Graduates of the College of Education are in teaching and educational leadership positions throughout the state. As of Fall 1999, the college will be housed in a new facility that will include "semi-smart" classrooms, production laboratories, and three distance learning sites. Graduate assistantships and minority scholarships are available to qualified students. Special programs include teacher preparation in gifted education, teaching the visually impaired, and teaching the hearing impaired.

Teacher Preparation Program Information

The following programs are 4 year programs:
Early Childhood Education, Middle Childhood Education, Secondary Education, Special Education (Deaf Education)

The following programs are 5th year programs:
K-12 Education (Art, French, German, Spanish, Music), Secondary Education (Art, Biology, Business, Chemistry, English/Language Arts, General Science, Mathematics, Social Studies), Special Education (Visually Impaired)

University of Arkansas at Monticello

The University of Arkansas at Monticello is a small, comprehensive public institution serving the population in the Mississippi River delta region of southeast Arkansas. One of the major components of the mission of the College of Education at UAM is to provide teachers to the schools in the region. The college's programs are based on three components: knowledge (of content, children, adults, communities, and technology), pedagogy (the ability to share this knowledge with others, as well as an understanding of learning styles), and the equitable treatment of all children.

Just the facts...

University of Arkansas at Monticello
School of Education
P.O. Box 3595, UAM
Monticello, AR 71655
(870) 460-1062
Website: www.uamont.edu
Profile: Rural, Small, Co-Ed
UG Tuition: $70.00/cr. hr. in-state; $92.00/cr. hr. out-of-state
G Tuition: $84.00/cr. hr. in-state; $113.00 cr. hr. out-of-state
Off Campus Programs: No

Clinical Experiences

Field experiences begin with a sophomore level introduction to education course and continue through an internship course. Requirements range from observation and tutoring in the early courses to teaching lessons to entire classes in later courses. Placements for all field experiences are made only in professional development schools within partner districts. The culminating field experience in the curriculum is the full-year internship for seniors (Internship I and II) at a professional development school site.

Noteworthy

The Minority Teacher Grant is designed to provide scholarships to African American freshman and sophomore students who are interested in pursuing a career in teaching. Participating students may receive up to $1,000 per academic year for two years and must agree to sign a statement of interest to teach.

Teacher Preparation Program Information

The following programs are 4 year programs:
Early Childhood Education, Elementary Education, K-12 Education (Art, French, Music, Physical Education, Reading, Spanish), Middle School Education (English, Mathematics, Science, Social Studies), Secondary Education (Biology, Business, Chemistry, English/Language Arts, General Science, Health, Mathematics, Physical Sciences, Physical Education, Physics, Social Studies), Special Education

The following programs are post-baccalaureate programs:
Early Childhood Education, K-12 Education (French, Reading, Spanish), Middle School Education (English, Mathematics, Science, Social Studies), Secondary Education (General Science)

The following programs are 5th year programs:
Elementary Education, Secondary Education

University of Arkansas at Pine Bluff

The University of Arkansas at Pine Bluff is committed to the preparation of teachers who have a basic philosophy of education and who are dedicated to excellence in service to persons from all ethnic backgrounds and socioeconomic levels. The School of Education trains teachers and human service professionals to meet the educational challenges of an ever-changing society. The four major components of the teacher education program at the University of Arkansas at Pine Bluff are social/cultural/human diversity, community and global awareness, professional growth, and professional education. The faculty strive to produce graduates who are promoters of academic excellence in their future students.

Just the facts...

University of Arkansas at Pine Bluff
School of Education
1200 North University Drive
P.O. Box 4986
Pine Bluff, AR 71611
(870) 543-8256
Website: www.uapb.edu
Profile: Rural, Small, Co-Ed
UG Tuition: $70.00/cr. hr. in-state; $162.00/cr. hr. out-of-state
G Tuition: $84.00/cr. hr. in-state; $197.00/cr. hr. out-of-state
Off Campus Programs: No

Clinical Experiences

Field-based experiences create opportunities for candidates to develop effective working relationships and collaborative efforts with P-12 professionals. These experiences are sequenced so that candidates are involved in a variety of activities throughout their professional program of study. Candidates' responsibilities increase as they progress from early field experiences at the freshman level to a twelve-week student teaching experience.

Noteworthy

The University of Arkansas at Pine Bluff is a historically black land grant institution whose original mission was teacher education. The School of Education provides scholarships from the Arkansas Department of Higher Education, Alumni Scholarships, and a variety of scholarships from other sources. The University of Arkansas at Pine Bluff attracts students from all over the world. The diversity of students and faculty at the University of Arkansas at Pine Bluff serves to strengthen teacher candidates' exposure, involvement, and experience with many different cultures and racial and ethnic groups.

Teacher Preparation Program Information

The following programs are 4 year programs:
Early Childhood Education, Elementary Education, K-12 Education (Reading), Secondary Education (Agriculture, Art, Biology, Business, Chemistry, English/Language Arts, General Science, Mathematics, Physical Education, Social Studies, Trade & Industrial, Vocational Agriculture, Vocational Home Economics/Job Training)

The following programs are 5th year programs:
Elementary Education, Secondary Education (English, General Science, Mathematics, Physical Education, Social Studies)

University of Central Arkansas

The University of Central Arkansas has prepared teachers and other school personnel since 1907, when it was established as the Arkansas State Normal School to prepare teachers for the state. The College of Education seeks to ensure that graduates possess a strong background in the liberal arts and competence in the content and professional roles they plan to assume. Candidates' work, reflecting their professional and pedagogical knowledge, is kept in an electronic portfolio that is used for licensure purposes.

Just the facts...

University of Central Arkansas
College of Education
201 Donaghey Avenue
Conway, AR 72035
(501) 450-3175
Website: www.coe.uca.edu
Profile: Suburban, Medium, Co-Ed
UG Tuition: $129.50/cr. hr. in-state; $212.75/cr. hr. out-of-state
G Tuition: $145.00/cr. hr. in-state; $298.00/cr. hr. out-of-state
Off Campus Programs: No

Clinical Experiences

Clinical experiences are required in all programs beginning in the sophomore year. These experiences are divided into three levels that allow students to assume greater responsibilities prior to student teaching. Elementary and special education candidates have extended field experiences in professional development schools during their junior and senior years (a similar program is being developed for secondary education students). The college strives to place candidates in culturally diverse and rural, suburban, and urban schools.

Noteworthy

Two priorities of the college are recruiting and retaining minorities and integrating technology into the curriculum. An array of programs and services are available for minority students, including a five-week Summer Academy that serves as a "bridge" program for African American high school students entering the university. Two clinical instructors provide individual and group assistance to faculty and students in the use of technology. They maintain two computer classrooms, one drop-in computer laboratory, a state-of-the-art multimedia classroom, and a distance education facility.

Teacher Preparation Program Information

The following programs are 4 year programs:
Early Childhood Education, Elementary Education, K-12 Education (Art, Physical Education), Secondary Education (Biology, Business, Chemistry, English/Language Arts, General Science, Health, Mathematics, Physical Education, Physical Sciences, Physics, Social Studies, Vocational Marketing, Vocational Home Economics/Consumer Homemaking), Special Education (Mild Handicapped, Moderate and Profound Handicapped, Severe Emotional Disturbance)

The following programs are post-baccalaureate programs:
Early Childhood Education, Elementary Education, K-12 Education (Art, Physical Education), Secondary Education (Biology, Business, Chemistry, English/Language Arts, General Science, Health, Mathematics, Physical Education, Physical Sciences, Physics, Social Studies, Vocational Marketing, Vocational Home Economics/Consumer Homemaking), Special Education (Mild Handicapped, Moderate and Profound Handicapped, Severe Emotional Disturbance)

University of the Ozarks

The overall goal of the teacher education program at the University of the Ozarks is to graduate qualified, competent, and inclusive professional educators. This process begins by providing qualified candidates with a broad liberal arts education, advanced knowledge in one or more disciplines, and a comprehensive working knowledge of teaching and learning. Candidates then apply and refine their professional skills during a variety of structured field experiences.

Just the facts...

University of the Ozarks
Division of Education
415 College Avenue
Clarksville, AR 72830
(501) 979-1331
Website: www.ozarks.edu
Profile: Rural, Small, Co-Ed
UG Tuition: $3,875.00/semester
Off Campus Programs: No

Clinical Experiences

The field experience component of the teacher preparation program at the University of the Ozarks is designed to be the integrating thread that meshes theoretical and pedagogical knowledge into applied practice. All of the specialty areas within the program are highly field-based and include observation, tutorial, practica, and directed teaching experiences. Candidates complete a 60-hour practicum as juniors. Student teaching is a full semester for candidates in all licensure areas.

Noteworthy

A strong emphasis on field experience and on working with children from diverse backgrounds and with special needs has made Ozarks' education program a trendsetter among colleges and universities. In addition to P-12 licenses, teacher candidates can receive special education licensure, as well as coaching and reading endorsements. The performance-based curriculum is organized around a professional portfolio. The curriculum meets state standards which match INTASC guidelines. Graduates of the teacher education program leave Ozarks fully prepared to work with *all* children.

Teacher Preparation Program Information

The following programs are 4 year programs:

Early Childhood Education, K-12 Education (Art, Music, Physical Education), Middle School Education (English, Mathematics, Science, Social Studies), Secondary Education (Art, Biology, Business, English/Language Arts, Health, Mathematics, Physical Education, Social Studies), Special Education (Concurrent Licensure)

The following programs are post-baccalaureate programs:

Early Childhood Education, K-12 Education (Art, Music, Physical Education), Middle School Education (English, Mathematics, Science, Social Studies), Secondary Education (Art, Biology, Business, English/Language Arts, Health, Mathematics, Physical Education, Social Studies), Special Education (Concurrent Licensure)

California State University—Bakersfield

California State University–Bakersfield is designated as a Hispanic institution and provides opportunities for pre-professional and graduate preparation in education. The mission of the School of Education is to provide educational leadership to its increasingly diverse region. The university seeks to produce student-centered graduates who are (1) effective with students from diverse backgrounds; (2) able to apply and evaluate current research, pedagogy, and technology; and (3) committed to their continuous professional and personal development.

Just the facts...

California State University—Bakersfield
School of Education
Bakersfield, CA 93311-1099
(805) 664-2219
Website: www.csubak.edu/
Profile: Suburban, Medium, Co-Ed
UG Tuition: $651.00/quarter
G Tuition: $651.00/quarter
Off Campus Programs: Yes

Clinical Experiences

All teacher preparation programs require multiple kinds of experiences including work with students from diverse cultural and linguistic backgrounds. In some programs, teacher preparation takes place entirely within local elementary schools. Guidance is provided by both faculty from the university and faculty at the school site. Elementary education candidates have several supervised clinical experiences including tutoring, reading, and student teaching during two quarters. Candidates working in the professional development school are involved in supervised field experiences during all three quarters of their program. Secondary education candidates complete two quarters of student teaching.

Noteworthy

Programs in the School of Education prepare candidates to become teachers of second language learners and diverse populations. The School of Education is using technology in its programs to facilitate distance learning. There are various scholarships available through the Office of Financial Aid & Scholarships for students in School of Education programs. California's Assumption Program Loans for Education (APLE) and Cal-T grants are designed to encourage outstanding students to become teachers and serve in critical teacher shortage areas in California public elementary and secondary schools.

Teacher Preparation Program Information

The following programs are 4 year programs:
Blended 4 year liberal studies program with multiple subject credential

The following programs are post-baccalaureate programs:
Elementary Education, Secondary Education (Selected Majors), Special Education (Adaptive Physical Education, Developmental Disabilities/Handicaps, Learning Disability, Severe Behavioral Disabilities/Handicaps)

California State University—Dominguez Hills

California State University—Dominguez Hills prepares candidates to work with culturally and linguistically diverse students in urban environments. Candidates work toward (1) ensuring educational equity for all learners, (2) developing sensitivity toward and effectiveness with learners from diverse backgrounds, (3) learning the appropriate and creative uses of independent and collaborative experiential learning, (4) incorporating multicultural and global perspectives in their practice, (5) achieving personal growth through reflection and self-evaluation, (6) learning to critically analyze theory and research, (7) developing skills in assessing performance, and (8) achieving technological literacy.

Just the facts...

California State University—Dominguez Hills
School of Education
1000 East Victoria Street
Carson, CA 90747
(310) 243-3510
Website: www.csudh.edu
Profile: Urban, Large, Co-Ed
UG Tuition: $753.00/sem. in-state; $3,705.00/sem. out-of-state
G Tuition: $792.00/sem. in-state; $3,744.00/sem. out-of-state
Off Campus Programs: Yes

Clinical Experiences

Candidates work under the direction of one or more experienced teachers in an urban setting during their student teaching experience. Candidates participate in a classroom full-time for one semester and also have the support of a university supervisor and a seminar where student teaching problems are discussed and resolved. Candidates who are employed in the schools on emergency credentials receive support and supervision from university faculty for two semesters. Programs are available in partnership with local school districts to provide support for beginning teachers.

Noteworthy

Several scholarships are available for candidates during their student teaching semester in addition to other scholarships and a forgivable loan program. The university works very closely with school districts in the Los Angeles Basin and provides opportunities for teachers who have emergency credentials to obtain a basic credential while teaching full-time. The School of Education's Urban Learning Resources Center, Reading Center, and Computer Lab provide resources for both preservice and working teachers.

Teacher Preparation Program Information

The following programs are post-baccalaureate programs:

Elementary Education/Multiple Subjects Credential, K-12 Education, Secondary Education/Single Subject Credential (Art, English/ Language Arts, Health, Mathematics, Music, Physical Education, Sciences, Social Studies, Spanish)

California State University—Fresno

The School of Education and Human Development at California State University—Fresno is organized around the theme "Making a Difference in a Diverse Society: Leadership for a New Millenium." CSU—Fresno is committed to developing candidates' knowledge, skills, and values so that they may become educational leaders in a diverse and technologically complex society. Graduates enter the profession as teachers, administrators, counselors, and educational specialists. Teacher education programs include a B.A. degree in an academic subject and approximately 34 units of professional preparation which can be taken, in part, as electives toward the degree or as postbaccalaureate units.

Just the facts...

California State University—Fresno
School of Education & Human Development
5005 N. Maple Avenue
Fresno, CA 93740-8025
(209) 278-0210
Website: http://caracas.soehd.csufresno.edu/
Profile: Urban/rural, Large, Co-Ed
UG Tuition: $897.00/sem. in-state; $4,587.00/sem. out-of-state
G Tuition: $936.00/sem. in-state; $4,628.00/sem. out-of-state
Off Campus Programs: Yes

Clinical Experiences

Clinical experiences are carefully designed to effectively connect the university with area schools and communities. All teaching, specialist, and services credential programs contain substantial clinical and field components. Student teachers are supervised and supported by classroom master teachers and university personnel. Special supplementary conferences and workshops provide additional information to candidates on various topics. Past workshops and conferences have focused on community agencies, civic responsibility, and character education. Each student teacher is given a minimum of two teaching placements at different school sites.

Noteworthy

Faculty in the School of Education and Human Development are actively involved in many special projects that both enrich learning and strengthen linkages with the community. Examples of these programs include the Fresno Family Counseling Center, a school-based clinic for counseling; the Turning Points Academy, which involves 150 high school students on campus for one semester; the Early Education Center structured under the Reggio Emilia model; a Parent Power Project for support of families who have children with learning problems; and a Center for Educational Research and Services that provides students and faculty with special opportunities to conduct research.

Teacher Preparation Program Information

The following programs are 4 year programs:
Elementary Education (Multiple Subject Credential-Cross Cultural Language and Academic Development-CLAD)—in process of approval and planned for implementation in Fall 1999.

The following programs are post-baccalaureate programs:
Early Childhood Education-CLAD, Elementary Education-CLAD, K-12 Education-CLAD, Secondary Education-CLAD (Agriculture, Art, Biology, Business, Chemistry, English, English/ESL, English/Speech, English/Theater Arts, French, Geoscience, Home Economics, Industrial Technology, Kinesiology, Mathematics, Music, Physics, Social Studies, Spanish), Special Education (Mild/Moderate Disabilities, Moderate/Severe Disabilities)

California State University—Fullerton

CSU Fullerton aspires to combine the best qualities of teaching and research universities where actively engaged candidates, faculty, and staff work collaboratively to expand knowledge. Undergraduate and graduate programs integrate professional studies with preparation in the arts and sciences, and are grounded in a solid base of theory and research. Candidates in the Multiple Subjects Program advance through the program in cohorts, which allow groups of candidates to work closely with small faculty teams. Single Subject candidates take methods courses and seminars taught by specialists in academic departments as well as general education courses taught by education faculty.

Just the facts...

California State University—Fullerton
School of Human Development
800 North State College
Fullerton, CA 92634
(714) 278-3311
Website: http://hdcs.fullerton.edu
Profile: Urban, Large, Co-Ed
UG Tuition: $792.00/sem. in-state; $246.00/cr. hr. out-of-state
G Tuition: $792.00/sem. in-state; $246.00/cr. hr. out-of-state
Off Campus Programs: Yes

Clinical Experiences

All candidates engage in clinical experiences before entry and through each phase of their program. Multiple Subject, Single Subject, and Special Education candidates begin with a 30-hour field observation in their prerequisite coursework before progressing through two semesters of student teaching. Special Education student teachers complete a general education and special education assignment. The early childhood program includes student teaching in both infant/toddler and preschool settings. TESOL candidates wishing to teach EDL at the kindergarten through university levels are able to fulfill the student teaching component in their own classes or under the supervision of a master teacher.

Noteworthy

CSU Fullerton has received special awards for its Bilingual Cross-Cultural Language Academic Development certificate, Early Childhood Special Education specialist program, Master of Science in Education with a concentration in Computer Education, and its Center for Collaboration for Children. CSU Fullerton offers expanded programs for part-time candidates and a professional internship track for candidates already teaching in the public schools on an emergency basis.

Teacher Preparation Program Information

The following programs are 4 year programs:
Blended Teacher Education Program for Multiple Subject Candidates

The following programs are post-baccalaureate programs:
Multiple Subject Credential (Credential in Cross Cultural Language Academic Development/CLAD), Credential in Bilingual Cross Cultural Language Academic Development/BCLAD), Single Subject Credential (Art, Business, English, Foreign Languages, Life Sciences, Mathematics, Physical Education, Physical Sciences, Music/Instrumental, Music/Choral, Social Studies, Theater), Special Education (Early Childhood, Mild/Moderate Disabilities, Moderate/Severe Disabilities)

California State University—Hayward

CSU Hayward believes the preparation of teachers is an all-university responsibility. The School of Education and Allied Studies works to prepare collaborative leaders who are prepared to work in a highly technological and diverse world. All programs emphasize collaboration, equity and diversity, professional integrity, critical inquiry, and continuous improvement. Prospective elementary school teachers pursue an interdisciplinary Liberal Studies major. Future secondary teachers complete subject matter preparation programs in their chosen field.

Just the facts...

California State University—Hayward
School of Education
Hayward, CA 94542
(510) 885-3942
Website: www.edschool.csuhayward.edu
Profile: Suburban, Large, Co-Ed
UG Tuition: $373.00-$583.00/quarter unit in-state
G Tuition: $387.00-$609.00/quarter unit in-state
Foreign/non-resident tuition $164 per unit in addition to above fees.
Off Campus Programs: Yes

Clinical Experiences

Candidates for basic teaching credentials must successfully complete three quarters of field experience. Currently, 65 percent of candidates complete their field experience requirements while teaching under "internship credentials" (interns are the "teacher of record" in the classroom and earn salaries equivalent to other beginning teachers). All interns work closely with an Intern Support Teacher, who is a veteran teacher on-site. Multiple Subject student teachers complete three distinct assignments, working with different master teachers each quarter.

Noteworthy

Candidates are admitted and complete the program in cohorts of 30. Each cohort has a faculty leader who arranges field placements and mentors candidates. The cohort system provides excellent peer support for candidates. Partnerships have been established with several school districts. Candidates in partnership teams complete all courses at sites in one of the partner school districts. Most of these courses are team-taught by a university professor and a practicing classroom teacher.

Teacher Preparation Program Information

The following programs are post-baccalaureate programs:
Bilingual Teaching, Elementary Teaching, Secondary Teaching (English, Mathematics, Music, Physical Education, Science, Social Studies)

California State University—Los Angeles

The Charter School of Education at Cal State LA, the first "charter" school of education in the nation, is recognized as a premier urban school of education. Located on one of the most culturally diverse university campuses in the country, it is uniquely suited to meeting the new challenges created by the demographic, economic, and sociological shifts within today's public school systems. All of its programs emphasize inquiry, reflection, and professional practice. Graduates are prepared to intelligently use their knowledge of linguistic and cultural diversity to transform schools into successful learning environments.

Just the facts...

California State University, Los Angeles
Charter School of Education
5151 State University
Los Angeles, CA 90032
(323) 343-4300
Website: www.calstatela.edu/academic
Profile: Urban, Large, Co-Ed
UG Tuition: $363.00/quart. in-state; $164.00/cr. hr. out-of-state
G Tuition: $363.00/quart. in-state; $164.00/cr. hr. out-of-state
Off Campus Programs: No

Clinical Experiences

All programs in the Charter School require early and frequent field-based experiences planned to allow the candidate to gain experience and transfer theory into practice. Activities include observation and classroom participation at school sites, student teaching full-time for two quarters, clinical experiences under the supervision of teachers and practitioners on-site, and graduate field work for advanced credentials and master's degree programs. Carefully selected and trained university school supervisors collaborate to provide continuous support and feedback to candidates.

Noteworthy

The structure of the Charter School encourages innovation in curriculum and research. Noteworthy programs are the integrated Model Teacher Education Program, the Literacy Cluster focusing on improved teacher preparation in reading and the language arts, the Los Angeles Accelerated School that implements the Accelerated School Reform model developed by Henry Levin at Stanford University, and the Program Evaluation Research Collaborative. The university has a comprehensive Financial Aid Office and offers many scholarships; the Charter School also offers eighteen scholarships based on need and academic achievement.

Teacher Preparation Program Information

The following programs are 4 year programs:*
Multiple Subject Credential (teaching in K-12 self-contained classrooms), Single Subject Credential (teaching the following subjects in K-12 classrooms: Art, Biological Science, Chemistry, English, Foreign Languages, Geoscience, Health Science, Industrial & Technology Education, Mathematics, Music, Physics, Social Science), Special Education (Early Childhood, Mild/Moderate Disabilities, Moderate/Severe Disabilities, Physical & Health Impairments, Vision Impairments)

The following programs are 5th year programs:
Multiple Subject Credential (teaching in K-12 self-contained classrooms), Single Subject Credential (teaching the following subjects in K-12 classrooms: Art, Biological Science, Chemistry, English, Foreign Languages, Geoscience, Health Science, Industrial & Technology Education, Mathematics, Music, Physics, Social Science), Special Education (Early Childhood, Mild/Moderate Disabilities, Moderate/Severe Disabilities, Physical & Health Impairments, Vision Impairments)

*California is returning to undergraduate programs for teacher education. The 4 year programs listed above will be offered by January 2000.

California State University—Northridge

California State University—Northridge, which just celebrated its fortieth anniversary, is one of the largest teacher preparation institutions in California. The College of Education promotes reflection, critical thinking, and excellence in teaching through interdisciplinary studies in an inclusive learning community. Its graduates are well-educated persons who view themselves as lifelong learners and who are prepared to practice in an ever-changing, multicultural world. Graduates assume leadership and service roles in educational programs and institutions. The faculty is committed to excellence in teaching, scholarship, and collaboration with the community and professions.

Just the facts...

California State University—Northridge
School of Education
18111 Nordhoff Street
Northridge, CA 91330
(818) 677-2590
Website: www.csun.edu
Profile: Urban, Large, Co-Ed
UG Tuition: $753.00/sem. in-state; $164.00/cr. hr. out-of-state
G Tuition: $792.00/sem. in-state; $246.00/cr. hr. out-of-state
Off Campus Programs: Yes

Clinical Experiences

CSUN requires 45 hours of participation with school-age children in a formal situation prior to application for admission to the teacher preparation program. All courses include participation in classroom situations. Student teaching, under the guidance of an experienced mentor teacher, is the candidate's final clinical experience. Two student teaching assignments are required at different grade levels and with diverse student bodies. University supervisors regularly visit the student teacher's classroom not only to observe and evaluate, but also to assist and support the prospective teacher.

Noteworthy

California's Assumption Program Loans for Education (APLE) is available for persons completing a teacher preparation program. Graduates teaching for three years in either a teacher shortage area or in a low income area are eligible for up to $11,000 in loan forgiveness. CSUN has a number of intern and pre-intern programs to assist persons hired on emergency permits in connection with California's severe shortage of teachers. Technology is an important component of the teacher preparation programs. While all CSUN teacher preparation programs are designed as post-baccalaureate programs leading to licensure, it is possible with careful planning to obtain a bachelor's degree and a credential simultaneously.

Teacher Preparation Program Information

The following programs are 4 year programs:
K-12 Education (Art, Bilingual, ESL, Health, Physical Education), Secondary Education (English/Language Arts, French, German, Health, Mathematics, Music, Physical Education, Science, Social Studies, Spanish)

The following programs are post-baccalaureate programs:
Special Education (Adaptive Physical Education, Communication Disorders, Early Childhood, Gifted/Talented, Hearing Impaired, Mild Learning/Behavioral Disability, Moderate Needs)

The following programs are 5 year programs:
Elementary Education, Secondary Education (Art, Business, English/Language Arts, French, German, Health, Mathematics, Music, Physical Education, Science, Social Studies, Spanish)

The following programs are 5th year programs:
Elementary Education (Reading), Secondary Education (English/Language Arts, German, Mathematics, Science, Social Studies), Special Education (Early Childhood, Gifted/Talented, Speech/Language Disabilities)

California State University—San Marcos

The College of Education at CSUSM prepares candidates to (1) design and deliver effective instruction, (2) create learning environments that are specifically suited to his or her class, (3) take into account how children learn and show what they learn in a variety of ways, and (4) critically analyze curricula, instruction, and societal influences on teaching and learning. The faculty believe that teaching is an intellectual, ethical, political, and critically reflective endeavor. All candidates learn how to teach students successfully, with issues of learner diversity and first and second language learning emphasized throughout the curriculum.

Just the facts...

California State University—San Marcos
College of Education
San Marcos, CA 92096-0001
(760) 750-4311
Website: www.csusm.edu/coe/
Profile: Suburban, Medium, Co-Ed
UG Tuition: $753.00/semester full-time; $459/semester part-time
Off Campus Programs: No

Clinical Experiences

All CSUSM professional education programs are field-based and emphasize a variety of planned, early field experiences prior to advanced student teaching. Candidates work with experienced educators in schools throughout North San Diego County, as well as in South Riverside and South Orange Counties. A minimun of 45 hours of field experience is required for entry into teacher education programs. Student teaching places candidates in diverse school settings. Methods courses integrate coursework with field experiences.

Noteworthy

All professional education programs at CSUSM are cohort-based; students enter a program in cohort groups of 25 and complete the program together. This practice develops a learning community among candidates, and models professional practice in effective schools. The Distinguished Teacher in Residence program brings outstanding classroom teachers to the university to serve as teacher education faculty for rotating two-year terms. The education of diverse learners, including English language learners, is emphasized in all CSUSM teacher education programs.

Teacher Preparation Program Information

The following programs are post-baccalaureate programs:

Bilingual options are available for each program: Middle Level Education, Multiple Subjects/Elementary Education, Secondary Education (English, Mathematics, Science, Social Science, Spanish), Special Education (Concurrent and Stand Alone options)

California State University—Stanislaus

CSU Stanislaus is dedicated to the preparation of teachers and school service personnel who value diversity and multicultural education. The education unit includes basic programs to prepare Multiple Subject, CLAD (Crosscultural, Language, Academic Development), Bilingual CLAD, Special Education, and Single Subject Credential Program teacher candidates. The knowledge base in each program has a core that focuses on subject matter content, second language learning, and literacy. Bilingual CLAD candidates must be able to read, write, and speak English and either Spanish, Cambodian, Hmong, or Lao.

Just the facts...

California State University, Stanislaus
School of Education
801 West Monte Vista Avenue
Turlock, CA 95382
(209) 667-3145
Website: www.csustan.edu/acadprog/
Profile: Rural, Medium, Co-Ed
UG Tuition: $539.00/0-6 units; $854.50/7 or more units in-state
G Tuition: $556.50/0-6 units; $889.50/7 or more units out-of-state
Foreign/non-resident tuition $246 per unit in addition to above fees.
Off Campus Programs: Yes

Clinical Experiences

Field experiences are required in prerequisite and teacher preparation courses. The Single Subject Credential Program is field-based; candidates work in cohorts and spend an entire academic year at high school and middle school off-campus sites. Internships in which candidates teach in a school district while finishing credential requirements are available for Multiple Subject teacher candidates who demonstrate exceptional ability and experience. Student teachers experience directly the cultural, linguistic, ethnic, and socio-economic diversity of the region.

Noteworthy

A blended, or integrated, multiple subject credential program is planned to start in the fall of 1999. Teacher preparation will begin at the undergraduate level as a joint venture between the School of Education and the College of Arts, Letters, and Sciences. CSU Stanislaus has recently added internship components to its Multiple Subject CLAD/BCLAD and Administrative Services credential programs. Candidates for the M.A. in education may now complete a concentration in education technology. Other M.A. concentrations are education administration, elementary education, multilingual education, reading/language arts, school counseling, secondary education, and special education.

Teacher Preparation Program Information

The following programs are post-baccalaureate programs:
Multiple Subject/Elementary Education (Cross-Cultural Language Academic Development, Bilingual Cross-Cultural/Spanish, Bilingual Cross-Cultural/South East Asian), Single Subject/Secondary Education (Art, English, Mathematics, Modern Languages, Music, Physical Education, Science, Social Science)

The following programs are 5 year programs:
K-12 Education (Liberal Studies), Secondary Education (Art, English/Language Arts, Mathematics, Modern Languages, Music, Physical Education, Science, Social Science), Special Education (Mild/Moderate Disabilities, Moderate/Severe Disabilities)

Loyola Marymount University

Loyola Marymount University is a private Catholic University founded in the Jesuit and Marymount traditions. As a modern Catholic institution, LMU is faithful to the values of the Catholic tradition. As a university, LMU is committed to excellence in teaching and scholarship, and the free and unencumbered exchange of ideas. The School of Education emphasizes a student-centered collaborative environment where individuals are valued and respected, cultural responsiveness and social justice are promoted, theory and practice are integrated, emerging technologies are embraced, and the development of moral, intellectual, and responsible leaders is a priority.

Just the facts...

Loyola Marymount University
School of Education
7900 Loyola Boulevard
Los Angeles, CA 90045-8425
(310) 338-2863
Website: www.lmu.edu
Profile: Suburban, Medium, Co-Ed
UG Tuition: $8,551.00/semester
G Tuition: $500.00/credit hour
Off Campus Programs: No

Clinical Experiences

In teacher preparation programs, candidates are required to perform a series of classroom observations over several courses, eventually culminating in practice lessons and, finally, the student teaching experience. The semester-long student teaching experience includes both seminars and weekly observations by the university supervisor. Student teaching sites represent a wide diversity of cultures and are carefully reviewed to meet the individual needs and characteristics of the candidates, as well as to meet program goals.

Noteworthy

LMU places a high priority on the personal relationship between faculty and candidates and on student support organizations. Technology is also a strong component of LMU's programs. Many opportunities are available for need-based financial aid, academic merit scholarships, and targeted grants. Programs include the Los Angeles Collaborative for Teacher Excellence grant for math and science teaching, a federal grant that supports candidates pursuing special education teaching, a Catholic educator's grant, and an assumption loan program for candidates committed to working with students in inner cities and underprivileged areas.

Teacher Preparation Program Information

The following programs are 4 year programs:
Elementary Education (K-6), Secondary Education (English/Language Arts, French, Mathematics, Social Studies, Spanish), Special Education (Mild/Moderate Disabilities)

The following programs are post-baccalaureate programs:
Elementary Education (K-6), Secondary Education (English/Language Arts, French, Mathematics, Social Studies, Spanish), Special Education (Mild/Moderate Disabilities)

The following programs are 5 year programs:
Special Education (Mild/Moderate Disabilities)

The following programs are 5th year programs:
Special Education (Mild/Moderate Disabilities), Specialized Programs (Bilingual/Bicultural Education, Child and Adolescent Literacy, General Education, MAT programs, TESOL/Multicultural Education)

San Diego State University

The College of Education at San Diego State University has prepared teachers for over 100 years, and has recently made a priority of responding to the need to increase the number of teachers for the nation's schools. It places emphasis on the preparation of educators and other human development personnel for culturally and linguistically diverse community and school settings. The college is involved in research and scholarship efforts contributing to the field and provides public service and technical assistance to the local community and local agencies. In addition to initial teacher preparation programs, San Diego State University offers a wide range of master's and doctoral degrees.

Just the facts...

San Diego State University
College of Education
5300 Campanile Drive
San Diego, CA 92182-1154
(619) 594-6091
Website: www.sdsu.edu
Profile: Urban, Large, Co-Ed
UG Tuition: $612.00/semester in-state
G Tuition: $633.00/semester in-state
(Out-of-state students add an additional $246.00/credit hour)
Off Campus Programs: Yes

Clinical Experiences

Prospective candidates are required to complete an early field experience in their area of study in an ethnically diverse classroom. Full-time candidates are normally placed in cohort programs at professional development schools. Student teaching is required during two semesters and usually involves two different placements. On-site master teachers and university faculty provide supervision. Candidates receive both individual supervision and meet in small group seminars that focus on the student teaching experience.

Noteworthy

The College of Education has been a finalist for or named one of the three most distinguished programs in teacher education in North America by the Association of Teacher Educators four times in ten years. Two of the last seven National Teachers of the Year are graduates of the College of Education. For over 25 years, teacher education programs have been site-based at local schools. The College of Education offers credential programs in flexible formats to meet the needs of part-time students and interns.

Teacher Preparation Program Information

The following programs are 4 year programs:
Vocational Education (for secondary and post-secondary education programs)

The following programs are post-baccalaureate programs:
K-12 Education (Art, Biology, Business, Chemistry, French, Geosciences, German, Latin, Mathematics, Music, Physical Education, Physics, Social Science, Spanish), Special Education (Adaptive Physical Education, Early Childhood, Hearing Impaired, Mild/Moderate Handicapped, Moderate & Severe Disabilities, Physical & Health Impairments)

San Francisco State University

Each department of the College of Education at San Francisco State University has a unique focus, but each shapes its curricula to prepare candidates to work in a multicultural world and to engage in innovative practice. All programs are based on excellence in teaching and clinical services, and a commitment to research and scholarship focused on the integration of services to schools and community agencies. The College of Education prepares candidates to serve as socially committed educational leaders and advocates, to contribute to the knowledge base in the profession, particularly in the area of urban education, and to use technology effectively to improve education and community services.

Just the facts...

San Francisco State University
College of Education
1600 Holloway Avenue
San Francisco, CA 94132-4158
(415) 338-2687
Website: www.sfsu.edu/educ
Profile: Urban, Large, Co-Ed
UG Tuition: $991.00/sem. in-state; $1,237.00/sem. out-of-state
G Tuition: $991.00/sem. in-state; $1,237.00/sem. out-of-state
Off Campus Programs: Yes

Clinical Experiences

All teacher education programs at SFSU have strong school-based components. Students actively participate in local schools from their first semester of enrollment. In some instances, university courses are taught at school sites. Student teaching assignments are carefully made based on candidate needs. Placements include urban, inner city, and suburban sites.

Noteworthy

Strong components of SFSU's teacher preparation programs include second language acquisition and strategies for working with children whose first language is not English. The majority of SFSU students work, and there are opportunities for financial aid and student loans. A variety of alternative programs are offered, including programs for re-entry students and teachers who need to complete additional coursework to be fully credentialed.

Teacher Preparation Program Information

The following programs are post-baccalaureate programs:

K-12 Education (Art, Chinese, Music, Physical Education, Spanish), Middle School Education, Secondary Education (Art, Biology, Chemistry, Consumer and Family Science/Home Economics, English/Language Arts, General Science, Mathematics, Physical Education, Physics, Science, Social Studies), Special Education (Adaptive Physical Education, Developmental Disabilities/Handicaps, Early Childhood, Hearing Impaired, Learning Disability, Multiple Disabilities/Handicaps, Physical Disabilities/Handicaps, Severe Behavioral Disabilities/Handicaps)

The following programs are 5th year programs:

Early Childhood Education, Elementary Education (Language Arts, Mathematics), K-12 Education (Art, Chinese, Music, Physical Education, Spanish), Middle School Education, Secondary Education (Art, Biology, Chemistry, Consumer and Family Science/Home Economics, English/Language Arts, General Science, Mathematics, Physical Education, Physics, Science, Social Studies), Special Education (Adaptive Physical Education, Developmental Disabilities/Handicaps, Early Childhood, Hearing Impaired, Learning Disability, Multiple Disabilities/Handicaps, Physical Disabilities/Handicaps, Severe Behavioral Disabilities/Handicaps, Speech/Language Disabilities, Visually Impaired)

San Jose State University

The College of Education at San Jose State University prepares well qualified professionals for careers in teaching, school administration, special education, and instructional technology. There are many ways to earn a teaching credential at San Jose State. Students may choose an integrated four-year program, a traditional fifth year of study and field experience, on-site internships, or field-based collaborative programs. San Jose State also offers a master's degree for educational professionals and students with long-term career goals who plan to earn a doctoral degree.

Just the facts...

San Jose State University
College of Education
One Washington Square
San Jose, CA 95192-0071
(408) 924-3600
Website: www.sjsu.edu
Profile: Urban, Large, Co-Ed
UG Tuition: $1,008.00/semester in-state
G Tuition: $792.00/semester in-state
Out-of-State UG & G Tuition $1,008.00 + ($246.00 x num. of units)
Off Campus Programs: No

Clinical Experiences

The standard credential program requires one semester of student teaching and classroom experiences. The internship option is a two-year, full-time, paid internship. This program gives the prospective teacher a beginning teacher's salary and full responsibility in the classroom in a supportive, team-oriented atmosphere. In partnership with the schools, San Jose State has developed field-based experiences for the prospective teacher. Other experiences include a newly developed, innovative science and math education program, and school redesign and systemic reform projects designed to improve the quality of education for all students (especially minority and non-English speaking students).

Noteworthy

The College of Education offers state-of-the-art computer labs, software, and equipment. Computer instruction designed for teachers is offered through the instructional technology department. San Jose State offers evening, weekend, and on-line courses. The College of Education actively recruits students from minority and economically disadvantaged populations. San Jose State offers BCLAD (bilingual culture, language, and academic development) credentials in Vietnamese, Spanish, and Chinese. A variety of scholarships, tuition assistance programs, forgiveable loans, and stipends are available. Continued professional development is enhanced through San Jose State's many certificate programs.

Teacher Preparation Program Information

The following programs are 4 year programs:
Child Development, Creative Arts Education, Environmental Studies Education, Liberal Studies Education, Natural Science Education, Social Science Education

The following programs are post-baccalaureate programs:
Deaf Education, Multiple Subject CLAD (Culture, Language, and Academic Development), Multiple Subject BCLAD (Chinese, Spanish, Vietnamese), Multiple Subject Learning Handicapped Program, Special Education (Mild/Moderate Disabilities, Moderate/Severe Disabilities)

The following programs are 5 year programs:
Child Development

University of the Pacific

The University of the Pacific is the oldest chartered university in California. The mission of the Bernerd School of Education is to prepare thoughtful, reflective professionals for service to diverse populations. Faculty direct their efforts toward researching the present and future needs of schools and the community and fostering intellectual and ethical development through personalized learning experiences. The programs emphasize the developmental process of learning how to be a thoughtful teacher. The university encourages candidates to begin their freshman year in a program combining bachelor's degree study and teaching credential coursework.

Just the facts...

University of the Pacific
Bernerd School of Education
3601 Pacific Avenue
Stockton, CA 95211
(209) 946-2683
Website: www.uop.edu
Profile: Urban, Medium, Co-Ed
UG Tuition: $9,500.00/semester
G Tuition: $594.00/credit hour
Off Campus Programs: Yes

Clinical Experiences

Candidates complete either sixteen weeks of student teaching in districts in Stockton or paid internships with local districts for a full school year. Candidates in the Multiple Subject (elementary teaching) program can learn in one of seven professional development school sites. Candidates begin field-based experiences in the sophomore year and can, with careful planning, complete their bachelor's degree and preliminary credential in four years. Strong clinical experiences are also a part of the Single Subject (secondary teaching) program.

Noteworthy

New funding from the state legislature provides Cal Grants and assumption of loan opportunities for teacher candidates from California. Undergraduate financial aid includes scholarships, grants, California grants, work-study, and/or loans. The School of Education awards a limited number of Project 30 scholarships to new undergraduates.

Teacher Preparation Program Information

The following programs are 4 year programs:
Elementary Education (Elementary Education K-6), K-12 Education (Bilingual), Secondary Education (English/Language Arts, Mathematics, Music, Physical Education, Science, Social Studies, Spanish), Special Education (Communication Disorders)

The following programs are post-baccalaureate programs:
Special Education (Adaptive Physical Education, Learning Disability, Mental Retardation, Mild Learning/Behavioral Disability, Moderate Needs, Severe Behavioral Disabilities/Handicaps)

The following programs are 5 year programs:
Elementary Education (Elementary Education K-6), K-12 Education (Bilingual), Secondary Education (English/Language Arts, Mathematics, Music, Physical Education, Science, Social Studies, Spanish), Special Education (Learning Disability, Mental Retardation, Mild Learning/Behavioral Disability, Moderate Needs, Severe Behavioral Disabilities/Handicaps, Speech/Language Disabilities)

The following programs are 5th year programs:
Special Education (Communication Disorders, Adaptive Physical Education, Learning Disability, Mental Retardation, Mild Learning/Behavioral Disability, Moderate Needs, Severe Behavioral Disabilities/Handicaps, Speech/Language Disabilities)

Adams State College

Nestled between two rugged mountain ranges at an altitude of 7,500 feet, Adams State College is located in the largest alpine valley in North America. It is the only institution in all of southern and western Colorado to offer master's degrees and endorsement programs in teacher education and school counseling. ASC has a strong and clearly defined rural mission. With this in mind, an underlying theme of programs in the School of Education is access to education for all. ASC has the highest rate of graduation for minorities of all colleges in the state.

Just the facts...

Adams State College
School of Education
210 Richardson Hall
Alamosa, CO 81102
(719) 587-7936
Website: www.adams.edu
Profile: Rural, Small, Co-Ed
UG Tuition: $75.00/cr. hr. in-state; $280.00/cr. hr. out-of-state
G Tuition: $90.00/cr. hr. in-state; $336.00/cr. hr. out-of-state
Off Campus Programs: Yes

Clinical Experiences

The faculty believe that realistic experiences in a variety of K-12 settings are a critical part of teacher preparation. These experiences begin early in the candidate's program, as ASC believes that potential teachers should have an opportunity to practice the art and science of teaching as they evaluate their own interest in and fitness for the profession. Most student teachers at ASC are supervised by full-time faculty in the Department of Teacher Education. Students are usually placed in schools within the San Luis Valley, although provisions are made for placements elsewhere. The student teaching experience is a full semester (fifteen weeks) in duration.

Noteworthy

Technological innovation and distance education are important components of the teacher education programs. ASC will be offering more courses in the future via Internet and supported by CD-ROM and other technologies. With assistance from various academic departments, the School of Education orchestrates professional development programs and courses for thousands of teachers in Colorado and neighboring states. The largest project on the horizon for teacher education is the building of a technologically sophisticated, public elementary school in the heart of the ASC campus. Adams State College expects to fully implement a field-based elementary program by the fall of 2000.

Teacher Preparation Program Information

The following programs are post-baccalaureate programs:
Early Childhood Education, Elementary Education, K-12 Education (Bilingual, ESL), Secondary Education, Special Education (Moderate Needs)

Colorado State University

The School of Education at Colorado State University offers initial teacher endorsement areas emphasizing secondary preparation (grades 7-12), with K-12 programs in art, music, and physical education. Colorado State University is the only state institution in Colorado that provides vocational teacher licensing and credentialing programs. All programs are based on the idea that the teacher is a facilitator of student success, which reflects the faculty's belief that the educator's role has changed from that of a mere presenter of information to one as a facilitator of the total learning process.

Just the facts...

Colorado State University
School of Education
209 Education Building
Fort Collins, CO 80523-1588
(970) 491-5292
Website: www.colostate.edu
Profile: Suburban, Large, Co-Ed
UG Tuition: $1,467.00/sem. in-state; $5,078.00/sem. out-of-state
G Tuition: $1,638.00/sem. in-state; $5,283.00/sem. out-of-state
Off Campus Programs: No

Clinical Experiences

Field experiences are infused throughout the curricula. Supervision takes place under the direction of qualified university and clinical faculty. Candidates must document 20 hours of educational contact with school-aged children before they are admitted to the teacher education program. Then, candidates participate in a series of planned and supervised field experiences which are integrated into the coursework. All candidates participate in a professional development school experience as an essential component of their instructional methods and assessment course. Student teaching is a full-time, semester-long experience.

Noteworthy

Education faculty at CSU are engaged in professional development schools at five Colorado high schools, including an alternative school. Faculty involvement in these schools ensures that the teacher preparation program is grounded in "real-world" practice. Colorado State University is a member of the National Network for Educational Renewal and the Colorado Partnership for Educational Renewal. CSU offers Project Promise, a program for non-traditional, older candidates who plan to teach in the areas of math, science, social studies, and English. Annually, 20 candidates are admitted into Project Promise.

Teacher Preparation Program Information

The following programs are 4 year programs:

K-12 Education (Art, Music, Physical Education), Secondary Education (Agriculture, Biology, Biology/Natural Resources, Business, Chemistry, Consumer & Family Studies, English, French, General Sciences, Geology, German, Mathematics, Marketing, Physics, Social Studies, Spanish, Speech/Theatre, Technology, Trade & Industry, Adult Technical Education)

The following programs are post-baccalaureate programs:

K-12 Education (Art, Music, Physical Education), Secondary Education (Agriculture, Biology, Biology/Natural Resources, Business, Chemistry, Consumer & Family Studies, English, French, General Sciences, Geology, German, Mathematics, Marketing, Physics, Social Studies, Spanish, Speech/Theatre, Technology, Trade & Industry, Adult Technical Education)

The following programs are 5th year programs:

K-12 Education (Art, Music, Physical Education), Secondary Education (Agriculture, Biology, Biology/Natural Resources, Business, Chemistry, Consumer & Family Studies, English, French, General Sciences, Geology, German, Mathematics, Marketing, Physics, Social Studies, Spanish, Speech/Theatre, Technology, Trade & Industry, Adult Technical Education)

Metropolitan State College of Denver

Since 1971, the Metropolitan State College of Denver has been a comprehensive, baccalaureate degree-granting, urban college that offers arts and sciences and professional and business courses to a diverse student population. The faculty of the education program strive to provide teacher candidates with every possible opportunity for success. All courses and field experiences expose candidates to a wide variety of theories, models, and practices, helping candidates to both develop their decision making skills as teachers and to work with a wide range of students in a broad spectrum of settings.

Just the facts...

Metropolitan State College of Denver
Department of Teacher Education and Cert.
Campus Box 8
P. O. Box 173362
Denver, CO 80217-3362
(303) 556-2978
Website: www.mscd.edu
Profile: Urban, Large, Co-Ed
UG Tuition: $69.90/credit hour
UG Tuition: $286.40/credit hour
Off Campus Programs: No

Clinical Experiences

Candidates must move through four "gates" intended to monitor their progress: provisional admission, formal admission, eligibility for student teaching, and recommendation for licensure. Candidates are guided through this process by campus advisors, the Director of Clinical Services, and student teaching supervisors. Candidates are placed in early field experiences prior to student teaching. MSCD has partnerships with selected public schools that serve as sites for field-based experiences. A minimum of thirteen weeks is required for student teaching.

Noteworthy

The Education Resource Center supports students and faculty in the teacher education programs with a state-of-the-art computer laboratory, audio-visual resources, and other materials for coursework and field experiences. Metropolitan's Child Development Center is a preschool laboratory that serves as a training facility for candidates enrolled in early childhood and other educational programs. The Teachers for Colorado Program, a collaborative initiative with surrounding school districts, provides scholarship and support services to minority students who wish to become teachers.

Teacher Preparation Program Information

The following programs are 4 year programs:
Early Childhood Education, Elementary Education, K-12 Education (Art, Music, Physical Education), Secondary Education (Art, Biology, English/Language Arts, French, German, Industrial Arts, Mathematics, Physical Education, Science, Social Studies, Spanish, Speech), Special Education (Moderate Needs)

The following programs are post-baccalaureate programs:
Early Childhood Education, Elementary Education, K-12 Education (Art, Music, Physical Education), Secondary Education (Art, Biology, English/Language Arts, French, German, Industrial Arts, Mathematics, Physical Education, Science, Social Studies, Spanish, Speech), Special Education (Moderate Needs)

University of Colorado at Boulder

The UCB teacher education program provides qualified students with preparation in liberal arts, academic disciplines, and professional knowledge. The program focuses on the nature of schools and their communities and knowledge of teaching and learning through coursework and field experiences designed to prepare candidates for the increasingly complex demands of teaching in a diverse society. The program emphasizes research-based approaches to teaching and learning, multiculturalism, education equity, partnerships with local schools, and professionalism. Graduates are reflective thinkers, effective decision makers, and enthusiastic collaborators.

Just the facts...

University of Colorado At Boulder
School of Education
Boulder, CO 80309-0249
(303) 492-6937
Website: www.colorado.edu
Profile: Suburban, Large, Co-Ed
UG Tuition: $1,200.00/sem. in-state; $7,500.00/sem. out-of-state
G Tuition: $1,700.00/sem. in-state; $7,500.00/sem. out-of-state
Off Campus Programs: Yes

Clinical Experiences

Field experiences provide practical applications of course content and consist of both early practica and student teaching. Practica are an integral part of all required education courses and involve placements in community and school settings. Each placement requires four to eight hours of work in the field each week. Student teaching requires a full-day, full-time commitment in a school for a full semester. University personnel monitor candidate performance in practica and student teaching experiences. Each candidate must complete one field experience in a school with a diverse student population.

Noteworthy

Noteworthy programs include the teacher education scholarship program (fifteen annual awards totaling over $9,000), the K-12 Partnership in Education Program (for preservice, novice, and experienced teacher preparation), the Professional Enrichment Program (for experienced teachers wishing to obtain a master's degree integrating research and practice), the Partner Schools Project (providing university/school collaboration in the creation of education renewal), and the BUENO Center for Multicultural Education (providing research, training, and service projects emphasizing cultural pluralism in universities, schools, and other agencies in the Rocky Mountain region).

Teacher Preparation Program Information

The following programs are 4 year programs:
Elementary Education, K-12 Education (Music), Secondary Education (English/Language Arts, French, German, Italian, Japanese, Latin, Mathematics, Russian, Science, Social Studies, Spanish)

The following programs are post-baccalaureate programs:
Elementary Education, K-12 Education (Music), Secondary Education (English/Language Arts, French, German, Italian, Japanese, Latin, Mathematics, Russian, Science, Social Studies, Spanish)

The following programs are 5th year programs:
Elementary Education, Secondary Education (English/Language Arts, Mathematics, Science, Social Studies)

University of Colorado at Colorado Springs

The University of Colorado at Colorado Springs is one of four campuses in the University of Colorado system. CU-Colorado Springs emphasizes a broad range of liberal arts and sciences, and provides professional and graduate programs. CU-Colorado Springs is the system's "growth campus"—in the past two years, the university has opened residence halls, a state-of-the-art classroom building, and a new family development center. The School of Education, located in newly constructed facilities, offers teacher, principal, and administrator licensure and graduate programs in curriculum and instruction, counseling and human services, educational leadership, and special education.

Just the facts...

University of Colorado at Colorado Springs
School of Education
Columbine Hall 3023
1420 Austin Bluffs Pkwy.
Colorado Springs, CO 80918
(719) 262-4996
Website: www.uccs.edu/~educatio
Profile: Urban, Medium, Co-Ed
UG Tuition: $92.00/cr. hr. in-state; $364.00/cr. hr. out-of-state
G Tuition: $121.00/cr. hr. in-state; $420.00/cr. hr. out-of-state
Off Campus Programs: No

Clinical Experiences

Each program offered by the School of Education utilizes field experiences in local schools and community settings. The community offers opportunities for teacher candidates to interact with ethnically and culturally diverse populations as well as within urban, suburban, and rural settings. The initial teacher preparation programs require early field experiences so that prospective teachers can apply their experiences to the theories and methods of teaching.

Noteworthy

The School of Education delivers the only university-based alternative licensure program in the state. This program provides unique avenues to the teaching profession for prospective students with unique life experiences. In addition, the School of Education offers initial licensure for special education teachers at the undergraduate level as part of a cooperative degree program with the College of Letters, Arts, and Sciences. Curriculum and instruction graduate programs include educational and corporate computing, reading, and gifted and talented education.

Teacher Preparation Program Information

The following programs are 4 year programs:
Distributed Studies/Special Education

The following programs are post-baccalaureate programs:
Elementary Education, Secondary Education (English, Mathematics, Science, Social Studies, Spanish), Special Education (Moderate Needs, Severe Needs/Affective, Severe Needs/Cognitive)

The following programs are 5th year programs:
Elementary Education, Secondary Education (English, Mathematics, Science, Social Studies, Spanish)

University of Colorado at Denver

Degree and licensing programs in the University of Colorado at Denver's School of Education prepare candidates for leadership roles in professional practice. The education curriculum has been developed through the study of the responsibilities of practicing education professionals, and the knowledge and skills that graduates will need for outstanding performance in their professional roles. Candidates acquire expertise in planning, organizing, motivating, and supporting learning throughout the community. Graduates foster innovation and change within learning organizations.

Just the facts...

University of Colorado at Denver
School of Education
Campus Box 106
P. O. Box 173364
Denver, CO 80217-3364
(303) 556-4387
Website: http://soe.cudenver.edu
Profile: Urban, Large, Co-Ed
G Tuition: $196.00/cr. hr. in-state; $739.00/cr. hr. out-of-state
Off Campus Programs: Yes

Clinical Experiences

Most teacher candidates seeking initial teacher licensure are full-time and all begin as a cohort in January, taking courses that require concurrent structured observations in schools. During the following school year, they complete three residencies in partner schools. The first and second residencies occur in the fall for two days per week and the third residency occurs during the spring for four days per week. By the end of the spring semester, teacher candidates have assumed roles as scholars, instructors, student advocates, professionals, and leaders, and are licensed. Candidates then complete ten credit hours during their first and/or second year of teaching, fulfilling the requirements for the master's degree.

Noteworthy

The graduate initial teacher education program is offered in collaboration with fourteen partner schools at the high school, middle school, and elementary school levels. School of Education faculty members spend a day per week in these schools to fulfill four partner school functions: teacher preparation, professional development, exemplary education, and research and inquiry into problems of practice in the schools. UCD is a member of the National Network for Educational Renewal. Out-of-state students may enroll in an off-campus program and pay in-state tuition.

Teacher Preparation Program Information

The following programs are 5th year programs:

Elementary Education, Secondary Education (English, Foriegn Language, Mathematics, Science, Social Studies)

University of Northern Colorado

The State of Colorado has designated UNC as its primary institution for the preparation of educators at the undergraduate and graduate levels. Teacher preparation at UNC is a collaborative effort, involving faculty from the Colleges of Education, Arts and Sciences, Health and Human Services, and Performing and Visual Arts, and educators in P-12 partner schools. All teacher candidates complete an academic major in a liberal arts and sciences discipline, along with an innovative professional licensure program and a broad general studies program. Candidates are also prepared to use multimedia technology in their teaching through award-winning courses in educational technology.

Clinical Experiences

Candidates work under the supervision of UNC faculty in 24 partner schools in and near Greeley throughout their program of study. Many education courses are taught in the schools, with UNC faculty assisted by master teachers. Continuous field experiences begin as early as the sophomore year and no later than the first semester of the junior year, with candidates working in school settings from two to three days per week. Experiences in UNC's partner schools assist candidates in their transition from novices to licensed teachers. The program of study concludes with a one-semester, full-time student teaching experience under the joint supervision of a master teacher and a university professor.

Just the facts...

University of Northern Colorado
College of Education
Greeley, CO 80639
(970) 351-2817
Website: www.edtech.unco.edu
Profile: Small City, Large, Co-Ed
UG Tuition: $983.50/sem. in-state; $4,498.50/sem. out-of-state
G Tuition: $1,168.50/sem. in-state; $4,789.00/sem. out-of-state
Off Campus Programs: Yes

Noteworthy

UNC faculty are active nationally, and are in touch with the reality of P-12 schools. Education programs involve faculty from the liberal arts and sciences disciplines and the teacher education faculty who work with teacher candidates and P-12 school personnel, and who are involved in the development of standards and assessments for P-12 education. Advanced technology resources are provided; e-mail and Internet access is available from residence halls and numerous campus computer labs. Several scholarship programs are limited to teacher candidates. UNC sponsors several minority teacher recruitment and support initiatives.

Teacher Preparation Program Information

The following programs are 4 year programs:
Elementary Education, Middle School Education, P-12 Education (Art, Music, Physical Education), Secondary Education (Biology, Chemistry, Drama, Earth Science, English/Language Arts, French, Geography, German, History, Mathematics, Physics, Social Science, Spanish, Speech), Special Education

The following programs are post-baccalaureate programs:
Elementary Education, Middle School Education

The following programs are 5th year programs:
Special Education (Moderate Needs)

Central Connecticut State University

Central Connecticut State University, the oldest public institution of higher education in Connecticut, was established in 1849 to prepare teachers for Connecticut's schools. Its founder, Henry Bernard, later became the first U.S. Commissioner of Education. Central Connecticut State prepares teachers who know their subject matter and pedagogy, have the capacity to be leaders, and have the knowledge to develop positive learning communities in diverse and inclusive classrooms and schools.

Just the facts...

Central Connecticut State University
School of Education and Professional Studies
1615 Stanley Street
New Britain, CT, 06050
(860) 832-2101
Website: wwwse.ccsu.ctstateu.edu
Profile: Urban, Medium, Co-Ed
UG Tuition: 1,835.00/sem. in-state; $4,589.00/sem. out-of-state
G Tuition: $2,069.00/sem. in-state; $4,811.00/sem. out-of-state
Off-Campus Programs: No

Clinical Experiences

Clinical experiences provide candidates with numerous opportunities to observe, study, and practice in diverse settings and to hold leadership positions. Early experiences include service at community agencies, school-based observations, and work with individual students. Candidates work with individual students and in small group situations in regular classrooms and with special needs students who have been included in the classroom. Later field experiences focus on working in whole class situations teaching in a discipline (eg., literacy, math, science). Student teachers are expected to become involved in the school's learning community and to demonstrate collaborative and leadership skills.

Noteworthy

Teacher candidates have field experiences each semester of the four-semester, cohort-group professional program. Most field experiences are in schools that form the university's Network of Professional Development Schools. Students take technology coursework in the School of Education's recently constructed Center for Innovation in Teaching and Technology. Portfolio development tied to INTASC standards form the basis for admission and graduation from the program. The School of Education has highly developed minority recruitment initiatives, and is a member of the Urban Network for Improving Teacher Education and the Holmes Partnership.

Teacher Preparation Program Information

The following programs are 4 year programs:
Early Childhood Education, Elementary Education, K-12 Education (Art, Music, Physical Education, Technology Education), Middle Level Education, Secondary Education (Biology, Chemistry, Earth Science, English, French, General Science, German, History/Social Studies, Italian, Mathematics, Physics, Spanish)

The following programs are post baccalaureate programs:
Early Childhood Education, Elementary Education (K-6, Urban Strand), K-12 Education (Art, Music, Physical Education, Technology Education), Middle Level Education, Secondary Education (Biology, Chemistry, Earth Science, English, French, General Science, German, History/Social Studies, Italian, Mathematics, Physics, Spanish)

The following programs are 5th year programs:
Elementary Education, K-12 Education (TESOL)

University of Connecticut

The University of Connecticut's School of Education is an institution of researchers, teachers, and students devoted to advancing and transmitting knowledge, and translating research into practice. The Integrated Bachelor's/Master's program ensures that (1) the bachelor's and master's degrees are strongly linked, (2) all candidates take a set of core courses, (3) all candidates have diverse clinical experiences, (4) the core courses, clinical experiences, and seminars are linked and complementary, and (5) coursework focusing on grade level and content-specific pedagogy has been designed to emphasize the interdisciplinary nature of knowledge.

Just the facts...

University of Connecticut
School of Education
249 Glenbrook Road
Storrs, CT 06269-2064
(860) 486-3813
Website: www.education.uconn.edu
Profile: Suburban, Large, Co-Ed
UG Tuition: $2,141.00/sem. in-state; $6,528.00/sem. out-of-state
G Tuition: $2,559.00/sem. in-state; $6,649.00/sem. out-of-state
New England Regional Student Program: UG $3,212.00/sem. G $3,839.00/sem.
Off Campus Programs: No

Clinical Experiences

Over the course of the Integrated Bachelor's/Master's (IB/M) program, candidates complete the equivalent of six semesters of clinical experiences. Each semester, candidates are also enrolled in a small seminar with other candidates who are at the same phase in their IB/M program and who are working in the same school district during their clinical experiences. In these seminars, candidates are expected to talk and write about what they are doing and learning from their placements, and how their field experience relates to their university coursework.

Noteworthy

Professional Development Schools (PDS) and Partner Schools (PS) play an important role in the IB/M program at the University of Connecticut. The PDS/PS are the school districts in which all of the candidate's clinical experiences take place, and include rural, suburban, and urban school environments. The PDS/PS are committed to working collaboratively with the University of Connecticut in the simultaneous renewal of schools and teacher education. The School of Education at the University of Connecticut recently received a gift of 21 million dollars. The donor, Raymond Neag, is an alumnus of the university. This gift is the largest of its kind in the nation.

Teacher Preparation Program Information

The following programs are 5 year programs:
Elementary Education, K-12 Education (Agriculture, Bilingual, French, German, Music, Spanish), Secondary Education (Biology, Chemistry, Earth Science, English/Language Arts, General Science, History /Social Studies, Mathematics, Physics), Special Education

University of Hartford

The University of Hartford's professional educator preparation programs encourage candidates to examine the ways in which they make decisions and to increase both the quantity and quality of their sources of understanding. The university is committed to integrated services for children and families, and believes that the educators of the future will have to work in interdisciplinary teams. Toward that end, candidates from all programs in the college come together for some of their courses in order to appreciate one another's roles and to consider together how to solve some of the problems facing children and families.

Just the facts...

The University of Hartford
College of Education, Nursing and Health Professions
200 Bloomfield Avenue
West Hartford, CT 06117-1599
(860) 768-4520
Website: www.hartford.edu
Profile: Suburban, Medium, Co-Ed
UG Tuition: $8,190.00/semester
G Tuition: $265.00/credit hour
Off Campus Programs: No

Clinical Experiences

Undergraduates begin work in the field during their first semester. Graduate students are given assignments and projects in their courses that take them into the field as well. Field experiences are always connected to course content. Student teaching hours exceed the minimum required by the state, and are accompanied by a seminar. Candidates can work in urban, rural, and suburban settings, and benefit from the university's professional development school relationships with several area schools.

Noteworthy

The University of Hartford offers programs leading to dual licensure in elementary and special education, and in both segments of early childhood education (Birth - K and N - 3). Faculty and candidates are heavily involved in the community. The university has a formal partnership with an elementary school, a middle school, and a high school in Hartford. It is also involved in building a magnet school organized using Gardner's multiple intelligences theory in partnership with Hartford and five local communities.

Teacher Preparation Program Information

The following programs are 4 year programs:
Early Childhood Education, Elementary Education, K-12 Education (Music), Secondary Education (Biology, Chemistry, English/Language Arts, General Science, Mathematics, Physics, Social Studies), Special Education

The following programs are 5th year programs:
Early Childhood Education, Elementary Education, K-12 Education (Music), Secondary Education (Biology, Chemistry, English/Language Arts, General Science, Mathematics, Physics, Social Studies), Special Education

Delaware State University

Delaware State University is a comprehensive land-grant institution founded in 1890. The Department of Education has developed a knowledge base for candidates that is grounded in best practices that prepare teachers for tomorrow's classrooms. Graduates are knowledgeable about content and pedagogy, have interpersonal communications skills, are able to implement theories of teaching and learning, can implement meaningful assessments, can integrate technology into instruction, apply effective teaching strategies, and are able to teach diverse student populations in many settings.

Just the facts...

Delaware State University
Department of Education
1200 N. DuPont Highway
Dover, DE 19901-2277
(302) 739-4941 or (800) 638-6149
Website: www.dsc.edu
Profile: Urban, Medium, Co-Ed
UG Tuition: $1,487.00/sem. in-state; $3,361.00/sem. out-of-state
Off Campus Programs: No

Clinical Experiences

Four phases of field experiences are designed to assist the preservice teacher make the connection between theory and practice, assimilate the culture of teaching, and practice reflective teaching. Candidates learn how to function effectively in diverse class situations and work effectively with supervisors and peers. Preservice teachers receive support from the field experience coordinator, professors, and peers in every facet of their professional development. Student teaching is a fifteen-week experience.

Noteworthy

Preservice teachers work closely with faculty advisors, the director of student services, coordinator of field experiences, evaluation coordinator, and director of student teaching. A number of education clubs in the Department of Education provide different levels of learning experiences for candidates. A Student Advisory Council brings together preservice teachers from all of Delaware State's teacher education programs, and provides constant feedback to the Department of Education.

Teacher Preparation Program Information

The following programs are 4 year programs:
Early Care and Education, Primary Education, K-12 Education (Art, Music, Physical Education), Middle Level Education, Secondary Education (Agriculture, Biology, Business, Chemistry, Earth/Space/General Science, English, Foreign Language, Health, Mathematics, Physics, Social Studies, Occupational-Vocational Education), Special Education (Early Care and Education/Exceptional, Elementary, Secondary)

Catholic University of America

The Catholic University of America offers courses for teacher candidates taught by full-time faculty in small classes that closely integrate coursework and field experiences. Candidates in the Department of Education can choose from a wide variety of programs, including a non-degree licensure-only program and an Education Studies program, which prepares students for jobs in non-school settings. CUA's D.C. location makes it possible for candidates to intern at the Discovery Channel, U.S. Department of Education, Smithsonian Institution, National Geographic Society, American Red Cross, National Association for Women in Education, and the Children's Defense Fund, as well as in P-12 schools.

Just the facts...

The Catholic University of America
Department of Education
208 O'Boyle Hall
Washington, DC 20064
(202) 319-5805
Website: www.cau.edu
Profile: Urban, Medium, Co-Ed
UG Tuition: $8,250.00/semester
G Tuition: $668.00/credit hour
Off Campus Programs: No

Clinical Experiences

CUA takes advantage of the unique character of the Washington, D.C. area and its wide variety of public, private, and parochial schools. Early childhood and elementary education candidates keep journals that reflect their ability to connect theory with practice in the classroom. A weekly practicum and seminar takes place during the junior year. Candidates intern for two half-days each week and are exposed to the daily routines of the classroom. During the second professional semester, candidates intern for one full day and one half day every week. Student teaching is a fourteen-week experience.

Noteworthy

The Department of Education is noted for its emphasis on strong lines of communication between faculty and candidates. Candidates benefit from access to resources in six school districts located in three states and in many educational associations headquartered in the metropolitan Washington area. Just a few of these associations include the National Education Association, the National Association for the Education of Young Children, American Council on Education, and National Catholic Education Association. CUA education programs have been highly commended for integrating field experiences throughout students' program of study.

Teacher Preparation Program Information

The following programs are 4 year programs:
Early Childhood Education, K-12 Education (Art, Drama/Theater, French, German, Italian, Latin, Music, Spanish), Secondary Education (Art, Biology, Chemistry, English/Language Arts, Mathematics, Social Studies)

The following programs are post-baccalaureate programs:
Early Childhood Education, Elementary Education, K-12 Education (Art, Drama/Theater, ESL, French, German, Italian, Latin, Music, Spanish), Secondary Education (Art, Biology, Chemistry, Mathematics, Social Studies)

The following programs are 5 year combined programs:
Elementary Education

The following programs are 5th year programs:
Early Childhood Education, Elementary Education, K-12 Education (Art, Drama/Theater, ESL, French, German, Italian, Latin, Music, Spanish), Secondary Education (Art, Biology, Chemistry, English/Language Arts, Mathematics, Social Studies)

Gallaudet University

Gallaudet University is the world's only liberal arts university designed for deaf and hard of hearing persons. Established by Congress as a national college for the deaf in 1864, communication among faculty, staff, and students takes place through sign language and written and spoken English. Gallaudet has offered graduate instruction for training teachers of the deaf since 1891. At the undergraduate level, admission is restricted to deaf and hard of hearing students, except for a limited number of special students. Gallaudet's graduate programs are offered to both hearing and deaf or hard of hearing students.

Just the facts...

Gallaudet University
School of Education and Human Services, Fowler Hall 214
Washington, DC 20002
(202) 651-5520
Website: www.gallaudet.edu
Profile: Urban, Small, Co-Ed
UG Tuition: $3,001.50/semester
G Tuition: $3,301.00/semester
International Students: 50 percent surcharge for developing countries, 90 percent surcharge other countries
Off Campus Programs: No

Clinical Experiences

Gallaudet teacher preparation programs place candidates in practicum, internship, and student teaching sites all over the United States. Recently, several Gallaudet students obtained foundation support to complete student teaching experiences with deaf and hard of hearing students in the Philippines and China. In the U.S., where most of Gallaudet's clinical experiences take place, candidates learn and practice in a variety of settings, including day programs, residential schools for the deaf, and mainstream programs in public schools.

Noteworthy

As a recognized center of deaf culture, Gallaudet offers an incomparable setting for students pursuing a career in teaching and serving deaf populations. Gallaudet's faculty and staff, comprised of approximately one-fourth deaf professionals, provides excellent role models for the success of deaf professionals. Not only is the president of the university deaf, but so are two of its four vice presidents and a number of its deans. The professional education programs are a collaboration between the School of Education and Human Services and the College of Arts and Sciences.

Teacher Preparation Program Information

The following programs are 4 year programs:
Early Childhood Education, Elementary Education, Secondary Education (Biology, English, Mathematics, Physical Education, Social Studies)

The following programs are 5th year programs:
Deaf Education (Elementary, Family-Centered Early Education, Multiple Disabilities, Secondary Deaf Education)

George Washington University

Since its 1821 founding in the nation's capital, George Washington University has offered courses designed for those entering the teaching profession. A strong tradition of educational leadership and clinical practice, combined with continual assessment and guidance of the profession stand as key philosophies of GW's Graduate School of Education and Human Development. Currently, four concepts frame the coursework: reflective practice, research and scholarship, educational leadership, and community service. Three departments—Teacher Preparation and Special Education, Educational Leadership, and Counseling, Human and Organizational Study—offer a range of education programs.

Just the facts...

George Washington University
Graduate School of Education and Human Development
2134 G Street, N.W.
Room 101
Washington, DC 20052
(202) 994-6160
Website: www.gwu.edu
Profile: Urban, Large, Co-Ed
G Tuition: $680.00/credit hour
Off Campus Programs: Yes

Clinical Experiences

As a member of the Holmes Partnership, the school uses the fifth-year program format to prepare teachers. With this model, candidates can focus on appropriate pedagogical methods for the duration of their program. Actual classroom participation ranges from 800 to 1,500 hours depending on the selected program. Extensive clinical experiences occur due to a variety of partnerships with schools throughout the Washington D.C., Virginia, and Maryland metropolitan area. The only professional development school in the United States serving emotionally disturbed students is a partner with the GW Graduate School of Education and Human Development.

Noteworthy

The school's partnership network, Capital Educators, brings a vast array of opportunities to the school's candidates, facilitating clinical placements, standards alignment, and professional development. Due to GW's high quality programs, significant external funding allows innovative course offerings in school-related programs. Mid-career and transition programs serve individuals from other professions. The Infant and Early Childhood Special Education program is nationally recognized by the Council for Exceptional Children.

Teacher Preparation Program Information

The following programs are post-baccalaureate programs:

K-12 Education (Art, Bilingual Special Education, Emotional Disturbance, ESL), Secondary Education (Art, Biology, Chemistry, Earth Science, English/Language Arts, ESL, French, General Science, History, Mathematics, Physics, Science, Social Studies, Spanish)

The following programs are 5th year programs:

Elementary Education, K-12 Education (Art, Bilingual Special Education, Emotional Disturbance, ESL), Secondary Education (Art, Biology, Chemistry, Earth Science, English/Language Arts, ESL, French, General Science, History, Mathematics, Physics, Science, Social Studies, Spanish), Special Education (Bilingual, Emotional Disturbance, Infant and Early Childhood, Transition Special Education)

Howard University

Howard University is the most comprehensive, historically black university in the world, and is one of only 88 universities designated as a Level One research university by the Carnegie Foundation for the Advancement of Teaching. Teacher education has been part of the mission of Howard University since its inception. Howard's School of Education seeks to provide high quality educational experiences to candidates that enable them to assume leadership roles in the global community. The School of Education has a long history of providing educators for the world, and continues in that tradition by graduating professionals in all areas of school services.

Just the facts...

Howard University
School of Education
Washington, DC 20059
(202) 806-7340
Website: www.howard.edu
Profile: Urban, Large, Co-Ed
UG Tuition: $4,543.00/semester
G Tuition: $5,153.00/semester
Off Campus Programs: No

Clinical Experiences

Field experiences for teacher candidates begin in the freshman year with an Introduction to Teaching course. This experience is followed by several other opportunities to work in schools or other educational agencies. Student teacher interns and other interns are placed in private and public institutions in the Washington metropolitan area. The full-semester student teaching experience is preceded by a semester of methods courses with two days on campus for coursework and field placements in schools for the rest of the week. The School of Education has partnerships with the District of Columbia Schools and several local systems in Maryland and Virginia.

Noteworthy

Candidates benefit from the many opportunities available in Washington, D.C., including the ability to conduct research at the Library of Congress, the National Institutes of Mental Health, and the National Center for Education Statistics. The National Education Association and Council of the Great City Schools also provide research resources for the School of Education. Graduates of the School of Education are employed in early learning programs, public and private school systems, university-based research centers, federal and state government agencies, and private practice.

Teacher Preparation Program Information

The following programs are 4 year programs:
K-12 Education (French, Music, Physical Education, Spanish, Theater), Secondary Education (English, Mathematics, Science, Social Studies)

The following programs are post-baccalaureate programs:
Early Childhood Education, Elementary Education, Secondary Curriculum and Instruction, Special Education

The following programs are 5 year programs:
Early Childhood Education, Elementary Education

Bethune-Cookman College

Bethune-Cookman College is one of 41 historically black colleges and universities in the United States. It is affiliated with the United Methodist Church, and is guided by Christian principles. The Teacher Education Program seeks to prepare teachers qualified to instruct and prepare an increasingly diverse student population with a variety of educational, social, and health needs. The motto of Bethune-Cookman is "Enter to Learn, Depart to Serve." This emphasis on service carries over into the Teacher Education Program. Graduates demonstrate "Reflective practice, Essential knowledge, Assessment evaluation and Professionalism (REAP)."

Just the facts...

Bethune-Cookman College
Division of Education
640 Dr. Mary McLeod Bethune Blvd.
Daytona Beach, FL 32114
(904) 238-4098
Website: www.bethune.cookman.edu
Profile: Urban, Small, Co-Ed
UG Tuition: $4,023.50/semester
Off Campus Programs: Yes

Clinical Experiences

Clinical experiences are provided for candidates beginning in their freshman year. Candidates progress through four different levels of experiences: observation; observation and participation; observation, participation, and tasks; and observation, participation, tasks, and teaching. Clinical experiences include fifteen hours of observation, 25 hours of participation, 80 hours of clinical tasks, and twelve weeks of student teaching. Candidates are assigned by the college to a variety of school and social service settings that reflect the diversity of the Volusia County communities.

Noteworthy

Since 1993, Bethune-Cookman has graduated 20 nominees for the Sallie Mae Outstanding Beginning Teacher Award. The Teacher Education program has received funding from the Florida Department of Education, the Ford Foundation, Mobil Oil, NASA, and the U.S. Department of Education. Since 1993, the program has emphasized the recruitment and retention of African American men. Project MODEL is designed to train African American men to teach in preschool handicapped classes, and project PACE is designed to recruit and train Latina and African American women to teach children with disabilities.

Teacher Preparation Program Information

The following programs are 4 year programs:

Biology Education (6-12), Business Education (6-12), Chemistry Education (6-12), Elementary Education (1-6), English Education (6-12), Exceptional Student Education (Specific Learning Disabilities, Varying Exceptionalities), French Education(6-12), Music Education (K-12), Physical Education (K-8, 6-12), Physics Education (7-12), Religious Education (K-12), Social Science Education (6-12), Spanish Education (6-12), Speech Communication Education (6-12)

Florida A&M University

Using a strong liberal arts program as its base, Florida A&M University offers courses of study to educate students to meet the challenges of a rapidly-changing world through a commitment to lifelong learning, and to provide a sound foundation for advanced study. The College of Education emphasizes an integrated approach to preparing teachers and other school personnel, with coursework, clinical experiences, and support services that complement one another.

Just the facts...

Florida A&M University
College of Education
300A Gore Education Center
Tallahassee, FL 32307
(850) 599-3482
Website: www.famu.edu
Profile: Urban, Large, Co-Ed
UG Tuition: $66.03/cr. hr. in-state; $263.25/cr. hr. out-of-state
G Tuition: $130.84/cr. hr. in-state; $436.23/cr. hr. out-of-state
Off Campus Programs: Yes

Clinical Experiences

Clinical experiences account for a minimum of 100 hours of in-school experiences and fourteen weeks of student teaching. In these field experiences, candidates assist classroom teachers in tutoring, diagnosing reading difficulties, developing learning centers, teaching lessons, and conducting collaborative research with teachers, principals, and university faculty.

Noteworthy

Several scholarships are offered by the College of Education in addition to those offered by the university. The College of Education conducts the Teacher Education Advisement and Progression Project, which is designed to aid students in meeting the requirements of admission into the teacher education program. The College of Education is involved in many innovative programs, including global student teaching, the Title I Migrant Workers Program, the Education of Homeless Children and Youth Project, the Black Male College Explorers Program, the Brain Research Program, the Accelerated School Project, Camp Adventure, and the Center for Teacher Renewal.

Teacher Preparation Program Information

The following programs are 4 year programs:
Elementary Education (1-6), K-12 Education (Art, Music), Physical Education (K-8), Secondary Education (Biology, Business, Chemistry, Drama, English, History, Mathematics, Physical Education, Physics, Political Science)

The following programs are post-baccalaureate programs:
Elementary Education (1-6), K-12 Education (Art, Music), Physical Education (K-8), Secondary Education (Biology, Business, Chemistry, Drama, English, History, Mathematics, Physical Education, Physics, Political Science)

Florida Atlantic University

Florida Atlantic University is a multicampus urban university on the southeast coast of Florida. The College of Education serves approximately 4,000 students with 115 faculty members divided among six academic departments. Programs in the College of Education emphasize the preparation of educators for its multiethnic, multilingual, economically and geographically diverse region. The programs in the College of Education include the study of liberal arts, pedagogy, cultural and linguistic diversity, technology, and content knowledge.

Just the facts...

Florida Atlantic University
College of Education
777 Glades Road
Boca Raton, FL 33431
(561) 297-3564
Website: www.fau.edu
Profile: Urban, Large, Co-Ed
UG Tuition: $67.42/cr. hr. in-state; $132.23/cr. hr. out-of-state
G Tuition: $264.64/cr. hr. in-state; $437.62/cr. hr. out-of-state
Off Campus Programs: No

Clinical Experiences

The College of Education has established eight professional development schools as well as numerous school/university partnerships for clinical placements of candidates. Teacher candidates are provided extensive clinical experience prior to student teaching. Thirty clinical hours are required as part of the introduction to the teacher preparation program. Various method courses require clinical experiences. Teacher candidates also complete a practicum prior to student teaching. The length of the practicum varies according to the candidate's program of study. Student teaching takes place for one semester, with an option for the candidate to student teach for a full year.

Noteworthy

The College of Education has established an ESOL/Elementary Education program in which graduates simultaneously gain ESOL endorsement and eligibility for elementary education licensure. The College of Education also participates in two experimental teacher education programs, the Teacher Education Alliance, which prepares teachers for Broward County urban schools, and the Genesis Project, a five-year program leading to both bachelor's and master's degrees and designed to prepare professional educators possessing a comprehensive elementary/secondary perspective in education.

Teacher Preparation Program Information

The following programs are 4 year programs:
Elementary Education/ESOL, Exceptional Student Education (Varying Exceptionalities), Secondary Education (Art, Biology, Chemistry, English, Foreign Language, Mathematics, Music, Physics, Social Studies)

The following programs are post-baccalaureate programs:
Secondary Education (Art, Biology, Chemistry, English, Foreign Language, Mathematics, Music, Physics, Social Studies)

The following programs are 5 year programs:
Genesis Program (*includes Elementary Education and one Secondary Education area*)

The following programs are 5th year programs:
Elementary Education, Exceptional Student Education (Learning Disabilities, Emotional Handicaps, Mental Retardation, Varying Exceptionalities), PK/Primary Education (Age 3-Grade 3), Curriculum and Instruction/Secondary Education (Art, Biology, Chemistry, English, Foreign Language, Mathematics, Music, Physics, Social Studies)

Florida International University

Florida International University is located in one of the most dynamic, artistically expressive, and cosmopolitan cities in the United States—and the gateway to Latin America and the Caribbean. The College of Education's mission is to prepare professionals that are competent, creative, and knowledgeable. FIU believes that the fundamental purpose of education is to nourish the inherent possibilities of human potential by fostering individual empowerment, interconnectedness, and change. Candidates are prepared to effect learning and change in diverse populations, and in technologically equipped classrooms and schools. FIU uses portfolio assessment to judge candidates' knowledge and performance.

Just the facts...

Florida International University
College of Education
University Park, ZEB 329
Miami, FL 33199
(305) 348-3222
Website: www.fiu.edu/~coe
Profile: Urban, Large, Co-Ed
UG Tuition: $64.76/cr. hr. in-state; $129.57/cr. hr. out-of-state
G Tuition: $261.98/cr. hr. in-state; $434.96/cr. hr. out-of-state
Off Campus Programs: No

Clinical Experiences

Candidates are provided early opportunities to observe, plan, and practice in a variety of settings. Clinical and field-based experiences include focused observations, interviews with education professionals, case studies, teaching individuals and groups, diagnostic assessments, and instructional material preparation. Candidates assist in the classroom. In consultation with exemplary practitioners, candidates develop evidence of their professional growth and its impact on P-12 student learning. Candidates are engaged in a fourteen-week student teaching experience.

Noteworthy

The College of Education has developed several programs, including FOCUS (preparing elementary education teachers for inner-city schools), PAC (encouraging minority students to pursue higher education in math and science), and the Peace Corps Project (enabling returning volunteers to earn licensure and master's degrees while working with "at-risk" children and in high-need subject areas). The College of Education has been recognized by the Council of Great City Schools for its commitment to urban education, and was awarded an American Association of Colleges for Teacher Education 1998 Best Practices Award.

Teacher Preparation Program Information

The following programs are 4 year programs:
Elementary Education, K-12 Education (Art, French, Music, Spanish), Secondary Education (Biology, Chemistry, Consumer & Family Science/Home Economics, English, Health Occupations, Mathematics, Physical Education, Physics, Social Studies, Vocational Industrial Education), Special Education (Emotionally Disturbed, Learning Disability, Mental Retardation)

The following programs are 5th year programs:
Art Education, English Education, Mathematics Education, Modern Languages Education, Music Education, Science Education, Social Studies Education, Special Education (Varying Exceptionalities)

Florida State University

Florida State University, a land grant institution, has faculty in eight of its colleges and schools who are involved with the preparation of school personnel. Florida State University strives to prepare educational leaders. The faculty believe that leaders must foster high academic standards and content mastery, possess technological literacy, think globally and address issues of diversity, engage in scientific inquiry, maintain collaborative partnerships with other professionals, and value lifelong learning. The university believes that all of its students should acquire a solid grounding in the liberal arts and an understanding of human learning and behavior.

Just the facts...

Florida State University
College of Education
236 Stone Building
Tallahassee, FL 32306-4450
(850) 644-6885
Website: www.fsu.edu
Profile: Suburban, Large, Co-Ed
UG Tuition: $69.48/cr. hr. in-state; $291.34/cr. hr. out-of-state
G Tuition: $138.83/cr. hr. in-state; $482.39/cr. hr. out-of-state
Off Campus Programs: Yes

Clinical Experiences

Beginning with freshman-level courses, candidates engage in school-based and/or education-related clinical placements that provide opportunities to understand the educational system and student diversity. Candidates engage in pre-internship experiences during their junior and senior years prior to a fifteen-week long internship. Partnership placements are made in settings that allow candidates to engage in educational experiences with varying and diverse student populations. The length of each pre-internship experience varies according to the candidate's program and needs. Internship placements are made in one of five area educational centers throughout the state.

Noteworthy

Colleges and schools involved with teacher education at Florida State University offer several scholarship opportunities, including departmental endowed scholarships and distinguished university fellowships. Candidates benefit from university services such as individual advising and mentoring. Florida State University is home to one of the state's research laboratory schools—Florida State University School. This educational setting offers a rich environment for practical experiences in teaching and research with K-12 students. The College of Education sponsors *Your Voice*, a television talk show highlighting diversity issues.

Teacher Preparation Program Information

The following programs are 4 year programs:

Early Childhood Education, Elementary Education, K-12 Education (Art, French, German, Health, Latin, Music, Physical Education, Spanish), Middle School Education (Mathematics, Science, Social Studies), Secondary Education (Biology, Biology/Chemistry, Biology/Earth-Space Science, Biology/Psychology, Chemistry, Earth-Space Science, English, Home Economics, Physics, Physics/Chemistry, Physics/Earth-Space Science, Mathematics, Mathematics/Physics, Mathematics/Statistics), Special Education (Mentally Handicapped, Visually Impaired)

The following programs are 5 year programs:

Emotionally Handicapped/Specific Learning Disabilities/Varying Exceptionalities

The following programs are 5th year programs:

Speech-Language Impaired

Stetson University

Teacher education at Stetson University covers a wide range of subjects and career opportunities related to teaching and learning. The study of education includes such areas as teaching methods, awareness of cultural differences, organization of curricula or levels of education, educational systems, and the policies and finances of educational institutions. The Department of Teacher Education, part of the College of Arts and Sciences, includes professional education degree programs that meet requirements for licensure by the Florida Department of Education. Through the Jessie Ball duPont endowed chair, candidates are prepared to work with multicultural and diverse populations.

Just the facts...

Stetson University
Department of Teacher Education
421 Woodland Boulevard
Deland, FL 32720-2779
(904) 822-7070
Website: www.stetson.edu/departments/ed
Profile: Suburban, Small, Co-Ed
UG Tuition: $15,850.00/year
G Tuition: $370.00/credit hour
Off Campus Programs: No

Clinical Experiences

Starting with foundation courses, candidates spend time observing and participating in schools. Field experience placements are made with regard to the diversity of school faculty and population and the opportunity to observe and be mentored by teachers using best practices. In each foundation course, candidates are assigned to different schools, allowing a breadth of experience. Junior year elementary majors are exposed to two different elementary schools and secondary majors to a middle and high school for field experiences. All schools afford prospective teachers with the opportunity to observe and participate with culturally diverse and exceptional populations.

Noteworthy

The Department of Teacher Education has an outstanding faculty with wide experience in public and private teaching and particular expertise in elementary education, reading, multicultural education, exceptional student education, technology, and educational leadership. They come from some of the nation's most distinguished universities. At Stetson, students find small classes with dedicated teachers who take a personal interest in each student. Stetson offers modern facilities and equipment, and most importantly, access to newly developing knowledge and innovations in the rapidly changing world of education.

Teacher Preparation Program Information

The following programs are 4 year programs:
Adult Education, Elementary Education, K-12 Education (Music), Secondary Education (English/Language Arts, Mathematics, Social Science)

The following programs are post-baccalaureate programs:
Special Education (Developmental Disabilities/Handicaps, Gifted/Talented, Learning Disability)

The following programs are 5th year programs:
Elementary Education, Secondary Education (English/Language Arts)

University of Central Florida

The College of Education at the University of Central Florida places a high priority on teaching, advisement, and student success. The teacher education component of a candidate's studies at UCF addresses the professional knowledge and practical experience future teachers need in order to successfully teach children and youth in public school and private school settings. Graduates are reflective learners who develop positive interpersonal relationships with others. They can demonstrate subject matter knowledge, professional knowledge, and professional commitment.

Just the facts...

University of Central Florida
College of Education
PO Box 161992
Orlando, FL 32816
(407) 823-5529
Website: www.pegasus.cc.ucf.edu
Profile: Urban, Large, Co-Ed
UG Tuition: $64.32/cr. hr. in-state; $261.54/cr. hr. out-of-state
G Tuition: $129.13/cr. hr. in-state; $434.52/cr. hr. out-of-state
Off Campus Programs: Yes

Clinical Experiences

A variety of clinical experiences in schools is offered, beginning with tutoring, continuing with a junior year internship semester, and ending with a senior year internship semester. Special clinical experience opportunities are available at the Orlando Science Center, Walt Disney World, Celebration School, and the U.S. Space Camp. Professional development schools offer unique opportunities for internships (the college is a member of the National Holmes Partnership). Internships provide for the development of teaching skills, knowledge, and the competencies required for the successful classroom teacher. Student responsibilities range from service as an assistant teacher to teaching full-time.

Noteworthy

Over 90 percent of the college's graduates are employed in education positions. The Education Complex, where most education courses take place, includes a state-of-the-art Multimedia Technological Center, student computer labs, a Curriculum Materials Center, an Education Student Services Office, a gym, and a snack bar. The College of Education is committed to "preparing the teachers of tomorrow, today." Candidates interact with faculty who know what it means and what it takes to be a good teacher.

Teacher Preparation Program Information

The following programs are 4 year programs:

Early Childhood Education, Elementary Education, K-12 Education (Art, French, Spanish, Music) PreSchool/PreK-Primary, Secondary Education (Biology, Chemistry, English/Language Arts, Mathematics, Physical Education, Physics, Social Studies, Business), Special Education (Learning Disability, Mentally Handicapped, Emotionally Handicapped)

The following programs are 5th year programs:

Art Education, Elementary Education, Biology Education, Chemistry Education, English Education, Mathematics Education, Music Education, Physics Education, Social Studies Education, Special Education (Varying Exceptionalities)

University of Florida

Since 1905, the University of Florida has prepared teachers and other school personnel. PROTEACH, an intensive, five-year program leading to a Master's of Education degree, is based on the belief that effective teachers are reflective, committed to educational equity and student empowerment, and believe knowledge is constructed by students and that classroom practice is developed through the interaction of student perspectives and experiences with the act of teaching. The university also offers four year programs in agriculture education, art education, music education, physical education, and health science education.

Just the facts...

University of Florida
College of Education
140 Norman Hall
P.O. Box 117040
Gainesville, FL 32611-7040
(352) 392-0726
Website: www.coe.ufl.edu
Profile: Suburban, Large, Co-Ed
UG Tuition: $68.40/cr. hr. in-state; $290.26/cr. hr. out-of-state
G Tuition: $137.75/cr. hr. in-state; $481.31/cr. hr. out-of-state
Off Campus Programs: No

Clinical Experiences

PROTEACH candidates begin tutoring individual children in a variety of classroom and community settings as freshmen. Clinical experiences in the junior and senior year allow candidates in elementary, special education, and unified early childhood education to participate in individual, small group, and whole class instruction under the direct supervision of an experienced classroom teacher. Student teaching occurs in the fifth year of the degree program for a period of twelve to fifteen weeks. Candidates in the four-year preparation programs complete practica prior to student teaching in the final semester of their senior year.

Noteworthy

In Fall 1999, a new five year Unified Elementary Education degree program will begin. This program is designed to prepare teachers with dual emphasis in elementary and mild disabilities. All graduates will be prepared to work with students whose native language is not English, and will receive elementary licensure with an ESOL endorsement. The purpose of the program is to prepare teachers who can create and maintain productive classrooms for diverse student populations, and who can work collaboratively with others to educate all children, including those who have traditionally been labeled "hard to teach" or "hard to manage."

Teacher Preparation Program Information

The following programs are 4 year programs:
Agriculture Education, Art Education, Health Education, Music Education, Physical Education

The following programs are 5 year combined programs:
Elementary Education, Special Education (Behavior Disorders, Learning Disabilities, Mental Retardation, Physical Impairments), Unified Early Childhood/Early Childhood Special Education

The following programs are 5th year programs:
Elementary Education, Reading, Secondary Education (Biology/Chemistry, English, French, Mathematics, Physics, Social Studies, Spanish), Special Education (Behavior Disorders, Learning Disabilities, Mental Retardation, Physical Impairments)

University of Miami

The University of Miami School of Education has prepared teachers since 1929. The faculty is committed to a knowledge base for preservice teachers focused on a strong liberal arts foundation with a subject matter specialization, knowledge of pedagogy, and knowledge of students and society. Teacher candidates graduate with a major in Education as well as a second major within the College of Arts and Sciences. This curriculum has been reviewed by a panel of distinguished educators to ensure that future teachers receive a solid liberal arts education as well as the knowledge necessary for effective teaching.

Just the facts...

University of Miami
School of Education
P.O. Box 248065
Coral Gables, FL 33124
(305) 284-3711
Website: www.education.miami.edu
Profile: Urban, Large, Co-Ed
UG Tuition: $815.00/credit hour
Off Campus Programs: No

Clinical Experiences

Candidates obtain diverse clinical experiences in the Dade County Public Schools, the fourth-largest school system in the country. Courses in methodology are often taught on-site at the university's professional development schools (PDSs). These PDSs are technologically well-equipped and are administered by dynamic leaders who are committed to working with candidates and faculty. A professor-in-residence is readily available at these sites to assist candidates. Clinical experiences culminate in a fifteen-week long associate teaching internship.

Noteworthy

Florida Future Educator Association scholarships are available to incoming freshmen and transfer students. Special funding to provide scholarships in secondary science, mathematics, and English education are also available. The School of Education offers its students a dual career path which enables graduates to pursue graduate study and career opportunities related to their liberal arts major and/or their education major. Because of the extensive work of faculty in research, candidates have many opportunities to become involved in local, state, and national issues affecting education.

Teacher Preparation Program Information

The following programs are 4 year programs:
Elementary Education, Music Education, Secondary Education (Biology, Chemistry, English, Mathematics, Science), Special Education

The following programs are 5th year programs:
Early Childhood Special Education, Elementary Education, Special Education K-12, TESOL K-12

University of North Florida

The College of Education and Human Services prepares professionals to live in a pluralistic society and to create communities focused on the improvement of teaching and learning. The faculty helps undergraduate candidates examine their values and beliefs. Undergraduate candidates also develop their knowledge in the liberal arts and sciences and their area of specialization while learning about pedagogy and practice. Graduate-level candidates develop their skills in their field of specialization while expanding their understanding of disciplined inquiry and the social contexts of teaching and learning.

Just the facts...

University of North Florida
College of Education and Human Services
4567 St. Johns Bluff Road, S.
Jacksonville, FL 32224-2645
(940) 620-2520
Website: www.unf.edu
Profile: Urban, Large, Co-Ed
UG Tuition: $71.89/cr. hr. in-state; $293.75/cr. hr. out-of-state
G Tuition: $141.24/cr. hr. in-state; $484.80/cr. hr. out-of-state
Off Campus Programs: No

Clinical Experiences

UNF is committed to providing teacher candidates, counselors, and school leaders with a variety of field-based experiences. Undergraduate programs include field experiences that start in the freshman or sophomore year and culminate in a term-long internship. The university offers clinical experiences in a variety of settings, including a set of urban professional development schools, which provide interns with the added benefits of on-site supervision by resident clinical faculty. At the graduate level, candidates continue to participate in a variety of clinical experiences.

Noteworthy

Programs in the College of Education and Human Services combine academic rigor and strong field-based experiences. Alumni are recognized as some of the most outstanding teachers throughout Florida. The faculty includes nationally and internationally recognized experts in fields such as multicultural education, education and technology, assessment, and learning and cognitive development. The college focuses on addressing issues related to urban education and to the use of urban professional development schools.

Teacher Preparation Program Information

The following programs are 4 year programs:
Elementary Education (PK-Primary, Grades 1-6, Physical Education), K-12 Education (Art, Music), Middle School Education (Social Studies, English, Mathematics, Science), PreSchool/PreK-Primary, Secondary Education (Biology, Chemistry, English, Mathematics, Physical Education, Physics, Social Sciences), Special Education (Emotional Conflict, Hearing Impaired, Learning Disability, Mentally Impaired)

The following programs are post-baccalaureate programs:
Elementary Education, K-12 Education (Art, Music), Middle School Education, Secondary Education (Mathematics, Science, Social Studies), Special Education (Emotional Conflict, Hearing Impaired, Learning Disability, Mentally Impaired)

The following programs are 5th year programs:
Elementary Education, Secondary Education (English/Language Arts), Special Education (Emotional Conflict, Gifted/Talented, Hearing Impaired, Learning Disability, Mentally Impaired)

University of South Florida

The University of South Florida's College of Education embraces the dual mission of improving today's schools and inventing tomorrow's schools. The College of Education is committed to preparing highly-skilled professionals from diverse backgrounds who are knowledgeable in their content field, technologically proficient, skilled in creating productive learning environments and experiences for all students, and ready to lead the continuing reinvention of schools to meet the needs of a changing society.

Just the facts...

University of South Florida
College of Education
4202 E. Fowler Avenue
EDU 208B
Tampa, FL 33620
(813) 974-3400
Website: www.coedu.usf.edu
Profile: Urban, Large, Co-Ed
UG Tuition: $69.53/cr. hr. in-state; $266.75/cr. hr. out-of-state
G Tuition: $134.34/cr. hr. in-state; $439.73/cr. hr. out-of-state
Off Campus Programs: No

Clinical Experiences

Most teacher education programs in the College of Education offer two early field experiences or practica and a final internship. These experiences provide students a wide range of opportunities to connect theory with practice under the supervision of university and school-based faculty. The clinical experiences encompass a wide variety of age groups within the candidate's area of focus. Strict eligibility requirements ensure sound preparation for each candidate before their final internship.

Noteworthy

The College of Education enjoys strong collaborative relationships with several school districts, including seven professional development schools. Through the Florida Fund for Minority Teachers, the College of Education offers scholarships to minority students interested in teacher education programs. The SunCoast Area Teacher Training program, the honors program of the College of Education, includes more than 500 students each year with average SAT/ACT scores above the 80th percentile.

Teacher Preparation Program Information

The following programs are 4 year programs:
Early Childhood Education, Elementary Education, Physical Education (K-8), K-12 Education (Art, Dance, French, German, Italian, Latin, Music, Russian, Spanish), Secondary Education (Biology, Business, Chemistry, Drama/Theater, English/Language Arts, Industrial Arts, Mathematics, Physical Education, Physics, Social Science, Technology Education), Special Education (Mentally Retardation, Specific Learning Disability, Severe Behavioral Disorders)

The following programs are 5th year programs:
Elementary Education, K-12 Education (Art, French, German, Music, Spanish), Secondary Education (Biology, Business, Chemistry, English, Mathematics, Physical Education, Physics, Social Science), Special Education (Behavioral Disorders, Mental Retardation, Specific Learning Disability, Varying Exceptionalities)

University of West Florida

The University of West Florida has a tradition of preparing quality educators to fill a variety of roles in the public schools. The College of Education has a dedicated faculty and staff who are sincerely interested in providing an outstanding educational experience for all COE students, and who are committed to preparing students to be successful in their chosen profession and to be empowered, life-long learners. Through a program combining general education studies, specialty studies, and professional studies, candidates are prepared to serve as empowered, professional educators.

Just the facts...

University of West Florida
College of Education
11000 University Parkway
Pensacola, FL 32514-5753
(850) 474-2769
Website: www.uwf.edu
Profile: Suburban, Medium, Co-Ed
UG Tuition: $77.44/cr. hr. in-state; $293.39/cr. hr. out-of-state
G Tuition: $140.79/cr. hr. in-state; $484.35/cr. hr. out-of-state
Off Campus Programs: Yes

Clinical Experiences

Teacher candidates complete approximately 300 hours of field experiences designed to provide them with the opportunity to demonstrate their ability to write lesson plans, deliver individualized instruction, and manage the classroom in a relevant field setting. Candidates also learn to infuse both multimedia and telecommunications into their teaching. Candidates are provided with exemplary role models, in both field placements and seminars. Student teaching is a full-semester experience.

Noteworthy

The Office of Student Financial Assistance coordinates a comprehensive program of scholarships, grants, part-time employment, and loans available through federal, state, and university funds. Two significant scholarship/forgivable loan programs for teacher education candidates are available in Florida—the Critical Shortage program (for special education candidates) and the Florida Fund for Minority Teachers. Students receiving these scholarships must teach in a Florida public K-12 school in the funded field for a specific time or the scholarship is converted into a non-forgivable loan for which the state must be reimbursed.

Teacher Preparation Program Information

The following programs are 4 year programs:
Elementary Education, K-12 Education (Art, Music), Middle School Education (English, Mathematics, Science, Social Studies), Secondary Education (Mathematics, Physical Education), Special Education (Learning Disability, Mentally Impaired, Severe Behavioral Disabilities/Handicaps)

Albany State University

Albany State University has prepared teachers and other school personnel since 1917. The College of Education is committed to ensuring that its graduates will be humane, knowledgeable, highly-qualified teachers who are skilled in facilitating learning, motivating children, and solving instructional problems in multicultural settings. ASU College of Education graduates possess sound content knowledge and management skills, combined with appropriate methodology and technology skills. The College of Education operates a number of computer labs, electronic classrooms with access to the Internet, and a Curriculum Materials Resource Center, all of which are used exclusively by teacher education students.

Clinical Experiences

Candidates engage in approximately 350 to 400 hours in a school setting prior to student teaching. Pre-student teaching experiences are required, such as the "September School Experience," in which all senior-level candidates participate. These candidates are assigned for two weeks to a coordinating teacher for pre-planning and the first week of class at a neighboring P-12 school. Clinical experiences culminate with fifteen weeks of student teaching in area public school classrooms.

Just the facts...

Albany State University
College of Education
504 College Drive
Albany, GA 31705
(912) 430-4715
Website: www.asurams.edu
Profile: Urban, Medium, Co-Ed
UG Tuition: $1,088.00/sem. in-state; $3,698.00/sem. out-of-state
G Tuition: $1,223.00/sem. in-state; $3,000.00/sem. out-of-state
Off Campus Programs:No

Noteworthy

Candidates enrolled in the School of Education may receive scholarships from the Hope Teacher Scholarship, Promise Teacher Scholarship, Southern Foundation Initiative, the Payton-Noble Scholarship, and the Common Ground Consortium Education fellowship program. The College of Education operates one of the ten Education Technology Centers in Georgia, in partnership with the Georgia State Department of Education. In addition, the college manages and operates three child development centers providing early childhood education for children from ages six weeks to five years old. Many education classes are offered via distance learning or the Web.

Teacher Preparation Program Information

The following programs are 4 year programs:
Early Childhood Education, Health & Physical Education and Recreation, Middle Grades Education, Secondary Education (Science Education), Special Education

The following programs are post-baccalaureate programs:
Early Childhood Education, Health & Physical Education and Recreation, Middle Grades Education, Secondary Education (Science Education), Special Education

The following programs are 5 year programs:
Early Childhood Education, Health & Physical Education and Recreation, Middle Grades Education, Secondary Education (English, Mathematics, Music, Science Education), Special Education (Behavioral Disorders, Interrelated and Learning Disabilities)

Armstrong Atlantic State University

The College of Education at Armstrong Atlantic, located in historic Savannah, Georgia, offers a variety of degree programs designed for the preparation of competent teachers who are committed to excellence in the profession and who are prepared to ensure success for all students. The College of Education aspires to provide prospective teachers with proficiency in the content area they plan to teach, appropriate learning theory and methodology, and the abilities and skills that will enable them to teach students from a variety of cultural and economic backgrounds, as well as those children with special needs.

Just the facts...

Armstrong Atlantic State University
College of Education
11935 Abercorn Street
Savannah, GA 31419-1997
(912) 927-5398
Website: www.armstrong.edu
Profile: Suburban, Medium, Co-Ed
UG Tuition: $217.00/sem. in-state; $435.00/sem. out-of-state
G Tuition: $228.00/sem. in-state; $478.00/sem. out-of-state
Off Campus Programs: Yes

Clinical Experiences

Clinical experiences at Armstrong Atlantic are incorporated into the majority of education classes. Clinical experiences prepare candidates to recognize and address the educational, emotional, psychological, and behavioral needs of pupils from all backgrounds. These experiences are structured to ensure that preservice teachers have a multidimensional experience with a variety of grade levels and socioeconomic groups. Although clinical hours vary by program, teacher candidates spend between 700 to 1,000 hours in the classroom during their clinical experiences at Armstrong Atlantic State University.

Noteworthy

The College of Education has several outstanding programs that have gained national recognition. The DeWitt Wallace-Reader's Digest Pathways to Teaching Program recruits, screens, and selects minority scholars who are employed by the local school district, and prepares them for professional licensure. The Troops to Teachers Program recruits former military personnel with strong backgrounds in mathematics, science, and management to enter the field of teaching. Armstrong also has a Teacher Induction Program in which a full time director works with graduates to provide support during their first year of teaching.

Teacher Preparation Program Information

The following programs are 4 year programs:
Early Childhood Education, K-12 Education (Art, Health/Physical Education, Music), Middle Grades Education, Secondary Education (Biology, Business, Chemistry, English, History, Mathematics, Political Science, Social Science), Special Education (Psychology with teacher certification in Behavior Disorders)

The following programs are post-baccalaureate programs:
Early Childhood Education, K-12 Education (Art, Health/Physical Education, Music), Middle Grades Education, Secondary Education (Biology, Business, Chemistry, English, General Science, History, Mathematics, Political Science, Social Science)

The following programs are 5th year programs:
Special Education (Behavioral Disorders)

Augusta State University

Augusta State University has been preparing educators since 1925. The faculty in the College of Education works with faculty from the College of Arts and Sciences as well as public school partners to prepare teachers with the "understanding for teaching" and the ability to "teach for understanding." Programs for initial teacher preparation revolve around INTASC model state licensing principles, which establish a set of expectations for beginning teacher competence. Graduates have thorough preparation in their selected discipline as well as extensive clinical and field experiences in public schools.

Just the facts...

Augusta State University
College of Education
2500 Walton Way
Augusta, GA 30910
(706) 737-1499
Website: www.aug.edu
Profile: Urban, Medium, Co-Ed
UG Tuition: $995.00/sem. in-state; $3,603.00/sem. out-of-state
G Tuition: $1,130.00/sem. in-state; $4,130.00/sem. out-of-state
Off Campus Programs: No

Clinical Experiences

Candidates spend more than 800 hours in classrooms working with children, allowing them to function "like a teacher with six months experience" when they begin their first teaching assignment. Each course in the preparation program has an in-school field component, usually in one of 27 professional development school partners. In the Apprenticeship Experience, the candidate spends fifteen weeks full-time in a classroom under the mentorship of a master teacher. Activities in clinical and field experiences are recorded and stored electronically as part of the candidate's comprehensive portfolio.

Noteworthy

Graduates from ASU are highly sought for employment in public schools locally, in the state of Georgia, and in the southeastern United States. The HOPE scholarship provides funds for tuition and other expenses to future educators. All programs are offered in an extremely technology-rich environment which includes a variety of instructional hardware and software support. ASU operates a two-way interactive television studio which allows broadcasts to public school settings for both candidate support and inservice activities. Candidates from ASU consistently score higher on PRAXIS I and II examinations than the state average.

Teacher Preparation Program Information

The following programs are 4 year programs:
Early Childhood Education, Middle School Education, Secondary Education (Biology, Chemistry, English/Language Arts, Mathematics, Physics, Political Science, Social Studies), Special Education

The following programs are post-baccalaureate programs:
Early Childhood Education, Middle School Education, Secondary Education (Biology, Chemistry, English/Language Arts, Mathematics, Physics, Political Science, Social Studies), Special Education

The following programs are 5th year programs:
Early Childhood Education, Middle School Education, Secondary Education (English/Language Arts, Mathematics, Political Science, Social Studies), Special Education

Berry College

The purpose of the Berry College Charter School of Education is to produce teachers who are developers of human potential. Teachers who are prepared by Berry faculty are encouraged to improve the quality of their classrooms through reading, research, experience, communication with colleagues, and creative thinking. The teacher education program at Berry offers a curriculum that emphasizes a rigorous liberal arts foundation, an understanding of American and world cultures, substantive school-based coursework, and the effective uses of technology.

Just the facts...

Berry College
School of Education and Human Sciences
5019 Berry College
Mount Berry, GA 30149-0279
(706) 236-1717
Website: www.berry.edu
Profile: Rural, Small, Co-Ed
UG Tuition: $5,450.00/semester
G Tuition: $146.00/credit hour
Off Campus Programs: No

Clinical Experiences

Berry strives to customize field experiences so that candidates receive the opportunity to teach in a variety of schools—rural, urban, suburban, and, in some cases, international. For all field experiences, including the year-long student teaching experience, candidates are supervised by both cooperating teachers and Berry faculty. Some field experiences are available in the Berry Elementary School, a K-6 school on campus, which boasts a high-achieving student body and an award-winning faculty. Other field experiences are available in a variety of elementary, middle, and high schools in the local area. Candidates can participate in diverse cultural experiences during a special May session.

Noteworthy

Berry's relationship with area schools is mutually supportive and many Berry faculty spend one day a week working in local schools. Berry students who become licensed teachers also receive an ESOL (teaching English to speakers of other languages) endorsement. The goal of Berry College is to provide an outstanding education for students from all economic backgrounds. The college provides more than $9.4 million to students through financial aid and work-study programs. Several scholarships are unique to the School of Education. Berry is consistently ranked as one of America's best schools of education and a best value.

Teacher Preparation Program Information

The following programs are 4 year programs:
Early Childhood Education/P-5, K-12 Education (Art, French, German, Health and Physical Education, Music, Spanish), Middle Grades Education/4-8, Secondary Education/7-12 (Biology, Chemistry, English, History, Mathematics, Physics, Political Science, Social Studies)

The following programs are post-baccalaureate programs:
K-12 Education (Art, ESOL, French, German, Music, Spanish), Secondary Education (Biology, Chemistry, Consumer & Family Science/Home Economics, English/Language Arts, History, Mathematics, Political Science, Social Studies)

The following programs are 5th year programs:
Early Childhood Education/P-5, Middle Grades Education/4-8, Reading, Secondary Education/7-12

Clark Atlanta University

The School of Education's mission is to produce school personnel who will be critical thinkers and change agents committed to serving historically disadvantaged groups, particularly in urban environments. Teacher candidates are prepared to improve academic performance and the educational quality of life for all learners. Graduates are technologically literate, adaptable to a changing multicultural and pluralistic society, and act as advocates who make a positive difference in the lives of urban youth.

Just the facts...

Clark Atlanta University
School of Education
223 James P. Brawley Drive, SW
Atlanta, GA 30314
(404) 880-8505
Website: None
Profile: Urban, Medium, Co-Ed
UG Tuition: $4,825.00/semester
G Tuition: $403.00/credit hour
Off Campus Programs: No

Clinical Experiences

The School of Education initiates its teacher candidates by placing them in school settings for one semester of class observations, individual tutoring, and microteaching. Additional clinical experiences are provided through courses in teaching methods during which candidates rotate to observe in different grade levels. The capstone experience for teaching candidates is a ten-week internship/student teaching experience in which the student teacher takes responsibility for a class under the supervision of a faculty advisor.

Noteworthy

The School of Education provides program enrichment with field trips, seminars and workshops with guest speakers drawn from organizations nationwide, and the opportunity for students to attend regional conferences. Students are given additional support through computer-based tutorials in mathematics and communication skills.

Teacher Preparation Program Information

The following programs are 4 year programs:
Early Childhood Education P-5, Middle Grades Education 4-8, P-12 Education (Art, Health & Physical Education, Music), Secondary Education 7-12 (Business, English, Foreign Language, History, Mathematics, Science, Social Studies)

The following programs are post-baccalaureate programs:
Early Childhood Education P-5, Middle Grades Education 4-8, P-12 Education (Health & Physical Education), Secondary Education 7-12 (Business, English, Mathematics, Science, Social Studies)

The following programs are 5 year programs:
Middle Grades Mathematics 4-8, Secondary Mathematics 7-12

The following programs are 5th year programs:
Early Childhood Education P-5, Middle Grades Education 4-8, Seconday Education 7-12 (English, Foreign Languages, History, Mathematics, Science, Social Studies), Special Education (Behavioral Disorders, Learning Disabilities, Mental Handicaps)

Clayton College & State University

At Clayton College & State University, the Middle Level Teacher Education Program is a collaborative partnership with the School of Arts and Sciences and local school systems. The faculty is committed to in-depth content preparation, effective use of technology, and teamwork. Candidates are admitted as members of a cohort group, and they participate in a carefully planned sequence of courses and school-based activities that prepare them for careers in teaching. Clayton's emphasis on frequent field-based experiences in multiple settings provides candidates with the experience they need to work with all types of students in all environments. The program emphasizes continuous assessment of candidate performance.

Just the facts...

Clayton College & State University
Office of Teacher Education
School of Arts & Sciences
5900 North Lee Street
Morrow, GA 30260-0285
(770) 961-3578
Website: www.clayton.edu
Profile: Suburban, Medium, Co-Ed
UG Tuition: $1,312.00/sem. in-state; $3,922.00/sem. out-of-state
Off Campus Programs: No

Clinical Experiences

The program allows candidates an early entry into a variety of school-based experiences and culminates with a year-long internship that follows the school system calendar. Candidates take education classes in middle schools where they are taught by middle school faculty and administrators. These school-based classes allow interaction with middle school students and teachers, and provide a realistic view of learning and teaching. During the senior year, candidates intern in a middle school classroom, gaining an understanding of middle level learners, curriculum, and local support staff. This experience involves working with the entire middle school community.

Noteworthy

All candidates have laptop computers with access to the Web, multimedia, word processing, and spreadsheet programs. CCSU prides itself on encouraging candidates to examine their own learning styles, to work in collaborative teams, and to think critically while actively engaging in learning. Students participate in local and state conferences that support middle level education. Pedagogy is taught by classroom teachers who relate content to actual classroom practices.

Teacher Preparation Program Information
The following programs are 4 year programs:
Middle Level Education

Columbus State University

At Columbus State, faculty in the College of Education guide candidates as they become professional educators. The faculty recognizes that new teachers must begin and finish their own journeys of learning in order to master the content knowledge, teaching repertoires, and habits of practice displayed by accomplished professional educators. Members of the faculty are skillful guides ready to show the way. Yet they celebrate the individuality, the diversity, and the ability of the next generation of teachers to make the journey.

Just the facts...

Columbus State University
College of Education
4225 University Avenue
Columbus, GA 31907-5645
(706) 568-2045
Website: www.colstate.edu
Profile: Urban, Medium, Co-Ed
UG Tuition: $84.00/cr. hr. in-state; $301.00/cr. hr. out-of-state
G Tuition: $95.00/cr. hr. in-state; $345.00/cr. hr. out-of-state
Off Campus Programs: No

Clinical Experiences

A medium-sized institution in a city of over two-hundred thousand people, Columbus State University has long made available in-depth field experiences to its undergraduate candidates. Early childhood majors work in preschool, primary, and intermediate grade settings. Secondary education majors have no fewer than four field experiences prior to student teaching. Student teaching is fifteen weeks; the first five weeks is a half-day placement. Graduate students may work in clinical roles in well-known summer programs in mathematics and science education.

Noteworthy

A distinguished College of Education faculty provides leadership in Georgia, the Southeast, and nationally among those working to ensure better schools and better teachers. The early childhood program (grades Pre-5), the largest CSU education major, has been noted as an outstanding teacher preparation program. Art, music, and theater education majors benefit from the university's close affiliation with well-known performing artists. The Columbus Regional Mathematics Collaborative (CRMC), a recognized center of excellence, is a catalyst for innovation in this field. The School Counseling program has earned CACREP accreditation.

Teacher Preparation Program Information

The following programs are 4 year programs:
Early Childhood Education, K-12 Education (Art, Drama/Theater, Music, Physical Education/Health), Middle School Education (Generalist), Secondary Education (English/Language Arts, General Science, History, Mathematics, Social Studies), Special Education (Mental Retardation)

The following programs are post-baccalaureate programs:
Early Childhood Education, K-12 Education (Art, Drama/Theater, ESL, Music, Physical Education/Health), Middle School Education (Generalist), Secondary Education (English/Language Arts, General Science, History, Mathematics, Social Studies), Special Education (Early Childhood, Gifted/Talented, Learning Disability, Mental Retardation, Severe Behavioral Disabilities/Handicaps)

Fort Valley State University

Fort Valley State University is a unit of the University System of Georgia, and is one of three historically black colleges and universities in the system. It is located in central Georgia, 90 miles south of Atlanta. The College of Education enrolls about one-third of the univesity's 3,000 students. Degree programs are offered in seven teacher education fields at the undergraduate level. Three master's degrees and one specialist degree are also offered.

Just the facts...

Fort Valley State University
College of Education
1005 State University Drive
Fort Valley, GA 31030
(912) 825-6365
Website: www.fvsu.edu
Profile: Rural, Small, Co-Ed
UG Tuition: $1,108.00/sem. in-state; $3,718.00/sem. out-of-state
G Tuition: $1,243.00/sem. in-state; $4,243.00/sem. out-of-state
Off Campus Programs: Yes

Clinical Experiences

Teacher candidates complete clinical experiences beginning in their sophomore year. Courses in the program are blocked so that teacher candidates spend most of their junior and senior year engaged in clinical experiences in Fort Valley State University's partner schools. The culminating experience is the semester-long student teaching requirement.

Noteworthy

All teacher education programs engage candidates in service volunteer programs. These programs are sponsored and held throughout the Middle Georgia community. Students with exceptional high school credentials are eligible for the Presidential scholarship, which covers all university costs. All of Fort Valley State University's students are encouraged to participate in international experiences, including student teaching.

Teacher Preparation Program Information

The following programs are 4 year programs:
Agriculture Education, Early Childhood Education, Family & Consumer Science Education, Middle Grades Education, P-12 Education (French, Health & Physical Education, Mathematics)

Georgia College and State University

Georgia College and State University is Georgia's only public liberal arts institution. The John H. Lounsbury School of Education's programs are based on the belief that educators are "Architects of Change." The faculty believes that educators must be change agents in schools and communities. All programs build on a strong foundation of liberal studies and the key themes of critical thinking, communication, diversity, and content preparation with interdisciplinary understanding. The teacher preparation programs develop candidates' professional ethics, classroom management skills, and ability to put theory into practice. There is a strong focus on interdisciplinary, integrated studies and international education.

Just the facts...

Georgia College and State University
The John H. Lounsbury School of Education
CBX 070
Milledgeville, GA 31061-0490
(912) 445-4546
Website: www.gac.peachnet.edu
Profile: Rural, Medium, Co-Ed
UG Tuition: $1,032.00/sem. in-state; $3,262.00/sem. out-of-state
G Tuition: $1,128.00/sem. in-state; $3,612.00/sem. out-of-state
Off Campus Programs: Yes

Clinical Experiences

All initial teacher preparation programs, with the exception of Music Education, are field-based. Candidates in early childhood, middle grades, health and physical education, and special education spend 20 hours a week in the public schools over a two-year period. The secondary program (at the graduate level) places candidates in public schools for half-days during a one-year program, which leads to a Master of Arts in Teaching. All candidates have multiple experiences at different grade levels and in different schools and neighborhoods. University coursework is taken in the afternoons after the field-based experience.

Noteworthy

All initial teacher preparation programs (except Music Education) are offered in cohorts—candidates begin and end the program together. A faculty member is assigned as a mentor and leader to each cohort. The mentor/leader teaches, advises, counsels, and supervises candidates in their assignments in the public schools. The School of Education prides itself on its focus on integrating theory and practice, which ensures that graduates are prepared for real-world classrooms. The one-year MAT program requires candidates to have a major in a specific secondary or K-12 teaching area or its equivalent. It was designed and is administered by faculty from Education and Arts/Sciences.

Teacher Preparation Program Information

The following programs are 4 year programs:
Early Childhood Education, K-12 Education (Music, Physical Education/Health), Middle School Education (Language Arts, Mathematics, Science, Social Studies), Special Education (Interrelated)

The following programs are 5th year programs:
K-12 Education (Art, French, Spanish), Secondary Education (Biology, English/Language Arts, History, Mathematics, Political Science, Science, Social Science), Special Education (Behavior Disorders, Interrelated, Learning Disability, Mental Retardation)

Georgia Southern University

Georgia Southern University has prepared teachers since 1906. The university's first priority is teaching, and it has an established reputation for preparing teachers and other school professionals to be reflective educators for diverse learners. Through a wide range of learning experiences, candidates become competent in five areas: knowledge of educational foundations, knowledge of content field, knowledge of curriculum, knowledge of learners, and knowledge of pedagogy. Candidates' programs benefit from the teacher preparation faculty's collaboration with P-12 educators and arts and sciences faculty.

Just the facts...

Georgia Southern University
College of Education
P.O. Box 8013
Statesboro, GA 30460-8013
(912) 681-5648
Website: www.gasou.edu
Profile: Suburban, Large, Co-Ed
UG Tuition: $72.00/credit hour
G Tuition: $83.00/credit hour
Off Campus Programs: Yes

Clinical Experiences

Clinical experiences begin with the Pre-Professional Block, in which candidates enroll concurrently in three core education courses and spend 20 hours in public school classrooms. Structured observations and participation occur and an admissions portfolio is developed. Each education program contains a sequence of field experiences that culminate in a fifteen-week student teaching experience. Candidates learn from placements with master "demonstration teachers" who model exemplary practice. Field experiences take place in a variety of schools and with a variety of students.

Noteworthy

The College of Education Advisement Center provides candidates with personal and comprehensive advisement. State-of-the-art computer labs, portable media stations, a production-quality video studio, two distance learning classrooms, and a service-oriented Instructional Resources Center facilitate technology integration into teaching and learning. A new College of Education building is currently under construction. Georgia Southern graduates score well above the statewide average on Georgia teacher licensure examinations.

Teacher Preparation Program Information

The following programs are 4 year programs:
Early Childhood Education (P-K), K-12 Education (Art, French, German, Health & Physical Education, Music, Spanish), Middle School Education, Secondary Education (Business, Consumer & Family Science/Home Economics, English/Language Arts, Mathematics, Science, Social Studies, Technology Education), Special Education

The following programs are post-baccalaureate programs:
Early Childhood Education, P-12 Education (Art, French, German, Health & Physical Education, Music, Spanish) Middle School Education, Secondary Education (Business, Consumer & Family Science/Home Economics, English/Language Arts, General Science, Mathematics, Social Studies, Technology Education), Special Education

The following programs are 5 year programs:
P-12 Education (French, German, Spanish, Music), Middle School Education, Secondary Education (English/Language Arts, Mathematics, Science, Social Studies)

Georgia Southwestern State University

The mission of the School of Education at Georgia Southwestern is to prepare and develop teachers who meet the needs of diverse student populations in all educational settings. The faculty strives to produce new teachers who are skilled, reflective decision makers. All programs include an emphasis on five principles: strong content-knowledge standards, collaboration, diversity, technology, and assessment and reflective evaluation. All teaching faculty in the School of Education have advanced degrees and extensive public school teaching experience. The School of Education is housed in a modern facility which also includes the Early Childhood Center, a diagnostic reading facility, and continuing education facilities.

Just the facts...

Georgia Southwestern State University
School of Education
800 Wheatley Street
Americus, GA 31709-4693
(912) 931-2145
Website: www.gsw.peachnet.edu
Profile: Rural, Small, Co-Ed
UG Tuition: $865.00/sem. in-state; $3,475.00/sem. out-of-state
G Tuition: $1,000.00/sem. in-state; $4,000.00/sem. out-of-state
Off Campus Programs: No

Clinical Experiences

The School of Education believes that field experiences are essential to all teacher preparation programs. Many courses have field experience requirements as an integral part of the course and/or as out-of-class requirements. Collaboration with area schools as professional partners enables candidates to observe and participate in classrooms beginning with the Introduction to Education course and continuing through the final field experience—student teaching. Student teachers practice their skills as reflective decision makers under the direction of an experienced licensed teacher in a public school for fifteen weeks and a total of twelve semester credit hours.

Noteworthy

The School of Education enjoys a reputation for producing excellent teachers, as evidenced by its graduates' successful completion of Georgia licensure examinations, and by surveys of employers, which indicate high satisfaction with the quality of the university's teacher preparation programs and graduates. The Outreach program of the School of Education assists in the development of educational programs to meet the needs of working students who are "place-bound" through the use of technology to provide alternative methods of instruction and through collaboration with other universities and local education agencies.

Teacher Preparation Program Information

The following programs are 4 year programs:
Early Childhood Education, K-12 Education (Art, French, Health & Physical Education, Music, Spanish), Middle School Education, Secondary Education (Biology, Chemistry, English/Language Arts, Mathematics, Social Studies/History), Special Education (Intellectual Disabilities, Learning Disabilities)

The following programs are post-baccalaureate programs:
K-12 Education (Art, French, Health & Physical Education, Music, Spanish), Secondary Education (Biology, Chemistry, English/Language Arts, Mathematics, Social Science/History)

The following programs are 5 year programs:
Early Childhood Education, Special Education (Intellectual Disabilities, Learning Disabilities)

The following programs are 5th year programs:
K-12 Education (Reading), Special Education (Severe Behavioral Disabilities/Handicaps)

Georgia State University

The College of Education, one of the Southeast's largest, prepares teachers, counselors, school psychologists, and administrators. The Professional Education faculty—an organization of faculty from the College of Education, College of Arts and Sciences, and local schools—prepares candidates as leaders, thinkers, and agents of change who are grounded in content, theory, and practice. Candidates are educated in the arts, humanities, and sciences. They master content knowledge and are skilled in creating effective learning environments. Graduates integrate assessment, planning, and instructional and leadership skills.

Just the facts...

Georgia State University, College of Education
Atlanta, GA 30303
(404) 651-2525
Website: www.gsu.edu
Profile: Urban, Large, Co-Ed
UG Tuition: $86.00/cr. hr. in-state; $344.00/cr. hr. out-of-state (*Plateau rates: $1,161.00/sem. in-state $4,644.00/sem. out-of-state above 13.5 credit hours*)
G Tuition: $106.00/cr. hr. in-state; $424.00/cr. hr. out-of-state (*Plateau rates: $1,336.50/sem. in-state $5,346.00/sem. out-of-state above 13.5 credit hours*)
Off Campus Programs: No

Clinical Experiences

All initial teacher preparation programs are field-based, beginning with the first professional education course. Candidates are placed in schools as they take each course. Methods course experiences provide candidates the opportunity to put into practice ideas and strategies that they are currently learning. Full-time student teaching caps all programs in the final year. Candidates gain experience in inner-city, urban, and suburban public schools, at different grade levels appropriate to their fields, under the intense supervision of university and school faculty.

Noteworthy

Early childhood programs at the College of Education have been cited for exemplary practice. The university offers one of only six deaf-blind programs in the United States. The College of Education is involved in projects through its Center for Urban Educational Excellence, including the B.E. Mays Lecture, the Peachtree Urban Writing Project, and the Urban Atlanta Coalition Compact funded by the Annenberg Foundation. The university has international projects with Cote d'Ivoire, Egypt, and the European Teacher Education Network. The College of Education has a state-of-the art instructional technology center and a reading recovery program.

Teacher Preparation Program Information

The following programs are 4 year programs:
Early Childhood Education P-5, Middle School Education 4-8, P-12 Education (Art, Health & Physical Education, Music), Secondary Education (English, French, German, Latin, Mathematics, Science, Social Science, Spanish)

The following programs are post-baccalaureate programs:
P-12 Education (ESL)

The following programs are 5th year programs:
Early Childhood Education P-5, Secondary Education (English, Mathematics, Science, Social Studies), P-12 Education (Art), Special Education (Communication Disorders, Deaf-Blind, Early Childhood, Emotional and Behavioral Disorders, Gifted/Talented, Hearing Impairment, Interrelated Special Education, Learning Disabilities, Mental Retardation, Orthopedically Impaired, Visually Impaired)

Kennesaw State University

KSU teacher education faculty are committed to quality undergraduate and graduate teacher preparation grounded in the liberal arts tradition. The teacher education program is an "all-university" endeavor, involving four colleges and eleven departments. All education programs, developed and implemented through collaboration between departments within the colleges of Education and Arts and Sciences, integrate strong academic preparation, pedagogical study, and school-based professional experiences. Graduates are committed to professional growth and excellence through scholarship, service, and research, and are able to serve the needs of diverse learners in a dynamic, pluralistic, and technological society.

Just the facts...

Kennesaw State University
Bagwell College of Education
1000 Chastain Road
Kennesaw, GA 30144-5591
(770) 423-6117
Website: www.kennesaw.edu/education
Profile: Urban, Large, Co-Ed
UG Tuition: $840.00/sem. in-state; $2,231.00/sem. out-of-state
Off Campus Programs: No

Clinical Experiences

KSU believes that intensive clinical and field experiences are essential to its teacher preparation programs. Each program area (P-12) includes multiple clinical and field-based experiences. The undergraduate programs include approximately 500 hours of experiential applications in each program; some include more hours. Supervision of these experiences is provided by classroom teachers and College of Education faculty who have content-specific expertise in the discipline. Candidates are able to observe, plan, and practice in settings that provide diversity in ethnicity, socioeconomic status, and exceptionalities.

Noteworthy

Numerous scholarships are available to assist education majors: the Durden Family Scholarship, Phi Delta Kappa Scholarship, Paul Douglas Teaching Scholarship, and the Retired Teachers Scholarship to name just a few. The College's Teacher Education Advisement Center offers support to new students. The Teacher Resource and Activity Center (TRAC) provides a curriculum library, textbooks, and other state-of-the-art instructional materials, and provides workshops and seminars for inservice and preservice teachers. The TRAC Technology Learning Center is a laboratory for enhancing technology skills.

Teacher Preparation Program Information

The following programs are 4 year programs:
Early Childhood Education, Elementary Education, K-12 Education (Art, French, Music, Physical Education, Spanish), Middle School Education (English, Mathematics, Science, Social Studies), Secondary Education (English/Language Arts, Mathematics, Science, Social Studies)

Morris Brown College

Morris Brown College is a private, co-educational undergraduate college founded in 1881 by the African Methodist Episcopal (A.M.E.) Church. Located in the heart of Atlanta, Georgia, Morris Brown has a student body of almost 2,000 students from 36 states and 23 foreign countries. Its academic programs offer baccalaureate degrees in more than 40 different areas, preparing graduates for entry-level employment, graduate or professional study, and public and military service. Morris Brown College's teacher preparation program focuses on early childhood education (grades P-5).

Just the facts...

Morris Brown College
Department of Education
643 Martin Luther King Jr. Drive NW
Atlanta, GA 30314
(404) 220-0207
Website: None
Profile: Urban, Small, Co-Ed
UG Tuition: $7,301.50/semester
Off Campus Programs: No

Clinical Experiences

Teacher candidates must participate in a total of 360 hours of practica experiences prior to student teaching. These experiences include a minimum of three traditional experiences in elementary school settings (grades P-5). In addition, a minimum of two non-traditional practica experiences are required in settings other than public schools (i.e., public and private child care centers, shelters, community agencies). Candidates are also encouraged to participate in service learning activities and the Elementary Science Education Partner (ESEP) program. ESEP allows the teacher candidate to work with elementary school teachers in implementing hands-on service activities in the classroom.

Noteworthy

The Department of Education has a rural and international student teaching program; candidates may conduct their student teaching experience abroad if they choose. The teacher education program at Morris Brown College is a member of the Consortium for Overseas Teaching (COST), and has an agreement with the Ministry of Education in Bermuda. Several rural student teaching collaboratives are set up around the state of Georgia. Candidates may participate in two education organizations on campus: the Student Association for Teacher Education and Kappa Delta Pi.

Teacher Preparation Program Information

The following programs are 4 year programs:
Early Childhood Education (P-5)

North Georgia College & State University

The Teacher Education Program at North Georgia College and State University prepares teachers for their roles as facilitators of instruction, decision makers, and leaders in their learning communities. Candidates become positive role models and educated citizens ready to contribute to society through their profession. The faculty believe that teachers must know their subject matter and be able to employ the best instructional strategies to make that subject matter meaningful to their students. Students apply for the teacher education program in the second semester of their sophomore year. Graduates are extremely successful in obtaining teaching jobs in the rapdily-growing north Georgia area.

Just the facts...

North Georgia College and State University
School of Education
Dahlonega, GA 30597
(706) 864-1533
Website: www.ngc.peachnet.edu
Profile: Rural, Medium, Co-Ed
UG Tuition: $72.00 cr. hr. in-state; $290.00 cr. hr. out-of-state
G Tuition: $83.00 cr. hr. in-state; $333.00 cr. hr. out-of-state
Off Campus Programs: No

Clinical Experiences

Each semester of the professional education sequence includes field placements based on content area and student diversity. In the first semester, placements and clinical experiences are in math and science. In the second semester, these experiences are in social science, language arts, and reading. In the third and fourth semesters, early childhood, middle school, and special education candidates complete a full internship in one school. All placement sites are involved in a professional partner school network in the School of Education's service area.

Noteworthy

All early childhood, middle school, and special education candidates complete an emphasis area in reading, which includes coursework in the teaching of reading, reading diagnosis and remediation, and reading in the content areas. Early childhood majors also complete at least twelve semester hours of mathematics. Candidates in the 7-12 and P-12 programs complete a course in the teaching of reading in the content area. Endorsements in ESOL and Preschool Handicapped are being developed so that candidates can graduate with dual licensure, thus increasing their skills and their employability.

Teacher Preparation Program Information

The following programs are 4 year programs:
Early Childhood Education, K-12 Education (Art, French, Music, Physical Education, Spanish), Middle Grades Education, Secondary Education (Biology, English/Language Arts, Mathematics, Science, Social Studies), Special Education (Interrelated)

The following programs are post-baccalaureate programs:
K-12 Education, Middle Grades Education, Secondary Education, Special Education

Spelman College

The Department of Education at Spelman College educates competent, self-confident teacher-leaders who are committed to education in urban, multicultural, and international communities. Faculty and staff believe that teacher-leaders are knowledgeable, innovative role models for all children. Candidates learn to empathize with all children and to use positive classroom instruction to encourage them to participate effectively in a democracy.

Just the facts...

Spelman College
Education Department
350 Spelman Lane, SW
P.O. Box 63
Atlanta, GA 30314
(404) 223-7687
Website: www.spelman.edu
Profile: Urban, Small, Women
UG Tuition: $4,500.00/semester
Off Campus Programs: No

Clinical Experiences

Many field experiences provide learning opportunities for candidates. Experiences are carefully designed so that candidates are prepared to work with culturally diverse populations. Candidates must complete both early field experiences and a twelve-week student teaching experience in urban schools. Early field experiences begin with observation, mentoring, and tutoring, and conclude with active participation in instructional activities in curriculum and methods courses.

Noteworthy

Although teacher preparation coursework at Spelman includes urban, multicultural and technological components, the Department of Education also offers specific courses in multicultural education, media and technology, and advocacy in urban schools. Spelman requires its teacher candidates to spend many hours in P-12 schools developing their instructional skills and immersing themselves in the cultures of diversely-populated communities. Graduates become skillful teacher-leaders who are sensitive to the needs of all of their students and who are willing to provide service to the communities in which they teach.

Teacher Preparation Program Information

The following programs are 4 year programs:
Early Childhood Education, P-12 Education (Art, French, Music, Spanish), Secondary Education (Biology, Chemistry, Economics, English/Language Arts, French, History, Mathematics, Political Science, Spanish)

State University of West Georgia

The State University of West Georgia prepares education professionals through exemplary teaching, scholarship, and service. The mission of the College of Education is to provide excellence in preparation of professionals for a variety of settings, to foster an innovative learning community, and to empower a faculty committed to teaching and the dissemination of knowledge. All undergraduate degree programs combine a strong liberal arts core, content major, professional education coursework with appropriate specializations, and practical field experiences. Teacher candidates take most of their classes in the Education Center, which features state-of-the-art instructional technology.

Just the facts...

State University of West Georgia
College of Education
Carrollton, GA 30118
(770) 836-6570
Website: www.westga.edu/coe/
Profile: Rural, Medium, Co-Ed
UG Tuition: $53.00/cr. hr. in-state; $177.00/cr. hr. out-of-state
G Tuition: $58.00/cr. hr. in-state; $196.00/cr. hr. out-of-state
Off Campus Programs: Yes

Clinical Experiences

West Georgia has three levels of field experiences: introductory, mid-level, and internship, which develop candidates' professional knowledge, skills, and attitudes. Field experiences include a variety of settings that include culturally diverse and exceptional populations, and incorporate observation, demonstration, practice, and feedback. All experiences address INTASC model state licensing standards in a sequence of placements that allow candidates to apply their knowledge base and teaching skills in diagnostic and prescriptive ways. All experiences stress the importance of learning about organizational structures and how beginning teachers become contributing members of the school environment.

Noteworthy

Special initiatives of the College of Education—including an External Degree Program, Professional Development School network, Child Development Center, and Distance Education program—provide excellent learning opportunities for candidates. The College of Education has been designated by the Georgia Department of Education as a technology training site for the region's public school educators. The Education Complex houses two computer/multimedia labs, nine multimedia classrooms, portable multimedia workstations, and distance learning classrooms.

Teacher Preparation Program Information

The following programs are 4 year programs:
Early Childhood Education, K-12 Education (Art, French, Music, Spanish), Middle School Education, Secondary Education (Business, Earth Science, English/Language Arts, History, Mathematics, Science, Social Studies), Special Education (Mental Retardation)

The following programs are post-baccalaureate programs:
Early Childhood Education, K-12 Education (Art, ESL, French, Music, Spanish), Middle School Education, Secondary Education (Business, English/Language Arts, Mathematics, Science, Social Studies), Special Education (Gifted/Talented, Learning Disability, Severe Behavioral Disabilities/Handicaps)

University of Georgia

The University of Georgia Peabody School of Education was founded in 1908 and grew into the College of Education in 1932. Since then, it has become one of the largest and most diverse institutions of its kind in the country. The College of Education provides research-based programs that offer a balance between content knowledge and practical skills. All programs strive to ensure that candidates are ready to work in diverse environments. Along with its mission of producing quality educators, the College of Education also assists P-12 schools in the improvement of teaching and learning and assists agencies and organizations in creating ongoing learning opportunities in their communities.

Just the facts...

The University of Georgia
College of Education
G-3 Aderhold Hall
Athens, GA 30602
(706) 542-3866
Website: www.coe.uga.edu
Profile: Rural, Large, Co-Ed
UG Tuition: $1,465.00/sem. in-state; $4,930.00/sem. out-of-state
G Tuition: $1,645.00/sem. in-state; $5,650.00/sem. out-of-state
Off Campus Programs: No

Clinical Experiences

Supervised observation/participation in cooperative schools is required of most candidates for a degree leading to professional licensure. The degree of required participation in pre-student teaching laboratory experiences varies extensively among different teacher preparation programs. Formal student teaching varies from ten to fifteen semester hours by teacher preparation field. A variety of clinics and laboratories operated by the College of Education provide useful experiences for candidates; these include the Reading Clinic, the Learning Disabilities Clinic, the Speech and Hearing Clinic, and the Student Development Laboratory.

Noteworthy

As part of a Land Grant institution, the College of Education is committed to blending teaching, scholarship, and outreach as exemplified by its participation in a state-wide P-16 initiative to foster higher student achievement. Unique to the state of Georgia is the HOPE scholarship (Helping Outstanding Pupils Educationally) which pays semester tuition, fees, and $100 toward books for Georgia students who maintain a 3.0 overall GPA. Multicultural education is stressed in the College of Education through an annual multicultural conference, faculty and student development seminars, and the development of a Multicultural Education Resources Center. Technology is integrated throughout the programs at the college.

Teacher Preparation Program Information

The following programs are 4 year programs:
Early Childhood Education (Grades 1-5, Kindergarten, Preschool), Middle School Education/4-8, P-12 Education (Art, Dance, French, German, Health Promotion and Education, Latin, Music, Physical Education, Spanish), Secondary Education/7-12 (Agriculture, Biology, Business, Chemistry, Earth Science, Economics, English, Family and Consumer Sciences, General Science, Geography, Health Occupations, Marketing, Mathematics, Physics, Political Science, Social Sciences, Technology, Trade and Industrial), Special Education

The following programs are 5th year programs:
Master of Arts, Master of Education, Master of Art Education, Master of Music Education

Valdosta State University

Since 1906, Valdosta State University has been committed to providing quality education for future educational professionals. The faculty strive to prepare teachers to meet the many challenges they will face by providing a strong background in subject matter and encouraging candidates to become a community of learners. The College of Education provides an educational environment where students fully participate in and take responsibility for their learning process, where collaboration is the norm, and where technology is fully integrated into the learning process. The college also promotes the full development of human potential and prepares professionals to meet the needs of all learners.

Clinical Experiences

Field and clinical experiences are an integral part of all programs. The College of Education maintains a close collaborative relationship with schools, community groups, and businesses in South Georgia. Candidates have the opportunity to develop teaching skills in many real life situations, and are supported by college faculty throughout their programs. Juniors and seniors spend a significant amount of time with master teachers in the public schools. Cooperative internships in instructional technology, psychology, speech and language pathology, and educational leadership assist candidates in applying knowledge gained in coursework.

Just the facts...

Valdosta State University
College of Education
Valdosta, GA 31698
(912) 333-5925
Website: www.valdosta.peachnet.edu
Profile: Rural, Medium, Co-Ed
UG Tuition: $1,101.00/sem. in-state; $3,711.00/sem. out-of-state
G Tuition: $1,236.00/sem. in-state; $4,236.00/sem. out-of-state
Off Campus Programs: No

Noteworthy

The College of Education operates fifteen classrooms equipped with multimedia teaching stations and twenty-one labs with state-of-the-art computers including Internet access and satellite download capabilities within the building. All students are given e-mail accounts, and are required to take an introductory computer course that gives them the skills to use technology to promote their own learning. The College of Education supports candidates by maintaining an Advising Center, offering a study skills course, and promoting the many scholarship programs available to future education professionals.

Teacher Preparation Program Information

The following programs are 4 year programs:

Early Childhood Education, K-12 Education (Art, French, Health and Physical Education, Music, Spanish), Middle School Education, Secondary Education (Business, English/Language Arts, Mathematics, Science, Social Studies, Vocational Trade & Industrial), Special Education

The following programs are post-baccalaureate programs:

Early Childhood Education, K-12 Education (French, Health and Physical Education, Music, Spanish), Middle School Education, Secondary Education (Business, English/Language Arts, Mathematics, Science, Social Studies)

The following programs are 5 year programs:

Special Education (Early Intervention Special Education, Mild Disabilities and Severe Disabilities)

The following programs are 5th year programs:

Early Childhood Education, K-12 Education (Art, Health and Physical Education, Music, Reading, Spanish), Middle School Education, Secondary Education (Business, English/Language Arts, Mathematics, Science, Social Studies, Vocational Trade & Industrial), Special Education (Early Intervention Specialist, Mild Disabilities, Severe Disabilities)

Boise State University

The State Board of Education has designated teacher education as a primary area of emphasis for Boise State University. The College of Education, with four departments and five centers, is strongly supported by the university. Undergraduates are expected to demonstrate their ability to plan instructional lessons based on student demographics in a classroom, teach appropriate lessons, effectively integrate technology into the learning process, and assess student learning. Graduate programs, including an Ed.D. in Curriculum and Instruction, focus on developing effective leaders in education. All coursework provides candidates with insight into the complexities of teaching and learning.

Clinical Experiences

Clinical experiences are an essential part of every candidate's education once a major is declared. These experiences provide rich learning opportunities for candidates as well as assistance to classroom teachers and their students. Each experience includes the following attributes: it takes place under the direction of a faculty mentor; it requires active participation, it is carefully planned, and it is associated with a particular required teacher education course. Working with at-risk children receives special emphasis.

Just the facts...

Boise State University
College of Education
1910 University Drive
Boise, ID 83725
(208) 426-1134
Website: http://coehp.idbsu.edu/
Profile: Urban, Large, Co-Ed
UG Tuition: $1,236.00/sem. in-state; $4,176.00/sem. out-of-state
G Tuition: $1,510.00/sem. in-state; $4,450.00/sem. out-of-state
Off Campus Programs: No

Noteworthy

The College of Education receives in excess of $2 million each year in external funding to provide direct services to public schools, teachers, and support programs for first generation college students. Many faculty have received awards for their teaching, scholarship, and service to schools at both the state, regional, and national levels. The College of Education received a national award from the Council for Advancement and Support of Education for placing over 2,500 recycled computers in public school classrooms over the past three years. Boise State University benefits from the J.A. and Kathryn Albertson Foundation's generous funding for the improvement of public education in Idaho.

Teacher Preparation Program Information

The following programs are 4 year programs:
Early Childhood Education, Elementary Education (Bilingual/ESL, General), K-12 Education (French, German, Music, Physical Education, Reading, Spanish), Secondary Education 5-12 (Anthropology, Art, Biology, Chemistry, Communications, Earth Science, Economics, English/Language Arts, History, Mathematics, Physical Education, Physics, Political Science, Social Studies, Sociology, Technology Education, Theatre Arts), Special Education (Mild/Severe Disabilities)

The following programs are post-baccalaureate programs:
Early Childhood Education, Elementary Education (Bilingual/ESL, General), K-12 Education (French, German, Music, Physical Education, Reading, Spanish), Secondary Education 5-12 (Anthropology, Art, Biology, Chemistry, Communications, Earth Science, Economics, English/Language Arts, History, Mathematics, Physical Education, Physics, Political Science, Social Studies, Sociology, Technology Education, Theatre Arts), Special Education (Mild/Severe Disabilities)

The following programs are 5 year combined programs:
Secondary Education (Technology Education)

The following programs are 5th year programs:
Curriculum and Instruction (Secondary Licensure)

Idaho State University

The Idaho State University College of Education builds all of its educator preparation programs on the philosophy "by teaching we learn." The College of Education's approach to preparing education professionals is standards-driven, assessment-informed, learner-centered, and collaborative. Teacher candidates are involved in a continual cycle of practice, reflection, and evaluation that provides them with many opportunities to learn and receive feedback regarding their professional practice. Graduates have the knowledge and skills essential for practicing teachers and school specialists.

Just the facts...

Idaho State University
College of Education
Box 8059
Pocatello, ID 83209-0009
(208) 236-2783
Website: www.isu.edu
Profile: Suburban, Large, Co-Ed
UG Tuition: $1,295.00/sem. in-state; $4,415.00/sem. out-of-state
G Tuition: $1,565.00/sem. in-state; $4,685.00/sem. out-of-state
Off Campus Programs: Yes

Clinical Experiences

Candidates in the teacher education program complete over 200 hours of field experience in schools and classrooms in addition to a semester-long student teaching assignment. Candidates in advanced programs, including school psychology, educational administration, school counseling, special education, and speech pathology, complete internship and practicum experiences related to their field of preparation. An early childhood laboratory school is housed in the College of Education.

Noteworthy

Upon application for admission to Idaho State University, all students are automatically registered for scholarship and grant support. As part of the teacher education program, candidates take courses in a state-of-the-art computer laboratory and complete an electronic portfolio documenting their accomplishments as beginning teachers. At the graduate level, the Idaho State University College of Education offers a mentoring program for accomplished teachers seeking National Board certification.

Teacher Preparation Program Information

The following programs are 4 year programs:

Early Childhood Education, Elementary Education, K-12 Education (Art, Dance, Drama/Theater, French, German, Literacy, Music, Physical Education, Spanish, Special Education), Secondary Education (Art, Biology, Business, Chemistry, Consumer & Family Science/Home Economics, Economics, Earth Science, English, General Science, Health, History, Mathematics, Music, Physical Education, Physical Sciences, Physics, Political Science, Social Science, Sociology, Spanish, Special Education, Speech Communication, Theater, Vocational Education), Special Education (Hearing Impaired)

Lewis-Clark State College

Lewis Clark State College is a four-year liberal arts college established in 1893. Teacher preparation is a major emphasis of the college. The faculty is committed to preparing competent, caring teachers who have the knowledge and abilities to be effective in helping students learn. Lewis Clark State College offers an integrated, performance-based program that seeks to promote high quality in teaching through a combination of coursework, collaborative instruction, community partnerships, and performance assessments.

Just the facts...

Lewis-Clark State College
Division of Education
500 8th Avenue
Lewiston, ID 83501-2898
(208) 799-2260
Website: www.lcsc.edu
Profile: Rural, Medium, Co-Ed
UG Tuition: $1,022.00/sem. in-state; $2,636.00/sem. out-of-state
Off Campus Programs: Yes

Clinical Experiences

Candidates participate in multiple school-based experiences with teachers who demonstrate best practices. Field experiences begin with a 40-hour practicum and culminate with a year-long internship. These experiences provide candidates with opportunities to explore the connection between theory and practice and to work with students from culturally diverse and exceptional populations. Candidates gain confidence and competence through frequent interaction with skilled practitioners.

Noteworthy

Lewis Clark State College's teacher preparation program builds on the benefits of a small college environment: personal attention, small classes, and student-centered accommodations. To enhance their chances of success, teacher candidates become members of learning cohorts. The Division of Education provides a technology-rich learning environment that includes a model classroom and fully integrated technology instruction. Recently, the division was awarded an $800,000 grant by the J.A. and Kathryn Albertson Foundation to reinvent its teacher education program in anticipation of 21st century needs. The division is home to Idaho's only chapter of Kappa Delta Pi. A number of scholarships are available for teacher candidates.

Teacher Preparation Program Information

The following programs are 4 year programs:
Elementary Education K-8, K-12 Education (Physical Education/Health), Secondary Education (English/Language Arts, General Science, Mathematics, Physical Education/Health, Social Studies, Speech/Theatre)

The following programs are post-baccalaureate programs:
Elementary Education K-8, K-12 Education (Physical Education/Health), Secondary Education (English/Language Arts, General Science, Mathematics, Physical Education/Health, Social Studies, Speech/Theatre), Special Education

Northwest Nazarene College

Educator preparation at Northwest Nazarene College is built on the idea that schools must be involved in preparing citizens for a democratic society. Graduates are prepared to view the education system broadly as a community that includes social workers, parents, police officers, other community members, teachers, counselors, and administrators who serve as important figures in a child's education.

Just the facts...

Northwest Nazarene College
Teacher Education
623 Holly Street
Nampa, ID 83686
(208) 467-8258
Website: www.nnc.edu
Profile: Suburban, Small, Co-Ed
UG Tuition: $363.00/quarter
G Tuition: $170.00/quarter
Off Campus Programs: Yes

Clinical Experiences

Clinical experiences are a strength of the teacher preparation programs at NNC. Each clinical/field experience is tied to the various professional education courses taken by candidates. Candidates begin with a 30-hour field experience as part of the introduction to teaching course taken in the freshman year. Elementary education majors conclude with a year-long internship as part of the faculty in a professional development school. This internship integrates instruction with practice in settings supervised by K-6 and higher education faculty. Prior to student teaching, secondary education majors complete five field experiences.

Noteworthy

NNC has a long-standing reputation for producing quality educators. Faculty enjoy a close working relationship with public and private school administrators and teachers in the area and with the state department of education. Faculty members have significant experience in K-12 settings and are involved in professional and accreditation organizations. NNC has received a three-year grant which enables the college to work with area school districts to implement professional development schools that will improve the way new teachers are prepared and the way practicing teachers teach.

Teacher Preparation Program Information

The following programs are 4 year programs:

Elementary Education, Secondary Education** (Art, Biology, Chemistry, Computer Science, English, Health, History, Kinesiology, Mathematics, Music, Physical Science, Physics, Psychology, Social Science, Sociology, Spanish)

** Some programs leading to secondary education licensure may take more than four years to complete, depending on the candidate's choice of first and second teaching fields. Candidates must choose a first and second teaching field.

University of Idaho

Teacher preparation programs at the University of Idaho are built on the theme of the teacher as reflective practicioner, researcher, and leader. Candidates in the College of Education's initial preparation programs develop an inquiry approach to teaching and learning that enables them to enhance their practice in the classroom. At the advanced level, research and leadership skills extend candidates' reflection on their practice into action research that results in improved education for all students. Program graduates assume school leadership roles in classroom, support, and administrative roles.

Just the facts...

University of Idaho
College of Education
Moscow, ID 83844
(208) 885-6772
Website: www.coe.uidaho.edu
Profile: Rural, Large, Co-Ed
UG Tuition: $971.00/sem. in-state; $3,871.00/sem. out-of-state
G Tuition: $1,241.00/sem. in-state; $4,141.00/sem. out-of-state
Off Campus Programs: Yes

Clinical Experiences

Candidates at the basic and advanced levels are involved in early and frequent experiences with and in P-12 schools. The first field experience for candidates in initial preparation programs is completed in their sophomore year. This is followed by a series of field placements where students practice and reflect on skills developed through their content and methodology classes. The culminating experience is a semester of student teaching. At the advanced level, internships are required in all programs.

Noteworthy

The College of Education provides a technology-rich environment where school personnel use computers for multimedia presentations, the integration of technology into curriculum development, and classroom demonstrations. Several math, science, and foreign language programs provide candidates with the opportunity to work in classroom settings in teaching and research roles. The Idaho Center on Disabilities and Human Development offers candidates practica, internships, work, and research in the field of developmental disabilities. These and other College of Education centers provide unique teaching and learning programs for candidates.

Teacher Preparation Program Information

The following programs are 4 year programs:
Elementary Education, K-12 Education (Art, Music, Physical Education), Secondary Education (Agriculture, Art, Biology, Bookkeeping, Business, Chemistry, Consumer & Family Science/Home Economics, Earth Science, Economics, English/Language Arts, Foreign Languages, Geography, Health, History, Industrial Technology, Mathematics, Physical Education, Physical Sciences, Physics, Political Science, Psychology, Social Studies, Sociology, Speech, Trade & Industrial, Vocational Agriculture, Vocational Business Office, Vocational Marketing, Vocational Home Economics/Consumer Homemaking, Vocational Trade & Industrial), Special Education

The following programs are post-baccalaureate programs:
Elementary Education, K-12 Education (Art, Music, Physical Education), Secondary Education (Agriculture, Art, Biology, Business, Chemistry, Consumer & Family Science/Home Economics, Earth Science, Economics, English/Language Arts, Foreign Languages, Geography, Health, History, Industrial Technology, Mathematics, Physical Education, Physical Sciences, Physics, Political Science, Psychology, Social Studies, Sociology, Speech, Vocational Agriculture, Vocational Business Office, Vocational Marketing, Vocational Home Economics/Consumer Homemaking), Special Education

The following programs are 5th year programs:
Elementary Education, K-12 Education (Art, Music, Physical Education), Secondary Education (Agriculture, Art, Biology, Business, Chemistry, Consumer & Family Science/Home Economics, Earth Science, Economics, English/Language Arts, Foreign Languages, Geography, Health, History, Industrial Technology, Mathematics, Physical Education, Physical Sciences, Physics, Political Science, Psychology, Social Studies, Sociology, Speech, Vocational Agriculture, Vocational Business Office, Vocational Marketing, Vocational Home Economics/Consumer Homemaking), Special Education

Augustana College

Augustana is a private, selective college of the liberal arts and sciences, located on 115 wooded acres overlooking the Mississippi River in Rock Island, Illinois, which is part of the Quad Cities metro area. Augustana's education majors develop a thorough knowledge of teaching theory in a context that includes a wide range of practical experience. Annual planning and assessment meetings with local educators assure that the teacher education program provides prospective teachers with the skills necessary to meet the complete spectrum of classroom challenges.

Just the facts...

Augustana College
Education Department
639 38th Street
Rock Island, IL 61201
(309) 794-7259
Website: edgarrett@augustana.edu
Profile: Urban, Small, Co-Ed
UG Tuition: $5,339.00/term
Off Campus Programs: No

Clinical Experiences

Clinical experience begins with the first course in the education sequence and is incorporated throughout the entire curriculum. Candidates are supervised by experienced education faculty and typically exceed the 100 hours of classroom work required by the Illinois State Board of Education. This extensive clinical experience is a powerful learning tool and ensures that prospective teachers are well prepared. The Quad Cities is a multicultural community large enough to offer every type of school—rural, urban, public, private and parochial. At the same time, it is small enough to ensure easy access to student teaching locations. Augustana works with local school systems to offer a full range of clinical and teaching experiences.

Noteworthy

Augustana College typically attracts students with strong social concerns. One priority of the education department is to prepare teachers who individualize instruction while coping successfully with the realities of modern educational systems. Consistent with this philosophy, the faculty treat candidates as individuals with distinct talents and needs as they learn to do the same for their own future students. All candidates work closely with a faculty adviser to help plan course schedules. The department's strong emphasis on preparation for graduate study provides the edge for advanced work in education.

Teacher Preparation Program Information

The following programs are 4 year programs:

Elementary Education, K-12 Education (Art, Music), Middle School Education, Secondary Education (Art, Biology, Chemistry, Earth Science, English/Language Arts, French, Geography, German, Mathematics, Physics, Political Science, Psychology, Sociology, Spanish)

Bradley University

Bradley University has prepared teachers and other school personnel since 1897. The faculty of the College of Education and Health Sciences is committed to preparing leaders in the human services professions. The Department of Teacher Education's primary mission is the preparation of "educational leaders and informed decision makers." Candidates are expected to become change agents who can effect a difference in student learning. The small class sizes at Bradley and individualized faculty attention help ensure that graduates are ready to successfully launch their teaching careers.

Just the facts...

Bradley University
College of Education and Health Sciences
1501 West Bradley Avenue
Peoria, IL 61625
(309) 677-3180
Website: www.bradley.edu
Profile: Urban, Medium, Co-Ed
UG Tuition: $6,620.00/semester
G Tuition: $359.00/credit hour
Off Campus Programs: No

Clinical Experiences

Practicum experiences in the schools begin the freshman year and continue each year of the program, increasing in responsibility. All of the clinical experiences are within the greater Peoria area and provide candidates with diverse placements in urban, suburban, and rural schools. All candidates have both university and school mentors. The university has professional development school partners at each level—early childhood, primary, middle school, and high school. Teacher education students have the opportunity to collaborate with other professionals and students in counseling, administration, and health care areas.

Noteworthy

Academic and talent scholarship awards, need-based awards, and awards directed to minority students are available. The teacher education program has had a placement record of nearly 100 percent in recent years. All elementary and early childhood education majors complete a double major in a liberal arts academic field. These majors are interdisciplinary in nature, and the options include middle school mathematics, general science, the humanities, and social studies. Graduates take on leadership roles in teaching, counseling, administration, and health care. An alumnus was named "First-Year Teacher of the Year" in Georgia in 1997.

Teacher Preparation Program Information

The following programs are 4 year programs:
Early Childhood Education, Elementary Education (Humanities Specialist, Language Arts, Mathematics, Science, Social Studies), K-12 Education (French, German, Music, Spanish), Kindergarten Education, Middle School Education (English, Mathematics, Science, Social Studies), Secondary Education (Art, Biology, Chemistry, Consumer & Family Science/Home Economics, Earth Science, English/Language Arts, General Science, History, Mathematics, Physics, Political Science, Psychology, Science, Science/Home Economics, Social Studies, Sociology, Speech, Theatre), Special Education (Developmental Disabilities/Handicaps, Learning Disability, Severe Behavioral Disabilities/Handicaps)

The following programs are 5th year programs:
Curriculum and Instruction, Special Education (Learning Disability)

Chicago State University

The College of Education at Chicago State University has prepared teachers for the nation's urban schools since it was founded in 1867 as an experimental teacher training school. The university prepares knowledgeable and competent educators who are dedicated to serving the education needs of students of varying abilities and backgrounds and are committed to improving the nation's schools and teaching profession. The College of Education's diverse student body and faculty reflect the diversity of the Chicago metropolitan area. All education programs include extensive site-based experiences, are standards-based, include school partnerships, incorporate comprehensive assessments, and integrate technology.

Just the facts...

Chicago State University
College of Education
9501 S. King Drive
Chicago, IL 60628
(773) 995-2472
Website: www.csu.edu
Profile: Urban, Medium, Co-Ed
UG Tuition: $89.50/cr. hr. in-state; $268.50/cr. hr. out-of-state
G Tuition: $94.50/cr. hr. in-state; $283.50/cr. hr. out-of-state
Off Campus Programs: No

Clinical Experiences

All education programs heavily emphasize clinical experiences. Pre-student teaching clinical experiences are site-based, and include observation, teacher-assistance, tutoring, and small-group instruction. All programs offer at least one required site-based course. Special field-based programs in early childhood education, elementary education, bilingual education, special education, and secondary education offer their professional curriculum in the field, fully integrating theory and practice. Student teaching is a full sixteen-week experience.

Noteworthy

Many services are available to assist education students. Teacher candidates are eligible to apply for the Minority Teachers in Illinois and DeBolt Teacher Shortage Scholarships. Four computer labs are housed in the College of Education to help integrate technology in the curriculum and improve the delivery of instruction. Special field-based programs are offered at the undergraduate and graduate levels for initial licensure: undergraduate programs in elementary education, bilingual education, special education, and secondary education; and Teachers for Chicago and Troops to Teachers, which are master's/intern programs for career-changing candidates.

Teacher Preparation Program Information

The following programs are 4 year programs:
Bilingual Elementary Education, Early Childhood Education, Elementary Education, K-12 Education (Physical Education, Special Education/EMH), Secondary Education (Art, Biology, Business, Chemistry, English, Geography, History, Industrial Technology, Mathematics, Music, Physical Education, Spanish)

The following programs are post-baccalaureate programs:
Bilingual Elementary Education, Early Childhood Education, Elementary Education, K-12 Education (Physical Education, Special Education/EMH), Secondary Education (Art, Biology, Business, Chemistry, English, Geography, History, Industrial Technology, Mathematics, Music, Physical Education, Spanish)

The following programs are 5th year programs:
Early Childhood Education, Elementary Education, Secondary Education (Art, Biology, Business, Chemistry, English, Geography, History, Industrial Technology, Mathematics, Music, Physical Education, Spanish)

Concordia University

Concordia University, a university of the Lutheran Church, Missouri Synod, has prepared teachers since 1856. The faculty in the College of Education is committed to delivering education programs in which educators are competent (highly knowledgeable and skilled), care for their pupils and the profession, and serve with dedication and professionalism. The College of Education is committed to ensuring that graduates have a strong liberal arts background, are able to use technology effectively, and recognize the strengths of a diverse society.

Just the facts...

Concordia University
Teacher Education
7400 Augusta
River Forest, IL 60305-1499
(708) 209-3437
Website: www.curf.edu
Profile: Suburban, Small, Co-Ed
UG Tuition: $286.00/credit hour
G Tuition: $336.00/credit hour
Off Campus Programs: No

Clinical Experiences

Clinical experiences at Concordia are an essential part of every prospective teacher's education. Methods classes are taught by professors in clinical settings. The pre-clinical hours are closely supervised and provide learning in a wide variety of settings and grade levels. Student teaching is done in a variety of sites both locally and throughout the nation and in two international settings. Concordia maintains formal professional development partnerships with three schools in the Chicago area. Student teaching assignments are available in both public and private settings. Concordia is also dedicated to providing clinical experiences in large, urban settings.

Noteworthy

Concordia University has a long history of service to the church and to the urban schools in Chicago and the surrounding region. Graduates from Concordia's teacher education programs are sought-after for their expertise, high level of commitment, and willingness to serve. A graduate from Concordia University was the major investigator for the Third International Mathematics and Science Study. Concordia continues its commitment to urban schools with innovative programs for preparing effective urban educators.

Teacher Preparation Program Information

The following programs are 4 year programs:
Early Childhood Education, Elementary Education, K-12 Education (Art, German, Reading), Middle School Education, Secondary Education (Art, Earth Science, English/Language Arts, General Science, Mathematics, Physical Sciences, Physical Education, Political Science, Psychology)

The following programs are 5 year programs:
Early Childhood Education, Elementary Education, K-12 Education (Art, German, Reading), Secondary Education (Earth Science, English/Language Arts, General Science, Mathematics, Physical Sciences, Physical Education, Political Science, Psychology)

The following programs are 5th year programs:
Early Childhood Education, Elementary Education (Language Arts, Mathematics, Science, Social Studies), K-12 Education (Art, German, Reading), Middle School Education, Secondary Education (Art)

DePaul University

DePaul University is one of the nation's largest Catholic institutions of higher learning. The two main campuses are located in downtown Chicago and Lincoln Park on the city's north side, and there are suburban campuses in DesPlaines, Lake County, Naperville, and Oak Forest. The School of Education is committed to educating students to become urban, professional, and multicultural educators. The program strives to graduate candidates who can integrate theory and practice, weigh and choose multiple perspectives, and promote lifelong student learning.

Just the facts...

DePaul University
School of Education
2320 N. Kenmore Avenue
Chicago, IL 60614
(773) 325-7740
Website: www.depaul.edu/~educate
Profile: Urban, Large, Co-Ed
UG Tuition: $275.00/credit hour
G Tuition: $320.00/credit hour
Off Campus Programs: Yes

Clinical Experiences

Clinical experiences include a minimum of 100 hours in schools, both in city and suburban areas. Candidates work with youth in classroom settings, tutoring projects, recreational venues, and the university's reading laboratory. Buses leave DePaul every morning during the school year to take teacher candidates to Chicago public schools. The schools have requested the university's assistance in raising student achievement levels. Experiences are directly linked to courses taken at the university; often, the entire class works in the same school, allowing for a great deal of interaction among candidates, K-12 students, and teachers and administrators. Candidates participate in eleven weeks of full-time student teaching.

Noteworthy

Opportunities to participate in DePaul's outreach programs and to tutor children or otherwise engage in hands-on, mentored practice are integral experiences in the educator preparation programs. One important outreach program is the DePaul Prep Academy, designed to help talented, inner-city, middle-school children develop skills and knowledge necessary to make the transition to, and succeed in, high school and beyond.

Teacher Preparation Program Information

The following programs are 4 year programs:

Early Childhood Education, Elementary Education K-8, K-12 Education (Music, Physical Education), Secondary Education 6-12 (Biology, Chemistry, Computer Science, English, French, Geography, German, History, Mathematics, Physics, Social Studies, Spanish)

The following programs are post-baccalaureate programs:

Early Childhood Education, Elementary Education, K-12 Education (Music, Physical Education), Secondary Education (Biology, Chemistry, Computer Science, English, French, Geography, German, History, Mathematics, Physics, Social Studies, Spanish)

The following programs are 5th year programs:

Early Childhood Eduation, Elementary Education, Secondary Education, Special Education (Learning Disabilities, Social and Emotional Disorders)

Eastern Illinois University

The College of Education and Professional Studies at EIU is committed to the idea that educators must have the knowledge bases to be able to effectively plan and manage educational environments that maximize student learning. Knowledge of how individuals learn, subject area competence, pedagogical knowledge, and understanding how schools function in society are essential. All programs educate students to become creators and managers of effective educational environments as they integrate their knowledge of students, subjects, strategies, and societies.

Just the facts...

Eastern Illinois University
College of Education and Professional Studies
1420 Buzzard Building
Charleston, IL 61920
(217) 581-2524
Website: www.eiu.edu
Profile: Rural, Large, Co-Ed
UG Tuition: $1,616.00/sem. in-state; $3,804.00/sem. out-of-state
G Tuition: $1,676.00/sem. in-state; $3,986.00/sem. out-of-state
Off Campus Programs: No

Clinical Experiences

Clinical experiences in the teacher education program move candidates from general experiences (observations, short-term participations) to more focused practice (micro-teaching, on-site teaching projects), culminating in a semester of full-time student teaching or an advanced practicum. Experiences are systematically selected based on program content, grade level, learner types, and cultural and demographic diversity. The selection is performed by trained university supervisors who take into consideration the needs of the candidate and the practices at a given site.

Noteworthy

The College of Education and Professional Studies is making good use of its recently completed $13 million building renovation project. The new building, Buzzard Hall, provides a beautiful, modern learning facility with state-of-the-art technology in its offices, classrooms, and laboratories. EIU has developed a network of professional development schools where students have access to new instructional technology, help from additional instructors, and exposure to a large variety of effective instructional strategies. The College of Education and Professional Studies is dedicated to quality programs, has a highly qualified and dedicated faculty, and a clinically intensive, contemporary curriculum.

Teacher Preparation Program Information

The following programs are 4 year programs:
Early Childhood Education, Elementary Education, Middle School Education (Art, English, Family & Consumer Sciences, History, Mathematics, Physical Education, Social Studies, Technology Education), Secondary Education (Art, Biological Sciences, Business, Chemistry, English, Family & Consumer Sciences, Foreign Languages, Health Studies, History, Mathematics, Music, Physical Education, Physics, Social Sciences, Speech Communication, Technology, Theater Arts), Special Education (Early Childhood Disabilities, Mild/Moderate Disabilities)

The following programs are post-baccalaureate programs:
Early Childhood Education, Elementary Education, Middle School Education (Art, English, Family & Consumer Sciences, History, Mathematics, Physical Education, Social Studies, Technology Education), Secondary Education (Art, Biological Sciences, Business, Chemistry, English, Family & Consumer Sciences, Foreign Languages, Health Studies, History, Mathematics, Music, Physical Education, Physics, Social Sciences, Speech Communication, Technology, Theater Arts), Special Education (Early Childhood Disabilities, Mild/Moderate Disabilities)

The following programs are 5 year programs:
Communication Disorders and Sciences

Elmhurst College

Elmhurst's Department of Education programs are designed to develop teachers who are caring, creative, and skilled in using a variety of teaching methods and technologies in the classroom. Graduates understand student growth and development, are able to organize and manage learning groups, and can creatively design learning experiences based upon lesson objectives and students' needs and developmental levels. Program graduates are committed to a classroom culture of inclusion that meets the needs of diverse students with varying abilities.

Just the facts...

Elmhurst College
Education Department
190 Prospect Street
Elmhurst, IL 60126-3296
(630) 617-3545
Website: www.elmhurst.edu
Profile: Suburban, Small, Co-Ed
UG Tuition: $6,435.00/semester
Off Campus Programs: No

Clinical Experiences

Clinical experiences are an integral component of the Education Department's teacher education programs. During a candidate's first course in professional education, he or she is asked to file a field experience plan. Candidates have the option of applying to the Satellite Program (*see Noteworthy*), or design a field experience of their own that would include a mentor teacher(s) and that would lend itself to evaluation. Student teaching is the culminating experience of each teacher education program.

Noteworthy

The Satellite Program is a collaborative program of the Education Department and 58 area schools. It is designed to strengthen candidates' clinical experiences. Candidates in the program are linked to satellite schools and are assigned to mentor teachers who support and assist them in structured, monitored, and varied clinical experiences. The Teacher Technology Program requires candidates to demonstrate proficiency in basic and advanced technology competencies and integrate them into lesson plans. The London, England Experience provides candidates with clinical opportunities to work in schools abroad during the January Term.

Teacher Preparation Program Information

The following programs are 4 year programs:
Early Childhood Education, Elementary Education, K-12 Education (Art, Music, Physical Education), Secondary Education (Biology, Chemistry, English/Language Arts, French, Geography, German, History, Mathematics, Physical Education, Physics, Political Science, Psychology, Sociology, Spanish, Speech/Theatre), Special Education (Learning Disabilities/Behavior Disorders)

The following programs are post-baccalaureate programs:
Early Childhood Education, Elementary Education, K-12 Education (Art, Music, Physical Education), Secondary Education (Biology, Chemistry, English/Language Arts, French, Geography, German, History, Mathematics, Physical Education, Physics, Political Science, Psychology, Sociology, Spanish, Speech/Theatre), Special Education (Learning Disabilities/Behavior Disorders)

The following programs are 5th year programs:
Early Childhood Special Education

Illinois State University

Illinois State University has a historic and enduring commitment to educate teachers who will be responsive to the moral and intellectual demands that a democratic society places on them. Established in 1857 to prepare teachers, ISU is currently the sixth largest producer of educators in the nation. Programs in the teacher education unit are built on "Realizing the Democratic Ideal." Graduates aspire to teach everyone, especially those who have been or are in danger of being excluded from the educational system. Graduates possess a strong, positive, professional identity.

Just the facts...

Illinois State University
College of Education
Campus Box 5300
Normal, IL 61790-5300
(309) 438-5415
Website: www.ilstu.edu
Profile: Urban, Large, Co-Ed
UG Tuition: $101.25/cr. hr. in-state; $303.75/cr. hr. out-of-state
G Tuition: $102.25/cr. hr. in-state; $306.75/cr. hr. out-of-state
Off Campus Programs: No

Clinical Experiences

Candidates complete at least 100 hours in schools prior to student teaching for ten full weeks or longer. Clinical experiences in Illinois' only state-funded P-12 laboratory schools complement those available in local schools and in year-long professional development school sites at the elementary or middle school level in several locations. Special education sequences are field-based. Secondary majors teach in districts throughout the state. Unique clinical experiences in urban, suburban, and rural Illinois, as well as in Texas, Florida, Mexico, and England, are available.

Noteworthy

Illinois State University's graduates have a high rate of employability as teachers, administrators, and school personnel throughout the state and the nation. Although ISU prepares large numbers of teachers, each one receives personal attention from its caring, dedicated faculty. The university has scholarships and undergraduate teaching assistantships for education students in each college. Illinois State University is a member of the Holmes Partnership. Faculty and teacher candidates are active in state education policy initiatives.

Teacher Preparation Program Information

The following programs are 4 year programs:
Early Childhood Education, Elementary Education (including Bilingual Education, Spanish), K-12 Education (Art, Business, Music, Physical Education), Middle School Education, Secondary Education (Agriculture, Biology, Business, Chemistry, Consumer & Family Science/Home Economics, English/Language Arts, French, Geography, German, Health, History, Industrial Technology, Mathematics, Physical Education, Physics, Social Science, Spanish, Speech, Theatre), Special Education (Educable Mentally Disabled, Hearing Impaired, Learning Disabilities-Social Emotional Disorders, Physical Disabilities, Trainable Mentally Disabled, Visual Disabilities), Speech Communication

The following programs are post-baccalaureate programs:
Early Childhood Education, Elementary Education (including Bilingual Education, Spanish), K-12 Education (Art, Business, Music, Physical Education), Middle School Education, Secondary Education (Agriculture, Biology, Business, Chemistry, Consumer & Family Science/Home Economics, English/Language Arts, French, Geography, German, Health, History, Industrial Technology, Mathematics, Physical Education, Physics, Social Science, Spanish, Speech, Theatre), Special Education (Educable Mentally Disabled, Hearing Impaired, Learning Disabilities-Social Emotional Disorders, Physical Disabilities, Trainable Mentally Disabled, Visual Disabilities), Speech Communication

The following programs are 5th year programs:
Reading

Northern Illinois University

Northern Illinois University, the fourth-largest public comprehensive university in the state, has been dedicated to teacher education from its founding in 1895. The Northern Illinois University "community of learners" includes scholars, education professionals, and teacher candidates working together to build on knowledge, practice, and reflection to produce exemplary educators. Candidates develop their strengths in creative and critical thinking, scholarship, and caring in a diverse community that supports lifelong learning.

Just the facts...

Northern Illinois University
Associate Provost
Lowden Hall 307
De Kalb, IL 60115
(815) 753-0494
Website: www.niu.edu
Profile: Rural, Large, Co-Ed
UG Tuition: $146.30/cr. hr. in-state; $350.30/cr. hr. out-of-state
Off Campus Programs: Yes

Clinical Experiences

Clinical experiences are essential to NIU's teacher education program and are combined with methods and content courses. Time spent in field experiences exceed the hours required by the state. Candidates are placed with experienced, well-trained teachers. Many placements are in partnership schools. These sites expose candidates to excellent teaching practices, action research opportunities, and technology-rich experiences from beginning observations through student teaching. Student teaching is a sixteen-week long experience.

Noteworthy

NIU offers teacher education students many scholarship opportunities. Technology plays an important role in teacher preparation, and the university and the College of Education have made major investments in computer laboratories and "smart" classrooms, all hooked to a fiber-optic network infrastructure. Specialized language learning laboratories, distance education, and multimedia computing facilities are also available. Over one dozen teachers from NIU's education programs have won state and national teaching honors in the past several years. The current Teacher of the Year is pursuing a graduate degree and further certification from the College of Education.

Teacher Preparation Program Information

The following programs are 4 year programs:

Early Childhood Education, Elementary Education, K-12 Education (Art, Physical Education), Secondary Education (Biology, Chemistry, English, Family Consumer & Nutrition Sciences, French, General Science, Geology, German, Health Education, History, Mathematics, Physical Sciences, Physics, Sciences, Spanish, Theatre Arts), Special Education (Deaf and Hard of Hearing, Developmental Disabilities/Multiply Disabled, High-Incidence Disabilities, Vision Impairments)

Roosevelt University

The College of Education prepares teachers, prinicipals, and counselors for the modern day challenges of Chicago metropolitan schools. Committed to reflective practice and transformational leadership, faculty prepare candidates to become facilitators, leaders, learners, and researchers in whatever professional role they pursue. Excellent collaboration with the colleges of arts and sciences, music, business, and continuing education enables candidates to combine content studies with a comprehensive array of pedagogical experiences. Roosevelt has been long committed to diversity and social responsibility.

Just the facts...

Roosevelt University
College of Education
430 South Michigan Avenue
Chicago, IL 60605
(312) 341-3701
Website: www.roosevelt.edu
Profile: Urban, Medium, Co-Ed
UG Tuition: $380.00/credit hour
G Tuition: $445.00/credit hour
Off Campus Programs: No

Clinical Experiences

Teacher candidates are required to participate in a full range of field experiences that begin with observing classrooms and helping to teach and critique lessons. Clinical experiences culminate with full immersion in student teaching assignments. Earlier clinical experiences focus on course content and enable candidates to transfer theoretical knowledge into the life of teachers and students within schools. In addition to the acquisition of a caring perspective and working knowledge of schools and classrooms at various levels of education, strong emphasis is placed on the development of respect and understanding of the diverse experiences and backgrounds of students.

Noteworthy

Special programs offered by the College of Education include the Metropolitan Elementary Teacher Academy, the Masters of Arts in Leadership, and the Chicago Alliance Leadership for Learning (MA in Educational Administration). Roosevelt is student-centered, featuring committed faculty, excellent advising, small class sizes, field-based courses, classes in the evenings and on weekends, extensive financial aid opportunities, and relatively low tuition. The College of Education enjoys several university/school partnerships, and prides itself on its metropolitan focus and its ability to offer multicultural experiences to its candidates.

Teacher Preparation Program Information

The following programs are 4 year programs:
Early Childhood Education, Elementary Education, Secondary Education (Business, English, French, General Science, Mathematics, Social Studies, Spanish, Theatre Arts)

The following programs are 5th year programs:
Early Childhood Education, Elementary Education, Secondary Education (Business, English, General Science, Mathematics, Social Studies, Spanish, Theatre Arts)

Southern Illinois University at Carbondale

Southern Illinois University at Carbondale has been involved in teacher education since its founding in 1847. It has since evolved into a multipurpose, comprehensive university. SIUC has continued its commitment to the preparation of teachers. The College of Education has designed its programs incorporating three basic components—a broad liberal arts education, in-depth study in an area of specialization, and training in pedagogy, technology, and practicum experiences.

Just the facts...

Southern Illinois University at Carbondale
College of Education
Carbondale, IL 62901
(618) 453-2415
Website: www.siu.edu
Profile: Rural, Large, Co-Ed
UG Tuition: $92.70/cr. hr. in-state; $278.10/cr. hr. out-of-state
G Tuition: $98.80/cr. hr. in-state; $296.40/cr. hr. out-of-state
Off Campus Programs: No

Clinical Experiences

Candidates in SIUC's teacher education program spend several semesters in public school classrooms completing practicum and student teaching experiences. Candidates begin their field experiences by spending a full day a week in a classroom as part of their "Introduction to Reflective Teaching Practice" course. A second semester is spent in classrooms as an integral component of the class "Classroom Management and Discipline." Finally, candidates complete their teacher education experiences with a full sixteen-week semester of student teaching. Candidates are placed in professional development centers for their clinical experiences.

Noteworthy

Technology plays a major role in the preparation of future teachers at SIUC. The Microcomputer Laboratory, the Teaching Skills Laboratory, and the Instructional Technology Laboratory all provide opportunities for candidates to learn how to integrate technology into their teaching. The Professional Development Center facilitates candidates' entry into the teaching profession by encouraging their involvement in schools. The College of Education is currently revising many of its programs to ensure that candidates meet the standards established by national content specialty organizations (such as the standards of the National Council of Teachers of Mathematics and the Council for Exceptional Children).

Teacher Preparation Program Information

The following programs are 4 year programs:

Early Childhood Education, Elementary Education (Mathematics, Science, Social Studies), K-12 Education (Art, French, German, Music, Physical Education, Spanish), Secondary Education (Agriculture, Art, Biology, Business, English, Health, History, Mathematics, Science, Science/Home Economics, Social Studies, Vocational Business Office), Special Education (Learning Disability, Severe Behavioral Disabilities/Handicaps, Speech-Language Disabilities)

The following programs are post-baccalaureate programs:

Early Childhood Education, Elementary Education (Mathematics, Science, Social Studies), K-12 Education (Art, French, German, Music, Physical Education, Spanish), Secondary Education (Agriculture, Art, Biology, Business, English, Health, History, Mathematics, Science, Science/Home Economics, Social Studies, Vocational Business Office), Special Education (Learning Disability, Severe Behavioral Disabilities/Handicaps, Speech-Language Disabilities)

Southern Illinois University Edwardsville

The theme for professional education programs at Southern Illinois University Edwardsville is the "Teacher as an Inquirer-Professional." The faculty in the School of Education is committed to the idea that teachers must perform as professionals, and as professionals, they must base their decisions on continuous inquiry into best practice. Programs emphasize six areas: knowledge application and development, instructional process, learners and learning, contexts of education, interpersonal relationships, and professional relationships.

Just the facts...

Southern Illinois University Edwardsville
School of Education
Box 1049
Edwardsville, IL 62026-1049
(618) 650-3350
Website: www.siue.edu
Profile: Suburban, Large, Co-Ed
UG Tuition: $1,040.00/sem. in-state; $3,121.00/sem. out-of-state
G Tuition: $1,144.00/sem. in-state; $3,432.00/sem. out-of-state
Off Campus Programs: No

Clinical Experiences

Faculty in the School of Education believe that candidates should engage in numerous supervised activities with children. The teacher education program combines on-campus instruction in professional courses with off-campus clinical practice in classrooms. The university is strategically located in a metropolitan area which provides a wealth of diversity for candidates' clinical experiences. In addition, the university is collaborating with area school districts to implement quality professional development schools.

Noteworthy

Teacher candidates have access to a wide array of technologies as they learn to use technology in K-12 classrooms. Education students may be eligible for the State of Illinois Scholarships which include the David A. DeBolt Teacher Shortage Scholarship and Minority Teachers of Illinois Scholarship, among others. Candidates are also given preference for some university-based scholarships.

Teacher Preparation Program Information

The following programs are 4 year programs:
Early Childhood Education, Elementary Education, K-12 Education (Art, Music, Physical Education), Secondary Education (Biology, Chemistry, English, French, German, General Science, Health, History, Physical Education, Physics, Mathematics, Spanish, Speech Communications), Special Education (Emotional Disturbance, Learning Disabled, Mental Retardation)

The following programs are post-baccalaureate programs:
Early Childhood Education, Elementary Education, K-12 Education (Art, Music, Physical Education), Secondary Education (Biology, Chemistry, English, French, German, General Science, Health, History, Physical Education, Physics, Mathematics, Spanish, Speech Communications), Special Education (Emotional Disturbance, Learning Disabled, Mental Retardation)

The following programs are 5 year programs:
Speech and Language Disabilities

The following programs are 5th year programs:
Early Childhood Education, Elementary Education, K-12 Education (Art, Music, Physical Education), Secondary Education (Biology, Chemistry, English, French, German, General Science, Health, History, Physical Education, Physics, Mathematics, Spanish, Speech Communications), Special Education (Emotional Disturbance, Learning Disabled, Mental Retardation)

Western Illinois University

Western Illinois University has been preparing teachers since 1899. The unifying goal of the WIU teacher education programs is the integration of a thorough knowledge of subject content with effective teaching skills. This goal emphasizes not only teaching content but also understanding the ethical nature of educational decision making, perceiving the implications of diversity, and using technology appropriately. Graduates are committed to a continual process of educational inquiry, practice, and reflection throughout their teaching careers.

Just the facts...

Western Illinois University
College of Education
#1 University Circle
Macomb, IL 61455
(309) 298-1690
Website: www.wiu.edu
Profile: Rural, Large, Co-Ed
UG Tuition: $91.00/cr.hr. in-state; $182.00/cr. hr. out-of-state
G Tuition: $1,188.00/sem. in-state; $2,376.00/sem. out-of-state
Off Campus Programs: Yes

Clinical Experiences

WIU provides candidates with early and diverse field experiences. Clinical experiences provide candidates with the opportunity to carefully examine their career choice as well as to explore and use best practices in teaching. Diverse experiences are available to candidates through student teaching, in the use of technology to provide diverse experiences, and participation in a two-week May interim session in which candidates are placed in schools in the Quad Cities area. These opportunities provide candidates with the ability to teach culturally diverse students as well as students with special needs.

Noteworthy

The Illinois State Board of Education invited Western Illinois University to participate in the redesign of the state's teacher education programs. WIU requires candidates in teacher education to develop "progressive learning" portfolios to demonstrate their ability to teach and to demonstrate the multiple methods and strategies they have learned in their programs. Candidates share their portfolios with their peers and with faculty. These portfolios provide evidence that candidates are able to meet state and national performance standards.

Teacher Preparation Program Information

The following programs are 4 year programs:

Early Childhood Education, Elementary Education, Elementary Bilingual/Bicultural Education , K-12 Education (Art, Music, Physical Education), Secondary Education (Agriculture, Art, Biology, Chemistry, English, French, Geography, History, Industrial Education and Technology, Mathematics, Physical Education, Physics, Political Science, Psychology, Spanish, Speech), Special Education (Learning Disabilities, Mentally Retarded-Educable or Trainable, Social/Emotional Disorders)

The following programs are post-baccalaureate programs:

Early Childhood Education, Elementary Education, Elementary Bilingual/Bicultural Education , K-12 Education (Art, Music, Physical Education), Secondary Education (Agriculture, Art, Biology, Chemistry, English, French, Geography, History, Industrial Education and Technology, Mathematics, Physical Education, Physics, Political Science, Psychology, Spanish, Speech), Special Education (Learning Disabilities, Mentally Retarded-Educable or Trainable, Social/Emotional Disorders)

Wheaton College

Wheaton College has a commitment to do all things "For Christ and His Kingdom." The college integrates faith and learning in its effort to maintain academic excellence and promote the evangelical Christian faith. Wheaton's Teacher Education Program prepares teachers who function as social, moral, and pedagogical "Agents of Change" and become actively involved in finding ways to alleviate the conditions that keep the nation from effectively educating all students.

Just the facts...

Wheaton College
Department of Education
501 College Avenue
Wheaton, IL 60187
(630) 752-5041
Website: www.wheaton.edu
Profile: Suburban, Small, Co-Ed
UG Tuition: $7,180.00/semester
Off Campus Programs: No

Clinical Experiences

The Department of Education offers candidates a variety of clinical experiences. In the first year, candidates participate in a multicultural practicum through various ministries. Subsequent experiences include teacher assistance, methods practica, and student teaching. Opportunities for suburban, urban, and foreign student teaching are available. A new clinical school project has been initiated.

Noteworthy

Wheaton College is an evangelical Christian college that integrates the Christian faith into all endeavors. In addition to a solid liberal arts preparation, all teacher candidates also complete a series of courses in the Bible and theology. The Wheaton education program attracts a national student body and offers a variety of opportunities for involvement. Education graduates take positions in public education, private Christian education, and missionary projects. An accelerated Master of Arts in Teaching program is available.

Teacher Preparation Program Information

The following programs are 4 year programs:
Elementary Education, K-12 Education (Art, Music, Physical Education), Secondary Education 6-12 (Biology, Chemistry, English/Language Arts, French, German, Mathematics, Physical Education, Physical Sciences, Physics, Political Science, Psychology, Social Studies, Spanish)

The following programs are 5th year programs:
Secondary Education 6-12 (Biology, Chemistry, English, French, Geology, German, History, Mathematics, Physical Education, Physics, Political Science, Social Science, Spanish)

Anderson University

The teacher education program at Anderson University strives to develop students who will become analytic, reflective, and caring professionals. The curriculum is built on a strong liberal arts component coupled with a conceptual framework emphasizing knowledge of self, students, schools, communities, and teaching. Candidates develop a global perspective and learn how to be competent and effective in their classrooms. Graduates use technological skills effectively, understand the role of the school in a democratic society, value and respect the individual student, and implement critical inquiry in their classrooms.

Just the facts...

Anderson University
School of Education
1100 East Fifth Street
Anderson, IN 46012
(765) 641-4400
Website: www.anderson.edu/academics/educ/index.html
Profile: Suburban, Small, Co-Ed
UG Tuition: $6,535.00/sem. in-state; $546.00/cr. hr. out-of-state
Off Campus Programs: No

Clinical Experiences

Clinical experiences are required for all candidates. Activities include observing, participating, tutoring, teaching small groups, and full-time student teaching. Candidates experience diversity through clinical experiences that include urban and suburban schools and placements in schools serving different socioeconomic groups. Candidates work with a range of grade levels and content areas. Opportunities are available for student teaching in an urban life experience, a suburban placement in an experimental partnership school, and an overseas experience in an international school.

Noteworthy

The School of Education, in collaboration with a local school system, was awarded a technology grant from Apple Computer. The grant was one of only ten awarded nationwide. The project provides for joint research by elementary and college students to build awareness of local culture and will culminate in a published book on the history of the local county. The project has been recognized by the Smithsonian and is part of the Collection on Information and Technology Innovations at the National Museum of American History. The grant included extensive equipment and software for both the public school and the university.

Teacher Preparation Program Information

The following programs are 4 year programs:
Elementary Education, K-12 Education (Art, Music, Physical Education, Reading, Curriculum & Instruction), Middle School Education (English, Mathematics, Science, Social Studies), Secondary Education (Art, Biology, Chemistry, Economics, Curriculum & Instruction, English/Language Arts, French, General Science, German, Health, Journalism, Mathematics, Music, Physical Education, Physical Sciences, Physics, Political Science, Psychology, Science, Social Studies, Sociology, Spanish, Speech)

The following programs are post-baccalaureate programs:
Elementary Education, K-12 Education (Art, Music, Physical Education), Middle School Education (English, French, German, Mathematics, Reading, Science, Social Studies, Spanish), Secondary Education (Art, Biology, Chemistry, Economics, English/Language Arts, French, General Science, German, Health, Mathematics, Music, Physical Education, Physical Science, Physics, Political Science, Social Studies, Spanish, Speech)

Ball State University

Ball State University's Teachers College, a member of the Holmes Partnership, is committed to preparing outstanding professional educators and human service providers, supporting their induction and continuing education, promoting research and development in their fields, and influencing policy to enhance their efforts. Distinctive features of the program include personal attention from a diverse faculty of teacher-scholars, field-based assignments in a variety of settings where best practices are exhibited, and emphasis on civic responsibility, international/multicultural experiences, innovation, and performance assessment.

Just the facts...

Ball State University
Teachers College
2000 University
Muncie, IN 47306
(765) 285-5251
Website: www.bsu.edu/teachers
Profile: Urban, Large, Co-Ed
UG Tuition: $1,727.00/sem. in-state; $4,658.00/sem. out-of-state
G Tuition: $1,817.00/sem. in-state; $4,748.00/sem. out-of-state
Off Campus Programs: Yes

Clinical Experiences

Early and continuous field experiences are an integral part of teacher preparation. Ball State has the only laboratory school in Indiana, the K-12 Burris School. The laboratory school and a growing number of professional development school partnerships offer candidates unique opportunities to observe, participate, and student teach in urban, suburban, and rural settings. Unique opportunties include an urban semester program, a year-long paid internship, summer experiences abroad, and a year in residence at the Indiana School for the Deaf.

Noteworthy

Teaching majors represent one of the largest majors in the University Honors College. Student education organizations provide opportunities for student leadership and professional development. Teaching majors are required to complete meaningful service learning activities and prove their technological competence. A performance-based assessment system for teachers is being designed to encourage and to help candidates prepare to apply for National Board Certification. Scholarships and assistantships are available for undergraduate and graduate students, with an endowed fund providing support for research and travel for graduate students.

Teacher Preparation Program Information

The following programs are 4 year programs:
Early Childhood Education, Elementary Education, K-12 Education (Art, Music, Physical Education), Secondary Education (Business, Consumer & Family Science/Home Economics, English/Language Arts, Health, Journalism, Mathematics, Science, Social Studies, Speech, Trade & Industrial, Vocational Marketing, Vocational Home Economics/Consumer Homemaking, Vocational Home Economics/Job Training, Vocational Trade & Industrial), Special Education (Hearing Impaired, Multiple Disabilities/Handicaps, Severe Behavioral Disabilities/Handicaps)

The following programs are post-baccalaureate programs:
Early Childhood Education, Elementary Education, K-12 Education (Art, Music, Physical Education), Secondary Education (Art, Biology, Business, Chemistry, Consumer & Family Science/Home Economics, Earth Science, Economics, English/Language Arts, General Science, Geography, Health, Journalism, Mathematics, Physics, Political Science, Psychology, Science, Social Studies, Sociology, Speech, Trade & Industrial, Vocational Business, Vocational Marketing, Vocational Trade & Industrial), Special Education (Adaptive Physical Education, Early Childhood, Hearing Impaired, Learning Disability, Physical Disabilities/Handicaps, Severe Behavioral Disabilities/Handicaps)

Bethel College

Bethel College was founded in 1947 as a Christian liberal arts college by the Missionary Church, a denomination with roots in both the Mennonite and Methodist traditions. It is a growing, dynamic, progressive institution dedicated to its mission as an evangelical Christian college, to its founding denomination, and to the local community. Candidates prepare for public and private school teaching by completing a major in their area of interest along with professional education courses. The Division of Education has the largest number of majors in the college, and job placement rates for its graduates are high.

Just the facts...

Bethel College
Division of Education
1001 W. McKinley Avenue
Mishawaka, IN 46545
(219) 257-3501
Website: www.bethel-in.edu
Profile: Urban, Small, Co-Ed
UG Tuition: $5,750.00/semester
Off Campus Programs: No

Clinical Experiences

Work in schools begins during the first education courses candidates take, as early as their freshman year. Field/clinical experiences provide opportunities to work in rural, urban, private, and public schools. The Division of Education has established partnerships with four of the school corporations in Saint Joseph county and often places students in the Elkhart county school system as well. Partnerships with area schools provide a valuable opportunity to develop teaching skills in "real world" situations.

Noteworthy

Various scholarships are available for candidates, including special minority scholarships and a Divisional Assistantship for a junior or senior student interested in assisting faculty members with special projects. Candidates are invited to join the Bethel College branch of the Association for Childhood Education International (BC-ACEI). The BC-ACEI is service-oriented and participates in projects for children and their families. There are also opportunities for candidates to travel with that group to the Annual International Study Conference. Several graduates work in international and home mission schools.

Teacher Preparation Program Information

The following programs are 4 year programs:

Elementary Education, K-12 Education (Music, Physical Education), Secondary Education (Biology, Business, Chemistry, English/Language Arts, Mathematics, Physical Education, Physics, Science, Social Studies)

The following programs are post-baccalaureate programs:

Elementary Education, K-12 Education (Music, Physical Education), Secondary Education (Biology, Business, Chemistry, English/Language Arts, Mathematics, Physical Education, Physics, Science, Social Studies)

Butler University

The College of Education at Butler University was created in 1930 when Butler's Department of Education, established in 1919, and the Teachers College of Indianapolis, founded in 1892, were combined. The major purposes of the College of Education are (1) preparing teachers, supervisors, counselors, and administrators for positions in P-12 education, and (2) providing services to schools, educational organizations and agencies and the general community through surveys, consultative services, research, cooperative studies, and clinical services.

Just the facts...

Butler University
College of Education
4600 Sunset Avenue
Indianapolis, IN 46208
(317) 940-9752
Website: www.butler.edu
Profile: Urban, Medium, Co-Ed
UG Tuition: $8,140.00/semester
G Tuition: $220.00/credit hour
Off Campus Programs: No

Clinical Experiences

Butler's education program provides an early introduction to the profession of teaching. Candidates are encouraged to explore teaching as early as the first semester of the freshman year. This introduction to teaching ranges from learning about lesson plans, parent conferences, and curriculum, to recognizing and adapting to the needs and characteristics of individual students. Candidates are supported by cohort groups of peers, professors, graduates, and professionals in the field of education. Clinical experiences culminate in two different student teaching experiences.

Noteworthy

The College of Education is moving toward performance-based programs in all areas. Most of its programs are delivered in professional development P-12 school partnerships. A number of college partnerships afford candidates opportunities to learn within a community of education professionals. For example, the Indiana Technology Learning Center, a three-way partnership, provides access to state-of-the-art technology and a variety of constituencies learning how to use technology to improve student learning.

Teacher Preparation Program Information

The following programs are 4 year programs:
Early Childhood Education, Elementary Education, Kindergarten-Primary Education/K-3, K-12 Education (Music, Physical Education), Middle Grades Education/5-9 (Language Arts, Mathematics, Science, Social Studies), Secondary Education (Biology, Chemistry, English, French, German, Journalism, Latin, Mathemathics, Physics, Radio-TV, Social Studies, Spanish, Speech Communications and Theatre)

DePauw University

The DePauw Teacher Education Program offers comprehensive field experiences and professional preparation emphasizing issues as well as pedagogy for future K-12 teachers. DePauw prepares the "Teacher as a Professional Leader and Educator." After a holistic education steeped in the liberal arts, interdisciplinary knowledge, and professional studies, graduates are expected to have attained the characteristics of a professional educator through their demonstration of critical thinking, effective communication, collaborative skills, advocacy for public education, and commitment to excellence in education.

Just the facts...

DePauw University
Department of Education
7 Asbury Hall
Greencastle, IN 46135
(765) 658-4812
Website: www.depauw.edu
Profile: Rural, Small, Co-Ed
UG Tuition: $8,825.00/semester
Off Campus Programs: No

Clinical Experiences

Candidates participate in field-based and laboratory experiences throughout their program. Field settings and mentors are selected to provide exposure to varied curricular programs, teaching styles, and diverse learners. Candidates participate in multicultural environments and in rural, urban, and suburban settings. University and public school faculty collaborate to design field experiences, and some university classes meet at public school sites. Candidates may design month-long off-campus winter-term internships where they can obtain in-depth experiences in special classroom settings in any location.

Noteworthy

The integration of technology throughout the Teacher Education Program is a major focus at DePauw. Funds are being sought for the development of a state-of-the-art facility to model the application of technology in teaching. Faculty have initiated funded technology projects involving university students and public school participants. Professional collaborations have been developed to provide on-site experiences and mentoring for science education, literacy, technology, and middle school curriculum. Graduates have been successful in obtaining teaching positions in both public and private schools that emphasize unique curricular programs.

Teacher Preparation Program Information

The following programs are 4 year programs:

Elementary Education, K-12 Education (Art, Music, Physical Education), Middle School Education (English, Mathematics, Science, Social Studies), Secondary Education (Art, Biology, Chemistry, Earth Science, Economics, English/Language Arts, Geography, Mathematics, Physical Education, Physics, Political Science, Psychology, Sociology)

The following programs are post-baccalaureate programs:

K-12 Education (Art, Music, Physical Education), Middle School Education (English, Mathematics, Science, Social Studies), Secondary Education (Art, Biology, Chemistry, Earth Science, Economics, English/Language Arts, Geography, Mathematics, Physical Education, Physics, Political Science, Psychology, Sociology)

Franklin College

The education program at Franklin College prepares future teachers and teacher-leaders to be competent, caring decision makers. Over one-fourth of the student body is affiliated with the teacher education program. Past and present college administrators at Franklin refer to the Education Department as "one of the four jewels in the crown," because they consider it to be one of the college's top-quality departments. The Education Department honors its roots in the liberal arts tradition while also working to help candidates gain the necessary tools to establish a professional career in the 21st century classroom.

Just the facts...

Franklin College
Education Department
501 East Monroe
Franklin, IN 46131
(317) 738-8253
Website: www.franklincoll.edu
Profile: Suburban, Small, Co-Ed
UG Tuition: $6,485.00/semester
Off Campus Programs: No

Clinical Experiences

All courses are designed to help future teachers be effective with children, and all include a field experience component. Visits to schools begin during the fall semester of the sophomore year in both the elementary and secondary programs. Each field experience assignment is usually in a different school, district, and grade level. Candidates experience inclusion and multicultural classrooms, and overseas or unique sites within the United States can be provided for candidates with particular interests. Franklin is proud of its close, personal supervision of field experiences by college personnel who were formerly P-12 teachers.

Noteworthy

In addition to the many opportunities for candidates to learn how to teach by practicing in real classrooms, Franklin is proud of the high job placement rates achieved by recent graduates of the elementary, middle, and secondary programs. Such career success reflects the high standards met by the candidates and the excellent reputation held by the program. Future projects are planned that will enable candidates to become leaders in multiple campus-wide education projects.

Teacher Preparation Program Information

The following programs are 4 year programs:
Elementary Education, Elementary Music Education, Elementary Reading Education, K-12 Education (Physical Education), Middle School Education (General Science, Language Arts, Mathematics, Social Studies, Middle School Reading Education), Secondary Education/5-12 or 9-12 (Biology, Chemistry, Economics, English, French, General Science, Journalism, Mathematics, Physical Education, Health and Safety, Physics, Political Science, Psychology, Reading, Sociology, Spanish, United States History, World Civilization)

Goshen College

At Goshen College teaching and learning involve dynamic interaction between students, teachers and content matter. Learning experiences are built from the life experiences of both students and teachers. The college seeks to graduate teachers who (1) thoroughly comprehend the content they teach, (2) build learning communities based on the diversity of students' backgrounds and the ways in which they learn, (3) flexibly employ a wide variety of teaching and assessment strategies, (4) manage classrooms effectively, (5) sense a strong call to serve, and (6) continually reflect on their teaching.

Just the facts...

Goshen College
Department of Education
Goshen, IN 46526
(219) 535-7440
Website: www.goshen.edu
Profile: Rural, Small, Co-Ed
UG Tuition: $6,160.00/semester
Off Campus Programs: Yes

Clinical Experiences

All candidates participate in a wide range of public school settings with students of diverse racial, cultural, and linguistic backgrounds. Candidates also have the opportunity to participate on campus in a laboratory kindergarten and in a preschool center. More than two-thirds of Goshen College education students choose to participate in a study-service semester, frequently as assistants in schools in other countries such as Costa Rica, Dominican Republic, Ivory Coast, and Germany.

Noteworthy

Education faculty maintain close contact with educators in local schools, keep current with the realities of classroom teaching, and collaborate with teachers in classroom research. Peace education and global education are strong emphases within the education department and throughout the college. Education students frequently elect minors in peace studies, intercultural studies or Teaching English to Speakers of Other Languages (TESOL). Students have opportunities to learn about other cultures first-hand and to develop conversational skill in Spanish, French or German through a three-month study-service term abroad.

Teacher Preparation Program Information

The following programs are 4 year programs:
Early Childhood Education, Elementary Education, K-12 Education (Art, ESL, French, German, Health, Music, Physical Education, Spanish), Kindergarten Education, Middle School Education (English, Mathematics, Science, Social Studies), Secondary Education (Art, Biology, Business, Chemistry, Economics, English/Language Arts, General Science, Health, Mathematics, Physical Education, Physical Sciences, Physics, Political Science, Psychology, Sociology, Speech, Theatre)

The following programs are post-baccalaureate programs:
Early Childhood Education, Elementary Education, K-12 Education (Art, ESL, French, German, Spanish, Health, Music, Physical Education), Kindergarten Education, Middle School Education (English, Mathematics, Science, Social Studies), Secondary Education (Art, Biology, Business, Chemistry, Economics, English/Language Arts, General Science, Health, Mathematics, Physical Education, Physical Sciences, Physics, Political Science, Psychology, Sociology, Speech, Theatre)

Hanover College

Founded in 1827, Hanover College is a small, private, four-year liberal arts institution located on scenic bluffs overlooking the Ohio River near historic Madison, Indiana. It is the oldest private college in Indiana and is located on 650 acres with 34 major buildings. The Education Department offers elementary (1-6) and secondary (5-12) programs leading to initial teacher licensure. The faculty collaborates to provide programs that prepare committed, competent, culturally responsive, and critically reflective new educators. A professor-to-student ratio of one-to-fifteen enables the development of strong mentor relationships among faculty and student learning groups.

Just the facts...

Hanover College
Education Department
P.O. Box 890
Hanover, IN 47243-0890
(812) 866-7390
Website: www.hanover.edu
Profile: Rural, Small, Co-Ed
UG Tuition: $10,175.00/year
Off Campus Programs: No

Clinical Experiences

Elementary education majors complete practica in local schools as part of their art, music, and physical education courses in their first and second years in college. In their third year, they complete practica in integrated learning and teaching in academic disciplines, direct writers' workshops, conduct classroom-based research projects, and lead community service programs. Sixteen weeks of student teaching are completed during the fall of the senior year, followed by a final practicum in inclusive education and assisted technologies for exceptional children. Secondary education majors complete several practica and student teach in the fall or winter terms of their senior year.

Noteworthy

Elementary and secondary education majors are required to pass comprehensive examinations in the winter term of their senior year. Proficiency in a foreign language is required of all Hanover graduates; this feature is especially important to new educators preparing for a multilingual, multicultural classroom. Richter Grants and other travel grants are available to support international learning and teaching. Creative uses of technology are integrated throughout the general liberal arts degree requirements and are higlighted in teacher preparation courses. Hanover places student teachers in both traditional and non-traditional sites. The Spicer-Phillips Multicultural Program supports student teacher placement in urban areas.

Teacher Preparation Program Information

The following programs are 4 year programs:

Elementary Education (Generalist 1-6), K-12 Education (Physical Education, Visual Arts), Secondary Education/5-12 (Biology, Chemistry, Earth Science, English, French, German, Mathematics, Physical Education, Physical Science, Physics, Social Studies (a primary area with two supporting areas from U.S. History, World Civilization, or Government), Spanish, Speech Communication/Theatre, Visual Arts)

Huntington College

As a church-related college, Huntington prepares candidates to teach in both public and Christian schools. The college has chosen the theme of "Teacher as Effective Steward" as its education program model. Taken from the Parable of the Talents in Matthew 25, this model stresses the importance of effective teachers being responsible managers of four critical areas of education: knowledge, student characteristics, the learning environment, and instructional methods. Responsible stewardship also applies to the crucial educational issues of multiculturalism, technology, and assessment.

Just the facts...

Huntington College
Department of Education
2303 College Avenue
Huntington, IN 46750-1299
(219) 359-4231
Website: www.huntington.edu
Profile: Suburban, Small, Co-Ed
UG Tuition: $6,125.00/semester
G Tuition: $215.00/credit hour
Off Campus Programs: No

Clinical Experiences

A distinguishing feature of the education program at Huntington is the "junior block" in which all elementary methods courses are scheduled. The university component of these courses finishes a month early both semesters of the junior year, and a daily, all-morning field experience is provided for the remaining month. Candidates also take a multicultural practicum during the college's January term, in which they spend full days in urban schools. Candidates work in the field every semester they are enrolled in the education program, ensuring wide exposure to different grade levels and teaching and learning styles.

Noteworthy

The education program is the biggest in the college, and enrollments in both the department and the college are growing. Yet the atmosphere is intimate—professors and students establish strong bonds, and professors get to know every student. The junior block courses and field experiences build solid teamwork and professionalism. Candidates enter the junior block program as typical college sophomores and leave as experienced instructors, eager and ready to move into student teaching. In their job hunts, graduates can claim significant classroom experiences at multiple grade levels in urban, suburban, and rural environments.

Teacher Preparation Program Information

The following programs are 4 year programs:

Elementary Education, K-12 Education (Art, Health, Music, Physical Education), Kindergarten Education, Middle School Education (English, Mathematics, Science, Social Studies), Secondary Education (Biology, Business, Chemistry, English/Language Arts, General Science, Health, Mathematics, Physical Education, Physical Sciences, Physics, Political Science, Psychology, Science, Social Studies, Sociology)

Indiana State University

Founded in 1865, Indiana State University has a long and distinguished tradition of preparing teachers. Part of this tradition is evident in the theme of the university's educator preparation programs—"Becoming a Complete Professional." The education programs are built on the belief that education professionals, including teachers, must demonstrate a balance across three fundamental areas: (1) their expertise as professionals, (2) the admirable qualities they exemplify as people, and (3) their contributions as members of the communities they serve.

Just the facts...

Indiana State University
School of Education
Terre Haute, IN 47809
(812) 237-2888
Website: www.indstate.edu/soe/
Profile: Urban, Large, Co-Ed
UG Tuition: $1,662.00/sem. in-state; $4,126.00/sem. out-of-state
G Tuition: $143.00/cr. hr. in-state; $325.00/cr. hr. out-of-state
Off Campus Programs: Yes

Clinical Experiences

Candidates have frequent opportunities to apply the knowledge and skills they are learning in classes on-campus to practical settings. Prior to student teaching, these experiences are likely to be in several of the sixteen elementary, middle, and high schools with which the university has a formal partnership in the Terre Haute and Indianapolis areas. For the semester-long student teaching experience, most candidates are placed somewhere in Indiana so they can receive support from faculty members based in Terre Haute.

Noteworthy

Though candidates benefit from the small classes and close student/faculty contact of a moderate-sized university, they also have the advantage of being at an institution that offers master's and doctoral programs preparing speech-language pathologists, school counselors and psychologists, and curriculum specialists. In addition, they gain confidence from knowing that a large percentage of Indiana's school principals and superintendents, who hire teachers, are aware of the strengths of Indiana State University's teacher education programs because they too received degrees or educator licenses at Indiana State.

Teacher Preparation Program Information

The following programs are 4 year programs:
Early Childhood Education, Elementary Education, K-12 Education (Art, Music, Physical Education), Kindergarten/Primary Education, Secondary Education (Business, English/Language Arts, Family & Consumer Science/Home Economics, French, German, Health, Latin, Mathematics, Science, Social Studies, Spanish, Technology Education, Vocational Home Economics/Consumer Homemaking, Vocational Trade & Industrial), Special Education (Mild Disabilities/Handicaps, Severe Behavioral Disabilities/Handicaps, Speech/Language Disabilities)

Indiana University at Bloomington/ Indianapolis

The School of Education at Indiana University is uniquely organized to fulfill its mission of preparing future educators. At Bloomington, faculty members, graduate and undergraduate students, P-12 teachers, and administrators have worked together to redesign the preservice program. The program at Indianapolis features an award-winning curriculum aligned with and based on Interstate Teacher Assessment and Support Consortium (INTASC) model state licensing standards for beginning teachers.

Just the facts...

Indiana University at Bloomington/Indianapolis
School of Education
Wendell W. Wright Education Building
201 North Rose Avenue, Room 4130
Bloomington, IN 47405-1006
(812) 856-8501
Website: http://education.indiana.edu
Profile: Urban, Large, Co-Ed
UG Tuition: $1,813.00/sem. in-state; $5,933.00/sem. out-of-state
G Tuition: $153.00/cr. hr. in-state; $445.00/cr. hr. out-of-state
Off Campus Programs: Yes

Clinical Experiences

Early field experiences allow candidates to explore teaching careers. When candidates begin their student teaching, they have the option of choosing from a wide variety of schools, communities, and international settings. Candidates enthusiastically report that these experiences provide personal and professional enrichment and give them an insight and better understanding of community and world diversity. All candidates are expected to complete a full semester of student teaching. Additionally, a student teaching seminar provides them the opportunity to reflect upon their experiences and their developing skills.

Noteworthy

At Bloomington, the School of Education is housed in a new building with modern classrooms, access to technology, and facilities for distance education. The Center on Learning and Technology has been established to design and conduct research on educational applications of technology. The School of Education offers about 25 classes delivered to remote locations using interactive video conferencing facilities. Technology has also become a hallmark of the teaching and research agenda of many faculty. The School of Education takes pride in its faculty, many of whom are internationally recognized scholars.

Teacher Preparation Program Information

The following programs are 4 year programs:
Early Childhood Education, Kindergarten-Primary Education, Elementary Education, K-12 Education (Art, Music, Physical Education, Special Education), Secondary Education 5-12 (Bilingual, Biology, Chemistry, Chinese, Earth Science, English, ESL, French, German, Health, Japanese, Journalism, Mathematics, Physics, Russian, Social Studies, Spanish, Speech and Theatre)

The following programs are post-baccalaureate programs:
Elementary Education, Special Education, Secondary Education (Bilingual, Biology, Chemistry, Chinese, Earth Science, English, ESL, French, German, Health, Japanese, Journalism, Mathematics, Physics, Russian, Social Studies, Spanish, Speech and Theatre)

The following programs are 5th year programs:
Elementary Education, Media Education, Secondary Education (Bilingual, Biology, Chemistry, Chinese, Earth Science, English, ESL, French, German, Health, Japanese, Journalism, Mathematics, Physics, Russian, Social Studies, Spanish, Speech and Theatre), Special Education

Indiana University East

The Division of Education at Indiana University East has been designed to develop professionals in the field who (1) are well-grounded in knowledge essential to being an informed instructional decision maker, (2) have the ability and desire to make reflective decisions on issues critical to education, (3) use the best available research to guide their practice, (4) have attained a high level of competency needed to be effective/reflective beginning teachers, (5) are capable of integrating technology throughout the curriculum, and (6) bring a pluralistic perspective to all dimensions of education. The faculty strives to produce teachers who are reflective scholars, instructional leaders, and global citizens.

Just the facts...

Indiana University East
Division of Education
2325 Chester Boulevard
Middlefork Hall
Richmond, IN 47374
(765) 973-8211
Website: www.iue.indiana.edu
Profile: Small, Co-Ed
UG Tuition: $94.10/cr. hr. in-state; $244.20/cr. hr. out-of-state
G Tuition: $124.60/cr. hr. in-state; $283.70/cr. hr. out-of-state
Off Campus Programs: No

Clinical Experiences

Clinical experiences are integrated with foundations and methods courses so that preservice teachers are engaged in critical thinking about schooling from the beginning of their professional preparation. Preservice teachers are involved in diverse settings that allow for their autonomy in the classroom as they increase their understanding. Methods courses are taught on-site and in conjunction with pre-student teaching field experiences so that decision making, leadership, creativity, and self-confidence develop at an appropriate pace and with ample support.

Noteworthy

A primary innovation of the Division of Education is the Teacher Mentor Program, which supports preservice teachers as they make the transition from the university through the first year of teaching. One-on-one mentoring, seminars, symposiums, and teaching resources are part of the services provided. The Curriculum Resource Center specializes in multicultural resources as well as simulations and "hands-on" teaching materials.

Teacher Preparation Program Information

The following programs are 4 year programs:
Elementary Education, Middle School Education (English, General Science, Language Arts, Mathematics, Science, Social Studies), Secondary Education (Biology, Chemistry, Earth Science, Economics, English/Language Arts, General Science, Geography, History, Mathematics, Physical Sciences, Physics, Political Science, Psychology, Sales, Science, Social Studies, Sociology)

The following programs are post-baccalaureate programs:
Elementary Education, Middle School Education (English, General Science, Language Arts, Mathematics, Science, Social Studies), Secondary Education (Biology, Chemistry, Earth Science, Economics, English/Language Arts, General Science, Geography, History, Mathematics, Physical Sciences, Physics, Political Science, Psychology, Sales, Science, Social Studies, Sociology)

Indiana University Kokomo

Located 45 miles north of Indianapolis, Indiana University Kokomo serves a mixed industrial and rural region. As part of the Indiana University School of Education, the Division of Education offers courses and programs meeting the standards of the university as a whole. Although most of its candidates are in the undergraduate program in elementary education, the campus also offers post-baccalaureate work toward licensure in selected secondary areas. The program, based on the Professional Educator Model, requires a balance of broad liberal arts education, specialized content knowledge, and reflective field practice.

Just the facts...

Indiana University Kokomo
Division of Education
2300 South Washington
P.O. Box 9003
Kokomo, IN 46904-9003
(765) 455-9441
Website: www.iuk.edu
Profile: Suburban, Medium, Co-Ed
UG Tuition: $94.10/cr. hr. in-state; $244.20/cr. hr. out-of-state
G Tuition: $124.60/cr. hr. in-state; $283.70/cr. hr. out-of-state
Off Campus Programs: No

Clinical Experiences

From the freshman to the senior year, clinical experiences are an important part of the Indiana University Kokomo undergraduate program, ranging from simple classroom observations to methods course practica requiring intensive teaching experiences. Clinical experiences carry with them expectations of reflective field practice and organization into a portfolio of evidence reflecting the competency of the beginning teacher practicioner. Practicum experiences are supervised by full-time university faculty, who also supervise many of the student teachers.

Noteworthy

Indiana University Kokomo responds to the needs of the local community while maintaining and infusing state and national standards and perspectives in its education programs. Education faculty, advisors, and staff members are in close contact with candidates and are readily available for consultation. Candidates enjoy the placement services and many other benefits of Indiana University at large; most courses in education transfer readily to other Indiana University campuses. Technology is expected to play an increasingly important role in the delivery of diverse instruction among the eight Indiana University campuses.

Teacher Preparation Program Information

The following programs are 4 year programs:
Elementary Education

The following programs are post-baccalaureate programs:
Elementary Education (Language Arts, Mathematics, Reading, Science, Social Studies), Kindergarten Education, Middle School Education (English, Mathematics, Science, Social Studies), Secondary Education (Biology, English/Language Arts, General Science, Mathematics, Physical Sciences, Social Studies)

The following programs are 5th year programs:
Pending approval for Fall 1999: Secondary Education (English, Mathematics, Science, Social Studies)

National Council for Accreditation of Teacher Education

Indiana University Northwest

Indiana University Northwest is an urban commuter university. The mission of the Division of Education at IUN is to provide quality educational programs through degrees, courses, and services to the region. The Division of Education provides the knowledge, skills, and experiences that prospective and inservice teachers need to demonstrate and practice effective teaching, and prepares educators who are technically and ethically sound. All full-time faculty members have Ph.Ds or Ed.Ds.

Just the facts...

Indiana University Northwest
Division of Education
3400 Broadway
Gary, IN 46408
(219) 980-6515
Website: www.iun.indiana.edu
Profile: Urban, Medium, Co-Ed
UG Tuition: $94.10/cr. hr. in-state; $244.20/cr. hr. out-of-state
G Tuition: $122.50/cr. hr. in-state; $283.70/cr. hr. out-of-state
Off Campus Programs: No

Clinical Experiences

Clinical experiences are an integral component of the teacher education program. IUN's proximity to urban, suburban, and rural areas provides candidates with rich experiences in diverse settings serving children and adolescents from many ethnic and economic groups. Candidates also work with students who have special needs or disabilities. Faculty teaching the methods courses are directly involved with the management of the corresponding clinical experiences, providing extensive feedback and support to candidates through site visits and comments in candidates' journals.

Noteworthy

IUN's Urban Teacher Education Program is a nationally recognized university-school partnership. Limited graduate fellowships are available through the Division of Education. Undergraduate scholarships are available for education majors through the Office of Admissions and Financial Aid.

Teacher Preparation Program Information

The following programs are 4 year programs:
Elementary Education, Secondary Education (Biology, Chemistry, Earth Science, Economics, English, French, General Science, Government, Mathematics, Physical Science, Psychology, Sociology, Spanish, United States History, World Civilization)

Indiana University-Purdue University Fort Wayne

Indiana University-Purdue University Fort Wayne was established to bring excellence in higher education to northeastern Indiana. The faculty in the School of Education are committed to the development of a performance-based teacher preparation program. The School of Education ensures that graduates have a strong general studies background and develop comprehensive skills using technology, meeting the needs of diverse learners, and creating a positive learning environment.

Just the facts...

Indiana University—Purdue University Fort Wayne
School of Education
2101 Coliseum Boulevard East
Fort Wayne, IN 46805-1499
(219) 481-4146
Website: www.ipfw.edu
Profile: Urban, Large, Co-Ed
UG Tuition: $97.60/cr. hr. in-state; $235.85/cr. hr. out-of-state
G Tuition: $125.85/cr. hr. in-state; $277.95/cr. hr. out-of-state
Off Campus Programs: No

Clinical Experiences

All candidates have field-based experiences within a range of school settings with culturally diverse populations. Candidates must participate in a minimum of three field experiences in a variety of settings prior to student teaching. These placements extend over a two-year period of time. Close and frequent supervision is provided by both school and university personnel to ensure opportunities for structured feedback and reflection on candidates' performance.

Noteworthy

Candidates have an opportunity to benefit from the rich variety of school settings available in Fort Wayne. During the past few years, the School of Education and the Fort Wayne Community Schools have established the PreK-16 Collaborative which has led to a close integration of the teacher preparation program with the school system. The Collaborative has developed a variety of specialized programs that enable candidates to work in the schools while completing their training. The Collaborative has received substantial financial support from the local business community and is seeking additional grants.

Teacher Preparation Program Information

The following programs are 4 year programs:

Elementary Education, K-12 Education (Drama/Theater, French, German, Music, Spanish), Secondary Education (Biology, Chemistry, Earth Science, Economics, English/Language Arts, General Science, Mathematics, Physical Sciences, Physics, Political Science, Psychology, Science, Social Studies, Sociology, Speech)

The following programs are post-baccalaureate programs:

Elementary Education, K-12 Education (Drama/Theater, French, German, Music, Spanish), Secondary Education (Biology, Chemistry, Earth Science, Economics, English/Language Arts, General Science, Mathematics, Physical Sciences, Physics, Political Science, Psychology, Science, Social Studies, Sociology, Speech)

Indiana University South Bend

The faculty and staff of the Division of Education at Indiana University South Bend promote the development of dedicated "students of learning" who are prepared to be educational decision makers throughout their professional careers. Close links between theory and practice in field and laboratory experiences are integral to all of the teacher education programs. Because of the regional nature of the Indiana University South Bend campus and the student population it serves, teacher education courses are offered during morning, afternoon, and evening hours. Extensive course offerings are also available during the summer semester.

Just the facts...

Indiana University South Bend
Division of Education
1700 Mishawaka Avenue
P.O. Box 7111
South Bend, IN 46634-7111
(219) 237-4339
Website: http://iusb.edu
Profile: Urban, Medium, Co-Ed
UG Tuition: $92.10/cr. hr. in-state; $120.90/cr. hr. out-of-state
G Tuition: $252.05/cr. hr. in-state; $293.05/cr. hr. out-of-state
Off Campus Programs: Yes

Clinical Experiences

Clinical experience offerings are carefully designed in order to link theory learned in coursework with real world practice. Candidates begin working with teachers in the field early in their progression from general studies to advanced methodology courses. Candidates interact with youth in urban, suburban, and rural settings. Faculty supervise these experiences in cooperation with outstanding practitioners. Student teaching is the capstone experience for all teacher education candidates. Outstanding local practitioners serve as field supervisors for the many clinical experiences required of teacher candidates.

Noteworthy

Classes are offered in day and evening formats. Scholarships are available for outstanding students. Faculty are experienced classroom teachers and nationally known scholars. Indiana University is a regional institution with international connections. Global perspectives are increasingly a part of programs in the Division of Education. The Division's Center for Global Education has been successful in bringing two Fulbright Scholars to the Division within the past two academic years.

Teacher Preparation Program Information

The following programs are 4 year programs:
Elementary Education, Secondary Education (English, Foreign Language, Mathematics, Science, Social Studies), Special Education (Mild Disabilities)

The following programs are post-baccalaureate programs:
Elementary Education, Secondary Education (English, Foreign Language, Mathematics, Science, Social Studies), Special Education (Mild Disabilities)

Indiana University Southeast

The Division of Education's mission is to develop high quality educational professionals who stimulate the continual renewal of schools within a multicultural society. Graduates will have the knowledge and skills that enable them to respond proactively, with care and intelligence, toward individuals and communities. The Division of Education has been graduating high quality educators for over 25 years. Growth in the quantity and quality of its graduates is anticipated by the faculty for many years to come.

Just the facts...

Indiana University Southeast
Division of Education
4201 Grant Line Road
New Albany, IN 47150
(812) 941-2385
Website: www.ius.indiana.edu
Profile: Urban, Medium, Co-Ed
UG Tuition: $94.10/cr. hr. in-state; $244.20/cr. hr. out-of-state
G Tuition: $124.60/cr. hr. in-state; $283.70/cr. hr. out-of-state
Off Campus Programs: No

Clinical Experiences

Clinical experiences are an integral part of every course in the program. Between 100 and 180 hours are spent in clinical environments prior to student teaching. Many courses have long-standing relationships with local schools where inservice professionals have become partners with the university in the preparation of educators. The experiences are also designed to provide variety, culture and ages so that graduates are prepared for a professional life in schools of the future as well as the present.

Noteworthy

The campus and community environment in which the Division of Education functions contributes to the special feel of its programs. The campus mission is to be a challenging, innovative, and supportive learning community committed to the intellectual and social growth of students, to the cultural and economic well-being of both Southern Indiana and the Greater Louisville metropolitan area, and to the advancement of knowledge in the context of a global society.

Teacher Preparation Program Information

The following programs are 4 year programs:
Elementary Education, Secondary Education (Biology, Chemistry, Earth Science, English/Language Arts, Mathematics, Social Studies), Special Education (Developmental Disabilities & Handicaps, Learning Disability, Severe Behavioral Disabilities & Handicaps)

The following programs are post-baccalaureate programs:
Kindergarten Education

Indiana Wesleyan University

The Education Program at Indiana Wesleyan University emphasizes a strong knowledge base supported by opportunities to apply and examine theory within instructional settings. The undergraduate "Teacher as Decision Maker" conceptual model prepares teacher candidates in eight interdependent areas: content/subject matter expertise, personal development, professional development, rights and responsibilities, methodology, management of time, classroom and behavior, communication, and global and multicultural perspectives. The Masters in Education "Teacher as Agent of Change" model emphasizes instructional effectiveness and reflective leadership.

Clinical Experiences

Clinical experiences in the teacher education program at Indiana Wesleyan are designed to place candidates in situations where they gradually move from observer to participant, ultimately assuming the role of classroom instructor. All candidates have their first field experience early in their preparation programs, and spend a significant amount of time during their sophomore and junior years preparing for student teaching. The student teaching experience is sixteen weeks, divided into two eight-week placements.

Just the facts...

Indiana Wesleyan University
Division of Education
4201 South Washington Street
Marion, IN 46953-9980
(765) 677-2221
Website: www.indwes.edu
Profile: Suburban, Medium, Co-Ed
UG Tuition: $5,361.00/semester
G Tuition: $195.00/credit hour
Off Campus Programs: Yes

Noteworthy

Indiana Wesleyan University is a Christ-centered academic community committed to changing the world by developing students in character, scholarship and leadership. Candidates in the teacher education program are equipped for lifelong learning and service by incorporating a Christian value system in their teaching. Excellence in classroom performance is emphasized through integrating faith and learning in university courses and applying knowledge and skills in field experiences.

Teacher Preparation Program Information

The following programs are 4 year programs:
Elementary Education, K-12 Education (Art, Music, Physical Education), Secondary Education (Art, Biology, Chemistry, Chemistry/Biology, English/Language Arts, Mathematics, Mathematics/Computers, Physical Education, Social Studies), Special Education (Emotional/Behavioral Disability, Learning Disability, Mild Disabilities, Mild Intellectual Disabilities)

The following programs are post-baccalaureate programs:
Elementary Education (Language Arts, Mathematics, Science, Social Studies), Kindergarten Education

Manchester College

Manchester College prepares teachers of ability and conviction within a campus environment emphasizing faith, learning, and service. The program prepares new teachers who demonstrate competency in each of the model state licensing principles developed by the Interstate Teacher Assessment and Support Consortium (INTASC). Manchester is committed to a strong liberal arts program with a global perspective, including opportunities for international study. The small campus and frequent contact with faculty ensure the development of each new teacher as a unique individual.

Just the facts...

Manchester College
Teacher Education
604 East College Avenue
North Manchester, IN 46962
(219) 982-5056
Website: www.manchester.edu
Profile: Rural, Small, Co-Ed
UG Tuition: $6,235.00/semester
Off Campus Programs: No

Clinical Experiences

Most teacher education candidates at Manchester are in public school classrooms each of their four years at the college. Field experiences are concurrent with education classes and are offered in rural, small town, and urban schools. These experiences are carefully designed to move from observation to full teaching responsibilities as candidates gain skills. Student teachers open the academic year in their school classrooms, and elementary education candidates continue work in this classroom throughout the fall. Student teaching is a full spring semester, in two placements, with a supportive on-campus seminar.

Noteworthy

Technology is integrated throughout education courses; all students have Internet access. Preservice teachers learn conflict resolution skills. During the elementary methods block, candidates spend a full week in an open concept school and another in an inner-city school. The Student Education Association provides additional professional development and volunteer opportunities. Graduates from Manchester include a state school superintendent, an education advisor to a governor, and numerous professors, school administrators, and teachers—educators of ability and conviction.

Teacher Preparation Program Information

The following programs are 4 year programs:

Elementary Education, K-12 Education (Art, Music, Physical Education), Secondary Education (Art, Biology, Chemistry, English/Language Arts, French, German, Mathematics, Physical Education, Physics, Spanish, Speech, Theatre), Kindergarten Education, Junior High/Middle School Education, Special Education (Adapted Physical Education, Mildly Mentally Handicapped)

Marian College

Marian College is a Catholic, co-educational liberal arts college of about 1,300 students guided by the Franciscan values of dignity of the individual, responsible stewardship, reconciliation, and peace and justice. The Education Department is committed to the intellectual, spiritual, moral, and social development of beginning teachers. The department encourages service learning, effective collaboration with families in schools, and mentoring activities. The program theme is "Teacher as Model and Mentor: Ever Teaching, Ever Learning, Ever Changing."

Just the facts...

Marian College
Department of Education
3200 Cold Spring Road
Indianapolis, IN 46222
(317) 955-6091
Website: www.marian.edu
Profile: Urban, Small, Co-Ed
UG Tuition: $6,517.00/semester
Off Campus Programs: No

Clinical Experiences

The teacher education program provides multiple clinical experiences in urban, suburban, ethnically diverse, private, and public schools from the first year the candidate is in the program. Full-time faculty advise candidates throughout their experiences. Candidates in the secondary education program take methods courses with current teachers in the field in a specially designed program. Clinical experiences provide candidates with opportunities to teach lessons and observe child development. The experiences become increasingly more focused throughout the four years. Candidates conclude their program with one semester of student teaching.

Noteworthy

Candidates have opportunities to develop service learning projects, work with schools and families in special projects, participate in mentoring activities with students in the Indianapolis area, and participate in special programs like Family Math and Family Science. A recently acquired million-dollar grant to work with urban middle school students will provide additional opportunities for students in the areas of math, science, and writing. Technology is embedded in coursework to ensure preparation for teaching in technologically-rich schools

Teacher Preparation Program Information

The following programs are 4 year programs:
Early Childhood Education, Elementary Education, K-12 Education (Art, Music), Secondary Education (Art, Biology, English, French, German, Health, Mathematics, Music, Physical Education, Social Studies, Spanish)

Oakland City University

Oakland City University has prepared teachers since 1885. The School of Education is a collaborative learning community dedicated to academic knowledge, technological skills, pedagogical proficiency, lifelong learning, the promotion of Christian ethical and moral values, the enhancement of candidates' intellectual, spiritual, and social development, and community service through positive leadership. Oakland's teacher candidates are evaluated by performance-based assessments appropriate to the area in which they plan to specialize. The education programs are designed to meet the continuously changing needs of society.

Just the facts...

Oakland City University
School of Education
143 Lucretia Street
Oakland City, IN 47660-1099
(812) 749-1232
Website: www.oak.edu
Profile: Rural, Small, Co-Ed
UG Tuition: $300.00/credit hour
Off Campus Programs: No

Clinical Experiences

Education majors enjoy a wide variety of clinical experiences beginning with an introduction to education and culminating with student teaching. Candidates are afforded a range of diverse cultural experiences including work in Amish schools, parochial and public schools, rural and urban schools, year-round schools, and the Qualla Boundary of the Eastern Tribe of the Cherokee Nation Schools. Student teachers are visited at least four times by faculty during their student teaching experience. Faculty and classroom supervisors work together to ensure candidates' success.

Noteworthy

The School of Education at Oakland City University is home to nearly 50 percent of all liberal arts students on campus. Classes have a seventeen-to-one student/teacher ratio. Education faculty have an open door policy. Students come and visit the faculty on a regular basis. Twenty outreach scholarships are available for students along with a variety of other financial aid packages. A new state-of-the-art computer lab with Internet access is available for all education majors to use. Education graduates from Oakland City can be found in nearly every school in southern Indiana.

Teacher Preparation Program Information

The following programs are 4 year programs:

Elementary Education, K-12 Education (Health, Music, Physical Education), Kindergarten Education, Middle School Education (English, Mathematics, Science, Social Studies), Secondary Education (Art, Biology, Business, English/Language Arts, General Science, Health, Mathematics, Physical Education, Physical Sciences, Social Studies, Vocational Business Office), Special Education (Multiple Disabilities/Handicaps)

The following programs are post-baccalaureate programs:

Elementary Education, K-12 Education (Health, Music, Physical Education), Kindergarten Education, Middle School Education (English, Mathematics, Science, Social Studies), Secondary Education (Art, Biology, Business, English/Language Arts, General Science, Health, Mathematics, Physical Education, Physical Sciences, Social Studies, Vocational Business Office), Special Education (Multiple Disabilities/Handicaps)

Purdue University

Purdue University has prepared teachers and other school personnel since 1908. The School of Education is dedicated to the development of education professionals who think critically and reflectively, teach effectively by integrating content and pedagogy, adapt instruction to diverse learners, and use current and emerging technologies. Graduates are committed to lifelong learning and continuing professional development through inquiry, reflection on practice, quality performance, and service to their students.

Just the facts...

Purdue University
School of Education
1440 Liberal Arts & Education Building
West Lafayette, IN 47907-1440
(765) 494-2336
Website: www.soe.purdue.edu
Profile: Urban, Large, Co-Ed
UG Tuition: $94.25/cr. hr. in-state; $237.00/cr. hr. out-of-state
G Tuition: $122.50/cr. hr. in-state; $278.25/cr. hr. out-of-state
Off Campus Programs: Yes

Clinical Experiences

Professional education courses and their related field experiences take place on-site in diverse classrooms. The progress of the teacher candidate is monitored in close collaboration with university faculty members and school personnel. Teacher candidates' clinical experiences encourage discovery, the integration of content knowledge and pedagogical knowledge, and reflective practice. Professional development schools are central to the success of the clinical experience at Purdue University. Areas of concentration include early childhood, middle childhood, early adolescence, adolescence/young adulthood, and a comprehensive array of teaching disciplines.

Noteworthy

Faculty, students, and K-12 colleagues are redesigning the School of Education's elementary and secondary education curricula with an emphasis on performance-based standards, the individual development of children, learning and motivation, multiculturalism, issues in exceptional needs, and educational technology. Purdue University offers students the opportunity to participate in international study abroad programs in more than 30 countries. The School Mathematics and Science Center develops partnerships between scientists, science educators, master teachers, and students to enhance the education of preservice teachers and science, mathematics, engineering, and technology majors.

Teacher Preparation Program Information

The following programs are 4 year programs:

Early Childhood Education, Elementary Education, Exceptional Needs, Middle School & Secondary Education (Agriculture, Anthropology, Biology, Chemistry, Consumer & Family Sciences, Earth/Space Science, Economics, English/Language Arts, French, General Science, Geography, German, Global Civilization, Government, Mathematics, Physical Education & Health, Physics, Psychology, Russian, Sociology, Spanish, Speech Communication & Theatre, Technology, United States History, Visual Arts, Vocational Education)

The following programs are post-baccalaureate programs:

Early Childhood Education, Elementary Education, Exceptional Needs, Middle School & Secondary Education (Agriculture, Anthropology, Biology, Chemistry, Consumer & Family Sciences, Earth/Space Science, Economics, English/Language Arts, French, General Science, Geography, German, Global Civilization, Government, Mathematics, Physical Education & Health, Physics, Psychology, Russian, Sociology, Spanish, Speech Communication & Theatre, Technology, United States History, Visual Arts, Vocational Education)

Purdue University Calumet

Purdue University Calumet is a regional campus of Purdue University. Purdue Calumet, however, has full autonomy over all its undergraduate programs. The School of Education embodies three basic themes: constructing theory, developing practice, and fostering relationships. A candidate must be grounded in theory, be able to apply the theory, and share with and learn from the community in order to be a successful teacher. Education programs are strong in the liberal arts and sciences, and offer candidates both theoretical and practical education experiences.

Just the facts...

Purdue University Calumet
Teacher Education
2235-171st Street
Hammond, IN 46323-2094
(219) 989-2335
Website: http://www.education.calumet.purdue.edu
Profile: Urban, Medium, Co-Ed
UG Tuition: $94.25/cr. hr. in-state; $237.00/cr. hr. out-of-state
G Tuition: $122.50/cr. hr. in-state; $278.25/cr. hr. out-of-state
Off Campus Programs: No

Clinical Experiences

Candidates are given the opportunity to observe, tutor, and micro-teach in the field during their courses. Professional development school (PDS) sites work with Purdue Calumet to offer these clinical experiences. PDS sites provide effective experiences for candidates as they integrate their knowledge and skills during their practica and student teaching. As part of a new initiative, the School of Education has created a Teacher-In-Residence (TIR) position. The TIR is a veteran classroom teacher who is assigned to the faculty of the School of Education for a year. The TIR is assigned a full course load and is intstrumental in assisting the School of Education with curriculum development.

Noteworthy

Purdue Calumet is able to place candidates in classrooms that display a wide range of socioeconomic, ethnic, and racial diversity. Graduates of the School of Education are expected to be advocates for all learners, promoting consistently positive interaction with children and families. Purdue Calumet is involved with and supports local community groups working to promote quality education, including the Urban Superintendents' Steering Committee, the Urban Principals Center, a cohort doctoral program, and the Northwest Indiana Secondary Principals Study Council.

Teacher Preparation Program Information

The following programs are 4 year programs:

Elementary Education (Kindergarten), K-12 Education (Computers, Reading), Middle School Education (English/Language Arts, French, German, Mathematics, Science, Social Studies, Spanish), Secondary Education (Biology, Chemistry, Economics, English, French, General Science, German, History, Mathematics, Physics, Political Science, Psychology, Science, Social Studies, Sociology, Spanish) Special Education (Learning Disabilities, Mildly Mentally Handicapped, Seriously Emotionally Handicapped)

The following programs are post-baccalaureate programs:

Elementary Education (Kindergarten), K-12 Education (Computers, Reading), Middle School Education (English/Language Arts, French, German, Mathematics, Science, Social Studies, Spanish), Secondary Education (Biology, Chemistry, Economics, English, French, General Science, German, History, Mathematics, Physics, Political Science, Psychology, Science, Social Studies, Sociology, Spanish) Special Education (Learning Disabilities, Mildly Mentally Handicapped, Seriously Emotionally Handicapped)

Saint Joseph's College

The Teacher Education Program at Saint Joseph's College is administered by a campus-wide Teacher Education Committee and members of the Education Department. Saint Joseph prepares candidates by providing them with first-hand professional experiences and the best professional knowledge about teaching, learning, and schooling in order for them to serve others and society within a Christian framework. The undergraduate program prepares future teachers with a strong liberal arts background, an early and wide range of field experiences, and an in-depth investigation of subject matter disciplines.

Just the facts...

Saint Joseph's College
Education Department
P.O. Box 935
Rensselaer, IN 47978-0889
(219) 866-6242
Website: www.saintjoe.edu
Profile: Rural, Small, Co-Ed
UG Tuition: $6,735.00/semester
Off Campus Programs: No

Clinical Experiences

Saint Joseph's believes that candidates should have early and wide-ranging field experiences. Beginning in the freshman year, elementary education majors spend time in local schools observing and working with classroom teachers and their pupils. Seven field experiences, one per term, must be completed prior to student teaching. Professional teachers in local public and parochial schools provide varied opportunities for candidates. P-12 classroom teachers work cooperatively with the college's education faculty in making sure that candidates see theory put into practice.

Noteworthy

The nationally acclaimed CORE program, which all candidates complete, is the hallmark of Saint Joseph's. Faculty from the Arts, Sciences, Humanities, Business, and Education divisions collaborate and team-teach in this single, integrated program that extends over the four undergraduate years. Throughout this academic program faculty develop the cognitive and communication abilities of candidates, including oral, written, and critical thinking skills. Connections between the CORE program and the academic major are stressed as candidates are exposed to different modes of inquiry in the search for truth.

Teacher Preparation Program Information

The following programs are 4 year programs:
Early Childhood Education, Elementary Education (Computer Science, Language Arts, Mathematics, Mild Disabilities, Reading, Science, Social Studies), K-12 Education (Music, Physical Education), Kindergarten Education, Middle School Education (English, Mathematics, Science, Social Studies, Speech/Theatre), Secondary Education (Biology, Business, Chemistry, Computer Science, Earth Science, Economics, English/Language Arts, French, General Science, German, Health, Mathematics, Physical Education, Physical Sciences, Physics, Political Science, Psychology, Science, Social Studies, Sociology, Spanish, Speech, Theatre), Special Education (Early Childhood, Learning Disability)

The following programs are post-baccalaureate programs:
Early Childhood Education, Elementary Education (Computer Science, Language Arts, Mathematics, Mild Disabilities, Reading, Science, Social Studies), Kindergarten Education, Middle School Education (English, Mathematics, Science, Social Studies, Speech/Theatre), Secondary Education (Computer Science, French, General Science, German, Health, Physical Sciences, Physics, Spanish), Special Education (Early Childhood, Learning Disability)

Saint Mary-of-the-Woods College

Saint Mary-of-the-Woods College (SMWC) is the oldest Catholic liberal arts college for women in the United States. Founded in 1840 by the Sisters of Providence, SMWC is dedicated to preparing women for complex roles in society. The Department of Education offers a wide range of undergraduate teacher education programs built upon the liberal arts and oriented toward professional goals. The mission of the faculty is to prepare competent, caring, professional teachers who can teach subject matter in ways that their students can understand and apply to their world.

Just the facts...

Saint Mary-of-the-Woods College
Department of Education
Saint Mary Of The Woods, IN 47876
(812) 535-5159
Website: http://woods.smwc.edu
Profile: Rural, Small, Women
UG Tuition: $6,580.00/semester
G Tuition: $300.00/credit hour
Off Campus Programs: No

Clinical Experiences

Candidates are required to complete a variety of field experiences that occur in a developmental sequence. In their first year, candidates complete ten hours of observation in a range of educational settings. In their sophomore year, candidates complete an initial field experience in which they are assigned duties as a teaching assistant. As juniors, candidates complete a second field experience in which they complete lesson plans and teach small groups of students. As seniors, candidates complete sixteen weeks of student teaching in two eight-week placements.

Noteworthy

Since 1973, SMWC has offered its teacher education programs in both the traditional resident student format as well as the external degree format. In the external degree format, candidates come to campus for an orientation program and meet with professors to arrange coursework. Subsequently, candidates return to the campus for one day at the beginning of each semester to meet with professors and arrange coursework. Coursework is completed at home, with regular feedback provided by professors. Field experiences must generally take place within 200 miles of SMWC in order to ensure proper supervision.

Teacher Preparation Program Information

The following programs are 4 year programs:
Early Childhood Education, Elementary Education, K-12 Education (Art, Music), Middle School Education (English, French, Mathematics, Science, Social Studies, Spanish, Visual Arts), Secondary Education (Art, English, French, Mathematics, Science, Social Studies, Spanish), Special Education (Learning Disability, Mildly Mentally Handicapped)

The following programs are post-baccalaureate programs:
Early Childhood Education, Elementary Education, K-12 Education (Art, Music), Kindergarten Education, Middle School Education (English, French, Mathematics, Science, Social Studies, Spanish, Visual Arts), Secondary Education (Art, English, French, Mathematics, Science, Social Studies, Spanish), Special Education (Learning Disability, Mildly Mentally Handicapped)

Saint Mary's College

Saint Mary's College is an academic community where women develop their talents and prepare to make a difference. Saint Mary's promotes a life of intellectual vigor, aesthetic appreciation, religious sensibility, and social responsibility. The college insists on a liberal arts foundation for all its students. The Education Department is committed to developing and maintaining a teacher preparation program that empowers educators as decision makers and leaders. The Education Department has incorporated the goals established by the National Association for Multicultural Education into its programs.

Just the facts...

Saint Mary's College
Education Department
320 Madeleva Hall
Notre Dame, IN 46556-5001
(219) 284-4485
Website: www.saintmarys.edu
Profile: Urban, Small, Women
UG Tuition: $8,000.00/semester
Off Campus Programs: No

Clinical Experiences

Candidates are required to complete one hundred hours of clinical and field-based experiences prior to student teaching. These experiences are provided to develop the ability of the candidate to apply a variety of data collection techniques, interact with different age groups and cultures, use a variety of assessment and evaluation techniques, study and analyze effective models of classroom management, and develop appropriate classroom management and discipline skills. Candidates complete one semester of full-time student teaching.

Noteworthy

The undergraduate teacher education program offers the elementary education major, a reading minor, bilingual/bicultural endorsement, computer endorsement, kindergarten endorsement, and a junior high/middle school endorsement. Secondary education, junior high/middle school education, visual art education, and music education programs are also offered. Candidates' performance is assessed and professional growth is evaluated through continuing portfolio development culminating in the student teaching portfolio.

Teacher Preparation Program Information

The following programs are 4 year programs:
Elementary Education, K-12 Education (Art, Music), Junior High/Middle School Education, Secondary Education

The following programs are post-baccalaureate programs:
Junior High/Middle School Education (Biology, Business, Chemistry, English/Language Arts, History, Mathematics, Physics, Political Science, Psychology, Social Studies, Sociology,), Secondary Education

Taylor University

Taylor University seeks to develop competent, caring, and reflective teachers prepared for world service. The university believes that teachers who have experienced a vigorous professional preparation within the framework of evangelical Christian values will have a profound influence on the students they teach in public, private, and overseas schools. A comprehensive liberal arts curriculum provides the foundation for subject matter competence as well as lifelong learning, leadership, and continued growth in the teaching profession.

Just the facts...

Taylor University
Department of Education
236 W. Reade Avenue
Upland, IN 46989-1001
(765) 998-5147
Website: www.tayloru.edu
Profile: Rural, Small, Co-Ed
UG Tuition: $7,120.00/semester
Off Campus Programs: No

Clinical Experiences

Clinical experiences with a strong multicultural emphasis are considered a vital part of teacher preparation at Taylor. These experiences begin during candidates' first professional education course and continue through their senior year. The culmination of these professional experiences occurs during the senior year in sixteen weeks of full-time student teaching. Opportunities are available for overseas student teaching after interested candidates complete ten weeks of student teaching in the United States.

Noteworthy

Because Taylor University is a two-campus institution with sites in Upland and Fort Wayne, clinical experiences are available in both urban and rural settings. Practica in inner city schools are available at the Fort Wayne campus, and an urban semester, also on the Fort Wayne campus, is in the developmental stages. The Educational Technology Center, on the Upland campus, offers state-of-the-art technology and production services to prospective teachers.

Teacher Preparation Program Information

The following programs are 4 year programs:
Elementary Education, K-12 Education (Art, Music, Physical Education), Secondary Education (English/Language Arts, French, Mathematics, Physical Education, Science, Social Studies, Spanish, Speech Communication and Theatre, Visual Arts)

University of Evansville

The University of Evansville's teacher preparation program is based on candidates receiving a strong foundation in liberal arts and professional preparation. The education programs reflect the view that teachers are decision makers who facilitate learning through their understanding of teaching, learner diversity, and instructional technology. Portfolios and performance-based assessment are used to evaluate candidate progress. Graduates of the program understand the importance of, and have a commitment to continued personal growth.

Just the facts...

University of Evansville
College of Education and Health Sciences
1800 Lincoln Avenue
Evansville, IN 47722-0011
(812) 479-2368
Website: www.evansville.edu
Profile: Urban, Small, Co-Ed
UG Tuition: $6,800.00/semester
G Tuition: $375.00/credit hour
Off Campus Programs: No

Clinical Experiences

The university has extensive working relationships with the community and public and private K-12 schools. A minimum of three pre-student teaching intern experiences are provided for candidates enrolled in elementary and middle school/secondary school programs. Candidates in the special education program participate in five intern placements. All intern placements are arranged to enable partnering among interns and are supervised by university faculty and classroom teachers familiar with the university's program goals and expectations.

Noteworthy

Education students are encouraged to spend a semester at the University of Evansville's Harlaxton College in Grantham, England. During this semester, educational coursework and field experiences are offered in British schools. All students in the professional education program participate in Collaborative Learning and Service Learning. Collaborative learning teams are composed of a freshman, sophomore, and junior student, with the junior student serving as team leader. The goal of the program is to facilitate mentoring, support, and academic work cooperation. The design and implementation of a service learning project is a curriculum component of all junior level field placement experiences.

Teacher Preparation Program Information

The following programs are 4 year programs:

Elementary Education, K-12 Education (Art, Health, Music, Physical Education), Middle School Education (Computer Instruction, English, French, Mathematics, Science, Social Studies, Spanish), Secondary Education (Biology, Chemistry, Earth Science, Economics, English/Language Arts, French, General Science, German, Health, Mathematics, Physical Education, Physical Sciences, Physics, Political Science, Psychology, Science, Social Studies, Spanish), Special Education (Learning Disability, Mild Disabilities, Multiple Disabilities/Handicaps, Physical Disabilities/Handicaps, Severe Behavioral Disabilities/Handicaps, Severe Disabilities)

University of Indianapolis

The University of Indianapolis has been preparing teachers for 100 years. The teacher education programs at the University of Indianapolis strive to prepare teachers for professional service and leadership. The relationship between pedagogy and a strong liberal arts/content area background is stressed throughout the program. The university focuses on four key components: knowing subject content and how to teach it, life-long learning, reflection on practice, and a commitment to students and learning.

Just the facts...

University of Indianapolis
School of Education
1400 East Hanna Avenue
Indianapolis, IN 46227
(317) 788-3285
Website: www.uindy.edu
Profile: Urban, Medium, Co-Ed
UG Tuition: $6,500.00/semester
G Tuition: $216.00/credit hour
Off Campus Programs: No

Clinical Experiences

The university has a highly respected professional development school partnership with a local school district. Field experiences are built into the program from the first year, and include experiences in urban, rural, and suburban districts. The experiences expand so that beginning with the third year, methods courses are taught on-site in schools. These courses are collaboratively planned and taught by university faculty and teachers within the schools. Collaboratively planned internships are offered with the Indianapolis Children's Museum and the Indianapolis Zoo.

Noteworthy

The teacher education program includes ongoing candidate assessment. Feedback to candidates includes regular input from practicing professionals. Candidates use technology in courses throughout the curriculum. Web-based courses, technology-facilitated distance-learning courses, and Internet connections with preservice teachers all over the world benefit candidates at the University of Indianapolis. Performance-based assessments are an integral part of the overall program.

Teacher Preparation Program Information

The following programs are 4 year programs:
Elementary Education (Language Arts), K-12 Education (Art, French, Music, Physical Education, Reading, Spanish), Middle School Education (English, Mathematics, Science, Social Studies), Secondary Education (Agriculture, Art, Business, Chemistry, Earth Science, Economics, Language Arts, Mathematics, Physical Education, Physics, Political Science, Psychology, Social Studies, Sociology)

University of Saint Francis

The University of Saint Francis offers three undergraduate education majors—elementary, secondary, and special education. Elementary education majors must minor in physical education, visual arts, special education, or reading. The teacher education curriculum provides a quality academic program that fosters the formation of religious, moral and ethical values; encourages the lifelong pursuit of learning; and develops a sense of community. The three major components in the preparation of teachers at the university are (1) general education, (2) professional education in the prospective teacher's chosen area, and (3) professional clinical experiences.

Just the facts...

University of Saint Francis
Department of Education
2701 Spring Street
Fort Wayne, IN 46808
(219) 434-7442
Profile: Urban, Small, Co-Ed
UG Tuition: $340.00/cr.hr. in-state; $350.00/cr. hr. out-of-state
Off Campus Programs: No

Clinical Experiences

Clinical experiences begin in the candidate's freshman year, and provide opportunities for them to teach both in private and public schools in diverse settings. Candidates benefit from the unique pairing of regular and special education faculty in seminar and field placements. Methods classes provide additional "hands-on" teaching experiences. Clinical experiences culminate with ten to fifteen weeks of student teaching.

Noteworthy

Excellent financial aid packages, including work-study options, and a "third-year tuition-free" policy make Saint Francis an affordable private university. Alumni seeking a second degree are granted half-tuition scholarships. Individual attention, small class sizes, and a caring faculty are hallmarks of Saint Francis. Student teaching is supervised by full-time faculty in the candidate's field. Graduate students complete internships and practica in diverse community settings. Several university/community collaborations provide multiple opportunities for service learning.

Teacher Preparation Program Information

The following programs are 4 year programs:

Elementary Education (Grades 1-6, Non-departmentalized 7-8), K-12 Education (Visual Arts), Secondary Education (Biology, Business, Chemistry, English, General Science, Health and Safety, Psychology, Sociology, United States History, Visual Arts, World Civilization), Special Education (Emotionally Handicapped, Mild Disabilities)

University of Southern Indiana

Teacher education programs at the University of Southern Indiana emphasize principles of teaching and learning applied to the daily work of teachers. The program's goal is to graduate teacher candidates who meet state and national standards for effective teaching. Candidates learn to integrate their content, professional, and pedagogical knowledge and skills to create meaningful learning experiences for all students. The university's reflective teaching model includes four themes—experiential learning, multiple perspectives, critical inquiry, and construction of knowledge—and rests on established and contemporary research, the wisdom of practice, and emerging education policies and practices.

Clinical Experiences

Clinical experiences are integral to all programs, beginning with the first required education course and culminating with student teaching. Some courses are taught in partnership schools, where university faculty and candidates participate in the curriculum at the school site. Through these experiences, candidates demonstrate knowledge, skills, and dispositions for teaching. Faculty use evaluative information from field experiences in assessing candidates' progress in meeting program requirements.

Just the facts...

University of Southern Indiana
School of Education and Human Services
8600 University Boulevard
Evansville, IN 47712
(812) 464-1811
Website: http://magic.usi.edu
Profile: Suburban, Medium, Co-Ed
UG Tuition: $87.75/cr. hr. in-state; $215.25/cr. hr. out-of-state
G Tuition: $129.25/cr. hr. in-state; $259.75/cr. hr. out-of-state
Off Campus Programs: No

Noteworthy

Candidates develop and apply computer applications for teaching, use the Internet and multimedia resources, create electronic portfolios, and are prepared to integrate technology in elementary, middle, and high schools. The university has provided leadership in educational technology for schools and teachers throughout southern Indiana. There are no graduate students who teach undergraduates—all classes are taught by professional faculty. Approximately 76 percent of all university classes enroll 32 or fewer students. The eighteen to one student/faculty ratio offers all the benefits of a private university at a public university cost. The university also offers a teacher placement service.

Teacher Preparation Program Information

The following programs are 4 year programs:
Elementary Education, K-12 Education (Art, Physical Education), Secondary Education (Art, Biology, Business, Chemistry, Earth Science, Economics, English/Language Arts, General Science, Mathematics, Physical Education, Political Science, Psychology, Science, History, French, German, Spanish)

The following programs are post-baccalaureate programs:
Elementary Education (Reading), K-12 Education (Reading), Kindergarten Education, Middle School Education (Art, English, Mathematics, Physical Education, Science, Social Studies), Secondary Education (Drama/Theater, Geography, Health, Physical Sciences, Physics, Vocational Business)

Valparaiso University

Valparaiso's Department of Education prepares future educators who have strong academic backgrounds, broad knowledge of child and adolescent development and effective teaching practices, extensive experiences in K-12 classrooms, and caring and reflective attitudes. The faculty is committed to preparing educators to teach tomorrow's students—children and young people with diverse cultural, ethnic, and language backgrounds and different academic achievement levels.

Just the facts...

Valparaiso University
Department of Education
Miller Hall
Valparaiso, IN 46383
(219) 464-5077
Website: www.valpo.edu
Profile: Suburban, Medium, Co-Ed
UG Tuition: $7,700.00/semester
G Tuition: $215.00/credit hour
Off Campus Programs: No

Clinical Experiences

Valparaiso University prospective teachers have extensive field experiences beginning in the sophomore year. Junior level elementary education candidates learn and teach for 200 hours in an elementary school with a diverse population during a semester that is a combination of university-based and school-based instruction and experience. Secondary education candidates learn and teach for five weeks in a middle school with a diverse population where they participate fully in adviser/advisee sessions and interdisciplinary teams. All candidates have ten to twelve weeks of full-time student teaching experience in their final year.

Noteworthy

Extensive collaboration between university faculty and regional elementary and secondary educators provides candidates with programs distinguished by strong links between theory and practice. Regional educators are fully involved with university faculty in planning, implementing, and coordinating learning experiences for candidates in classrooms, with children's families, and in the community. Valparaiso's location offers future teachers opportunities to participate in professional development activities that range from environmental study at the Indiana Dunes National Lakeshore to cultural studies at Chicago-area museums.

Teacher Preparation Program Information

The following programs are 4 year programs:
Elementary Education, K-12 Education (Art, Music, Physical Education), Middle School Education (Art, Biology, Chemistry, English, French, German, Latin, Mathematics, Music, Physical Education, Science, Social Studies, Spanish), Secondary Education (Art, Biology, Chemistry, Economics, English/Language Arts, French, Geography, German, Latin, Mathematics, Music, Physical Education, Physics, Political Science, Psychology, Science, Social Studies, Sociology, Spanish), Special Education (Learning Disability)

The following programs are post-baccalaureate programs:
Special Education (Learning Disability, Mildly Mentally Handicapped, Severe Behavioral Disabilities/Handicaps)

The following programs are 5 year programs:
Elementary Education, K-12 Education (Art, Music, Physical Education), Middle School Education (Art, Biology, Chemistry, French, German, Latin, Music, Physical Education, Spanish), Secondary Education (Art, Biology, Chemistry, Economics, English/Language Arts, French, Geography, German, Latin, Mathematics, Music, Physical Education, Physics, Political Science, Psychology, Science, Social Studies, Sociology, Spanish), Special Education (Learning Disability)

The following programs are 5th year programs:
Special Education (Mildly Mentally Handicapped)

Graceland College

Faculty at Graceland College believe that the effective teacher is a professional proficient in content knowledge, pedagogy, reflective thinking, interpersonal skills, and technology. Candidates are immersed in the belief that teaching is a helping profession. In their senior year, candidates compile portfolios that demonstrate their attainment of professional teaching competencies.

Just the facts...

Graceland College
Teacher Education
700 College Avenue
Lamoni, IA 50140
(515) 784-5252
Website: www.graceland.edu
Profile: Rural, Small, Co-Ed
UG Tuition: $5,600.00/semester
Off Campus Programs: Yes

Clinical Experiences

All teacher candidates complete a minimum of twelve consecutive weeks of senior-level student teaching. Student teaching is preceded by at least 90 hours of junior-level practicum or internship experiences and 22 hours of sophomore-level field experiences. Junior-level practicums or internships are completed during a three-week January term. Diverse settings for clinical experiences are encouraged. A yearly Prospectus of Teacher Education Graduates describing each candidate's clinical experiences is available on the college's Website.

Noteworthy

In 1997, the North Central Regional Laboratory selected Graceland as an exemplary college as a result of its integration of technology into the curriculum. A complete description of the Graceland technology model is provided on the college's Website. Technology integration begins in the Introduction to Education course where candidates learn skills for teaching with the Internet, communicating with e-mail, and developing a digital résumé/portfolio using Hyperstudio. All education courses include technology modules related to the teaching of curriculum content.

Teacher Preparation Program Information

The following programs are 4 year programs:
Early Childhood Education, Elementary Education (Language Arts, Multi-Categorical Special Education, Reading, Science), K-12 Education (Art, Multi-Categorical Special Education, Music, Physical Education), Middle School Education, Secondary Education (Art, Biology, Chemistry, Economics, English/Language Arts, General Science, German, Health, History, Mathematics, Multi-Categorical Special Education, Music, Physical Sciences, Physics, Political Science, Psychology, Sociology, Spanish, Speech Communication/Theatre)

Luther College

The education major at Luther offers candidates many options in preparation for the teaching profession. Thorough classroom instruction, combined with extensive field experience, prepares candidates for careers in elementary or secondary teaching. Special adjunct programs for elementary education majors offer preparation for endorsements in academic areas, early childhood, reading, special education, English as a second language, and middle school. Methods classes are closely integrated with the activities of actual elementary and secondary classrooms. College faculty work side by side with elementary and secondary teachers in these courses, and many class meetings take place in schools rather than on campus.

Just the facts...

Luther College
Education Department
700 College Drive
Koren Building
Decorah, IA 52101-1045
(319) 387-1544
Website: www.luther.edu
Profile: Small, Co-Ed
UG Tuition: $20,275.00/year
Off Campus Programs: No

Clinical Experiences

Luther believes that field experience—working with real students in real classrooms—is the cornerstone of an effective teacher education program. A systematic sequence of field-based classroom opportunities supplements and enriches the coursework on campus. Very early in candidates' training, clinical experience in an elementary or secondary classroom gives them an opportunity to test their potential for teaching. The culmination of the program is a full semester of student teaching. College supervisors visit the classrooms during this semester to observe performance and make constructive suggestions. Additional teaching methods are also discussed in a small group format during the clinical semester.

Noteworthy

Luther enjoys great success in placing its graduates in teaching positions in all 50 states and a number of foreign countries. The Luther College Career Development Center and the Department of Education produce the *Teacher Candidate Brochure* which is mailed to school districts each spring to introduce graduates to schools that are looking for new teachers. The Career Development Center offers a full range of services, including credential preparation and service, individual career counseling and advising, workshops, and other career-related resources. Graduates also utilize the UNI CareerLink WebRegistration and WebResume System, which connects them to educational employers.

Teacher Preparation Program Information

The following programs are 4 year programs:

Early Childhood Education, Elementary Education (Language Arts, Mathematics, Science, Social Studies), K-12 Education (Art, Drama/Theater, ESL, French, German, Latin, Music, Physical Education/Health, Reading, Spanish), Kindergarten Education, Secondary Education (Art, Biology, Business, Chemistry, English/Language Arts, General Science, Health, Learning Disability, Mathematics, Physical Education/Health, Physical Sciences, Physics, Political Science, Psychology, Science, Social Studies, Sociology), Special Education (Multiple Disabilities/Handicaps)

Morningside College

Morningside College is rooted in a strong liberal arts tradition affiliated with the Methodist Church. The college strives to integrate the arts and sciences and professional programs to provide teacher candidates with an interdisciplinary approach to education. A new interdisciplinary core curriculum is an example of this commitment. The primary mission of teacher education at Morningside College is to prepare teachers who will provide the highest quality education for all their students. The undergraduate programs provide a solid foundation for beginning teachers.

Just the facts...

Morningside College
Department of Education
1501 Morningside College
Sioux City, IA 51106
(712) 274-5106
Website: www.morningside.edu
Profile: Urban, Small, Co-Ed
UG Tuition: $5,718.00/semester
G Tuition: $160.00/credit hour
Off Campus Programs: No

Clinical Experiences

Morningside works collaboratively with area schools to improve the quality of teacher education. Candidates complete extensive field experiences, including student teaching in area classrooms in the Sioux Community Schools, Sergeant Bluff-Luton Schools, Westwood Community School District, Lawton-Bronson Community Schools, and Woodbury Central School District. Practicums in Early Childhood Education may be done at the Morningside College Child Care Center, located on the college campus, which provides child care for students, faculty, and local residents.

Noteworthy

The Education Placement Bureau assists graduates in finding teaching positions by maintaining graduates' credential files, sending files to potential applicants, assisting graduates in locating postions, and providing training in résumé development and interviewing skills. The Educational Resource Center includes a large collection of curriculum materials and resources for candidates and faculty to use in courses and field experiences. Activity books, manipulatives, software, and teacher periodicals are included in the collection. Computers and work space are available, as well as educational and media equipment that may be checked out by candidates.

Teacher Preparation Program Information

The following programs are 4 year programs:

Early Childhood Education, Elementary Education, K-12 Education (Art, French, Music, Physical Education, Reading, Spanish), Secondary Education (Biology, Business, Chemistry, English/Language Arts, Mathematics, Physics, Psychology, Social Studies), Special Education (Behavior Disordered, Mild/Moderate Mental Disabilities, Multicategorical Resource Teaching Programs/Mild)

The following programs are post-baccalaureate programs:

Early Childhood Education, Elementary Education, K-12 Education (Art, Coaching, French, Music, Physical Education, Reading, Spanish), Secondary Education (Biology, Business, Chemistry, English/Language Arts, Mathematics, Physics, Psychology, Social Studies), Special Education (Behavior Disordered, Mild/Moderate Mental Disabilities, Moderate/Severe Mental Disabilities, Multicategorical Resource Teaching Programs/Mild, Multicategorical Self-Contained)

Northwestern College

Northwestern College's teacher education model is the "teacher as servant." The college serves students in the name of Jesus Christ with the expectation that they too will seek to offer themselves in Christian service as they go forth to teach others. Northwestern emphasizes a well-rounded experience and intellectual and emotional wholeness. The Teacher Education Program is based on the belief that effective teaching results from research and knowledge of teaching and learning.

Just the facts...

Northwestern College
Department of Education
101 7th Street, SW
Orange City, IA 51041
(712) 737-7031
Website: www.nwciowa.edu
Profile: Rural, Small, Co-Ed
UG Tuition: $5,650.00/semester
Off Campus Programs: No

Clinical Experiences

Northwestern's emphasis on content and pedagogical knowledge is put into practice in various pre-teaching and teaching experiences in the field. All professional education courses have field experience components in area K-12 schools. A full-semester student teaching experience is available in traditional area schools as well as in diverse cultural settings. There is a field experience requirement in a multicultural area prior to student teaching.

Noteworthy

In addition to the basic programs in elementary and secondary education, special programs are provided in education for special needs children, reading, early childhood, and middle school. The Department of Education enjoys excellent facilities and a faculty committed to intergration of faith and learning. Most graduates pursue public school careers; however, an increasing number are entering private Christian schools.

Teacher Preparation Program Information

The following programs are 4 year programs:

Early Childhood Education, Elementary Education, K-12 Education (Drama/Theater, French, Health, Music, Physical Education, Reading, Spanish), Middle School Education, Secondary Education (Art, Business, Chemistry, English/Language Arts, General Science, Health, Physical Education, Physical Sciences, Physics, Political Science, Sociology), Special Education (Learning Disability, Multiple Disabilities/Handicaps)

Wartburg College

The Teacher Education Program at Wartburg combines general education, specialty content, and professional core coursework to develop effective and reflective preservice teachers. Candidates learn about assessment, instructional strategies, and planning; study ethics and student learning; practice collaboration; and plan for their continuing education and professional development. Programs are offered in elementary and secondary teaching and are designed to be completed in four years.

Just the facts...

Wartburg College
Education Department
222 9th Street
Waverly, IA 50677
(319) 352-8226
Website: www.wartburg.edu
Profile: Rural, Small, Co-Ed
UG Tuition: $7,070.00/semester
Off Campus Programs: No

Clinical Experiences

The Teacher Education Program provides early and continuing field experiences in rural and urban settings. As early as their first year at Wartburg, candidates become involved in teaching activities. Before graduation, all teacher education candidates must complete a 25-hour experience with children from cultures significantly different from their own. Placements are available in Denver and New York City, as well as in Wartburg's surrounding communities. Elementary education candidates student teach for fourteen weeks in two different placements. Secondary education candidates student teach for twelve weeks.

Noteworthy

Wartburg College is affiliated with the Evangelical Lutheran Church of America. Wartburg is recognized for the Waterloo Teachers Project, designed to provide an undergraduate teacher education experience/degree for over thirty American ethnic students in nearby Waterloo. Wartburg's commitment to leadership, ethics, global/multicultural perspectives, and "living your learning" initiatives are hallmarks of the college.

Teacher Preparation Program Information

The following programs are 4 year programs:

Elementary Education (Language Arts, Mathematics, Reading, Science, Social Studies), K-12 Education (Art, French, Health, Music, Physical Education, Spanish), Kindergarten Education, Secondary Education (American History, Art, Biology, Chemistry, Earth Science, Economics, English/Language Arts, General Science, Health, Mathematics, Music, Physical Education, Physical Sciences, Physics, Psychology, Political Science, Sociology, World History)

Baker University

Teacher candidates at Baker University become effective educators who are able to create learning environments that enable all children to develop the essential skills, knowledge, attitudes, and values for the 21st century. The Department of Education at Baker has defined five essential areas that prospective teachers in its educator preparation programs must develop: professional knowledge, problem solving skills, effective communication skills, technological literacy, and the ability to become life-long learners and active community participants. The Department of Education emphasizes integrating theory with practice and linking coursework to the real world.

Just the facts...

Baker University
Department of Education
8th and Grove, Box 65
Baldwin City, KS 66006-0065
(785) 594-6451
Website: www.bakeru.edu
Profile: Rural, Small, Co-Ed
UG Tuition: $5,650.00/semester
G Tuition: $190.00/credit hour
Off Campus Programs: Yes

Clinical Experiences

Baker University takes pride in providing candidates with a wide variety of field experiences prior to student teaching. Pre-student teaching field experience requirements include such experiences as observing and assisting in classrooms, working with children who have disabilities, tutoring students, assisting with school activities, assisting teachers with before school planning, attending faculty meetings, and participating in the process of improving schools. A required urban field experience practicum provides prospective teachers with the opportunity to gain invaluable experience working in diverse school settings.

Noteworthy

Baker University's Department of Education was recently recognized by the Kansas Association of Elementary School Principals with its top award, citing Baker for providing exceptional support to education in the local community. Baker's education programs focus on effective practice and leadership skills using faculty who are effective former practitioners able to integrate their valuable experiences with theory. Faculty members boast of an average of sixteen years of teaching/administration experience in the public schools. A number of adjunct faculty in the Department of Education are also employees in the public schools, further strengthening the link between the university and P-12 classrooms.

Teacher Preparation Program Information

The following programs are 4 year programs:
Elementary Education, K-12 Education (Art, Music, Physical Education), Secondary Education (Biology, Business, Chemistry, English, French, General Mathematics, General Science, German, Health, History/Government, Journalism, Mathematics, Physical Education, Physical Science, Physics, Psychology, Sociology/Anthropology, Spanish, Speech Communication/Theatre)

Benedictine College

Programs in the Department of Education call upon future teachers and administrators to recognize their roles as developers of community—the learning community that is within classrooms and schools as well as the communities outside their walls. Graduates build fellowship with students, families, and members of the local community. Benedictine graduates strive to develop individuals who will assume responsibility for building a healthy community locally, nationally, and globally. Grounded in a Benedictine liberal arts tradition, the education programs advocate the pursuit of human dignity and social responsibility.

Just the facts...

Benedictine College
Department of Education
1020 North 2nd Street
Atchison, KS 66002
(913) 367-5340
Website: www.benedictine.edu
Profile: Rural, Small, Co-Ed
UG Tuition: $5,770.00/semester
Off Campus Programs: No

Clinical Experiences

Candidates progress through a series of field experiences that develop insights and standards for building a learning community. Each experience requires candidates to become actively involved in discovery teaching, learning, decision making, and self-assessment. The Department of Education is engaged in collaborative partnerships with schools and school districts to carry out mutually beneficial activities. School faculty serve as clinical supervisors of candidates and collaborate with Benedictine faculty in providing mentored teaching and learning opportunities that encourage discovery, application, and self-reflection.

Noteworthy

Small classes enable candidates and faculty to work together on projects that can make a difference in schools. Faculty/candidate teams engage in research and showcase their findings at regional conferences and in publications. Creative, community-based learning projects, designed by candidates, bring together people of all ages in projects that benefit the local and global community. Online telemonitoring is one way that candidates work together and receive guidance from K-12 teachers and college faculty. The Teacher Education Laboratory enables education majors and practicing teachers to co-develop hands-on multimedia projects for K-12 students. Graduates of the program are highly respected and quickly offered jobs.

Teacher Preparation Program Information

The following programs are 4 year programs:

Elementary Education, K-12 Education (Music, Physical Education/Health), Secondary Education (Biology, Chemistry, Computer Studies, Drama, English/Language Arts, French, Spanish, General Science, History, Journalism, Latin, Mathematics, Physical Sciences, Physics, Political Science, Psychology, Social Studies, Spanish), Special Education (Mental Retardation)

Bethany College

Faculty members at Bethany College believe that America needs teachers who bring to the classroom the wisdom derived from wide-ranging life experiences, the confidence that comes from solid grounding in the subjects they will teach, and the professional communication skills gained from the study of pedagogy. Bethany College's Teacher Education Program prepares beginning teachers who understand the nature of their contributions to their students, who will stand as exemplars to their students, colleagues and communities, and who will continue to grow and develop throughout their careers.

Just the facts...

Bethany College
Education Department
421 North First Street
Lindsborg, KS 67456
(785) 227-3311
Website: www.bethanylb.edu
Profile: Rural, Small, Co-Ed
UG Tuition: $5,620.00/semester
Off Campus Programs: No

Clinical Experiences

An introduction to teaching seminar allows candidates to experience life in a K-12 classroom their freshman year. A full-time, month-long practicum is required of all candidates during the sophomore year. Secondary teaching majors complete an additional 30 hours of field experience during their junior year prior to their student teaching experience. Elementary education majors complete practica in various methods courses throughout their program. All education majors complete a student teaching experience from twelve to sixteen weeks in length. Added endorsements for middle level and special education require an additional six-week experience.

Noteworthy

Bethany offers an interrelated special education endorsement program for candidates, which leads to licensure in educable mental retardation, learning disabilities, and behavior disorders. Other endorsement offerings include an early childhood special education program, and middle-level programs in mathematics, social studies, language arts, and general studies. Bethany is the only NCATE-accredited teacher preparation program in Kansas to offer special education at the baccalaureate level.

Teacher Preparation Program Information

The following programs are 4 year programs:
Elementary Education, K-12 Education (Art, Health & Physical Education, Music, Physical Education), Secondary Education (Behavioral Sciences, Biology, Business, Chemistry, English, Health & Physical Education, Mathematics, Social Studies), Special Education (Behavior Disorders, Educable Mental Retardation, Learning Disabilities)

The following programs are post-baccalaureate programs:
Elementary Education, Kindergarten Education, K-12 Education (Art, Health & Physical Education, Music, Physical Education), Secondary Education (Behavioral Sciences, Biology, Business, Chemistry, English, Health & Physical Education, Mathematics, Social Studies), Special Education (Behavior Disorders, Educable Mental Retardation, Learning Disabilities)

Emporia State University

Founded in 1863 as Kansas State Normal School, Emporia State University has grown into a comprehensive university providing leadership in quality instruction, scholarship, and service. The university provides programs of national distinction in education and library and information management. Students enjoy Emporia's attractive, small campus, strong general education program, opportunities for personal contacts with faculty, and a wide range of social and academic activities.

Just the facts...

Emporia State University
The Teachers College
1200 Commercial Street
Emporia, KS 66801-5087
(316) 341-5367
Website: www.emporia.edu
Profile: Rural, Medium, Co-Ed
UG Tuition: $991.00/sem. in-state; $3,173.00/sem. out-of-state
G Tuition: $1,150.00/sem. in-state; $3,006.00/sem. out-of-state
Off Campus Programs: No

Clinical Experiences

All programs at Emporia's Teachers College require extensive field experience. To be admitted into the teacher education program, candidates must complete a 100-hour volunteer program. Further clinical and field-based experiences are integrated throughout the program. The Teachers College maintains six professional development schools in Olathe and Emporia, Kansas. Its professional development school model offers a collaborative, 100 percent field-based, year-long clinical school experience for elementary education candidates.

Noteworthy

The Teachers College and Emporia State maintain an active state, regional, and national agenda and have received five national awards for excellence. The Teachers College is a member of several education reform initiatives, including the Project 30 Alliance, the Renaissance Group, and the Teacher Education Council of State Colleges and Universities. Emporia State is home to the National Teachers Hall of Fame. The campus operates two on-campus lab schools, Butcher Elementary School and the Child Development Center, and maintains the Great Plains Center for National Teacher Certification through the Jones Institute for Educational Excellence.

Teacher Preparation Program Information

The following programs are 4 year programs:

Elementary Education, K-12 Education (Art, ESL, French, Health, Music, Physical Education, Spanish), Middle School Education, Secondary Education (Art, Biology, Bookkeeping, Business, Chemistry, Computer Science, History, Journalism, Earth Science, Economics, English/Language Arts, General Science, Geography, Health, Mathematics, Physical Education, Physical Sciences, Physics, Political Science, Psychology, Social Studies, Sociology, Steno/Typing/Keyboard, Vocational Business Office), Special Education (Mental Retardation)

The following programs are post-baccalaureate programs:

Elementary Education, K-12 Education (Art, ESL, French, Health, Music, Physical Education, Spanish), Middle School Education, Secondary Education (Art, Biology, Bookkeeping, Business, Chemistry, Computer Science, History, Journalism, Earth Science, Economics, English/Language Arts, General Science, Geography, Health, Mathematics, Physical Education, Physical Sciences, Physics, Political Science, Psychology, Social Studies, Sociology, Steno/Typing/Keyboard, Vocational Business Office), Special Education (Mental Retardation)

Fort Hays State University

The primary mission of the College of Education at Fort Hays State University is to prepare P-12 educators who have a strong general education background, and who understand the contemporary role of the profession of teaching and the organizational system of the school. Graduates are knowledgeable in content and curriculum planning; are able to use instructional strategies for effective learning; value and use theory and research for effective teaching; have comprehensive knowledge of human growth and development; understand themselves and are sensitive to cultural difference and global perspectives; and are skilled in technology and communications.

Clinical Experiences

Candidates participate in a variety of field experiences teaching diverse students at small- to medium-sized schools. Learning is planned and monitored by university faculty and cooperating classroom teachers in order to maximize candidates' achievement. The relationship of field experiences to coursework is amplified through seminars, candidate journals, and teaching portfolios. Student teaching varies from twelve to sixteen weeks depending on the program selected by the teacher candidate.

Just the facts...

Fort Hays State University
College of Education
600 Park Street
Hays, KS 67601-4099
(785) 628-5866
Website: www.fhsu.edu
Profile: Rural, Medium, Co-Ed
UG Tuition: $67.55/cr. hr. in-state; $213.05/cr. hr. out-of-state
G Tuition: $93.60/cr. hr. in-state; $248.25/cr. hr. out-of-state
Off Campus Programs: Yes

Noteworthy

Teacher preparation programs at FHSU are becoming more field-based and partnership-oriented. Elementary education majors may choose an intensive field-based program providing over 1,000 hours of hands-on experience or a more traditional program providing extensive coursework in special needs and cultural diversity. FHSU maintains on-campus and off-campus programs staffed by permanent faculty. Increasing varieties of instructional delivery in the teacher education programs make technology use a priority.

Teacher Preparation Program Information

The following programs are 4 year programs:
Elementary Education, K-12 Education (Art, Music, Physical Education), Secondary Education (Biology, Business, Chemistry, Earth-Space Science, English, French, General Science, German, History, Mathematics, Physical Science, Physics, School Nursing, Sociology, Spanish, Speech Communication, Technology Studies)

Friends University

For nearly 100 years, Friends University has been providing a liberal arts education for students of all ages and denominations. As a nondenominational Christian university, Friends incorporates learning within the context of the Christian faith. The university is committed to a central core of arts and sciences. Friends was named one of the "100 Best College Buys" for two years in a row based on its academic quality and low tuition cost. Education Department candidates enjoy modern classrooms in a beautifully renovated turn-of-the-century building, a computer lab, and an education curriculum library.

Just the facts...

Friends University
Division of Education
2100 West University Street
Wichita, KS 67213
(316) 295-5824
Website: www.friends.edu
Profile: Urban, Small, Co-Ed
UG Tuition: $5,200.00/semester
G Tuition: $326.90/credit hour
Off Campus Programs: Yes

Clinical Experiences

Friends University sponsors varied clinical experiences for teacher education candidates. A professional development school arrangement for Early Childhood majors has been developed, as has a high school site for secondary methods instruction. Many courses in the Education Department include a required clinical placement component, and a full-time semester of student teaching is completed by all candidates. Friends works closely with an organization known as Communities and Schools to place candidates in diverse school settings for field experiences.

Noteworthy

The Teacher Education Department at Friends University sponsors an exchange each spring with two British universities, the University of Central England and the University of Exeter. During spring break, teacher candidates travel to England, are housed in British university students' homes, visit local schools, and end the trip with a long weekend in London. During their Easter holiday, the same British university students come to Wichita, see the Midwest, and visit U.S. schools. Friends is also known for its Summer Workshops for Teachers, which regional school teachers attend as they continue their own learning about quality teaching.

Teacher Preparation Program Information

The following programs are 4 year programs:
Early Childhood/Elementary Education, Elementary Education, K-12 Education (Art, Music, Physical Education, Spanish), Secondary Education (Biology, Business, Chemistry, English, General Science, Mathematics, Social Science)

The following programs are 5th year programs:
Master of Arts in Teaching (various areas)

National Council for Accreditation of Teacher Education

Kansas State University

Kansas State University, the oldest land grant institution in the country, has prepared professional educators for more than 100 years. The College of Education is dedicated to preparing educators to be knowledgeable, ethical, caring decision makers in the context of teaching and learning in P-12 classrooms. The College of Education is engaged in a number of professional partnerships that contribute to a culture of inquiry and continual renewal.

Just the facts...

Kansas State University
College of Education
Bluemont Hall
Manhattan, KS 66506-5301
(785) 532-5525
Website: www.educ.ksu.edu
Profile: Suburban, Large, Co-Ed
UG Tuition: $68.05/cr. hr. in-state; $289.00/cr. hr. out-of-state
G Tuition: $101.00/cr. hr. in-state; $329.75/cr. hr. out-of-state
Off Campus Programs: No

Clinical Experiences

Teacher education candidates complete a sequence of clinical experiences over a period of two years, most of which are in professional development schools (PDSs). Based upon the success of the elementary education PDS model initiated in 1989, the PDS concept has been expanded into the middle and secondary education levels. Clinical experiences planned and facilitated by university faculty and clinical instructors address school, classroom, and student diversity, and help candidates attain professional teaching skills. Most students complete a full semester of student teaching.

Noteworthy

The College of Education is committed to addressing the needs of diverse constituents and is dedicated to education reform. Nationally recognized for successful school, university, and community partnerships, the curriculum reflects a collaborative and collegial approach to preservice teacher preparation. A high priority is placed on preparing graduates to use technology in the classroom. The Honors program recognizes high-achieving students and provides opportunities for independent research projects.

Teacher Preparation Program Information

The following programs are 4 year programs:

Early Childhood Education, Elementary Education, K-12 Education (Art, French, German, Music, Spanish), Middle Level Education (English, Home Economics, Mathematics, Science, Social Studies), Secondary Education (Agriculture, Art, Biology, Business, Chemistry, Earth Science, English/Language Arts, Mathematics, Physical Sciences, Physics, Political Science, Social Studies, Vocational Agriculture, Vocational Home Economics)

The following programs are post-baccalaureate programs:

Early Childhood Education, Elementary Education, K-12 Education (Art, French, German, Music, Spanish), Middle Level Education (English, Home Economics, Mathematics, Social Studies, Science), Secondary Education (Agriculture, Art, Biology, Business, Chemistry, Earth Science, English/Language Arts, Mathematics, Physical Sciences, Physics, Political Science, Social Studies, Vocational Agriculture, Vocational Home Economics)

Pittsburg State University

Pittsburg State University has been preparing teachers since 1903. The faculty in the College of Education is dedicated to ensuring that candidates become competent, committed, and caring professionals. The College of Education fulfills its mission by advocating and modeling the use of techniques, pedagogies, and technologies that promote innovation and lifelong learning.

Just the facts...

Pittsburg State University
College of Education
1701 South Broadway
Pittsburg, KS 66762
(316) 231-4517
Website: www.pittstate.edu
Profile: Rural, Medium, Co-Ed
UG Tuition: $1,050.00/sem. in-state; $3,232.00/sem. out-of-state
G Tuition: $1,209.00/sem. in-state; $3,065.00/sem. out-of-state
Off Campus Programs: Yes

Clinical Experiences

Clinical experiences are an important part of the teacher education program at Pittsburg State University. Candidates are introduced to field experiences in Pre-Professional Lab I. A second pre-lab experience follows, and an elective third pre-lab is available for candidates minoring in early childhood, special education, middle level, or multicultural education. Other clinical experiences include practica in reading, special education, math, and science methods. Student teaching is a sixteen-week field experience, during which candidates return to campus for eight full-day seminars.

Noteworthy

The College of Education has several new projects that involve new facilities and new programs; it has completed renovation of its classrooms to accommodate mediated instruction, and it has built a new Instructional Resource Center that boasts new equipment and additional funding for continually updated materials. The College of Education is also planning to formalize its professional development school partnerships, is working toward the goals and objectives established by the Teacher Education Unit Multicultural Committee, and is implementing a technology plan.

Teacher Preparation Program Information

The following programs are 4 year programs:

Early Childhood Education, Elementary Education, K-12 Education (Art, French, Music, Physical Education, Spanish, Special Education/Mental Retardation), Middle Level Education (English, Industrial Technology, Mathematics), Secondary Education (Biology, Chemistry, Computer Studies, Drama, English, French, General Industrial Technology, General Science, Journalism, Mathematics, Physical Science, Physical Education, Physics, Psychology, Social Studies, Spanish, Special Education/Mental Retardation, Speech Communication, Vocational Home Economics)

National Council for Accreditation of Teacher Education

Saint Mary College

Saint Mary College—a Catholic, liberal arts college with a commitment to developing in its graduates value-centered lives of learning, service, and character—provides a long and distinguished history of teacher preparation. The education department is dedicated to liberal, professional preparation for teaching. Students seek self-understanding through critical reflection, reading, discussion, collaborative projects, and experiences in area schools. They explore provocative questions to enhance their communication skills and understanding of content in order to make a difference in the lives of their future students and in the global community.

Just the facts...

Saint Mary College
Department of Education
4100 South 4th Trafficway
Leavenworth, KS 66048-5082
(913) 758-6116
Website: www.smcks.edu
Profile: Urban, Small, Women
UG Tuition: $5,425.00/semester
Off Campus Programs:Yes

Clinical Experiences

Field experiences are a vital part of the teacher education program. From initial observations of the entire school culture in a variety of schools to more focused experiences, candidates work closely with a cooperating teacher and complete a full semester of student teaching in professional development schools. Reflection and analysis of knowledge and practice brings a breadth and depth to understanding the diversity of children's needs. Teacher candidates practice working with individual learning styles and creating a positive classroom climate as they grow in awareness of students' varying cultural backgrounds.

Noteworthy

Saint Mary College offers day programs at its campus and an evening/weekend degree completion program in K-9 teacher preparation sites in Kansas City. The teacher education program has a comprehensive technology and assessment plan, infused into the coursework. The plan culminates in the development of teacher candidate portfolios that include evidence of progressively sophisticated learning and performance.

Teacher Preparation Program Information

The following programs are 4 year programs:

Elementary Education K-9, Secondary Education (Biology, Chemistry, English/Journalism, History/Political Science, Mathematics, Theater)

University of Kansas

The School of Education's Professional Teacher Preparation Program prepares caring, competent, qualified professionals who can use effective practices to educate students with diverse strengths and needs. Candidates benefit from a strong liberal arts education and a field-based pedagogical program. Candidates graduate with a basic belief in the uniqueness, dignity, and worth of the individual; a comprehensive knowledge of the subject matter they will teach; critical, research-based skills in teaching methodology; and an understanding of the school and its role in society.

Just the facts...

University of Kansas
School of Education
112 Bailey Hall
Lawrence, KS 66045-2330
(785) 864-3726
Website: www.soe.ukans.edu
Profile: Suburban, Large, Co-Ed
UG Tuition: $68.05/cr. hr. in-state; $283.00/cr. hr. out-of-state
G Tuition: $101.00/cr. hr. in-state; $329.75/cr. hr. out-of-state
Off Campus Programs: No

Clinical Experiences

Candidates participate in clinical experiences throughout their five years of study. Although candidates do not enter the program until their junior year, they engage in field experiences in pre-education courses as freshmen and sophomores. As juniors and seniors, candidates participate in methods courses with field-based components. In their fifth year, as graduate students, candidates spend a total of twenty weeks in student teaching and internship experiences, which may take place in professional development schools.

Noteworthy

The University of Kansas's School of Education is ranked as the nation's 22nd best graduate education school by *U.S. News and World Report*; the Department of Special Education is ranked number one. The Professional Teacher Preparation Program consists of a four-year baccalaureate program followed by a licensure year during which candidates work toward graduate degrees, student-teach for six weeks, take graduate-level education courses for ten weeks, and spend fourteen weeks in internships. The School of Education awards over $200,000 in scholarships annually.

Teacher Preparation Program Information

The following programs are 4 year programs:
Early Childhood Education

The following programs are 5 year programs:
Art Education, Elementary Education, Elementary-Middle Education, Health Education, K-12 Education, Middle/Secondary Education (Biology, Chemistry, Earth and Space Science, English/Language Arts, Foreign Language, General Science, Mathematics, Physical Science, Physics, Social Studies), Music Education, Physical Education, Secondary Education (Biology, Chemistry, Earth and Space Science, English/Language Arts, Foreign Language, General Science, Mathematics, Physical Science, Physics, Social Studies)

Washburn University of Topeka

Washburn, an urban university, prepares teachers for urban, rural, and suburban settings. Faculty work closely with the Brown Foundation (an outgrowth of the 1954 Brown v. Topeka Board of Education Supreme Court decision) to prepare candidates for diverse teaching positions. Faculty are dedicated to developing reflective educators who have strengths in the arts and sciences as well as an extensive repertoire of teaching skills. Washburn takes pride in its average class size of eighteen students, its balance of traditional and non-traditional students, and an educational climate that values excellent teaching.

Just the facts...

Washburn University
Department of Education
1700 Southwest College Avenue
Topeka, KS 66621
(785) 231-1010
Website: www.wuacc.edu/cas/education
Profile: Urban, Medium, Co-Ed
UG Tuition: $100.00/cr. hr. in-state; $218.00/cr. hr. out-of-state
G Tuition: $131.00/cr. hr. in-state; $270.00/cr. hr. out-of-state
Off Campus Programs: No

Clinical Experiences

Washburn provides candidates with multiple opportunities to apply skills acquired in the college classroom when working with students in area schools. Candidates participate in two early field experiences and several field-based practica as part of their methods courses. Student teaching includes a series of seminars. Candidates are placed with excellent classroom teachers in a variety of culturally diverse settings. Student teacher supervisors report that Washburn teacher candidates enter student teaching with exceptional levels of confidence and well-developed skills.

Noteworthy

Washburn University is a public school with a private school atmosphere. Its endowment fund ranks nineteenth out of 156 public institutions. Financial support for education students has tripled in the past five years. Complementing its urban mission, Washburn participates with the Yale University Child Study Center and the Topeka Public Schools in a partnership called the Comer School Development Program. A wide variety of technology resources is available to candidates, and faculty integrate technology into their instruction.

Teacher Preparation Program Information

The following programs are 4 year programs:
Early Childhood Education, Elementary Education, K-12 Education (Art, Music, Physical Education), Secondary Education (Biology, Business, Chemistry, Computer Science, English/Language Arts, French, General Science, German, History, Journalism, Mathematics, Physical Education, Physics, Psychology, Social Studies, Spanish, Speech)

The following programs are post-baccalaureate programs:
Secondary Education (Computer Science, General Science, Journalism, Political Science, Social Studies, Speech)

Wichita State University

Wichita State University's College of Education is located in the largest city in Kansas. This setting provides a wide range of resources, contacts with businesses and schools, and employment and internships for teacher candidates. Undergraduate teacher candidates are prepared to be nurturing professionals who are knowledgeable of and sensitive to the needs of learners. Graduate programs are grounded in scholarly inquiry and theory related to professional practice.

Just the facts...

Wichita State University
College of Education
1845 Fairmont
Campus Box 131
Wichita, KS 67260-0131
(316) 978-3301
Website: www.twsu.edu
Profile: Urban, Large, Co-Ed
UG Tuition: $83.85/cr. hr. in-state; $293.90/cr. hr. out-of-state
G Tuition: $115.45/cr. hr. in-state; $339.95/cr. hr. out-of-state
Off Campus Programs: No

Clinical Experiences

Each semester, faculty teams work with partner teachers in public and private schools to ensure that undergraduate candidates are engaged in classroom field experiences designed to support the campus program. Elementary, middle level, and high school teacher candidates have the opportunity to work and study in one of three professional development schools. Advanced programs in curriculum and instruction, special education, and educational administration provide site- or field-based programs.

Noteworthy

The College of Education operates one of the largest cooperative education programs in the nation. Candidates have the opportunity to work in paid paraprofessional positions in the public schools for up to three semesters before beginning student teaching.

Teacher Preparation Program Information

The following programs are 4 year programs:

Elementary Education, K-12 Education (Art, French, Music, Physical Education, Spanish), Secondary Education (Biological Sciences, Chemistry, English/Language Arts, Mathematics, Physical Sciences, Physics, Social Sciences)

National Council for Accreditation of Teacher Education

Bellarmine College

Bellarmine College prepares teachers to use their knowledge and skills to devise new methods of reasoning and new strategies of action to better help students learn. The School of Education trains teacher candidates to exercise their powers to change society for the better. Programs are based on the idea that the successful teacher is a reflective learner.

Just the facts...

Bellarmine College
Department of Education
2001 Newburg Road
Louisville, KY 40205-0167
(502) 452-8191
Website: www.bellarmine.edu
Profile: Suburban, Small, Co-Ed
UG Tuition: $5,800.00/semester
G Tuition: $360.00/credit hour
Off Campus Programs: No

Clinical Experiences

Clinical experiences are significant components of all teacher preparation programs at Bellarmine. These experiences begin early with classroom observations in the candidate's freshman year. One hundred and fifty hours of clinical and field experience must be completed prior to one semester of student teaching. These hours are spent in public, private, and/or parochial schools. Bellarmine College continues to expand its collaborative training programs with area schools.

Noteworthy

Bellarmine currently is working in conjunction with area public schools to provide training for current teachers who wish to work in the special education field. Bellarmine continues to develop new collaborations to take advantage of special training opportunities in science and math, so that candidates can hone their content knowledge and their classroom management skills simultaneously. The Accelerated Master of Arts in Teaching is a cohort program designed for non-traditional, adult students. Classes are offered at night and on weekends. Bellarmine prides itself on its small community atmosphere and its ability to produce graduates ready to succeed in the global marketplace.

Teacher Preparation Program Information

The following programs are 4 year programs:
Elementary Education (Language Arts, Mathematics, Science, Social Studies), K-12 Education (Art, Music), Middle School Education (English, Mathematics, Science, Social Studies), Secondary Education (Art, Biology, Chemistry, Science/Home Economics, English/Language Arts, General Science, Mathematics, Science, Social Studies), Special Education (Learning and Behavior Disorders)

The following programs are 5th year programs:
Elementary Education P-5 (English/Communications, Fine Arts, Mathematics, Science, Social and Behavioral Studies, Special Education), Middle School Education 5-9 (English/Communications, Mathematics, Science, Social and Behavioral Studies, Special Education)

Berea College

Founded in 1855, Berea College is a private, non-denominational, liberal arts college of 1,500 students located in the Appalachian foothills. Berea College focuses its efforts on serving the people of the Appalachian region. All Berea students receive a tuition-free education supported in part through its student labor program. A strong general studies program combined with intensive study in the major leads to licensure in elementary, middle level, or secondary education. The elemenary and middle level programs are five-year programs; secondary preparation requires four years and a January term.

Just the facts...

Berea College
Education Studies Department
CPO 2354
Berea, KY 40404
(606) 986-4341
Website: www.berea.edu
Profile: Rural, Small, Co-Ed
UG Tuition: Tuition-Free (see at left)
Off Campus Programs: No

Clinical Experiences

Theory and practice are integrated at Berea. Course-related clinical experiences begin with the introductory seminar. All candidates are required to have the equivalent of a month-long extended clinical experience prior to admission to the professional school terms. A full fifth year of professional experience is required for candidates preparing to teach in the elementary or middle grades; one semester and a January term of professional experience are required for candidates seeking secondary licensure.

Noteworthy

Careful advising and continuous assessment are integral to Berea's program and are reflected in the comprehensive and rigorous education portfolio developed by each candidate.

Teacher Preparation Program Information

The following programs are 4 year programs:
K-12 Education (Art, French, German, Health, Latin, Music, Physical Education, Spanish), Secondary Education (Biology, Child & Family Studies/Home Economics for Grades 5-12, English/Language Arts, Mathematics, Physical Sciences, Social Studies)

The following programs are 5 year programs:
Elementary Education, Middle School Education (English, Mathematics, Science, Social Studies)

National Council for Accreditation of Teacher Education

Eastern Kentucky University

Eastern Kentucky University has been long-committed to the preparation of teachers and other school personnel who function effectively in a culturally diverse society and who are able to meet the needs of all students. Each teacher candidate at Eastern Kentucky University makes progress through the program by applying knowledge to practice through performance-based learning experiences.

Just the facts...

Eastern Kentucky University
College of Education
421 Bert Combs Building
521 Lancaster Avenue
Richmond, KY 40475-3102
(606) 622-3515
Website: www.eku.edu
Profile: Suburban, Large, Co-Ed
UG Tuition: $1,095.00/sem. in-state; $3,015.00/sem. out-of-state
G Tuition: $1,195.00/sem. in-state; $3,315.00/sem. out-of-state
Off Campus Programs: No

Clinical Experiences

In addition to their instructional and student teaching experiences, EKU's teacher education candidates benefit from over 500 hours of observation and classroom experiences at the pre-primary, elementary, middle, and high school levels. Before beginning the student teaching experience, candidates spend time every year in structured experiences in the Model Laboratory School (see *Noteworthy* for a description of this school).

Noteworthy

The Model Laboratory School, the largest nursery-12 laboratory school in the nation, is operated as a department of the College of Education to fulfill several purposes: (1) to provide quality and innovative education for its 700-plus students; (2) to provide preservice education for prospective teachers; (3) to serve as an experimental testing ground for curriculum development and dissemination; and (4) to serve as a demonstration site for elements of school reform in Kentucky.

Teacher Preparation Program Information

The following programs are 4 year programs:

Early Childhood Education, Elementary Education, K-12 Education (Art, French, German, Health, Music, Physical Education, Spanish), Middle School Education (English, Mathematics, Science, Social Studies), Secondary Education (Biology, Business, Consumer & Family Science/Home Economics, English/Language Arts, Geography, History, Mathematics, Physical Education, Physical Sciences, Social Studies, Technology, Vocational Trade & Industrial), Special Education (Developmental Disabilities/Handicaps, Early Childhood, Hearing Impaired, Learning Disability, Multiple Disabilities/Handicaps, Physical Disabilities/Handicaps, Severe Behavioral Disabilities/Handicaps)

Kentucky State University

The Kentucky State University Teacher Education Program's theme "Teachers as Liberators Through Education" reflects the liberal arts mission of the university. Future teachers at KSU engage in learning experiences within liberal studies, specialty studies, and professional studies that foster diversity, technology, intellectual vitality, self reflection, and evaluation. The elementary and secondary educational programs provide the knowledge, skills, and attitudes necessary to teach and prosper in a multicultural, highly technological society. The teacher education program encourages minority students and others to pursue a career in education through recruitment efforts and scholarships.

Just the facts...

Kentucky State University
Division of Education and Human Services
Hathaway Hall 215
Frankfort, KY 40601
(502) 227-5916
Website: www.kysu.edu
Profile: Urban, Small, Co-Ed
UG Tuition: $960.00/sem. in-state; $2,880.00/sem. out-of-state
G Tuition: $1,060.00/sem. in-state; $3,180.00/sem. out-of-state
Off Campus Programs: No

Clinical Experiences

Field-based and clinical experiences are selected to provide opportunities for candidates to observe, plan, and practice in a variety of settings appropriate to the professional role for which they are being prepared. Candidates complete a minimum of 150 clock hours in clinical and field-based activities prior to their enrollment in the supervised teaching program. Candidates are given an increasing amount of responsibility in planning and implementing instruction as they progress through the program. Tutoring, observing, critiquing, and micro-teaching are all important parts of candidates' field experiences.

Noteworthy

A survey published in the *Louisville Courier Journal* revealed that KSU graduates received the highest marks of all teacher education graduates in Kentucky in classroom preparation, establishment of positive learning environments, communication of high expectations, and multiple teaching strategies. The Birth Through Primary certification program includes 21 hours in Special Education. Special programs include the Teacher Recruitment Leadership Summer Institute, the Governors Minority College Preparation Program, Title III Preservice Professional Development, Exceptional Education, and the National Youth Sports Program.

Teacher Preparation Program Information

The following programs are 4 year programs:

Early Childhood Education, Elementary Education, K-12 Education (Art, Music, Physical Education), Secondary Education (Biology, English, History, Mathematics, Social Studies)

The following programs are post-baccalaureate programs:

Early Childhood Education, Elementary Education, K-12 Education (Art, Music, Physical Education), Secondary Education (Biology, English, History, Mathematics, Social Studies)

Morehead State University

Morehead State believes that teachers are architects who design environments where students can learn and develop the skills they need to succeed in an ever-changing world. Candidates in teacher education are acquainted with the nature of learning and the various strategies for teaching in their specialty area. Candidates learn how to diagnose and prescribe according to the individual needs of their students, and they discover how to transform academic information into interesting, stimulating learning experiences.

Just the facts...

Morehead State University
College of Education and Behavioral Science
100 Ginger Hall
Morehead, KY 40351
(606) 783-2040
Website: www.morehead-st.edu
Profile: Rural, Medium, Co-Ed
UG Tuition: $1,135.00/sem. in-state; $3,055.00/sem. out-of-state
G Tuition: $1,235.00/sem. in-state; $3,355.00/sem. out-of-state
Off Campus Programs: Yes

Clinical Experiences

All degree programs in the College of Education and Behavioral Science provide relevant and exciting supervised on- and off-campus internships, practicums, or clinical and field experiences that link classroom learning with professional exploration. Teacher education is field-based, requiring 150 hours of clinical and field experiences prior to the professional (student teaching) semester. Experiences involve observation and participation sequenced by tutorial, group instruction, and the application of Kentucky Teacher, Administrator, and Counselor Standards. All experiences support course requirements, diversity, and effective teaching practices.

Noteworthy

Students have an opportunity to work side-by-side with nationally and regionally recognized faculty scholars. Morehead teacher candidates enjoy high rates of job placement after graduation and successful admission to graduate and professional schools. CEBS students also have an opportunity to earn a commission as a Second Lieutenant through the Department of Military Science.

Teacher Preparation Program Information

The following programs are 4 year programs:
Interdisciplinary Early Childhood Education, Elementary Education, P-12 Education (Art, French, Health, Music, Physical Education, Spanish), Middle School Education (Agriculture, Biological Sciences, Business & Marketing, English, Family & Consumer Science, Industrial Technology, Mathematics, Physical Sciences, Social Studies), Secondary Education (Agriculture, Biological Sciences, Business & Marketing, English, Family & Consumer Science, Industrial Technology, Mathematics, Physical Sciences, Social Studies), Special Education (Learning and Behavior Disorders, Moderate and Severe Disabilities)

The following programs are post-baccalaureate programs:
Elementary Education, P-12 Education (Art, French, Music, Spanish), Middle School Education (Agriculture, Biological Sciences, Business & Marketing, English, Family & Consumer Science, Industrial Technology, Mathematics, Social Studies), Secondary Education (Agriculture, Biological Sciences, Business & Marketing, English, Family & Consumer Science, Industrial Technology, Mathematics, Social Studies)

Murray State University

Murray State University began its existence as a normal school, later became a teachers college, and achieved comprehensive regional university status more than thirty years ago. It is ranked as one of the south's top public schools in *U.S. News and World Report*'s *America's Best Colleges* (1998), and is rated in the prestigious "very competitive" category in *Barron's Profiles of American Colleges*. Working within the context of school reform nationally and in Kentucky, the teacher education faculty have produced a program for candidates that is relevant and responsive to emerging needs in education.

Just the facts...

Murray State University
Dean's Office—Education
P.O. Box 9
Murray, KY 42071-0009
(502) 762-3817
Website: www.murraystate.edu
Profile: Rural, Medium, Co-Ed
UG Tuition: $1,150.00/sem. in-state; $3,070.00/sem. out-of-state
G Tuition: $1,250.00/sem. in-state; $3,370.00/sem. out-of-state
Off Campus Programs: No

Clinical Experiences

Teacher education programs are performance-based and continually assess candidates as they progress through the system. From the very first professional course, candidates complete tasks in public school classrooms, and all candidates engage in full-time student teaching before completing their programs. College and public school instructors work together to guide candidates through an extensive set of field experiences. A comprehensive portfolio system provides a means for documenting the field and clinical experiences of each candidate.

Noteworthy

Murray State University is located in the lakes region of west Kentucky. Proximity to the lakes provides candidates with unique opportunities in environmental education, science education, and biological and watershed research. Murray State's extensive use of distance learning technology and technology-rich interactive television classrooms—both on-campus and in 23 off-campus sites—provides both instruction and unique opportunities for candidates related to advising, supervision, consultation, observation, and assessment of candidates working in the field.

Teacher Preparation Program Information

The following programs are 4 year programs:

Early Childhood Education, Elementary Education, K-12 Education (Art, French, German, Health, Music, Physical Education, Spanish), Middle School Education (English, Mathematics, Science, Social Studies), Secondary Education (Agriculture, Art, Biology, Business, Chemistry, Consumer & Family Science/Home Economics, Earth Science, Economics, English/Language Arts, Geography, Health, Mathematics, Physical Education, Physical Sciences, Physics, Political Science, Social Studies, Trade & Industrial, Vocational Trade & Industrial), Special Education (Learning Behavior Disorders)

Northern Kentucky University

Northern Kentucky University's School of Education faculty is dedicated to preparing teachers who have the ability to reflect and learn from their experiences and from those of their students. The university features a strong liberal arts program. The School of Education is the largest department on campus and is well-respected in the university and in area communities. The teacher education program features continual assessment so that candidates are aware of their proficiencies in relation to the program standards.

Just the facts...

Northern Kentucky University
School of Education
Highland Heights, KY 41099-0800
(606) 572-5365
Website: www.nku.edu
Profile: Suburban, Large, Co-Ed
UG Tuition: $1,110.00/sem. in-state; $3,030.00/sem. out-of-state
Off Campus Programs: No

Clinical Experiences

Northern Kentucky University believes that experience is a good teacher. Therefore, candidates are involved in the schools from their first education courses (usually starting in the late sophomore or early junior years) all the way through their student teaching experience. NKU typically places over 150 student teachers per semester in schools in fifty school districts in Kentucky, Ohio, and Indiana.

Noteworthy

Northern Kentucky University is the newest of Kentucky's eight regional universities. Located in the greater Cincinnati metropolitan area, NKU enjoys many partnerships with regional schools, providing candidates with the opportunity for experiences in rural, urban, and suburban settings. NKU graduates have one of the highest first time passing rates for the PRAXIS exam in Kentucky. Candidates report high satisfaction with the training they receive. Schools employing NKU graduates are impressed by their knowledge and high-quality preparation for the classroom.

Teacher Preparation Program Information

The following programs are 4 year programs:
Early Childhood Education, Elementary Education, K-12 Education (Art, French, Health, Music, Physical Education, Spanish), Kindergarten Education, Middle School Education (English, Mathematics, Science, Social Studies), Secondary Education (Biology, English/Language Arts, Mathematics, Physical Sciences, Social Studies), Special Education (Learning Disability)

The following programs are post-baccalaureate programs:
Early Childhood Education, Elementary Education, K-12 Education (Art, French, Health, Music, Physical Education, Spanish), Kindergarten Education, Middle School Education (English, Mathematics, Science, Social Studies), Secondary Education (Biology, English/Language Arts, Mathematics, Physical Sciences, Social Studies), Special Education (Learning Disability)

Spalding University

In keeping with Spalding University's pioneer spirit of service and its tradition of collaborative commitment to the development of the individual, the School of Education prepares educators who possess intellectual understanding, a holistic perspective, and professional skills to lead others to the maximum use of their potential for lifelong learning in a multicultural society. Spalding believes that all educators are leaders, and prides itself on giving individualized attention to each student.

Just the facts...

Spalding University
School of Education
851 South Fourth Street
Louisville, KY 40203
(502) 585-7121
Website: www.spalding.edu
Profile: Urban, Small, Co-Ed
UG Tuition: $5,300.00/semester
G Tuition: $350.00/credit hour
Off Campus Programs: No

Clinical Experiences

Through mentoring, service learning, diverse field and laboratory experiences, guided teaching projects, and mini-teaching of thematic units, Spalding teacher candidates receive a well-rounded look at schools in the community and surrounding counties. From their first foundations class, candidates are out in the field—learning, growing, shaping, and ultimately becoming excellent teachers. Candidates are encouraged to choose their own cooperating teachers, which allows them to choose a master teacher as a mentor with whom they share similar educational philosophies and teaching and learning styles.

Noteworthy

In the spring 1999 semester, Spalding launched a program leading to national certification as a pre-primary teacher in Montessori schools. This program directly responds to local and state interest in Montessori education and may be completed in conjunction with the Interdisciplinary Early Childhood Education, Early Elementary, or Liberal Studies programs.

Teacher Preparation Program Information

The following programs are 4 year programs:

Interdisciplinary Early Childhood Education and Special Education (Birth-Kindergarten), Elementary Education (Primary-Grade 5), Middle Grades Education (Grades 5-9), Secondary Education (Grades 8-12)

The following programs are post-baccalaureate programs:

Interdisciplinary Early Childhood Education and Special Education (Birth-Kindergarten), Montessori (Early Childhood)

The following programs are 5th year programs:

Interdisciplinary Early Childhood Education and Special Education (Birth-Kindergarten), Elementary Education (Primary-Grade 5), Middle Grades Education/Grades 5-9 (English, Mathematics, Science, Social Studies), P-12 Education (Art, Business/Grades 5-12), Secondary Education/Grades 8-12 (Biological Sciences, Business, English, Mathematics, Physical Sciences)

University of Kentucky

The University of Kentucky's College of Education was founded in 1923 in response to Kentucky's growing need for professional teachers. Now the College of Education prepares teachers, counselors, administrators, health promotion personnel, and higher education leaders. As a part of the university's land grant mission, the College of Education is dedicated to advancing knowledge, professionalism, and education policies to serve Kentucky's citizens. The College of Education takes pride in preparing educators who meet Kentucky's professional teaching standards and who make thoughtful decisions in today's changing schools.

Just the facts...

University of Kentucky
College of Education
103 Dickey Hall
Lexington, KY 40506-0017
(606) 257-2813
Website: www.uky.edu
Profile: Suburban, Large, Co-Ed
UG Tuition: $1,508.00/sem. in-state; $4,188.00/sem. out-of-state
G Tuition: $1,638.00/sem. in-state; $4,578.00/sem. out-of-state
Off Campus Programs: Yes

Clinical Experiences

Teacher education candidates participate in extensive clinical experiences early in their programs. These experiences link theory and practice in elementary, middle, and high school classrooms. Professional development schools provide the backdrop for these experiences. At these schools, candidates work in teams with school personnel and university faculty to plan and implement curriculum, assessment, and school policies. Teacher education faculty and school personnel also collaborate on teacher education courses taught at these schools.

Noteworthy

Reports from principals, resource teachers, and teacher educators who work with University of Kentucky teacher education graduates during their first year of teaching indicate that graduates are extremely well-prepared to meet the challenges of today's schools. Many graduates have won teaching awards in school, district, state, and national competitions. Graduates are also actively recruited to assume leadership roles at various levels. Innovative programs include the Teacher Opportunity Program, the Masters with Initial Certification Program, and the Overseas Student Teaching Program.

Teacher Preparation Program Information

The following programs are 4 year programs:
Interdisciplinary Early Childhood Education, Elementary Education, K-12 Education (Art, Health, Music, Physical Education), Middle School Education (English/Communication, Mathematics, Science, Social Studies), Grades 5-12 Education (Vocational Agriculture, Vocational Family & Consumer Sciences), Special Education (Developmental Disabilities/Handicaps, Emotional Conflict, Learning Disability, Mental Retardation, Mild Learning/Behavioral Disability, Moderate and Severe Disabilities/Handicaps)

The following programs are post-baccalaureate programs:
Interdisciplinary Early Childhood Education, Elementary Education, Special Education (Developmental Disabilities/Handicaps, Emotional Conflict, Learning Disability, Mental Retardation, Mild Learning/Behavioral Disability, Moderate and Severe Disabilities/Handicaps)

The following programs are 5 year programs:
K-12 Education (French, German, Latin, Russian, Spanish), Grades 5-12 Education (Business and Marketing, Vocational Agriculture, Vocational Family & Consumer Sciences), Secondary Education (Biological Science, English, Mathematics, Physical Sciences, Social Studies)

The following programs are 5th year programs:
Interdisciplinary Early Childhood Education, K-12 Education (French, German, Latin, Russian, Spanish), Grades 5-12 Education (Business and Marketing, Vocational Agriculture, Vocational Family & Consumer Sciences), Secondary Education (Biological Sciences, English, Mathematics, Physical Science, Social Studies), Special Education (Moderate and Severe Disabilities)

University of Louisville

Modeled after successful pilot programs developed over a five-year period, the University of Louisville Teacher Education Programs feature a professional year that leads to both a Master of Arts in Teaching and eligibility for a license to teach in Kentucky schools. Based on the belief that teachers must have a strong grounding in the liberal arts and sciences, U of L programs require that applicants earn a bachelor's degree in an academic major in addition to completing coursework necessary to be licensed in a teaching major. U of L provides candidates with the same kind of hands-on, performance-based experiences they will later design for their students.

Just the facts...

University of Louisville
School of Education
Belknap Campus
Louisville, KY 40292
(502) 852-6411
Website: www.louisville.edu
Profile: Urban, Large, Co-Ed
UG Tuition: $1,460.00/sem. in-state; $4,140.00/sem. out-of-state
G Tuition: $1,590.00/sem. in-state; $4,530.00/sem. out-of-state
Off Campus Programs: No

Clinical Experiences

Candidates enter teacher education as a cohort and have courses and field experiences together. For their professional year, candidates are assigned to P-12 schools, most of which are within U of L's professional development school network of more than twenty sites. Through case studies and action research, candidates are encouraged to study and reflect on what they are observing and practicing. Candidates also are involved in service learning as a way to better understand the complex communities in which they will teach.

Noteworthy

Collaboration with local schools is comprehensive and effective. The School of Education's design and delivery of its curriculum, including the use of performance assessment and technology in teaching, are exemplary. Scholarship support totals more than $275,000 per year at the undergraduate and professional year levels, and includes support through the Minority Teacher Recruitment Project.

Teacher Preparation Program Information

The following programs are 4 year programs:
Vocational Health Occupation, Vocational Trade & Industrial, Music Education

The following programs are 5 year programs:
Early Childhood Education, Elementary Education, K-12 Education (Art, French, German, Russian, Spanish, Health, Music, Physical Education), Middle School Education (English, Mathematics, Science, Social Studies), Secondary Education (Biology, Business, English/Language Arts, Mathematics, Physical Sciences, Social Studies)

The following programs are 5th year programs:
Early Childhood Education, Special Education (Learning and Behavior Disorders)

Western Kentucky University

Western Kentucky University has been preparing teachers since 1906 and counts among its alumni about fifteen percent of the new teachers employed in Kentucky. In addition to programs leading to licensure as classroom teachers, Western offers degree and non-degree programs leading to licensure in school counseling, administration, and psychology. All programs are performance-based and feature continuous assessment. Recognizing the diverse roles of school personnel, Western Kentucky University prepares and develops professionals who can facilitate high levels of student learning.

Just the facts...

Western Kentucky University
College of Education and Behavioral Sciences
Bowling Green, KY 42101
(502) 745-4662
Profile: Rural, Large, Co-Ed
Website: www.wku.edu
UG Tuition: $92.00/cr. hr. in-state; $252.00/cr. hr. out-of-state
G Tuition: $134.00/cr. hr. in-state; $369.00/cr. hr. out-of-state
Off Campus Programs: Yes

Clinical Experiences

All candidates in initial teacher preparation programs are required to complete a minimum of 150 hours of clinical and field placements prior to a twelve-week student teaching experience. Placements are provided in settings that are characterized by diversity, and selected courses are currently being taught in school-based settings that provide opportunities for teacher candidates to integrate theory and practice. At the graduate level, several programs of study include a specified practicum/internship component.

Noteworthy

The teacher education unit at Western has established a minority teacher recruitment program to promote the recruitment and retention of teacher candidates from ethnic minority groups. Since its inception in 1993, there has been a significant increase in the number of individuals from ethnic minority groups admitted to and matriculating through the teacher education program. This effort is supported by both institutional and BellSouth Foundation funding. Western is currently pursuing funding to develop a program that recruits minority individuals wishing to complete a program leading to an administrator's license.

Teacher Preparation Program Information

The following programs are 4 year programs:
Elementary Education, P-12 Education (Art, French, German, Health, Music, Physical Education, Spanish), Middle School Education (English/Language Arts, Mathematics, Science, Social Studies), Secondary Education/5-12 (Agriculture, Business & Marketing, Family & Consumer Science, Industrial Technology, Vocational Education), Secondary Education/8-12 (Biology, English/Language Arts, Mathematics, Physical Science) Special Education (Communication Disorders, Learning and Behavioral Disorders, Moderate and Severe Disabilities)

The following programs are post-baccalaureate programs:
Elementary Education, P-12 Education (Art, ESL, French, German, Health, Music, Physical Education, Reading and Writing, Spanish), Middle School Education (English/Language Arts, Mathematics, Science, Social Studies), Secondary Education/5-12 (Agriculture, Business & Marketing, Family & Consumer Science, Industrial Technology, Vocational Education), Secondary Education/8-12 (Biology, Computer Science, Driver's Education, Mathematics, Physical Science, Social Studies) Special Education (Gifted, Learning and Behavioral Disorders, Moderate and Severe Disabilities)

The following programs are 5th year programs:
Early Childhood Education

Grambling State University

Grambling State University was originally created for the purpose of meeting the educational, cultural, and social needs of individuals in the surrounding area. Grambling adheres to the philosophy that education is the cornerstone of a creative, enlightened, participative and responsive society. The College of Education is committed to providing experiences that contribute to the professional development of teacher education majors. These experiences include coursework, library and field research, seminars, professional conferences, and a variety of field-based experiences that translate theory into practice.

Just the facts...

Grambling State University
College of Education
P.O. Drawer A
Grambling, LA 71245
(318) 274-2231
Website: www.gram.edu
Profile: Rural, Medium, Co-Ed
UG Tuition: $1,044.00/sem. in-state; $2,019.00/sem. out-of-state
G Tuition: $1,044.00/sem. in-state; $2,019.00/sem. out-of-state
Off Campus Programs: No

Clinical Experiences

Through the professional laboratory experiences program, candidates pursue a wide range of observation/participation experiences totaling a minimum of 100 hours prior to student teaching. Clinical experiences are designed to prepare competent professionals who know and understand teaching, learning, and learners at various stages of development. Student teaching is a full semester, all-day experience required for each teaching major.

Noteworthy

Several services in the College of Education support the educational process through research, community service, program development, consultation, technical assistance and professional service, including: the University Magnet Schools; the Center for Field Services and Research; the Educational Resource Center; the Office of Professional Laboratory Experiences; and the Centralized Advisement, Referral and Evaluation (CARE) Center. The College offers NTE Preparation Workshops conducted by college and laboratory school faculty and content area faculty from other departments at Grambling.

Teacher Preparation Program Information

The following programs are 4 year programs:
Early Childhood Education, Elementary Education, K-12 Education (Art, French, Music), Secondary Education (Art, Biology, Business, Home Economics, English, Mathematics, Physical Education, Social Studies), Special Education (Early Childhood)

The following programs are post-baccalaureate programs:
Early Childhood Education (Generalist, N-K, 1-3), K-12 Education (French, Music), Special Education (Mild/Moderate Elementary Dual, Mild/Moderate Secondary, Non-Categorical Early Childhood Dual)

Louisiana State University and A&M College

LSU offers three paths to teacher licensure: (1) a five-year elementary or fifth-year secondary/K-12 program leading to certification and a master's degree; (2) a four-year elementary or secondary/K-12 program leading to licensure and a bachelor's degree; and (3) an elementary or secondary/K-12 alternate post-baccaluareate licensure program. In all courses, candidates learn to integrate theory and approaches to teaching and learning. Candidates test their ideas in a variety of field experiences, and are expected to become reflective practitioners.

Just the facts...

Louisiana State University and A&M College
College of Education
221 Peabody Hall
Baton Rouge, LA 70803-4707
(225) 388-1258
Website: www.ednet.lsu.edu
Profile: Urban, Large, Co-Ed
UG Tuition: $1,354.00/sem. in-state; $3,154.00/sem. out-of-state
G Tuition: $1,357.00/sem. in-state; $3,157.00/sem. out-of-state
Off Campus Programs: Yes

Clinical Experiences

The teacher education program is highly clinically based. All clinical experiences in the elementary education program and almost all in the secondary/K-12 program are organized and conducted in the University Laboratory School and in more than twenty professional development school sites. Internships and student teaching in both four- and five-year programs include placement in at least two sites: one urban and one suburban. Candidates work both in pairs and as individual teachers. Weekly seminars accompany the final field experience.

Noteworthy

The five-year elementary and the fifth-year secondary/K-12 programs are designed to prepare future education leaders. Both programs have selective admission, require a thoughtful school-based research project, and culminate in a master's degree as well as licensure. The professional team that organizes and maintains these programs includes graduate faculty professors, highly experienced university-based clinical professors, and selected school-based clinical adjunct professors. Graduates of these programs are highly sought after, and many of them have won various teaching awards, particularly as the "best new teacher in the school district."

Teacher Preparation Program Information

The following programs are 4 year programs:
Early Childhood Education, Elementary Education, K-12 Education (Art, French, Latin, Music, Physical Education/Health, Spanish), Kindergarten Education, Secondary Education (Agriculture, Biology, Chemistry, English/Language Arts, General Science, Mathematics, Physics, Social Studies, Vocational Home Economics/Consumer Homemaking, Vocational Home Economics/Job Training, Vocational Trade & Industrial)

The following programs are post-baccalaureate programs:
Elementary Education, K-12 Education (Art, French, Physical Education/Health, Spanish), Secondary Education (Biology, Chemistry, English/Language Arts, General Science, Mathematics, Physics, Social Studies, Speech)

The following programs are 5 year programs:
Elementary Education

The following programs are 5th year programs:
Early Childhood Education, K-12 Education (Art, French, Latin, Physical Education/Health, Spanish), Secondary Education (Biology, Chemistry, English/Language Arts, General Science, Mathematics, Physics, Social Studies)

Louisiana State University in Shreveport

LSUS College of Education majors are prepared for future work as teachers in elementary, secondary, or special education, and as administrators, school service personnel, psychologists, physical education instructors or exercise specialists. Programs at the College of Education are guided by a broad-based curriculum that is liberally reinforced with attention to technology, assessment, diversity, and societal needs.

Just the facts...

Louisiana State University in Shreveport
College of Education
One University Place
Shreveport, LA 71115
(318) 797-5381
Website: www.lsus.edu
Profile: Urban, Medium, Co-Ed
UG Tuition: $1,115.00/sem. in-state; $2,785.00/sem. out-of-state
G Tuition: $1,265.00/sem. in-state; $3,165.00/sem. out-of-state
Off Campus Programs: No

Clinical Experiences

Clinical experiences begin in the sophomore year, and are managed throughout the program so that candidates have experiences in widely diverse school settings. Two school districts that include many different types of schools provide laboratory settings on a contractual basis. These districts' close working partnership with the College of Education provides LSUS students with valuable practical experiences to ready them for the challenges of teaching.

Noteworthy

Since 1978, 97 percent of LSUS teacher education graduates have passed the National Teacher's Examination on their first try, and 100 percent of graduates of the school psychology program who seek employment are successful. Technology is integrated in all teacher education programs, and the College of Education has taken a leading role in helping schools in northwest Louisiana to use technology effectively as a tool in the classroom.

Teacher Preparation Program Information

The following programs are 4 year programs:
Elementary Education, K-12 Education (Art, Music, Physical Education/Health), Secondary Education (Biology, Chemistry, English/Language Arts, French, Mathematics, Physics, Social Studies, Spanish)

The following programs are post-baccalaureate programs:
Elementary Education, K-12 Education (Art, Music, Physical Education/Health), Secondary Education (Biology, Chemistry, English/Language Arts, French, Mathematics, Physics, Social Studies, Spanish)

The following programs are 5 year programs:
Elementary Education, K-12 Education (Art, Music, Physical Education/Health), Secondary Education (Biology, Chemistry, English/Language Arts, French, Mathematics, Physics, Social Studies, Spanish)

National Council for Accreditation of Teacher Education

Louisiana Tech University

Since its founding in 1894, Louisiana Tech University has been committed to the preparation of educators. The College of Education faculty has designed and implemented programs to prepare educators who are effective communicators with strong content knowledge, professional identities, and competence in applying research to produce effective teaching and enhanced student learning. All coursework and experiences are organized to enable candidates to demonstrate increasing levels of proficiency in all aspects of their programs.

Just the facts...

Louisiana Tech University
College of Education
P.O. Box 3163 TS
Ruston, LA 71272
(318) 257-3712
Website: www.LaTech.edu
Profile: Rural, Large, Co-Ed
UG Tuition: $665.00/sem. in-state; $789.00/sem. out-of-state
G Tuition: $665.00/sem. in-state; $789.00/sem. out-of-state
Off Campus Programs: Yes

Clinical Experiences

Clinical experiences are carefully linked to coursework and vary widely according to candidates' majors and interests. Experiences begin during the freshman year, allowing candidates to observe at multiple grade levels to determine their teaching preferences. As candidates progress, they spend extended periods of time in classrooms through practica guided and supported by college supervisors. Clinical experiences culminate with student teaching or an internship in a public P-12 school setting on an all-day basis for a quarter, under the supervision of cooperating master teachers and university faculty.

Noteworthy

A campus laboratory school gives candidates an opportunity to observe master teachers and receive important feedback regarding planning for varying student needs and interests. A math and science children's discovery center, The IDEA Place, serves as a field trip destination for surrounding schools. Education majors participate as children explore hands-on activities. NSF Teaching Scholars assist in math and science activities such as planning exhibits for The IDEA Place and making presentations at state, regional, and national conferences.

Teacher Preparation Program Information

The following programs are 4 year programs:
Early Childhood Education, Elementary Education, K-12 Education (Art, French, Health, Music, Physical Education), Secondary Education (Agriculture, Business, Biology, Chemistry, Consumer & Family Science/Home Economics, Earth Science, English/Language Arts, General Science, Mathematics, Physics, Social Studies), Special Education

The following programs are post-baccalaureate programs:
Elementary Education, Secondary Education (Agriculture, Business, Biology, Chemistry, Consumer & Family Science/Home Economics, Earth Science, English/Language Arts, General Science, Mathematics, Physics, Social Studies)

The following programs are 5th year programs:
Elementary Education, K-12 Education (Art, French, Health & Physical Education, Music), Secondary Education (Business, Biology, Chemistry, Earth Science, English/Language Arts, General Science, Mathematics, Physics, Social Studies) Special Education

McNeese State University

Programs of study in teacher education at the Burton College of Education are based on the idea that teachers are professional educators who value lifelong learning and instill this value in their students. Teacher candidates are prepared in general knowledge, professional education studies, and specialty studies. Programs emphasize practical applications of knowledge, critical thinking, learner diversity, technology, respect for individual differences, and comprehensive assessment of teaching and learning.

Just the facts...

McNeese State University
Burton College of Education
P.O. Box 93255-MSU (102 Farrar Hall)
Lake Charles, LA 70609-3255
(318) 475-5432
Website: www.mcneese.edu
Profile: Urban, Medium, Co-Ed
UG Tuition: $1,048.00/sem. in-state; $3,268.00/sem. out-of-state
G Tuition: $1,028.00/sem. in-state; $3,248.00/sem. out-of-state
Off Campus Programs: No

Clinical Experiences

Field experiences begin with introductory teacher education courses and continue throughout the remainder of the teacher education program for approximately 300 hours prior to the student teaching experience. Student teaching is an all-day experience for a total of fifteen weeks. Field experiences and student teaching take place in approved private or public school settings within a nine-parish area.

Noteworthy

Teacher education programs in the Burton College of Education are provided financial support by a $1,000,000 endowment from the Burton Foundation. Annual interest generated from the endowment and state funding are used to finance a variety of initiatives in the College of Education.

Teacher Preparation Program Information

The following programs are 4 year programs:

Early Childhood Education, Elementary Education, Health and Human Performance, Secondary Education (Art, Biology, Business, Chemistry, English/Language Arts, Foreign Language, Mathematics, Social Studies, Speech), Special Education

Nicholls State University

Nicholls State is a comprehensive, regional university serving South Central Louisiana. It is located in the heart of "Cajun country," an area rich in tradition and culture. Nicholls State University's teacher education program prepares future professional elementary and secondary teachers as well as school specialists. Faculty members believe that the teacher is a decision maker with broad-based general and content knowledge; knowledge of pedagogy; and the ability to plan, implement, and evaluate the effectiveness of the learning process.

Just the facts...

Nicholls State University
College of Education
Box 2053
Thibodaux, LA 70310
(504) 448-4325
Website: http://server.nich.edu
Profile: Rural, Medium, Co-Ed
UG Tuition: $1,068.00/sem. in-state; $2,688.00/sem. out-of-state
G Tuition: $1,058.00/sem. in-state; $2,688.00/sem. out-of-state
Off Campus Programs: No

Clinical Experiences

Field experiences for teacher education candidates begin during their first professional course (typically in the sophomore year). Field experiences intensify in number and in type as the candidate progresses. Prior to student teaching, candidates have over 100 hours of field experience. Student teaching is an "all-day, every day" experience for an entire semester. At a minimum, candidates spend at least 270 hours in the elementary or secondary classroom with at least 180 of these hours spent in actual teaching. Candidates may also gain experience observing or teaching in the Summer Elementary Enrichment Program on campus.

Noteworthy

The College of Education enjoys a strong professional relationship with the area education community. Housed on the campus is the Region III Louisiana State Department of Education Service Center. This Center sponsors professional development programs in cooperation with the College of Education. In addition, Region III and the College of Education have collaborated in the successful acquisition of numerous grants. Of special note is the Systemic Plan for Science and the Goals 2000 preservice and professional development initiatives.

Teacher Preparation Program Information

The following programs are 4 year programs:
Elementary Education, K-12 Education (Art, Physical Education), Secondary Education (Biology, Business, Chemistry, Consumer & Family Science/Home Economics, Earth Science, English/Language Arts, General Science, Mathematics, Physical Sciences, Psychology, Social Studies), Special Education (Speech/Language Disabilities)

The following programs are post-baccalaureate programs:
Elementary Education, K-12 Education (Art, Physical Education), Secondary Education (Biology, Business, Chemistry, Consumer & Family Science/Home Economics, Earth Science, English/Language Arts, General Science, Mathematics, Physical Sciences, Psychology, Social Studies), Special Education (Speech/Language Disabilities)

Northeast Louisiana University

The College of Education and Human Development at Northeast Louisiana University is committed to a conceptual framework that features interactive learning and integrates general studies, content studies, and professional/pedagogical studies and integrative studies, linked together by sequential, structured clinical and field experiences. Each graduate becomes a learning facilitator who demonstrates effective knowledge, skills, and performance in effective planning, management, learning enhancement, evaluation, and collaboration.

Just the facts...

Northeast Louisiana University
College of Education and Human Development
Monroe, LA 71209
(318) 342-1235
Website: www.nlu.edu
Profile: Urban, Large, Co-Ed
UG Tuition: $962.00/sem. in-state; $2,163.00/sem. out-of-state
G Tuition: $962.00/sem. in-state; $2,135.00/sem. out-of-state
Off Campus Programs: No

Clinical Experiences

Clinical and field experiences are integrated throughout all programs and are introduced gradually and systematically. All programs culminate with an extended field experience. Undergraduate programs conclude with an eighteen-week semester of full-time student teaching under the supervision of a master teacher in a school with a diverse range of students. Culminating field experiences for graduate programs are designed according to specialization area and often entail supervised internships.

Noteworthy

Several types of scholarships are available to teacher education majors in addition to TOPS, which is available to all Louisiana high school students who qualify. The College of Education and Human Development boasts two new state-of-the-art computer facilities, desktop conferencing equipment, and a distance learning education classroom equipped with compressed video, and Internet links in all classrooms. Cypress Point University School, NLU's latest professional development school, has become the first year-round school in the region.

Teacher Preparation Program Information

The following programs are 4 year programs:
Early Childhood Education, Elementary Education, K-12 Education (Art, Physical Education, Reading, Music), Secondary Education (Biology, Chemistry, Science/Home Economics, Earth Science, English/Language Arts, French, General Science, Mathematics, Physics, Social Studies, Spanish, Speech)

The following programs are post-baccalaureate programs:
Early Childhood Education

The following programs are 5 year programs:
Special Education

National Council for Accreditation of Teacher Education

Northwestern State University of Louisiana

The College of Education at Northwestern prepares beginning teachers who are models for learning and who can demonstrate pedagogical, general, and specialized knowledge. Candidates learn problem-solving, creative and critical thinking, and decision-making skills. The College of Education strives to meet the needs and interest of schools, educational agencies, and communities by developing well-trained teachers, providing leadership services, demonstrating good models of teaching, and developing ancillary school and university personnel.

Just the facts...

Northwestern State University of Louisiana
College of Education
Natchitoches, LA 71497
(318) 357-6288
Website: http://www.nsula.edu
Profile: Rural, Medium, Co-Ed
UG Tuition: $1,183.50/sem. in-state; $2,145.00/sem. out-of-state
G Tuition: $1,128.50/sem. in-state; $2,145.00/sem. out-of-state
Off Campus Programs: No

Clinical Experiences

During their first two years, teacher candidates primarily observe and document activities in the teaching/learning environment and study child/adolescent development. As candidates enroll in more advanced professional education and specialized academic courses, they learn to apply their knowledge in planning, implementing, and evaluating teaching in public school classrooms. In the final professional semester, the student teaching component brings together knowledge and practice, and prepares candidates for their future roles.

Noteworthy

The university and the College of Education offer placement support in a variety of ways. The staff of Student Support Services presents workshops on résumé writing, interviewing skills and other issues related to job seeking and job keeping. Bulletin boards in the Teacher Education Center display postings of job announcements. The Teacher Job Fair, held annually in April on the NSU campus, offers education majors an opportunity to interview with prospective employers. Several campus organizations are geared toward education majors, including Kappa Delta Pi, the Student Council for Exceptional Children, and the Student Louisiana Education Association.

Teacher Preparation Program Information

The following programs are 4 year programs:
Early Childhood Education, Elementary Education, K-12 Education (Art, Music, Physical Education/Health), Secondary Education (Biology, Business, Chemistry, English/Language Arts, General Science, Mathematics, Physics, Social Studies, Speech, Vocational Home Economics/Consumer Homemaking), Special Education (Mild/Moderate Handicapped)

The following programs are post-baccalaureate programs:
Elementary Education (Computer Science), K-12 Education (Art, Computer Science, Music, Physical Education/Health, Reading), Kindergarten Education, Secondary Education (Biology, Business, Chemistry, Computer Science, Driver Ed/Safety, English/Language Arts, General Science, Journalism, Mathematics, Physics, Social Studies, Speech, Vocational Home Economics/Consumer Homemaking), Special Education (Adaptive Physical Education, Gifted/Talented, Mild/Moderate Handicapped)

The following programs are 5th year programs:
Special Education (Gifted/Talented)

Southeastern Louisiana University

Southeastern Louisiana University believes that educators must master four sets of skills: planning, implementation, management, and evaluation. Faculty members believe that successful teaching depends on being able to make a smooth transition from one function to another. Courses in general education, specialty areas, and professional education ensure that candidates have knowledge of effective communication and foundations of teaching.

Just the facts...

Southeastern Louisiana University
College of Education
P.O. Box 10671
Hammond, LA 70402
(504) 549-2311
Website: www.selu.edu
Profile: Rural, Large, Co-Ed
UG Tuition: $964.00/sem. in-state; $1,632.00/sem. out-of-state
G Tuition: $959.00/sem. in-state; $1,632.00/sem. out-of-state
Off Campus Programs: No

Clinical Experiences

Southeastern Louisiana University has a strong commitment to providing candidates with practical experiences throughout their preparation. Candidates are involved in field-based experiences beginning in their sophomore year. Methods courses provide an opportunity to plan, implement, manage, and evaluate actual teaching experiences in a variety of school settings. In student teaching, candidates accumulate a minimum of 180 hours of teaching experience under the supervision of a classroom teacher.

Noteworthy

The College of Education works through various projects to reform teacher education practices. Four projects in the areas of math and science reform are part of the Louisiana Systemic Initiatives Program. One collaborative program in English is a part of the National Writing Project. An Early Literacy Initiative is funded through the Louisiana Department of Education. A K-3 Reading and Math reform program is funded through the Board of Regents. The Teacher Scholars leadership development program is a cooperative program between Southeastern Louisiana University and local parish school systems.

Teacher Preparation Program Information

The following programs are 4 year programs:

Elementary Education, K-12 Education (Art, Music, Physical Education/Health, Special Education), Secondary Education (Biology, Chemistry, English/ Language Arts, French, Mathematics, Physics, Science, Social Studies, Spanish, Vocational Home Econ./Consumer Science), Special Education (Speech/ Language Disabilities)

The following programs are post-baccalaureate programs:

Alternative Certification Programs: Art Education, Biology, Chemistry, Elementary Education, English, Family & Consumer Sciences, French, Mathematics, Music Education, Physical Education/Health, Physics, Social Studies, Spanish, Speech, Special Education

National Council for Accreditation of Teacher Education

Southern University and A&M College

The primary mission of the College of Education is to offer undergraduate and graduate programs for the preparation of teachers and other education specialists. Faculty engage in teaching, research, and other scholarly activities, as well as perform community and professional services. Teacher candidates learn to integrate general content knowledge and professional and pedagogical knowledge to create successful learning experiences. Administrators and faculty emphasize effective teaching practices, scholarly inquiry, continuous professional development, and active involvement in the world of practice.

Just the facts...

Southern University and A&M College
College of Education
P. O. Box 9983
Baton Rouge, LA 70813
(504) 771-2290
Website: www.subr.edu
Profile: Urban, Large, Co-Ed
UG Tuition: $1,104.00/sem. in-state; $2,394.00/sem. out-of-state
G Tuition: $1,098.00/sem. in-state; $2,018.00/sem. out-of-state
Off Campus Programs: Yes

Clinical Experiences

Practica and student teaching experiences are designed to develop candidates' skills through practice of competency in the art of teaching. Success in student teaching requires that the teacher candidate perform at a high level of excellence in practice and instructional activities. To perform at such a level, teacher candidates must bring to student teaching a certain level of competence in order that their performance will not prove a detriment to the development of the children in the classroom. Southern University and A&M College prepares candidates who have this level of competence prior to student teaching.

Noteworthy

Southern takes part in Louisiana's alternative certification initiation, which provides opportunities for people with non-education degrees to become licensed public school teachers. Candidates for this program must have a bachelor's degree from an accredited institution with an overall grade point average of 2.5. More information about this program is available from the College of Education.

Teacher Preparation Program Information

The following programs are 4 year programs:
Elementary Education (Elementary Education K-8), K-12 Education (Foreign Language, Music, Physical Education), Secondary Education (Biology, Chemistry, English/Language Arts, Mathematics, Physics, Social Studies, Vocational Agriculture), Special Education (Hearing Impaired, Mild/Moderate Disabilities)

The following programs are post-baccalaureate programs:
Elementary Education, Secondary Education

University of New Orleans

The University of New Orleans is located in one of America's most interesting cities—Mardi Gras and the Louisiana Jazz and Heritage Festival take place right in its back yard. Both New Orleans and UNO are big enough to offer everything a student needs but small enough to be personal and easily accessible. UNO offers future teachers a setting rich in diversity and steeped in culture. After graduation, students may continue their education at UNO in Louisiana's largest graduate programs. Students may choose from a full complement of master's degrees and doctoral degrees in curriculum and instruction, special education, educational administration, and counselor education.

Just the facts...

University of New Orleans
College of Education
Lakefront
New Orleans, LA 70148
(504) 280-6251
Website: www.uno.edu
Profile: Urban, Large, Co-Ed
UG Tuition: $1,181.00/sem. in-state; $3,944.00/sem. out-of-state
G Tuition: $1,181.00/sem. in-state; $3,944.00/sem. out-of-state
Off Campus Programs: No

Clinical Experiences

Undergraduate candidates begin classroom visits in their sophomore year and add frequency and depth in classroom involvement continuously up to and through a fifteen-week student teaching experience. Post-baccalaureate candidates have an internship option. Approximately one-half of all student teachers work in Urban Partnership for Teacher Development sites in a mentor-coaching environment. A major part of every licensure program is now taught on location in urban classrooms.

Noteworthy

The College of Education has won state, regional, and national awards for innovative programs related to university-school collaborations. It houses a satellite center for the Accelerated Schools Project, and its Teacher Education Council combines the faculty forces of all four of its departments to integrate teacher preparation across disciplines with a particular focus on combining the traditionally discrete domains of general and special education.

Teacher Preparation Program Information

The following programs are 4 year programs:

Elementary Education, K-12 Education (Instrumental and Vocal Music, Physical Education/Health), Secondary Education (Biology, Chemistry, Earth Science, English, French, German, Mathematics, Social Studies, Spanish)

The following programs are post-baccalaureate programs:

Elementary Education, K-12 Education (Instrumental and Vocal Music, Physical Education/Health), Secondary Education (Biology, Chemistry, Earth Science, English, French, German, Mathematics, Social Studies, Spanish)

The following programs are 5th year programs:

Early Childhood Education, Special Education (Early Intervention, Mild/Moderate Disabilities, Severe Behavioral Disabilities)

National Council for Accreditation of Teacher Education

University of Southwestern Louisiana

The College of Education at the University of Southwestern Louisiana strives for excellence in teacher education. Its programs incorporate contemporary and seminal research on the foundations of education, pedagogical knowledge and skills, field and clinical experiences, and modern technologies. Faculty relationships within the professional community are strong. The College of Education addresses these components to produce master teachers who are prepared to serve as leaders and decision makers in our nation's schools.

Just the facts...

University of Southwestern Louisiana
College of Education
East University Avenue
Lafayette, LA 70504-0240
(318) 482-6678
Website: www.usl.edu/
Profile: Urban, Large, Co-Ed
UG Tuition: $998.75/sem. in-state; $3,614.75/sem. out-of-state
G Tuition: $1,005.75/sem. in-state; $3,621.75/sem. out-of-state
Off Campus Programs: No

Clinical Experiences

Courses scheduled within the first/second year of each program provide an early introduction to the world of practice and introduce candidates to College of Education regulations and procedures, issues in education, and a foundation of professional knowledge. Reading practica in the third or fourth year continue to provide opportunities for applied learning and "real world" experience. Student teaching is an all-day semester-long experience guided by master teachers and university faculty.

Noteworthy

The pass rate for University of Southwestern Louisiana students on the National Teacher's Exam averaged 98 percent from 1990-1995 and has been 100 percent for the past four years. The College of Education is a collaborative partner in the School-to-Work initiative. The University of Southwestern Louisiana offers the state's only master's program in Education of the Gifted, and its Educational Technology Review Center was the first of its kind in the state. The University of Southwestern Louisiana's athletic teams are called "Ragin' Cajuns," a moniker deemed the "most unique" in the nation.

Teacher Preparation Program Information

The following programs are 4 year programs:
Elementary Education, K-12 Education (Health and Physical Education, Music), Secondary Education (Art, English, French, General Science and Biology, Mathematics, Social Studies, Spanish, Speech), Special Education (Early Intervention, Mild/Moderate, Speech/Language/Hearing), Vocational Education (Agriculture, General Business, Industrial Arts, Vocational Home Economics/Family & Consumer Science)

The following programs are post-baccalaureate programs:
Early Childhood Education, Elementary Education, Kindergarten Education, K-12 Education (Art, French, Spanish, Health, Health and Physical Education, Music), Secondary Education (Art, Chemistry, Computer Literacy, Computer Science, Earth Science, English, French, General Science and Biology, Journalism, Mathematics, Physics, Social Studies, Spanish, Speech), Special Education (Adaptive Physical Education, Early Intervention, Mild/Moderate, Speech/Language/Hearing), Vocational Education (Agriculture, General Business, Industrial Arts, Vocational Home Economics/Family & Consumer Science)

Xavier University of Louisiana

Upon its founding by the Sisters of the Blessed Sacrament in 1915, Xavier University accepted the sacred privilege and social responsibility of preparing well-qualified teachers. Today, it remains the only historically black and Catholic university in the country. The Division of Education prepares educators who possess professional abilities integrated with a humanities-oriented liberal arts education. Xavier University's teacher education programs are based on the core concepts of values, culture, spirituality, knowledge, and skills. Graduates are self-directed, and can adjust to the changing needs of schools.

Just the facts...

Xavier University of Louisiana
Division of Education
7325 Palmetto Street
New Orleans, LA 70125
(504) 483-7536
Website: www.xula.edu
Profile: Urban, Medium, Co-Ed
UG Tuition: $4,250.00/semester
G Tuition: $200.00/credit hour
Off Campus Programs: No

Clinical Experiences

Beginning with the first course in the program and continuing to the semester of student teaching, candidates are exposed to diverse school settings and various grade levels. The experiences are designed to help candidates reflect on their career choices, become acquainted with the processes of teaching and learning, learn classroom management and instructional planning skills, and understand communication and interaction between teachers and students in the classroom.

Noteworthy

Candidates are guided by faculty advisors (usually professors with expertise in the candidates' intended specialties) throughout their studies at Xavier. All education candidates meet with the faculty as a group three times a semester to review program procedures and any changes forthcoming from the Louisiana State Department of Education. The Division of Education is working to increase the number of science and mathematics teachers by offering funds to assist candidates in the graduate degree programs for math and science education. Candidates majoring in elementary education (1-8) are provided additional training specific to middle school education.

Teacher Preparation Program Information

The following programs are 4 year programs:

Early Childhood Education, Elementary Education (Grades 1-8), K-12 Education (Art, Music/Vocal and Instrumental, Health/Physical Education, Special Education), Secondary Education (Biology, Chemistry, English/Language Arts, French, Mathematics, Social Studies, Spanish)

The following programs are post-baccalaureate programs:

Early Childhood Education, Elementary Education, Secondary Education (Alternate Certification), Special Education

University of Maine

The University of Maine has provided a century of progressive leadership in preparing confident, creative educators in the fields of elementary, secondary, and physical education with a broad range of concentration options. As part of Maine's land-grant institution, the College of Education and Human Development has statewide responsibility for educational professional development, research, and service. This distinction gives candidates the advantage of learning alongside faculty who help shape and address the issues, needs, and policy of educational practice and reform.

Just the facts...

University of Maine
College of Education
141 Shibles Hall
Orono, ME 04469
(207) 581-2420
Website: www.ume.maine.edu/~cofed/
Profile: Rural, Large, Co-Ed
UG Tuition: $129.00/cr. hr. in-state; $365.00/cr. hr. out-of-state
G Tuition: $194.00/cr. hr. in-state; $548.00/cr. hr. out-of-state
Off Campus Programs: No

Clinical Experiences

The professional development program is conducted in partnership with K-12 schools, where UMaine faculty, candidates, public school teachers, and students work and learn together. In the first two years, candidates complete liberal arts and concentration requirements, plus two education field experiences, gain technological competency, and begin a portfolio documenting their development as teachers. The last two years focus on methods courses and extensive experience in schools, including a full semester of student teaching.

Noteworthy

Candidates are surrounded by innovation. The College of Education is home of the National Center for Student Aspirations, seven state and regional research/service centers, Maine's National Writing Project, a nursery school and kindergarten, and a state-of-the-art computer lab. Undergraduates benefit from the same outstanding faculty and instruction that gained the college's Secondary Education Program a top 25 ranking in *U.S. News & World Report*'s 1998 *America's Best Graduate Schools*. Faculty are nationally recognized, award-winning researchers, teachers, and authors.

Teacher Preparation Program Information

The following programs are 4 year programs:

Early Childhood Education, Elementary Education, K-12 Education (Art, French, German, Physical Education, Spanish), Secondary Education (Biology, Chemistry, Earth Science, English/Language Arts, General Science, Mathematics, Physical Education, Physics, Science)

University of Maine at Farmington

The University of Maine at Farmington, founded in 1863, is Maine's first institution of higher education. Selective admissions limits enrollment to 2,000 students, which ensures individualized attention for each student. The student/faculty ratio is sixteen to one. In its 1999 *America's Best Colleges* guidebook, *U.S. News and World Report* selected UMF as the top public liberal arts college in the North. The conceptual framework for teacher education at UMF ensures that teacher candidates are strongly grounded in the liberal arts, including the discipline of education, and are reflective practitioners who will continue to expand their teaching effectiveness throughout their careers.

Just the facts...

University of Maine at Farmington
College of Education, Health & Rehabilitation
104 Main Street
Farmington, ME 04938-1993
(207) 778-7153
Website: www.umf.maine.edu
Profile: Rural, Small, Co-Ed
UG Tuition: $1,695.00/sem. in-state; $4,140.00/sem. out-of-state
Off Campus Programs: No

Clinical Experiences

Starting in either their first or second year at UMF, all candidates begin observing, planning, and practice-teaching in a variety of settings appropriate to their future roles. All clinical experiences require weekly or biweekly seminars and/or conferences at which candidates reflect with each other and their instructors on observations and experiences encountered in the field. Journals, class assignments, and portfolio entries associated with field experiences support candidates in becoming reflective practitioners. Student teaching placements and internships are available throughout the state.

Noteworthy

At UMF, candidates benefit from close working relationships with a faculty small enough to know each student individually, yet large enough to represent various points of view and a wide range of disciplines. Faculty and candidates work side by side in programs and clinics for children with special needs, day care centers, nursery schools, family day care facilities, and public schools. Mutually beneficial ties are maintained with 28 regional school districts through the Western Maine Partnership for Educational Renewal. Courses in early childhood and special education are offered statewide via interactive television and other distance learning technologies to help meet personnel preparation needs in these areas.

Teacher Preparation Program Information

The following programs are 4 year programs:
Early Childhood Education, Elementary Education, K-12 Education (Health), Secondary Education (Biology, English, Mathematics, Mathematics/Computer Science, Physical Sciences, Science, Social Science), Special Education (Early Childhood, Emotional Disturbance, Learning Disability, Mental Retardation)

University of Southern Maine

Faculty members in USM's College of Education and Human Development believe that the process of teaching is actually a process of learning. Programs are based on the idea that effective teaching should be grounded in knowledge, experience, critical reflection, and a commitment to preparing children for an increasingly technology-driven, multicultural, and global society. The College of Education and Human Development is committed to providing experiences to teacher candidates that will promote a lifelong pursuit of learning.

Just the facts...

University of Southern Maine
College of Education and Human Development
119 Bailey Hall
Gorham, ME 04038
(207) 780-5371
Website: www.usm.maine.edu
Profile: Suburban, Large, Co-Ed
UG Tuition: $118.00/cr. hr. in-state; $327.00/cr. hr. out-of-state
G Tuition: $178.00/cr. hr. in-state; $491.00/cr. hr. out-of-state
Off Campus Programs: No

Clinical Experiences

The hallmark of USM's teacher preparation programs, whether at the undergraduate or post-baccalaureate level, is a full year of immersion in partner professional development schools. Coursework, supervision, and mentoring all occur within K-12 school and classroom settings, with university professors and clinical faculty sharing both formal instruction and supervision. The internship culminates in performance assessments integrating content and professional knowledge with demonstrated instructional skills evaluated by both university and school faculty.

Noteworthy

The strength of USM's programs is in the strong school-university partnerships it has developed with several area school districts and other post-secondary colleges belonging to the Southern Maine Partnership. Through its affiliation with several leading national reform networks such as the National Network for Educational Renewal and the Coalition for Essential Schools, the Southern Maine Partnership enables USM candidates to learn not only from university faculty, but from leaders in several outstanding schools across the region, ranging from urban sites with significant minority enrollments to small, rural communities.

Teacher Preparation Program Information

The following programs are 4 year programs:
K-12 Education (Art, Industrial Technology, Music)

The following programs are 5 year programs:
Elementary Education, Kindergarten Education, Middle School Education, Secondary Education (Biology, Chemistry, Mathematics, Physics)

The following programs are 5th year programs:
Elementary Education, K-12 Education (French, Spanish), Kindergarten Education, Middle School Education, Secondary Education (Biology, Chemistry, English/Language Arts, Mathematics, Physics, Social Studies), Special Education

Bowie State University

Established in 1865, Bowie State University (BSU) is the oldest historically black institution in Maryland and is among the oldest in the state. BSU aspires to produce graduates who are leaders among their peers in a global community, who think critically, value diversity, and are committed to the higher moral and ethical good. The university places special emphasis on excellence in teaching, and encourages research on teaching methodology and the learning process to improve instruction. Faculty members demonstrate excellence, scholarship, and creativity in their teaching and service to the university, the community, and their profession.

Just the facts...

Bowie State University
Department of Education
14000 Jericho Park Road
Bowie, MD 20715
(301) 464-7562
Website: www.bowiestate.edu
Profile: Suburban, Medium, Co-Ed
UG Tuition: $1,359.00/sem. in-state; $3,771.00/sem. out-of-state
G Tuition: $2,028.00/sem. in-state; $3,648.00/sem. out-of-state
Off Campus Programs: Yes

Clinical Experiences

Teacher education programs are grounded in practice to enable candidates to learn what the "real world" of teaching is all about. Candidates work with professional educators to develop, assess, and refine their skills over an extended period of time. Professional practice in the school setting enables candidates to learn to be reflective practitioners and researchers. In addition, the Department of Education has been engaged in a professional development school partnership with Bladensburg High School for the past four years.

Noteworthy

The University College of Excellence for all freshmen and sophomores provides a holistic, challenging, and enriching set of experiences that enhances critical thinking, problem solving, research, oral and written communications, and computer skills. Participation in professional development school activities has enabled faculty to engage in action research, to link theory with practice, and to collaborate in the writing of grants and proposals.

Teacher Preparation Program Information

The following programs are 4 year programss:
Early Childhood/Special Education (N-3/Infant-Grade 3), Elementary Education (Grades 1-6, Middle School), Secondary Education (Biology, Chemistry, English, History, Mathematics, Physics)

The following programs are post-baccalaureate programs:
Special Education 1-8 (Mild/Moderate Disabilities)

The following programs are 5 year programs:
Elementary Education, Secondary Education (English, Mathematics, Science, Social Studies)

National Council for Accreditation of Teacher Education

Coppin State College

The Division of Education at Coppin State College offers a variety of undergraduate and graduate programs designed primarily to prepare students for careers in teaching. An integral component of the Teacher Education Program is the development of candidates' understanding of the realities of our multicultural, interdependent world and their ability to work effectively with all students. Multicultural and global education are addressed in each major component of the programs. To prepare candidates to guide and instruct learners of all ages, each program is based on a core of general education courses.

Just the facts...

Coppin State College
Division of Education
2500 West North Avenue
Baltimore, MD 21216
(410) 383-5530
Website: www.coppin.umd.edu
Profile: Urban, Medium, Co-Ed
UG Tuition: $1,587.00/sem. in-state; $3,933.00/sem. out-of-state
G Tuition: $140.00/cr. hr. in-state; $240.00/cr. hr. out-of-state
Off Campus Programs: No

Clinical Experiences

All candidates participate in planned field experiences designed to introduce them to the nature of the learner, the curriculum, and the teaching/learning environment. Clinical experiences include school visits, observation/participation experiences, an intense twelve-week student teaching experience, and graduate-level practica and internship experiences. Some programs require semester-long, school-based experiences that combine theory and practice.

Noteworthy

College-wide computer laboratories are available to enhance the overall quality of teaching and learning. The Division of Education has an education technology center, which prepares elementary and secondary school teachers for teaching in today's technology-driven environment. The center focuses on developing technology skills of preservice and in-service teachers in community schools so they might improve learning through the infusion of technology into the instructional process. The Division of Education also has an Education Resource Center that houses K-12 multimedia instructional materials.

Teacher Preparation Program Information

The following programs are 4 year programs:
Early Childhood Education, Elementary Education, Secondary Education (Biology, English/Language Arts, History, Mathematics, Social Sciences), Special Education (Mild/Moderate Handicapped)

The following programs are post-baccalaureate programs:
Secondary Education (Biology, Chemistry, English/Language Arts, Mathematics, Social Sciences)

The following programs are 5th year programs:
Elementary Education, Secondary Education (Biology, English/Language Arts, Mathematics, Social Sciences)

Morgan State University

Morgan State University, a historically black institution, has been designated Maryland's Public Urban University. As an urban university, Morgan serves an ethnically and culturally diverse student body. Some of Maryland's best and brightest students are at Morgan State University. The School of Education and Urban Studies prepares professionals who are competent, sensitive, and socially aware. The teacher education programs are especially sensitive to urban issues and provide candidates with the opportunity to develop essential abilities for success in guiding the learning activities of students, particularly urban students.

Just the facts...

Morgan State University
School of Education
1700 East Cold Spring Lane
Baltimore, MD 21239
(443) 885-3385
Website: www.morgan.edu
Profile: Urban, Medium, Co-Ed
UG Tuition: $1,300.00/sem. in-state; $3,590.00/sem. out-of-state
G Tuition: $145.00/cr. hr. in-state; $260.00/cr. hr. out-of-state
Off Campus Programs: No

Clinical Experiences

The hallmark of Morgan's teacher education programs is early experience in real classrooms. Field experiences begin in the freshman year with candidate observation and participation in the Professional Education Centers, all of which are public schools within the city system. At the sophomore level, candidates analyze and develop case studies based on their observations. At the junior and senior levels, candidates proceed through peer-teaching, micro-teaching, and other work with small groups of students. During student teaching, the candidate gradually assumes responsibility for teaching an entire class of students.

Noteworthy

Graduates of the School of Education and Urban Studies use their understanding of individuals and groups to pursue successful social service careers with government agencies and businesses, as well as within schools. Morgan is currently implementing educational technology and media studies throughout its teacher education programs. Several courses teach candidates to integrate digital sound recording and digital video capture into multimedia instruction.

Teacher Preparation Program Information

The following programs are 4 year programs:
Elementary Education

The following programs are post-baccalaureate programs:
K-12 Education (Art, Music, Physical Education, Spanish), Secondary Education (Art, Biology, Business, Chemistry, English/Language Arts, Mathematics, Physical Education, Physics)

National Council for Accreditation of Teacher Education

University of Maryland—College Park

The College of Education at the University of Maryland is nationally ranked and recognized for its outstanding professional preparation programs. The College of Education, located near Baltimore and Washington, D.C., is committed to advancing the science and art of education through disciplined inquiry. Candidates are prepared to be educational leaders and decision makers through a knowledge base that stresses subject matter, curriculum, understanding of the learner, pedagogy, educational goals and assessment, and the social context of learning.

Just the facts...

University of Maryland—College Park
College of Education
3119 Benjamin Building
College Park, MD 20742-1121
(301) 405-2334
Website: www.umcp.umd.edu
Profile: Suburban, Large, Co-Ed
UG Tuition: $170.00/cr. hr. in-state; $434.00/cr. hr. out-of-state
G Tuition: $272.00/cr. hr. in-state; $400.00/cr. hr. out-of-state
Off Campus Programs: No

Clinical Experiences

UMCP has received national awards for its excellent clinical program. Field placements in early childhood, elementary, secondary, and special education range from half-day observation/participation to full-time student teaching. Teacher candidates are placed in schools with diverse student populations and accomplished mentor teachers. Student teaching is closely monitored by university supervisors and cooperating teachers to help candidates meet high performance standards. The College of Education is working with local school systems to design year-long internships in professional development schools.

Noteworthy

$32,000 is awarded annually in merit and need-based scholarships in amounts ranging from $500 to $1,000. A cluster of two or three courses is scheduled for freshmen to create a learning community; this clustering makes the College of Education a "small place" at the university. College Park Scholars: Advocates for Children is a living-learning option for talented candidates. College student organizations provide diverse outreach opportunities for candidates participating in volunteer and experiential activities in area schools, model campus programs, and the College of Education's nationally recognized Center for Young Children.

Teacher Preparation Program Information

The following programs are 4 year programs:
Early Childhood Education, Elementary Education, K-12 Education (Art, Health, Music, Physical Education), Secondary Education (Biology, Chemistry, Earth Science, English/Language Arts, Foreign Languages, Mathematics, Physics, Science, Social Studies)

The following programs are 5 year programs:
Special Education (Early Childhood, Educationally Handicapped, Secondary and Transition, Severe Disabilities)

The following programs are 5th year programs:
Elementary Education, Secondary Education (English/Language Arts, Mathematics, Science, Social Studies)

Boston College

The School of Education at Boston College, a Catholic and Jesuit University, endeavors to improve the human condition through education. Faculty pursue this goal through excellence and ethics in teaching, research, and service. Through research, the faculty seek to advance knowledge in their respective fields, to inform policy, and to improve practice. As teachers and scholars, they engage in collaborative school and community improvement efforts locally, nationally, and internationally. The School of Education will be named the Peter S. and Carolyn A. Lynch School of Education in recognition of the couple's endowment gift of more than ten million dollars, the largest individual gift ever made to Boston College.

Just the facts...

Boston College
School of Education, Campion Hall
140 Commonwealth Avenue
Chestnut Hill, MA 02467-3800
(617) 552-4200
Website: www.bc.edu/education
Profile: Urban, Large, Co-Ed
UG Tuition: $20,760.00/year
G Tuition: $626.00/credit hour
Off Campus Programs: No

Clinical Experiences

Undergraduate and graduate candidates engage in supervised practica appropriate to their program. All candidates participate in field placements. Practica experiences for licensure in teacher education are offered at either advanced provisional or standard levels. Placement sites for field experiences are located in Boston and neighboring areas. In addition to the local field sites, a limited number of placements in teaching are available in international and domestic settings, including Switzerland, Ireland, England, France, Scotland, Germany, Spain, and Mexico, and an Arizona Native American reservation.

Noteworthy

The Graduate School of Education at Boston College houses three research centers: the Center for the Study of Testing, Evaluation & Educational Policy; the Center for International Higher Education; and the Center for Child, Family, and Community Partnerships. The Urban Catholic Teacher Corps offers new teachers an opportunity to gain classroom experience in the inner city. The Donovan Program prepares teachers for urban schools; partial funding is available for competitive candidates. The Boston College Partnership is an interprofessional collaborative effort between the School of Education, other Boston College Professional schools, and the Boston Public Schools.

Teacher Preparation Program Information

The following programs are 4 year programs:

Early Childhood Education, Elementary Education, Elementary Education/Moderate Special Needs Education, Elementary Education/Intensive Special Needs Education, Secondary Education (Biology, Chemistry, Classical Humanities, English, French, Geology/Earth Science, History, Latin, Mathematics, Physics, Spanish), Special Needs Education

The following programs are 5th year programs:

Early Childhood or Secondary Teaching, Elementary Education, Low Incidence Disabilities (Severe Special Needs, Visually Impaired Studies, Deaf/Blindness and Multiple Disabilities Studies), Reading/Literacy Teaching, Teacher of Students with Special Needs (Grades P-9, Grades 5-12)

Bridgewater State College

Bridgewater State College was instituted in 1840 to prepare teachers. The School of Education and Allied Studies has adopted "Growth of the Professional Educator" as the model for its professional education programs. This model outlines a program that is student-oriented, knowledge-based, and designed for both campus and field-based experiences that develop knowledge and skill over time. The faculty believes that learners are active problem solvers, and programs are designed to prepare candidates to help students construct their own learning.

Just the facts...

Bridgewater State College
School of Education and Allied Studies
Bridgewater, MA 02325
(508) 697-1347
Website: www.bridgew.edu
Profile: Suburban, Medium, Co-Ed
UG Tuition: $47.92/cr. hr. in-state; $268.75/cr. hr. out-of-state
Off Campus Programs: No

Clinical Experiences

Candidates in the initial teacher preparation program spend a minimum of 80 hours in monitored field-based pre-practica including a variety of school settings and a variety of students. Much hands-on experience is provided at the campus PK-6 school. The student teaching experience is a minimum of 300 hours over fifteen weeks. Supervision and evaluation is provided by a college supervisor and a cooperating practitioner in the school. Candidates are clustered in communities selected by the college and in many cases with cooperating teachers who have had mentor training.

Noteworthy

The John Joseph Moakley Center for Technological Applications is devoted to servicing southeast Massachusetts with technology in education. A feature of the building is the Teacher Technology Center used by education candidates and cooperating practitioners associated with Bridgewater State College. The constructivist framework at Bridgewater State College moves prospective educators through professional development exercises that ensure they are ready to teach when they complete their initial licensure program and prepared to lead when they complete the clinical master's degree program.

Teacher Preparation Program Information

The following programs are 4 year programs:
Early Childhood Education, Elementary Education, K-12 Education (Art, Communication and Performing Arts, Health, Music, Physical Education, Spanish), Middle School Education (English, Mathematics, Science, Social Studies), Secondary Education (Biology, Chemistry, Earth Science, English/Language Arts, Mathematics, Physics, Social Studies), Special Education (Intensive Special Needs, Students with Special Needs)

The following programs are post-baccalaureate programs:
Early Childhood Education, Elementary Education, K-12 Education (Art, Communication and Performing Arts, Health, Music, Physical Education, Spanish), Middle School Education (English, Mathematics, Science, Social Studies), Secondary Education (Biology, Chemistry, Earth Science, English/Language Arts, Mathematics, Physics, Social Studies), Special Education (Intensive Special Needs, Students with Special Needs)

Fitchburg State College

At Fitchburg State College the preparation of professional educators rests on the following: the foundation of a strong liberal arts and science education; a depth of understanding in subject matter; the development of acceptable teaching practice; and a breadth of knowledge provided by a second major. Each of these components is undergirded by a knowledge base that contributes to the development of professional educators committed to helping children learn.

Just the facts...

Fitchburg State College
School of Education
160 Pearl Street
Fitchburg, MA 01420
(978) 665-3239
Website: www.fsc.edu
Profile: Urban, Medium, Co-Ed
UG Tuition: $635.00/sem. in-state; $2,975.00/sem. out-of-state
G Tuition: $140.00/credit hour
Off Campus Programs: Yes

Clinical Experiences

Clinical experiences give candidates the opportunity to demonstrate their pedagogical and content knowledge, skills, understanding, and collegial orientation. Candidates are provided the opportunity for supervised direct teaching. They are expected to implement education concepts and practices gained through earlier coursework and courses taken simultaneously with the clinical experiences. The quality of the candidate's field experience is jointly monitored by the college supervisor and the cooperating practitioner-mentor.

Noteworthy

Teacher preparation faculty and the technical support staff collaborate in establishing and maintaining an up-to-date technology infrastructure, so that education candidates can use technology and integrate it into their teaching. Each education program integrates aspects of multiculturalism and global perspectives in the curriculum. Support for candidates includes an academic advising center, computer facilities, a freshman readiness program, developmental skills and ESL programs, peer advising, tutorials, counseling, and health services.

Teacher Preparation Program Information

The following programs are 4 year programs:

Early Childhood Education, Elementary Education, Middle School Education, Secondary Education (Biology, Earth Science, English, History, Technology Education), Special Education (Moderate and Intensive)

Salem State College

Salem State College began as a training school for teachers in 1854. Grounded in the liberal arts, the preparation of teachers and other school personnel remains an important focus today. Programs in the School of Education combine the study of human development, sociocultural context, subject matter, pedagogy, and community partnerships. Assessment, communication, diversity, reflection, and technology are integrated throughout the candidates' coursework.

Just the facts...

Salem State College
School of Education
352 Lafayette Street
Salem, MA 01970-4589
(978) 542-6630
Website: www.salem.mass.edu
Profile: Urban, Medium, Co-Ed
UG Tuition: $125/cr. hr. in-state; $160/cr. hr. out-of-state
G Tuition: $160/cr. hr. in-state; $250/cr. hr. out-of-state
Off Campus Programs: Yes

Clinical Experiences

Clinical experiences evolve from the first education course through student teaching and into advanced programs. Reflective practice is a component of all field experiences. Education courses early in the program involve observation or tutoring experiences. The curriculum block requires half-days of field work, and student teaching is a full-semester commitment. The college assigns upper-level practica students a cooperating practitioner in the school in addition to a college supervisor. At least one school placement is in an urban school.

Noteworthy

Initial licensure programs at Salem State College are grounded in the arts and sciences. The college has three laboratory schools—two elementary level and one preschool. The unit has many community-based education grant programs that provide a service to the community and hands-on learning experiences for candidates. On campus, candidates are supported by an education computer laboratory, a Global Education Center, an Education Resource Library, a children's literature examination center, an Instructional Design Lab, and a summer reading clinic for children.

Teacher Preparation Program Information

The following programs are 4 year programs:
Early Childhood Education, Elementary Education, K-12 Education (Art, Physical Education), Middle School Education, Secondary Education (Biology, Chemistry, Earth Science, English/Language Arts, History, Mathematics, Social Studies)

The following programs are post-baccalaureate programs:
Early Childhood Education, Elementary Education, K-12 Education (Art, Physical Education), Middle School Education, Secondary Education (Biology, Chemistry, Earth Science, English/Language Arts, History, Mathematics, Social Studies)

The following programs are 5th year programs:
Early Childhood Education, Elementary Education, ESL Education, Middle School Education, Reading Education, Secondary Education (Biology, Chemistry, English/Language Arts, History, Mathematics), Special Education

University of Massachusetts Amherst

The University of Massachusetts Amherst prepares candidates for licensure, and develops practitioners who will become leaders in their schools. Programs in the School of Education explore the complexities of educational issues within their historical, organizational, and social context, making preparation meaningful and relevant to future educators. Although the educator preparation programs are centered in the School of Education, the university ensures that the preparation of teacher candidates is a campus-wide effort. Faculty from almost every school and college on campus are involved in the training of future teachers.

Just the facts...

University of Massachusetts Amherst
School of Education
124 Furcolo Hall
Amherst, MA 01003-3010
(413) 545-0233
Website: www.umass.edu/education
Profile: Rural, Medium, Co-Ed
UG Tuition: $1,002.00/sem. in-state; $4,476.00/sem. out-of-state
G Tuition: $110.00/cr. hr. in-state; $375.75/cr. hr. out-of-state
Off Campus Programs: No

Clinical Experiences

All educator preparation programs at the University of Massachusetts Amherst integrate field experiences in urban, suburban, and rural settings. The university is proud of its range of outstanding clinical and professional development school sites where candidates can learn how to teach. Observation, tutoring, working with small groups, full-semester student teaching, and internships provide a solid grounding for candidates in the world of practice.

Noteworthy

The University of Massachusetts Amherst has been listed in the top 50 graduate schools of education by *U.S. News and World Report* in three of the last four years. For the past three years, the university and the Springfield Public School System have been members of the Massachusetts Consortium for Initial Teacher Professional Development, a consortium of school, college, nonprofit, and state partners developing and implementing innovations in initial teacher preparation. A commitment to diversity, equity, and excellence infuse all programs.

Teacher Preparation Program Information

The following programs are 4 year programs:

Early Childhood Education, Elementary Education, P-12 Education (Art, Music), Middle School Education (Earth Science, English/Language Arts, General Science, History, Mathematics, Social Studies), Middle/Secondary School Education (Chinese, Consumer & Family Sciences/Home Economics, French, Italian, Japanese, Portuguese, Spanish), Secondary Education (Agriculture, Biology, Chemistry, Earth Science, English/Language Arts, History, Mathematics, Physics, Social Studies)

The following programs are post-baccalaureate programs:

Early Childhood Education, P-12 Education (Art, ESL, Music), Middle School Education (Earth Science, English/Language Arts, General Science, History, Mathematics, Social Studies), Middle/Secondary School Education (Chinese, Consumer & Family Sciences/Home Economics, French, Italian, Japanese, Portuguese, Spanish), Secondary Education (Agriculture, Biology, Chemistry, Earth Science, English/Language Arts, History, Mathematics, Physics, Social Studies)

The following programs are 5th year programs:

Early Childhood Education, Elementary Education, P-12 Education (Art, ESL, Music), Middle School Education (Earth Science, English/Language Arts, General Science, History, Mathematics, Social Studies), Middle/Secondary School Education (Chinese, Consumer & Family Sciences/Home Economics, French, Italian, Japanese, Portuguese, Spanish), Secondary Education (Agriculture, Biology, Chemistry, Earth Science, English/Language Arts, History, Mathematics, Physics, Social Studies), Special Education (Special Educaiion P-12)

University of Massachusetts Lowell

The Graduate School of Education at the University of Massachusetts Lowell fulfills a mission of striving for excellence in teaching, scholarship, and community service. The curriculum is unified across all programs as novice and experienced educators from diverse backgrounds share viewpoints and gain enhanced capabilities for teaching and educational leadership roles. All programs operate on a year-round, trimester schedule and support the professional development of beginning and experienced teachers who have a strong background in the liberal arts and sciences.

Just the facts...

University of Massachusetts Lowell
Graduate School of Education
One University Avenue
Lowell, MA 01854
(978) 934-4601
Website: www.uml.edu/College/Education
Profile: Urban, Large, Co-Ed
G Tuition: $89.46/cr. hr. in-state; $311.75/cr. hr. out-of-state
Off Campus Programs: No

Clinical Experiences

Observations and student teaching experiences are required of all candidates in the Graduate Program in Teaching. Prepracticum placements include both urban and suburban settings in professional development schools. Practicum school sites are chosen on the basis of the school's commitment to work with the faculty in developing experiences that reflect excellence of programs and curriculum along with innovative initiatives. Faculty are responsible for ensuring that the clinical experiences are congruent with the goals and concepts of the candidate's program.

Noteworthy

The University of Massachusetts Lowell is a technologically advanced campus with a specific mission for regional economic development. The Graduate School of Education is distinguished by strong partnership programs with local school systems, including an on-campus trilingual Demonstration School (serving ages three to grade four, Spanish, Khmer, and English languages), a Center for Field Services and Studies (sponsoring K-12 leadership and professional development), the Tsongas Industrial History Center (hosting 48,000 children annually for learning experiences), and ten years of successful distance education programming.

Teacher Preparation Program Information

The following programs are 5th year programs:
Elementary Education, Elementary/Middle School Education, Elementary/Early Childhood Education, Middle/Secondary Education (Biology, Chemistry, Earth Science, English, History, Mathematics, Physics, Social Studies)

Wheelock College

Wheelock College has been identified by a national education organization as one of the top ten teacher preparation institutions in the country. Wheelock prepares undergraduate and graduate students to teach children in diverse settings. Undergraduate teacher candidates choose a liberal arts major in the humanities, in math/science, in human development, or in the arts. They also select a professional concentration in early childhood or elementary teaching, and participate in a year-long course in human development.

Just the facts...

Wheelock College
Professional Studies Department
200 The Riverway
Boston, MA 02215-5200
(617) 879-2206
Website: www.wheelock.edu
Profile: Urban, Medium, Co-Ed
UG Tuition: $8,048.00/semester
G Tuition: $525.00/credit hour
Off Campus Programs: No

Clinical Experiences

Wheelock values the importance of field work and its dynamic integration within the classroom experience. Undergraduates have field placement opportunities beginning in the fall of their first year. Wheelock's extensive connections in the greater Boston community ensure a wide range of high-quality placements for candidates in child care and after-school settings, Head Start programs and museums, independent and public schools, and social service settings. Juniors, seniors, and graduate students have a choice of student teaching experiences in a variety of public and private settings.

Noteworthy

Wheelock is a member of the Colleges of the Fenway Consortium. Students at Wheelock and four other colleges cross-register for courses and share theater arts opportunities, library holdings, campus facilities, and joint social events. Connections, a community service learning program, provides opportunities for students at local schools, social service agencies, and through the America Reads tutoring program. Scholarships and financial aid are available for undergraduates. Internships and on-campus graduate assistantships are available for graduate students.

Teacher Preparation Program Information

The following programs are 4 year programs:
Early Childhood Education P-3, Early Childhood Education P-3/P-12 ESL, Elementary Education 1-6 (Elementary Education 1-6, Mathematics, Science), Elementary Education 1-6/P-12 ESL, Elementary Education 1-6/Special Education P-9

The following programs are 5 year programs:
Early Childhood Education P-3, Early Childhood Education P-3/Reading P-12, Early Childhood Education P-3/P-12 ESL, Elementary Education 1-6, Elementary Education 1-6/Reading P-12, Elementary Education 1-6/P-12 ESL, Special Education P-9/Elementary Education 1-6

The following programs are 5th year programs:
Early Childhood Education P-3, Early Childhood Education P-3/Reading P-12, Early Childhood Education P-3/P-12 ESL, Elementary Education 1-6, Elementary Education 1-6/Reading P-12, Elementary Education 1-6/P-12 ESL, Reading P-9, Special Education P-9/Elementary Education 1-6

Andrews University

The goal of Andrews University's teacher education program is to provide all candidates with a solid foundation of skills and knowledge necessary for success in their professions and for their growth as lifelong learners. To this end faculty combine their efforts toward developing people who (1) love learning and apply knowledge and theory to the practice of education; (2) apply principles of a Christian world view to their professions; (3) are effective in social relationships and serve with sensitivity and skill; (4) practice healthful living; and (5) effectively lead others toward fulfillment of their God-given potential.

Just the facts...

Andrews University
School of Education
Berrien Springs, MI 49104-0100
(616) 471-3481
Website: www.educ.andrews.edu
Profile: Rural, Small, Co-Ed
UG Tuition: $3,895.00/quarter
G Tuition: $290.00/credit hour
Off Campus Programs: No

Clinical Experiences

Trained within the Dimensions of Learning paradigm, Andrews' elementary preservice teachers engage in 700 clinical/field experience hours and secondary preservice teachers engage in over 800 clinical/field experience hours. These experiences include in-class observations; aiding teachers; lesson, unit, and semester planning; micro- and macro-teaching; small group tutoring; first day of school experience; and student teaching. All field experiences focus on reflective practice in diverse school settings.

Noteworthy

One noteworthy component of undergraduate teacher education is the First Days of School Experience program. The Leadership doctoral program is also a source of pride. It is student-centered, comptency-based, field-oriented, and flexible enough to meet a variety of student needs. It emphasizes servant leadership and draws from an excellent selection of national applicants. The relationship the school has to its sponsoring body (the worldwide Seventh-Day Adventist Church) allows Andrews to have one of the highest percentages of international students in higher education in the United States.

Teacher Preparation Program Information

The following programs are 4 year programs:

Elementary Education (Behavioral Science, Biology, Chemistry, General Science, Geography, History, Language Arts, Mathematics, Social Studies), K-12 Education (Art, French, German, Music, Physical Education, Reading, Spanish), Secondary Education (Behavioral Science, Biology, Chemistry, Computer Science, English, French, General Science, Geography, German, History, Mathematics, Physics, Political Science, Social Studies, Sociology, Spanish, Speech Communication, Technology Education)

The following programs are 5th year programs:

Biology Education, Elementary Education, English Education, English as a Second Language, History, Secondary Education

Calvin College

Calvin College has prepared teachers since 1920. The faculty is committed to preparing teachers who are reflective practitioners who know why they teach, what they teach, to whom they teach, how to teach, and how to evaluate the effectiveness of their teaching. Calvin College works to ensure that graduates have a strong liberal arts background in addition to a solid grounding in academic majors and minors from a Reformed Christian perspective.

Just the facts...

Calvin College
Teacher Education
3201 Burton SE
Grand Rapids, MI 49546
(616) 957-6214
Website: www.calvin.edu
Profile: Urban, Medium, Co-Ed
UG Tuition: $245.00/credit hour
G Tuition: $245.00/credit hour
Off Campus Programs: No

Clinical Experiences

Teacher candidates complete three levels of clinical experiences. The first level involves gaining practical school experience with students who are handicapped and students from different races and cultures. The second level involves an intensive pre-student teaching clinical experience where candidates are more involved in the classroom. The third level involves fourteen weeks of full-time, directed teaching.

Noteworthy

Calvin College has a student chapter of the Association for Supervision and Curriculum Development. Its purpose is to promote students' professional development with a major focus on issues, innovations, and promising practices in education. Education candidates are supported by a well-equipped Curriculum Center, Audio-Visual Laboratory, and Computer Center. A number of scholarships are available to qualified candidates.

Teacher Preparation Program Information

The following programs are 4 year programs:

K-12 Education (Art, French, German, Japanese, Music, Physical Education, Spanish), Secondary Education (Art, Biology, Chemistry, Earth Science, Economics, English/Language Arts, General Science, Geography, Health, Latin, Mathematics, Physical Education, Physical Sciences, Physics, Political Science, Psychology, Science, Social Studies, Sociology), Special Education (Developmental Disabilities/Handicaps)

The following programs are post-baccalaureate programs:

K-12 Education (Art, French, German, Japanese, Music, Physical Education, Spanish), Secondary Education (Art, Biology, Chemistry, Earth Science, Economics, English/Language Arts, General Science, Geography, Health, Latin, Mathematics, Physical Education, Physical Sciences, Physics, Political Science, Psychology, Science, Social Studies, Sociology), Special Education (Developmental Disabilities/Handicaps)

The following programs are 5th year programs:

Special Education (Learning Disability)

Central Michigan University

The primary mission of the College of Education and Human Services is to provide the highest quality undergraduate and graduate educational experiences that develop effective professionals, critical thinkers, and lifelong learners. Candidates will expand their understanding of themselves and their roles in a global society. Through a broad range of technological and human services, the college and its graduates, in collaboration with the constituencies they serve, will be proactive forces for improving the quality of life in the twenty-first century.

Just the facts...

Central Michigan University
College of Education, Health, and Human Services
307 Ronan Hall
Mount Pleasant, MI 48859
(517) 774-3079
Website: www.cmich.edu
Profile: Suburban, Large, Co-Ed
UG Tuition: $95.00/cr. hr. in-state; $249.05/cr. hr. out-of-state
G Tuition: $131.35/cr. hr. in-state; $260.60/cr. hr. out-of-state
Off Campus Programs: Yes

Clinical Experiences

The clinical experiences program provides quality placements in diverse educational settings in which candidates select the ideas and practices most appropriate for their professional development. Candidates benefit from collaborative supervision by university and school district faculties. Education candidates develop their professional practice based on concepts and knowledge with a learner-centered focus. They become reflective practitioners in diverse settings.

Noteworthy

Established in fall 1997, the Teacher Education Mentor and Information Center provides education candidates with ongoing mentor support. Candidates may receive immediate answers to questions about teacher education and assistance with portfolio development. The Center serves not only students who are either in the teacher education program or working toward being admitted to it, but also those students who are interested in knowing more about the programs prior to making a career decision.

Teacher Preparation Program Information

The following programs are 4 year programs:
Early Childhood Education, Elementary Education (Art, Biology, Chemistry, Chemistry-Physics, Computer Science, Dance, Earth Science, English, Geography, Health, History, Industrial Arts, Language Arts, Mathematics, Physics, Physical Sciences, Reading, Recreation, Science, Social Studies, Speech), K-12 Education (Dance, French, German, Industrial Technology, Japanese, Music, Physical Education, Reading, Spanish), Secondary Education (Art, Biology, Business, Chemistry, Earth Science, English/Language Arts, General Science, Geography, Health, Mathematics, Physical Education, Physical Sciences, Physics, Social Studies, Vocational Business Office, Vocational Health Occupation, Vocational Trade & Industrial), Special Education (Emotional Conflict, Mentally Impaired K-12, Speech/Language Disabilities)

The following programs are 5th year programs:
Early Childhood Education, Elementary Education (Chemistry, Health, Industrial Arts, Mathematics, Reading), K-12 Education (Music, Physical Education, Reading), Secondary Education (Chemistry, Health, Mathematics, Physical Education), Special Education (Emotional Conflict, Learning Disability, Mentally Impaired, K-12, Speech/Language Disabilities)

Eastern Michigan University

For almost 150 years, EMU has played a major state and national role in the preparation of teachers and other school personnel. It was among the first institutions in the country to prepare physical education teachers and special education teachers. EMU is the nation's largest producer of professional education personnel. EMU's teacher graduates are highly prized and are actively recruited by many out-of-state school districts. In the initial teacher preparation programs, EMU teacher educators produce knowledgeable professionals who are caring, reflective, decision makers in a culturally diverse and technological society.

Just the facts...

Eastern Michigan University
College of Education
117 Boone Hall
Ypsilanti, MI 48197-2212
(734) 487-1414
Website: www.emich.edu
Profile: Suburban, Large, Co-Ed
UG Tuition: $96.25/cr. hr. in-state; $254.00/cr. hr. out-of-state
G Tuition: $145.00/cr. hr. in-state; $339.00/cr. hr. out-of-state
Off Campus Programs: No

Clinical Experiences

Structured field experiences are offered at three points in the program prior to student teaching. Each of these experiences is related to a key course, so that field experience becomes a laboratory for that course. In addition, the structured field experiences are designed to give candidates an opportunity to participate in P-12 teaching/learning through assignments at different grade levels (upper and lower elementary, middle grades, and high school). Student teaching is a full-time, semester-long experience. EMU has partnerships with a number of schools, including seventeen in Detroit and others in suburban and small town settings.

Noteworthy

In addition to academic programs, the College of Education's Office of Collaborative Education works with numerous school districts in a variety of school improvement activities. Alumni are distinguished; a Pulitzer Prize winner, a National Teacher of the Year, seventeen winners of the $25,000 Milken Family Foundation National Educator Award, one of 20 members of the 1998 *USA Today* "All-USA Teacher First Team," numerous winners of various educator of the year awards, and several presidents and executives of major national professional organizations are graduates of Eastern Michigan University's College of Education.

Teacher Preparation Program Information

The following programs are 4 year programs:
Early Childhood Education, Elementary Education (Language Arts, Mathematics, Science, Social Studies), K-12 Education (Art, Japanese, Music, Physical Education, Technology), Secondary Education (Biology, Business, Chemistry, Computer Science, Earth Science, Economics, English, French, General Science, Geography, German, History, Industrial-Vocational, Marketing, Mathematics, Physics, Political Science, Psychology, Social Science, Sociology, Spanish, Speech, Vocational Business, Vocational Marketing), Special Education (Emotionally Impaired, Hearing Impaired, Mentally Impaired, Physically and Otherwise Health Impaired, Visually Impaired)

The following programs are post-baccalaureate programs:
Early Childhood Education, Elementary Education (Language Arts, Mathematics, Science, Social Studies), K-12 Education (Art, Music, Japanese, Physical Education, Technology), Secondary Education (Biology, Business, Chemistry, Computer Science, Earth Science, Economics, English, French, General Science, Geography, German, History, Industrial-Vocational, Marketing, Mathematics, Physics, Political Science, Psychology, Social Science, Sociology, Spanish, Speech, Vocational Business, Vocational Marketing), Special Education (Emotionally Impaired, Hearing Impaired, Mentally Impaired, Physically and Otherwise Health Impaired, Visually Impaired)

The following programs are 5 year programs:
Speech/Language Impaired

Grand Valley State University

The teacher preparation program prepares candidates with strong backgrounds in the liberal arts, familiarity with learning theory, and practical experience in diverse settings. Candidates major in academic disciplines and also complete the professional program. Education and subject area faculty teach courses and seminars in educational philopsophy, psychology, teaching strategies, and classroom organization and management. Graduate programs create opportunities for professional development by enhancing students' knowledge and their repertoire of instructional and administrative skills.

Just the facts...

Grand Valley State University
School of Education
One Campus Drive
Allendale, MI 49401-9403
(616) 895-2091
Website: www.gvsu.edu
Profile: Suburban, Large, Co-Ed
UG Tuition: $146.00/cr. hr. in-state; $151.00/cr. hr. out-of-state
G Tuition: $162.00/cr. hr. in-state; $330.00/cr. hr. out-of-state
Off Campus Programs: Yes

Clinical Experiences

Early exposure to classroom practices helps candidates better understand what a career in teaching would be like. Grand Valley has a long tradition of offering intensive field opportunities under the guidance of faculty mentors. Candidates have between two and four semesters of hands-on opportunities in school classrooms. These experiences help candidates become competent and confident professionals when they begin their careers.

Noteworthy

Teacher Education is a medium-sized program comfortably housed in one wing of a new building. It offers small classes, close faculty contact, and active student organizations. Several scholarships are available to full-time and part-time students. The Minority Teacher Education Center also offers financial assistance, summer internships, and academic support for students interested in urban teaching careers. Unique opportunities for post-baccalaureate licensure are also available for a select cohort at the graduate level, in addition to a wide range of education master's degrees.

Teacher Preparation Program Information

The following programs are 4 year programs:
Elementary Education (Foreign Language, Language Arts, Mathematics, Science, Social Studies), K-12 Education (Art, Music, Physical Education), Middle School Education (English, Foreign Language, Mathematics, Science, Social Studies), Secondary Education (Art, Biology, Chemistry, Earth Science, Economics, English/Language Arts, Foreign Language, Geography, Health, Mathematics, Physical Education, Physics, Political Science, Psychology, Social Studies, Sociology), Special Education (Hearing Impaired, Mentally Impaired, Severe Behavioral Disabilities/Handicaps)

The following programs are post-baccalaureate programs:
Elementary Education (Foreign Language, Language Arts, Mathematics, Science, Social Studies), K-12 Education (Art, Music, Physical Education), Middle School Education (English, Foreign Language, Mathematics, Science, Social Studies), Secondary Education (Art, Biology, Chemistry, Earth Science, Economics, English/Language Arts, Foreign Language, Geography, Health, Mathematics, Physical Education, Physics, Political Science, Psychology, Social Studies, Sociology), Special Education (Hearing Impaired, Mentally Impaired, Severe Behavioral Disabilities/Handicaps)

Hope College

The Teacher Education Program at Hope College is developmental; it recognizes that students come to the program with varying degrees of readiness, experience and resolve, rather like an uncut gem—rough around the edges, but brimming with possibility. Students encounter courses that are keyed to three different levels—choosing teaching, learning how to teach, and applying teaching. The Teacher Education Program is intertwined with the general education liberal arts program of the College. Candidates explore their own learning styles and belief systems in order to verify their calling to the profession.

Just the facts...

Hope College
Education Department
41 Graves Place
P.O. Box 9000
Holland, MI 49422-9000
(616) 395-7740
Website: www.hope.edu
Profile: Urban, Small, Co-Ed
UG Tuition: $7,690.00/semester
Off Campus Programs: No

Clinical Experiences

Beginning with the first education class, teacher candidates have co-requisite field placement experiences that are integrated with the college coursework. This enables prospective teachers to connect research and theory to professional practice. Prior to student teaching, candidates complete 120-150 hours in field placements. Student teaching is eleven weeks of full-time teaching. Special Education majors have two student teaching semesters, one in general education and the other in special education. Candidates in the field are guided by a dedicated and skilled group of mentor teachers in area schools.

Noteworthy

The Education Department has developed a unique program which brings two area public school teachers on campus as Half-Time Professors. These teachers bring their expertise in special education and secondary education to the college classroom on a daily basis while teaching half-time in their K-12 school assignments. May term opportunities take candidates to Liverpool, England, Rosebud Indian Reservation in South Dakota, or rural Northern Michigan to teach for three weeks in local schools. Candidates also have leadership opportunities in on-campus professional organizations.

Teacher Preparation Program Information

The following programs are 4 year programs:

Elementary Education (English, Fine Arts, Language Arts, Science, Social Studies, Spanish), K-12 Education (Art, Dance, Music, Physical Education), Secondary Education (Biology, Chemistry, Spanish, Latin, Earth Science, English, French, German, History, Mathematics, Physical Education, Physics, Political Science, Social Studies), Special Education (Learning Disability, Emotionally Impaired)

The following programs are post-baccalaureate programs:

Elementary Education (English, Fine Arts, Language Arts, Science, Social Studies, Spanish), K-12 Education (Art, Dance, Music, Physical Education), Secondary Education (Biology, Chemistry, Spanish, Latin, Earth Science, English, French, German, History, Mathematics, Physical Education, Physics, Political Science, Social Studies), Special Education (Learning Disability, Emotionally Impaired)

Madonna University

Madonna University was founded in 1937 by the Felician Sisters of Livonia, Michigan, as a liberal arts college committed to public service. Consistent with the University's mission, teachers are prepared for both public and private schools. Madonna University stresses Christian humanistic values, intellectual inquiry, and a respect for diversity. The Teacher Education program strives to prepare teachers for today's schools who are caring, competent, and professional.

Just the facts...

Madonna University
Education Department
36600 Schoolcraft Road
Livonia, MI 48150-1173
(734) 432-5655
Website: www.munet.edu
Profile: Suburban, Medium, Co-Ed
UG Tuition: $207.00/credit hour
G Tuition: $260.00/credit hour
Off Campus Programs: No

Clinical Experiences

Madonna University's teacher education program integrates field experiences and classroom instruction at every level. Program candidates are required to successfully complete a field experience course prior to formal admission to the program. Subsequent field experiences require contact with culturally diverse students and students with special needs. Candidates must successfully complete a teaching practicum prior to admission to the student teaching practicum; a university supervisor observes candidate performance. Student teaching is fifteen weeks in length for initial licensure.

Noteworthy

Madonna's teacher education program is proud of its reputation as a rigorous program for preservice teachers. Over the last decade, Madonna has developed quality master's level programs in Educational Leadership, Literacy Education, and Learning Disabilities. Madonna has offered a unique bilingual residential program for Taiwanese teachers in Educational Leadership. Last year, Madonna (in collaboration with the Archdiocese of Detroit) introduced a new master's program in Catholic School Leadership.

Teacher Preparation Program Information

The following programs are 4 year programs:

Early Childhood Education, Elementary Education (Elementary Education K-6, Language Arts, Mathematics, Science, Social Studies), K-12 Education (Art, Japanese, Music, Reading), Secondary Education (Art, Biology, Chemistry, Consumer & Family Science/Home Economics, English/Language Arts, Spanish, General Science, History, Journalism, Mathematics, Music, Occupational Work, Physics, Political Science, Science, Social Studies, Sociology, Speech, Trade & Industrial, Vocational Health Occupation, Vocational Home Economics/Consumer Homemaking, Vocational Trade & Industrial)

The following programs are post-baccalaureate programs:

Elementary Education (Elementary Education K-6, Language Arts, Mathematics, Science, Social Studies), K-12 Education (Art, Japanese, Music, Reading), Literacy Education, Middle School Education (5-8 Certification, English, Spanish, General Science, Language Arts, Mathematics, Music, Science, Social Studies, Speech, Visual Arts), Secondary Education (Art, Biology, Chemistry, Consumer & Family Science/Home Economics, English/Language Arts, Spanish, General Science, History, Journalism, Mathematics, Music, Occupational Work, Physics, Political Science, Science, Social Studies, Sociology, Speech, Trade & Industrial, Vocational Health Occupation, Vocational Home Economics/Consumer Homemaking, Vocational Trade & Industrial), Special Education (Learning Disabilities)

Marygrove College

Marygrove's goals of competence, compassion, and commitment are also the requisite attributes of an effective teacher. The education programs seek to combine technical skill and knowledge with guided experiences that, together, will foster educational professionalism. Marygrove challenges students to be self-directed learners, to adapt to changes, and to foster understanding and sensitivity to issues of diversity. Teacher candidates are invited to use their deepening understanding of themselves as learners and as future teachers to share their insights with each other and with the faculty so that the entire learning community can grow.

Just the facts...

Marygrove College
8425 West McNichols Road
Detroit, MI 48221
(313) 927-1457
Website: www.marygrove.edu
Profile: Urban, Medium, Co-Ed
UG Tuition: $347.00/credit hour
G Tuition: $347.00/credit hour
Off Campus Programs: No

Clinical Experiences

Prospective teachers take their first clinical experience in conjunction with the course "The Teaching Profession" in an elementary or secondary school setting. Appropriate field experiences are included in all methods courses. All candidates student teach for fifteen weeks. An additional ten-week full-time professional lab experience is required for special education and/or child development majors.

Noteworthy

The Marygrove Griots program was launched to increase the number of African American male teachers in Detroit schools. *Griot* is the West African word for storyteller. The program began in 1998, targeting African American males who had earned bachelor's degrees and were seeking teacher licensure. Benefits of the program include a weekend college format (allowing students to substitute teach or maintain their current employment while attending classes), "on-the-job" student teaching, and a mentor program. In the fall of 1999, Marygrove will welcome transfer students as well as a new class of post-baccalaureate students to the Griot program.

Teacher Preparation Program Information

The following programs are 4 year programs:
Elementary Education (Art, Early Childhood, Dance, English, French, General Science, Humanities, Language Arts, Mathematics, Music, Social Studies, Special Education), Secondary Education (Art, Biology, Chemistry, Computer Information Systems, Dance, Economics, English, French, History, Humanities, Mathematics, Music, Political Science, Social Studies, Special Education)

The following programs are post-baccalaureate programs:
Marygrove Griots Program (see *Noteworthy* for details)

Northern Michigan University

Northern Michigan University's teacher education faculty are committed to developing an academic community in which prospective teachers may demonstrate the knowledge and skills needed to become reflective and effective decision makers and practitioners. This philosophy is derived from the premise that teachers must be educated in the arts and sciences, be articulate communicators, serve for the common good, love learning, and seek knowledge about themselves.

Just the facts...

Northern Michigan University
Department of Education
1401 Presque Isle
Marquette, MI 49855-5348
(906) 227-2728
Website: www.nmu.edu
Profile: Rural, Medium, Co-Ed
UG Tuition: $112.00/cr. hr. in-state; $210.00/cr. hr. out-of-state
G Tuition: $135.00/cr. hr. in-state; $215.00/cr. hr. out-of-state
Off Campus Programs: No

Clinical Experiences

Candidates observe and work with children in area school classrooms for at least 33 hours early in the program. Advanced candidates have additional opportunities in nearly every education class for work with students one-on-one and in groups. Several education classes meet in assigned classrooms in area schools to observe good teaching, to enhance opportunities to collaborate with practicing teachers, and to provide ample opportunities to apply what's being learned with school children.

Noteworthy

Methods courses are blocked over two semesters. Instructors work in teams to (1) connect the subject matter in each course in ways which enable candidates to see connections among subjects; (2) model collaborative teaching; (3) provide opportunities for candidates to apply what they are learning in elementary classrooms; and (4) provide a smooth transition into the student teaching experience. Graduates have an exceptionally good record in passing mandatory subject area tests. They have scored above the statewide average on MTTC tests in 29 of the 33 majors and minors offered.

Teacher Preparation Program Information

The following programs are 4 year programs:

Elementary Education (English, Language Arts, Mathematics, Science, Social Studies), K-12 Education (Art, Computer Science, Music, Physical Education), Secondary Education (Art, Biology, Business, Chemistry, Computer Science, Earth Science, Economics, English/Language Arts, French, General Science, Geography, Health, Mathematics, Physical Education, Physics, Political Science, Psychology, Social Studies, Sociology, Spanish), Special Education (Mentally Impaired)

The following programs are post-baccalaureate programs:

Elementary Education (English, Language Arts, Mathematics, Science, Social Studies), K-12 Education (Art, Computer Science, Music, Physical Education), Secondary Education (Art, Biology, Business, Chemistry, Computer Science, Earth Science, Economics, English/Language Arts, French, General Science, Geography, Health, Mathematics, Physical Education, Physics, Political Science, Psychology, Social Studies, Sociology, Spanish), Special Education (Mentally Impaired)

Oakland University

The School of Education and Human Services at Oakland University provides many innovative educational programs for undergraduate and graduate study. The educational programs provide a strong theoretical knowledge base plus experiential learning opportunities so that graduates are extremely well prepared for their chosen professional area. Fundamental to Oakland's program is the concept of a team approach to education and school improvement. Partnership initiatives between university and urban and rural school personnel benefit area K-12 educators and provide candidates with a model of the 21st century educator.

Just the facts...

Oakland University
School of Education
Rochester, MI 48309-4494
(248) 370-3050
Website: www.oakland.edu
Profile: Suburban, Large, Co-Ed
UG Tuition: $115.25/cr. hr. in-state; $339.50/cr. hr. out-of-state
G Tuition: $214.20/cr. hr. in-state; $474.15/cr. hr. out-of-state
Off Campus Programs: Yes

Clinical Experiences

Elementary education candidates have four or more field experiences for a minimum of thirty hours each prior to student teaching. Student teaching is fifteen weeks, full-time, under the supervision of a cooperating teacher and a university supervisor. Secondary education candidates have two field experiences prior to student teaching. Student teaching consists of a full academic year (September through June) with a minimum teaching assignment of two class periods in the fall semester and three class periods in the winter semester.

Noteworthy

Faculty and staff are involved in urban partnerships with many individual schools and in collaborative efforts with two school districts, including an urban teacher licensure program in Pontiac and the Oak Park Business Education Alliance. Faculty contribute to the advancement of new knowledge in their fields through action research, service in professional organizations, publishing in journals, and providing consultation to area professionals. The school sponsors the North American Center for Teacher Training in New Zealand's Beginning School Mathematics program, a Reading Recovery program, the Institute for Action Research, the Lowry Child Development Center, and two career counseling centers.

Teacher Preparation Program Information

The following programs are 4 year programs:
Elementary Education

The following programs are post-baccalaureate programs:
Elementary Education (Language Arts, Mathematics, Science, Social Studies)

The following programs are 5 year programs:
K-12 Education (Music), Secondary Education (Biology, Chemistry, English/Language Arts, French, German, History, Mathematics, Physics, Spanish)

Saginaw Valley State University

The mission of the College of Education at Saginaw Valley State University is to prepare teacher candidates in initial teacher preparation and advanced programs. Initial programs include elementary education, secondary education, special education (emotionally impaired and learning disabled), and an endorsement in bilingual education. Advanced programs include Master of Arts in Teaching degrees in elementary, middle school, and secondary classroom teaching, early childhood education, special education, reading education, math and science education, and Master of Education degrees in administration and supervision. At both coursework levels, candidates engage in clinical and field-based experiences.

Clinical Experiences

Clinical experiences are a vital component of Saginaw Valley State University's teacher preparation program. Candidates engage in early and in-depth field components in urban, suburban, and rural settings in the service area of the university. All professional courses require extensive fieldwork as part of the course requirements. Preservice teachers work with K-12 students through tutoring, through interview experiences, and by preparing lessons and teaching. Supervision of candidates during these experiences is fulfilled by tenured classroom teachers, the College of Education's team of clinical field supervisors, and professional coursework professors.

Just the facts...

Saginaw Valley State University
College of Education
2250 Pierce Road
University Center, MI 48710-0001
(517) 790-5648
Website: www.svsu.edu
Profile: Rural, Medium, Co-Ed
UG Tuition: $118.15/cr. hr. in-state; $215.50/cr. hr. out-of-state
G Tuition: $158.50/cr. hr. in-state; $311.30/cr. hr. out-of-state
Off Campus Programs: No

Noteworthy

The Saginaw Valley State University College of Education offers its students a wide range of support services and enrichment opportunities—specialized advising, a Math/Science Center, Teacher Resource Center, Early Childhood Resource Center, up-to-date computer labs, and courses offered through interactive television. Recently, the College of Education Building became the official home for the Society for the Preservation of Michigan Special Education History. This center is believed to be a one-of-a-kind collection of historical memorabilia for special education in the United States.

Teacher Preparation Program Information

The following programs are 4 year programs:
Elementary Education K-6, K-12 Education (Art, French, Music, Physical Education/Health, Spanish), Secondary Education (Art, Biology, Chemistry, English, French, History, Mathematics, Physical Education, Physics, Science, Spanish, Speech)

The following programs are post-baccalaureate programs:
Elementary Education K-6, K-12 Education (Art, French, Music, Physical Education/Health, Spanish), Secondary Education (Art, Biology, Chemistry, English, French, History, Mathematics, Physical Education, Physics, Science, Spanish, Speech)

The following programs are 5 year programs:
Special Education (Emotional Conflict, Learning Disabilities)

Spring Arbor College

Spring Arbor, an evangelical Christian college affiliated with the Free Methodist Church, is committed to academic excellence. Through the influence of an affirming academic community where a faculty of Christian scholars integrates faith with experiential learning, students develop intellectually, grow as persons, and are challenged by the call to vibrant Christian service. The Teacher Certification Program seeks to give its students a grasp of key concepts and teaching skills, based on psychological and sociological principles applied to the theory and practice of teaching.

Just the facts...

Spring Arbor College
School of Education
106 Main Street
Spring Arbor, MI 49283
(517) 750-6409
Website: www.arbor.edu
Profile: Suburban, Small, Co-Ed
UG Tuition: $5,500.00/semester
G Tuition: $200.00/credit hour
Off Campus Programs: Yes

Clinical Experiences

Education candidates are required to complete 120 hours of pre-student teaching experiences through the completion of an introduction to teaching course and a field experience seminar. Candidates gain experience through observing and participating in P-12 schools. Clinical and field experiences assist candidates in becoming reflective practitioners and provide a forum for discussion of issues related to the profession of teaching. All experiences prepare Spring Arbor College student teachers for a highly successful internship.

Noteworthy

Spring Arbor College is actively involved in site-based methods courses. Many candidates learn their methodology for the teaching of reading and language arts, science, math, and social studies in actual P-8 settings. Numerous partnerships exist with area schools to enhance the learning of both college interns and the P-8 students. Noting the success of the P-8 site-based methods courses, the School of Education is developing a similar approach for the secondary program. The School of Education has added new courses to the curriculum focusing on instructional technology and the diverse learner. Spring Arbor will soon be seeking NCATE accreditation for its advanced programs.

Teacher Preparation Program Information

The following programs are 4 year programs:

Early Childhood Education, Elementary Education, K-12 Education (Art, Music, Spanish), Secondary Education (Art, Biology, Chemistry, English/Language Arts, Mathematics, Physical Education, Physics, Political Science, Psychology, Social Studies)

The following programs are post-baccalaureate programs:

Early Childhood Education, Elementary Education, K-12 Education (Art, Music, Spanish), Secondary Education (Art, Biology, Chemistry, English/Language Arts, Mathematics, Physical Education, Physics, Political Science, Psychology, Social Studies)

Wayne State University

Wayne State University is committed to excellence in the preparation of urban educators who are reflective, innovative professionals. The College of Education prepares candidates who have the commitment and competence to help people acquire the knowledge, skills, and understanding necessary to establish successful careers in a complex, changing society. The College has a long history of involvement in schools, agencies, and institutions that employ its graduates. All of its programs are aligned with current research findings, professional and specialty area standards, and policies of the Michigan Department of Education.

Clinical Experiences

Candidates complete two to four field experiences depending on their program area. Elementary candidates are in schools five half-days a week for two semesters of pre-student teaching, followed by one semester of full-day student teaching. Secondary candidates have one semester of pre-student teaching followed by a semester of student teaching. Special education, early childhood, and bilingual education candidates have two semesters of pre-student teaching and two semesters of student teaching. An instructor on-site teaches a co-requisite class and observes candidates as they work with students.

Just the facts...

Wayne State University
College of Education
Detroit, MI 48202-3489
(313) 577-1605
Website: www.coe.wayne.edu
Profile: Urban, Large, Co-Ed
UG Tuition: $111.00/cr. hr. in-state; $251.00/cr. hr. out-of-state
G Tuition: $178.00/ cr. hr. in-state; $370.00/cr. hr. out-of-state
Off Campus Programs: No

Noteworthy

Wayne State is located in the heart of Detroit's metropolitan cultural center, which offers ethnic diversity, world-renowned historical and cultural exhibitions, and a variety of research and educational opportunities for candidates. A wide variety of scholarships and work opportunities are available. Computer laboratories, a curriculum services center, a video-editing suite, a research support lab for assisting faculty and candidates in conducting research, and a counseling center are available resources for candidates.

Teacher Preparation Program Information

The following programs are 4 year programs:
Early Childhood Education, Elementary Education (English, French, Language Arts, Mathematics, Science, Social Studies, Spanish), K-12 Education (Art, Dance, Music, Physical Education), Secondary Education (Biology, Business, Chemistry, Home Economics, Economics, English, General Science, Geography, Geology, Mathematics, Physical Education, Physics, Political Science, Science, Social Studies, Trade & Industrial, Vocational Business Office, Vocational Health Occupation, Vocational Home Economics/Consumer Homemaking), Special Education (Mentally Impaired)

The following programs are post-baccalaureate programs:
Elementary Education, Secondary Education

The following programs are 5th year programs:
Early Childhood Education, Elementary Education (English, French, Language Arts, Mathematics, Science, Social Studies, Spanish), K-12 Education (Art, Dance, Music, Physical Education), Secondary Education (Biology, Business, Chemistry, Economics, English, French, Geography, Geology, German, Group Science, Home Economics, Italian, Language Arts, Latin, Mathematics, Physical Education, Physics, Political Science, Russian, Science, Spanish, Social Studies, Trade & Industrial, Vocational Business Office, Vocational Health Occupation, Vocational Home Economics/Consumer Homemaking)

Western Michigan University

The teacher educaton programs at Eastern Michigan University prepare educators who are reflective practitioners. Reflective practitioners continually build, examine, and extend knowledge about learners, the content of schooling, and the contexts in which teaching and learning occur while simultaneously renewing teaching practice. Reflective practitioners come to understand over time how to create and modify classroom practices to meet the needs of diverse learners. The goal is to create conditions in which responsible and deliberate teaching and learning can occur.

Just the facts...

Western Michigan University
College of Education
2306 Sangren Hall
Kalamazoo, MI 49008-5190
(616) 387-2960
Website: www.wmich.edu
Profile: Urban, Large, Co-Ed
UG Tuition: $110.95/sem. in-state; $141.75/sem. out-of-state
G Tuition: $281.75/sem. in-state; $344.30/sem. out-of-state
Off Campus Programs: Yes

Clinical Experiences

Clinical experiences are supported by partnerships between the College of Education and school Cluster Sites. A Cluster Site is a real-life laboratory where education candidates can experience the diversity and challenges faced by teachers today. Throughout their coursework, candidates participate in studying, practicing, and reflecting about teaching and learning in the context of partner schools. School district stakeholders collaborate with university faculty, sharing knowledge and understanding about research, curriculum, and practice.

Noteworthy

During student teaching, partnerships with the College of Education and Cluster Sites open doors for collaborative teaching and learning. University faculty and public school teachers meet regularly and contribute to school, district, and college program planning, development, and implementation. At individual Cluster Sites, experienced teachers guide candidates and engage with them in co-teaching, studying, and reflecting on their roles. University supervisors participate in classrooms and with site teachers and candidates to create a community of learners who explore best teaching and learning practices.

Teacher Preparation Program Information

The following programs are 4 year programs:

Early Childhood Education, Elementary Education, K-12 Education (Art, Drama/Theater, Health, Music, Physical Education), Secondary Education (Biology, Business, Chemistry, Consumer & Family Science/Home Economics, Earth Science, English/Language Arts, French, General Science, Geography, German, Health, Latin, Mathematics, Physical Education, Physics, Political Science, Science, Science/Home Economics, Social Studies, Spanish, Trade & Industrial, Vocational Business Office, Vocational Marketing, Vocational Home Economics/Consumer Homemaking, Vocational Trade & Industrial), Special Education (Emotional Conflict, Learning Disability, Mentally Impaired, Speech/Language Disabilities, Visually Impaired)

The following programs are post-baccalaureate programs:

Early Childhood Education, Elementary Education, Middle School Education

Augsburg College

The mission of Augsburg College is to nurture future leaders in service to the world by providing high-quality educational opportunities based in the liberal arts and shaped by the faith and values of the Christian Church in a vital metropolitan setting and an intentionally diverse campus community. The Augsburg College Education Department commits itself to developing future teachers who foster student learning and success by being knowledgeable in their fields, being capable in pedagogy, being ethical in practice, nurturing self-worth, embracing diversity, thinking reflectively, and collaborating effectively.

Just the facts...

Augsburg College
Department of Education
2211 Riverside Avenue
Minneapolis, MN 55454-1351
(612) 330-1130
Website: www.augsburg.edu/education
Profile: Urban, Small, Co-Ed
UG Tuition: $7,311.75/semester
Off Campus Programs: No

Clinical Experiences

Each term, candidates will have a fieldwork placement that is directly tied to the courses they are taking. Prospective teachers are exposed to the rich student diversity in the Minneapolis area. Opportunities also exist for suburban or rural placements and full-year internships. Fieldwork begins in the first semester of study, continues each term, and is designed to create highly skilled teachers.

Noteworthy

The department maintains several "teacher of color" grant programs. Teacher education courses and several secondary education majors are available in a weekend college format. The department has been recognized by the governor of Minnesota and by the American Association of Colleges for Teacher Education for its work in the area of service learning. Recent projects include "Goals 2000" and "America Reads" activities. Teacher candidates prepare a program portfolio before they may progress to student teaching.

Teacher Preparation Program Information

The following programs are 4 year programs:

Elementary Education, K-12 Education (Art, French, German, Health, Music, Physical Education), Middle School Education (Science), Secondary Education (Biology, Chemistry, English/Language Arts, Mathematics, Physical Sciences, Physics, Social Studies, Spanish)

The following programs are post-baccalaureate programs:

Elementary Education, K-12 Education (Art, French, German, Health, Music, Physical Education), Middle School Education (Science), Secondary Education (Biology, Chemistry, English/Language Arts, Mathematics, Physical Sciences, Physics, Social Studies, Spanish)

Bemidji State University

Bemidji State University was founded for the purpose of preparing teachers. This emphasis continues today through the university's commitment to its education students: to provide them with meaningful learning experiences and to prepare them for the educational challenges of the next century. Graduates from Bemidji State University are conversant with issues focusing on teacher competence, accountability, and educational reform; are grounded in a content and pedagogical knowledge base; and are ready to adapt to and use changing technologies in the classroom.

Just the facts...

Bemidji State University
Professional Studies
1500 Birchmont Drive, Northeast
Bemidji, MN 56601
(218) 755-3734
Website: www.bemidji.msus.edu
Profile: Rural, Medium, Co-Ed
UG Tuition: $47.00/cr. hr. in-state; $101.00/cr. hr. out-of-state
Off Campus Programs: Yes

Clinical Experiences

Student teaching and other clinical experience opportunities exist at the pre-kindergarten and kindergarten levels as well as at the elementary, middle, and secondary levels. Fifty-three schools in northern Minnesota offer teacher candidates from Bemidji quality student teaching experiences. Other areas of Minnesota are open to Bemidji's teacher candidates, and teaching abroad programs are available. Additionally, Bemidji State University's internship program provides education majors with an alternative experience that involves a year of student teaching within a four-year program of study.

Noteworthy

Many scholarships are available to teacher candidates at Bemidji. New freshmen may apply for a full-tuition scholarship if they ranked in the top ten percent of their graduating class and achieved an ACT score of 28 or above. The Department of Professional Education offers courses at the Arrowhead University in Hibbing, Grand Rapids, and Virginia (MN), and at Metropolitan State University in Minneapolis and St. Paul. The Class Act Lab School, a program funded by the Minnesota Department of Children, Families, and Learning, offers relevant classroom experiences in public schools beginning in the teacher candidate's first year at Bemidji.

Teacher Preparation Program Information

The following programs are 4 year programs:
Elementary Education, Secondary Education (Biology, Chemistry, Earth Science, English, French, Health, Industrial Technology, Mathematics, Science, Social Studies, Spanish, Theatre)

The following programs are post-baccalaureate programs:
Elementary Education (Early Childhood), Secondary Education (Biology, Chemistry, Earth Science, English, French, Health, Industrial Technology, Mathematics, Science, Social Studies, Spanish, Theatre)

National Council for Accreditation of Teacher Education

Bethel College

Bethel College is a liberal arts college with a decidedly Christian emphasis. Equidistant from the downtown centers of St. Paul and Minneapolis, candidates are easily able to learn by serving others in an urban setting as well as in the surrounding suburbs. As the state of Minnesota adjusts to K-12 graduation standards, Bethel College is preparing teachers to lead "results-oriented" classrooms. Bethel College graduates serve as teachers and administrators across the nation and around the world.

Just the facts...

Bethel College
Education Department
3900 Bethel Drive
Saint Paul, MN 55112
(651) 638-6149
Website: www.bethel.edu
Profile: Suburban, Small, Co-Ed
UG Tuition: $6,920.00/semester
G Tuition: $370.00/credit hour
Off Campus Programs: No

Clinical Experiences

Beginning with the sophomore year, education candidates are involved in a field experience every semester of their enrollment. The initial courses focus on observing the role of the teacher as the instructional leader. Later courses require the candidate to tutor a small group or teach lessons to an entire class. Bethel College is committed to providing real world experiences for pre-professional teachers as they progress toward licensure.

Noteworthy

Bethel College is committed to encouraging candidates to be the most astute scholars and leaders they can be, recognizing that leadership in schools is contingent upon having bright and concerned individuals develop creative solutions to the challenges of life. Ultimately, however, it is the ability to persuade others that produces results. Through service learning activities, candidates are given the chance to influence communities through action as well as words.

Teacher Preparation Program Information

The following programs are 4 year programs:
Early Childhood Education, Elementary Education, K-12 Education (Art, Health, Music, Physical Education), Secondary Education (English/Language Arts, Life Science, Mathematics, Physical Sciences, Social Studies, Spanish)

The following programs are post-baccalaureate programs:
Elementary Education, K-12 Education, Secondary Education

College of St. Benedict & St. John's University

The College of Saint Benedict (CSB) and Saint John's University (SJU) are two liberal arts colleges located in Central Minnesota. CSB is a college for women and SJU is a college for men. The students of these two colleges share a common education, as well as co-educational social, cultural, and spiritual programs. The liberal arts education provided by CSB/SJU is rooted in Catholic and Christian tradition and guided by Benedictine principles, which stress cultivation of the love of God, neighbor, and self through the art of listening, worship, and balanced living. Teacher candidates are broadly educated, have a command of content and pedagogy, demonstrate professionalism, and understand and care about others.

Just the facts...

College of St. Benedict & St. John's University
Education Department
37 South College Avenue
Saint Joseph, MN 56374-2099
(320) 363-5709
Website: www.csbsju.edu
Profile: Rural, Medium, Co-Ed
UG Tuition: $7,712.00/semester
Off Campus Programs: No

Clinical Experiences

Potential teacher candidates who request admittance into the K-6, 5-12, or K-12 education program at CSB/SJU must complete a pre-admission classroom experience which is designed to show them the "real world" of the teaching profession. Often students choose to complete this experience during January Term, which is a three-week period during the month of January when students can complete intensive study in a variety of areas. Candidates are involved in many different educational settings as they take their subject area methods courses (e.g., science, math, reading). Teacher candidates' programs culminate in a sixteen-week student teaching experience prior to graduation.

Noteworthy

The Education Department at CSB/SJU enjoys a very positive reputation in the state of Minnesota. When students and graduates are asked to evaluate their preparation for teaching, they invariably give credit to the faculty members of the department and state that they are the program's greatest asset. Principals and supervisors/mentors of CSB/SJU education graduates are constantly impressed with the preparation of those who are hired into their schools. The placement rate of education graduates is consistently high and is currently at 96 percent.

Teacher Preparation Program Information

The following programs are 4 year programs:

Elementary Education (Elementary Education K-6), K-12 Education (Art, French, German, Music, Spanish), Secondary Education (Biology, Chemistry, English/Language Arts, Mathematics, Physics, Social Studies)

The following programs are post-baccalaureate programs:

Elementary Education (Elementary Education K-6), K-12 Education (Art, French, German, Music, Spanish), Secondary Education (Biology, Chemistry, English/Language Arts, Mathematics, Physics, Social Studies)

National Council for Accreditation of Teacher Education

College of Saint Catherine

The College of Saint Catherine is a Catholic, liberal arts college for women with a focus on developing leadership qualities within a social justice mission and a strong intellectual tradition. Extending the college's mission, the education department's programs prepare effective educators by integrating the liberal arts within the professional sequence, providing a theoretical and clinical foundation in education methodology, developing ethical leaders with a global perspective, and fostering dispositions for lifelong learning.

Just the facts...

College of Saint Catherine
Education Department
2004 Randolph Avenue
Saint Paul, MN 55105
(651) 690-6610
Website: www.stkate.edu
Profile: Urban, Medium, Women
UG Tuition: $440.00/credit hour
G Tuition: $350.00/credit hour
Off Campus Programs: No

Clinical Experiences

Before being formally admitted to the education sequence, candidates complete at least 30 hours of fieldwork in a school setting. The entry-level fieldwork is completed in an introduction to education course, which includes classroom observation, tutoring individuals or small groups, and assisting the classroom teacher. Additional fieldwork experiences take place during the more advanced education methods courses. Student teaching, which is ten weeks in duration, occurs after a candidate has completed all of the methods courses.

Noteworthy

The College of Saint Catherine is situated on 110 acres in the middle of a residential area in the city of St. Paul in Minnesota. Because the College is located in an urban area, there are many fieldwork and student teaching environments from which to choose, including urban, suburban, rural, public, and private schools. This diversity allows a rich variety of experiences for education candidates. As the largest Catholic women's college in the country, St. Catherine provides a special spiritual and ethical grounding that prepares its graduates to lead and influence others.

Teacher Preparation Program Information

The following programs are 4 year programs:
Early Childhood Education, Elementary Education, K-12 Education (Art, Music, Physical Education), Kindergarten Education, Secondary Education (Art, Biology, Chemistry, Consumer & Family Science/Home Economics, English/Language Arts, Mathematics, Physical Education, Physical Sciences, Physics, Science/Home Economics, Social Studies)

The following programs are post-baccalaureate programs:
Early Childhood Education, Elementary Education, K-12 Education (Art, Music, Physical Education), Kindergarten Education, Secondary Education (Art, Biology, Chemistry, Consumer & Family Science/Home Economics, English/Language Arts, Mathematics, Physical Education, Physical Sciences, Physics, Science/Home Economics, Social Studies)

Concordia College

Concordia College has a long history of teacher preparation. With more than twenty percent of its student body seeking licensure to teach, teacher education is a significant part of the campus. All candidates complete a strong liberal arts component. This emphasis on both the professional and the liberal arts aspects of teacher education recognizes the intellectual and the spiritual responsibilities of the teacher. Concordia provides schools with teachers who are highly competent in subject matter knowledge and methods of effective teaching, and who approach their profession with a sense of Christian vocation.

Just the facts...

Concordia College
Department of Education
901 South Eighth Street
Moorhead, MN 56562
(218) 299-3910
Website: www.cord.edu
Profile: Suburban, Small, Co-Ed
UG Tuition: $6,275.00/semester
Off Campus Programs: No

Clinical Experiences

Every component of the teacher preparation program at Concordia College includes clinical and practical experiences and includes opportunities to work in diverse settings. Candidates have multiple options for student teaching, including programs on reservations, urban student teaching, and overseas experiences in Europe and the Pacific Rim. The annual May Seminar Abroad allows candidates to complete clinical experiences in Europe and to compare education in other countries with that in the United States.

Noteworthy

The methods program for elementary and middle school foreign languages, offered each summer, attracts teachers from around the country to study methodologies for teaching foreign languages at those grade levels and to gain licensure. Of note are significant collaborations with area schools and the integration of global education throughout the teacher preparation program.

Teacher Preparation Program Information

The following programs are 4 year programs:

Elementary Education (Elementary Education K-6), K-12 Education (Art, French, German, Latin, Music, Physical Education, Russian, Spanish), Kindergarten Education, Secondary Education (Art, Biology, Business, Chemistry, Consumer & Family Science/Home Economics, Earth Science, English/Language Arts, French, German, Spanish, Health, Mathematics, Music, Physical Education, Physical Sciences, Physics, Social Studies, Speech, Vocational Home Economics/Consumer Homemaking)

Concordia University

The mission of Concordia University, St. Paul, a university of The Lutheran Church—Missouri Synod, is to prepare students for thoughtful and informed living, for dedicated service to God and humanity, and for enlightened care of God's creation. Teacher education at Concordia University focuses on teaching as a decision-making activity, viewed both as a process and a result that empowers new educators to know what they do and why they do it. Personal and professional decisions reflect candidates' theoretical knowledge, subject matter knowledge, teaching skills, and attitude.

Just the facts...

Concordia University
College of Education
275 North Syndicate Street
Saint Paul, MN 55104
(651) 641-8200
Website: www.csp.edu
Profile: Urban, Small, Co-Ed
UG Tuition: $9,401.00/semester
G Tuition: $200.00/credit hour
Off Campus Programs: No

Clinical Experiences

Prior to admission, candidates must submit a portfolio and be formally interviewed. Teacher candidates are required to complete two student teaching experiences. The first experience is coordinated with teaching methods. During this semester, candidates are in classes half of the day and in teaching situations the other half of the day. This semester is arranged so candidates receive both a morning and afternoon teaching experience. The second experience is a ten-week, full-day student teaching position. Student teachers are required to complete an action-research project during this semester.

Noteworthy

Concordia University recently initiated a BA completion/teacher licensure program for paraeducators. The goal of this program will be to meet the growing needs of Southeast Asians, Latinos, and other minority groups. Concordia University offers a special program geared to working adults. This program, Teacher Education at Convenient Hours (TEACH), enables candidates to attend afternoon and evening classes. Candidates also student teach. This program is provided to all candidates in any of the post-baccalaureate programs.

Teacher Preparation Program Information

The following programs are 4 year programs:
Early Childhood Education, Elementary Education, K-12 Education (Art, Music, Physical Education), Secondary Education (English/Language Arts, Life Science, Mathematics, Social Studies)

The following programs are post-baccalaureate programs:
Early Childhood Education, Elementary Education, K-12 Education (Art, Music, Physical Education), Kindergarten Education, Middle School Education, Secondary Education (English/Language Arts, Life Science, Mathematics, Social Studies)

The following programs are 5th year programs:
Early Childhood Education (MA in Education emphasis)

Gustavus Adolphus College

Gustavas Adolphus teacher education programs are held in high regard as being successful and progressive. Core values include service, democracy, interdisciplinary learning, reflective growth, and collaborative teaching. The teacher education programs rely on a sound liberal arts education, focused learning within a disciplinary emphasis, and carefully articulated and highly experiential professional preparation in teaching. Candidates develop personal philosophies and an extensive repertoire of instructional strategies, and work with students from diverse age groups, cultures, and ability levels.

Just the facts...

Gustavus Adolphus College
Department of Education
800 West College Avenue
Saint Peter, MN 56082
(507) 933-7457
Website: www.gac.edu
Profile: Rural, Small, Co-Ed
UG Tuition: $460.00/credit hour
Off Campus Programs: No

Clinical Experiences

Clinical experiences are integrated throughout Gustavus' teacher education programs. A month-long, full-time experience begins candidates' programs. Practicum experiences are a part of all blocked courses. Two service-learning requirements (one with students with disabilities and one with students from diverse cultures), and a fourteen-week student teaching experience are also part of candidates' programs. Candidates are placed in Gustavus partnership schools in urban, suburban, and rural communities. Part of the student teaching experience may be completed abroad.

Noteworthy

Gustavus has an array of school partnerships. The Gustavus program is a selective, high-quality program with clear and well-articulated goals for candidates. The Department of Education supports students who want to study and travel internationally. "English School and Family" is a January term course that involves a month of study in schools and homes in England. International student teaching options to such places as Australia, England, and New Zealand also are selected by some candidates. Placement rates for graduates are very high.

Teacher Preparation Program Information
The following programs are 4 year programs:
Elementary Education, K-12 Education (Art, Drama/Theater, French, German, Music, Physical Education, Spanish), Secondary Education (Biology, Chemistry, Communication Arts/Literature, Earth & Space Science, Health, Mathematics, Physics, Social Studies, Theatre/Dance)

Hamline University

Hamline's education department has adopted the theme of "developing reflective practice in an urban, multicultural context" for its teacher preparation programs. The education department believes that future teachers educated in this context will be better prepared to teach in a variety of settings. In this way, the education program serves as a bridge to teaching in urban, rural, suburban, and international educational environments. Teacher candidates do not major in education, but complete a full liberal arts major in the field of their choice. Completion of the professional education sequence, taken in addition to the major, leads to a Minnesota teaching license.

Just the facts...

Hamline University
Department of Education
1536 Hewitt Avenue
Saint Paul, MN 55104
(651) 523-2241
Website: www.hamline.edu
Profile: Urban, Medium, Co-Ed
UG Tuition: $7,560.00/semester
Off Campus Programs: Yes

Clinical Experiences

Hamline is committed to building reflective practice through an urban, multicultural field-based program. Clinical experiences are integrated throughout the program and are closely tied to the sequence of courses leading to a teaching license. Candidates are assigned as teachers' assistants and tutors in the core courses of the program, in clinicals that range between 32 and 35 hours over eight or ten weeks. Micro teaching experiences are tied to the methods courses and student teaching ranges between twelve and sixteen weeks.

Noteworthy

The teacher education program at Hamline assures that candidates are able to incorporate national and state standards into their instruction upon completion of the program. Candidates learn to use technology as a tool for teaching and learning in Hamline's Teacher Education Technology and Curriculum Center. The program takes advantage of Hamline's location in St. Paul-Minneapolis, and the rich diversity that characterizes these cities. Candidates are able to further develop their skill in working with diverse student populations by taking part in the HOST program, which allows candidates to complete a portion of their student teaching overseas.

Teacher Preparation Program Information

The following programs are 4 year programs:
Elementary Education, K-12 Education (Music, Physical Education), Secondary Education (Biology, Chemistry, English/Language Arts, French, German, Mathematics, Physics, Social Studies, Spanish)

The following programs are post-baccalaureate programs:
Elementary Education, K-12 Education (ESL, Music, Physical Education), Secondary Education (Biology, Chemistry, English/Language Arts, French, German, Mathematics, Physics, Social Studies, Spanish)

Minnesota State University, Mankato

The College of Education at Minnesota State University, Mankato prepares professionals to function effectively within complex systems marked by diversity, interdependence, and accelerating change. These professionals practice reflective inquiry. The programs involve collaborative relationships between interdisciplinary general education and the academic disciplines. Teacher candidates acquire professional skills and knowledge. All programs within the College of Education are structured around national standards, and emphasize demonstration of current knowledge in educational technology.

Just the facts...

Minnesota State University, Mankato (formerly Mankato State Univ.)
College of Education
MSU Box 52
P.O. Box 8400
Mankato, MN 56002-8400
(507) 389-5445
Website: www.mankato.msus.edu
Profile: Suburban, Large, Co-Ed
UG Tuition: $83.85/sem. in-state; $187.45/sem. out-of-state
G Tuition: $128.15/sem. in-state; $202.80/sem. out-of-state
Off Campus Programs: Yes

Clinical Experiences

Clinical experiences begin with the first course in the teacher education program. Candidates continue this applied experience at increasing levels of responsibility throughout their professional preparation. Experiences with school-age children in culturally diverse and inclusive educational settings are required. Student teachers are clustered in school settings for enhanced supervision and collegiality. Professional internship components are also an area of emphasis within Minnesota State University, Mankato's graduate progams preparing school administrators, library media specialists, and special educators.

Noteworthy

The Center for School-University Partnerships collaborates with sixteen area K-12 school districts, sponsoring major school improvement initiatives and providing a highly successful intern-mentor program for beginning teachers. This school-university partnership continues in the area of instructional technology through the Electronic Academy and three major distance learning programs. The college houses one of the nation's few graduate programs in experiential education. Minnesota State University, Mankato's Children's House is an accredited regional day care/preschool facility.

Teacher Preparation Program Information

The following programs are 4 year programs:
Elementary Education (Art, Computer Science, Mathematics, Music, Physical Education, Science, Social Studies), K-12 Education (Art, Health, Music, Physical Education), Middle School Education (Science), Secondary Education (Consumer & Family Science/Home Economics, Earth Science, English/Language Arts, French, General Science, German, Life Science, Mathematics, Physical Sciences, Social Studies, Spanish, Speech, Technology Education)

The following programs are post-baccalaureate programs:
Early Childhood Education, K-12 Education (Reading), Kindergarten Education, Middle School Education (English, Mathematics, Science, Social Studies), Special Education (Adaptive Physical Education, Early Childhood, Learning Disability, Moderate & Severe Disabilities, Severely Behavioral Disabilities/Handicaps)

The following programs are 5 year programs:
K-12 Education (Art, Health, Music, Physical Education), Secondary Education (Consumer & Family Science/Home Economics, Earth Science, English/Language Arts, French, General Science, German, Life Science, Mathematics, Physical Sciences, Social Studies, Spanish, Speech, Technology Education), Special Education (Adaptive Physical Education, Early Childhood)

Moorhead State University

Moorhead State University offers baccalaureate and master's degrees in the art and science of teaching. The mission of the teacher education unit at MSU is to prepare future teachers who are literate, grounded in the liberal studies, skilled in instruction, and dedicated to inclusive education for all learners. Graduates are characterized by their commitment to lifelong learning. They will provide leadership that maximizes their students' opportunity to participate in a technological, diverse, and rapidly changing society.

Just the facts...

Moorhead State University
College of Education and Human Services
1104 7th Avenue South
Moorhead, MN 56563
(218) 236-2095
Website: www.moorhead.msus.edu
Profile: Suburban, Medium, Co-Ed
UG Tuition: $100.53/cr. hr. in-state; $204.26/cr. hr. out-of-state
G Tuition: $145.23/cr. hr. in-state; $219.83/cr. hr. out-of-state
Off Campus Programs: No

Clinical Experiences

All teacher candidates have at least a 40-hour sophomore experience, an 80-hour junior experience, and a 400-hour student teaching experience. In practice, many candidates complete additional field experiences plus many classroom observations. Virtually all field experiences in the unit have a concurrent class that significantly increases the quality of the learning experience, allowing for reflection by candidates and feedback from both the course instructor and the candidates' peers.

Noteworthy

Education programs at MSU allow candidates to explore teaching through both the traditional experiences and innovative and exemplary centers for learning. These include the MSU Regional Science Center devoted to environmental study, a nationally recognized Early Education Center, state-of-the-art technology, an outstanding Curriculum Library, the nation's largest Student Teaching Abroad program, and field experience opportunities across the state and the nation.

Teacher Preparation Program Information

The following programs are 4 year programs:
Early Childhood Education, Elementary Education, K-12 Education (Art, ESL, Drama/Theater, Health, Music, Physical Education, Reading, Spanish), Secondary Education (Biology, Chemistry, English/Language Arts, General Science, Health, Mathematics, Physical Sciences, Physics, Science, Social Studies), Special Education (Developmental Disabilities/Handicaps, Early Childhood, Emotional/Behavioral Disorders, Learning Disability, Multiple Disabilities/Handicaps, Physical and Health Disorders)

The following programs are post-baccalaureate programs:
Kindergarten Education, Special Education (Adaptive Physical Education, Developmental Disabilities/Handicaps, Early Childhood, Learning Disability, Multiple Disabilities/Handicaps, Severe Behavioral Disabilities/Handicaps)

The following programs are 5th year programs:
Early Childhood Education, Elementary Education, Special Education

Saint Cloud State University

Saint Cloud State University's College of Education prepares high-quality teachers, administrators, scholars, and other school, community, and business professionals. The College of Education prepares transformative professional educators—educators who are open to life-long learning; cultivate and use higher order thinking; are positive and proactive in addressing life's opportunities, problems, and challenges; and contribute meaningfully to the evolution of democratic society. As candidates are prepared to become transformative professional educators, they will participate in designing their learning opportunities, take responsibility for their own learning, and work with faculty and peers to assess their progress.

Clinical Experiences

The College of Education has a long and rich history in pioneering field-related professional experiences. Supervised, professional clinical experiences are integral to the development of professional educators. Candidates enrolled in teacher preparation programs are involved early and often in varied field settings including urban, suburban, and rural sites across Minnesota. Additional opportunities for student teaching exist in Arizona and several international sites. Various models of field experiences are available for teacher candidates ranging from traditional ten-week experiences to year-long internships.

Just the facts...

Saint Cloud State University
College of Education
720 Fourth Avenue South
Saint Cloud, MN 56301-4498
(320) 255-3023
Website: http://condor.stcloudstate.edu
Profile: Suburban, Large, Co-Ed
UG Tuition: $82.80/sem. in-state; $186.50/sem. out-of-state
G Tuition: $127.00/sem. in-state; $201.00/sem. out-of-state
Off Campus Programs: No

Noteworthy

A number of unique programs exist at Saint Cloud State including a Teacher of Color Program, Urban Teaching partnerships, international opportunities, and faculty and student exchanges at an international level. In 1998, the College of Education received an award from the American Association of Colleges for Teacher Education for best practice in support of diversity and multiculturalism. Saint Cloud State University offers the best of both worlds—a campus that's big enough to support excellent faculty, resources, and programs, yet small enough to offer students the opportunity to develop and grow in a closely knit community.

Teacher Preparation Program Information

The following programs are 4 year programs:
Early Childhood Education, Elementary Education, K-12 Education (Art, Drama/Theater, French, German, Health, Industrial Technology, Music, Physical Education, Spanish), Kindergarten Education, Secondary Education (Biology, Chemistry, Earth Science, English/Language Arts, General Science, Mathematics, Physics, Social Studies), Special Education (Developmental Disabilities/Handicaps, Learning Disability, Severe Behavioral Disabilities/Handicaps)

The following programs are post-baccalaureate programs:
Early Childhood Education, Kindergarten Education, Middle School Education (English, Mathematics, Science, Social Studies), Special Education (Early Childhood)

The following programs are 5th year programs:
Early Childhood Education, Special Education (Developmental Disabilities/Handicaps, Early Childhood, Learning Disability, Severe Behavioral Disabilities/Handicaps)

Saint Olaf College

Graduates of Saint Olaf's teacher education program have participated in studies and experiences in professional education, liberal arts, and a concentrated study within at least one major field. The Department of Education emphasizes both the professional and liberal arts aspects of teacher education. Because the intellectual and spiritual responsibilities of the teacher are so great, Saint Olaf strives to prepare teachers who are professional, of the highest competence in subject matter and techniques, and who approach their profession with dedication and conviction.

Just the facts...

Saint Olaf College
Department of Education
Northfield, MN 55057-1098
(507) 646-3245
Website: www.stolaf.edu
Profile: Rural, Small, Co-Ed
UG Tuition: $7,435.00/semester
Off Campus Programs: No

Clinical Experiences

Every candidate is required to complete 40-60 hours of clinical preservice experience in a K-12 setting and twelve weeks of student teaching. Preservice sites are centered primarily in area schools, but include opportunities in suburban and urban sites in St. Paul-Minneapolis. Saint Olaf has ten student teaching centers (four urban, four suburban, two rural) within 50 miles of campus, an urban cooperative option with the Associated Colleges of the Midwest in Chicago, a bilingual Spanish option in Texas, and four international options in India, Hong Kong, and Korea.

Noteworthy

Saint Olaf offers a unique January Interim clinical practicum program. The January Interim program for sophomores places them in schools and classrooms of their choice and is intended to assist them in deciding if teaching is for them. Three additional January Interim programs place candidates in multicultural environments in Chicago, Minneapolis, or Hawaii. These interim programs are led by faculty and provide intensive practicum experiences and seminars.

Teacher Preparation Program Information

The following programs are 4 year programs:
K-12 Education (Art, Dance, ESL, French, German, Latin, Music, Physical Education, Spanish), Secondary Education (Biology, Chemistry, English/Language Arts, Mathematics, Physics, Social Studies)

The following programs are 5 year programs:
Elementary Education (*cooperative with University of St. Thomas in St. Paul, Minnesota—four and a half year program*)

University of Minnesota—Duluth

The University of Minnesota—Duluth (UMD) provides undergraduate degrees in early childhood, elementary, and secondary education; licensure programs in special education; and graduate programs in psychology, communication disorders, and early childhood and special education. The College of Education and Human Service Professions emphasizes reflection, diversity, collaboration, and empowerment. The College opened a new professional development lab school in fall 1998 with an arts integration focus, and plans to research the impact of integrating the arts into academic core areas.

Just the facts...

University of Minnesota—Duluth
College of Education and Human Service Professions
10 University Drive
Duluth, MN 55812-2496
(218) 726-7131
Website: www.d.umn.edu/cehspsa/
Profile: Urban, Medium, Co-Ed
UG Tuition: $1,500.00/quart. in-state; $4,000.00/quart. out-of-state
G Tuition: $1,710.00/quart. in-state; $3,350.00/quart. out-of-state
Off Campus Programs: No

Clinical Experiences

Clinical experiences are an integral part of many courses in UMD's education programs. In the early childhood, elementary, and special education programs, candidates are in field-based practica for a minimum of one year while they are completing education coursework prior to their student teaching experience. Candidates may be placed for student teaching in rural schools in northern Minnesota, in urban schools in St. Paul-Minneapolis, or abroad in countries such as New Zealand and Sweden.

Noteworthy

The education program at UMD has an endowed professorship in American Indian Education and a strong commitment to preparing teachers to work with American Indian students and families. Faculty model collaboration by team-teaching, and several have won outstanding teaching awards. The education faculty members are leaders in using technology in teaching courses on campus as well as in distance learning. The campus provides support for undergraduate candidates for research opportunities in collaboration with faculty. Scholarship support is available to increase the number of candidates of color. UMD will move to a semester-based system in fall 1999.

Teacher Preparation Program Information

The following programs are 4 year programs:
Early Childhood Education, Elementary Education (Elementary Education K-6), K-12 Education (Art, Music, Physical Education), Middle School Education (Science), Secondary Education (Biology, Earth Science, English/Language Arts, French, German, Health, Mathematics, Physical Sciences, Social Studies, Spanish), Special Education (Communication Disorders)

The following programs are post-baccalaureate programs:
Early Childhood Education, Elementary Education (Elementary Education K-6), K-12 Education (Art, ESL, Music, Physical Education), Middle School Education (Science), Secondary Education (Biology, Earth Science, English/Language Arts, French, German, Health, Mathematics, Physical Sciences, Social Studies, Spanish), Special Education (Communication Disorders, Learning Disability, Severe Behavioral Disabilities/Handicaps)

The following programs are 5th year programs:
Special Education (Communication Disorders)

University of Minnesota at Morris

At the University of Minnesota at Morris candidates can pursue the study of education and its role in society (separate from teacher licensure programs); complete a major and teaching licensure in elementary education; prepare to teach one or more liberal arts subjects at the secondary school level; and/or prepare for graduate study in education. Division of Education programs are enhanced through faculty commitment to personalized instruction, use of current instruction technologies, and opportunities for student and faculty participation in multicultural and international educational experiences.

Just the facts...

The University of Minnesota at Morris
Division of Education
East 4th Street and College Avenue
Morris, MN 56267
(320) 589-6400
Website: www.mrs.umn.edu
Profile: Rural, Small, Co-Ed
UG Tuition: $93.90/quarter in-state; $277.00/quarter out-of-state
Off Campus Programs: No

Clinical Experiences

During student teaching, the Division assures that candidates have experiences in cultural settings different from those with which they are familiar. Approximately two-thirds of candidates complete their student teaching outside of the university's local service area. Approximately one-half of candidates teach in Asia, Africa, Eastern and Western Europe, and Central and South America. Placements are also available in several cities in the United States. Student teaching offers candidates an opportunity to develop professional talents, an understanding of alternative approaches to educational practice, and an appreciation of different cultural lifestyles.

Noteworthy

Global Student Teaching is a signature program of the University of Minnesota at Morris. Through this program, and in cooperation with other colleges, the university offers teacher education students from many colleges the opportunity to complete their teaching practice in different communities in the United States and throughout the world.

Teacher Preparation Program Information

The following programs are 4 year programs:
Elementary Education, K-12 Education (Art, Music), Secondary Education (Biology, Chemistry, Earth Science, English, French, German, Life Science, Mathematics, Physical Sciences, Social Science, Spanish, Speech, Speech/Theatre, Theatre Arts)

The following programs are post-baccalaureate programs:
Elementary Education, K-12 Education (Art, Music), Kindergarten Education, Secondary Education (Biology, Chemistry, Earth Science, English, French, German, Life Science, Mathematics, Physical Sciences, Social Science, Spanish, Speech, Speech/Theatre, Theatre Arts)

University of Minnesota—Twin Cities

Teacher education has been central to the mission of the College of Education and Human Development since its founding in 1905. The college is committed to preparing professionals who assume leadership positions at the local, state, national, and international levels. As an urban land-grant institution, the University of Minnesota uses its teacher education programs as a vehicle for advancing the reform of educational practice in Minnesota and preparing educators to work in classrooms of students with diverse abilities, creeds, languages, nationalities, races, and economic backgrounds.

Just the facts...

University of Minnesota—Twin Cities
College of Education and Human Development
178 Pillsbury Drive, Southeast
104 Burton Hall
Minneapolis, MN 55455-0211
(612) 625-6501
Website: www.coled.umn.edu
Profile: Urban, Large, Co-Ed
UG Tuition: $90.65/cr. hr. in-state; $267.45/cr. hr. out-of-state
G Tuition: $123.70/cr. hr. in-state; $247.40/cr. hr. out-of-state
Off Campus Programs: No

Clinical Experiences

Clinical experiences comprise one-third of the initial licensure program. Along with the foundations of education and content pedagogy, the in-school experiences are designed to develop the knowledge, skills, and abilities necessary for beginning teachers and are included throughout the program. The college works closely with the schools and teachers to assist preservice teachers as they take on increasing responsibilities within the classrooms. Throughout their clinical experiences, candidates engage in reflection on their teaching strengths as well as areas for improvement.

Noteworthy

The teacher preparation programs require candidates to enter the college with completed baccalaureate degrees in the content area. The college operates twelve- to fifteen-month cohort programs designed to prepare educators who can adapt to and lead change in both urban and rural educational settings. The college supports collaborative partnerships with a range of agencies in addition to school partners, including community, health, social work, and businesses. University of Minnesota graduates are sought for their high level of preparation, quality of teaching, and leadership abilities.

Teacher Preparation Program Information

The following programs are 4 year programs:
K-12 Education (Music), Secondary Education (Agriculture)

The following programs are post-baccalaureate programs:
Kindergarten Education, Middle School Education, Special Education

The following programs are 5th year programs:
Early Childhood Education, Elementary Education, K-12 Education (Art, Chinese, Industrial Technology, Physical Education, Second Languages and Cultures [ESL, French, German, Italian, Japanese, Russian, Spanish]), Secondary Education (Agriculture, Consumer & Family Science/Home Economics, Earth Science, English/Language Arts, Life Science, Mathematics, Physical Sciences, Social Studies)

University of Saint Thomas

The School of Education at the University of Saint Thomas develops creative, reflective educators dedicated to the success of all learners. Since 1885, Saint Thomas has been a leader in offering values-centered, career-oriented eduation. Saint Thomas prepares teachers who are continuing learners, global citizens, scholarly professionals, instructional leaders, curriculum specialists, effective communicators, and collaborative agents of change. Advanced education programs in curriculum, special education, and administration prepare leaders for a rapidly changing and increasingly complex society.

Just the facts...

University of Saint Thomas
School of Education
2115 Summitt Avenue
Mail #CHC 131
Saint Paul, MN 55105-1096
(651) 962-5200
Website: www.soe.stthomas.edu/websoew/
Profile: Urban, Large, Co-Ed
UG Tuition: $492.00/credit hour
G Tuition: $321.00/credit hour
Off Campus Programs: Yes

Clinical Experiences

Candidates gain hands-on experience in K-12 classrooms at three stages of the program. During extensive clinical experiences at the beginning and middle of each program, candidates observe and orient themselves to classroom teaching. The capstone of the program is an intensive student teaching experience. Candidates benefit from Saint Thomas' long-standing ties to K-12 schools. New school-university partnerships include a lab school collaboration with an innovative K-12 magnet school opening adjacent to Saint Thomas.

Noteworthy

In 1999, the School of Education will move to a new, state-of-the-art facility in downtown Minneapolis. The building will provide technology-rich classrooms, a fully-developed curriculum lab, an award-winning children's literature collection, and a home for a new children's literature quarterly. Candidates benefit from being part of a diverse urban learning community—with programs for new teachers and for seasoned educators, for candidates in gifted and special education, leadership, and learning technology—without sacrificing personal attention and service.

Teacher Preparation Program Information

The following programs are 4 year programs:
Elementary Education, K-12 Education (French, German, Spanish, Health, Physical Education, Reading), Kindergarten Education, Secondary Education (Biology, Earth Science, English/Language Arts, Mathematics, Physical Sciences, Physics, Social Studies, Speech, Speech/Theatre)

The following programs are post-baccalaureate programs:
Elementary Education, K-12 Education (French, German, Spanish, Health, Physical Education), Kindergarten Education, Secondary Education (Biology, Earth Science, English/Language Arts, Mathematics, Physical Sciences, Physics, Social Studies, Speech, Speech/Theatre)

The following programs are 5 year programs:
Elementary Education, K-12 Education (French, German, Spanish, Health, Physical Education), Kindergarten Education, Secondary Education (Biology, Earth Science, English/Language Arts, Mathematics, Physical Sciences, Physics, Social Studies, Speech, Speech/Theatre)

The following programs are 5th year programs:
Elementary Education, K-12 Education (French, German, Spanish, Health, Physical Education), Kindergarten Education, Secondary Education (Biology, English/Language Arts, Mathematics, Physical Sciences, Physics, Social Studies, Speech, Speech/Theatre)

Winona State University

First home of the National Education Association, Winona State University is the oldest teacher preparation institution west of the Mississippi. In Ernest Boyer's *Smart Parents Guide to College* (1996), WSU was cited as a model institution for helping good teachers become better teachers. Recently, WSU was mentioned as one of the best college buys in *The Student Guide to America's Best College Buys* (1997-1998). WSU's graduates enter their professional roles with the essential knowledge, skills, experiences, critical insights, and inquiry necessary to be effective educators committed to career-long professionalism.

Just the facts...

Winona State University
College of Education
Winona, MN 55987-5838
(507) 457-5570
Website: www.winona.msus.edu
Profile: Rural, Medium, Co-Ed
UG Tuition: $84.10/cr. hr. in-state; $188.35/cr. hr. out-of-state
G Tuition: $129.15/cr. hr. in-state; $203.95/cr. hr. out-of-state
Off Campus Programs: Yes

Clinical Experiences

Teacher candidates engage in a broad array of field experiences, beginning as early as their first year in the program, with the intent of exposing them to the many roles and responsibilities of teachers, and the many rewards and realities of teaching. Experiences occur both in schools and in the community, and include working with students in an urban and a rural setting. Teacher candidates also have opportunities to work with students from different cultures and student with exceptionalities. Candidates may also choose to enter a field-based program at the Rochester campus.

Noteworthy

The College of Education offers several unique programs and initiatives. Since the fall of 1998, all of WSU's students have had the opportunity to participate in the Laptop University project called LUNIAC (Laptop Universal Access). The eventual goal for this project is for every student to have a laptop computer, updated software, and 24-hour access to the Internet. WSU students also have access to an electronic portfolio service called WINGS (Winona Graduate Skills). The electronic portfolio contains the usual information about education, employment experience, and references, but can also contain photography, charts, sound, animation, and video.

Teacher Preparation Program Information

The following programs are 4 year programs:
Elementary Education, K-12 Education (Art, French, German, Health, Music, Physical Education, Spanish, Speech), Middle School Education (Science), Secondary Education (Business, Earth Science, English/Language Arts, Life Science, Mathematics, Physical Sciences, Social Studies), Special Education (Developmental Disabilities/Handicaps, Learning Disability)

The following programs are 5th year programs:
Special Education (Developmental Disabilities/Handicaps, Learning Disability)

Alcorn State University

The primary objectives of the School of Education and Psychology at Alcorn State are to identify and attract people of intellectual and moral integrity; to promote content competency in teaching and sound scholarship through a series of specialized courses and experiences; to develop in prospective teachers a broad understanding of the learner and the teaching-learning process; to guide and supervise teacher candidates through a series of professional laboratory experiences culminating with directed teaching; and to provide the teacher education student and non-teaching student with formal and informal educational experiences that will enable them to develop a meaningful philosophy of education.

Clinical Experiences

The teacher education unit selects field experiences, including student teaching and internships, to provide candidates with meaningful learning experiences. Candidates are placed in school settings in which cultural differences due to race, socioeconomic status, sex, urban/rural settings, and geographic location are evident. Candidates enrolled in the teacher education unit are involved in early field-based experiences at the initial level and internships and practicum experiences at the advanced level.

Just the facts...

Alcorn State University
School of Education and Psychology
P.O. Box 989
Lorman, MS 39096
(601) 877-6149
Website: www.alcorn.edu
Profile: Rural, Medium, Co-Ed
UG Tuition: $1,254.63/sem. in-state; $1,358.88/sem. out-of-state
G Tuition: $713.11/sem. in-state; $882.61/sem. out-of-state
Off Campus Programs: No

Noteworthy

Support services, such as the Center for Excellence in Teacher Education, the Curriculum Resource Center, the Media Center in the library, and various computer laboratories and resource centers throughout the university contain equipment and materials essential to support teaching and scholarship. Some of these facilities have been recently upgraded and are equipped with various on-line research indices and multimedia equipment.

Teacher Preparation Program Information

The following programs are 4 year programs:
Elementary Education (Elementary Education K-6, Elementary Education K-8), K-12 Education (Industrial Technology, Physical Education, Physical Education/Health), Secondary Education (Agriculture, Biology, Bookkeeping, Business, Chemistry, English/Language Arts, Health, History, Mathematics, Music, Physical Education, Trade & Industrial, Vocational Home Economics/Consumer Homemaking, Vocational/Industry Arts, Vocational Trade & Industrial), Special Education (Learning Disability, Mental Retardation, Multiple Disabilities/Handicaps)

The following programs are post-baccalaureate programs:
Elementary Education (Elementary Education K-6, Elementary Education K-8), K-12 Education (Physical Education), Secondary Education (Health, Physical Education), Special Education (Learning Disability, Mental Retardation, Multiple Disabilities/Handicaps)

Delta State University

Delta State University was founded in 1924 as a teachers college. In addition to the original Bachelor of Science degree in Education, education degrees include preparation for teaching in the sciences, arts, music, and business. Advanced training for school personnel is also offered. All programs prepare graduates to function professionally as they address societal, educational, and personal needs. The School of Education operates collaboratively with the other schools of the university, university staff, and outside agencies to produce graduates who will be effective in the field of human learning and services. Faculty demonstrate the professional competencies and skills expected of teacher candidates.

Just the facts...

Delta State University
School of Education
P.O. Box 3121
Cleveland, MS 38733
(601) 846-4400
Website: www.deltast.edu
Profile: Rural, Medium, Co-Ed
UG Tuition: $1,298.00/sem. in-state; $2,773.00/sem. out-of-state
G Tuition: $1,298.00/sem. in-state; $2,773.00/sem. out-of-state
Off Campus Programs: No

Clinical Experiences

Arrangements with area schools provide pre-teaching school visits and placement of student teachers, interns, and students doing practicum work. University supervision is provided during all clinical and laboratory experiences. Those preparing to teach in secondary schools receive supervision from both education and content area faculty. Full-time master's level administrator preparation students spend 38 weeks in clinical experiences that are integrated with leadership instruction.

Noteworthy

The School of Education hosts a 34-member educational consortium, the Delta Area Association for the Improvement of Schools (DAAIS), that encompasses the geographic region of Mississippi known as the Delta. All activities of DAAIS are the result of collaboration among school districts, Delta State University, the Mississippi Department of Education, and other entities that have an interest in education in the Delta. School of Education faculty and staff provide leadership for the majority of professional development activities and technical assistance provided through DAAIS.

Teacher Preparation Program Information

The following programs are 4 year programs:

Elementary Education (Elementary Education K-8), K-12 Education (Art, Music, Physical Education/Health), Secondary Education (Biology, Consumer & Family Science/Home Economics, English/Language Arts, French, German, Mathematics, Physical Sciences, Social Studies, Spanish), Special Education (Mild Learning/Behavioral Disability, Severe Behavioral Disabilities/Handicaps)

Jackson State University

Jackson State University, a public, co-educational institution, seeks to develop persons who can and will assume prominent roles in societal growth and change, and who view effective education as indispensable to the well-being of society. The university attracts academically gifted and non-traditional students who pursue programs in such fields as business, education, science, and technology. It is committed to providing quality instruction that will guide students in acquiring essential knowledge and skills. The School of Education believes that effective education requires responsive education. The teacher education program ensures that graduates are able to use appropriate teaching strategies.

Clinical Experiences

Clinical and field-based experiences are designed for all professional roles and are planned, evaluated, and modified based on findings from research questions. They stimulate teacher candidates' interests and include observations, hands-on activities, research, and practice teaching. Candidates are provided opportunities to test and confirm their interests while developing new skills and enhancing existing skills and talents through a systematic five-level process ranging from 40 to 420 hours. Candidates are guided by mentors and university, school, and agency personnel in a variety of settings and clinical schools.

Just the facts...

Jackson State University
School of Education
1400 John R. Lynch Street
Jackson, MS 39217
(601) 968-2433
Website: www.jsums.edu
Profile: Urban, Medium, Co-Ed
UG Tuition: $1,344.00/sem. in-state; $2,773.00/sem. out-of-state
G Tuition: $1,344.00/sem. in-state; $2,773.00/sem. out-of-state
Off Campus Programs: No

Noteworthy

The School of Education features an outstanding faculty, prepares trainers of Reading Recovery, and assists schools through its Regional Service Center, consortia, and partnerships. Teacher candidates have access to the latest technology and individualized services provided through the School of Education's Center for Excellence, computer laboratories, technology laboratory, electronic classroom for distance learning, teaching and learning center, and student support services. Graduates are placed in schools and agencies throughout the nation. Teacher scholarships are available.

Teacher Preparation Program Information

The following programs are 4 year programs:
Elementary Education (Elementary Education K-8), K-12 Education (Health, Music, Physical Education), Secondary Education (Biology, Business, Chemistry, English, Mathematics, Science, Social Studies, Speech, Technology Education), Special Education (Gifted/Talented, Hearing Impaired, Mild Learning/Behavioral Disability, Physical Disabilities/Handicaps)

The following programs are post-baccalaureate programs:
Secondary Education (Computer Science, Driver Ed/Safety, French, Spanish)

The following programs are 5th year programs:
Early Childhood Education, K-12 Education (Reading)

Millsaps College

The Millsaps College Teacher Education Program emphasizes leadership, scholarship, and research in service. The program strives to develop teachers who can integrate theory and practice and who can think critically about their practice. The program introduces candidates to the variety of opportunities the profession offers for service. The importance of the liberal arts in education, the need for reflection on teaching and professional practice, and the belief that the competent teacher education graduate is one who can think, act, and teach in a morally responsible manner are integrated throughout the Millsaps College Teacher Education Program.

Just the facts...

Millsaps College
Department of Education
1701 North State Street
Jackson, MS 39201-001
(601) 974-1353
Website: www.millsaps.edu
Profile: Urban, Small, Co-Ed
UG Tuition: $9,394.00/semester
Off Campus Programs: No

Clinical Experiences

Carefully crafted and supervised field experiences are distinctive features of Millsaps College Teacher Education. Each course emphasizes the importance of scholarship and competence in teaching and is designed to cultivate candidate knowledge of his or her chosen discipline, child development, school culture, and professional attitude and conduct. Clinical experiences are characterized by on-site classroom experience, interactions with school personnel, research and study of school culture, course lecture and discussion, and peer and self-performance-based evaluation.

Noteworthy

Teacher education leads to initial licensure in Elementary Education, Secondary Education, Art Education, Music Education, and Performing Arts Education. A candidate may elect to complete additional courses to be eligible to receive supplemental licensure in Special Education, Computer Applications, Remedial Reading, and Gifted Education. Millsaps prides itself on its emphasis on active learning, liberal arts, counseling and mentoring, and self-assessment.

Teacher Preparation Program Information

The following programs are 4 year programs:

Elementary Education, K-12 Education (Art, Drama/Theater, French, Latin, Music, Spanish), Secondary Education (Biology, Chemistry, Earth Science, English/Language Arts, General Science, Mathematics, Physics, Social Studies)

Mississippi College

The mission of the Mississippi College School of Education is to provide a caring Christian environment where teacher candidates acquire knowledge in the behavioral sciences, teaching and learning, and health and human sciences. The School of Education provides the general education, professional studies, field and clinical experience, research skill development, and technological foundation required for each graduate and undergraduate program. These components generate the knowledge, dispositions, and skills necessary to render appropriate services to God and others in a professional environment while meeting all local, state, and national performance standards.

Just the facts...

Mississippi College
School of Education
Box 4009
Clinton, MS 39058
(601) 925-3250
Website: www.education.mc.edu
Profile: Rural, Medium, Co-Ed
UG Tuition: $263.00/credit hour
G Tuition: $276.00/credit hour
Off Campus Programs: No

Clinical Experiences

Clinical experiences at Mississippi College begin with a pre-teaching field experience that is taken as a co-requisite course with the first professional education course. The clinical experiences are an integral part of professional education courses. The clinical experiences are located in culturally diverse educational environments within a fifty-mile radius of the campus that includes the metropolitan Jackson area. Student teaching is for a full semester and includes seminars and classroom management activities.

Noteworthy

Mississippi College offers scholarships for candidates in the School of Education. Programs integrate the use of computers and other technology in the classroom. Clinical and field experiences for elementary and special education candidates have been redesigned into a sequential program including reading and content/methods blocks that lead into a professional semester. The directed teaching experience has been expanded from twelve to sixteen weeks. The Mississippi College Teacher Assistant Program (MCTAP) has been recognized by Recruiting New Teachers, Inc. as an exemplary model for recruiting and preparing minority candidates for service in high need areas.

Teacher Preparation Program Information

The following programs are 4 year programs:

Elementary Education, K-12 Education (Art, Music), Secondary Education (Biology, Business, Chemistry, Computer Science, Consumer & Family Science/Home Economics, English, French, Mathematics, Physics, Social Studies, Spanish, Speech), Special Education (Mild/Moderate Handicapped)

Mississippi State University

The first course in education at Mississippi State University (MSU) was taught 96 years ago in 1903. Since then, the alumni of what is now the College of Education at MSU have become educational leaders and advocates for excellence in Mississippi's public schools and classrooms. Approximately 24 percent of all Mississippians licensed to practice their profession in a public school are graduates of the College of Education. Approximately 60 percent of the university's bachelor level teacher education graduates are employed in Mississippi public schools within a year of graduation. Over three-fourths of the alumni of the College of Education are employed in educational agencies or institutions.

Just the facts...

Mississippi State University
College of Education
P.O. Box 9710
Mississippi State, MS 39762-9710
(601) 325-3717
Website: www.msstate.edu
Profile: Rural, Large, Co-Ed
UG Tuition: $125.75/cr. hr. in-state; $129.25/cr. hr. out-of-state
G Tuition: $167.50/cr. hr. in-state; $172.25/cr. hr. out-of-state
Off Campus Programs: Yes

Clinical Experiences

Every student in the College of Education takes classes focused on preparing them for the world of practice. Teacher candidates at MSU participate in pre-student teaching field-based methods classes. Student teaching is the culminating field experience of the teacher education program in which teacher candidates work full-time for sixteen weeks in a placement with one school supervisor or full-time in two eight-week placements with different age groups and two school supervisors. A requirement for all students in clinical courses is the completion of a professional portfolio documenting and demonstrating their knowledge and skills.

Noteworthy

The College of Education is the university's third-largest college and offers the university's largest undergraduate major (elementary education) and graduate major (counselor education). The Mississippi Public Education Forum recognized the Elementary Education Senior Block Field Experience with a 1996 Award for Excellence. The College of Education Center for Educational Partnerships works with over two-thirds of the state's school districts on projects such as the Writing/Thinking Project, the Mississippi World Class Teacher Project, the Educational Design Institute, and the America Reads Project. External funds for research exceed $8 million.

Teacher Preparation Program Information

The following programs are 4 year programs:

Elementary Education, K-12 Education (Music, Physical Education), Secondary Education (Agriculture, Biology, Chemistry, Consumer & Family Science/Home Economics, English/Language Arts, French, General Science, German, Mathematics, Physics, Social Studies, Spanish), Special Education, Technology Education

Mississippi University for Women

The Mississippi University for Women has prepared teachers since 1885. MUW prepares teachers who can make decisions that promote student learning. Candidates learn about human development and the process of learning in teacher preparation programs that emphasize the individual and cultural differences among learners. Graduates of MUW's teacher education programs learn to reflect critically and creatively on their own knowledge and performance, and they actively seek out continued professional growth.

Just the facts...

Mississippi University for Women
Division of Education and Human Science
P.O. Box W-1637
Columbus, MS 39701
(601) 329-7175
Website: www.muw.edu
Profile: Rural, Medium, Co-Ed
UG Tuition: $106.50/cr. hr. in-state; $231.00/cr. hr. out-of-state
G Tuition: $142.00/cr. hr. in-state; $308.00/cr. hr. out-of-state
Off Campus Programs: Yes

Clinical Experiences

Mississippi University for Women's field-based experiences are planned so that the knowledge, theories, and practices taught in the teacher education courses are applied in meaningful ways throughout the program. Candidates begin the series of four levels of field experience in the introductory education course and conclude with the fourteen-week student teaching experience. This sequence of experiences moves candidates from identifying the decisions that teachers make to making instructional and management decisions themselves. All field experiences are in public school settings where candidates are able to observe and work with students who are culturally and racially diverse.

Noteworthy

In its eleventh annual *America's Best Colleges* guide, *U.S. News and World Report* named Mississippi University for Women first among the best public regional liberal arts colleges in the South. For the fourth consecutive year, MUW has ranked in the top five for academic reputation among Southern liberal arts colleges. Teacher candidates at MUW work directly with students at the university's Demonstration School and many other professional development sites in the area. Education majors also have the opportunity to be involved in the Mississippi Hall of Master Teachers, an awards recognition for exemplary public school teachers, and the Institute for First Year Teachers, a support network for beginning teachers.

Teacher Preparation Program Information

The following programs are 4 year programs:
Elementary Education, K-12 Education (Art, Music, Physical Education), Secondary Education (Biology, Chemistry, Consumer & Family Science/Home Economics, English/Language Arts, Mathematics, Social Studies), Special Education

Mississippi Valley State University

In serving the Delta region, Mississippi Valley State University provides educational, cultural, and support services for a diverse population. The institution's impact extends beyond the Delta, however, as evidenced by the achievement of many of its graduates at the state, regional and national level. The faculty at MVSU believes that schools should provide the opportunity, knowledge, and skills for students to become active learners and participants in a democratic society. Teacher candidates at MVSU are not trained to become classroom lecturers. Instead, they become learning guides for students.

Just the facts...

Mississippi Valley State University
Department of Education
14000 Highway 82 West
Itta Bena, MS 38941-1400
(601) 254-3619
Website: www.mvsu.edu
Profile: Rural, Small, Co-Ed
UG Tuition: $72.00/cr. hr. in-state $104.25/cr. hr. out-of-state
G Tuition: $97.00/cr. hr. in-state $139.00/cr. hr. out-of-state
Off Campus Programs: No

Clinical Experiences

Candidates in the education program begin their clinical experiences in their freshman year and are actively involved in practice through senior-year student teaching. Each candidate begins as a teacher's aide, and his or her experiences increase in depth and responsibility as he or she progresses. The early clinical experiences offered by MVSU provide candidates with a real-world view of a classroom, and enable them to make sensible career choices.

Noteworthy

The faculty develops many collaborative ventures with area businesses and public schools. The teacher preparation programs provide many field experiences that expose candidates to rural, Delta classrooms. To respond to the acute teacher shortage in the region, the state of Mississippi has established the William Winter scholarship program which is designed to attract more young people into teaching. The state also offers Critical Needs Teacher Loans/Scholarships, which are written off if participating candidates teach in critical needs areas after graduation.

Teacher Preparation Program Information

The following programs are 4 year programs:
Elementary Education, K-12 Education (Music), Kindergarten Education, Secondary Education (Biology, English/Language Arts, Mathematics, Physical Education, Social Studies)

The following programs are 5th year programs:
Elementary Education, K-12 Education (Music, Physical Education), Secondary Education (Biology, English, Mathematics, Social Studies)

University of Mississippi

Since its creation in 1903, the School of Education has been dedicated to the preparation of effective leaders who serve in schools, homes, and the community. The School of Education promotes critical inquiry, reflection, and social action through interdisciplinary studies. Students, faculty, and staff learn and work in a climate of professional productivity that values relevancy, diversity, involvement, ownership, and accountability. Graduates are prepared to work in a changing and multicultural world in leadership roles in educational programs and institutions, health and social institutions, and the private sector.

Just the facts...

The University of Mississippi
School of Education
University, MS 38677
(601) 232-7063
Website: www.olemiss.edu/depts/educ_school/
Profile: Rural, Medium, Co-Ed
UG Tuition: $1,527.00/sem. in-state; $3,078.00/sem. out-of-state
G Tuition: $1,527.00/sem. in-state; $3,078.00/sem. out-of-state
Off Campus Programs: No

Clinical Experiences

Professional development schools serve as the sites for clinical experiences for the professional education programs. Teachers, principals, and counselors at the PDS sites serve as clinical instructors. Collaboration between professional education faculty and clinical instructors results in seamless professional preparation programs that guide candidates from theory to practice. Teacher candidates begin their professional preparation courses during the junior year of study and participate in intensive field experiences in professional development school sites under the direction of university supervisors and clinical instructors. These experiences culminate in the senior year with a student teaching semester.

Noteworthy

Teacher education majors have the opportunity to participate in the William Winter Loan/Scholarship Program. Funds are provided to Mississippi residents in the form of a low-interest loan. Candidates who teach in Mississippi upon completion of their degree are released from repayment of the loan. In addition, candidates have the opportunity to use the Learning Plus program. This self-paced computer program allows users to diagnose their strengths and weaknesses in reading, writing, and mathematics, and provides supplemental instruction.

Teacher Preparation Program Information

The following programs are 4 year programs:
Elementary Education K-8, K-12 Education (Art, Music, Special Education), Secondary Education (Biology, Chemistry, English, Foreign Languages, Mathematics, Physics, Social Studies)

The following programs are 5th year programs:
Secondary Education (Biology, Chemistry, English, Foreign Languages, Mathematics, Physics, Social Studies)

University of Southern Mississippi

Since 1912, The University of Southern Mississippi has prepared teachers, originally for Mississippi's rural schools. Today, USM educates teachers to teach in some of the fastest growing areas of the Southeast. Graduates serve as classroom teachers, school district personnel, educational leaders, and researchers at both the state and national levels. The university, under its "practitioner-to-scientist" framework, strives to develop graduates who possess theoretical and technical competence, effective communication skills, an appreciation of diversity, a commitment to lifelong learning, and a sensitivity to standards of ethical conduct.

Just the facts...

University of Southern Mississippi
Professional Education Unit
Southern Station, Box 5023
Hattiesburg, MS 39406-5023
(601) 266-4568
Website: www.usm.edu
Profile: Urban, Large, Co-Ed
UG Tuition: $1,435.00/sem. in-state; $2,986.00/sem. out-of-state
G Tuition: $1,435.00/sem. in-state; $2,986.00/sem. out-of-state
Off Campus Programs: Yes

Clinical Experiences

Early clinical experiences encourage candidates to observe the impact of technological and societal changes on schools, and also allow candidates the opportunity to incorporate current technology and multicultural perspectives in practice lessons. Candidates must apply knowledge from coursework during their field experiences, in their teaching portfolios, and in their student teaching. Student teachers complete two experiences with students from different grade levels in a variety of schools with diverse populations. Also, teacher candidates may participate in a clinical setting abroad. Each semester a few student teachers are selected to conduct their supervised field experience in England.

Noteworthy

Critical-needs area scholarships for tuition and board are available for resident and non-resident undergraduates who agree to teach in Mississippi for two to four years. The university's Summer Program for Graduate Education offers master's degree programs that may be completed in two summers along with six or more semester hours of independent study, practica/internship, and/or transfer credit completed outside of the summer sessions. The Career Planning and Placement department conducts annual Education Recruitment Days when school district recruiters throughout the United States come to campus to interview candidates.

Teacher Preparation Program Information

The following programs are 4 year programs:

Elementary Education (Elementary Education K-8), K-12 Education (Art, Computer Instruction, Dance, Health, Music, Physical Education), Secondary Education (Biology, Business, Chemistry, Consumer & Family Science/Home Economics, English/Language Arts, French, General Science, German, Mathematics, Physics, Social Studies, Spanish, Speech, Vocational Trade & Industrial), Special Education (Hearing Impaired)

Central Missouri State University

Central Missouri State University has prepared teachers and other school personnel since 1871. Central's faculty and administration are committed to preparing educators to translate sound theory into effective practice, believing that reflective practice is essential to that process. Central's students experience a strong liberal arts focus in University Studies, which is guided by the university's focus on communicating, thinking, interacting, and valuing. Candidate competencies in these areas are further integrated across the academic majors and professional studies.

Just the facts...

Central Missouri State University
College of Education and Human Services
Lovinger 203
Warrensburg, MO 64093
(660) 543-4272
Website: www.cmsu.edu
Profile: Rural, Large, Co-Ed
UG Tuition: $91.00/cr. hr. in-state; $182.00/cr. hr. out-of-state
G Tuition: $137.00/cr. hr. in-state; $274.00/cr. hr. out-of-state
Off Campus Programs: No

Clinical Experiences

Central provides field experiences to candidates beginning in their sophomore year. Candidates subsequently have multiple field experiences embedded in a variety of courses to connect theory and effective practice. In the junior year, candidates may intern in a professional development school, taking a course or courses designed and taught collaboratively on-site by university and school faculty. Candidates complete the student teaching capstone experience in the senior year.

Noteworthy

Central's four-year program represents a total university commitment to teacher education. Programs are continuously updated to ensure quality. Special attention is given to placing candidates in a variety of school settings with diverse student populations. Candidates enjoy multiple opportunities to learn how to best use technology in teaching and learning. Faculty are successful teachers who enjoy working with students, as do academic and department advisors. Central has an excellent record of graduates securing teaching positions.

Teacher Preparation Program Information

The following programs are 4 year programs:
Early Childhood Education, Elementary Education, Middle School Education (Language Arts, Mathematics, Science, Social Science), K-9 Education (Art, Health, Physical Education), K-12 Education (Art, French, German, Music/Instrumental, Music/Vocal, Physical Education, Spanish), Secondary Education (Agriculture, Art, Business, English, Industrial Technology, Mathematics, Physical Education, Social Science, Speech/Theater, Unified Science/Biology, Unified Science/Chemistry, Unified Science/Earth Science, Unified Science/Physics, Vocational Family & Consumer Science), Special Education (Early Childhood, Mild/Moderate Behavior Disordered, Mild/Moderate Learning Disabled, Mild/Moderate Mentally Handicapped, Severely Developmentally Disabled)

The following programs are post-baccalaureate programs:
Early Childhood Education, Elementary Education, Middle School Education (Language Arts, Mathematics, Science, Social Science), K-9 Education (Art, Health, Physical Education), K-12 Education (Art, French, German, Music/Instrumental, Music/Vocal, Physical Education, Spanish), Secondary Education (Agriculture, Art, Business, English, Industrial Technology, Mathematics, Physical Education, Social Science, Speech/Theater, Unified Science/Biology, Unified Science/Chemistry, Unified Science/Earth Science, Unified Science/Physics, Vocational Family & Consumer Science), Special Education (Early Childhood, Mild/Moderate Behavior Disordered, Mild/Moderate Learning Disabled, Mild/Moderate Mentally Handicapped, Severely Developmentally Disabled)

Drury College

The motto of the Drury College teacher education program is "Dedicated Teachers Make the Difference." At Drury, the preparation of teachers is grounded not only in the academic disciplines, but also in a partnership with the public schools. Drury strives to instill a level of dedication and personal commitment in its graduates. Graduates are reflective, thinking professionals who have a vision of schools as places of energy, creativity, commitment and decency for all children.

Just the facts...

Drury College
Department of Education
900 North Benton
Springfield, MO 65802
(417) 873-7271
Website: www.drury.edu
Profile: Urban, Medium, Co-Ed
UG Tuition: $5,270.00/semester
G Tuition: $170.00/credit hour
Off Campus Programs: Yes

Clinical Experiences

Drury College participates with the Springfield Public School System and the Yale University Child Study Center in the Developmental School Program. Field experiences are concentrated in a center-city elementary and a middle school. Several of the methods courses are taught at the school site. Children from the Development Schools come to the Drury College campus each week for classes in technology, physical education, and academic enrichment. Student teaching is an eleven-week experience.

Noteworthy

The Drury College Center for Pre-College Programs and Gifted Education has fifteen years of service and leadership with gifted students. Each summer, as many as 700 gifted students from five to seventeen years of age study in Drury's gifted programs. The Drury College symposia for teachers of the gifted attracts national leaders as presenters. Drury College is a partner in the Yale University School Development Program. The Gerald Brooks Scholarship provides tuition assistance for minority students seeking initial teacher licensure. The Ollie Allen Graduate Fellowship provides full tuition for minority and international students admitted to the Masters in Education degree program.

Teacher Preparation Program Information

The following programs are 4 year programs:
Elementary Education (Elementary Education K-6), K-12 Education (Art, Music), Secondary Education (Art, Biology, Chemistry, Drama/Theatre, English/Language Arts, French, German, History, Journalism, Music, Physical Education, Physics, Spanish, Speech)

The following programs are post-baccalaureate programs:
Elementary Education (Elementary Education K-6), K-12 Education (Art, Music), Secondary Education (Art, Biology, Chemistry, Drama/Theatre, English/Language Arts, French, German, History, Journalism, Music, Physical Education, Physics, Spanish, Speech)

The following programs are 5th year programs:
Elementary Education (Elementary Education K-6), Middle School Education (5-8 Certification), Advanced Physical Education, Secondary Education, Special Education (Gifted/Talented)

Evangel University

Teacher education is a top priority at Evangel University. The Education Department is the largest academic department at Evangel. Through its programs, the Education Department endeavors to provide for the spiritual, intellectual, cultural, physical, and emotional development of the teacher. The college is committed to a program that prepares caring, committed, and competent teachers who will shape the nation's future. All education majors receive a strong liberal arts background. The Evangel University teacher eduation graduate is one who is dedicated to the improvement of and service to the student, the community, and the world.

Just the facts...

Evangel University
Education Department
1111 North Glenstone
Springfield, MO 65802
(800) EVANGEL
Website: www.evangel.edu
Profile: Urban, Small, Co-Ed
UG Tuition: $4,000.00/semester
Off Campus Programs: No

Clinical Experiences

The clinical experiences of education majors at Evangel University are vital to their preparation as professional educators. All candidates are placed in numerous practicums emphasizing the teaching of math, science, language arts, and social studies. Special placements are provided in daycare settings, Head Start programs, preschools, and special education settings. Evangel's partnership with a local elementary school provides opportunities for tutoring, reading instruction, mentoring, and observation.

Noteworthy

All education majors at Evangel enroll in an educational technology course that includes integration of the Internet in classroom settings, the use of presentation software such as Powerpoint, and the preparation of computer-based, self-instructional packages for students. Candidates demonstrate practical application of these skills; various teaching methods courses throughout the program require development of technology skills. Candidates prepare portfolios that showcase these skills.

Teacher Preparation Program Information

The following programs are 4 year programs:

Early Childhood Education, Elementary Education, K-12 Education (Art, French, Music, Physical Education, Spanish), Middle School Education (English, Mathematics, Science, Social Studies), Secondary Education (Art, Biology, Business, Chemistry, English/Language Arts, General Science, Mathematics, Physical Education, Science, Social Studies, Speech/Drama), Special Education (Learning Disability, Mentally Impaired, Severe Behavioral Disabilities/Handicaps)

The following programs are post-baccalaureate programs:

Early Childhood Education, Elementary Education, K-12 Education (Art, French, Music, Physical Education, Spanish), Middle School Education (English, Mathematics, Science, Social Studies), Secondary Education (Art, Biology, Business, Chemistry, English/Language Arts, General Science, Mathematics, Physical Education, Science, Social Studies, Speech/Drama), Special Education (Learning Disability, Mentally Impaired, Severe Behavioral Disabilities/Handicaps)

Harris-Stowe State College

Harris-Stowe State College, a historically black institution, has prepared classroom teachers for 140 years. The college is located in the heart of St. Louis. The teacher education programs prepare teachers for inner city and suburban schools. The college strives to train effective teachers for a democratic and diverse society. Students are drawn to the rapidly expanding campus from the entire metro St. Louis area. Diverse international groups are also attracted to study in the Harris-Stowe teacher preparation program. The overall program theme "effective teachers for a diverse society" reflects the college's unique history, characteristics, and commitment to training teachers for urban schools in the new millenium.

Just the facts...

Harris-Stowe State College
Teacher Education
3026 Laclede Avenue
Saint Louis, MO 63103
(314) 340-3361
Website: ww.hssc.edu
Profile: Urban, Small, Co-Ed
UG Tuition: $83.00/cr. hr. in-state; $163.51/cr. hr. out-of-state
Off Campus Programs: No

Clinical Experiences

Teacher education programs at Harris-Stowe State College are characterized by site-based or "in-school" experiences at racially and ethnically diverse schools. Many classes are held in schools where cohorts of candidates have the opportunity to integrate theory and practice in classrooms. Student teacher cohorts become members of the school community, participating in staff meetings, parent conferences, and classroom instruction. All teacher candidates are strongly supported and mentored by college faculty, teachers, and school administrators.

Noteworthy

Harris-Stowe State College is a member of the National Network of Educational Renewal in partnership with Maryville University. As a result, unique opportunities—such as student leadership programs—are available to candidates. Other collaborative efforts include classes held at the St. Louis Science Center and the Pathways to Teaching Program. Most teacher candidates receive financial assistance. Technology for the classroom environment is emphasized with hands-on experiences in "smart classrooms" and in a new technology center. Faculty members create personal and supportive relationships with all candidates.

Teacher Preparation Program Information

The following programs are 4 year programs:
Early Childhood Education, Elementary Education, Middle School Education, Secondary Education

The following programs are post-baccalaureate programs:
Middle School Education (Mathematics, Science, Social Studies), Secondary Education (Biology, English/Language Arts, Mathematics, Social Studies), Special Education (Emotional/Behavioral Disability, Gifted/Talented, Learning Disability, Mental Retardation)

Lincoln University

Lincoln University prepares teachers to make professional decisions based on knowledge and best practice. Teacher education at Lincoln focuses on having students learn to plan, implement, and evaluate instruction while keeping in mind the needs of the individual student, the classroom community, and the content appropriate for the age level. The department is committed to using technology effectively in elementary, middle, and secondary classrooms. Candidates compile portfolios composed of papers, video clips, and resources for teaching.

Just the facts...

Lincoln University
Department of Education
820 Chestnut Street
Jefferson City, MO 65102
(573) 681-5250
Website: www.lincolnu.edu
Profile: Rural, Medium, Co-Ed
UG Tuition: $92.00/cr. hr. in-state; $184.00/cr. hr. out-of-state
G Tuition: $117.00/cr. hr. in-state; $234.00/cr. hr. out-of-state
Off Campus Programs: No

Clinical Experiences

Candidates participate in clinical experiences beginning in their sophomore year. Structured experiences are offered in several courses and an individually designed experience of at least fifteen hours must be completed before the junior year. A total of at least 100 hours in school settings is required prior to student teaching. Student teaching is done at two levels (either primary and intermediate, intermediate and middle school, middle school and high school, or elementary and secondary for K-12 majors). Student teaching may be completed in Kansas City or St. Louis with prior agreement.

Noteworthy

Education majors have the opportunity to attend and make presentations at state, regional, and national professional conferences during their tenure at the university. The university's partnerhsip with Scholastic Books, Inc. allows prospective teachers the opportunity to work with the most current curriculum materials.

Teacher Preparation Program Information

The following programs are 4 year programs:

K-12 Education (Art, Music, Physical Education), Secondary Education (Biology, Business, Chemistry, English/Language Arts, General Science, Mathematics, Physics), Special Education (Learning Disability, Mental Retardation)

Maryville University

Maryville University prepares beginning teachers in early childhood, elementary, middle level, secondary, and K-12 art education. The university also offers programs for experienced teachers and those who wish to become administrative leaders in the schools. A strong liberal arts education forms the basis for the preparation of teachers within the School of Education. All programs are designed to enable educators to reflect deeply upon the moral and ethical dimensions of schooling in a social and political democracy.

Just the facts...

Maryville University
School of Education
13550 Conway Road
Saint Louis, MO 63141
(314) 529-9466
Website: www.maryvillestl.edu
Profile: Suburban, Medium, Co-Ed
UG Tuition: $4,740.00/semester
G Tuition: $345.00/credit hour
Off Campus Programs: No

Clinical Experiences

Maryville's Teacher Education programs are highly field-based. A freshman clinical experience is offered for all potential teacher candidates. In the sophomore year, candidates enroll in the first "education block" of coursework which includes clinical experiences three mornings each week. Each subsequent semester, candidates are required to combine clinical experiences with courses on campus. Teacher education candidates typically spend about 300 hours in the field prior to student teaching. The Master of Arts with an emphasis in Secondary Teaching and Inquiry engages candidates in intensive field work.

Noteworthy

Maryville University, together with Harris-Stowe State College and the partner schools of each institution, is a member of the Metropolitan St. Louis Consortium for Educational Renewal. Maryville currently works with four partner/professional schools: an early childhood center, an elementary school, and two high schools. In conjunction with the high schools, Maryville offers a fifth year master's degree in secondary teaching and inquiry that prepares beginning high school teachers in English, social studies, mathematics, and the sciences. Scholarships and loans are available for qualified candidates, especially in mathematics, science, and early childhood education.

Teacher Preparation Program Information

The following programs are 4 year programs:
Elementary Education, K-12 Education (Art), Middle School Education

The following programs are post-baccalaureate programs:
Middle School Education

The following programs are 5 year programs:
Early Childhood Education, Elementary Education, Middle School Education

The following programs are 5th year programs:
Secondary Education (Biology, Chemistry, English/Language Arts, Mathematics, Science, Social Studies)

Missouri Southern State College

The mission of the Teacher Education Department at Missouri Southern State College is to prepare instructional decision makers who teach children to live, play, study, and grow to adulthood in a culturally diverse society. MSSC believes that those who can teach children to adapt and flourish in an ever-changing world will help improve everyone's quality of life. Faculty and staff help teacher candidates (1) identify their values; (2) embrace their responsibility to their future students, to themselves, to the teaching profession, and to society; and (3) develop the knowledge necessary to help their future students reach their full potential.

Just the facts...

Missouri Southern State College
School of Education
3950 East Newman Road
Joplin, MO 64801-1595
(417) 625-9314
Website: www.mssc.edu
Profile: Urban, Medium, Co-Ed
UG Tuition: $73.50/cr. hr. in-state; $147.00/cr. hr. out-of-state
Off Campus Programs: No

Clinical Experiences

Candidates have multiple field opportunities, beginning in the sophomore year. Junior block classes teach candidates to function in a performance-based teacher evaluation (PBTE) system that includes peer and faculty review of practice in micro-teaching labs before a 32 hour internship in area schools. Student teaching builds upon the instructional decision making PBTE program model used in many area schools. All student teachers visit Kansas City to enhance their understanding of urban education and cultural diversity.

Noteworthy

MSSC prides itself on its close faculty/candidate working relationships and the infusion of technology into the teacher education curriculum. Candidates work with application and productivity software and can record their teaching portfolios on CD-ROMs. Employers give positive reviews to graduates from MSSC's teacher education programs; one district gives hiring preference to MSSC's graduates. Placement rates approach 100 percent. MSSC has the lowest tuition in the state, making teacher education at MSSC the best value in Missouri.

Teacher Preparation Program Information

The following programs are 4 year programs:
Early Childhood Education, Elementary Education, K-12 Education (Art, ESL, Music, Physical Education, Reading, Spanish), Middle School Education (English, Mathematics, Science, Social Studies), Secondary Education (Business, English/Language Arts, Mathematics, Social Studies, Speech/Theatre, Unified Science), Special Education (Behavior Disorders, Learning Disability, Cross-Categorical, Mentally Impaired)

The following programs are post-baccalaureate programs:
Early Childhood Education, Elementary Education, K-12 Education (Art, ESL, Music, Physical Education, Reading, Spanish), Middle School Education (English, Mathematics, Science, Social Studies), Secondary Education (Business, English/Language Arts, Mathematics, Social Studies, Speech/Theatre, Unified Science), Special Education (Behavior Disorders, Learning Disability, Cross-Categorical, Mentally Impaired)

Missouri Western State College

The philosophy of the teacher education program at MWSC is "teachers learn to teach by teaching." MWSC's teacher education program is based on three concepts: (1) candidates' early exposure to the profession prior to a firm commitment to the program, (2) the development of instructional and educational expertise under professional guidance, and (3) the integration of theory with actual experience in real teaching situations. MWSC uses this approach to develop well-prepared teachers who have the experience to develop the confidence, poise, and expertise needed to meet the challenges of the profession.

Just the facts...

Missouri Western State College
Education Department
4525 Downs Drive, A 122
Saint Joseph, MO 64507-2294
(816) 271-4332
Website: www.mwsu.edu
Profile: Urban, Medium, Co-Ed
UG Tuition: $107.00/credit hour
G Tuition: $179.00/credit hour
Off Campus Programs: No

Clinical Experiences

A three-phase, three-semester professional education sequence offers candidates a rich opportunity for clinical experiences under the direction of qualified cooperating teachers and college supervisors. The three semesters complement a broad education curriculum and provide a blend of classroom theory with the realities of teaching in a selected grade level. Clinical experiences usually take place during candidates' sophomore, junior, and senior years.

Noteworthy

Missouri Western's low student-faculty ratio allows instructors to work closely with candidates to help them achieve personal success. The award-winning education faculty use animated and interactive teaching styles that encourage student participation at all levels. MWSC has several state-of-the-art multimedia classrooms, and requires all elementary education candidates to take an educational technology course. Many scholarships are available to qualified teacher education candidates. MWSC collaborates with regional professional development schools.

Teacher Preparation Program Information

The following programs are 4 year programs:

Early Childhood Education, Elementary Education, K-12 Education (Art, French, Music, Physical Education, Spanish), Middle School Education (English, Mathematics, Science, Social Studies), Secondary Education (Biology, Chemistry, English/Language Arts, Mathematics, Social Studies, Speech/Theatre), Special Education (Cross-Categorial, Early Childhood)

Northwest Missouri State University

The Teacher Education Program at Northwest Missouri State University is built on the idea of the teacher as a facilitator of lifelong learning in a world of diversity and change. Northwest emphasizes the importance of staying current in a field of study; making use of new technology; defining and solving problems in teaching; making reflective pedagogical decisions; becoming involved with professional development activities; working with professional and scholarly organizations; maintaining flexibility in one's teaching; and becoming a lifelong learner.

Just the facts...

Northwest Missouri State University
College of Education and Human Services
Maryville, MO 64468
(660) 562-1671
Website: www.nwmissouri.edu
Profile: Rural, Medium, Co-Ed
UG Tuition: $90.75/cr. hr. in-state; $157.75/cr. hr. out-of-state
G Tuition: $112.75/cr. hr. in-state; $197.00/cr. hr. out-of-state
Off Campus Programs: No

Clinical Experiences

Clinical experiences are an exciting and important area of the teacher education program at Northwest. On campus, the Horace Mann School, an elementary school for pre-kindergarten through sixth grade, offers unique hands-on teaching experience for Northwest education majors through observation and practica throughout their undergraduate coursework. Clinical experiences are also offered in Northwest's K-12 Professional Development Partner Schools. Candidates learn about diversity through work in schools with students from many different backgrounds.

Noteworthy

Northwest has placed over 1,500 new desktop computers in residence hall rooms. More than 50 electronic classrooms across campus provide access to cutting-edge technology in addition to an array of general and specialized computer laboratories. Northwest has received several awards for its high quality, including the Missouri Quality Award. Several scholarships are available for candidates. On-campus organizations allow teacher candidates to get involved, including the Student Council for the Exceptional Child, Koncerned Individuals Dedicated to Service (KIDS), the Student Missouri State Teachers Association, Kappa Delta Pi, and a student chapter of the International Reading Association.

Teacher Preparation Program Information

The following programs are 4 year programs:
Early Childhood Education, Elementary Education, K-12 Education (Art, French, Music, Spanish), Middle School Education (English, Mathematics, Science, Social Studies), Secondary Education (Biology, Business, Chemistry, Earth Science, English, Health, Mathematics, Physical Education, Physics, Social Studies, Speech/Theatre, Vocational Agriculture, Vocational Home Economics/Consumer Homemaking), Special Education (Developmental Disabilities/Handicaps, Early Childhood, Learning Disability, Multiple Disabilities/Handicaps)

The following programs are post-baccalaureate programs:
Early Childhood Education, Elementary Education, Secondary Education

Saint Louis University

Saint Louis University's teacher education programs are housed within the College of Public Service—the newest college within the university. The teacher education programs prepare reflective practitioners and socially responsible educational leaders who seek truth and knowledge for service to and for humanity. Candidates are provided the opportunity to develop leadership and service skills and become capable critical thinkers, problem solvers, and decision makers. All teacher education programs are guided by a commitment to diversity and social justice. Saint Louis University prides itself on the combination of academic excellence and field experience it offers to future educators.

Clinical Experiences

Practicum experiences are provided through a wealth of multifaceted on and off-campus sites and culminate in the student teaching experience. The Department of Educational Studies provides practicum and student teaching experiences in urban, suburban, and rural settings, and through its professional development school. Both diagnostic and teaching experiences are offered beginning in the undergraduate education programs. Diagnostic and therapeutic experiences across the life span are emphasized in Communication Disorders and Counseling and Family Therapy coursework.

Just the facts...

Saint Louis University
Department of Educational Studies
3750 Lindell Boulevard
Saint Louis, MO 63108
(314) 977-2510
Website: www.slu.edu
Profile: Urban, Medium, Co-Ed
UG Tuition: $7,470.00/semester
G Tuition: $4,320.00/semester
Off Campus Programs: No

Noteworthy

The education programs are housed in a newly renovated facility at the heart of campus life. Program highlights include multiple practica opportunities and three State of Missouri recognized exemplary programs. The Department of Communications Disorders offers over 30 practica opportunities and internships with stipends at the master's level. Graduates exceed the national average on the National Examination in Speech-Language Pathology and the National Teacher's Examination. Graduate stipends or fellowships are available in all programs.

Teacher Preparation Program Information

The following programs are 4 year programs:
Early Childhood Education, Elementary Education (K-6 Certification), Middle School Education (5-8 Certification, English, French, German, Language Arts, Mathematics, Social Studies, Spanish), Secondary Education (English/Language Arts, French, German, History, Mathematics, Social Studies, Spanish), Special Education (Behavior Disorders, Early Childhood, Learning Disability, Mental Retardation)

The following programs are 5th year programs:
Communication Sciences Disorders (Speech/Language Disabilities)

Southeast Missouri State University

The College of Education offers instruction in programs that prepare teachers, school administrators, and counselors to be competent professional educators. These programs include a strong general education component; skill in the art of teaching; integrated field-based experiences; knowledge in a specialty area with a commitment to the professional development school concept; and birth to grade twelve collaboration. Master's degree programs in teacher education, educational administration, and counseling provide opportunities for advanced study.

Just the facts...

Southeast Missouri State University
College of Education
One University Plaza
Cape Girardeau, MO 63701
(573) 651-2123
Website: www.semo.edu
Profile: Rural, Medium, Co-Ed
UG Tuition: $93.30/cr. hr. in-state; $179.30/cr. hr. out-of-state
G Tuition: $105.30/cr. hr. in-state; $196.30/cr. hr. out-of-state
Off Campus Programs: No

Clinical Experiences

Clinical experiences are a significant part of all education programs at Southeast Missouri State University. Candidates engage in a series of activities, from observing and assisting a teacher several hours a week to student teaching all day for fourteen weeks. The emphasis is placed on diverse experiences in the undergraduate programs and candidates are placed in rural and urban schools with pupils from diverse backgrounds. Candidates can elect to participate in either the block program setting or in a professional development school.

Noteworthy

The Elementary Education Program received the American Association of State Colleges and Universities (AASCU) Christa McAuliffe Showcase in Excellence Award for its innovative teacher preparation curriculum in 1989 and again in 1994 for the KSAM hands-on science and mathematics program. The program has been designated as exemplary by the state of Missouri's State Board of Education and was recognized in 1994 by the White House Teach America program for its contributions to the advancement of national education priorities. Southeast is a member of the prestigious Renaissance Group, aimed at improving education for teachers.

Teacher Preparation Program Information

The following programs are 4 year programs:
Early Childhood Education, Elementary Education, K-12 Education (Art, French, Music, Physical Education), Middle School Education (English, Mathematics, Science), Secondary Education (Biology, Business, Chemistry, Earth Science, English/Language Arts, Mathematics, Physics, Social Studies, Speech/Theatre, Vocational Consumer & Family, Industrial Technology), Special Education (Behavior Disorders, Learning Disability, Mentally Impaired)

Truman State University

Since 1867, Truman State University has maintained a tradition of excellence in teacher education. The Master of Arts in Education program is the first extended teacher preparation program in the state of Missouri and one of a select few in the Midwest. The MAE is the only initial teacher licensure program offered at Truman State University. Students admitted into the MAE must first complete a bachelor of science or bachelor of arts degree in a liberal arts and sciences field. The program is designed to be completed in either one or two summer sessions and one academic year, or two academic years. In addition to the initial teacher preparation MAE programs, an M.A. is offered in speech pathology.

Clinical Experiences

The internship experience can be either an unpaid one-semester internship or, with faculty approval, a paid year-long internship. In the latter internship, the MAE candidate is hired as a teacher of record by a public school. The intern signs a contract and is paid by the public school to fill a full-time teaching position while completing the internship requirement. The MAE program encourages internship placements in diverse settings which include schools in the St Louis and Kansas City regions. Internships may also be arranged in rural school settings.

Just the facts...

Truman State University
Division of Education
Violette Hall 2300
100 East Normal
Kirksville, MO 63501-4221
(660) 785-4383
Website: www2.truman.edu/ed/
Profile: Rural, Medium, Co-Ed
UG Tuition: $142.00/cr. hr. in-state; $251.00/cr. hr. out-of-state
G Tuition: $151.00/cr. hr. in-state; $268.00/cr. hr. out-of-state
Off Campus Programs: No

Noteworthy

The five basic components of the MAE program include the undergraduate degree, graduate pedagogical coursework, advanced content in the teaching specialty coursework, a semester or year-long internship in a public school, and a research component. The research component can be one of three options: a case study analyzing action research conducted during the internship, a graduate thesis, or a publishable journal article.

Teacher Preparation Program Information

The following programs are 5th year programs:

Elementary Education, K-12 Education (Art, French, Health, Music, Physical Education, Spanish), Secondary Education (Biology, Chemistry, English/ Language Arts, Journalism, Mathematics, Physics, Political Science, Social Studies, Speech and Theater), Special Education (Learning Disability, Mentally Impaired, Mild/Moderate Behaviorally Disordered)

University of Missouri at Kansas City

The initial teacher preparation program at the University of Missouri at Kansas City is based on the concept of the teacher as a thoughtful decision maker who applies knowledge gained from both practice and theory to improve teaching and learning. The program seeks to prepare teachers who have a strong liberal arts education and who are well-grounded in their content field(s); who demonstrate the development of pedagogical skills; and who possess a professional commitment to education.

Just the facts...

University of Missouri at Kansas City
School of Education
5100 Rockhill Road
Kansas City, MO 64110-2499
(816) 235-2236
Website: www.umkc.edu
Profile: Urban, Large, Co-Ed
UG Tuition: $147.60/cr. hr. in-state; $403.20/cr. hr. out-of-state
G Tuition: $181.70/cr. hr. in-state; $508.20/cr. hr. out-of-state
Off Campus Programs: No

Clinical Experiences

The four-semester professional sequence includes intensive field experiences during each semester. Elementary and middle level candidates have opportunities to work in the university's evolving partnership schools. Field experiences emphasize urban and culturally diverse settings; however, candidates spend time in a variety of settings. Prior to admission to student teaching, candidates are required to complete a program portfolio that is reviewed by faculty as well as by candidates in the Education Administration program, who provide guidance to teacher candidates in the development of job portfolios.

Noteworthy

Candidates in secondary education earn a B.A. in their content field as well as in Education. Candidates are admitted in cohort groups; collegial sharing and feedback are emphasized. Although the program is developed around a four-semester professional sequence, there are part-time options and an accelerated option for students in Secondary Education who have already earned a baccalaureate degree in their teaching field. A variety of scholarships are available in the School of Education for teacher candidates.

Teacher Preparation Program Information

The following programs are 4 year programs:
Early Childhood Education, Elementary Education, Middle School Education (English, Mathematics, Science, Social Studies)

The following programs are post-baccalaureate programs:
Early Childhood Education, Elementary Education, K-12 Education (French, German, Physical Education, Spanish), Middle School Education (English, Mathematics, Science, Social Studies), Secondary Education (Art, English/Language Arts, Mathematics, Physical Education, Science), Special Education (Behavioral Disabilities, Learning Disability)

University of Missouri at Saint Louis

With its community partners, the School of Education at the University of Missouri at St. Louis is creating the 21st century school of education—a responsive, field-based, collaborative approach to preparing educators to serve a dynamic, technologically advanced, and diverse community. The faculty and staff believe that a strong nation depends on a high correlation between what is being taught in the classroom, how teachers are prepared, and the demands of the workplace. As the largest provider of educators in the state, the university has a special mission to provide equal access to education for all children.

Just the facts...

University of Missouri at Saint Louis
School of Education
8001 Natural Bridge Road
Saint Louis, MO 63121
(314) 516-5109
Website: www.umsl.edu
Profile: Suburban, Large, Co-Ed
UG Tuition: $128.00/cr. hr. in-state; $384.00/cr. hr. out-of-state
G Tuition: $162.50/cr. hr. in-state; $489.10/cr. hr. out-of-state
Off Campus Programs: Yes

Clinical Experiences

Candidates attend selected classes on-site in one of the School's Professional Development School partnerships. A wide range of partner schools are represented, from middle-income urban to affluent suburban settings. Candidates observe and interact early and often with practicing K-12 professionals and their students during regular classtime work. Candidates also may choose to tutor or develop teaching units in one of several year-round precollegiate programs serving grades five through twelve. These extensive field experiences prepare candidates well for their fourteen-week student teaching assignments.

Noteworthy

The School of Education at the University of Missouri at St. Louis proudly seats ten endowed professorships held by nationally renowned experts in their respective fields. Three positions are held by outstanding professors in science education, another in Technology and Learning. Candidates are exposed to informal cultural and scientific education resources, including music education with the St. Louis Symphony; science education with the St. Louis Science Center, St. Louis Zoo, and Missouri Botanical Garden; and art education with the St. Louis Art Museum.

Teacher Preparation Program Information

The following programs are 4 year programs:
Early Childhood Education, Elementary Education, K-12 Education (Drama/Theater, French, German, Music, Physical Education, Spanish), Middle School Education (English, Mathematics, Science, Social Studies), Secondary Education (Biology, Business, Chemistry, English/Language Arts, Mathematics, Physical Education, Physics, Political Science, Psychology, Social Studies, Sociology, Steno/Typing/Keyboard), Special Education (Learning Disability, Severe Behavioral Disabilities/Handicaps)

The following programs are post-baccalaureate programs:
Early Childhood Education, Elementary Education, K-12 Education (Drama/Theater, French, German, Music, Physical Education, Spanish), Middle School Education (English, Mathematics, Science, Social Studies), Secondary Education (Biology, Business, Chemistry, English/Language Arts, Mathematics, Physical Education, Physics, Political Science, Psychology, Social Studies, Sociology, Steno/Typing/Keyboard), Special Education (Learning Disability, Severe Behavioral Disabilities/Handicaps)

Washington University

At Washington University, teacher education programs are designed to produce teachers who take an inquiry-oriented approach to education. Because teaching is a complex and changing activity, the university sees teacher education as an ongoing problem-solving process as opposed to a search for the "one best way." Candidates are expected to develop the ability and the inclination to look at educational policy and classroom decision making from multiple perspectives. Candidates are also expected to raise questions about the purposes, processes, and inequities of current systems.

Just the facts...

Washington University
Department of Education
Campus Box 1183
One Brookings Drive
Saint Louis, MO 63130-4899
(314) 935-6730
Website: www.wustl.edu
Profile: Urban, Medium, Co-Ed
UG Tuition: $950.00/credit hour
G Tuition: $950.00/credit hour
Off Campus Programs: No

Clinical Experiences

Washington's three required clinical experiences begin with an early placement in the Educational Psychology course. Candidates then practice methodology in field placements connected to methods courses. The final placement is a professional semester of integrated coursework and student teaching. Faculty who teach professional semester courses supervise student teachers who are clustered in field sites. This practice creates a strong support group for candidates, helping candidates link ideas from campus instruction with the realities of classroom teaching. Field placements are available in urban and suburban schools, including the university's two partner schools.

Noteworthy

A required action-research project enables student teachers to learn how to identify instructional problems, take action, collect pertinent classroom data, and modify instruction based on the results of investigation. School-university partnership sites at suburban and urban schools provide rich field experience placements for candidates. There is a low four to one candidate/faculty supervision ratio. Student teaching experiences include videoanalysis, weekly supervision conferences, and peer group meetings. Candidates are instructed in content areas by world-class scholars in the College of Arts and Sciences.

Teacher Preparation Program Information

The following programs are 4 year programs:
Elementary Education, K-12 Education (Art, French, German, Japanese, Latin, Russian, Spanish), Middle School Education (English, Mathematics, Science, Social Studies), Secondary Education (Art, Biology, Chemistry, Earth Science, English/Language Arts, Mathematics, Physics, Social Studies)

The following programs are post-baccalaureate programs:
K-12 Education (Art, French, German, Japanese, Latin, Russian, Spanish), Middle School Education (English, Mathematics, Science, Social Studies), Secondary Education (Art, Biology, Chemistry, Earth Science, English/Language Arts, Mathematics, Physics, Social Studies)

The following programs are 5th year programs:
Elementary Education, K-12 Education (Art, French, German, Japanese, Latin, Russian, Spanish), Middle School Education (English, Mathematics, Science, Social Studies), Secondary Education (Art, Biology, Chemistry, Earth Science, English/Language Arts, Mathematics, Physics, Social Studies), Special Education (Hearing Impaired)

Montana State University—Billings

The mission of the College of Education and Human Services is to prepare competent, caring and committed professionals for Montana's schools and human service programs; to conduct socially significant research to improve the human condition; to provide community services aimed at improving the quality of life experienced by Montanans; and to provide graduate education designed for the continuing development of professionals. Teacher education at MSU—Billings addresses four themes: human development, social consciousness, decision making and problem solving, and professional development.

Just the facts...

Montana State University—Billings
College of Education and Human Services
1500 North 30th Street
Billings, MT 59101-0298
(406) 657-2285
Website: www.msubillings.edu
Profile: Urban, Medium, Co-Ed
UG Tuition: $190.25/cr. hr. in-state; $360.25/cr. hr. out-of-state
G Tuition: $204.75/cr. hr. in-state; $374.75/cr. hr. out-of-state
Off Campus Programs: No

Clinical Experiences

MSU—Billings incorporates field experiences throughout undergraduate and graduate education, beginning in the sophomore year. During their education methods studies, candidates have the opportunity to apply their coursework in school settings. The Professional Semester includes student teaching and a capstone seminar. The college has partnerships with a number of area schools, each with a different focus, including community health; technology development; mentoring for early career science and math teachers; inclusion of students with disabilities; and American Indian culture.

Noteworthy

MSU—Billings has a number of scholarship opportunities for candidates who are majoring in education. Awards are available up to $2,500 for one academic year. Scholarships include the Henrietta Adams Memorial for female elementary education majors; the Harold S. Alterowitz Academic Excellence Award for physical education majors graduating with honors; the Professor Ken Card Scholarship for full-time special education majors; and the College of Education and Human Services Graduate Alumni Excellence Award for an education or human services leader in Montana. Contact the college for additional schoalrship information.

Teacher Preparation Program Information

The following programs are 4 year programs:

Elementary Education, K-12 Education (Art, Music, Physical Education/Health, Spanish, Special Education), Secondary Education (Biology, Chemistry, English, History, Mathematics, Social Studies)

The following programs are 5th year programs:

Elementary Education, K-12 Education (Art, Music, Physical Education/Health, Spanish, Special Education), Secondary Education (Biology, Chemistry, English, History, Mathematics, Social Studies)

National Council for Accreditation of Teacher Education

Montana State University—Bozeman

The College of Education, Health and Human Development seeks to improve understanding of education practices, human development, and health through teaching, research and service. Teacher education candidates in the college are highly motivated and dedicated to academics and preparing for their future careers. Programs focus on building knowledge; considering the importance of community and social influences on learning and the schools; and emphasizing relationships with the students, teachers, parents, and community.

Just the facts...

Montana State University—Bozeman
College of Education
250 Reid Hall
Bozeman, MT 59717
(406) 944-6752
Website: www.montana.edu
Profile: Rural, Large, Co-Ed
UG Tuition: $117.55/cr. hr. in-state; $299.65/cr. hr. out-of-state
G Tuition: $131.55/cr. hr. in-state; $313.65/cr. hr. out-of-state
Off Campus Programs: No

Clinical Experiences

All potential teacher candidates have an in-school experience as freshmen to acquaint them with the classroom from the perspective of a teacher. This is followed by a paraprofessional experience in the junior year completed at the same time as various methods courses. In the senior year, candidates take one semester of student teaching. Candidates in the elementary teacher education program are required to do additional volunteer work with children before being admitted into the professional program. Candidates may choose to complete their student teaching in-state, out-of-state, or in the United Kingdom, New Zealand, or Australia.

Noteworthy

On average, MSU—Bozeman teacher education candidates consistently score higher on the Pre-Professional Skills Test than do candidates from other education programs nationally. Advising for freshman and sophomore elementary teacher education candidates is done through an advising center. The center uses a peer advising format that helps candidates through their first two years. Faculty serve as advisors/mentors during the junior and senior years. A Teacher Resource Center with the latest in teaching materials provides candidates with additional resources to use throughout their teacher education program.

Teacher Preparation Program Information

The following programs are 4 year programs:

Early Childhood Education, Elementary Education, K-12 Education (Art, French, German, Health Enhancement, Music, Spanish), Secondary Education (Agriculture, Art, Biology, Chemistry, English, Family & Consumer Science, General Science, Health Enhancement, History, Mathematics, Physical Sciences, Physics, Science, Social Studies, Technology)

University of Montana

Programs in the School of Education are organized to promote the development of a learning community and incorporate three basic themes: integration of knowledge and experience; cooperation among participants; and inclusivity, caring, and respect for others. Graduates demonstrate competence in their subject matter and value the integration of knowledge and practice; gain intellectual skills leading to reflection, creativity, and risk-taking in their professional lives; and develop a sense of self-worth and a respect for the uniqueness of others, effective communication skills, and a commitment to life-long learning.

Just the facts...

University of Montana
School of Education
Missoula, MT 59812-1295
(406) 243-4911
Website: www.umt.edu
Profile: Urban, Large, Co-Ed
UG Tuition: $1,388.00/sem. in-state; $3,838.00/sem. out-of-state
G Tuition: $1,250.00/sem. in-state; $3,264.00/sem. out-of-state
Off Campus Programs: No

Clinical Experiences

All candidates complete three separate field experiences, including a full semester of student teaching. Two sections per year of the introductory field experience are school site-based, one for elementary education majors and one for secondary education majors. Candidates take on increasing responsibility in their field experiences as they progress through the program. Elementary education candidates complete an intensive, field-based semester of methods coursework prior to student teaching. In addition, two laboratory preschools are available on campus, including one for early intervention serving children with disabilities.

Noteworthy

Candidates experience interdisciplinary instruction in preparation for teaching at elementary and secondary levels. To fulfill professional and general education requirements all candidates complete coursework in applied professional ethics. For secondary licensure candidates, an optional Master's/licensure program for post-baccalaureate students is available. Seven endowed scholarships are available to teacher education candidates. Candidates have access to two multimedia computer labs, a Teacher Resource Center, and a newly renovated science/mathematics instructional center. The Montana TALES project (Technology and Learning in Every School) provides partnerships with fourteen school districts.

Teacher Preparation Program Information

The following programs are 4 year programs:
Elementary Education (Elementary Education K-8), K-12 Education (Art, Drama/Theater, ESL, French, German, Latin, Health, Music, Physical Education, Russian, Spanish), Secondary Education (Biology, Business, Chemistry, Earth Science, Economics, English/Language Arts, General Science, Geography, History, Mathematics, Physical Education, Physics, Political Science, Psychology, Social Studies, Sociology), Special Education

The following programs are post-baccalaureate programs:
Elementary Education (Elementary Education K-8), K-12 Education (Art, Drama/Theater, ESL, French, German, Latin, Health, Music, Physical Education, Russian, Spanish), Secondary Education (Biology, Business, Chemistry, Earth Science, Economics, English/Language Arts, General Science, Geography, History, Mathematics, Physical Education, Physics, Political Science, Psychology, Social Studies, Sociology), Special Education

Western Montana College

Western Montana College has been dedicated to excellence in teacher education from its founding in 1893. Excellence in undergraduate instruction is the primary goal of the college, enhanced by close candidate-faculty relationships and inter-disciplinary courses. The hallmarks of education at Western are small-group instruction, field-based experience, interdis-ciplinary teaching and research, a commitment to lifelong learning, and a spirit of collegiality. Western continues to focus on partnerships between P-12 schools and the college in edu-cating future teachers, and emphasizes teachers' understand-ing of the communities they serve.

Just the facts...

Western Montana College
Division of Education
710 South Atlantic Street
Dillon, MT 59725-3598
(406) 683-7325
Website: www.wmc.edu
Profile: Suburban, Small, Co-Ed
UG Tuition: $1,228.00/sem. in-state; $3,529.00/sem. out-of-state
Off Campus Programs: Yes

Clinical Experiences

Western's clinical experiences feature a wide variety of rural and urban schools for hands-on experiences. The Professional Development School in Butte, Montana, offers elementary methods classes at the school site, team-taught by college and school faculty. Rural elementary and secondary schools bring their students to the college regularly for enrichment experi-ences designed and taught by teacher candidates. A new inter-national placement program arranges student teaching experi-ences in New Zealand and Australia for interested candidates.

Noteworthy

Western prides itself on over 100 years of service to teaching, with more than 80 percent of its students graduating with education degrees. The education program includes a quality liberal arts program. Located at the southwestern tip of Big Sky Country, the region surrounding the college is rich in Western history. The region provides numerous outdoor rec-reational activities including fishing, hunting, boating, down-hill and cross-country skiing, backpacking, horseback riding, and camping.

Teacher Preparation Program Information

The following programs are 4 year programs:

K-12 Education (Art, Library, Reading, Physical Education/Health), Elementary Education (Early Childhood Education), Secondary Education (Biology, Business, Chemistry, Computer Science, Drama, Earth Science, English/Language Arts, General Science, History, Industrial Technology, Mathematics, Physical Sciences, Social Sciences)

Chadron State College

Chadron State College's professional teacher preparation program is designed to produce visionary leaders. Graduates are aware of the best contemporary educational research and development. The program consists of general studies, specialty studies, and professional studies. Professional studies focus on communication, critical thinking, evaluation, professionalism, human relations, leadership, and methodology. With an enrollment of approximately 3,500 CSC offers a university education in a personalized environment. The college has a long standing tradition of preparing graduates who have a strong grasp of the fundamentals of teaching.

Just the facts...

Chadron State College
Department of Education
1000 Main
Chadron, NE 69337
(308) 432-6330
Website: www.csc.edu
Profile: Rural, Medium, Co-Ed
UG Tuition: $59.50/cr. hr. in-state; $119.00/cr. hr. out-of-state
G Tuition: $74.50/cr. hr. in-state; $149.00/cr. hr. out-of-state
Off Campus Programs: No

Clinical Experiences

Candidates in the teacher education program observe, plan, and practice their skills in a variety of clinical and field-based experiences. Candidates must complete 100 hours of field experiences before student teaching. Elementary education candidates can observe and participate in middle school, elementary, and rural sites. Secondary education candidates observe and participate within their areas of specialization. Student teaching is a sixteen-week experience supervised by both college and public school personnel.

Noteworthy

Chadron State's teacher education program includes in its curriculum a two-day cultural immersion field experience on South Dakota's Pine Ridge Indian Reservation. During this field experience, candidates spend their time touring and observing at public and private elementary, secondary, and post-secondary reservation schools. Candidates meet with school administrators, teachers, students, and parents in an effort to learn if and how things are done differently on the Reservation. Candidates hear presentations on such topics as Lakota culture and religion and the dying art of Lakota storytelling; candidates also participate in a traditional Native American meal.

Teacher Preparation Program Information

The following programs are 4 year programs:

Early Childhood Education, Elementary Education, K-12 Education (Art, Computer Science, Drama/Theater, Health, Industrial Technology, Music, Physical Education), Middle School Education (English, Industrial Technology, Mathematics, Social Studies), Secondary Education (Art, Biology, Business, Chemistry, Consumer & Family Science/Home Economics, Driver Education/Safety, Earth Science, Economics, English/Language Arts, General Science, Health, History, Mathematics, Occupational Work, Physical Education, Physical Sciences, Physics, Political Science, Science/Home Economics, Social Studies, Sociology, Trade & Industrial, Vocational Business Office), Special Education (Adaptive Physical Education, Mild Disabilities)

National Council for Accreditation of Teacher Education

Concordia University

The teacher education program at Concordia University is organized under the themes of teaching, leading, and learning. It includes interpretation of divine revelation and the application of philosophy, educational research, and best educational practice as program sources. The general studies component contributes to the development of effective Christian living in each candidate. The professional and specialty studies components consist of field experiences, student teaching, and core courses which provide essential knowledge and skills to all education candidates.

Just the facts...

Concordia University
Education Governance/Basic Programs
800 North Columbia Avenue
Seward, NE 68434
(402) 643-3651
Website: www.ccsn.edu
Profile: Rural, Small, Co-Ed
UG Tuition: $5,655.00/semester
G Tuition: $127.00/credit hour
Off Campus Programs: No

Clinical Experiences

At the initial level, all elementary and secondary candidates complete in excess of 100 field experience hours prior to student teaching. Candidates completing additional field endorsements are assigned field experiences in their endorsement area. Each candidate completes a minimum of fourteen weeks of student teaching in two or more settings. Field experience journals are completed by candidates and evaluated by school-based personnel as well as course instructors.

Noteworthy

Concordia is a residential college where nearly all full-time students live in on-campus residence halls. Concordia students establish close relationships with each other that often last a lifetime. Student activities and entertainment options provide students with opportunities for relaxation and personal growth outside the classroom. The school's academic support services are available for students who need extra assistance with their studies. Education scholarships are offered to select students who have demonstrated outstanding leadership in high school.

Teacher Preparation Program Information

The following programs are 4 year programs:

Early Childhood Education, Elementary Education, K-12 Education (Art, Health, Music, Physical Education), Middle Level Education, Secondary Education (Biology, Business, Chemistry, Coaching, Computer Science, English/Language Arts, Geography, German, Health, History, Industrial Technology, Mathematics, Music, Natural Science, Physical Education, Physical Sciences, Physics, Religious Studies, Science/Home Economics, Social Studies, Spanish, Speech/Drama), Special Education (Mild/Moderate Handicapped)

The following programs are post-baccalaureate programs:

Early Childhood Education, Elementary Education, K-12 Education (Art, Health, Music, Physical Education), Middle Level Education, Secondary Education (Biology, Business, Chemistry, Coaching, Computer Science, English/Language Arts, Geography, German, Health, History, Industrial Technology, Mathematics, Music, Natural Science, Physical Education, Physical Sciences, Physics, Religious Studies, Science/Home Economics, Social Studies, Spanish, Speech/Drama), Special Education (Mild/Moderate Handicapped)

Creighton University

Creighton University enrolls more than 6,000 students annually and has been ranked first among Midwestern universities for three consecutive years by *U.S. News & World Report*. The Department of Education is one of 22 departments housed in the College of Arts and Sciences. All teacher education programs at Creighton are a harmonious blend of theory and practical experience. This experience includes serving as tutors, teachers' aides, and student teachers in the Omaha metropolitan public and private schools. Each program is designed with one primary goal—to produce the best teachers possible.

Just the facts...

Creighton University
Education Department
2500 California Plaza
Omaha, NE 68178-0106
(402) 280-2820
Website: www.creighton.edu
Profile: Urban, Medium, Co-Ed
UG Tuition: $6,429.00/semester
G Tuition: $402.00/credit hour
Off Campus Programs: No

Clinical Experiences

Beginning with the foundations course in education, candidates are introduced to elementary, special education, and secondary classrooms. During the sophomore and junior years, candidates spend more than 120 hours interacting with students in settings that are ethnically and socioeconomically diverse. The culminating experience in student teaching occurs during one semester (fifteen weeks) in two settings. Student teachers work under the direction of master cooperating teachers and are mentored by university supervisors.

Noteworthy

Candidates who complete the teacher education program at Creighton are highly sought after by local, national, and international schools. The current placement rate for graduates is 93 percent. The department offers three endowed scholarships, one of which is designated specifically for minority applicants. Faculty members in the Department of Education have served as elementary and secondary principals, classroom teachers, and school counselors, and bring a wealth of theoretical and practical knowledge to their classrooms.

Teacher Preparation Program Information

The following programs are 4 year programs:
Elementary Education (Elementary Education K-6), K-12 Education (Art), Secondary Education (Biology, Chemistry, English/Language Arts, French, German, History, Journalism, Latin, Mathematics, Physics, Political Science, Psychology, Social Science, Sociology, Spanish, Speech, Theatre)

The following programs are post-baccalaureate programs:
Secondary Education

Dana College

The teacher education faculty at Dana College takes pride in working individually with undergraduates in a caring, nurturing environment. The faculty believes that program graduates should be scholars and facilitators who enhance the self-worth of their students. A scholar has mastered the basic skills and knowledge associated with liberally educated people and understands how new information is created and adapted to the contemporary world. A facilitator evaluates, plans, and manages the school environment to encourage students to learn independently and cooperatively.

Just the facts...

Dana College
Education Department
College Drive
Blair, NE 68008
(402) 426-7280
Website: www.dana.edu
Profile: Rural, Small, Co-Ed
UG Tuition: $5,565.00/semester
Off Campus Programs: No

Clinical Experiences

As early as their freshman year, candidates begin working in the public schools. Candidates serve as Teacher Assistants in area public schools during their freshman, sophomore, and junior years. Several courses included interaction and/or service projects with youth in K-12 settings as part of the course requirements. Student teaching takes place in both urban and rural settings during the fall semester and interim session. While working with younger pupils, candidates are encouraged to link general education and pedagogical course content with best teaching practice. Many times that connection is made through reflective essays and/or Internet dialogue with course instructors.

Noteworthy

Dana College offers many opportunities for students to experience leadership roles. Teacher education candidates are encouraged to join the Student Education Association of Nebraska (SEAN). Dana's chapter of SEAN is a pre-professional program that meets monthly to discuss current topics in education. Another exciting feature of Dana's education program is the Horizon Shuttle and Mission Control Center. Both candidates and public school children use this unique opportunity to infuse technology into a problem-solving curriculum during the school year and in the summer.

Teacher Preparation Program Information

The following programs are 4 year programs:
Elementary Education, K-12 Education (Art, Music), Secondary Education (Biology, Chemistry, English/Language Arts, History, Modern Languages, Physical Education, Social Studies, Speech/Theatre), Special Education

The following programs are post-baccalaureate programs:
Elementary Education, K-12 Education (Art, Music), Secondary Education (Biology, Chemistry, English/Language Arts, History, Modern Languages, Physical Education, Social Studies, Speech/Theatre), Special Education

Doane College

Teacher preparation has been a part of Doane's mission since its founding in 1873. Building on a liberal arts foundation, teacher education students take classes on and off campus; participate in a variety of practicum experiences; and have opportunities to travel in the United States and abroad as part of the total Doane program. Doane guarantees all teacher education students employment upon graduation and assistance through the first year of teaching. Doane offers a warranty on its graduates to their employing school districts that ensures expertise in teaching. Doane maintains nearly a 100 percent teacher placement rate.

Just the facts...

Doane College
Department of Education
1014 Boswell
Crete, NE 68333
(800) 333-6263
Website: www.doane.edu
Profile: Rural, Small, Co-Ed
UG Tuition: $5,900.00/semester
G Tuition: $130.00/credit hour
Off Campus Programs: Not at undergraduate level

Clinical Experiences

All preservice candidates complete five semesters of practicum experiences in a variety of settings before student teaching. Doane maintains close relationships with both urban and rural school districts to ensure students experience all educational settings. Candidates work as sophomores and juniors in the Doane/Crete Professional Development School and in the Lincoln Public schools. Student teaching takes place for a minimum of fourteen weeks. Mentors are assigned to candidates in the practicum experiences. Graduate student candidates may complete research requirements in their own classrooms, if they wish.

Noteworthy

Doane believes that education doesn't end upon graduation. All education majors enroll in twelve hours of graduate credit immediately following graduation, which extends their knowledge of teaching and learning. Doane supports graduates during their first year of teaching. Beginning teachers are assigned a mentor in the school, and Doane faculty visit the new teachers. Doane also maintains contact with graduates and their principals in order to receive feedback to help Doane constantly improve its teacher preparation program.

Teacher Preparation Program Information

The following programs are 4 year programs:

Early Childhood Education, Elementary Education, K-12 Education (Art, ESL, Music, Physical Education, Special Education-Mild/Moderate), Middle Grades Education, Secondary Education (Biology, Business, Chemistry, Computer Science, Drama, English, French, German, History, Language Arts/English, Mathematics, Natural Science, Physical Science, Physics, Political Science, Social Science, Spanish)

Hastings College

Hastings College strives to provide an environment that challenges students to develop the intellectual, critical, creative, and communicative skills that provide the basis for learning, personal growth, and expression. The teacher education program at Hastings College trains teachers who bring to the classroom confidence born of excellent training and experience. Candidates benefit from extensive field experience and personalized instruction in small classes with experienced professors. Hastings' programs are field-based in partner schools in the local area and emphasize performance-based assessment. The department and the college are members of the Nebraska Network for Educational Renewal.

Just the facts...

Hastings College
Department of Teacher Education
7th and Turner
Hastings, NE 68901
(402) 461-7426
Website: www.hastings.edu/
Profile: Rural, Small, Co-Ed
UG Tuition: $5,729.00/semester
G Tuition: $166.00/credit hour
Off Campus Programs: No

Clinical Experiences

Candidates complete more than 800 hours of on-site laboratory, clinical, and student teaching experience. Opportunities are available to work in diverse school settings such as Eagle Rock School in Estes Park, Colorado, the Urban Life Center in Chicago, and inner-city schools in Omaha and Kansas City. Teacher candidates have participated in school visits to Japan and other countries. Additional pre-student teaching and post-student teaching practica are available as options in a variety of school settings.

Noteworthy

Hastings College is a member of the Nebraska Network for Educational Renewal. Extensive partnership activities engage candidates with Arts and Sciences faculty and master teachers in partner schools. Candidates experience extensive engagement with the use of technology to assist in developing skills to apply to the classroom. Hastings' professors visit graduates at their new teaching positions to offer encouragement and support and to solicit suggestions for the strengthening of the teacher education program.

Teacher Preparation Program Information

The following programs are 4 year programs:
Elementary Education (Elementary Education K-8), K-12 Education (Art, ESL, Music, Physical Education), Secondary Education (Art, Biology, Business, Chemistry, English/Language Arts, German, General Science, History, Journalism, Mathematics, Music, Physical Education, Physical Sciences, Physics, Psychology, Science, Social Studies, Sociology, Spanish, Speech), Special Education (Mild Learning/Behavioral Disability)

The following programs are post-baccalaureate programs:
Elementary Education (Elementary Education K-8), K-12 Education (Art, ESL, Music, Physical Education), Secondary Education (Art, Biology, Business, Chemistry, English/Language Arts, German, General Science, History, Journalism, Mathematics, Music, Physical Education, Physical Sciences, Physics, Psychology, Science, Social Studies, Sociology, Spanish, Speech), Special Education (Mild Learning/Behavioral Disability)

The following programs are 5 year programs:
Elementary Education (Elementary Education K-8), K-12 Education (Art, Drama/Theater 6-12, ESL, German, Music, Physical Education, Spanish), Secondary Education (Art, Biology, Business, Chemistry, English/Language Arts, German, General Science, History, Journalism, Mathematics, Music, Physical Education, Physical Sciences, Physics, Psychology, Science, Social Studies, Sociology, Spanish, Speech), Special Education (Mild Learning/Behavioral Disability)

Nebraska Wesleyan University

Nebraska Wesleyan University is an independent, undergraduate, liberal arts institution located in Lincoln, Nebraska. Nebraska Wesleyan University is recognized for its academic excellence. It is classified as one of 163 highly selective national liberal arts colleges by the Carnegie Foundation for the Advancement of Teaching. *U.S. News and World Report* includes Nebraska Wesleyan among its list of the top 159 national liberal arts colleges. Only 38 of these institutions are located west of the Mississippi River. Nebraska Wesleyan is one of 140 colleges and universities selected for the John Templeton Foundation Honor Roll of Character-Building Colleges.

Just the facts...

Nebraska Wesleyan University
Department of Education
5000 Saint Paul Avenue
Lincoln, NE 68504-2796
(402) 465-2304
Website: www.nebrwesleyan.edu
Profile: Urban, Small, Co-Ed
UG Tuition: $5,886.00/semester
Off Campus Programs: No

Clinical Experiences

Nebraska Wesleyan prides itself on the quality and quantity of field experiences that are part of its program. Each semester, from the time a student considers a major in education through student teaching, the candidate has numerous and progressive opportunities to work with students in schools and other community settings. A minimum of 100 hours of working with youth is required before student teaching. Teacher candidates are encouraged to complete part of their student teaching assignment in an international setting. Candidates have the opportunity to student teach in Australia, England, Germany, India, Ireland, New Zealand, Scotland, Taiwan, or Wales.

Noteworthy

The Nebraska Wesleyan University Education Department offers three majors: Elementary Education, Middle Grades Education, and Special Education. The Education Department also participates in four interdisciplinary majors which include Comprehensive Social Studies, Language Arts, Natural Science, and Physical Science. It also offers K-12 and Grades 7-12 certification programs. Students who rank in the top half of their graduating class or earn an ACT composite score of 20 or SAT combined score of 800 are invited to apply for admission to Nebraska Wesleyan. Fifty-five percent of first-year students in 1998 graduated in the top one-fourth of their high school classes. The average ACT score for first-year students is 24.1.

Teacher Preparation Program Information

The following programs are 4 year programs:

Elementary Education, K-12 Education (Art, French, German, Music, Physical Education, Spanish), Middle School Education, Secondary Education (Art, Biology, Business, Coaching, Economics, English/Language Arts, History, Mathematics, Natural Science, Physical Education, Physical Sciences, Physics, Political Science, Psychology, Social Studies, Sociology, Speech/Theatre), Special Education

The following programs are post-baccalaureate programs:

Elementary Education, K-12 Education (Art, French, German, Music, Physical Education, Spanish), Middle School Education, Secondary Education (Art, Biology, Business, Coaching, Economics, English/Language Arts, History, Mathematics, Natural Science, Physical Education, Physical Sciences, Physics, Political Science, Psychology, Social Studies, Sociology, Speech/Theatre), Special Education

National Council for Accreditation of Teacher Education

Peru State College

Peru State College, founded as a teachers' college, prepares teachers to serve the region, the state, and the nation. The faculty view the K-12 teacher as a rational and effective decision maker with a cognitive knowledge base in learning theory, child and adolescent growth, educational planning, diversity, exceptional learners, technology, curriculum development, and human relations. Peru State's goal is to impart to every graduate a professional disposition to be a lifelong learner and role model.

Just the facts...

Peru State College
Division of Education
P.O. Box 10
Peru, NE 68421-0010
(402) 872-2258
Website: www.peru.edu
Profile: Rural, Small, Co-Ed
UG Tuition: $59.50/cr. hr. in-state; $119.00/cr. hr. out-of-state
G Tuition: $74.50/cr. hr. in-state; $149.00/cr. hr. out-of-state
Off Campus Programs: Yes

Clinical Experiences

Required clinical experiences include a minimum of 100 hours working with master teachers and their students before a full semester of student teaching. Faculty teaching methods courses monitor accompanying practica, and student teachers are observed in their classrooms a minimum of once every other week. In both practica and student teaching, candidates are encouraged to experiment with what they are learning about their chosen profession. They receive direct and immediate feedback in order to consider alternative techniques, correct mistakes, and reflect on their experiences. Candidates, cooperating teachers, and supervisors work toward the goal of developing competent professionals.

Noteworthy

Teacher candidates at Peru State are given a great deal of individual attention, and are advised by full-time education faculty. The education programs reflect current theory, research, and practice in the field and include hands-on experience with instructional technology and, in the near future, teaching in a distance learning classroom. Peru State's graduates are hired across the nation because they are ready, eager, and able to start their first teaching positions at graduation.

Teacher Preparation Program Information

The following programs are 4 year programs:

Early Childhood Education, Elementary Education, K-12 Education (Art, Music, Physical Education), Middle School Education, Secondary Education (Biology, Business, Chemistry, English/Language Arts, History, Industrial Technology, Mathematics, Natural Science, Physical Education, Physical Science, Psychology, Social Science, Sociology), Special Education (Mild/Moderate Handicapped, Preschool Handicapped)

The following programs are post-baccalaureate programs:

Early Childhood Education, Elementary Education, K-12 Education (Art, Music, Physical Education), Middle School Education, Secondary Education (Biology, Business, Chemistry, English/Language Arts, History, Industrial Technology, Mathematics, Natural Science, Physical Education, Physical Science, Psychology, Social Science, Sociology), Special Education (Mild/Moderate Handicapped, Preschool Handicapped)

Union College

Union College, a Seventh-Day Adventist liberal arts college, has prepared K-12 teachers for over 100 years. Education faculty believe that it is God's desire for humans to develop their full potential. Union College's goal is to provide opportunities that will encourage its teacher candidates to develop their own mental, physical, social, and spiritual capabilities while learning the skills necessary to foster the development of their future students' potential. Union College works cooperatively with Canadian University College to offer a joint teacher education program on its LaCombe, Canada, campus.

Just the facts...

Union College
Division of Human Development
3800 South 48th Street
Lincoln, NE 68506
(402) 486-2522
Website: www.ucollege.edu
Profile: Suburban, Small, Co-Ed
UG Tuition: $430.00/credit hour
Off Campus Programs: Yes

Clinical Experiences

A minimum of 100 hours of clinical experience is required before student teaching begins. These clinical experiences begin the first semester of the freshman year when prospective education majors devote twenty hours of time as classroom aides in regular classrooms. During their sophomore year, candidates spend five days with youth on the Pine Ridge Reservation in South Dakota. Junior year candidates gain 40 hours of experience with students with disabilities. Additionally, teacher candidates regularly volunteer for overseas, one-year service projects. Student teaching requires fourteen weeks of full-time work during candidates' senior year.

Noteworthy

The college provides a first-year teacher induction program that includes monthly telephone contact with college faculty and regular mentor assistance. Technology is an integral part of the program, and a computer monitor with free Internet access is available to every student in his or her dorm room. The elementary program specializes in multigrade education. All majors perform seven hours of their student teaching in a two-teacher, one-room, all eight grades lab school.

Teacher Preparation Program Information

The following programs are 4 year programs:

Elementary Education, K-12 Education (Music), Middle School Education (English, Mathematics, Religious Studies, Science, Social Studies), Secondary Education (Art, Biology, Business, Chemistry, English/Language Arts, History, Mathematics, Physics, Religious Studies, Social Studies)

National Council for Accreditation of Teacher Education

University of Nebraska at Kearney

Professional education programs at the University of Nebraska at Kearney are based upon an enduring commitment to quality public education. This commitment recognizes the role of public education in the American democratic experience. Central to the instructional program is the belief that all students can be successful learners. Graduates understand the disciplines they teach; create learning experiences that make subject matter meaningful; use their knowledge to work effectively with all students; use assessment strategies to continually improve learning and teaching; deal positively with issues of diversity; and work effectively with parents and other educators to enhance students' achievement.

Just the facts...

University of Nebraska at Kearney
College of Education
Education Center Room 101
Kearney, NE 68849
(308) 865-8502
Website: www.unk.edu
Profile: Rural, Large, Co-Ed
UG Tuition: $67.00/cr. hr. in-state; $125.00/cr. hr. out-of-state
G Tuition: $83.00/cr. hr. in-state; $157.00/cr. hr. out-of-state
Off Campus Programs: Yes

Clinical Experiences

Professional education programs for initial licensure include clinical experiences in six elementary partner and two middle partner schools. There are also clinical experiences in many other schools in Nebraska with whom the university has long collaborated. All preservice teachers must spend at least 100 hours prior to student teaching working with children and/or youth in community and school settings. Student teaching is one semester. Clinical settings are selected to represent the cultural, rural/urban, and economic diversity of the region. In addition, clinical experiences take place in settings that serve diverse K-12 student populations whenever possible. Candidates are mentored by cooperating teachers in the schools.

Noteworthy

The University of Nebraska at Kearney/Kearney Public Schools Partnership involves K-12 teachers and administrators in the preparation of future teachers through guided practice in extensive field experiences. Candidates work with master teachers in partner schools who collaborate with UNK faculty in the teacher preparation program. This collaboration reflects a commitment by UNK to work with K-12 schools in improving its teacher education program. In addition, candidates have an opportunity to work with faculty whose expertise in reading is recognized statewide. UNK is one of 22 Reading Recovery sites in the United States.

Teacher Preparation Program Information

The following programs are 4 year programs:
Early Childhood Education, Elementary Education (Generalist K-6, Physical Education), K-12 Education (Art, ESL, Health & Physical Education, Music), Middle Grades Education/Grades 4-9, Secondary Education/Grades 7-12 (Basic Business, Biology, Business, Chemistry, Coaching, Diversified Occupations, Driver Education, Economics, English, Family & Consumer Sciences, Family & Consumer Sciences Related Occupation, French, Geography, German, Health, History, Mathematics, Marketing, Physical Education, Physical Science, Physics, Political Science, Psychology, Social Science, Sociology, Spanish, Speech Communication, Speech/Theatre, Theatre), Special Education (Adapted Physical Education, Mild/Moderate Disabilities, Preschool Handicapped, Vocational Special Needs)

The following programs are post-baccalaureate programs:
Early Childhood Education, Elementary Education (Generalist K-6, Physical Education), K-12 Education (Art, ESL, Health & Physical Education, Music), Middle Grades Education/Grades 4-9, Secondary Education/Grades 7-12 (Basic Business, Biology, Business, Chemistry, Coaching, Diversified Occupations, Driver Education, Economics, English, Family & Consumer Sciences, Family & Consumer Sciences Related Occupation, French, Geography, German, Health, History, Mathematics, Marketing, Physical Education, Physical Science, Physics, Political Science, Psychology, Social Science, Sociology, Spanish, Speech Communication, Speech/Theatre, Theatre), Special Education (Adapted Physical Education, Mild/Moderate Disabilities, Preschool Handicapped, Vocational Special Needs)

The following programs are 5th year programs:
Special Education (Behavior Disorders)

University of Nebraska at Lincoln

Teachers College at UNL, founded in 1908, seeks to conduct exemplary professional preparation programs, carry out useful research, improve education, embrace diversity, and support the learning of all students. The College trains its candidates to be scholars and practitioners. It establishes a strong link between research and practice, and models for teacher candidates the trait of active and reflective inquiry. Graduates are especially strong not only in content expertise and pedagogical skills, but also at inquiring about and analyzing their own educational practices.

Just the facts...
University of Nebraska at Lincoln
Teachers College
231 Mable Lee Hall
Lincoln, NE 68588-0234
(402) 472-5400
Website: www.unl.edu/tcweb/
Profile: Urban, Large, Co-Ed
UG Tuition: $2,968.00/sem. in-state; $6,951.00/sem. out-of-state
G Tuition: $2,485.00/sem. in-state; $5,572.00/sem. out-of-state
Off Campus Programs: No

Clinical Experiences

The Elementary Education program includes five required clinical experiences, The Middle Level Education program includes four required clinical experiences, and the Secondary programs include two required clinical experiences. Many methods courses include a clinical experience component. The first clinical experience takes place in a developmental psychology course. Student teaching is a full-time sixteen-week experience. Employers of UNL's graduates consistently emphasize the value of the clinical experiences offered by UNL.

Noteworthy

All undergraduate students are admitted as Pre-Education majors, and must submit an application portfolio after completing 42 credit hours of required courses. Admission to Teachers College as a Pre-Education major does not guarantee admission to a teacher education program. Admission to teacher education is selective and identifies those potential candidates with a demonstrated record of professional promise. UNL has a new honors program which accepts 25 freshman students from Teachers College each year.

Teacher Preparation Program Information

The following programs are 4 year programs:
Early Childhood Education, Elementary Education, K-12 Education (Art, French, German, Music, Physical Education, Physical Education/Health, Spanish), Middle School Education, Secondary Education (Agriculture, Biology, Business, Chemistry, Consumer & Family Science/Home Economics, Earth Science, Economics, English, French, Geography, German, Health, Industrial Technology, Mathematics, Natural Science, Physical Education, Physical Sciences, Physics, Political Science, Social Science, Sociology, Spanish, Speech, Speech/Drama, Theatre, Trade & Industrial, Vocational Home Economics/Consumer Homemaking), Special Education (Mild Disabilities, Moderate/Profound Handicapped)

The following programs are post-baccalaureate programs:
K-12 Education (ESL), Secondary Education (Biology, Chemistry, Coaching, Computer Science, Earth Science, Economics, Geography, Health, Physical Education, Physics, Political Science, Sociology, Trade & Industrial, Speech, Speech/Drama, Theatre)

The following programs are 5 year programs:
Special Education (Hearing Impaired)

National Council for Accreditation of Teacher Education

University of Nebraska at Omaha

The College of Education at the University of Nebraska at Omaha promotes excellence in education through instruction, research, and service. The college prepares individuals in a wide range of professional education programs. Through research, the college adds to the knowledge base on teaching by learning and disseminating new information. The college provides service to the professions, the university, the community, and the nation, thereby improving the conditions under which individuals work, live, and grow. The College of Education sees the teacher as the orchestrator of the learning environment.

Just the facts...

University of Nebraska at Omaha
College of Education
Kayser Hall
Omaha, NE 68182-0163
(402) 554-2717
Website: www.unocoe.unomaha.edu
Profile: Urban, Large, Co-Ed
UG Tuition: $75.70 cr. hr. in-state; $204.00 cr. hr. out-of-state
G Tuition: $94.25 cr. hr. in-state; $225.00 cr. hr. out-of-state
Off Campus Programs: No

Clinical Experiences

Clinical experiences accompany and complement coursework throughout the candidate's program. The college, situated in a metropolitan area, enjoys a close working relationship with community schools, agencies, health care providers, businesses, and government. These partnerships enrich teaching, research, and service within the college, and provide students with unique learning and employment opportunities. Every teacher candidate experiences placements with exceptional populations and culturally diverse students. Student teaching is a sixteen-week experience.

Noteworthy

The Metropolitan Omaha Educational Consortium (MOEC) consists of seven public school districts and the College of Education. This unique relationship has led to the development and expansion of the following programs: a model teacher induction program; a minority intern program which has grown from four students to thirty-five; a strong infusion of technology in all basic programs; and a mentor training program for master teachers. A number of scholarship programs have been created specifically for teacher education candidates at the entry level, for student teachers, and for minority students seeking teacher certification.

Teacher Preparation Program Information

The following programs are 4 year programs:
Early Childhood Education, Elementary Education, K-12 Education (Art, French, German, Health, Music, Physical Education, Spanish), Secondary Education (Art, Biology, Business, Chemistry, Geography, Health, Mathematics, Physical Education, Physics, Social Studies), Special Education (Hearing Impaired, Mild/Moderately Handicapped)

Wayne State College

Wayne State College is proud of its long tradition of excellence in teacher education. Starting as the Nebraska Normal School in 1891, it has been producing outstanding educators ever since. The Division of Education encourages the use of theory, research, and experiences to inquire and reflect on teaching practices that help students develop their potential as citizens in a democracy. Wayne State College offers teacher preparation programs that encourage the development of well-rounded educators.

Just the facts...

Wayne State College
Division of Education
136 Brandenburg
Wayne, NE 68787
(402) 375-7389
Website: www.wsc.edu
Profile: Rural, Medium, Co-Ed
UG Tuition: $59.50/cr. hr. in-state; $119.00/cr. hr. out-of-state
G Tuition: $74.50/cr. hr. in-state; $149.00/cr. hr. out-of-state
Off Campus Programs: No

Clinical Experiences

The Division of Education offers many clinical experiences appropriate to the needs of individual candidates. Experiences are designed by college faculty and field partners in order to ensure an intensive learning experience. Advancing through Wayne State teacher education programs requires increasingly sophisticated field performance. To ensure this development, clinical experiences are closely monitored by college faculty and field partners. Students move through four "benchmark points" tied to clinical performance en route to being licensed as a teacher.

Noteworthy

Wayne State College is a member of the Nebraska Network for Educational Renewal (NeNER), which is part of John Goodlad's larger National Network for Educational Renewal (NNER). The Education Division has formalized partnerships with several K-12 schools in keeping with the NNER agenda. The division is also a partner with the Nebraska Schools at the Center Initiative, a program designed to encourage school-work that advances both individual academic achievement and community well-being.

Teacher Preparation Program Information

The following programs are 4 year programs:

Early Childhood Education, Elementary Education (Elementary Education K-6), K-12 Education (Art, Music, Physical Education/Health), Secondary Education (Art, Biology, Business, Chemistry, Consumer & Family Science/Home Economics, English/Language Arts, French, German, Geography, History, Mathematics, Music, Physical Education, Physical Sciences, Natural Science, Sociology, Spanish, Speech, Trade & Industrial), Special Education (Mild/Moderate Handicapped)

National Council for Accreditation of Teacher Education

University of Nevada at Las Vegas

UNLV's College of Education is a dynamic academic unit characterized by quality instruction, innovative partnerships with the community, and strong and steady growth. Particular attention is focused on preparing professionals for diverse educational settings and on contributing to educational and pedagogical knowledge through scholarly endeavors. The College provides leadership in both the art and science of educational practice, and is committed to creating an inclusive learning environment that values and promotes diversity.

Just the facts...

University of Nevada at Las Vegas
College of Education
4505 Maryland Parkway
Box 453001
Las Vegas, NV 89154-3001
(702) 895-3374
Website: www.unlv.edu
Profile: Urban, Large, Co-Ed
UG Tuition: $69.00/cr. hr. in-state; $2,885.00/sem. out-of-state
G Tuition: $93.00/cr. hr. in-state; $2,885.00/sem. out-of-state
Off Campus Programs: Yes

Clinical Experiences

Field-based and clinical experiences include classroom observation opportunities, practica, pre-student teaching, and student teaching. UNLV's Fifth Year Program, the Urban Teaching Partnership, is a full field-based program established in two elementary schools and one high school. Student teaching is considered a full-day experience for one semester. Candidates have the option to student teach in the summer because of the year-round schools in the area. Candidates may select urban, suburban, and rural settings for their field placements.

Noteworthy

The college has won national recognition for its teacher education program, Cultural Diversity Bridge to Academic Success. Several college facilities and centers serve the needs of the southern Nevada community while also providing candidates a living laboratory to develop their skills in counseling, administration, and teaching. Candidates from the College of Education's undergraduate programs attain a 90 percent placement rate.

Teacher Preparation Program Information

The following programs are 4 year programs:
Early Childhood Education, Elementary Education (Physical Education), K-12 Education (Drama/Theater, French, German, Music, Physical Education, Science, Social Studies, Spanish), Secondary Education (Anthropology, Art, Biology, Business, Chemistry, Communication, Earth Science, English/Language Arts, General Science, Health, History, Journalism, Mathematics, Music, Physical Education, Physical Sciences, Physics, Political Science, Psychology, Science, Social Studies, Spanish, Theatre, Vocational Home Economics/Job Training)

The following programs are post-baccalaureate programs:
Elementary Education (Physical Education), K-12 Education (Drama/Theater, ESL, French, German, Music, Physical Education, Reading, Spanish), Secondary Education (Anthropology, Art, Biology, Business, Chemistry, Communication, Earth Science, English/Language Arts, General Science, Health, History, Journalism, Mathematics, Music, Physical Education, Physical Sciences, Physics, Political Science, Psychology, Science, Social Studies, Spanish, Theatre, Vocational Home Economics/Job Training), Special Education (Adaptive Physical Education)

The following programs are 5th year programs:
Elementary Education, Secondary Education

University of Nevada at Reno

The College of Education at the University of Nevada at Reno believes that a professional educator loves learning, develops a large font of knowledge, is reflective, and values democracy and multiculturalism. Initial teacher licensure can be obtained through the traditional four-year program for elementary and special education majors or through a four and one-half year program for secondary and elementary/special education dual majors. Individuals with bachelor's degrees can enroll in either a post-baccalaureate or Master of Education/First Time Licensure program.

Just the facts...

University of Nevada at Reno
College of Education
Reno, NV 89557-0029
(702) 784-4345
Website: www.unr.edu
Profile: Urban, Large, Co-Ed
UG Tuition: $69.00/cr. hr. in-state; $144.00/cr. hr. out-of-state
G Tuition: $93.00/cr. hr. in-state; $190.00/cr. hr. out-of-state
Off Campus Programs: No

Clinical Experiences

Teacher education programs at UNR are field-based. Candidates complete field experiences in a variety of school settings ranging from a minimum of 60 hours in the secondary education program to over 300 hours in the dual elementary/special education program prior to their student internship. The student internship is the culminating experience lasting a full semester which occurs under the supervision of a master teacher.

Noteworthy

The College of Education moved into a new 110,000 square foot building in August 1997. The building has high-tech classrooms, computer labs, auditoriums, and a conference center. Lounge and study areas with Internet connections offer education majors comfortable places to study. A student advising center offers the opportunity for students to obtain information and advisement on a drop-in basis from qualified individuals. Numerous scholarships are available for education majors through the university's scholarship office.

Teacher Preparation Program Information

The following programs are 4 year programs:
Elementary Education, Special Education

The following programs are post-baccalaureate programs:
Elementary Education, Elementary/Special Education Dual, Secondary Education, Special Education

The following programs are 4 1/2 programs:
K-12 Education (Music, Physical Education), Elementary/Special Education Dual, Secondary Education (Biology, Business, Chemistry, Consumer & Family Science/Home Economics, English/Language Arts, French, General Science, German, Health, History, Industrial Arts, Journalism, Mathematics, Physical Education, Physical Sciences, Physics, Science, Social Studies, Spanish, Speech, Theatre, Trade & Industrial, Vocational Agriculture, Vocational Business Office, Vocational Home Economics/Consumer Homemaking, Vocational Trade & Industrial)

National Council for Accreditation of Teacher Education

Keene State College

Keene State College's teacher education programs emphasize social responsibility and ethics development, family interaction, integrated knowledge, and collaboration in a community of learners. The education major is designed to provide students with intensive professional preparation based on a model which infuses theories and practices from developmental, special education, and technological perspectives into all course and field work. Undergraduates complete (1) general studies, (2) a non-education major, and (3) an education major or teacher licensure option.

Just the facts...

Keene State College
Division of Professional and Graduate Studies
229 Main Street
Keene, NH 03435-2611
(603) 358-2301
Website: www.keene.edu
Profile: Rural, Medium, Co-Ed
UG Tuition: $1,810.00/sem. in-state; $4,460.00/sem. out-of-state
G Tuition: $175.00/cr. hr. in-state; $205.00/cr. hr. out-of-state
Off Campus Programs: No

Clinical Experiences

Candidates are in the field throughout the entire sequence of professional education courses. They visit and observe at field sites and complete projects. All candidates complete a methods course with a concurrent field placement for a minimum of ten hours. Candidates are supervised and evaluated by classroom teachers and faculty. Student teachers are placed in approved sites for a full semester and are supervised and evalauted by a designated teacher who is the on-site supervisor. The Child Development Center and Wheelock School provide on-campus clinical experiences with children from three months through fifth grade.

Noteworthy

Service learning projects are an important aspect of the education programs at Keene State College. Faculty choose appropriate service learning projects that will help candidates connect theory to real life situations. These projects are built into course requirements. The Institute on Emotional Disabilities conducts in-service workshops and seminars for professional educators working with students with EDB and provides opportunities for best practice research in schools. Each October for more than 20 years, the KSC Children's Literature Festival presents internationally recognized writers and illustrators of books for children and adolescents.

Teacher Preparation Program Information

The following programs are 4 year programs:

Early Childhood Education, Elementary Education, K-12 Education (Music, Physical Education), Middle School Education (Mathematics), Secondary Education (Biology, Earth Science, English, French, Geography, History, Mathematics, Social Studies, Sociology, Spanish, Vocational Trade & Industrial)

Plymouth State College

Plymouth State College has been training teachers since it opened in 1871. *Barron's Best Buys* and *Money* magazine recently noted Plymouth State for its resources, a talented and dedicated faculty, remarkable support services and a diverse curriculum, all of which are offered at a fraction of the cost of a private school education. The teacher preparation program at Plymouth State College provides prospective teachers with a solid foundation in theory, practice, and the flexibility to adapt to today's diverse classrooms.

Just the facts...

Plymouth State College
MSC #38 Education Department
17 High Street
Plymouth, NH 03264
(603) 535-2285
Website: www.plymouth.edu
Profile: Rural, Medium, Co-Ed
UG Tuition: $1,620.00/sem. in-state; $4,370.00/sem. out-of-state
G Tuition: $232.00/cr. hr. in-state; $254.00/cr. hr. out-of-state
Off Campus Programs: No

Clinical Experiences

Teacher candidates majoring in early childhood education (0-9 years of age), elementary education (5-13 years of age), and secondary education (12-17 years of age) have many opportunities to observe and participate in public and private schools. Candidates also work in other settings with children and families. In their first year, most teacher candidates begin observing and working in local public schools. Each department offers unique field experiences to provide candidates with many opportunities to work with children.

Noteworthy

Plymouth State College has a number of scholarships available to education majors. On campus, the Center for Professional Educational Partnerships supports programs linking schools throughout the state. Plymouth State College offers a number of different student support programs that assist candidates in their academic growth and development. Students have the opportunity to select their academic advisor and work closely with this person to develop their program of study.

Teacher Preparation Program Information

The following programs are 4 year programs:
Early Childhood Studies (Integrated Arts, Reading, Special Education), Childhood Studies/K-8 (Integrated Arts, Middle School, Reading, Special Education), K-12 Education (Art, Foreign Languages, Health/Physical Education/Recreation, Music & Theatre), Middle/Junior High School Education (Mathematics, Social Science), Secondary Education (English/Communications, English/Literature, English/Writing, Mathematics, Natural Science/Biology, Natural Science/Environmental Biology, Natural Science/Physical Science, Social Science)

The following programs are post-baccalaureate programs:
Early Childhood Studies (Integrated Arts, Reading, Special Education), Childhood Studies/K-8 (Integrated Arts, Middle School, Reading, Special Education), K-12 Education (Art, Foreign Languages, Health/Physical Education/Recreation, Music & Theatre), Middle/Junior High School Education (Mathematics, Social Science), Secondary Education (English/Communications, English/Literature, English/Writing, Mathematics, Natural Science/Biology, Natural Science/Environmental Biology, Natural Science/Physical Science, Social Science)

University of New Hampshire

The Department of Education at UNH prepares beginning teachers who demonstrate excellence in classroom practice and who will become education leaders. Candidates master subject matter and professional knowledge, and acquire a good grounding in general education with an understanding of diverse cultures and environments. Candidates complete a baccalaureate degree outside of education and apply for graduate study, which includes a full-year internship leading to an M.Ed. or M.A.T. degree and licensure. Candidates in some majors may choose a basic four-year program for licensure.

Just the facts...

University of New Hampshire
Department of Education
College of Liberal Arts
Morrill Hall
Durham, NH 03824-3595
(603) 862-2310
Website: www.unh.edu
Profile: Rural, Large, Co-Ed
UG Tuition: $3,250.00/sem. in-state; $7,638.00/sem. out-of-state
G Tuition: $2,720.00/sem. in-state; $7,080.00/sem. out-of-state
Off Campus Programs: Yes

Clinical Experiences

At UNH candidates spend 65 hours in local classrooms before deciding if they want to pursue a career in education. A year-long internship is part of the final stage of the five-year program. UNH faculty members collaborate with school practitioners in intern supervision within professional development schools and internship cluster sites. Another field-based option for candidates is Live, Learn and Teach—a seven-week program for prospective teachers to learn how to design experiential and community-based curricula. This curricula is team-taught by participants during a five-week summer school program for area youth.

Noteworthy

UNH provides opportunities for experiential, interdisciplinary, and international educational experiences. Faculty have developed community-based science and technology, mentoring, literacy, and school-to-work programs. They are involved in research and exchange programs in Belize, Italy, England, Japan, and Brazil. Up to 40 graduate scholarships are available through the department. The department houses a computer lab with multimedia capabilities. Ninety percent of UNH graduates find teaching jobs within a year of graduating. They remain in teaching longer than the national average.

Teacher Preparation Program Information

The following programs are 4 year programs:
K-12 Education (Music), Nursery/Kindergarten Education, Middle School Education (Mathematics), Secondary Education (Agriculture, Mathematics, Trade & Industry, Vocational Education)

The following programs are 5 year programs:
Elementary Education, K-12 Education (Art, ESL, Music, Physical Education), Middle School Education (Mathematics), Secondary Education (Agriculture, Biology, Chemistry, Earth Science, English, French, General Science, German, Mathematics, Physics, Russian, Social Studies, Spanish, Trade & Industry, Vocational Education)

The following programs are 5th year programs:
Early Childhood Education, Elementary Education, K-12 Education (Art, ESL, Music, Physical Education), Middle School Education (Mathematics), Secondary Education (Agriculture, Biology, Chemistry, Earth Science, English, French, General Science, German, Mathematics, Physics, Russian, Social Studies, Spanish, Trade & Industry, Vocational Education), Special Education

College of New Jersey

The School of Education at The College of New Jersey lives by the motto of "creating exemplary professionals." This framework guides the work of faculty and permeates courses and professional experiences in all programs. Its philosophy supports the creation of an active, reflective, and interactive exemplary educator. Five themes support and define this framework within the programs: knowledge and inquiry; excellence in practice; multiculturalism, diversity, and inclusion; multiple contexts and communities; and leadership and advocacy. The School of Education emphasizes focused programs of study and collaborative approaches to learning and teaching.

Just the facts...

The College of New Jersey
School of Education
Dean's Office
P.O. Box 7718
Ewing, NJ 08628-0718
(609) 771-2100
Website: www.tcnj.edu/~educat/
Profile: Suburban, Medium, Co-Ed
UG Tuition: $5,318.00/sem. in-state; $8,248.00/sem. out-of-state
Off Campus Programs: No

Clinical Experiences

Field experiences progress from observation to participation to the assumption of responsibility for complex tasks. Under on-site supervision from college faculty, most experiences occur in the School of Education's Professional Development School Network—a diverse array of twelve school districts within a thirty-mile radius of the college. The Network provides experiences in multicultural and diverse settings and interaction with members of varying neighborhoods and larger societal communities.

Noteworthy

The College of New Jersey has numerous undergraduate and graduate international education initiatives that reflect New Jersey's multicultural, multilingual population. Programs include global student teaching, student exchanges, study abroad, certification for the international teacher, and master's degree programs in English as a Second Language, Elementary Education, Secondary Education, and Educational Leadership. The College of New Jersey is committed to the international education of educators; to developing global competence in all its students by broadening individual horizons; and to learning more about what constitutes effective education in differing contexts and cultures.

Teacher Preparation Program Information

The following programs are 4 year programs:

Early Childhood Education, Elementary Education, K-12 Education (Art, Music, Physical Education/Health, Technology), Secondary Education (Biology, Chemistry, English/Language Arts, Mathematics, Physics, Social Studies, Spanish), Special Education (Deaf and Hard of Hearing)

The following programs are post-baccalaureate programs:

Elementary Education, K-12 Education (ESL, Health, Music), Secondary Education (Biology, Chemistry, English/Language Arts, Mathematics, Physics, Social Studies, Spanish), Teacher Certification for International Schools

Kean University

Kean University has prepared educators since 1855. The mission of the School of Education is to prepare informed, dynamic professionals who have the prerequisite knowledge, skills, and values to be effective in diverse settings. Graduates think creatively and critically, can design instruction to suit different learning styles, recognize and respect individual and cultural differences, can establish professional and collaborative relationships, are committed to lifelong learning, and are advocates for quality schooling for all.

Just the facts...

Kean University
School of Education
Morris Avenue
Union, NJ 07083
(908) 527-2136
Website: www.kean.edu
Profile: Urban, Large, Co-Ed
UG Tuition: $1,976.00/sem. in-state; $2,784.00/sem. out-of-state
G Tuition: $2,963.00/sem. in-state; $3,655.00/sem. out-of-state
Off Campus Programs: No

Clinical Experiences

All undergraduate teacher candidates at Kean complete a three-level sequence of field experiences in the schools. Candidates complete a guided pre-admission field experience in their sophomore year, a supervised pre-professional field experience in their junior year, and a full semester student teaching/internship. During the student teaching experience, a university supervisor visits the candidate every other week to provide support and feedback. Candidates keep journals and complete professional portfolios during their student teaching experience. Candidates in graduate programs complete appropriate practica and internships.

Noteworthy

The School of Education at Kean University is committed to diversity and partnerships with the education and business community. Diversity is reflected in the student body, faculty composition, curriculum, and field experiences. The School has special scholarships for paraprofessionals from underrepresented groups and several award-winning pre-college programs to encourage students to pursue teaching careers. The School of Education has a large number of collaborative programs with surrounding school districts designed to promote the simultaneous renewal of the schools and the University.

Teacher Preparation Program Information

The following programs are 4 year programs:
Early Childhood Education, Elementary Education, Elementary Education Bilingual, K-12 Education (Art, Music, Physical Education, Health/Physical Education, Technology), Secondary Education (Biology, Chemistry, Earth Science, English, Mathematics, Social Studies, Spanish), Special Education (Teacher of the Handicapped), Teacher of the Deaf

The following programs are post-baccalaureate programs:
Early Childhood Education, Elementary Education, Elementary Education Bilingual, English as a Second Language, K-12 Education (Art, Music, Physical Education, Health/Physical Education, Technology), Secondary Education (Biology, Chemistry, Earth Science, English, Mathematics, Social Studies, Spanish), Special Education (Teacher of the Handicapped), Teacher of the Deaf

The following programs are 5th year programs:
Elementary Education

Montclair State University

The award-winning Montclair State University Teacher Education Program enhances a liberal arts background and an academic major with an innovative sequence of professional course work and clinical experiences that emphasize critical thinking. The program is associated with four national teacher education networks that seek renewal in teacher education and the schools. Candidates formally apply for admission during their sophomore year through the Center of Pedagogy. The Center encourages scholarship in the art and science of teaching.

Just the facts...

Montclair State University
College of Education and Human Services
Montclair, NJ 07043
(973) 655-5167
Website: www.montclair.edu
Profile: Suburban, Large, Co-Ed
UG Tuition: $100.15/cr. hr. in-state; $154.55/cr. hr. out-of-state
G Tuition: $200.50/cr. hr. in-state; $257.35/cr. hr. out-of-state
Off Campus Programs: No

Clinical Experiences

Prior to student teaching, two field placement courses afford opportunities for candidates to observe and team teach in urban and suburban schools. Candidates also must complete some of their clinical experience in an urban setting. In the professional semester, candidates combine the study of pedagogy with extensive classroom practice that is supported by mentors and university supervisors. Selected university courses are held at professional development schools, which provide settings for ongoing interaction among university instructors, school faculty, and prospective teachers.

Noteworthy

Under the coordination of the Center of Pedagogy, twenty public school districts have formed a partnership with the university to become the New Jersey Network for Educational Renewal. Collaboratively, the schools and the Center foster critical thinking, enculturate youth in a political and social democracy, and prepare prospective teachers to become stewards of best educational practice. In addition, the program is supported by the Curriculum Resource Center, which maintains an extensive collection of professional books, texts, curriculum guides, computer applications and a model classroom.

Teacher Preparation Program Information

The following programs are 4 year programs:
Early Childhood Education (N-8), K-12 Education (Art, Biology, Business, Chemistry, English, English as a Second Language, French/German, Geoscience, Health and Physical Education, Home Economics, Italian, Latin, Mathematics, Music, Physics, Psychology, Social Studies, Spanish, Speech and Language Specialist, Speech and Theater, Technology)

The following programs are post-baccalaureate programs:
Early Childhood Education (N-8), K-12 Education (Art, Biology, Business, Chemistry, English, English as a Second Language, French/German, Geoscience, Health and Physical Education, Home Economics, Italian, Latin, Mathematics, Music, Physics, Psychology, Social Studies, Spanish, Speech and Language Specialist, Speech and Theater, Technology)

New Jersey City University

The College of Education at New Jersey City University is committed to meeting the educational, professional, personal, and cultural needs of its education majors. Dedicated to graduating well-rounded professionals, the College provides students with the skills needed to succeed in early childhood, elementary, secondary, and special education. New Jersey City University bases its education programs on a model designed to prepare educators ready to teach in urban environments. Candidates learn how to reflect on their own practice, acquire content knowledge, teach content knowledge effectively, and focus on the urban learner.

Just the facts...

New Jersey City University
College of Education
2039 Kennedy Boulevard
Professional Building 303
Jersey City, NJ 07305
(201) 200-2101
Website: www.njcu.edu
Profile: Urban, Medium, Co-Ed
UG Tuition: $136.50/cr. hr. in-state; $226.50/cr. hr. out-of-state
G Tuition: $221.75/cr. hr. in-state; $333.50/cr. hr. out-of-state
Off Campus Programs: Yes

Clinical Experiences

The junior practicum field experience provides weekly opportunities for candidates to observe interactions in urban schools, observe children at a variety of age and grade levels, and work with children under the guidance of a mentor teacher and a college supervisor. Student teaching is a full semester clinical experience, during which the candidate is responsible for the classroom under the supervision of a cooperating teacher and a college supervisor.

Noteworthy

Two scholarship programs at New Jersey City University, funded by the U.S. Department of Education, offer opportunities to teacher candidates. Project DIVISE, a full-time graduate program, is designed to enrich the experience of future minority Special Education teachers. Full-time graduate students are immersed in field experiences. Project Early Childhood Special Education addresses the critical need for well-trained early childhood special education teachers who are members of ethnically diverse cultures. This program has a strong interdisciplinary focus.

Teacher Preparation Program Information

The following programs are 4 year programs:
Early Childhood Education, Elementary Education, Health Education, K-12 Education (Art, Modern Language, Music), Secondary Education (Art, Biology, Chemistry, Earth Science, English, Mathematics, Music, Social Studies), Special Education

The following programs are post-baccalaureate programs:
Early Childhood Education, Elementary Education, Health Education, K-12 Education (Art, Modern Language, Music), Secondary Education (Art, Biology, Chemistry, Earth Science, English, Mathematics, Music, Social Studies), Special Education

The following programs are 5th year programs:
Bilingual/English as a Second Language, Early Childhood Education

Rider University

Committed to excellence, the School of Education keeps all its programs relevant to the changing needs of students, the professional communities it serves, and to society, by anticipating those needs and taking measures to meet them. This commitment to excellence is based on the belief that today's teacher must be able to demonstrate sensitivity to students, familiarity with curriculum, and a thorough knowledge of subject matter and the learning process. Rider University teacher preparation programs are grounded in current research on learning, curriculum, teaching, and exemplary practice of reflective teachers.

Just the facts...

Rider University
School of Education
2083 Lawrenceville Road
Trenton, NJ 08648-3099
(609) 896-5048
Website: www.rider.edu
Profile: Suburban, Medium, Co-Ed
UG Tuition: $530.00/credit hour
G Tuition: $329.00/credit hour
Off Campus Programs: No

Clinical Experiences

Each undergraduate education course is taught in conjunction with a semester-long field experience in a public school in which candidates work with an experienced classroom teacher and a Rider professor two half-days a week. Over the course of his or her professional preparation, each candidate is placed in a variety of grade levels in both urban and suburban schools. The capstone experience is a semester of student teaching. All graduate degree and licensure candidates complete related field experiences, ranging from 150 hours to 700 hours.

Noteworthy

The small faculty-candidate ratio and the developmental progression of field experiences support candidates' learning about teaching and permit individualized attention. A series of educational technology courses and well-equipped computer labs enhance candidates' communication and technology skills. Two scholarships, one for minority candidates and another for paraprofessionals in education who wish to advance their careers, are offered within the School. Faculty who publish in national and international journals work closely with candidates.

Teacher Preparation Program Information

The following programs are 4 year programs:

Elementary Education, K-12 Education (ESL, French, German, Music, Spanish), Secondary Education (Biology, Business, Chemistry, Earth Science, English/Language Arts, General Science, Marketing, Mathematics, Physical Sciences, Physics, Psychology, Science, Social Studies)

The following programs are post-baccalaureate programs:

Elementary Education, K-12 Education (French, German, Reading, Spanish), Secondary Education (Biology, Business, Chemistry, Earth Science, English/Language Arts, General Science, Marketing, Mathematics, Physical Sciences, Physics, Psychology, Science, Social Studies)

National Council for Accreditation of Teacher Education

Rowan University

The College of Education provides an intellectually rigorous and challenging environment for the professional preparation of education leaders. Built on a liberal education, Rowan's programs combine learning in diverse settings with personal and collective study that promotes professional achievement and personal fulfillment. Rowan's goal is to prepare educators who are effective communicators, instructors, curriculum planners, classroom managers, decision makers, problem solvers, advocates for cultural and learning diversity, technology users/producers, and scholars/professionals.

Just the facts...

Rowan University
College of Education
201 Mullica Hill Road
Glassboro, NJ 08028-1701
(609) 256-4750
Website: www.rowan.edu
Profile: Rural, Medium, Co-Ed
UG Tuition: $4,240.50/sem. in-state; $7,370.50/sem. out-of-state
G Tuition: $237.00/cr. hr. in-state; $358.00/cr. hr. out-of-state
Off Campus Programs: No

Clinical Experiences

Field experiences often begin in the freshman year, and increase in intensity and duration (from a one-day visit to a full semester of student teaching) as candidates progress through the program. Candidates are placed in a variety of schools in major urban settings, large suburban districts, and sparsely populated rural districts. Faculty members from various departments in the College of Education supervise closely candidates during all of their clinical experiences. The College of Education has partnerships and professional development schools in various settings, which provide many candidates with extensive collaborative clinical experiences.

Noteworthy

Rowan University has received recognition for its award-winning programs from several state and national organizations. The college provides support for its beginning teachers through the nationally recognized Thomas E. Robinson Beginning Teacher Induction Center. The college also has two outreach organizations that work closely with school districts: the Education Institute and the Curriculum Development Council.

Teacher Preparation Program Information

The following programs are 4 year programs:
Elementary Education, K-12 Education (Art, Drama/Theater, Music, Physical Education/Health, Reading Teacher, Spanish), Secondary Education (Biology, Bookkeeping, Business, Chemistry, English/Language Arts, Mathematics, Physical Sciences, Social Studies, Steno/Typing/Keyboard), Special Education

The following programs are post-baccalaureate programs:
Elementary Education, K-12 Education (Art, Drama/Theater, ESL, French, Music, Physical Education/Health, Reading Teacher, Spanish), Secondary Education (Biology, Bookkeeping, Business, Chemistry, English/Language Arts, Mathematics, Physical Sciences, Social Studies, Steno/Typing/Keyboard), Special Education

The following programs are 5 year programs:
Co-Teach (a dual certification program in Elementary and Special Education)

The following programs are 5th year programs:
Elementary Education, K-12 Education (ESL, French, Spanish), Secondary Education (Biology, Chemistry, English/Language Arts, Mathematics, Physical Sciences, Social Studies), Special Education

William Paterson University

The College of Education develops and administers the education components of the university's teacher education and school specialist programs. Every effort is made to relate student needs, program innovations, and interdisciplinary offerings to the contemporary world. To enhance its preservice and in-service course offerings, the college has established reciprocal relationships with the surrounding community.

Just the facts...

William Paterson University of New Jersey
College of Education
300 Pompton Road
Wayne, NJ 07470
(973) 720-2139
Website: www.wilpaterson.edu
Profile: Suburban, Medium, Co-Ed
UG Tuition: $2,075.00/sem. in-state; $230.00/cr. hr. out-of-state
G Tuition: $3,290.00/sem. in-state; $327.00/cr. hr. out-of-state
Off Campus Programs: No

Clinical Experiences

Field experiences are an essential part of all programs beginning with initial teacher education courses. A practicum experience consists of one or two sixteen-week placements. All undergraduates spend a minimum of 32 days in pre-student teaching field experiences. Student teaching is a sixteen-week, full-time experience. Placements are varied to include urban and suburban schools. A course in mentoring is offered to cooperating teachers who work with the candidates. Innovative programs include a Teacher Learning Collaborative with one-year placements in urban districts. Candidates, university supervisors, and cooperating teachers all have laptop computers and can communicate via e-mail.

Noteworthy

The undergraduate special education program has been newly revised from a categorical teacher preparation program to a cross-categorical program. Candidates benefit from the university's emphasis on tying field experience to designated methods courses, and its increase in the number of required practica from two to three. Collaboration with public schools is emphasized and demonstrated by four courses that are co-taught by university professors and practicing public school master teachers. The post-baccalaureate program is being revised to parallel the new undergraduate program and to be more distinct from the master's degree program.

Teacher Preparation Program Information

The following programs are 4 year programs:
Elementary Education, N-12 Education (Art, Biology, Earth Science, English, Mathematics, Music, Physical Education, Physical Education/Health, Physical Science, Social Studies, Spanish), Special Education

The following programs are post-baccalaureate programs:
Elementary Education, N-12 Education (Art, Biology, Earth Science, English, Mathematics, Music, Physical Education, Physical Education/Health, Physical Science, Social Studies, Spanish), Special Education

The following programs are 5th year programs:
N-12 Education (Bilingual/English as a Second Language, Language Arts, Mathematics, Reading), Special Education (Developmental Disabilities, Emotional Handicap, Learning Disabilities)

Eastern New Mexico University

The preparation of educators is at the center of Eastern New Mexico University's historic mission to its service region and vitally informs Eastern's instructional philosophy and practice in virtually every academic program. The College of Education and Technology prides itself on the extent to which faculty integrate research, theory, and practice as they prepare candidates to become reflective practitioners. Faculty teach candidates to combat bias and discriminatory practices, modify instruction for diverse learners, build strong relationships with parents, and build diverse communities of learners. The College of Education and Technology infuses technology into coursework, on-site work with children, and action-research projects.

Just the facts...

Eastern New Mexico University
College of Education and Technology
Station #25
Portales, NM 88130
(505) 562-2443
Website: www.enmu.edu
Profile: Rural, Medium, Co-Ed
UG Tuition: $876.00/sem. in-state; $3,255.60/sem. out-of-state
G Tuition: $978.00/sem. in-state; $3,351.00/sem. out-of-state
Off Campus Programs: Yes

Clinical Experiences

Candidates in professional education programs participate in a variety of field experiences that are designed to help them become effective teachers and school leaders. Since 1992, the college has tripled the number of field experiences required of teacher candidates. The field experience components of required courses provide candidates with opportunities to observe the application of theories; to engage in small-scale research projects; and to observe effective classroom practices. Candidates can complete field experiences in three professional development schools, in two cities.

Noteworthy

The newly renovated Education Building is equipped with state-of-the-art technology in all classrooms, computer laboratories, and an instructional television center. Distance education programs are available in bilingual education and special education. The College of Education operates the Center for Teaching Excellence, which provides action-research, professional development, and university/school partnership grants for improving teaching and learning throughout the state. The college houses the New Mexico Educational Software Clearinghouse and offers an elementary education degree at its Roswell, New Mexico, campus.

Teacher Preparation Program Information

The following programs are 4 year programs:
Early Childhood Education, Elementary Education (Bilingual, Family/Consumer Science), Secondary Education (Biology, Chemistry, Consumer & Family Science/Home Economics, Spanish, General Science, History, Mathematics, Physical Education, Physical Sciences, Physics, Psychology, Science, Social Studies, Sociology, Vocational Education), Special Education (Communication Disorders)

The following programs are post-baccalaureate programs:
Early Childhood Education, Elementary Education (Bilingual, Family/Consumer Science), Secondary Education (Biology, Chemistry, Consumer & Family Science/Home Economics, Spanish, General Science, History, Mathematics, Physical Education, Physical Sciences, Physics, Psychology, Science, Social Studies, Sociology, Vocational Education), Special Education (Communication Disorders)

New Mexico State University

The College of Education at New Mexico State University has an enrollment of about 2,300 students. The college is a charter member of the Holmes Group, a select group of major research institutions whose goal is improving teacher education. Graduates possess an intellectual foundation in fine arts, humanities, mathematics, natural sciences, and behavioral sciences. Graduates can assess student learning and are able to apply content and pedagogical knowledge in appropriate settings. Graduates demonstrate a knowledge of learners' needs and the ability to meet those needs.

Just the facts...
New Mexico State University
College of Education
Box 30001, Department 3AC
Las Cruces, NM 88003-8001
(505) 646-2498
Website: www.nmsu.edu
Profile: Rural, Large, Co-Ed
UG Tuition: $1,173.00/sem. in-state; $3,825.00/sem. out-of-state
G Tuition: $1,257.00/sem. in-state; $3,924.00/sem. out-of-state
Off Campus Programs: Yes

Clinical Experiences
The programs in the College of Education provide internships for candidates within public school settings, community colleges, university settings, and in non-public school settings. Long-term internships under the guidance of experienced faculty provide candidates with multiple opportunities to put educational principles into practice. Programs are designed to take advantage of the close relationship the college has with the public schools in the region and include numerous experimental and traditional internships.

Noteworthy
New Mexico State University is a Carnegie I research institution, and its strong commitment to scholarship influences all of its education programs. The College of Education is a national leader in bilingual and multicultural education. These themes are integrated throughout the course of study. The college offers one of the few early childhood programs that include degrees from the associate through doctoral level. The College of Education's Educational Research Center (ERC) assists faculty, staff, and candidates in locating outside funding sources, preparing grant proposals, and administering funds once they are received.

Teacher Preparation Program Information
The following programs are 4 year programs:
Early Childhood Education, Elementary Education (Bilingual, Language Arts, Mathematics, Science, Social Studies), K-12 Education (Bilingual, French, German, Music, Physical Education, Spanish), Middle School Education (English, Mathematics, Science, Social Studies), Secondary Education (Agriculture, Biology, Business, Chemistry, Consumer & Family Science/Home Economics, Earth Science, English/Language Arts, General Science, Mathematics, Physical Education, Physical Sciences, Science/Home Economics, Social Studies, Vocational Agriculture, Vocational Home Economics/Consumer Homemaking), Special Education (Developmental Disabilities/Handicaps, Early Childhood, Learning Disability, Multiple Disabilities/Handicaps, Severely Behavioral Disabilities/Handicaps)

The following programs are post-baccalaureate programs:
Elementary Education, K-12 Education (Reading), Secondary Education, Special Education

The following programs are 5th year programs:
Early Childhood Education, Elementary Education (Bilingual, Language Arts, Mathematics, Science, Social Studies), K-12 Education (Bilingual, French, German, Music, Reading, Spanish), Secondary Education (Agriculture, Biology, Business, Chemistry, Consumer & Family Science/Home Economics, Science/Home Economics, Earth Science, English/Language Arts, General Science, Mathematics, Physical Sciences, Social Studies, Vocational Agriculture, Vocational Home Economics/Consumer Homemaking), Special Education (Developmental Disabilities/Handicaps, Early Childhood, Hearing Impaired, Learning Disability, Multiple Disabilities/Handicaps, Severe Behavioral Disabilities/Handicaps)

National Council for Accreditation of Teacher Education

University of New Mexico

UNM's mission is to prepare teachers who (1) are committed to their students' education and well-being, (2) embrace the diversity of America's classrooms, and (3) serve as effective advocates for education and for children. The College of Education—located in one of the most culturally diverse regions in the country—is well-suited for this mission. The college has established a multidisciplinary Center for Teacher Education where university faculty, public school teachers and administrators, and others work collaboratively to prepare diverse populations of outstanding teacher candidates and then support them throughout their careers.

Just the facts...

The University of New Mexico
College of Education
Albuquerque, NM 87131
(505) 277-3190
Website: www.unm.edu
Profile: Urban, Large, Co-Ed
UG Tuition: $93.40/credit hour in-state
G Tuition: $103.10/credit hour in-state
Out-of-state (for 7th cr. hr.): UG add $1,907.45 + ($352.55 x additional cr. hrs.), G add $1,925.55 + ($363.45 x additional cr. hrs.)
Off Campus Programs: Yes

Clinical Experiences

Many candidates in the College of Education engage in service learning opportunities early in their college careers. Candidates enrolled in educator preparation programs spend a full year or more gaining invaluable experience in real classrooms. The college also offers a variety of licensure programs for post-baccalaureate candidates which engage them in integrated methods courses, clinical experiences, and mentoring relationships. In addition, the college offers graduates from its initial licensure programs the opportunity to engage in a paid intern program that leads to a variety of master's degrees.

Noteworthy

UNM is nationally known for its innovative and award-winning partnership programs with public school districts. These partnership programs and the other outstanding preparation programs in the Center for Teacher Education place the College of Education at the forefront of teacher preparation in the United States. High-quality education programs provide focused preparation in critical areas like literacy, science, special education, and technology. Intensive internships, mentoring, and lifelong networks for professional development and support are available to teacher candidates.

Teacher Preparation Program Information

The following programs are 4 year programs:
Early Childhood Education, Elementary Education, K-12 Education (Art, Health, Music, Physical Education, Special Education), Secondary Education (Biology, Chemistry, Earth Science, English/Language Arts, ESL, French, General Science, German, Mathematics, Russian, Social Studies, Spanish)

The following programs are post-baccalaureate programs:
Early Childhood Education, Elementary Education, K-12 Education (Art, Health, Music, Physical Education, Special Education), Secondary Education (Biology, Chemistry, Earth Science, English/Language Arts, ESL, French, General Science, German, Mathematics, Russian, Social Studies, Spanish)

The following programs are 5th year programs:
Early Childhood Education, Elementary Education, Secondary Education, Special Education, Speech/Language Disabilities

Western New Mexico University

The purpose of the School of Education at Western New Mexico University is to ignite and nurture a spirit of learning for both educator and student. Western New Mexico University prepares professional educators through a curriculum that supports collaborative learning. The School of Education recognizes and accepts diverse ideas, languages, and cultures; integrates theoretical knowledge into the world of practice through field-based experiences; and supports the idea that educators are proactive leaders. Graduates have a command of subject matter and demonstrate best practices in teaching.

Just the facts...

Western New Mexico University
School of Education
P.O. Box 680
Silver City, NM 88062
(505) 538-6416
Website: www.wnmu.edu
Profile: Rural, Small, Co-Ed
UG Tuition: $84.85/cr. hr. in-state; $271.85/cr. hr. out-of-state
G Tuition: $89.85/cr. hr. in-state; $276.85/cr. hr. out-of-state
Off Campus Programs: Yes

Clinical Experiences

Candidates are placed in the schools during their first semester in the teacher education program. Teacher candidates are expected to complete three major field experiences, the first two of which require 90 hours in the schools prior to student teaching. Student teaching is a semester-long full-time teaching experience. During the student teaching experience, candidates are supervised and assessed by clinical faculty/master teachers. Candidates are expected to complete professional portfolios which include a self-analyzed videotape of their teaching.

Noteworthy

Western New Mexico University's teacher preparation program immerses prospective teachers in culturally rich and diverse school environments. Field experience sites include schools with a majority of Hispanic students. Graduate programs include a Native American population of 35 percent.

Teacher Preparation Program Information

The following programs are 4 year programs:
Elementary Education, K-12 Education (Wellness and Movement Science), Secondary Education, Special Education (Mild/Moderate Disabilities, Severe Disabilities)

The following programs are post-baccalaureate programs:
Elementary Education, K-12 Education, Secondary Education, Special Education

The following programs are 5 year programs:
Master of Arts in Teaching

The following programs are 5th year programs:
Master of Arts in Teaching

National Council for Accreditation of Teacher Education

Buffalo State College

Buffalo State College is the largest of the thirteen four-year comprehensive colleges in the State University of New York system, and the only four-year college in the system situated in an urban metropolitan area. The four basic components of the undergraduate teacher education programs at Buffalo State are general education studies, foundational studies, curricular/content studies, and practica in teaching. Graduate programs are designed to ensure that graduates have the sound academic preparation that will lead them to become reflective practitioners.

Just the facts...

Buffalo State College
Faculty of Applied Science and Education
1300 Elmwood Avenue
Buffalo, NY 14222
(716) 878-4212
Website: www.buffalostate.edu
Profile: Urban, Large, Co-Ed
UG Tuition: $1,700.00/sem. in-state; $4,150.00/sem. out-of-state
G Tuition: $2,550.00/sem. in-state; $4,208.00/sem. out-of-state
Off Campus Programs: No

Clinical Experiences

Through field-based experiences, teacher candidates learn to design meaningful learning experiences for all students. Many of the experiences are designed so that candidates become acquainted with community educational programs early in their college career. Along with early on-site experiences, all teacher education programs require at least two practica experiences. Many courses are taught on-site, and all candidates have at least one urban placement for their student teaching experience. Teacher candidates work in a variety of communities, with students of different ages, and with culturally diverse and exceptional populations.

Noteworthy

Internships, independent study, special projects, and topics courses broaden candidates' intellectual horizons, provide candidates with non-conventional educational opportunities, and encourage candidates to work independently as they probe issues of particular interest to them. An All-College Honors Program is open to a select number of new students each year. Additional off-campus opportunities include study abroad, a national student exchange program, semester internships in Washington and Albany, and student teaching on a Southwestern reservation. Support and mentoring are available for freshmen.

Teacher Preparation Program Information

The following programs are 4 year programs:
Business Education, Business & Distributive Education, Elementary Education P-Grade 6, Elementary Education P-6 and Grades 7-9 Extension (English, French, General Science, Mathematics, Social Studies, Spanish), Exceptional Education, K-12 Education (Art), Secondary Education Grades 7-12 (Biology, Chemistry, Earth Science, English, French, Mathematics, Physics, Social Studies, Spanish), Technology Education, Vocational Technical Education

The following programs are post-baccalaureate programs:
Elementary Education

Fordham University

For over 80 years, the Graduate School of Education has focused on developing well-educated and well-trained teachers and other professionals for service in urban schools. The school reflects the Jesuit tradition of academic excellence and a dynamic balance between theory and practice. Small classes and an outstanding faculty contribute to candidates' success. The School of Education has developed strong partnerships with public and private schools and agencies, creating a broad range of internships, practica, and research opportunities. Fordham is nationally recognized for its preparation of educators for leadership roles in non-public schools.

Just the facts...

Fordham University
School of Education
113 West 60th Street
New York, NY 10023
(212) 636-6400
Website: www.fordham.edu
Profile: Urban, Large, Co-Ed
UG Tuition: $8,400.00/semester
G Tuition: $6,000.00/semester
Off Campus Programs: Yes

Clinical Experiences

Fordham's initial teacher education programs provide candidates exceptional opportunities to put theory into practice and to develop their teaching skills. Elementary education candidates in the Intern Fellowship program teach as interns for a full year. Candidates in the Master of Science in Teaching program and secondary education candidates student teach for a full semester. Candidates work with cooperating teachers, mentors, field specialists, and university faculty throughout their programs and participate in a seminar intended to guide their clinical experience and to develop their professional portfolios.

Noteworthy

Fordham's Intern Fellowship program for elementary education candidates provides paid internships or full scholarships that offset all tuition costs. Interns in the New York Public Schools complete their programs with a degree, state licensing, and a full year of teaching experience. The Master of Science in Teaching program for elementary candidates and the Master of Arts in Teaching program for secondary candidates are offered for full and part-time students. Need-based scholarships are available. Fordham's initial teacher education graduates in elementary education have 100 percent pass rates on the New York State teacher licensing exam.

Teacher Preparation Program Information

The following programs are post-baccalaureate programs:
Elementary Education, Secondary Education (Biology, English, Social Studies)

The following programs are post-baccalaureate programs:
Elementary Education, Secondary Education (Biology, English, Social Studies)

The following programs are 5th year programs:
Elementary Education, Secondary Education (Biology, English, Social Studies)

Hofstra University

Hofstra University prides itself in having an "all-university" approach to teacher education. Preparation in the content major, the liberal arts, and professional education are viewed as fundamental to a successful teaching career. The School of Education and Allied Human Services is dedicated to preparing teachers who are scholar/practitioners. Faculty and staff work with teacher candidates by modeling classroom practices that are reflective, participatory, and collaborative in the support of student learning. Freshmen who enroll in and after the fall of 1999 should expect to enter a five-year program leading to licensure with a master's degree.

Just the facts...

Hofstra University
School of Education & Allied Human Studies
216 Mason Hall
Hempstead, NY 11549
(519) 463-5740
Website: www.hofstra.edu
Profile: Suburban, Large, Co-Ed
UG Tuition: $420.00/credit hour
G Tuition: $442.00/credit hour
Off Campus Sites: No

Clinical Experiences

Teacher candidates must complete several clinical/field experiences in diverse area schools. New state certification requirements require all candidates to complete at least 150 hours of clinical experiences prior to full-time student teaching. Hofstra's teacher candidates consider this the most valuable experience in the program and regularly complete more clinical hours than required. Teacher candidates are carefully supervised by university faculty and cooperating teachers on-site.

Noteworthy

Hofstra University's School of Education and Allied Human Services is one of only four NCATE accredited institutions in the entire state of New York where more than 105 institutions are registered to prepare teachers. Teacher candidates at Hofstra have been recognized as National Student Teacher of the Year for 1997 and 1998 by the Association of Teacher Educators and Kappa Delta Pi. Hofstra students receive support and mentoring from faculty members in their first two years when employed in New York City area schools. Faculty members and students frequently conduct research together and present findings at national professional meetings.

Teacher Preparation Program Information

The following programs are 4 year programs:
Elementary Education, Elementary Bilingual Education, K-12 Education (Art), Business Education, Music Education, Physical Education, School Health Education, Secondary Education, Secretarial and Office Subjects Education

The following programs are 5th year programs:
Bilingual Elementary Education, Bilingual Secondary Education, Business Education, Early Childhood Special Education, Elementary Education, Health Education, Physical Education, Reading Teacher, Reading Teacher/Secondary Education, Special Education, Special Education & Art Therapy, Teacher of Speech & Hearing Handicapped, Teaching of English as a Second Language

Niagara University

Niagara University is a Catholic university founded in 1856 by the Vincentian Fathers and Brothers. The College of Education, in existence for over 60 years, considers a liberal arts foundation fundamental to the success of the educational practitioner. The undergraduate programs strive to prepare teachers in the theory, methods, and practice of effective instruction and the use of technology in regular and inclusive P-12 classrooms. The Graduate Division strives to produce qualified professionals who can assume leadership roles in education and other vocational or professional settings as teachers, counselors, and administrators.

Just the facts...

Niagara University
College of Education
Niagara University, NY 14109
(716) 286-8574
Website: www.niagara.edu
Profile: Suburban, Medium, Co-Ed
UG Tuition: $6,443.00/semester
G Tuition: $390.00/credit hour
Off Campus Programs: Yes

Clinical Experiences

All candidates for teacher licensure are required to observe the teacher-learning process and tutor in area schools through the University's Learn and Serve tutoring program. Coursework in each candidate's professional preparation sequence includes both observation and/or participation in learning activities. The emphasis in the field experiences is to ensure that candidates are exposed to and have experience with various methodological approaches to classroom practice. Three portfolios required for graduation provide evidence of the candidate's readiness to teach.

Noteworthy

Financial assistance is available through New York State, federal grants, and Niagara University funding. There are four-year half financial aid tuition packages for four minority students. The College of Education's graduate programs have two full scholarships available by application. The Niagara University, Niagara Falls, and Niagara Wheatfield School Districts partnership is funded by an America Reads grant to develop a tutor-training model incorporating technology into reading and writing programs at the K-5 grade level.

Teacher Preparation Program Information

The following programs are 4 year programs:

Elementary Education (Elementary Education K-6), Secondary Education (Biology, Business, Chemistry, English/Language Arts, French, General Science, Mathematics, Social Studies, Spanish), Inclusive/Special Education (Communication Disorders, Developmental Disabilities/Handicaps)

The following programs are 5th year programs:

Elementary Education (Elementary Education K-6), Secondary Education (Biology, Business, Chemistry, English/Language Arts, French, General Science, German, Mathematics, Social Studies, Spanish)

Appalachian State University

The faculty at Appalachian State University are committed to preparing excellent professionals for today's schools. Faculty and candidates form a community of inquirers who examine the nature of learning. Teaching and professional service are dynamic, goal-oriented, social activities that reflect the values of cultural diversity and solving social problems. Faculty and candidates believe learning is an active process of acquiring, assessing, and producing knowledge in a caring and respectful environment. New forms of teaching are explored through experimentation with technology. Faculty promote excellence in teaching, learning, scholarship, and professional service.

Just the facts...

Appalachian State University
Reich College of Education
Boone, NC 28608
(828) 626-2232
Website: www.appstate.edu
Profile: Rural, Large, Co-Ed
UG Tuition: $947.50/sem. in-state; $4,582.50/sem. out-of-state
G Tuition: $905.50/sem. in-state; $4,540.50/sem. out-of-state
Off Campus Programs: No

Clinical Experiences

Beginning early in their program, candidates participate in clinical experiences in diverse settings. Early field experiences involve candidates in tutoring experiences that acquaint them with different learning styles and with the role technology plays in teaching. Candidates participate in appropriate clinical and field-based experiences and are often placed in partnership schools. Programs culminate in fifteen weeks of full-time student teaching. International experiences are also available.

Noteworthy

The College of Education has the second-largest teacher education program in North Carolina; 98 percent of the students who graduate and seek licensure in North Carolina successfully obtain a license. The College of Education maintains one of the largest NC Teaching Fellows Programs (a $6,000 per year scholarship program), grants Reich Scholar Awards of $6,000 (undergraduates), provides technology support to over 85 schools in the ASU Public School Partnership, and maintains the only NC site for Fifth Dimension (5D), a unique technology-oriented, teaching and learning program that focuses on improving student performance. Terminal degrees are held by 98 percent of the faculty.

Teacher Preparation Program Information

The following programs are 4 year programs:

Birth-Kindergarten, Elementary Education (K-6), K-12 Education (Art, French, Health, Music, Physical Education, Spanish, Theatre Arts), Middle School Education (Language Arts, Mathematics, Science, Social Studies), Secondary Education (Biology, Chemistry, Earth Sciences, English, Mathematics, Physics, Social Studies, Vocational Business Education, Vocational Family & Consumer Science, Vocational Industrial Education, Vocational Marketing Education), Special Education (Learning Disabilities)

The following programs are post-baccalaureate programs:

Birth-Kindergarten, Elementary Education (K-6), K-12 Education (Art, French, Health, Music, Physical Education, Spanish, Theatre Arts), Middle School Education (Language Arts, Mathematics, Science, Social Studies), Secondary Education (Biology, Chemistry, Earth Sciences, English, Mathematics, Physics, Social Studies, Vocational Business Education, Vocational Family & Consumer Science, Vocational Industrial Education, Vocational Marketing Education), Special Education (Learning Disabilities)

Barton College

Barton College's teacher preparation program develops new professionals. The program nurtures candidates as they grow in skill throughout the program and their teaching career. Experiences are designed to develop cultural awareness, knowledge of content, decision-making abilities, confidence, and self-esteem. Using technology in instruction is an emphasis as the college prepares candidates for twenty-first century classrooms.

Just the facts...

Barton College
School of Education
P.O. Box 5000
Wilson, NC 27893-7000
(919) 399-6431
Website: www.barton.edu
Profile: Urban, Small, Co-Ed
UG Tuition: $5,015.00/semester
Off Campus Programs: No

Clinical Experiences

All teacher education majors have at least four practica leading up to a full semester of student teaching. These practica begin early in the candidate's college career and include work in classrooms in the intended licensure area. In addition, all candidates work in classrooms with disabled students and in classrooms emphasizing the teaching of reading. Candidates in two licensure areas—elementary education and education of the deaf and hard of hearing—spend one full day each week in their classrooms in the semester prior to student teaching.

Noteworthy

Barton College offers a number of scholarships to its students. The Ruth Patton Grady Scholarhip, awarded to an entering elementary education major each year, is valued at $5,000 (first preference is given to minority students). Barton has the only undergraduate education for the deaf and hard of hearing program on the Atlantic seaboard between Virginia and Florida. A school for the deaf just two miles away is a rich source of clinical experiences. Many teacher candidates at Barton receive licensure in more than one area, increasing their versatility and their breadth of knowledge and skills.

Teacher Preparation Program Information

The following programs are 4 year programs:
Elementary Education, K-12 Education (ESL, Physical Education, Spanish), Middle School Education (English, Mathematics, Science, Social Studies), Secondary Education (Art, Biology, English/Language Arts, Mathematics, Science, Social Studies), Special Education (Hearing Impaired)

The following programs are post-baccalaureate programs:
Elementary Education, K-12 Education (ESL, Physical Education, Spanish), Middle School Education (English, Mathematics, Science, Social Studies), Secondary Education (Art, Biology, English/Language Arts, Mathematics, Science, Social Studies), Special Education (Hearing Impaired)

Belmont Abbey College

Belmont Abbey College, a Catholic liberal arts institution, recognizes a responsibility to search for understanding in the context of the scriptural message and through the wisdom of the ages. This requires careful study of the human experience, together with reflection on, and reverence for God. The college exposes candidates to many of the world's major problems and helps them develop a responsible social consciousness guided by Catholic teaching. The college recognizes that intolerance hinders learning; therefore, Belmont Abbey benefits from the presence of people of different faiths, racial backgrounds, and cultures among its student body and faculty.

Just the facts...

Belmont Abbey College
Department of Education
Belmont, NC 28012-2795
(704) 825-6838
Website: www.belmontabbeycollege.edu
Profile: Rural, Small, Co-Ed
UG Tuition: $4,500.00/semester
Off Campus Programs: No

Clinical Experiences

The goal of the education program is to provide teacher candidates with the knowledge and skills necessary to plan and implement developmentally appropriate learning experiences for children and adolescents. Clinical preparation includes integrating theoretical study, a variety of selective field experiences, and systematic professional and personal reflection. Clinical field experiences begin in the earliest education classes, progressing from basic classroom observations through one-on-one student tutoring experiences, into teaching "teacher-planned" then "candidate-planned" lessons, on through the culminating experience of a semester-long student teaching experience.

Noteworthy

Belmont Abbey College has an excellent working relationship with local and regional K-12 schools. Many principals and teachers regularly request Belmont Abbey College student involvement in their student enrichment exercises (including classroom, individual tutoring assistance, and after-school assistance). Not only education majors are involved with local schools; students from other academic disciplines give of themselves and their time to assist K-12 students. Members of Kappa Delta Pi, an education honors society, provide books and supplemental materials to Catherine's House, a shelter for battered women and families that is supported by the Sisters of Mercy.

Teacher Preparation Program Information

The following programs are 4 year programs:

Elementary Education (K-6), Middle School Education (English/Language Arts, Social Studies), Secondary Education (English, Social Studies)

The following programs are post-baccalaureate programs:

Elementary Education (K-6), Middle School Education (English/Language Arts, Social Studies), Secondary Education (English, Social Studies)

Bennett College

Bennett College was founded in 1873 as a co-educational school and seminary by newly emancipated slaves. Since that time, Bennett has been named among the top ten institutions that produce African American graduates who later earn doctoral degrees. The September 1996 issue of *Money* magazine ranked Bennett College fifth in its list of "Best College Buys" among historically black colleges and universities. The teacher education faculty is committed to preparing teachers who will be successful in their areas of specialization, and who are prepared to meet challenges, celebrate diversity, and respond compassionately to their students.

Just the facts...

Bennett College
Department of Curriculum and Instruction
900 East Washington Street
Greensboro, NC 27401-3239
(336) 370-8672
Website: www.bennett.edu
Profile: Urban, Small, Women
UG Tuition: $11,430.00/semester
Off Campus Programs: No

Clinical Experiences

Faculty members directing Bennett College's teacher education program believe that theory learned in the classroom must be integrated with observation and practice in the schools in order for candidates to demonstrate and apply their knowledge and skills. Clinical experiences are carefully supervised, and often take place in the Guilford County school system, which includes a high percentage of culturally diverse students. Candidates must complete 120 hours of practicum experiences in the public schools before student teaching.

Noteworthy

Bennett College's teacher education program has collaborated with two liberal arts colleges, Greensboro College and Midway College, in faculty exchanges and student forums centered on topics in education. Teacher candidates have access to the NASA MASTAP Resource Center on campus, which provides state-of-the-art technology and multimedia equipment af particular use to future science and math teachers. The new Instructional Technology Center, funded by the Lilly Endowment, is designed to help candidates develop the skills they will need in instructional technology in order to gain licensure. Approximately 92 percent of Bennett College students receive some form of financial aid.

Teacher Preparation Program Information

The following programs are 4 year programs:

Elementary Education, K-12 Education (Music), Middle School Education, Secondary Education (Biology, English/Language Arts, Mathematics), Special Education (Mentally Handicapped, Specific Learning Disabilities)

Campbell University

Professional education programs have been offered at Campbell University since 1961. A carefully designed sequence of educational experiences blends the theoretical, professional, and practical aspects of teaching and learning in all of Campbell's education programs. Concepts and principles presented in the classroom are translated into practice by means of undergraduate field placements and graduate practica and internships. The faculty strives to develop education professionals who will be effective problem solvers in their education roles.

Just the facts...

Campbell University
School of Education
P.O. Box 369
Buies Creek, NC 27506
(910) 893-1630
Website: www.campbell.edu
Profile: Rural, Medium, Co-Ed
UG Tuition: $5,108.00/semester
G Tuition: $175.00/credit hour
Off Campus Programs: No

Clinical Experiences

Clinical experiences begin in candidates' sophomore year and continue throughout their programs of study. Teacher candidates move sequentially through a minimum of two early field experiences, a practicum, and student teaching. Candidates are placed with qualified cooperating teachers in a variety of educational settings. Field experiences are designed to provide practice in the application of the problem-solving process as appropriate to the student's developmental level and program area. University faculty work collaboratively with cooperating teachers to supervise and evaluate students in their field experiences.

Noteworthy

More than 3,000 professional educators in North Carolina are graduates of one or more of Campbell's programs. Three North Carolina Teachers of the Year and numerous recipients of state and local awards have been Campbell graduates. Two of Campbell's graduates recently won the Milken Award, a national award for exemplary principals. Recently, a new graduate was nominated for the Sally Mae Award for first-year teachers. Most of Campbell's graduates serve in rural eastern North Carolina. No candidate completing Campbell's teacher preparation program has been denied continuing licensure in North Carolina as a teacher in the last nine years.

Teacher Preparation Program Information

The following programs are 4 year programs:
Elementary Education (Elementary Education K-6), K-12 Education (French, Music, Physical Education, Spanish), Middle School Education (Language Arts/Social Studies), Secondary Education (Biology, English, Family & Consumer Science/Home Economics, Mathematics, Social Studies)

The following programs are post-baccalaureate programs:
Elementary Education (Elementary Education K-6), K-12 Education (Physical Education), Middle School Education (Language Arts/Social Studies), Secondary Education (English, Mathematics, Social Studies)

Catawba College

Catawba College, established in 1851, has a long history of preparing teachers. The teacher education faculty, supported college-wide by colleagues from other disciplines, is committed to preparing knowledgeable, problem-solving teachers for K-12 classrooms. A strong liberal arts background, deep disciplinary study, and understanding of both the science and art of teaching diverse learners are essential components of the program. Small student-professor ratios make possible the individual attention needed as teaching interns develop "reflective habits of mind."

Just the facts...

Catawba College
Teacher Education
2300 West Innes Street
Salisbury, NC 28144-2488
(704) 637-4461
Website: www.catawba.edu
Profile: Suburban, Small, Co-Ed
UG Tuition: $6,067.00/semester
Off Campus Programs: No

Clinical Experiences

Classroom internships in partnership schools are integrated into professional courses, begin early in the program, and culminate in a full semester of student teaching. Interns are placed in a variety of settings and grade levels as they progress through the clinical sequence. All who successfully complete the program demonstrate—both on-campus and in K-12 classroom settings—skill in using technology to enhance both teaching and learning. The fifteen-week student teaching experience involves the development of a professional portfolio and participation in a capstone seminar.

Noteworthy

Throughout the sequence of professional courses and related field experiences, candidates reflect on the relationship between theory and practice through journals, essays, and examinations. All junior interns participate in a two-semester instructional theory and design course, which is closely integrated with parallel methods courses. These methods courses include a substantial field component supervised by school- and college-based educators.

Teacher Preparation Program Information

The following programs are 4 year programs:
Elementary Education (Elementary Education K-6), K-12 Education (Music, Physical Education), Middle School Education (Language Arts, Mathematics, Science, Social Studies), Secondary Education (Biology, Chemistry, Comprehensive Science, English/Language Arts, Mathematics, Social Studies)

The following programs are post-baccalaureate programs:
Elementary Education (Elementary Education K-6), K-12 Education (Music, Physical Education, Reading), Middle School Education (Language Arts, Mathematics, Science, Social Studies), Secondary Education (Biology, Chemistry, Comprehensive Science, English/Language Arts, Mathematics, Social Studies)

Davidson College

Davidson College is a liberal arts institution emphasizing broad and deep academic preparation for undergraduates founded on the teaching excellence of its faculty. The professional education program seeks to develop teachers who are leaders in the academic development of secondary school students. Graduates serve as academic role models for candidates and P-12 students. Teacher candidates undertake a program of liberal studies, a rigorous academic major, and a sequence of professional studies leading to pedagogical proficiency.

Just the facts...

Davidson College
Department of Education
P.O. Box 1719
Davidson, NC 28036
(704) 892-2130
Website: www.davidson.edu
Profile: Suburban, Small, Co-Ed
UG Tuition: $21,189.00/year
Off Campus Programs: No

Clinical Experiences

Candidates participate in more than 70 hours of sequenced field experiences prior to student teaching. All experiences are carefully supervised. The student teaching experience is divided into two phases to ensure that candidates have the opportunity to teach different populations, and learn from a variety of mentors. Each student teacher's situation is unique, and the specific design of the two phases is created on an individual basis. Special attention is focused on teaching exceptional students and on understanding the diverse cultural backgrounds of students.

Noteworthy

Each year Davidson College offers one or more First Union Teaching Scholarships to a member or members of the entering freshman class. These merit scholarships may be retained for four years provided there is evidence that the recipient is actively exploring the teaching profession. For students with financial need who are interested in careers in education, Davidson offers the William B. Hight, Jr. Scholarship. The William B. Hight, Jr. Teaching Award is given each year to the senior who has demonstrated great potential for a successful career in teaching at the secondary level.

Teacher Preparation Program Information

The following programs are 4 year programs:
K-12 Education (French, Spanish), Secondary Education (English/Language Arts, Latin/9-12, Mathematics, Social Studies)

The following programs are post-baccalaureate programs:
K-12 Education (French, Spanish), Secondary Education (English/Language Arts, Latin/9-12, Mathematics, Social Studies)

Duke University

Duke University offers teacher preparation programs that lead to eligibility for licensure to teach on either the elementary (K-6) or secondary (9-12) level. The program is committed to producing liberally educated, reflective teachers who possess the intellectual background and ethical motivation to become leaders in their profession. The teacher preparation programs combine Duke's commitment to strong liberal arts majors with intensive field experiences, close personal contact with faculty, and a truly cooperative relationship with area schools. The resulting course of study leads to a multifaceted and complex understanding of the theory and practice of teaching.

Just the facts...

Duke University
Teacher Preparation
Box 90739
Durham, NC 27708-0739
(919) 660-3075
Website: www.duke.edu
Profile: Urban, Medium, Co-Ed
UG Tuition: $10,775.00/semester
G Tuition: $7,920.00/semester
Off Campus Programs: No

Clinical Experiences

Through the cooperation of local public and independent schools, a wide variety of experiences is available. Starting as early as the first year, candidates have the opportunity to observe diverse approaches to teaching and learning, to tutor individuals and small groups, to work with special children, and to implement social service projects. The final full-time internship is both a continuation and a culmination of the field-based experiences from earlier education courses, and takes place in a nurturing environment that allows student interns to engage in the kind of critical reflection and refinement of skill that leads to a successful teaching career.

Noteworthy

Duke's undergraduate liberal arts college is widely recognized as one of the country's best institutions of higher learning. Duke's achievement is based on the recruitment of a select group of truly distinguished faculty and the admission of an equally exceptional student body. The commitment to breadth and depth of study within majors develops new teachers who have sophisticated understanding in their fields. Candidates benefit from small classes, close contact with mentors in professional education, and a personalized series of experiences in area schools. These schools are as committed to the education of teachers as Duke candidates are to providing meaningful experiences for the young people they encounter.

Teacher Preparation Program Information

The following programs are 4 year programs:

Elementary Education, Secondary Education (Biology, Chemistry, Earth Science, English/Language Arts, General Science, Mathematics, Physical Sciences, Physics, Political Science, Psychology, Science, Social Studies, Sociology)

The following programs are post-baccalaureate programs:

Secondary Education (Biology, Chemistry, Earth Science, English/Language Arts, General Science, Mathematics, Physical Sciences, Physics, Political Science, Psychology, Science, Social Studies, Sociology)

East Carolina University

East Carolina University, as a public doctoral degree-granting institution, is committed to rich and distinctive undergraduate and graduate education, exemplary teaching, research and scholarship, public service, and human and intellectual diversity. The university is the third-largest institution in the University of North Carolina System. East Carolina University provides teacher candidates with a strong liberal arts foundation, multiple opportunities to work with schools and service agencies, and skills in the use of technology in the classroom.

Just the facts...

East Carolina University
School of Education
East Fifth Street
Greenville, NC 27858
(252) 328-4260
Website: www.ecu.edu
Profile: Rural, Large, Co-Ed
UG Tuition: $943.00/sem. in-state; $4,578.00/sem. out-of-state
Off Campus Programs: No

Clinical Experiences

A new model of teacher preparation was instituted in 1997 that requires a year-long senior experience in one of the eleven public school systems in the university's service area. The Senior Year Experience was jointly developed by university faculty and public school personnel. Prior to the Senior Year Experience, candidates work in public schools for three semesters observing, shadowing, and conducting small and large group instruction. The university has a Child Development Center where Birth through Kindergarten preservice teachers interact with children on a daily basis.

Noteworthy

East Carolina University received one of six BellSouth Foundation Re-Creating Teacher Education grants. This grant has helped foster increased partnership opportunities and professional development schools. Other program features include an assistive technology lab for students with special needs, and workshops provided to assist candidates preparing for the PRAXIS exams. East Carolina University offers accelerated alternative preparation programs for adults changing careers who wish to teach; a Math-Science Center for inservice teachers; and assistance in portfolio development and assessment for initial and continuing licensure.

Teacher Preparation Program Information

The following programs are 4 year programs:

Birth-Kindergarten Education, Elementary Education, K-12 Education (Art, Dance, Drama/Theatre, French, German, Music, Physical Education, Spanish), Middle School Education (English/Language Arts, Mathematics, Science, Social Studies), Secondary Education (Business, Consumer Science/Home Economics, English, Health, Marketing, Mathematics, Science, Social Studies), Special Education (Learning Disability, Mental Retardation, Severe Behavioral Disabilities/Handicaps, Speech/Language Disabilities)

The following programs are post-baccalaureate programs:

Birth-Kindergarten Education, Elementary Education, K-12 Education (Art, Dance, Drama/Theatre, French, German, Music, Physical Education, Spanish), Middle School Education (English/Language Arts, Mathematics, Science, Social Studies), Secondary Education (Business, Consumer Science/Home Economics, English, Health, Marketing, Mathematics, Science, Social Studies), Special Education (Learning Disability, Mental Retardation, Severe Behavioral Disabilities/Handicaps, Speech/Language Disabilities)

Elizabeth City State University

Elizabeth City State University (ECSU) develops citizens and leaders who participate fully in a diverse society. Graduates from the teacher education program are prepared to be competent practitioners who have both knowledge and a repertoire of skills to prepare their students for lifelong learning in a technologically oriented world. Candidates become decision makers through practice and reflection in a challenging and supportive environment. A combination of general studies, professional studies, and practica allows candidates to develop their knowledge and skills.

Just the facts...

Elizabeth City State University
Teacher Education
1704 Weeksville Road
Elizabeth City, NC 27909
(252) 335-3295
Website: http://tep.ecsu.edu
Profile: Rural, Medium, Co-Ed
UG Tuition: $844.00/sem. in-state; $4,002.00/sem. out-of-state
Off Campus Programs: No

Clinical Experiences

ECSU provides a graduated series of clinical/field-based experiences for its candidates. The initial experience is designed to assist students in determining whether teaching is the correct profession for them. Candidates spend 25 hours in a classroom in their specified area observing and participating in the class. Other early field experiences occur in conjunction with reading, classroom management, and methods courses. The culminating clinical experience is a twelve-week student teaching assignment. Plans are being finalized for a school-university partnership in the area of elementary education, in which teachers and university faculty will design coursework and clinical experiences for candidates.

Noteworthy

ECSU offers a Weekend/Evening Program to meet the needs of working people who want to earn a bachelor's degree. Most teacher preparation coursework, with the exception of student teaching, can be taken through this format. ECSU participates in the North Carolina Model Teacher Education Consortium, which provides coursework to teacher assistants and other school district employees who wish to become teachers, particularly those who will work in rural, northeastern North Carolina. Through the consortium, the state pays for textbooks, offers a stipend for student teachers, and covers the cost for all but forty dollars of each undergraduate course.

Teacher Preparation Program Information

The following programs are 4 year programs:

Elementary Education, K-12 Education (Art, Music, Physical Education), Middle School Education (English, Mathematics, Science, Social Studies), Secondary Education (Biology, Business, Chemistry, English/Language Arts, Mathematics, Social Studies, Technology Education), Special Education (Learning Disability, Mental Retardation)

The following programs are post-baccalaureate programs:

Elementary Education, K-12 Education (Art, Music, Physical Education), Middle School Education (English, Mathematics, Science, Social Studies), Secondary Education (Business, Chemistry, English/Language Arts, Mathematics, Technology Education), Special Education (Learning Disability, Mental Retardation)

Elon College

Founded in 1897, Elon College has continually focused on teacher preparation as one of its main programs of study. The education program blends a strong liberal arts general studies background with pedagogical studies and clinical experiences. Faculty engage candidates in active learning strategies to equip them with a body of content knowledge and a repertoire of teaching skills. Graduates are able to demonstrate skills in planning and preparation, delivery of instruction, and assessment of student learning in diverse learning settings. Throughout the program, candidates learn to use technology in teaching and learning.

Just the facts...

Elon College
Education Department
Campus Box 2165
Elon College, NC 27244
(336) 584-2355
Website: www.elon.edu
Profile: Suburban, Medium, Co-Ed
UG Tuition: $6,000.00/semester
G Tuition: $210.00/credit hour
Off Campus Programs: No

Clinical Experiences

Clinical experiences are an essential part of Elon College's teacher education program. Candidates begin clinical experiences with the first education course and continue clinical experiences throughout the program. Experiences progress from an initial observation experience to individual tutoring to small-group work to whole class teaching. The program culminates with a fourteen-week full-time student teaching experience.

Noteworthy

Elon College is one of fourteen campuses in the state of North Carolina participating in the North Carolina Teaching Fellows Program. This program, funded by the North Carolina General Assembly, is an innovative scholarship program designed to attract highly talented students into teaching with a special emphasis on increasing the number of males and minorities in teaching. At Elon College, this program provides a $13,000 scholarship each year.

Teacher Preparation Program Information

The following programs are 4 year programs:
Elementary Education, K-12 Education (French, Physical Education, Spanish), Middle School Education (English, Mathematics, Science, Social Studies), Secondary Education (Biology, Chemistry, English/Language Arts, Mathematics, Physics, Social Studies), Special Education (Learning Disability, Severe Behavioral Disabilities/Handicaps)

The following programs are post-baccalaureate programs:
Elementary Education, K-12 Education (French, Physical Education, Spanish), Middle School Education (English, Mathematics, Science, Social Studies), Secondary Education (Biology, Chemistry, English/Language Arts, Mathematics, Physics, Social Studies), Special Education (Learning Disability, Severe Behavioral Disabilities/Handicaps)

Fayetteville State University

Fayetteville State University, a public comprehensive university, has provided quality education since 1867. The School of Education educates and prepares individuals at the undergraduate and graduate levels for professions in the field of education, and provides leadership in teacher education throughout the region, state, and nation. The conceptual framework for the teacher education program is "The Educational Professional as a Facilitator of Learning." The faculty believe that the educator's main task is to engage students efficiently and effectively in the learning process. Graduates from Fayetteville's program are catalysts and motivators of learning who lead learners in discovery.

Just the facts...

Fayetteville State University
School of Education
1200 Murchison Road
Newbold Station
Fayetteville, NC 28301-4208
(910) 486-1265
Website: www.uncfsu.edu
Profile: Urban, Large, Co-Ed
UG Tuition: $1,726.00/semester
G Tuition: $1,498.00/semester
Off Campus Programs: Yes

Clinical Experiences

Candidates begin their early field experiences by focusing primarily on the school environment. Early field experiences are provided through laboratory experiences in area schools, and foundations of education and human development courses. Student teaching is the culmination of clinical experiences for all teacher education majors, supervised by both a university supervisor and a cooperating public school teacher. Continuous feedback and evaluation throughout all clinical experiences is key to developing candidates' knowledge and skills.

Noteworthy

Fayetteville State University provides a warranty for all of its teacher education graduates. The warranty provides assistance to graduates who are deemed unsatisfactory performers by their supervisors. Thus far, this warranty has never been invoked. A variety of academic support services are available to students in the School of Education, including an advisement center, computer laboratory, PRAXIS Laboratory, education majors meetings, and the Curriculum Learning Resource Laboratory. There are many scholarship award opportunities for teacher education majors. Numerous student organizations focus on issues in education.

Teacher Preparation Program Information

The following programs are 4 year programs:

Elementary Education, K-12 Education (Health, Music, Physical Education, Spanish), Middle School Education (5-8 Certification, Language Arts, Mathematics, Science, Social Studies), Secondary Education (Biology, English/Language and Literature, History, Mathematics, Marketing, Political Science, Sociology, Vocational Business), Special Education

The following programs are post-baccalaureate programs:

Elementary Education (Reading), K-12 Education (Health, Physical Education, Spanish), Middle School Education (5-8 Certification, Language Arts, Mathematics, Science, Social Studies), Secondary Education (Biology, English/Language and Literature, History, Mathematics, Marketing, Political Science, Sociology, Vocational Business), Special Education

The following programs are 5th year programs:

Elementary Education, Middle School Education (5-8 Certification, Language Arts, Mathematics, Science, Social Studies), Secondary Education (Biology, English/Language and Literature, History, Mathematics, Political Science), Special Education

Gardner-Webb University

The primary purpose of Gardner-Webb University is to provide learning of distinction in the liberal arts and in professional studies within a caring community based upon Christian principles and values. The School of Education attempts to fulfill this mission by preparing educators to formulate and apply research, facilitate the acquisition of knowledge, cultivate effective teaching, and serve the educational community. The teacher preparation program at Gardner-Webb seeks to empower candidates to take on the roles of theorist and practitioner through coursework, personal influence, field experiences, and modeling.

Just the facts...

Gardner-Webb University
Department of Education
Main Street
Boiling Springs, NC 28017
(704) 434-4406
Website: www.gardner-webb.edu
Profile: Rural, Medium, Co-Ed
UG Tuition: $5,095/semester
G Tuition: $178/credit hour
Off Campus Programs: Yes (graduate level only)

Clinical Experiences

Student teaching assignments and various field experiences required throughout the teacher education program are made in public schools within commuting distance from the university. Diversity of experiences and feedback from public school personnel and university staff help to make candidates ready for the classroom when they graduate. These experiences begin early in the sophomore year and conclude with the professional student teaching semester.

Noteworthy

The School of Education has formulated agreements with local community colleges to provide elementary education programs for teacher assistants in local school districts. Licensure-only candidates and candidates seeking additional licensure are welcomed and encouraged to seek admission. The master's degree programs in school administration and school counseling have attracted and successfully graduated a large and productive school personnel population.

Teacher Preparation Program Information

The following programs are 4 year programs:
Elementary Education, K-12 Education (French, Music, Physical Education, Spanish), Middle School Education, Secondary Education (Biology, Chemistry, Comprehensive Social Studies, English, Mathematics)

The following programs are post-baccalaureate programs:
Elementary Education, K-12 Education (French, Music, Physical Education, Spanish), Middle School Education, Secondary Education (Biology, Chemistry, Comprehensive Social Studies, English, Mathematics)

Greensboro College

The Greensboro College teacher education program is committed to cultivating teachers who are reflective practitioners. Studies and clinical experiences are designed to develop literate, articulate, intellectually independent, and professionally competent individuals. Active learning, critical reflection, and disciplined inquiry are central to this program as candidates gain understanding about learning and teaching. Theory and practice are combined to develop professional educators who are prepared to meet challenges, celebrate diversity, and respond compassionately and ethically to their students.

Just the facts...

Greensboro College
Teacher Education Program
815 West Market Street
Greensboro, NC 27401-1875
(336) 272-7102
Website: www.gborocollege.edu
Profile: Urban, Small, Co-Ed
UG Tuition: $5,400.00/semester
Off Campus Programs: No

Clinical Experiences

Field experiences are a valued and critical component of the program. A series of sequential settings has been designed to move prospective teachers from simple observation to the more complex aspects of instruction. Candidates will complete between 100 and 150 hours in field settings prior to entering a sixteen-week student teaching placement. An Early Field Experiences Seminar, which is also a program admission requirement, is offered in conjunction with beginning field experiences.

Noteworthy

The program has extensive partnership arrangements with area schools, enabling candidates to work with culturally and linguistically diverse populations. Collaboration with other colleges has enriched learning and teaching on the campus. Although Greensboro College is small, it offers licensure opportunities in many areas. Each year, the Proctor Special Education Scholarship is awarded to a student entering his or her senior year of study.

Teacher Preparation Program Information

The following programs are 4 year programs:

Elementary Education (Birth-Kindergarten), K-12 Education (Art, Drama/Theater, Music, Physical Education, Spanish), Middle School Education (English, Mathematics, Science, Social Studies), Secondary Education (Biology, English/Language Arts, Mathematics, Social Studies), Special Education (Learning Disability, Mental Retardation, Severe Behavioral Disabilities/Handicaps)

The following programs are post-baccalaureate programs:

Elementary Education (Birth-Kindergarten), K-12 Education (Art, Drama/Theater, Music, Physical Education, Spanish), Middle School Education (English, Mathematics, Science, Social Studies), Secondary Education (Biology, English/Language Arts, Mathematics, Social Studies), Special Education (Learning Disability, Mental Retardation, Severe Behavioral Disabilities/Handicaps)

Guilford College

The Education Studies Department at Guilford College seeks to develop educators who are committed to and capable of constructive action in contemporary society. The objectives of the program reflect the college's Quaker background, its liberal arts tradition, and multicultural and global perspectives. Graduates respect individual learners, build community, respond to the spiritual dimensions of learning and living, and assume responsibilities in their local, national, and global communities. The program emphasizes understanding educational issues from a global perspective using observation, practice, experimentation, and action research.

Just the facts...

Guilford College
Education Studies Department
5800 West Friendly Avenue
Greensboro, NC 27410
(336) 316-2270
Website: www.guilford.edu
Profile: Suburban, Small, Co-Ed
UG Tuition: $7,398.00/semester
Off Campus Programs: No

Clinical Experiences

Education majors begin their clinical experiences with tutorials and other experiences designed to broaden their perspectives on education. Midway through the program, candidates complete a cross-cultural internship and inquiry, usually in another country. This fieldwork requires examination of another education system as well as reflection on personal experiences in a different culture. The internship provides candidates with a foundation of first-hand knowledge of cultural diversity so that they can understand and relate more deeply to diversity when they enter the complex world of the classroom. In advanced coursework, candidates concentrate on clinical experiences in their specialty area.

Noteworthy

Central components of the program include tutorial sessions that engage candidates and faculty members in one-on-one interchanges in first and second year coursework; a portfolio review; a written and oral self-assessment presented by each candidate to the faculty; and a capstone experience in which candidates reflect on their teaching in relation to its theoretical grounding, and explore leadership roles they may assume in the future. Close faculty/candidate relationships are developed through tutorial sessions, peer-group learning, portfolio reviews, field supervision, and the advising system.

Teacher Preparation Program Information

The following programs are 4 or 4 1/2 year programs:
Elementary Education, K-12 Education (French, Spanish), Secondary Education (English/Language Arts, Social Studies)

High Point University

Founded in 1924, High Point University has prepared teachers for public schools since its inception. The program is based on interdisciplinary perspectives within a liberal arts tradition, and coordinates professional education experiences with candidates' acquisition of knowledge and skills in various academic disciplines. Graduates have an understanding of diverse student characteristics, the ability to maintain a positive learning environment, and a commitment to the well being of individual students and society. The faculty enjoys a collegial relationship with area public and private schools. Faculty are committed to organizing quality field experiences for candidates.

Just the facts...

High Point University
Teacher Education
833 Montlieu Avenue
High Point, NC 27262
(336) 841-9000
Website: www.highpoint.edu
Profile: Suburban, Medium, Co-Ed
UG Tuition: $5,020.00/semester
Off Campus Programs: No

Clinical Experiences

Candidates participate in clinical experiences beginning in their sophomore year. Clinical experiences differ in perspective and depth depending on the candidate's area of study. Experiences move from structured, professor-led experiences to independent student teaching. During the first semester of the sophomore year, the practicum is a carefully structured, guided experience in which an instructor accompanies candidates to various school settings. Other experiences involve working with at-risk students and exceptional children and working in small group tutoring situations. The spring semester of the senior year is a semester-long student teaching experience.

Noteworthy

Each year, over 90 percent of the graduates from the teacher education program are employed in North Carolina and across the United States. Four current school superintendents in North Carolina are graduates from High Point University. Candidates have the opportuntity to study during the fall semester of their junior year at Westminster College in Oxford, England. Westminster College, a teacher education college, provides innovative and enriching studies for candidates. High Point University's teacher education program received a grant from the Guilford County Schools, which enables candidates to be paid tutors at various schools in the district.

Teacher Preparation Program Information

The following programs are 4 year programs:

Elementary Education (Elementary Education K-6), K-12 Education (Art, Physical Education), Middle School Education (English, Language Arts, Mathematics, Science, Social Studies); Secondary Education (Biology, Chemistry, English/Language Arts, French, History, Mathematics, Social Studies, Spanish), Special Education (Behaviorally/Emotionally Handicapped, Gifted/Talented, Learning Disability, Mental Retardation)

The following programs are post-baccalaureate programs:

Elementary Education (Elementary Education K-6), K-12 Education (Art, Physical Education), Middle School Education (English, Language Arts, Mathematics, Science, Social Studies), Secondary Education (Biology, Chemistry, English/Language Arts, French, History, Mathematics, Social Studies, Spanish), Special Education (Behaviorally/Emotionally Handicapped, Gifted/Talented, Learning Disability, Mental Retardation)

Johnson C. Smith University

The primary purpose of the Department of Education is to prepare teachers for the public schools and other educational service agencies in a complex, technological, and multicultural age. The programs are based on the belief that teachers are professional decision makers in multifaceted roles. Candidates are prepared to make decisions in a variety of roles—as masters of content, diagnosticians, curriculum designers, instructors, managers, and child advocates.

Just the facts...

Johnson C. Smith University
Department of Education
100 Beatties Ford Road
Charlotte, NC 28216
(704) 378-1064
Website: www.jcsu.edu
Profile: Urban, Small, Co-Ed
UG Tuition: $3,213.00/semester
Off Campus Programs: No

Clinical Experiences

Clinical experiences include a focus on all of a student's direct school and community relationships. Candidates in elementary education are required to complete 100-130 hours in pre-student teaching experiences. Secondary education candidates complete 80-105 hours of pre-student teaching experiences.

Noteworthy

Diversity and technology are major components of the teacher education program, and are infused in each professional education course. Candidates develop an electronic portfolio to demonstrate their technology skills.

Teacher Preparation Program Information

The following programs are 4 year programs:
Elementary Education (Elementary Education K-6), K-12 Education (Health, Physical Education), Secondary Education (English/Language Arts, Mathematics, Social Studies)

The following programs are post-baccalaureate programs:
Elementary Education (Elementary Education K-6), K-12 Education (Health, Physical Education), Secondary Education (English/Language Arts, Mathematics, Social Studies)

Lees-McRae College

Lees-McRae College has distinguished itself as a teacher preparation institution by preparing competent, caring, and conscientious teachers. The programs are based on the concept of the teacher as a reflective mentor. The college strives to provide candidates with a strong background in teaching knowledge as well as the technological skills that will enable graduates to be effective in the classroom. Admission is selective, and graduates are mentored by faculty well into their careers.

Just the facts...

Lees-McRae College
Division of Education
P.O. Box 128
Banner Elk, NC 28604-0128
(828) 898-8781
Website: www.lmc.edu
Profile: Rural, Small, Co-Ed
UG Tuition: $5,040.00/semester
Off Campus Programs: Yes

Clinical Experiences

Clinical experiences begin early in the program of studies and culminate with the student teaching experience. Initial introduction begins with a period of observations and a gradual transition to teacher assisting at a professional development school or at specially selected school sites. Comprehensive assessments occur during these field experiences with increased emphasis placed on candidates' reflections about their experiences. Cooperating teachers for the clinical experiences are chosen because they are reflective mentors and have met specified teaching competencies.

Noteworthy

Lees-McRae notes its extensive mentoring of teacher candidates and graduates; one graduate pointed out with pride "the faculty mentors us to our graves." Graduates have a wide range of choices for employment opportunities, and are employed by school districts both locally and nationwide. Lees-McRae's education program has partnerships with various local schools to enhance the coursework and experiences of its teacher candidates.

Teacher Preparation Program Information

The following programs are 4 year programs:

Elementary Education (Mathematics, Science, Social Studies), K-12 Education (Dance, Drama/Theater, Physical Education), Middle School Education (English, Mathematics, Science, Social Studies), Secondary Education (Comprehensive Social Science, English/Language Arts, Mathematics, Physical Education, Social Studies)

The following programs are post-baccalaureate programs:

Elementary Education (Mathematics, Science, Social Studies), K-12 Education (Dance, Drama/Theater, Physical Education), Middle School Education (English, Mathematics, Science, Social Studies), Secondary Education (Comprehensive Social Science, English/Language Arts, Mathematics, Physical Education, Social Studies)

Lenoir-Rhyne College

Founded 108 years ago to prepare future teachers and ministers, Lenoir-Rhyne College is a member of the North Carolina Synod of the Evangelical Lutheran Church of America. The faculty is committed to developing thinking, reflective decision makers who facilitate learning. As reflective decision makers, education majors are encouraged to gain a foundation of knowledge in a liberal arts curriculum and then begin to develop an evolving philosophy regarding education today. Graduates have a strong liberal arts background and are able to use technology effectively in the P-12 classroom.

Just the facts...

Lenoir-Rhyne College
Teacher Education
P.O. Box 7219
Hickory, NC 28603
(704) 328-7189
Website: www.lrc.edu
Profile: Urban, Small, Co-Ed
UG Tuition: $5,268.00/semester
G Tuition: $5,268.00/semester
Off Campus Programs: No

Clinical Experiences

Beginning in their sophomore year, education candidates are introduced to interactive experiences in local public schools. Each experience focuses on working with students, teachers, and parents, and extends previous experiential learning. Through field experiences, candidates gain confidence acquired through familiarity with the classroom and practical application of course content. Several partnership schools provide exposure to large numbers of ethnic minority and low socioeconomic populations.

Noteworthy

Small student-faculty ratios allow for personal relationships that often extend beyond graduation. Scholarship awards are available through college, state, federal, and legacy funds as well as endowments and gifts. The Education Department has four state-of-the-art multimedia classrooms available to faculty and students. Graduates have received awards at the local, state, and national levels. One recent graduate has attained National Board certification, and others are pursuing this advanced level of certification as well.

Teacher Preparation Program Information

The following programs are 4 year programs:
Early Childhood Education, Elementary Education (Communications, Mathematics, Science, Social Studies), K-12 Education (Art, ESL, French, German, Latin, Music, Physical Education, Reading, Spanish), Middle School Education (Two of the following—Communications, Mathematics, Science, Social Studies), Secondary Education (Biology, Business, Chemistry, English/Language Arts, General Science, Mathematics, Physics), Special Education (Gifted/Talented, Hearing Impaired)

The following programs are post-baccalaureate programs:
Early Childhood Education, Elementary Education (Communications, Mathematics, Science, Social Studies), K-12 Education (Art, ESL, French, German, Latin, Music, Physical Education, Reading, Spanish), Middle School Education (Two of the following—Communications, Mathematics, Science, Social Studies), Secondary Education (Biology, Business, Chemistry, English/Language Arts, General Science, Mathematics, Physics), Special Education (Gifted/Talented, Hearing Impaired)

The following programs are 5th year programs:
Early Childhood Education

Livingstone College

Livingstone College's teacher education program is committed to ensuring that its graduates have a strong liberal arts background, are able to use technology effectively, and are able to work with all children in K-12 classrooms. The program is designed to support the development of teachers who will enter the classrooms prepared to make instruction meaningful to each student, who will make instructional decisions that involve selecting content and material, who will plan multiple teaching and learning activities, and who serve as advocates for the teaching profession.

Just the facts...

Livingstone College
Department of Education/Sports Management
701 West Monroe Street
Salisbury, NC 28144
(704) 638-5602/5600
Website: None
Profile: Rural, Small, Co-Ed
UG Tuition: $11,550.00/year
Off Campus Programs: No

Clinical Experiences

Clinical experiences are well planned and are offered in partnership with K-12 schools. Education faculty and teachers are central to this arrangement. The experiences are sequential and provide opportunities for prospective teachers to understand the complex lives of students in schools, and to plan, organize, and work with students in a positive classroom environment. Coursework ensures that during these experiences teacher candidates demonstrate theories and practices consistent with the objectives of the program. Clinical experiences begin in the freshman year and end with a full semester of student teaching.

Noteworthy

The teacher education program is committed to continuous and systematic program examination, development, and revision. The program has a strong theoretical foundation built on research, reflective teaching and learning, thoughtful analysis of national studies on education, solidly based strategies, and proven practice. Scholarships are awarded based on candidates' interests and academic achievement.

Teacher Preparation Program Information

The following programs are 4 year programs:

Elementary Education, K-12 Education (Music, Physical Education), Secondary Education (English, Mathematics, Social Studies)

The following programs are post-baccalaureate programs:

Elementary Education, K-12 Education (Music, Physical Education), Secondary Education (English, Mathematics, Social Studies)

Mars Hill College

Mars Hill College has offered a teacher education program since it became a senior college in 1962. The faculty are committed to a knowledge base that produces teachers who are "facilitators of optimal development" in their students. The School of Education and Leadership faculty model the characteristics of teachers who encourage and challenge students to reach maximum potential regardless of their background and abilities. The school has developed a very positive reputation for its teacher education graduates, who are actively sought for employment by public school systems.

Clinical Experiences

Prospective teachers enjoy quality hands-on experiences with schools, teachers, and students in western North Carolina. The elementary teacher preparation program requires a full-year internship in one public school classroom. Middle school candidates are also involved in a full year internship, although they are generally assigned to more than one classroom. Secondary and specialized subject candidates major in an academic area and spend one full semester in an assigned public school classroom. All four groups of candidates are involved in a three-week multicultural experience at the end of their senior year.

Noteworthy

Mars Hill College is a small college in the southern Appalachian area, and its location allows prospective teachers to experience both urban schools in Asheville and rural Appalachian schools. Alumni have assumed many roles in education including North Carolina State Board Chair, presidents of higher education institutions, superintendents, principals, and teachers at all levels. Graduates often continue their education to complete master's or doctoral degrees. Due to a large federal grant, computers and software are kept up to date. Scholarships and prospective teacher scholarship/loans are available for education candidates. Faculty are diverse in background and all have had public school experience.

Teacher Preparation Program Information
The following programs are 4 year programs:
Elementary Education, K-12 Education (Art, Drama/Theater, Music, Physical Education), Kindergarten Education, Middle School Education, Secondary Education (Biology, Chemistry, English/Language Arts, Mathematics, Social Studies)

Meredith College

Meredith College is the largest private women's college in the Southeast. The student-faculty ratio is fourteen to one, with an average class size of nineteen students. Through an emphasis on the liberal arts, career preparation, and personal development, Meredith women are challenged to excel. The Education Department is committed to the development of reflective practitioners who are able to evaluate critically the purposes of education; meet the needs of linguistically, socioeconomically, and culturally diverse school populations; and assume leadership roles in working with teacher colleagues to improve the education system.

Just the facts...

Meredith College
Department of Education
3800 Hillsborough Street
Raleigh, NC 27607
(919) 760-8315
Website: www.meredith.edu
Profile: Urban, Small, Women
UG Tuition: $4,420.00/semester
G Tuition: $260.00/credit hour
Off Campus Programs: No

Clinical Experiences

Field experiences are an integral component of the teacher preparation program. Early in the program, preservice teachers attend school board meetings to understand schooling from a system perspective and to begin to formulate effective strategies for school improvement and reform. Classroom field experiences provide opportunities to observe teachers and students, as well as the teaching of lessons under the direction of college faculty. The culminating field experience includes a year-long student teaching placement under the supervision of a cooperating teacher.

Noteworthy

The Education Department has entered into collaborative agreements with elementary and secondary schools. These partnerships allow for the exchange of faculty between the college and public schools and the use of public school classrooms for instructional purposes. These agreements also entail placing candidates with their cooperating teacher the semester before their student teaching experience. Residents of North Carolina are eligible for Teaching Fellows Scholarships and Prospective Teacher Scholarship/Loans.

Teacher Preparation Program Information

The following programs are 4 year programs:

Elementary Education, K-12 Education (Art, Dance, French, Music, Physical Education, Spanish, Theatre), Middle School Education (Language Arts, Mathematics, Science, Social Studies), Secondary Education (Biology, Business, Chemistry, English, Family & Consumer Sciences, Mathematics, Social Studies)

The following programs are post-baccalaureate programs:

Elementary Education, K-12 Education (Art, Dance, French, Music, Physical Education, Spanish, Theatre), Middle School Education (Language Arts, Mathematics, Science, Social Studies), Secondary Education (Biology, Business, Chemistry, English, Family & Consumer Sciences, Mathematics, Social Studies)

Methodist College

The faculty of the teacher education program at Methodist College believe the role of the teacher is to facilitate both learning and personal development. Candidates must demonstrate that they are attentive, genuine, understanding, respectful, knowledgeable, and communicative. Graduates understand the cognitive and affective development of their students; realize that learning is a complex process that requires interaction between curriculum, instruction, students, and the environment; and implement appropriate instructional strategies to create a positive learning environment in the classroom.

Just the facts...

Methodist College
Department of Education
5400 Ramsey Street
Fayetteville, NC 28311
(910) 630-7060
Website: www.methodist.edu
Profile: Suburban, Small, Co-Ed
UG Tuition: $5,950.00/semester
Off Campus Programs: No

Clinical Experiences

Three pre-student teaching field experience courses require a minimum of 90 hours total to be spent in classrooms. Field Experience I candidates must teach at least one lesson; Field Experience II candidates must teach at least two lessons; and Field Experience III candidates must teach at least three lessons. The ten-week student teaching experience involves an orientation and evaluation session for candidates, cooperating teachers, and college supervisors. Secondary or subject area candidates are assigned a college supervisor from their respective disciplines for the field experience courses and student teaching. Candidates are placed in public schools that reflect the culturally diverse population of the region.

Noteworthy

At Methodist College, students and academics are priorities. Smaller class sizes allow students the opportunity for more individual attention. Graduates have served as past presidents of the student division of the North Carolina Association of Educators and as effective teachers and administrators in school systems throughout the state. With careful planning and additional coursework, teacher candidates can earn a second certificate in reading or academically gifted education. There are many financial aid and scholarship opportunities for qualified students.

Teacher Preparation Program Information

The following programs are 4 year programs:
Elementary Education, K-12 Education (Art, French, Music, Physical Education, Spanish), Middle School Education (English, Mathematics, Science, Social Studies), Secondary Education (English/Language Arts, Mathematics, Science, Social Studies), Special Education (Learning Disability)

The following programs are post-baccalaureate programs:
Elementary Education, K-12 Education (Art, French, Music, Physical Education, Spanish), Middle School Education (English, Mathematics, Science, Social Studies), Secondary Education (English/Language Arts, Mathematics, Science, Social Studies), Special Education (Learning Disability)

Montreat College

Montreat College's teacher education program prepares teachers to be reflective communicators—instructional leaders who, through reflection, adjust content and method for a given audience, purpose, and context. Candidates master teaching and communications skills, and through methods courses, field experiences, practice, and feedback, they develop sound methodology. Graduates are introspective, open-minded, and thoughtful, and are able to create optimal learning environments for their students. Teacher candidates major in an academic discipline and take the education courses necessary for licensure.

Just the facts...

Montreat College
Division of Teacher Education
P.O. Box 1267
Montreat, NC 28757
(828) 699-8011
Website: www.montreat.edu
Profile: Suburban, Small, Co-Ed
UG Tuition: $5,222.00/semester
Off Campus Programs: No

Clinical Experiences

Candidates begin their field experiences in the freshman year with observation in the schools. Candidates graduate to tutoring, teaching short lessons, teaching full lessons, and teaching a two-week unit. The field experiences culminate in student teaching. All teaching is supervised by the candidates' faculty mentor who gives generous amounts of feedback. The program arranges field work to engage candidates in a diverse range of experiences in public, private, city, and rural schools, with honors and at-risk students.

Noteworthy

Montreat College's teacher education program has a student-faculty ratio of five to one; the college's overall student to faculty ratio is eleven to one. The college is a member of the Coalition for Christian Colleges and Universities and, as such, emphasizes the integration of Christian faith and learning. Montreat College is committed to preparing teacher candidates to use technology to improve student learning. Candidates work with faculty to teach current teachers in the public and private schools how to use technology for their own learning and teaching. Candidates are required to create both a teaching portfolio and a technology project (a prototype of a multimedia lesson).

Teacher Preparation Program Information

The following programs are 4 year programs:
Secondary Education (English/Language Arts, General Science, Mathematics, Social Studies)

The following programs are post-baccalaureate programs:
Secondary Education (English/Language Arts, General Science, Mathematics, Social Studies)

National Council for Accreditation of Teacher Education

North Carolina A&T State University

The School of Education at North Carolina A&T State University administers a quality educational program preparing candidates for 42 licenses at the undergraduate and graduate levels. The School of Education collaborates with two school districts using a professional development school model to prepare educational professionals as catalysts for learning. The professional development school partnership serves over 9,000 students and 130 teachers, and continues to grow each year. Teaching and learning is facilitated by extensive technology use by students and faculty. The faculty believes that an effective educator is one who promotes lifelong learning and the love of learning to students.

Clinical Experiences

Clinical experiences are driven by the professional development school partnership model. Field experiences for candidates are sequentially planned and tailored to the candidates' specialized areas of preparation, and designed to complement course objectives. Field experiences begin with the first course in education, with a major field experience in the middle of the program. The culminating field experience is the final year-long internship. In the first semester of the internship, candidates' field experiences are connected to methods courses. Student teaching takes place the entire second semester. Candidates may also conduct their student teaching in England or Germany.

Just the facts...

North Carolina A&T State University
School of Education
1601 East Market Street
Greensboro, NC 27411
(336) 334-7757
Website: www.ncat.edu
Profile: Urban. Medium, Co-Ed
UG Tuition: $840.00/sem. in-state; $4,475.00/sem. out-of-state
G Tuition: $840.00/sem. in-state; $4,475.00/sem. out-of-state
Off Campus Programs: No

Noteworthy

The School of Education student population is culturally, racially, and ethnically diverse. The student to instructor ratio is small, which provides time for meeting individual student needs and making progress assessments. In 1992 and 1993 the School of Education was cited by *Black Issues in Higher Education* for graduating more African Americans with B.S. degrees in education than any other institution in the nation. The School of Education has a systematic support system for assisting candidates for academic success that includes advisement, computer labs, and support staff. The School of Education is a campus leader in using technology for teaching.

Teacher Preparation Program Information

The following programs are 4 year programs:
Birth-Kindergarten Education, Elementary Education, K-12 Education (Art, Drama/Theater, French, Industrial Technology, Music, Physical Education), Secondary Education (Biology, Business, Chemistry, English/Language Arts, Mathematics, Physics, Social Studies, Vocational Agriculture, Vocational Home Economics/Consumer Homemaking, Vocational Trade & Industrial), Special Education (Cross-Categorial)

The following programs are post-baccalaureate programs:
Elementary Education, K-12 Education (Drama/Theater, French, Industrial Technology, Music, Physical Education, Reading), Secondary Education (Business, Chemistry, English/Language Arts, Mathematics, Physics, Social Studies, Vocational Agriculture, Vocational Home Economics/Consumer Homemaking, Vocational Trade & Industrial)

North Carolina Central University

North Carolina Central University, as the nation's first public liberal arts institution for African Americans, maintains a strong liberal arts tradition and commitment to academic excellence in a diverse educational and cultural environment. The university continues to serve its traditional clientele of African American students, but has expanded its commitment to meet the educational needs of a student body that is diverse in race and socioeconomic attributes. The School of Education provides preparation for teachers, administrators, counselors, speech language pathologists, and educational technologists who serve in public schools. Research and service are also central to the School of Education's mission.

Clinical Experiences

Clinical experiences begin in the candidate's sophomore year, and culminate in a year-long internship during the senior year. Pre-student teaching experiences include orientation to schools, children, and communities; planning; and teaching and evaluating students. Candidates observe and participate in school openings, closings, inter-sessions, parent conferences, extra-curricular activities, and support services. The program is designed to provide exposure to diverse school settings. Professional development schools have been established at the elementary level and at the Governor Morehead School for the Blind, and a middle school professional development school site is being planned.

Just the facts...

North Carolina Central University
School of Education
P.O. Box 19376
Shephard Station
Durham, NC 27707
(919) 560-6466
Website: www.soe.nccu.edu
Profile: Urban, Medium, Co-Ed
UG Tuition: $759.00/sem. in-state; $4,001.00/sem. out-of-state
G Tuition: $668.50/sem. in-state; $3,910.50/sem. out-of-state
Off Campus Programs: No

Noteworthy

The university established a master's degree program in Special Education-Visual Impairment in 1997. This program uses educational technology (interactive video, cable and satellite broadcast, computer-mediated instruction) to reach non-traditional learners and to address the severe shortage of teachers of visually impaired students. Three professional development school partnerships serve as training laboratories for candidates, research laboratories for faculty, and support services for students in public schools.

Teacher Preparation Program Information

The following programs are 4 year programs:

Elementary Education (Elementary Education K-6), K-12 Education (Art, Drama/Theater, French, Music, Physical Education, Spanish), Middle School Education (Language Arts, Mathematics, Science, Social Studies), Secondary Education (Biology, Chemistry, Consumer & Family Science/Home Economics, English/Language Arts, Mathematics, Physics, Social Studies)

The following programs are post-baccalaureate programs:

Elementary Education (Elementary Education K-6), K-12 Education (Art, Drama/Theater, French, Music, Physical Education, Spanish), Middle School Education (Language Arts, Mathematics, Science, Social Studies), Secondary Education (Biology, Physics, Social Studies)

North Carolina State University

North Carolina State University focuses on the preparation of middle grades and high school teachers, counselors, supervisors, school administrators, and school psychologists. Teacher education programs are designed to provide in-depth preparation in the candidate's subject matter area as well as intensive skill development in the teaching of their content field. From the freshman year, candidates are advised and mentored throughout their program by education faculty in the area in which they will be licensed. Faculty strive to prepare professionals who are dedicated to human improvement through education and who have demonstrated competence in the teaching/learning process.

Clinical Experiences

Candidates begin field experiences in the sophomore year, continue them in the junior year, and conclude with student teaching in the senior year. Experiences are centered in the candidate's subject area with supervision from faculty in that discipline as well as from cooperating teachers. Some field experiences are conducted within partnership schools. These experiences emphasize pre-service, beginning, and career teacher development. Experiences include observing; tutoring; conducting small group work and mini-lessons; and classroom teaching. Student teaching ranges from ten weeks to a full semester depending on the candidate's program.

Just the facts...

North Carolina State University
School of Education
208 Poe Hall, Box 7801
Raleigh, NC 27695-7801
(919) 515-7160
Website: www.ncsu.edu
Profile: Urban, Large, Co-Ed
UG Tuition: $1,182.00/sem. in-state; $5,765.00/sem. out-of-state
G Tuition: $1,185.00/sem. in-state; $5,768.00/sem. out-of-state
Off Campus Programs: No

Noteworthy

Instructional technology is an important part of education at all levels, and students and teachers in North Carolina public schools must now be able to demonstrate competence in using technology for teaching and learning. The Center for Learning Technologies coordinates the college's efforts in ensuring its faculty and students can not only demonstrate competence but lead in the use of technology in education. Housed within the College of Education are seven computing labs that are open to education candidates. The college offers numerous scholarship opportunities for entering freshmen and rising juniors and seniors.

Teacher Preparation Program Information

The following programs are 4 year programs:
K-12 Education (French, Spanish), Middle School Education (Language Arts, Mathematics, Science, Social Studies), Secondary Education (English, Mathematics, Science, Social Studies, Technology Education, Vocational Agriculture, Vocational Marketing, Vocational Health Occupations)

The following programs are post-baccalaureate programs:
Secondary Education (Agriculture, Mathematics, Science, Technology Education)

The following programs are 5 year programs:
Middle School Education (Language Arts, Social Studies), Reading, Marketing, Special Education (Behavior Disorders, Learning Disabilities, Mental Retardation), Secondary Education (Mathematics)

North Carolina Wesleyan College

North Carolina Wesleyan College, a small liberal arts college, has prepared teachers since the 1960s. The college is committed to working with students as they develop the skills needed to become responsible, productive members of a diverse society. Education faculty work closely with candidates as they progress through a sequence of education courses that build on the liberal arts, develop specific teaching skills, and provide opportunities for candidates to participate in several public school settings. The goal of the education program is the development of the knowledge and skills candidates need to become effective teachers who are reflective decision makers.

Just the facts...

North Carolina Wesleyan College
Education Department
3400 North Wesleyan Boulevard
Rocky Mount, NC 27804
(252) 985-5163
Website: www.ncwc.edu
Profile: Rural, Small, Co-Ed
UG Tuition: $4,072.00/semester
Off Campus Programs: No

Clinical Experiences

Clinical experiences begin in the sophomore year, continue through the junior year, and culminate in a semester of student teaching. School activities are coordinated so candidates experience the many roles teachers fulfill today. Candidates observe, tutor, complete case studies, teach small groups and whole classes, and work closely with teachers in three or more sites to provide opportunities to experience the diversity of schools. Elementary majors complete student teaching in both kindergarten and an elementary grade.

Noteworthy

The program provides personal attention and support to its teacher candidates, including traditional students, career changers, and those returning to school to gain provisional licenses. This mix of students is a strength of the program because students learn from each other's experiences. Candidates may complete internships that carry a college stipend. Many leadership opportunities are available on campus. Graduates of the program are readily employed, are recognized as well prepared and knowledgeable of current practices, and often assume leadership roles in their schools.

Teacher Preparation Program Information

The following programs are 4 year programs:
Elementary Education, Middle School Education (English, Mathematics, Science, Social Studies), Secondary Education (Biology, English/Language Arts, History, Mathematics, Social Studies)

The following programs are post-baccalaureate programs:
Elementary Education, Middle School Education (English, Mathematics, Science, Social Studies), Secondary Education (Biology, English/Language Arts, History, Mathematics, Social Studies)

Pfeiffer University

Pfeiffer University emphasizes service to the local and larger community. The faculty and staff believe that there is perhaps no greater area of service available to young people today than the teaching profession. Programs are based on the idea that teachers at the elementary, high school, and college levels have a direct influence on the future of the country. Candidates are prepared to inspire in their future students a dedication to intellectual pursuits and a sense of citizenship and responsibility. Teacher preparation at Pfeiffer is a concern of the entire faculty.

Just the facts...

Pfeiffer University
Department of Teacher Education
Misenheimer, NC 28109
(704) 463-1360
Website: www.pfeiffer.edu
Profile: Rural, Small, Co-Ed
UG Tuition: $5,115.00/semester
Off Campus Programs: No

Clinical Experiences

Pfeiffer believes that experiences in the schools are vital to the successful development of prospective teachers. Therefore, clinical experiences are incorporated throughout the program of studies. Candidates benefit from numerous clinical experiences, which include two 30-hour observation/assistant experiences; internships in the public schools of ten or more hours during most methods courses; and a full semester of student teaching.

Noteworthy

A letter from a parent of a Pfeiffer University student notes, "We are most happy with your concern with students, not only in their studies, but in their personal lives. The family environment seems very evident at Pfeiffer. It makes a parent feel confident knowing that the goals and dreams they hold for their children's future will be a reality due to the dedication and continuous support of faculty members."

Teacher Preparation Program Information

The following programs are 4 year programs:
Elementary Education (Elementary Education K-6), K-12 Education (Music, Physical Education), Secondary Education (English/Language Arts, Mathematics, Music, Physical Education, Social Studies), Special Education (Learning Disability, Severe Behavioral Disabilities/Handicaps)

The following programs are post-baccalaureate programs:
Elementary Education (Elementary Education K-6), K-12 Education (Music, Physical Education), Secondary Education (English/Language Arts, Mathematics, Physical Education, Social Studies), Special Education (Learning Disability, Severe Behavioral Disabilities/Handicaps)

Queens College

Professional education programs at Queens build on strong liberal studies and an emphasis on the role of the teacher as an independent learner. In the integrated core experience required of all Queens students, education majors learn to view academic topics as integrated rather than as separate and discrete categories. In the fall of the sophomore year, candidates begin field experiences in the public schools, applying theory to diverse classrooms under the supervision of teachers. The recently modified elementary major includes additional content knowledge requirements. Queens' small classes allow candidates to easily and effectively collaborate with their professors and other students.

Just the facts...

Queens College
Department of Education
1900 Selwyn Avenue
Charlotte, NC 28274
(704) 337-2565
Website: www.queens.edu
Profile: Urban, Medium, Co-Ed
UG Tuition: $9,500.00/year
G Tuition: $225.00/credit hour
Off Campus Programs: No

Clinical Experiences

Elementary education majors begin their clinical experiences in their sophomore year. At the secondary level, candidates are placed in departments in their licensure area for more than 30 hours before student teaching. Due to the good reputation of teacher training at Queens, teachers and administrators from the Charlotte-Mecklenburg system confidently welcome candidates into their schools. Candidates are systematically placed in schools where they gain a variety of experiences at several grade levels with diverse populations. They work with small groups, assess learning, plan for instruction, and teach lessons. Student teaching for both elementary and secondary candidates is a semester-long placement.

Noteworthy

Unique features of the education programs at Queens include small classes, close association with faculty members, early and varied field experiences, and invitations to be part of paid summer programs for literacy improvement. The newly designed undergraduate education major increases both candidates' academic requirements and their ability to plan and implement integrated learning experiences for K-6 students. The student teaching experience now includes an additional component which emphasizes working with diverse socio-economic populations. Plans also include an increased emphasis on teaching students with special needs in the regular classroom.

Teacher Preparation Program Information

The following programs are 4 year programs:
Elementary Education

The following programs are post-baccalaureate programs:
K-12 Education (French, Spanish, Music), Secondary Education (Biology, English/Language Arts, Mathematics, Social Studies)

The following programs are 5th year programs:
MAT Initial Licensure Elementary Education (K-6)

Saint Andrews Presbyterian College

The purpose of the Saint Andrews professional education program is to prepare learner-directed, proactive teachers. Saint Andrews' candidates believe and demonstrate that teachers are the single most important factor outside the home environment in effecting student learning and development. The curriculum is designed to develop in candidates the attitudes, content, experience, knowledge, and skills needed for a student-centered approach to teaching and learning.

Just the facts...

Saint Andrews Presbyterian College
Department of Education
1700 Dogwood Mile
Laurinburg, NC 28352
(910) 277-5340
Website: www.sapc.edu
Profile: Rural, Small, Co-Ed
UG Tuition: $18,540.00/year
Off Campus Programs: Yes

Clinical Experiences

Preservice teachers complete a series of field experiences beginning with the professional studies sequence of courses. These courses place candidates in a school setting to observe; they are designed to orient prospective teachers to the profession. Candidates also engage in a series of field-based experiences along with methods courses requiring them to work with small groups, tutor individual students, and teach whole group lessons. The final field-based experience is student teaching, which places candidates in two classroom settings at different grade levels during the semester.

Noteworthy

Saint Andrews is nationally recognized for its barrier-free campus and its commitment to accommodating students with physical challenges. The teacher education program supports and encourages physically challenged students preparing for careers in education. The Saint Andrews, Sandhill Campus Program offers evening and weekend classes leading to a bachelor's degree in elementary education in Pinehurst, North Carolina. The program is designed for the working adult who has returned to college to seek a career in teaching.

Teacher Preparation Program Information

The following programs are 4 year programs:
Elementary Education, K-12 Education (Physical Education)

The following programs are post-baccalaureate programs:
Elementary Education, K-12 Education (Physical Education)

Saint Augustine's College

Saint Augustine's College offers a strong liberal arts education that enables its students to grasp the skills required to function effectively in a world of enormous technological advances. Graduates have a strong commitment to community service. The Department of Education prepares future teachers using a conceptual framework based on mentoring. During this preparation, the student is exposed to the historical, philosophical, and sociological foundations of education; a scientific investigation of the human personality, behavior, and development; and an investigation of schools.

Just the facts...

Saint Augustine's College
Department of Education
1315 Oakwood Avenue
Raleigh, NC 27610-2298
(919) 516-4096
Website: www.st-aug.edu
Profile: Urban, Small, Co-Ed
UG Tuition: $2,444.00/semester
G Tuition: $2,444.00/semester
Off Campus Programs: No

Clinical Experiences

The Early Field Experience is a program designed to provide preservice teachers with first-hand exposure to the classroom setting. As a prerequisite to student teaching, the Early Field Experience enables candidates to better understand principles as they apply to the world of practice. The experience consists of 45 to 60 hours of observation, assistance, participation, and analysis under the guidance of an experienced teacher. Each teacher candidate participates in student teaching for a full semester (a minimum of fourteen weeks). The student teacher is paired with a licensed teacher who has at least three years of experience in the classroom.

Noteworthy

At the end of the 1998-1999 academic year, Saint Augustine's College will begin its one hundred and fifteenth year as an institution of higher learning. Throughout its existence, Saint Augustine's College has prepared and graduated more than 9,000 young men and women who have assumed leadership positions throughout the United States and the rest of the world. Saint Augustine's College is proud of its tradition of giving its students a quality foundation for critical thinking, character building, and leadership skills necessary for life-long living and learning.

Teacher Preparation Program Information

The following programs are 4 year programs:
Elementary Education, K-12 Education (Music, Physical Education), Secondary Education (Biology, Business, English/Language Arts, Mathematics, Social Studies), Special Education (Learning Disability)

The following programs are post-baccalaureate programs:
Elementary Education, K-12 Education (Music, Physical Education), Secondary Education (Biology, Business, English/Language Arts, Mathematics, Social Studies), Special Education (Learning Disability)

The following programs are 5th year programs:
Secondary Education (English/Language Arts, Mathematics, Social Studies)

Salem College

The early Moravians who settled in Salem, North Carolina, believed that young women deserved an education, and they began a school for girls in 1772 that has evolved into a nationally recognized academy and college. As early as the 1850s, Salem was preparing highly qualified, caring teachers. Salem students are encouraged to seek a firm foundation in the liberal arts, intellectual independence, creative and critical thinking abilities, and the knowledge and skills to solve problems. The Salem Department of Education is committed to promoting the cognitive development of each prospective teacher. Candidates engage in significant clinical experiences as they learn about content, theory, and research.

Just the facts...

Salem College
Department of Education
Winston Salem, NC 27108
(336) 721-2658
Website: www.salem.edu
Profile: Urban, Small, Co-Ed
UG Tuition: $173.75/credit hour
G Tuition: $195.00/credit hour
Off Campus Programs: No

Clinical Experiences

Prospective teachers at Salem participate in early field experiences and guided clinical work throughout the program. Many courses provide opportunities for working with small groups and individual students under the guidance of faculty members. Through a partnership with Konnoak School, Salem candidates work under the supervision of skilled teachers and gain real-life, practical experience in the classroom. As teaching interns, candidates receive guidance and support from school-based personnel and college faculty.

Noteworthy

At Salem, prospective teachers receive a solid foundation in promoting literacy development. The constructivist philosophy guides Salem's program, and the faculty emphasize literature-based, integrated instruction. The program also prepares candidates to meet the diverse needs of students. The graduate program is designed for students who are employed, and all classes meet in the evening. Candidates with undergraduates degrees can usually earn the master's degree with licensure in 18 months. Salem is a multi-age campus located in a beautiful, restored historic village. Scholarships and financial aid are available.

Teacher Preparation Program Information

The following programs are 4 year programs:
Elementary Education, K-12 Education (French, Spanish), Secondary Education (Biology, Chemistry, English/Language Arts, Mathematics, Social Studies), Special Education (Learning Disability)

The following programs are post-baccalaureate programs:
Early Childhood Education, Elementary Education, K-12 Education (French, Spanish), Secondary Education (Biology, Chemistry, English/Language Arts, Mathematics, Social Studies), Special Education (Learning Disability)

The following programs are 5 year programs:
Early Childhood Education, Elementary Education, Special Education (Learning Disability)

The following programs are 5th year programs:
Early Childhood Education, Elementary Education, Special Education (Learning Disability)

Shaw University

Shaw University is located just a few blocks from the state capitol in historic downtown Raleigh. It is the oldest African American college in the South, and among the oldest in the nation. The teacher education program at Shaw has been producing teachers and other educational leaders since 1878. The faculty are committed to preparing teachers who have a strong liberal arts background, and who are critical thinkers and problem solvers. The programs emphasize the development of the technological skills that are crucial to success in modern-day society.

Just the facts...

Shaw University
Department of Teacher Education
118 East South Street
Raleigh, NC 27601
(919) 546-8530
Website: Pending
Profile: Urban, Small, Co-Ed
UG Tuition: $5,334.00/semester
Off Campus Programs: Yes

Clinical Experiences

Clinical experiences at Shaw give candidates an opportunity to evaluate their interest and potential in the teaching profession. Candidates observe, plan, and practice instructional and professional duties in public school settings. They apply the critical thinking and problem solving strategies they have learned through their coursework to real-life classrooms. Three levels of field experiences take candidates from observation to student teaching or internships in schools.

Noteworthy

Candidates can take some classes through distance learning with the aid of videotapes. Satellite programming, supported by a grant from the U.S. Department of Education, includes instruction in topics such as current educational issues and curriculum changes. A PRAXIS Series lab provides assistance for candidates who wish to improve their performance on licensure tests. The Department of Education also runs a project funded by the Department of Health and Human Resources to provide an educational training program for Head Start and Early Head Start personnel. A project funded by NASA is designed to train qualified mathematics and science teachers.

Teacher Preparation Program Information

The following programs are 4 year programs:
Elementary Education, Secondary Education (Biology, English/Language Arts, Mathematics, Social Studies), Special Education

The following programs are post-baccalaureate programs:
Elementary Education, Secondary Education (Biology, English/Language Arts, Mathematics, Social Studies), Special Education

University of North Carolina at Asheville

The UNCA Department of Education operates under the guiding principle that effective educators are best prepared by a foundation in liberal arts. The goal of the Department of Education is to prepare teachers who (1) demonstrate exceptional content-based academic and educational expertise; (2) reflect the knowledge and skills essential to effective instructional practices; (3) recognize, accept, and promote the needs, aspirations, and potential of every student; and (4) demonstrate creativity, innovation, and ability as independent thinkers and problem solvers.

Just the facts...

The University of North Carolina at Asheville
Department of Education
One University Heights
Asheville, NC 28804-3299
(828) 251-6420
Website: www.unca.edu/education/
Profile: Urban, Medium, Co-Ed
UG Tuition: $946.00/sem. in-state; $4,155.00/sem. out-of-state
Off Campus Programs: No

Clinical Experiences

Candidates are engaged in a variety of pre-methods/student teaching clinical experiences, beginning with their first education course and ranging from 36 to 57 semester hours. Final methods course internships are completed under the supervision of the same school system teacher who will supervise the candidate's fifteen-week full-time student teaching experience. UNCA is engaged in forming partnerships with area schools that bring teachers to campus and present additional opportunities for candidates to observe and tutor in the public schools.

Noteworthy

UNCA provides an undergraduate liberal arts education and is the only university in the sixteen-campus University of North Carolina system designated as a public liberal arts institution. UNCA is also the only school in the University of North Carolina system that does not offer a major in education. Instead, teacher candidates major in a liberal arts/sciences discipline and a course of study leading to their specific area of licensure. Students at UNCA enjoy a low student-faculty ratio and education students have advisors in both education and their academic area. North Carolina residents can participate in the Teaching Fellows Program, a four-year fellowship program.

Teacher Preparation Program Information

The following programs are 4 year programs:

K-12 Education (Art, French, German, Reading, Spanish, Theater Arts), Middle School Education (English, Mathematics, Science, Social Studies), Secondary Education (Biology, Chemistry, English, History, Latin, Mathematics, Physics, Science, Social Studies)

University of North Carolina at Chapel Hill

The School of Education prepares educational leaders by conducting teaching, research, and service, and by assisting in the development of strong and effective public schools in the state. Undergraduate teacher education programs are offered in Child Development and Family Studies (birth-kindergarten), Elementary, and Middle Grades Education. Secondary Education and special subjects (foreign languages and music) are offered in a graduate-level fifth year M.A.T. program. Other graduate education programs are also offered.

Just the facts...

University of North Carolina at Chapel Hill
School of Education
CB #3500, Peabody Hall
Chapel Hill, NC 27599
(919) 966-7000
Website: www.unc.edu
Profile: Suburban, Large, Co-Ed
UG Tuition: $1,117.16/sem. in-state; $5,610.16/sem. out-of-state
G Tuition: $1,112.46/sem. in-state; $5,605.46/sem. out-of-state
Off Campus Programs: No

Clinical Experiences

Teacher candidates in the undergraduate programs have clinical experiences during each semester of their junior and senior years including a full semester of a professional teaching internship in their senior year. Elementary and middle grades internships are offered in the spring semester of the candidate's senior year, and in the fall and spring of the senior year for candidates in the child development and family studies program. The M.A.T. program is a twelve-month, full-time, school-based program that relies on partnerships between the public schools and the university, and that uses the reality of the classroom as the motivation for connecting theory and practice.

Noteworthy

The University of North Carolina at Chapel Hill's Office of Undergraduate Admissions is responsible for both freshman and transfer admissions. A freshman interested in pursuing a course of study in an education program must first be admitted to and enrolled in the General College. The student remains enrolled in the General College through the sophomore year and then may apply to transfer directly into the School of Education for the junior and senior years in one of the three undergraduate programs. Candidates are admitted to the School of Education as transfers from other university departments (other than General College) or other institutions on a very limited basis.

Teacher Preparation Program Information

The following programs are 4 year programs:
Early Childhood Education, Elementary Education, Middle School Education

The following programs are post-baccalaureate programs:
K-12 Education (ESL, Reading), Special Education (Learning Disability)

The following programs are 5th year programs:
K-12 Education (French, German, Japanese, Spanish, Music), Secondary Education (English/Language Arts, Latin, Mathematics, Science, Social Studies)

University of North Carolina at Charlotte

The University of North Carolina at Charlotte has been involved in the preparation of teachers, counselors, and school administrators for more than 25 years. Programs in the College of Education foster effective schooling and development of healthy, autonomous, lifelong learners. The mission of the College of Education is two-fold: to identify and create knowledge that addresses the developmental and educational needs of children, youth, and their families and to disseminate this knowledge through high-quality initial preparation and continuing education programs for professionals who seek to be exceptionally competent as teachers.

Just the facts...

University of North Carolina at Charlotte
College of Education
Charlotte, NC 28223
(704) 547-4707
Website: www.unuc.edu
Profile: Urban, Large, Co-Ed
UG Tuition: $919.00/sem. in-state; $4,554.00/sem. out-of-state
Off Campus Programs: No

Clinical Experiences

Clinical experiences in schools and classrooms that provide multiple opportunities to work with culturally diverse P-12 students are a critical part of all professional education programs. Preservice clinical experiences begin as early as the freshman year in some programs and in all programs by the sophomore year. Beginning activities involve classroom observations, and subsequent activities involve one-on-one and small and large group instruction. The culminating experience is a fifteen-week, full-time student teaching semester. All teacher education programs will soon incorporate student teaching in a year-long internship that spans the candidate's senior year.

Noteworthy

University-school teacher education partnerships enhance preservice, induction, and continuing professional development programs for teachers. Two model elementary classrooms, a computer classroom, a computer lab, and a faculty development lab provide up-to-date technology support. The Teaching Fellows program for talented North Carolina high school graduates and the Principal Fellows program for selected graduate students pursuing a master's degree in school administration are offered. A faculty development coordinating council supports teaching and research and coordinates mentoring and peer observation programs. The Office of Educational Outreach facilitates faculty involvement in schools.

Teacher Preparation Program Information

The following programs are 4 year programs:

Birth-Kindergarten Education, Elementary Education, K-12 Education (Art, Dance, French, German, Music, Spanish, Theatre), Middle Grades Education, Secondary Education (Biology, Chemistry, Earth Science, English, Mathematics, Physics, Social Studies), Special Education (Mental Disabilities)

The following programs are post-baccalaureate programs:

Birth-Kindergarten Education, Elementary Education, K-12 Education (Art, Dance, French, German, Music, Spanish, Theatre), Middle Grades Education, Secondary Education (Biology, Chemistry, Earth Science, English, Mathematics, Physics, Social Studies)

University of North Carolina at Greensboro

The School of Education at the University of North Carolina at Greensboro is committed to creating for students, faculty, and staff an environment that is grounded in mutual trust, shared responsibility, and open communication. The School of Education strives to make quality the common characteristic of all its endeavors with its faculty, students, academic programs, partnerships within the university, and partnerships with the public and private sectors.

Just the facts...

University of North Carolina at Greensboro
School of Education
P.O. Box 26171
Greensboro, NC 27402-6171
(336) 334-3407
Website: www.uncg.edu
Profile: Urban, Large, Co-Ed
UG Tuition: $508.00/sem. in-state; $4,652.00/sem. out-of-state
G Tuition: $381.00/sem. in-state; $3,489.00/sem. out-of-state
Off Campus Programs: No

Clinical Experiences

Beginning in 1991, UNCG's School of Education embraced the professional development school (PDS) model as an integral part of its preparation of prospective elementary and middle school teachers. Sophomores accepted into licensure programs in elementary or middle grades education become members of an inquiry team, take their methods courses as a cohort, and also participate in extensive field experiences for four consecutive semesters. Faculty leaders of the inquiry teams, methods faculty, and on-site teacher educators collaborate regularly to assess the progress of teacher candidates.

Noteworthy

UNCG participates in the North Carolina Teaching Fellows Program designed to attract high-quality students into teaching. Participants receive scholarship awards of $5,000 annually or up to four years. Currently, there are approximately 130 Teaching Fellows pursuing undergraduate teaching degrees at UNCG. The School of Education also offers undergraduates an opportunity to participate in an Educational Learning Community. Members of the Learning Community live together and complete a set of course experiences together. The Learning Community helps students form partnerships with others who share similar educational interests.

Teacher Preparation Program Information

The following programs are 4 year programs:
Early Childhood Education, Elementary Education, K-12 Education (Art, Drama/Theater, Dance, French, German, Health, Latin, Music, Physical Education, Spanish), Middle School Education (Mathematics, Science, Social Studies), Secondary Education (Art, Biology, Chemistry, English/Language Arts, Mathematics, Physical Education, Physics, Social Studies, Sociology, Vocational Marketing), Special Education (Hearing Impaired)

The following programs are post-baccalaureate programs:
K-12 Education (Art, French, German, Spanish), Secondary Education (Art, Biology, Chemistry, English/Language Arts, Mathematics, Physics), Special Education (Behavioral/Emotional Disorders, Learning Disability)

University of North Carolina at Pembroke

The University of North Carolina at Pembroke (UNCP) was originally founded in 1887 as an institution for the education of American Indians. The teacher education program at the UNCP is committed to providing preservice and inservice teachers and student support personnel with an understanding that the dynamic interrelationship among theory, practice, and reflection provides the foundation for continuous professional development. The teacher education program is also committed to influencing positive change in professional education systems through school/university partnerships, collaborative improvement projects, and continuing education opportunities.

Clinical Experiences

Clinical/field experiences, culminating in a full-semester student teaching experience, allow prospective teachers to explore the relationships among theory, practice, and reflection. The number of hours of field experience prior to student teaching varies from 45 to 96 hours depending on the program area. Experiences involve a range of activities appropriate to professional education and the specific program area. Experiences include such activities as observation, tutoring, assisting the teacher, data collection and related tasks. The quantity and quality of the field experiences progressively increase from initial experiences to an extensive set of experiences immediately preceding student teaching.

Just the facts...

The University of North Carolina at Pembroke
Office of Teacher Education
One University Drive
Pembroke, NC 28372
(910) 521-6221
Website: www.uncp.edu/education
Profile: Rural, Medium, Co-Ed
UG Tuition: $571.00/sem. in-state; $3,437.00/sem. out-of-state
G Tuition: $571.00/sem. in-state; $3,437.00/sem. out-of-state
Off Campus Programs: No

Noteworthy

The Teacher Education Program at the University of North Carolina at Pembroke is one of the selected programs for participation in the North Carolina Teaching Fellows Program. The highly competitive program provides selected students with $6,500 per year, for up to four years, as a loan for tuition and other costs which may be repaid by teaching in North Carolina. Each year of teaching experience provides a year of loan repayment.

Teacher Preparation Program Information

The following programs are 4 year programs:

Elementary Education (Birth-Kindergarten, Elementary Education K-6), K-12 Education (Art, Music, Physical Education), Middle School Education (Language Arts, Mathematics, Science, Social Studies), Secondary Education (Biology, English, Mathematics, Science, Social Studies), Special Education (Learning Disability, Mentally Impaired K-12)

The following programs are post-baccalaureate programs:

Elementary Education (Birth-Kindergarten, Elementary Education K-6), K-12 Education (Art, Music, Physical Education), Middle School Education (Language Arts, Mathematics, Science, Social Studies), Secondary Education (Biology, English, Mathematics, Science, Social Studies), Special Education (Learning Disability, Mentally Impaired K-12)

University of North Carolina at Wilmington

The Watson School of Education at the University of North Carolina at Wilmington is a community of scholars dedicated to teaching, learning, creating, and extending knowledge through research. The faculty strive to model effective teaching practices, provide a variety of understandings related to the field of education, encourage application of instructional strategies to field experiences, and enhance collaboration with public and private school systems through a variety of service activities and special programs. Candidates receive a strong liberal arts background and take courses in pedagogy that stress the infusion of technology.

Just the facts...

University of North Carolina at Wilmington
Watson School of Education
601 South College Road
Wilmington, NC 28403-3297
(910) 962-4142
Website: www.uncwil.edu
Profile: Suburban, Medium, Co-Ed
UG Tuition: $967.00/sem. in-state; $4,602.00/sem. out-of-state
G Tuition: $967.00/sem. in-state; $4,602.00/sem. out-of-state
Off Campus Programs: No

Clinical Experiences

The Watson School of Education has entered into professional development system collaborative agreements with ten school systems in the region. Students are required to complete extensive and developmentally sequential field experiences in professional development schools and to participate in regular site seminars that focus on instructional practices. In addition, candidates tutor children in reading and mathematics in the Ed Lab and engage in observation and teaching in placements at agencies that serve children and adolescents. Faculty are required to complete field rotations on a regular basis that provide support for candidates in the field. Partnership teachers receive training for their roles in mentoring candidates.

Noteworthy

Candidates in the Watson School of Education have access to a number of special services including the Ed Lab, Curriculum Materials Center, and Instructional Technology Center. The advising program in the Watson School is very strong, and all education majors are advised by full-time faculty members. A number of scholarships are available, including Teaching Fellows and Principal Fellows. Candidates have access to job placement services while completing their internships, and employment rates of graduates are very high. Watson School of Education graduates have received Teacher of the Year and Principal of the Year awards at the school, school system, regional, and state levels.

Teacher Preparation Program Information

The following programs are 4 year programs:

Early Childhood Education, Elementary Education (Elementary Education K-6), K-12 Education (French, Spanish, Music, Physical Education), Middle School Education (Language Arts, Mathematics, Science, Social Studies), Secondary Education (Biology, Chemistry, English/Language Arts, General Science, History, Mathematics, Physics, Science, Social Studies), Special Education (Behaviorally-Emotionally Handicapped, Learning Disability, Mental Retardation)

The following programs are post-baccalaureate programs:

Early Childhood Education, Elementary Education (Elementary Education K-6), K-12 Education (French, Spanish, Music, Physical Education), Middle School Education (Language Arts, Mathematics, Science, Social Studies), Secondary Education (Biology, Chemistry, English/Language Arts, General Science, History, Mathematics, Physics, Science, Social Studies), Special Education (Behaviorally-Emotionally Handicapped, Learning Disability, Mental Retardation)

National Council for Accreditation of Teacher Education

Wake Forest University

The Department of Education at Wake Forest University prepares teachers who become lifelong learners. The faculty believe that teachers learn about the skills and knowledge of their profession from their earliest preservice experience into the induction process and through their career development as master practitioners. The Department of Education has developed an atmosphere in which multiple approaches to practice and careful appraisal of research findings lead candidates to fashion their own teaching philosophy and classroom style.

Just the facts...

Wake Forest University
Department of Education
P.O. Box 7266
Winston Salem, NC 27109
(910) 759-5341
Website: www.wfu.edu
Profile: Suburban, Medium, Co-Ed
UG Tuition: $19,450/year
G Tuition: $16,300/year
Off Campus Programs: No

Clinical Experiences

Candidates' initial clinical experience is in an observation and reflection seminar. Candidates observe in a variety of school settings, allowing them to see many special student populations and a variety of teaching styles. Then they return to campus for a seminar led by a master teacher that focuses on special populations and other issues in the public schools. In their second clinical experience, candidates observe four master teachers who serve in the licensing areas offered by the university. Candidates also reflect on what they have observed through discussions with the master teachers and a university advisor. The student teaching experience lasts for fifteen weeks.

Noteworthy

Wake Forest is one of twelve North Carolina colleges and universities that take part in the Model Clinical Teaching Network. The Master Teacher Fellows program seeks academically talented and committed students who have a baccalaureate degree and no prior coursework in teacher education. During an intense fourteen-month period of study and field experience, Fellows engage in graduate work in their discipline; rotate through master teachers' classrooms; take part in an intensive six-week block of pedagogical courses; and teach for ten weeks in the local schools. All twenty-four Fellows are awarded full scholarships and an additional stipend.

Teacher Preparation Program Information

The following programs are 4 year programs:
Elementary Education, K-12 Education (French, German, Latin, Spanish), Secondary Education (Biology, Chemistry, English/Language Arts, Mathematics, Physics, Social Studies)

The following programs are post-baccalaureate programs:
K-12 Education (French, German, Latin, Spanish), Secondary Education (Biology, Chemistry, English/Language Arts, Mathematics, Physics, Social Studies)

The following programs are 5th year programs:
K-12 Education (French, Spanish), Secondary Education (Biology, Chemistry, English/Language Arts, Mathematics, Physics, Social Studies)

Warren Wilson College

Warren Wilson College is an independent, four-year liberal arts institution surrounded by the Blue Ridge Mountains near Asheville, North Carolina. The college has over 700 students enrolled in 32 majors/concentrations as well as interdisciplinary and integrated programs. The campus covers nearly 1,100 acres, including a farm and miles of forests and trails. The college's Triad Education Program combines academic study; participation in a campus-wide work program (all students work fifteen hours a week); and required community service. The teacher education program builds a professional knowledge repertoire that combines academics, work, and service, and prepares students to make a difference.

Clinical Experiences

Candidates observe schools, teachers, and children. They consider the roles of teachers and the ways that teachers' perceptions of and actions toward students can be shaped by school context. Fieldwork experiences are intended to help preservice teachers understand diversity issues. Candidates also receive an introduction to educational and classroom research through the questions that shape their observations. On campus, candidates can work in the Early Learning Center/Head Start Program. College service opportunities encourage candidates to be involved in schools and with children from their first year at Warren Wilson College.

Just the facts...

Warren Wilson College
Education Department
Box 9000
Asheville, NC 28815-9000
(828) 298-3325
Website: www.warren-wilson.edu
Profile: Rural, Small, Co-Ed
UG Tuition: $12,850/year
Off Campus Programs: No

Noteworthy

College academic requirements include studies in global issues. In 1997 the college inaugurated Warren Wilson World Wide, a program to subsidize cross-cultural or international travel for every qualified student in his or her junior year. A consortium of health care providers, business owners, early childhood educators, and concerned citizens is establishing the Mountain Area Child and Family Center (MACFC), a state of the art child development center located on campus. The MACFC will integrate the current Head Start program and care for 100 birth to preschool children.

Teacher Preparation Program Information

The following programs are 4 year programs:
Elementary Education, Secondary Education (Biology, English/Language Arts, Mathematics, Social Studies)

The following programs are post-baccalaureate programs:
Elementary Education, Secondary Education (Biology, English/Language Arts, Mathematics, Social Studies)

Western Carolina University

Western Carolina University's campus rests at the base of the Great Smoky and Blue Ridge Mountains. The College of Education and Allied Professions seeks to prepare professionals for the schools and colleges of the state and region and for other educational and service agencies. It also provides services to individuals, schools, and regional educational and professional agencies. It undertakes continuous evaluation to assure curricula and professional services of high quality, and coordinates the screening, selection, and counseling of candidates. The College of Education and Allied Professions trains candidates to become reflective decision makers.

Just the facts...

Western Carolina University
College of Education and Allied Professions
222 Killian Building
Cullowhee, NC 28723-9038
(828) 227-7311
Website: www.ceap.edu
Profile: Rural, Medium, Co-Ed
UG Tuition: $459.00/sem. in-state; $4,094.00/sem. out-of-state
G Tuition: $459.00/sem. in-state; $4,094.00/sem. out-of-state
Off Campus Programs: Yes

Clinical Experiences

All candidates complete a fifteen-week semester of full-time student teaching and a minimum of 22 hours per week in a public school classroom as a requirement in each of three professional education courses. Student teachers are supervised every other week by a university supervisor. The college has a school-university partnership with nine local schools. Selected teacher candidates spend the equivalent of two to three full days in a public school classroom during the first semester of a year-long internship. Candidates then spend a full semester as student teachers in the same classroom working with the same teacher.

Noteworthy

The College of Education and Allied Professions has produced three of the last six North Carolina State Teachers of the Year. According to *Yahoo* magazine, Cullowhee, home of Western Carolina University's College of Education and Allied Professions, has the distinction of being the most wired small town in North Carolina. Special centers in the college include the Reading Center, Office for Rural Education, Center for Mathematics and Science Education, Developmental Evaluation Center, Speech and Hearing Center, Office for School-University Partnerships, and Office of School Services. The university participates in the North Carolina Teaching Fellows Scholarship Program.

Teacher Preparation Program Information

The following programs are 4 year programs:
Elementary Education (Birth-Kindergarten), K-12 Education (Art, French, German, Music, Physical Education, Spanish), Middle School Education (English, Mathematics, Science, Social Studies), Secondary Education (Biology, English/Language Arts, Mathematics, Social Studies), Special Education

The following programs are post-baccalaureate programs:
Elementary Education (Birth-Kindergarten), K-12 Education (Art, French, German, Music, Physical Education, Spanish), Middle School Education (English, Mathematics, Science, Social Studies), Secondary Education (Biology, English/Language Arts, Mathematics, Social Studies), Special Education

Wingate University

Wingate University strives to promote academic excellence and leadership while educating students in a Christian environment. Students are encouraged to develop and expand their knowledge, their understanding of people, and their faith. The School of Education prepares educators who are thinking, ethical decision makers who can fulfill their roles as scientists (creating and following well-designed lesson plans) and artists (demonstrating creativity and flexibility). Candidates learn how to adapt their strategies and methods to meet both the needs of a large group and the special needs student within the same classroom.

Just the facts...

Wingate University
School of Education
Box 3065
Wingate, NC 28174-0157
(704) 233-8075
Website: www.wingate.edu
Profile: Urban, Small, Co-Ed
UG Tuition: $385.00/credit hour
G Tuition: $155.00/credit hour
Off Campus Programs: Yes

Clinical Experiences

Every course in the School of Education has a field component, ranging from twelve to fifteen hours in length. In some classes candidates serve as teacher aides; in others, they tutor or work one-on-one with learners. Candidates also work on case studies and with small groups, and gain actual teaching experience in methods courses prior to student teaching. Student teaching is a fourteen-week experience within the candidate's selected teaching field.

Noteworthy

In addition to on-campus courses and experiences, all students at Wingate have the opportunity for study/travel experiences in other countries (over 30 destinations in Europe, Asia, Africa, and South America in the last few years) under the tutelage of Wingate professors at no extra cost. Candidates in the School of Education have successfully competed for grants and fellowships at the local and state levels. The employment rate of graduates from the School of Education is between 90 and 100 percent. Graduates have often been named teacher of the year in their schools and counties. Other graduates have gone on to teach at the college level, and train and consult for textbook companies.

Teacher Preparation Program Information

The following programs are 4 year programs:
Elementary Education, K-12 Education (Art, Music, Physical Education, Reading), Middle School Education (Language Arts, Mathematics, Science, Social Studies), Secondary Education (Biology, English, Mathematics, Social Studies)

The following programs are post-baccalaureate programs:
Elementary Education, K-12 Education (Art, Music, Physical Education, Reading), Middle School Education (Language Arts, Mathematics, Science, Social Studies), Secondary Education (Biology, English, Mathematics, Social Studies)

The following programs are 5th year programs:
Elementary Education

National Council for Accreditation of Teacher Education

Winston-Salem State University

Winston-Salem State University is a historically black university and a member of the state-supported University of North Carolina System. Located in the Piedmont region of North Carolina, this undergraduate institution provides liberal arts and specialized education for approximately 2,900 students. The primary purpose of the teacher education program at Winston-Salem is to produce scholarly, thinking teachers who are prepared to be enlightened, thinking citizens. The program is designed to prepare education majors to be critical thinkers and to prepare them to help P-12 students become critical thinkers.

Just the facts...

Winston-Salem State University
Division of Education
Anderson Center, Room 254 B
601 Martin Luther King Drive
Winston Salem, NC 27110
(336) 750-2374
Website: www.wssu.edu
Profile: Urban, Small, Co-Ed
UG Tuition: $817.00/sem. in-state
UG Tuition: $4,026.00/sem. out-of-state
Off Campus Programs: No

Clinical Experiences

Prior to student teaching, candidates observe in at least two different school settings and gain experience with several cooperating teachers. Clinical experiences take place in professional development schools. The first level of clinical experience includes observing and tutoring small groups of children in the classroom. The second level of clinical experience requires candidates to teach several lessons and to develop lesson plans. The third level of clinical experience is a full-year internship, which includes a semester spent in a school working with a cooperating teacher and a semester of student teaching under the supervision of the same cooperating teacher.

Noteworthy

The Division of Education's Maya Angelou National Institute for the Improvement of Child and Family Education, a community-based comprehensive center of child and family development, develops family support programs; connects research, theory, and practice in education and outreach activities; and informs practicing professionals and policy makers regarding issues related to improving practices and professional preparation in education and human services. The center develops and coordinates clinical experiences with children and families for teacher candidates. Current projects include a parent education program and a study on the impact of government policies on the welfare of children and families in Forsyth County.

Teacher Preparation Program Information

The following programs are 4 year programs:
Birth-Kindergarten Education, Elementary Education, K-12 Education (Art, Music, Physical Education, Spanish), Middle School Education (English, Mathematics, Social Studies), Secondary Education (English/Language Arts, Mathematics, Social Studies), Special Education (K-12, Learning Disabilities)

The following programs are post-baccalaureate programs:
Birth-Kindergarten Education, Elementary Education, K-12 Education (Art, Music, Physical Education, Spanish), Middle School Education (English, Mathematics, Social Studies), Secondary Education (English/Language Arts, Mathematics, Social Studies), Special Education (K-12, Learning Disabilities)

Dickinson State University

Dickinson State University, with an enrollment of 1,800, is located in Dickinson, North Dakota, near the rugged and beautiful Badlands. With a population of more than 17,000, Dickinson is the hub of West River, North Dakota. Dickinson State continues its 80-year tradition of preparing quality teachers. Courses and clinical experiences are offered to help prospective teachers develop the knowledge and skills needed to be an effective elementary or secondary teacher.

Just the facts...

Dickinson State University
College of Education, Business, and Applied Sciences
291 Campus Drive
Dickinson, ND 58601
(701) 227-2151
Website: www.dsu.nodak.edu
Profile: Rural, Small, Co-Ed
UG Tuition: $1,098.00/sem. in-state; $1,190.00 to $2,628.00/sem. out-of-state (depending on state of origin)
Off Campus Programs: No

Clinical Experiences

Candidates in early field experience observe and participate in local schools. Microteaching experiences and an additional field experience provide candidates with opportunities to plan, implement, and evaluate lessons taught to peers as well as to local elementary or secondary students. The full-time, ten-week capstone student teaching experience in area schools provides many opportunities for candidates to continue to develop and refine teaching skills.

Noteworthy

The Department of Teacher Education is located in a newly renovated and expanded facility that includes classrooms, seminar rooms, department and faculty offices, a microteaching classroom with videotape equipment, an interactive video network classroom, Beck Auditorium, and the university art gallery. The West River Teacher Center provides professional development opportunities for area K-12 teachers and also serves as a valuable resource for teacher education students. Candidates have access to computer and other educational technologies, and learn to use those technologies in instructional settings.

Teacher Preparation Program Information

The following programs are 4 year programs:
Elementary Education, K-12 Education (Art, Music, Physical Education), Secondary Education (Art, Biology, Business, Chemistry, English/Language Arts, History, Mathematics, Science, Social Studies, Spanish, Speech/Theatre)

The following programs are post-baccalaureate programs:
Elementary Education, K-12 Education (Art, Music, Physical Education), Secondary Education (Art, Biology, Business, Chemistry, English/Language Arts, History, Mathematics, Science, Social Studies, Spanish, Speech/Theatre)

National Council for Accreditation of Teacher Education

Mayville State University

Mayville State University has prepared teachers since 1889. The teacher education faculty is committed to the belief that preservice teachers should develop the ability to reflect on and use research, theoretical knowledge, and effective teaching strategies and practices. The teacher education program ensures that all graduates have a strong liberal arts background, diverse learning experiences, and the ability to use technology effectively in instruction.

Just the facts...

Mayville State University
School of Education
330 3rd Street NE
Mayville, ND 58257
(701) 786-4828
Website: www.masu.nodak.edu
Profile: Urban, Small, Co-Ed
UG Tuition: $73.71/credit hour
G Tuition: $195.42/credit hour
Off Campus Programs: No

Clinical Experiences

Clinical experiences are an essential component of teacher education at Mayville State University. Each secondary education major has field-based clinical experiences in their methods classes, classes in evaluation, and classes specific to their major field of study. Elementary education majors have many opportunities for clinical practice, including a three-week nature study teaching program; a three-week clinical experience with fourth grade students; and a five-week experience teaching in regional school districts.

Noteworthy

Each Mayville student is furnished with a notebook computer and learns how to use the accompanying software. Candidates are required to make multimedia presentations using state-of-the-art equipment. Candidates have access to the state's largest Teacher Center, which includes classroom space; computer hook-ups; current classroom books; hands-on teaching materials; and statewide access to materials from seven other centers. Candidates also have access to a fourteen-acre Nature Study area located one mile from the university. The nature area includes a grassland area, a woodland area, an oxbow lake, and a nature trail.

Teacher Preparation Program Information

The following programs are 4 year programs:

Elementary Education (Mathematics), Secondary Education (Biology, Business, Chemistry, English/Language Arts, Health, Mathematics, Physical Education, Physical Sciences, Science)

Minot State University

Teacher Education at Minot State University, in its graduate and undergraduate programs, prepares teachers who will be reflective decision makers. Decision making builds from a knowledge base. From that base, teachers are able to draw conclusions, make inferences, internalize concepts, and act. Minot State's mission is to provide opportunities for teacher candidates to acquire the knowledge, skills, attitudes, and behaviors that will allow them to deliver quality learning experiences for diverse pupils in changing classroom environments.

Just the facts...

Minot State University
College of Education
500 University Avenue West
Minot, ND 58707
(701) 858-3150
Website: www.misu.nodak.edu
Profile: Rural, Medium, Co-Ed
UG Tuition: $1,120.35/sem. in-state; $2,757.35/sem. out-of-state
G Tuition: $1,426.35/sem. in-state; $3,574.35/sem. out-of-state
Off Campus Programs: No

Clinical Experiences

Undergraduate programs require field experiences in both rural and urban settings. Student teaching is a minimum of ten full weeks with an expectation that student teachers will be given full responsibility for the assigned classroom for at least 75 percent of the student teaching experience. Candidates who are seeking K-12 licensure complete an additional six weeks of student teaching in a kindergarten placement. Special Education candidates complete extensive practicums in appropriate school sites.

Noteworthy

Teacher candidates at Minot State University can receive a B.S.E. degree with a major in either Special Education (Education of the Mentally Handicapped) or Deaf Education. Students must take a double major in Elementary Education with this degree. Minot's Speech-Language Pathology program is well-known nationally and facilities for the programs in Speech-Language Pathology and School Psychology are among the best in the upper Midwest if not nationally. The North Dakota Center for Persons with Disabilities serves as a grant support office for many educationally related projects including one focused on Native American children with hearing loss and the Deafblind Services project.

Teacher Preparation Program Information

The following programs are 4 year programs:

Elementary Education (Elementary Education K-8), K-12 Education (Art, Music, Physical Education), Secondary Education (Biology, Business, Chemistry, Communication, Earth Science, Economics, English/Language Arts, French, German, History, Mathematics, Physical Sciences, Physics, Psychology, Social Studies, Sociology, Spanish), Special Education (Hearing Impaired, Mental Retardation)

The following programs are 5th year programs:

Special Education (Early Childhood, Learning Disability, Severe Multiple Disabilities/Handicaps)

North Dakota State University

Through the School of Education at North Dakota State University, candidates are prepared to be teachers, counselors, and school administrators capable of working effectively with diverse populations. Through course work and field experiences, candidates come to appreciate and are committed to cultural diversity and the elimination of inequitable instruction and institutional practices.

Just the facts...

North Dakota State University
School of Education
Family Life Center 210, NDSU
Fargo, ND 58105-5057
(701) 231-7202
Website: www.ndsu.nodak.edu
Profile: Urban, Medium, Co-Ed
UG Tuition: $115.34/cr. hr. in-state; $279.67/cr. hr. out-of-state
G Tuition: $124.09/cr. hr. in-state; $303.09/cr. hr. out-of-state
Off Campus Programs: Yes

Clinical Experiences

The School of Education places student teachers for a ten-week, full-time experience under the supervision of a qualified classroom teacher. Candidates can request specific student teaching sites, and every effort will be made to accommodate the requests. Candidates placed outside the metro area by request will pay the cost of university supervision. Candidates apply and are audited for eligibility one full semester prior to student teaching.

Noteworthy

The School of Education has initiated a program called Partners in Reasoned-Action Teacher Education (PIRATE) at an area middle school. Candidates with baccalaureate degrees in their teaching specialty fields may apply for the program so that they may complete teacher preparation largely on-site. The program evolved from alumni feedback suggesting increased field experiences, as well as an interest expressed by teachers, counselors, and administrators at the school to become more involved in the preparation of teachers. As NDSU's teacher education program moves toward more post-baccalaureate preparation, the PIRATE program has become a valuable model.

Teacher Preparation Program Information

The following programs are 4 year programs:
K-12 Education (Music, Physical Education), Secondary Education (Agriculture, Biology, Chemistry, Consumer & Family Science/Home Economics, Earth Science, English/Language Arts, French, General Science, Geography, German, History, Mathematics, Music, Physical Education, Physics, Social Studies, Sociology, Spanish, Speech)

The following programs are post-baccalaureate programs:
K-12 Education (Music, Physical Education), Secondary Education (Biology, Chemistry, Earth Science, English/Language Arts, French, General Science, Geography, German, History, Mathematics, Music, Physical Education, Physics, Social Studies, Sociology, Spanish, Speech)

The following programs are 5th year programs:
K-12 Education (Music, Physical Education), Secondary Education (Agriculture, Consumer & Family Science/Home Economics, English/Language Arts, General Science, History, Mathematics, Music, Physical Education)

University of North Dakota

UND's teacher education programs reflect the progressive tradition with a focus on individualized, developmentally appropriate curriculum; student-centered learning; interdisciplinary approaches to solving real problems; use of primary resources and the direct experience of learners; community involvement; and commitment to the school as a laboratory for democracy where diversity is valued, and humane and holistic approaches to teaching, learning, and assessment are fostered.

Just the facts...

University of North Dakota
College of Education and Human Development
Box 7189
Grand Forks, ND 58202-7189
(701) 777-2674
Website: www.und.nodak.edu
Profile: Urban, Large, Co-Ed
UG Tuition: $1,415.00/sem. in-state; $3,372.00/sem. out-of-state
G Tuition: $1,520.00/sem. in-state; $3,668.00/sem. out-of-state
Off Campus Programs: No

Clinical Experiences

Candidates in initial programs complete a minimum of two semester-long field experiences prior to sixteen weeks of student teaching at the elementary, middle, or secondary level. Candidates in early childhood and kindergarten education complete additional experiences. Field experiences for advanced candidates include practica, internships, and residencies that often involve work at a professional development school or the University Children's Center.

Noteworthy

UND is a member of the Knight Excellence in Education Network and NEA's network of exemplary professional development schools. The program is engaged in many partnerships including a state-wide middle grade initiative, technology partnerships and residencies with the Grand Forks Public Schools, the North Dakota Teacher Center Network, the North Dakota LEAD Center, and a full-service school initiative.

Teacher Preparation Program Information

The following programs are 4 year programs:
Early Childhood Education, Elementary Education (Early Childhood, Mathematics), K-12 Education (Music, Physical Education), Middle Level Education (English, Language Arts, Mathematics, Music, Physical Education, Science, Social Studies, Visual Arts), Secondary Education (Art, Biology, Business, Chemistry, Communication, Earth Science, English/Language Arts, French, Geography, German, Industrial Technology, Mathematics, Physical Education, Physics, Science, Social Studies, Spanish, Vocational Marketing)

The following programs are post-baccalaureate programs:
Early Childhood Education, Elementary Education (Early Childhood, Mathematics), K-12 Education (Music, Physical Education), Middle Level Education (English, Language Arts, Mathematics, Music, Physical Education, Science, Social Studies, Visual Arts), Secondary Education (Art, Biology, Business, Chemistry, Communication, Earth Science, English/Language Arts, French, Geography, German, Industrial Technology, Mathematics, Physical Education, Physics, Science, Social Studies, Spanish, Vocational Marketing)

The following programs are 5 year programs:
Special Education (Speech/Language Disabilities)

Valley City State University

The Valley City State University Division of Education and Psychology ensures a high-quality teacher education program based on established knowledge and practice as well as new research findings. The purpose of the program is to prepare teachers who can teach students of varying backgrounds and needs; are competent decision makers; and have skills in planning, implementing, and evaluating learning experiences. Graduates have learned that decision making is a reflective process and accept professional growth as an ongoing process.

Just the facts...

Valley City State University
Division of Education and Psychology
101 College Street, SE
Valley City, ND 58072
(701) 845-7191
Website: www.vcsu.nodak.edu
Profile: Rural, Small, Co-Ed
UG Tuition: $73.00/credit hour
G Tuition: $160.00/credit hour
Off Campus Programs: No

Clinical Experiences

Clinical experiences are designed to promote program goals and objectives and provide opportunities for candidates' professional growth. Experiences in the field begin during the introductory course in education; continue through practicum courses, methods courses, and microteaching; and culminate in student teaching. Preservice teachers may work with minority culture and exceptional students during the various phases of the field-based program.

Noteworthy

Candidates enter a progressive program of study and enter the teaching profession equipped to meet the complex challenges of the next century. Universal access to notebook computers helps candidates acquire highly developed technology skills and enables them to create CD-ROM portfolios as a program requirement. UPDATE, the education newsletter, highlights important information for teacher candidates. The annual Partners in Quality Conference, hosted by the VCSU Division of Education and Psychology, features a nationally known presenter. The conference brings together K-16 educators, preservice teachers, and parents to find improved ways to meet learner needs.

Teacher Preparation Program Information

The following programs are 4 year programs:
Elementary Education, K-12 Education (Art, Music, Physical Education), Secondary Education (Art, Biology, Business, Business Composite, Chemistry, English, General Science, Health, History, Mathematics, Music, Music Composite, Physical Education, Science Composite, Social Science Composite, Spanish, Technology, Technology Composite)

The following programs are post-baccalaureate programs:
Elementary Education, K-12 Education (Art, Music, Physical Education), Secondary Education (Art, Biology, Business, Business Composite, Chemistry, English, General Science, Health, History, Mathematics, Music, Music Composite, Physical Education, Science Composite, Social Science Composite, Spanish, Technology, Technology Composite)

Ashland University

Ashland University's education faculty prepare educators who (1) work cooperatively and collaboratively with the education community, (2) communicate clearly and effectively, (3) demonstrate understanding of human development, cultural diversity, socioeconomic influences and learning differences, (4) employ research in teaching, (5) use a variety of appropriate assessment techniques to enhance learning, (6) master appropriate disciplines to engage students in meaningful academic study, (7) integrate educational technology in the teaching and learning process, and (8) assume lifelong responsibility to grow academically, professionally, and personally.

Just the facts...

Ashland University
College of Education
103 Bixler Hall
401 College Avenue
Ashland, OH 44805
(419) 289-5365
Website: www.ashland.edu
Profile: Rural, Medium, Co-Ed
UG Tuition: $13,726.00/year
G Tuition: $275.00/credit hour
Off Campus Programs: Yes

Clinical Experiences

All education programs begin with exploratory experiences in the schools. Each year has successively more demanding clinical experiences in appropriate settings with collaborating schools. The twelve-week student teaching experience is designed to provide the student teacher with full responsibility for the classroom and a full range of experiences related to the teaching role. Experiences take place in rural, urban, and small town settings with a variety of student populations (cultural backgrounds and inclusion settings). Experiences are integrated with coursework that helps candidates interpret and reflect upon what they are learning.

Noteworthy

Ashland University emphasizes the development of the individual. Candidates benefit from a dual focus on liberal arts education and professional preparation. An introductory freshman year experience provides prospective teachers with the opportunity to explore their interest in the teaching profession. Financial aid is available to those who need it, and support systems for all students are strong. The relationships the College of Education has with local schools include service opportunities as well as traditional program experiences. The Becker Reading Center, a Reading Recovery Program, Saturday School, and the Wuliger Center provide further opportunities to interact with children.

Teacher Preparation Program Information

The following programs are 4 year programs:

Early Childhood Education, Middle Childhood Education (Language Arts, Mathematics, Science, Social Studies), Adolescent to Young Adult Education (Integrated Language Arts, Integrated Mathematics, Integrated Science, Integrated Social Studies, Life Science, Earth Science, Physical Science), Vocational Education (Integrated Business, Family & Consumer Sciences, Work and Family), P-12 Education (Art, French, Health, Music, Physical Education, Spanish, Theater), Intervention Specialist (Early Childhood, Mild/Moderate, Moderate/Intensive)

The following programs are post-baccalaureate programs:

Early Childhood Education, Middle Childhood Education (Language Arts, Mathematics, Science, Social Studies), Adolescent to Young Adult Education (Integrated Language Arts, Integrated Mathematics, Integrated Science, Integrated Social Studies, Life Science, Earth Science, Physical Science), Vocational Education (Integrated Business, Family & Consumer Sciences, Work and Family), P-12 Education (Art, French, Health, Music, Physical Education, Spanish, Theater)

Baldwin-Wallace College

Baldwin-Wallace College was founded in 1845 and has been preparing teachers for over 100 years. Its early heritage was firmly rooted in the pursuit of liberal arts. The faculty and staff of the Division of Education and the academic leadership of the college are committed to a strong program of teacher education which builds candidates' knowledge and skills. The program is based on six themes: educational philosophy, history, sociology, multicultural perspectives, implications for teaching and learning, and technology. The teacher education curriculum is based on the theme of "teacher as reflective decision maker" and includes numerous field experiences, seminars, class sessions, and assessments.

Just the facts...

Baldwin-Wallace College
Division of Education
275 Eastland Road
Berea, OH 44017
(440) 826-2168
Website: www.bw.edu
Profile: Suburban, Medium, Co-Ed
UG Tuition: $6,970.00/semester
G Tuition: $355.00/credit hour
Off Campus Programs: No

Clinical Experiences

Baldwin-Wallace College's Division of Education provides clinical experiences for the majority of the education courses it offers. Candidates benefit from working with master teachers in suburban, rural, and inner-city schools. Partnerships with area schools provide special mentors for methods courses and student teaching. Baldwin-Wallace education majors complete approximately 300 hours of clinical experience before starting their student teaching assignments. Multi-age licensure programs require experience at both a lower and upper grade level.

Noteworthy

Baldwin-Wallace College offers a range of support groups and clubs for future educators, including Teaching Together, Teaching in the Middle, Kappa Delta Pi, Phi Delta Kappa, and the Graduate Alumni/Student Association. In addition to numerous required clinical experiences, education majors are encouraged to seek additional experience through the Community Outreach Office via volunteer or paid internships.

Teacher Preparation Program Information

The following programs are 4 year programs:

Early Childhood Education, Multi-Age Education (French, German, Health, Music, Physical Education, Spanish, Visual Arts), Middle Childhood Education (Reading/Language, Mathematics, Science, Social Studies), Integrated Language Arts, Integrated Mathematics, Integrated Science, Integrated Social Studies, Life Sciences, Physical Sciences

The following programs are 5th year programs:

Early Childhood Education, Multi-Age Education (French, German, Health, Music, Physical Education, Spanish, Visual Arts), Middle Childhood Education (Reading/Language, Mathematics, Science, Social Studies), Integrated Language Arts, Integrated Mathematics, Integrated Science, Integrated Social Studies, Life Sciences, Physical Sciences

Bowling Green State University

Bowling Green State University has prepared teachers and other school personnel since it was established in 1910. The faculty of the College of Education and Human Development focus on the education of professionals who will positively impact the development of individuals, families, communities, schools, and other societal institutions. Further, the college's vision is to promote a dynamic community of lifelong learners and leaders. Programs are based on essential knowledge, established and current research findings, and sound professional practices.

Just the facts...

Bowling Green State University
College of Education and Human Development
444 Education Building
Bowling Green, OH 43403-0240
(419) 372-7401
Website: http://edhd.bgsu.edu/
Profile: Rural, Large, Co-Ed
UG Tuition: $2,327.00/sem. in-state; $4,951.00/sem. out-of-state
Off Campus Programs: No

Clinical Experiences

All teacher education programs follow a four-stage model for incorporating field and clinical experiences into the curriculum. The four stages of the model progress from "initial exploratory" to "structured-dependent" to "structured-independent" to "independent-generative." This approach provides a minimum of 300 hours of clinical experiences prior to student teaching. Candidates are exposed to various school settings including urban, suburban, and rural schools, and are provided experience with both culturally and linguistically diverse populations. Several programs within the College of Education and Human Development have initiated professional development school partnerships.

Noteworthy

Bowling Green's teacher education program is one of the largest and most respected in the country. The department of special education sponsors a number of highly successful summer programs for gifted students, including residential and extension programs. International student teaching opportunities are available in English-speaking schools in Montreal and Rio de Janeiro. Through the Martha Gesling Weber Reading Center, candidates are prepared to offer diagnostic and evaluation services as well as individualized instruction for elementary and secondary students. Educational psychology candidates provide tutoring services throughout the area through the Help-A-Child Tutoring Program.

Teacher Preparation Program Information

The following programs are 4 year programs:

Early Childhood Education, Middle Childhood Education (Language Arts, Mathematics, Science, Social Studies), Adolescent and Young Adult Education (Integrated Language Arts, Life Science, Integrated Mathematics, Physical Science, Integrated Science, Integrated Social Studies), Multi-Age Education (Art, French, German, Latin, Music, Physical Education, Russian, Spanish), Intervention Specialist (Hearing Impaired, Mild/Moderate Needs, Moderate/Intensive Needs), Vocational Education (Family & Consumer Sciences, Integrated Business, Industrial Technology, Marketing)

The following programs are post-baccalaureate programs:

Intervention Specialist (Hearing Impaired, Mild/Moderate Needs, Moderate/Intensive Needs)

National Council for Accreditation of Teacher Education

Capital University

The teacher education program at Capital University has a long-standing tradition of developing caring, competent, and committed professional educators for diverse communities of learners. Program objectives give attention to acquiring, processing, and organizing content knowledge for student learning; establishing environments conducive to communities of student learners; employing multiple strategies for facilitating student learning; and developing and participating as a professional. Teacher education at Capital is driven by the design of theory, practice, and reflection. Teacher candidates gain a strong liberal arts background.

Just the facts...

Capital University
Education Department
Renner Hall
Columbus, OH 43209-2394
(614) 236-6301
Website: www.capital.edu
Profile: Suburban, Medium, Co-Ed
UG Tuition: $7,630.00/semester
G Tuition: $7,630.00/semester
Off Campus Programs: No

Clinical Experiences

Clinical experiences are the essence of the practice component of the teacher education program's design, which includes theory, practice, and reflection. The program integrates two extensive daily field-based experiences within blocks of teacher education courses prior to student teaching for a semester, or an internship for two semesters. Experiences are conducted in rural, suburban, and urban settings under the daily supervision of cooperating teachers and the weekly supervision of university supervisors.

Noteworthy

Teacher education faculty have each had various experiences in public school settings that allow them to relate directly to the daily responsibilities of classroom teachers. Education faculty have received several of the highest honors and grants awarded by the university and professional organizations. Graduates of Capital's teacher education program have made significant contributions in the lives of others through a variety of positions—as classroom teachers, special education teachers, special area teachers, principals, supervisors, central office staff, superintendents, and faculty members and administrators at colleges and universities.

Teacher Preparation Program Information

The following programs are 4 year programs:

Early Childhood Education, Elementary Education, K-12 Education (Art, Drama/Theater, Health, Music, Physical Education, Reading), Middle School Education (Language Arts, Mathematics, Science, Social Studies), Adolescent to Young Adult Education (English/Language Arts, Life Sciences, Mathematics, Science, Social Studies), Special Education (Intervention Specialist)

The following programs are post-baccalaureate programs:

Early Childhood Education, Elementary Education, K-12 Education (Art, Drama/Theater, Health, Music, Physical Education, Reading), Middle School Education (Language Arts, Mathematics, Science, Social Studies), Adolescent to Young Adult Education (English/Language Arts, Life Sciences, Mathematics, Science, Social Studies), Special Education (Intervention Specialist)

Cleveland State University

Cleveland State University has prepared teachers and school personnel since 1966. The College of Education faculty is committed to preparing responsive, reflective professionals who are partners in learning. Teacher education graduates from the College of Education are known for abilities that reflect inquiry, partnership, contextualism, and professionalism. Inquiry and partnership guide the design of the program and candidate evaluations, and the professionalism that suffuses the program calls on candidates to be thoughtful, able to adapt, and learner-centered. Candidates work in both urban and suburban environments that reflect learner diversity.

Just the facts...

Cleveland State University
College of Education
1983 East 24th Street
Cleveland, OH 44115
(216) 687-3737
Website: www.csuohio.edu
Profile: Urban, Large, Co-Ed
UG Tuition: $1,800.00/sem. in-state; $3,600.00/sem. out-of-state
G Tuition: $2,626.00/sem. in-state; $5,252.00/sem. out-of-state
Off Campus Programs: No

Clinical Experiences

The College of Education has agreements with eleven school districts where it places candidates for their clinical experiences. Initial experiences involve observation, interviews, and visits to school settings. In practicum and student teaching experiences candidates are assigned to a cooperating teacher from a designated teaching area as well as to a university supervisor. All candidates have extensive urban experiences and all programs require a minimum of fifteen weeks of student teaching.

Noteworthy

Special programs in the College of Education include Tomorrow's Next Teachers (a minority student recruitment and retention effort that pairs candidates with individuals from the university or the community for assistance with personal, academic, and professional concerns), the Greater Cleveland Education Development Center and Northeast Regional Professional Development Center (which provide professional development for teachers throughout the area), and the Education Services Center (serving children with disabilities and providing clinical experiences to candidates and service to the community).

Teacher Preparation Program Information

The following programs are 4 year programs:

Early Childhood Education, K-12 Education (Art, French, Music, Physical Education, Spanish), Middle School Education (5-8 Certification, Language Arts, Mathematics, Science, Social Studies), Secondary Education (English/Language Arts, French, Mathematics, Social Studies, Spanish), Special Education (Mild/Moderate, Moderate/Intensive)

The following programs are post-baccalaureate programs:

Early Childhood Education, K-12 Education (Art, French, Music, Physical Education, Spanish), Middle School Education (5-8 Certification, Language Arts, Mathematics), Secondary Education (English/Language Arts, French, Mathematics, Social Studies, Spanish), Special Education (Early Childhood, Gifted/Talented, Mild/Moderate, Moderate/Intensive)

John Carroll University

John Carroll University's programs in teaching, counseling, and school leadership are grounded in the Jesuit view of education and seek to develop the Jesuit ideal of the educator. The faculty believe that the ideal educator is a lifelong learner who exercises personal influence in learning communities; views education as a vocation; and seeks knowledge in the arts and sciences. Teacher candidates study the contexts of education, child and adolescent development, curriculum and instruction, and professional responsibilities. Much of what candidates learn in the classroom is examined and experienced in the schools during the course of the program.

Just the facts...

John Carroll University
Department of Education and Allied Studies
20700 North Park Boulevard
Cleveland, OH 44118
(216) 397-4331
Website: www.jcu.edu
Profile: Suburban, Small, Co-Ed
UG Tuition: $441.00/credit hour
G Tuition: $450.00/credit hour
Off Campus Programs: No

Clinical Experiences

Clinical experiences in teacher preparation occur in three phases. In the early phase, candidates develop an awareness of teaching as a career; observe the work environment of the schools; and engage in one-to-one instructional interactions with children and youth. Observational skills are emphasized along with tutorial work in schools. Mid-phase experiences involve more in-depth, sustained opportunities to observe, plan, and practice in a wide range of instructional settings. Guided teaching and feedback on performance in real classrooms are stressed. In the final phase, candidates spend one full academic year in a single classroom placement.

Noteworthy

One distinguishing feature of the teacher education program is the emphasis on abundant experiences in schools. From the moment students express an interest in teaching as a professional career, they become involved in the everyday life of schools. Candidates frequently visit schools; participate in tutorial programs; engage in distance learning opportunities; take courses on-site in schools; practice teaching in a wide variety of classrooms; and interact with children and parents at school and community events.

Teacher Preparation Program Information

The following programs are 4 year programs:
Early Childhood Education, K-12 Education (French, German, Latin, Physical Education, Spanish), Middle School Education (English, Mathematics, Science, Social Studies), Secondary Education (Biology, English/Language Arts, Mathematics, Physical Education, Social Studies)

The following programs are post-baccalaureate programs:
Early Childhood Education, K-12 Education, Middle School Education, Secondary Education

The following programs are 5th year programs:
Elementary Education, Secondary Education, School-Based M.Ed. (year-long, full-time)

Kent State University

Kent State University's College and Graduate School of Education (CGSE) is committed to preservice teacher education programs that prepare inquiry-oriented, technologically sophisticated teachers. CGSE graduates can function in a professional learning community and as educational leaders in a pluralistic, information-age society. The CGSE faculty prepare candidates who are committed to the continuing study of their work in collaborative contexts that are (1) focused on educational practices characterized by active meaning-making, curriculum integration, and multicultural sensitivity; (2) informed by research; and (3) disciplined by an ongoing examination of knowledge and beliefs.

Just the facts...

Kent State University
College and Graduate School of Education
408 White Hall
Kent, OH 44242
(330) 672-2202
Website: www.educ.kent.edu
Profile: Suburban, Large, Co-Ed
UG Tuition: $217.00/cr. hr. in-state; $429.00/cr. hr. out-of-state
G Tuition: $230.75/cr. hr. in-state; $442.75/cr. hr. out-of-state
Off Campus Programs: No

Clinical Experiences

Beginning in the freshman year, teaching/learning experiences in school settings are an integral part of the teacher preparation curriculum for teacher candidates. These experiences are systematically arranged for teacher candidates in a combination of urban, suburban, and rural settings and with special needs populations. Each teacher candidate must successfully complete a student teaching experience, the length of which varies by program area. Student teachers are expected to observe the same school policies, daily schedules, and instructional expectations as regular classroom teachers. Student teachers are supported and guided by experienced classroom teachers and university supervisors.

Noteworthy

Kent State University is one of 37 universities nationally (and one of two universities in Ohio) to be classified as a Carnegie II research institution. The CGSE, with approximately 4,000 students, including nearly 600 at the Ph.D. level, is a charter member of the Holmes Group, now the Holmes Partnership. The Kent Educational Network for Tomorrow involves the CGSE with nine school systems and five human service agencies. Ameritech's Electronic University School Classroom, located in the university's Moulton Hall Technologies and Learning Center, provides state-of-the-art facilities for the teacher education program.

Teacher Preparation Program Information

The following programs are 4 year programs:

Early Childhood Education, K-12 Education (Art, Dance, French, German, Latin, Music, Physical Education, Russian, School Health, Spanish), Middle School Education (Language Arts, Mathematics, Science, Social Studies), Secondary Education (Earth Science, English/Language Arts, Integrated Science, Life Sciences, Life Science/Chemistry, Mathematics, Physical Sciences, Science, Social Studies, Vocational Business, Vocational Family & Consumer Sciences, Vocational Marketing, Vocational Trade & Industrial, Vocational Technology Education), Intervention Specialist (Gifted/Talented, Hearing Impaired, Mild/Moderate, Moderate/Intensive)

The following programs are post-baccalaureate programs:

Early Childhood Education, K-12 Education (Art, Dance, French, German, Latin, Music, Physical Education, Russian, School Health, Spanish), Middle School Education (Language Arts, Mathematics, Science, Social Studies), Secondary Education (Earth Science, English/Language Arts, Integrated Science, Life Sciences, Life Science/Chemistry, Mathematics, Physical Sciences, Science, Social Studies, Vocational Business, Vocational Family & Consumer Sciences, Vocational Marketing, Vocational Trade & Industrial, Vocational Technology Education), Intervention Specialist (Gifted/Talented, Hearing Impaired, Mild/Moderate, Moderate/Intensive)

The following programs are 5th year programs:

Some of these programs may take more than one year to complete: Early Childhood Education, K-12 Education (Art, Dance, ESL, French, German, Health, Latin, Library/Media, Music, Physical Education, Reading, Russian, Spanish), Secondary Education (Biology/Chemistry, Earth Science, English/Language Arts, Integrated Science, Life Sciences, Life Science/Chemistry, Mathematics, Physical Sciences, Social Studies, Vocational Family & Consumer Science, Vocational Business, Vocational Marketing, Vocational Trade & Industrial, Vocational Technology Education), Intervention Specialist (Early Childhood, Gifted/Talented, Hearing Impaired, Mild/Moderate Handicapped, Moderate/Intensive)

Miami University

Established in 1809, Miami University is the seventh-oldest state-assisted university in the nation and has had a role in the preparation of teachers since 1902. The School of Education and Allied Professions, offering a full complement of performance-based licensure programs, is currently organized into five departments and accounts for twelve percent of the university's enrollment. Miami University maintains three campuses; the main campus is in Oxford and two regional campuses are located in Hamilton and Middletown. The regional campuses offer carefully structured programs—equal to those at the main campus—of lower division undergraduate coursework and courses that lead to master's degrees.

Just the facts...

Miami University
School of Education
500 East High Street
Oxford, OH 45056
(513) 529-6418
Website: www.eap.muohio.edu
Profile: Rural, Large, Co-Ed
UG Tuition: $2,876.00/sem. in-state; $3,203.00/sem. out-of-state
G Tuition: $2,940.00/sem. in-state; $3,203.00/sem. out-of-state
Off Campus Programs: Yes

Clinical Experiences

Prospective educators in the School of Education and Allied Professions will find many opportunities to interact with children and youth throughout their program. Each experience provides candidates with opportunities to demonstrate success in the classroom. Clinical experiences are provided in a variety of settings—rural, urban, and suburban—and with a diverse range of learners from many cultural backgrounds. The culminating experience, the Senior Internship, is a full-semester opportunity to apply the knowledge and skills that characterize effective teaching.

Noteworthy

The Institute for Educational Renewal provides multiple opportunities for faculty and candidates to exercise shared responsibilty for the learning, development, and well being of children, youth, and families through partnerships established through the collaborative efforts of schools and health/human service organizations. Other centers in the School of Education include the Center for Education and Cultural Studies, the Center for Excellence in Mathematics and Science, the Center for Human Development, Learning and Teaching, the Family and Child Studies Center, and the Heckert Center for Children's Reading and Writing.

Teacher Preparation Program Information

The following programs are 4 year programs:
Early Childhood Education, K-12 Education (Art, French, German, Health, Latin, Music, Physical Education, Russian, Spanish), Middle School Education (English, Mathematics, Science, Social Studies), Secondary Education (Biology, Chemistry, Earth Science, English/Language Arts, General Science, Mathematics, Physical Sciences, Physics, Social Studies), Special Education (Developmental Disabilities/Handicaps, Early Childhood, Gifted/Talented, Learning Disability, Multiple Disabilities/Handicaps, Severe Behavioral Disabilities/Handicaps)

The following programs are post-baccalaureate programs:
Early Childhood Education, K-12 Education (Art, French, German, Health, Latin, Music, Physical Education, Russian, Spanish), Middle School Education (English, Mathematics, Science, Social Studies), Secondary Education (Biology, Chemistry, Earth Science, English/Language Arts, General Science, Mathematics, Physical Sciences, Physics, Social Studies), Special Education (Developmental Disabilities/Handicaps, Early Childhood, Gifted/Talented, Learning Disability, Multiple Disabilities/Handicaps, Severe Behavioral Disabilities/Handicaps)

Ohio Northern University

Ohio Northern University has prepared teachers since 1871. The Center for Teacher Education, established in 1991, offers licensure in fourteen areas. The teacher education program is designed to provide prospective teachers with the general education, subject area concentration, and professional education experiences that will ensure professional competency. The Center for Teacher Education is committed to ensuring that graduates have a strong liberal arts background.

Just the facts...

Ohio Northern University
Center for Teacher Education and Certification
525 South Main Street
Dukes Building
Ada, OH 45810
(419) 772-2118
Website: www.onu.edu
Profile: Rural, Small, Co-Ed
UG Tuition: $6,605.00/quarter
Off Campus Programs: No

Clinical Experiences

Candidates participate in 300 hours of supervised clinical experiences in a variety of settings before student teaching. Clinical experiences begin in the freshman year and are incorporated throughout the program. Qualified supervising teachers are engaged in professional development activities with the university and provide support during the student teaching experience. Candidates may complete their student teaching at the Antwerp International School (AIS). AIS offers a unique learning environment where students come from 40 countries around the globe and teachers represent twelve countries.

Noteworthy

The Center for Teacher Education operates a Child Development Center where all teacher education students complete supervised clinical experiences. The Instructional Technology Center is a resource for candidates as they become competent and confident in using technology in their teaching.

Teacher Preparation Program Information

The following programs are 4 year programs:

Early Childhood Education, Elementary Education, K-12 Education (Art, French, Health, Music, Physical Education, Spanish, Technology), Middle Childhood Education (English, Mathematics, Science, Social Studies), Secondary Education (English/Language Arts, Integrated Science, Life Science, Mathematics, Physical Science, Social Studies)

The following programs are post-baccalaureate programs:

Early Childhood Education, Elementary Education, K-12 Education (Art, French, Health, Music, Physical Education, Spanish, Technology), Middle Childhood Education (English, Mathematics, Science, Social Studies), Secondary Education (English/Language Arts, Integrated Science, Life Science, Mathematics, Physical Science, Social Studies)

National Council for Accreditation of Teacher Education

The Ohio State University

Since 1907 the College of Education at The Ohio State University has been a major center of teacher preparation in Ohio, and a recognized leader in elementary education, secondary education, school couseling, educational administration, and teacher education. Its programs and faculty have been consistently ranked among the best nationally. The College of Education's mission is to promote critical inquiry, dynamic teaching, and reflection, and to further social changes through systematic study, instruction, and service. Its purpose is to prepare school personnel who will develop, apply, impart, promote, and manage the learning essential to the future of society.

Clinical Experiences

The College of Education has partnerships with nineteen school districts in the metropolitan area where candidates experience field placements consisting of early experiences, observation, participation, and internships. Within the M.Ed. licensure program, candidates serve year-long internships in both urban and suburban districts that have been carefully selected and developed as teaching laboratories. Mentor teachers work with candidates to teach the strategies and methodology of successful teaching.

Just the facts...

The Ohio State University
College of Education
1945 North High Street
Columbus, OH 43210-1172
(614) 292-2581
Website: http://coe.ohio-state.edu
Profile: Urban, Large, Co-Ed
UG Tuition: $1,302.00/quart. in-state; $3,825.00/quart. out-of-state
G Tuition: $1,824.00/quart. in-state; $4,724.00/quart. out-of-state
Off Campus Programs: No

Noteworthy

The College of Eduation is a member of the Holmes Partnership, a consortium of leading universities dedicated to reforming teacher education. Faculty in the College of Education believe that Ohio State's emphasis on graduate degree/teacher licensure offers candidates the chance to master all of the components of teacher preparation—liberal arts, content, and teaching methodology—resulting in well-prepared teachers. Candidates can apply for more than $300,000 in scholarship and fellowship support available annually.

Teacher Preparation Program Information

The following programs are 4 year programs:
K-12 Education (Music), Secondary Education (Vocational Agriculture)

The following programs are 5th year programs:
Elementary Education, K-12 Foreign Language Education (Arabic, Chinese, French, German, Hebrew, Italian, Japanese, Latin, Russian, Spanish), Secondary Education (Biology, Chemistry, Consumer & Family Science, Earth Science, English/Language Arts, General Science, Mathematics, Social Studies & Global Education, Technology Education), Sensory Impairment, Special Education

Ohio University

Ohio University's College of Education is a professional college whose major goal is to prepare individuals for careers related to education. Many graduate and undergraduate programs are offered for teaching in elementary, middle, and high schools, and for positions in counseling, public school administration, and higher education administration. The College of Education strives to provide supportive and challenging experiences that develop education and human services professionals, and the communities they serve.

Just the facts...

Ohio University
College of Education
Athens, OH 45701
(740) 593-4400
Website: www.ohiou.edu
Profile: Rural, Large, Co-Ed
UG Tuition: $1,360.00/quart. in-state; $2,858.00/quart. out-of-state
G Tuition: $1,708.00/quart. in-state; $3,281.00/quart. out-of-state
Off Campus Programs: Yes

Clinical Experiences

Candidates begin their clinical experiences during their first quarter of education coursework, typically in the sophomore year. Successful student teaching represents the culmination of the program of professional preparation. Student teaching is a requirement for the Bachelor of Science in Education for individuals pursuing programs that lead to eligibility for teacher licensure. The student teaching experience is typically for one full quarter (ten weeks). The majority of candidates complete their student teching in the Athens area. Other opportunities are available through the Consortium for Overseas Student Teaching, and in other parts of Ohio and the United States.

Noteworthy

Since 1990 the College of Education, in conjunction with public schools in Ohio, has developed several partnerships that share five major goals: to improve P-12 education for all students; to provide increased field experience opportunities for preservice teachers; to create mentoring relationships for preservice teachers to learn with, and from, experienced inservice teachers; to support and encourage ongoing professional development for the college and partnership school faculty and administrators; and to study and learn about effective ways of developing and strengthening partnerships.

Teacher Preparation Program Information

The following programs are 4 year programs:
Early Childhood Education, Elementary Education (Early Childhood Education P-3), K-12 Education (French, German, Latin, Music, Physical Education, Russian, Spanish), Middle School Education (English, Mathematics, Science, Social Studies), Secondary Education (Biology, Business, Chemistry, Communication, Consumer & Family Science/Home Economics, Earth Science, English/Language Arts, Health, Mathematics, Physics, Science, Social Studies, Speech), Special Education (Developmental Disabilities/Handicaps, Early Childhood, Gifted/Talented, Learning Disability, Multiple Disabilities/Handicaps, Severe Behavioral Disabilities/Handicaps)

The following programs are post-baccalaureate programs:
Early Childhood Education, Elementary Education (Early Childhood Education P-3), K-12 Education (French, German, Latin, Music, Physical Education, Russian, Spanish), Middle School Education (English, Mathematics, Science, Social Studies), Secondary Education (Biology, Business, Chemistry, Communication, Consumer & Family Science/Home Economics, Earth Science, English/Language Arts, Health, Mathematics, Physics, Science, Social Studies, Speech), Special Education (Developmental Disabilities/Handicaps, Early Childhood, Gifted/Talented, Learning Disability, Multiple Disabilities/Handicaps, Severe Behavioral Disabilities/Handicaps)

The following programs are 5 year programs:
Special Education

Otterbein College

Otterbein College is committed to providing a coherent teacher education program that fosters critical reflection within a context of collaborative learning. Building on a liberal arts foundation that emphasizes multidisciplinary and interdisciplinary ways of knowing, the professional education department requires candidates to examine their values and actions. The Department of Education's mission is to build a community of lifelong learners who can respect diverse perspectives; make sound decisions based on complex data; and be responsive to the changing needs of children.

Just the facts...

Otterbein College
Department of Education
One Ottervein College
Westerville, OH 43081-2006
(614) 823-1214
Website: www.otterbein.edu
Profile: Suburban, Small, Co-Ed
UG Tuition: $15,648.00/year
G Tuition: $190.00/credit hour
Off Campus Programs: No

Clinical Experiences

Clinical experiences serve an important socialization function in Otterbein's teacher education program. They are based in schools and are designed to help prospective teachers decide whether teaching is an appropriate career choice, to develop skills in applying methods and management techniques, and to observe teachers executing various roles during the school day. Across the clinical experiences, candidates observe, plan, instruct, manage, and assess within the context of current practice. On-campus clinical experiences may include simulation activities and peer teaching.

Noteworthy

The Gahanna Jefferson Internship is designed to be a year-long internship in the Gahanna-Jefferson schools for qualified teacher candidates. The internship is taken from August to June and is very demanding of the intern's time. The first ten weeks follow the general student teaching schedule. For the remainder of the year candidates continue to team teach with their cooperating teachers. A student teaching experience in New Mexico is also available. This ten-week internship takes place at the McCurdy School in Espanola, a United Methodist-affiliated private K-12 school. This program provides a unique multicultural field experience for candidates.

Teacher Preparation Program Information

The following programs are 4 year programs:
Early Childhood Education, K-12 Education (Art, French, Health, Music, Physical Education, Spanish), Middle School Education (English, Mathematics, Science, Social Studies), Secondary Education (Biology, English/Language Arts, Mathematics, Physical Sciences, Social Studies), Special Education (Early Childhood)

The following programs are post-baccalaureate programs:
Early Childhood Education, K-12 Education (Art, French, Health, Music, Physical Education, Spanish), Middle School Education (English, Mathematics, Science, Social Studies), Secondary Education (Biology, English/Language Arts, Mathematics, Physical Sciences, Social Studies), Special Education (Early Childhood)

The following programs are 5th year programs:
Middle School Education (English, Mathematics, Science, Social Studies)

University of Akron

From its founding in 1870, the University of Akron has prepared educators. College of Education faculty believe that successful 21st century educators must possess skills in decision making, problem solving, and critical thinking that will enable them to understand, reflect on, and make decisions about practice. The college holds primary responsibility within the university for producing educational personnel for Ohio's schools and colleges. Education graduates contribute to the positive reform of education and strengthen the research and knowledge base of the discipline.

Just the facts...

University of Akron
College of Education
Zook Hall 210
Akron, OH 44325-4201
(330) 972-7680
Website: www.uakron.edu/education/
Profile: Urban, Large, Co-Ed
UG Tuition: $147.60/cr. hr. in-state; $342.60/cr. hr. out-of-state
G Tuition: $178.10/cr. hr. in-state; $333.10/cr. hr. out-of-state
Off Campus Programs: Yes

Clinical Experiences

Clinical and field-based experiences are an early and continuous part of the curriculum. Extensive experience is provided using computer technology to develop classroom teaching competency. Field experiences in urban, suburban, and rural settings include developmental teaching within college classrooms as a basis for practice teaching at school-based sites. Field experiences include a full semester of student teaching.

Noteworthy

The College of Education offers a developmental, integrated teacher education program which includes the following features: collaborative projects with schools and agencies; BECOME (Business Education Collaboration on Minorities in Education); advanced media technology and telecommunications in all programs; state-of-the-art teaching studios and multimedia, research, and curriculum laboratories; laboratories focusing on motor behavior and skill diagnosis; and a Center for Child Development.

Teacher Preparation Program Information

The following programs are 4 year programs:

Adolescent Young Adult Education/7-12 (Language Arts, Mathematics, Sciences, Social Studies), Early Childhood Education (P-3), Grades 4-12 Education (Family & Consumer Science, Integrated Business), K-12 Intervention Specialist (Mild/Moderate, Moderate/Intensive), Middle Childhood Education/4-9 (English, Mathematics, Science, Social Studies), P-12 Education (Dance, Drama/Theatre Arts, French, German, Health, Latin, Music, Physical Education, Spanish, Visual Arts)

The following programs are 5th year programs:

Adolescent Young Adult Education (7-12), P-12 Education, K-12 Education, Grades 4-12 Education

University of Cincinnati

The Cincinnati Initiative for Teacher Education provides standards-based teacher education in the areas of early childhood, middle childhood, adolescence to young adult, and special education. Programs are collaborative, with efforts from education faculty, arts and sciences faculty, county educational service centers, school districts, administrators, teachers, and a teachers' union. Candidates acquire in-depth subject matter knowledge, professional preparation, and extended, authentic teaching experiences. Candidates are supported by university faculty, master teachers, and institutional arrangements as they make their way through the demanding programs.

Just the facts...

University of Cincinnati
College of Education
Office of the Dean
P.O. Box 210002
Cincinnati, OH 45220-0002
(513) 556-2337
Website: www.education.uc.edu
Profile: Urban, Large, Co-Ed
UG Tuition: $1,503.00/quart. in-state; $3,712.00/quart. out-of-state
G Tuition: $1,856.00/quart. in-state; $3,502.00/quart. out-of-state
Off Campus Programs: No

Clinical Experiences

Clinical experiences are provided in professional development schools. Placements are made with experienced mentor teachers who are well-versed in the teacher education programs. Instead of student teaching experiences, year-long internships provide authentic classroom teaching experience with support from a professional team. Many internships, but not all, are paid positions.

Noteworthy

In the University of Cincinnati's five-year programs, candidates earn two bachelor's degrees: one in an academic discipline and one in education. The Cincinnati Initiative for Teacher Education (CITE) has been nationally recognized and has been featured in *Time* magazine, in the *New York Times Sunday Magazine*, and on NBC Nightly News. The National Commission on Teaching and America's Future recognizes CITE as a model for teacher education.

Teacher Preparation Program Information

The following programs are 4 year programs:
K-12 Education (Art, Music)

The following programs are 5 year programs:
Early Childhood Education (P-3), K-12 Education (French, German, Spanish), Middle Childhood Education (Language Arts, Mathematics, Science, Social Studies), Secondary Education (Earth Science, Integrated Language Arts, Integrated Mathematics, Integrated Science, Integrated Social Studies, Life Science, Physical Science)

The following programs are 5th year programs:
K-12 Education (Art, French, German, Music, Spanish), Middle Childhood Education (Language Arts, Mathematics, Science, Social Studies), Secondary Education (Earth Science, Integrated Language Arts, Integrated Mathematics, Integrated Science, Integrated Social Studies, Life Science, Physical Science), Special Education (Developmental Disabilities/Handicaps, Hearing Impaired, Learning Disability)

University of Dayton

The School of Education at the University of Dayton includes four departments: Teacher Education, Counselor Education & Human Services, Educational Administration, and Health & Sport Science. The mission of the School of Education is to become a learning community, to model that community, and to mentor others in their quest for community, all in the context of the Marianist tradition. All programs place emphasis on connecting the concrete and abstract in ways that engender critical reflection. Early field experiences in the P-12 classroom environment stress the importance of these clinical connections. The university also emphasizes the liberal arts.

Just the facts...

The University of Dayton
School of Education and Allied Professions
300 College Park
Dayton, OH 45469-0510
(937) 229-3146
Website: www.udayton.edu
Profile: Urban, Medium, Co-Ed
UG Tuition: $7,085.00/semester
G Tuition: $161.00/credit hour
Off Campus Programs: Graduate level only

Clinical Experiences

Clinical experiences are an integral part of each candidate's program. In their first semester, candidates begin clinical experiences in settings that include urban, suburban, public, private, and preschool settings. Prior to student teaching each candidate must log a minimum of 300 hours of education-related experiences in a variety of settings. When in the field, each candidate is assigned a peer mentor, an academic advisor, and an adult supervisor. The final field experience for each candidate is fifteen weeks of student teaching.

Noteworthy

The School of Education has a special professional development relationship with numerous area schools. The university makes special efforts to place future teachers with regular classroom teachers who are trained mentors as well as master teachers. A pre-student teaching experience places candidates in both a university classroom setting and a field setting. This practice allows candidates to immediately test in the field new skills learned in the classroom. State-of-the-art technology/media equipment is available to candidates. The School of Education provides special scholarships for under-represented students. The university has a variety of scholarship opportunities for qualified students.

Teacher Preparation Program Information

The following programs are 4 year programs:

Early Childhood Education, K-12 Education (Art, French, German, Health, Music, Physical Education, Reading, Spanish), Middle School Education (English, Mathematics, Science, Social Studies), Secondary Education (Biology, Chemistry, Earth Science, English/Language Arts, General Science, Mathematics, Physical Education, Physical Sciences, Physics, Social Studies), Special Education

The following programs are 5th year programs:

Early Childhood Education, K-12 Education (Art, Physical Education, Reading), Middle School Education (English, Mathematics, Science, Social Studies), Secondary Education (Earth Science, English/Language Arts, General Science, Mathematics, Physical Education, Physical Sciences, Physics, Social Studies), Special Education

University of Findlay

The University of Findlay's teacher education faculty are dedicated to developing lifelong learners who are reflective practitioners in a climate of change. Faculty have a deep philosophical and pragmatic commitment to experientially based active learning and meaningful field-based involvement with children and teachers in P-12 schools. The program is composed of professional knowledge, content area studies, and diverse liberal arts classes. Faculty also support and model the integration of technology across the curriculum. Teacher candidates are prepared to translate their professional understanding, personal beliefs, and experience into real world teaching situations.

Clinical Experiences

University of Findlay teacher candidates participate in field experiences during each of the four years of the program. Freshman observations are linked with three required classes. Sophomores participate in a six-week field assignment. The Junior Practicum, in conjunction with methods classes, places candidates in the field for six to eight weeks. Seniors participate in an eleven-week student teaching internship under the supervision of a cooperating teacher and a university supervisor. Experiences are assigned by age levels and content areas of desired licensure.

Just the facts...

University of Findlay
College of Education
1000 North Main Street
Findlay, OH 45840-3695
(419) 422-8313
Website: www.findlay.edu/
Profile: Rural, Medium, Co-Ed
UG Tuition: $311.00/credit hour
G Tuition: $230.00/credit hour
Off Campus Programs: Yes

Noteworthy

The University of Findlay is implementing an Early Childhood/Intergenerational Curriculum. Candidates may earn a two-year associate degree with opportunity to move into the early childhood education program as juniors. All participants will work in the Lifelong Educational Center, which is a collaboration between the University of Findlay, the Findlay City Schools, Winebrenner Village, and the Kerrington House. The Center brings senior citizens together with preschool and school age children in a unique intergenerational setting. Funding of over $1.5 million from gifts and grants has been received from FIPSE and the Ohio Department of Education.

Teacher Preparation Program Information

The following programs are 4 year programs:
Early Childhood Education, Middle Childhood Education, Special Education/Intervention Specialist (Mild/Moderate Disabilities), Adolescent/Young Adult Education (Earth Science, Integrated English/Language Arts, Integrated Mathematics, Integrated Science, Integrated Social Studies, Life Science, Physical Science), Multi-Age Education (Drama/Theater, Health, Japanese, Physical Education, Spanish, Visual Arts), Vocational Education (Integrated Business)

The following programs are post-baccalaureate programs:
Elementary Education

The following programs are 5th year programs:
Elementary Education

University of Toledo

The University of Toledo's College of Education and Allied Professions is committed to programs based on strong content, sound pedagogy, and social understanding. Candidates have the opportunity to prepare for roles as early childhood educators, middle childhood educators, adolescent educators, multi-age educators, and intervention specialist (special education) educators. Professional studies, normally taking place during the candidate's last three or four semesters, are completed in a modified cohort fashion. Candidates work together as a learning community with university faculty, school-based faculty, and other students. Candidates have the opportunity to earn a dual degree in their four-year program.

Just the facts...

University of Toledo
College of Education & Allied Professions
2801 West Bancroft Street
Toledo, OH 43606
(419) 530-2025
Website: www.utoledo.edu
Profile: Urban, Large, Co-Ed
UG Tuition: $2,082.00/sem. in-state; $5,047.00/sem. out-of-state
G Tuition: $2,953.00/sem. in-state; $5,917.00/sem. out-of-state
Off Campus Programs: No

Clinical Experiences

The College of Education and Allied Professions has worked closely with professional educators in the greater Toledo area to provide a number of diverse and high-quality experiences for candidates. The college regularly places candidates in over 100 different schools in the region. Several professional development schools are being established with urban, rural, and suburban districts. Candidates complete a minimum of a full-semester of student teaching/internship (sixteen weeks). Some programs such as adolescent education and early childhood education require additional time. In a typical program the candidate can expect to be in the schools approximately 200 hours prior to student teaching.

Noteworthy

The College of Education and Allied Professions hosts the national association of the Great City Colleges of Education and belongs to Alliance Thirty and the Holmes Partnership. The university, on a beautiful and dynamic campus, is large enough to have a comprehensive array of programs, yet small enough to provide personal attention to candidates. Candidates participate in several active professional honorary and social societies. Millions of dollars of external research and development funds have been granted to the university.

Teacher Preparation Program Information

The following programs are 4 year programs:
Early Childhood Education/P-3, Combination Regular/Special Education, Middle Childhood Education/4-8 (Language Arts, Mathematics, Science), Adolescent to Young Adult Education/7-12 (Earth Science, Integrated Langauge Arts, Integrated Mathematics, Integrated Social Studies, Life Science, Physical Science), Multi-Age Education/K-12 (French, German, Health, Music, Physical Education, Spanish, Visual Arts), Intervention Specialist/Special Education (Mild/Moderate, Moderate/Intensive, Visually Handicapped), Vocational Education/5-12 (Health Occupation, Trade & Industrial)

The following programs are post-baccalaureate programs:
Early Childhood Education/P-3, Combination Regular/Special Education, Middle Childhood Education/4-8 (Language Arts, Mathematics, Science), Adolescent to Young Adult Education/7-12 (Earth Science, Integrated Langauge Arts, Integrated Mathematics, Integrated Social Studies, Life Science, Physical Science), Multi-Age Education/K-12 (French, German, Health, Music, Physical Education, Spanish, Visual Arts), Intervention Specialist/Special Education (Mild/Moderate, Moderate/Intensive, Visually Handicapped), Vocational Education/5-12 (Health Occupation, Trade & Industrial)

The following programs are 5 year programs:
Early Childhood Intervention Specialist

The following programs are 5th year programs:
Elementary Education, Secondary Education (Chemistry, Biology, Earth Science, English, History, Mathematics, Physical Science, Physics, Social Studies), K-12 Education (Art, French, German, Music, Spanish), Special Education

Wright State University

The teacher preparation program at Wright State University began in 1971. In 1994, the National Education Association recognized the program as exemplary. Preservice teacher education candidates continue to receive exemplary prepration in pedagogical content knowledge; the use of technology to enhance instruction; and the ability to teach students from diverse cultural, special needs, and experiential backgrounds. Graduates are expected to provide meaningful and productive learning experiences for the students they teach, collaborate with administrators and colleagues in improving school practices, and contribute to advancing the profession.

Just the facts...

Wright State University
College of Education and Human Services
3640 Colonel Glenn Highway
Dayton, OH 45435
(937) 775-2821
Website: www.wright.edu
Profile: Urban, Large, Co-Ed
UG Tuition: $1,310.00/quarter
G Tuition: $1,703.00/quarter
Off Campus Programs: Yes

Clinical Experiences

Early in the teacher licensure program, candidates experience real classrooms where they are able to observe, interact, and work with children, and engage in reflective dialogue with classroom teachers, peers, and university faculty. Through these experiences, candidates become problem solvers and develop as professionals. Seven professional development schools (three high schools, one middle school, and three elementary schools) provide opportunities for candidates to learn from the best practices in the region. An early childhood center on campus provides opportunities to work with young children.

Noteworthy

The college houses an educational resource center with a collection of instructional materials, an instructional media production lab, computer lab, and conference facility. Faculty regularly contribute to the scholarly literature through their research and publications and participate in advancing the profession through participation with public schools and professional organizations. The College of Education and Human Services actively participates in educational reform and renewal through membership in the National Network for Educational Renewal, Holmes Group Partnership, and the Council of Great City Schools.

Teacher Preparation Program Information

The following programs are 4 year programs:
Early Childhood Education, Multi-Age Education (Health, Music, Physical Education), Vocational Education (General Vocational, Integrated Business, Marketing)

The following programs are 5 year programs:
Middle Childhood Education (Integrated Language Arts, Integrated Mathematics, Integrated Sciences, Integrated Social Studies), Adolescent/Young Adult Education (Earth & Space Sciences, Earth Science/Chemistry, Earth Science/Life Science, Earth Science/Physics, Language Arts, Life Sciences, Life Science/Chemistry, Life Science/Physics, Mathematics, Physical Sciences, Sciences, Social Sciences) Multi-Age Education (French, Spanish, Visual Arts)

The following programs are 5th year programs:
Elementary Education (Language Arts, Mathematics, Science, Social Studies), K-12 Education (Art, ESL, French, German, Reading, Spanish), Middle School Education (English, Mathematics, Science, Social Studies), Secondary Education (Art, Biology, Bookkeeping, Business, Chemistry, Consumer & Family Science/Home Economics), Special Education (Developmental Disabilities/Handicaps, Early Childhood, Gifted/Talented, Learning Disability, Multiple Disabilities/Handicaps, Severe Behavioral Disabilities/Handicaps)

Youngstown State University

The Beeghly College of Education's professional education programs at the initial and advanced levels are defined within a conceptual framework referred to as "Reflection in Action." This is translated into six program goals to develop professionals who are critical thinkers, problem solvers, decision makers, discerning counselors, lifelong learners, and active professionals. This conceptual framework functions to inform, to guide, and to inspire faculty and students by providing a central core of related ideas from which programs evolve, are explained, and are evaluated.

Just the facts...

Youngstown State University
College of Education
One University Plaza
Youngstown, OH 44555
(330) 742-3215
Website: www.ysu.edu
Profile: Urban, Large, Co-Ed
UG Tuition: $99.00/cr. hr. in-state; $210.00/cr. hr. out-of-state
G Tuition: $110.00/cr. hr. in-state; $222.00/cr. hr. out-of-state
(Note: Youngstown converts to a semester system in fall 2000)
Off Campus Programs: No

Clinical Experiences

All professional education courses require clinical and field experiences including observation, tutoring, small group instruction, teacher aiding, microteaching, and peer teaching. Experiences often take place in collaborative professional development schools. These professional development schools are located in both urban and suburban settings, and candidates have experiences in both settings. Prior to student teaching, candidates have a quarter-long blocked experience in the schools. Student teaching is at least one quarter in length; some programs require multiple student teaching experiences.

Noteworthy

The Beeghly College of Education operates the GOE (Generating Opportunities for Educators) program for minority students. In the GOE program minority students learn college and career survival skills through professional networks, work in community schools and weekend programs, and receive advising through a professional advising office; after successful completion of the first year, students are advised by the subject area faculty.

Teacher Preparation Program Information

The following programs are 4 year bachelor degree programs:
Early Childhood Education, Middle Childhood Education (Mathematics, Reading & Language Arts, Science, Social Studies), Multi-Age Education (Art, Drama/Theater, French, German, Health, Italian, Latin, Music, Physical Education, Russian, Spanish), Secondary Education (Earth Sciences, Life Sciences, Integrated Language Arts, Integrated Mathematics, Integrated Sciences, Integrated Social Studies, Physical Sciences), Vocational Education (Family & Consumer Sciences, Integrated Business), Special Education (Intervention Specialist-Mild/Moderate Disabilities, Intervention Specialist-Moderate/Intensive Disabilities)

The following programs are post-baccalaureate programs:
Early Education of Handicapped Children

Cameron University

Cameron University is an interactive university committed to preparing elementary, secondary, and K-12 teachers for the 21st century through an emphasis on field-based experiences. Programs combine the history of educational thought, knowledge of research, teaching strategies, professional skills, and practice to develop effective teachers. An innovative program for initial licensure leading to a Master of Arts in Teaching (CAMSTEP) is available for post-baccalaureate candidates. The Department of Education is dedicated to developing graduates who are competent, caring, and committed reflective decision makers and problem solvers.

Just the facts...

Cameron University
Department of Education
2800 West Gore Boulevard
Lawton, OK 73505
(580) 581-2320
Website: www.cameron.edu
Profile: Suburban, Medium, Co-Ed
UG Tuition: $63.65/cr. hr. in-state; $150.65/cr. hr. out-of-state
G Tuition: $78.65/cr. hr. in-state; $180.65/cr. hr. out-of-state
Off Campus Programs: No

Clinical Experiences

Clinical experiences begin with the first professional education course and continue each semester through student teaching. Experiences range in focus from directed observations to microteaching to supervised internships. Most interns are supervised by public school mentors. Elementary teacher candidates have two internship semesters, one in primary grades and one in intermediate grades. Secondary/K-12 teacher candidates may select a traditional program or a post-baccalaureate field-based program for initial licensure.

Noteworthy

The 3-T Tutoring Program is a service learning project in which teacher candidates volunteer to work with public school pupils. Open computer labs and instructional labs are available to students. Teacher candidates become proficient in using e-mail, the Internet, and software for classrooms. Candidates can become pen pals with elementary classes through the use of e-mail. Teaching portfolios are developed to demonstrate candidates' professional and pedagogical competencies.

Teacher Preparation Program Information

The following programs are 4 year programs:
Elementary Education, Elementary/Early Childhood Education, Elementary Education/Special Education (Mild/Moderate, Severe/Profound)

The following programs are 5th year programs:
K-12 Education (Art, French, Instrumental Music, Physical Education, Spanish, Vocal Music), Secondary Education (English, Mathematics, Science, Social Studies, Speech/Drama)

East Central University

By combining established research-based teaching principles of instruction along with instructional flexibility, East Central is meeting the challenge of preparing well qualified teachers. The faculty and staff believe that effective educators are reflective practitioners. School of Education graduates usually score in the top ten percent on the Oklahoma State Curriculum Exam. The teacher education program prepares candidates for a variety of occupations in public and private schools, institutions, business, industry, or hospitals. Early childhood, elementary, and special education candidates major in education; secondary education candidates major in their respective content fields.

Just the facts...

East Central University
School of Education
1000 East 14th Street
Ada, OK 74820
(580) 332-8000
Website: www.ecok.edu
Profile: Rural, Medium, Co-Ed
UG Tuition: $60.95/cr. hr. in-state; $147.95/cr. hr. out-of-state
G Tuition: $75.95/cr. hr. in-state; $177.95/cr. hr. out-of-state
Off Campus Programs: No

Clinical Experiences

East Central University's teacher preparation program requires candidates to complete three field experience courses and an internship. The three field experience courses are prerequisites for the student teaching semester, and each course is an integral part of one of the three respective "blocks" designed for a semester-cohort of candidates. Each of the three courses consists of 25 hours of observation and on-site experience in public schools. A satisfactory portfolio evaluation is required at the conclusion of each block.

Noteworthy

The teacher preparation structured block program emphasizes seamless integration of pedagogy and practice. Candidate portfolios designed to reflect individual competence allow each candidate to compile unique documentation based on individual strengths, self-awareness, and reflection. All candidates must demonstrate both computer literacy and "novice high level" competency in a second language. Continuous evaluation and feedback is provided to candidates by professors who are sensitive to the uniqueness of each individual.

Teacher Preparation Program Information

The following programs are 4 year programs:

Early Childhood Education, Elementary Education, K-12 Education (Art, Music, Physical Education), Secondary Education (Biology, Business, Chemistry, Consumer & Family Science, English/Language Arts, General Science, Geography, Mathematics, Physical Sciences, Physics, Political Science, Science, Social Studies, Sociology, Speech/Drama, Vocational Business Office, Vocational Consumer & Family Science), Special Education (Mild/Moderate Disabilities)

Langston University

Langston University is one of 117 historically black colleges and universities in the nation and the only one in Oklahoma. The Langston University School of Education and Behavioral Sciences develops reflective teachers who make wise decisions in the classroom. The teacher education program is based on a model of teacher decision making that is drawn largely from cognitive psychology. The faculty believe that teachers who make well-informed, appropriate decisions in the classroom are more likely to foster their students' learning, growth, and development.

Just the facts...

Langston University
School of Education and Behavioral Science
Sanford Hall, Room 202W
Langston, OK 73050
(405) 466-3382
Website: www.lunet.edu
Profile: Rural, Medium, Co-Ed
UG Tuition: $43.00-$55.50/cr. hr. in-state; $116.50-$137.00/cr. hr. out-of-state (*rate depends on division and campus*)
G Tuition: $58.00/cr. hr. in-state; $153.00/cr. hr. out-of-state
Off Campus Programs: Yes

Clinical Experiences

Beginning with entering freshmen, each candidate in the undergraduate program must have a minimum of 60 hours of pre-student teaching experiences in area schools. Candidates majoring in elementary education, special education, early childhood education, and health, physical education and recreation will complete as many as 50 additional hours in the public schools. Candidates student teach for sixteen weeks in two different assignments to ensure two different grade levels of teaching experience. Teaching seminars are conducted at school sites as well as on the main campus. Student teachers also attend workshops on topics such as careers and placement, multicultural education, and portfolio development.

Noteworthy

Special scholarships are available for teacher candidates, including a grant for African American males who agree to teach in an Olahoma urban school for at least two years; a matching grant from the Oklahoma Regents for Higher Education for male teacher candidates; and grants for future math, science, and special education teachers. During the past three years, four of Langston's graduates have been named "Outstanding Teacher of the Year." Langston has launched a professional school partnership with Thelma R. Parks Elementary School, and operates a collaborative project with Millwood Public School System and an Adopt-a-School program with Monroe Middle School.

Teacher Preparation Program Information

The following programs are 4 year programs:

Early Childhood Education, Elementary Education, Human Ecology, K-12 Education (Music), Middle School Education (English, Mathematics, Science), Secondary Education (English/Language Arts, Mathematics, Physical Education, Psychology, Science), Special Education (Learning Disability, Mental Retardation)

Northeastern State University

The College of Education at Northeastern State University has prepared students to become teachers in the public schools since 1909. The four academic departments in the College of Education provide instruction in courses that contribute to the general education, specialized education and professional education of students pursuing degree and/or licensure programs in virtually every area of teacher education. Programs are built on the belief that professional educators are facilitators of learning who emphasize multicultural perspectives, effective teaching practices, group learning strategies, reflective thinking, and technology.

Just the facts...

Northeastern State University
College of Education
Tahlequah, OK 74464
(918) 458-2092
Website: www.nsuok.edu
Profile: Rural, Medium, Co-Ed
UG Tuition: $60.00/cr. hr. in-state; $145.00/cr. hr. out-of-state
G Tuition: $75.00/cr. hr. in-state; $177.00/cr. hr. out-of-state
Off Campus Programs: Yes

Clinical Experiences

Northeastern State University has traditionally provided applied/field-based programs for teacher candidates. Candidates currently participate in three formal clinical/intern experiences, including a full semester student teaching internship. Candidates are mentored by teachers in the field as well as by university faculty in each of these experiences. Several program areas offer candidates opportunities to work and learn in professional development sites.

Noteworthy

Northeastern State University typically graduates the largest number of newly-licensed teachers in the state of Oklahoma, and graduates the largest number of Native American teachers in the United States. There are many opportunities for involvement in Native American schools and cultural activities. The College of Education offers an Oklahoma Residency Teacher Induction program for first-year teachers, and is involved in the America Reads program. Many educational scholarships are available to qualified candidates.

Teacher Preparation Program Information

The following programs are 4 year programs:
Early Childhood Education, Elementary Education, K-12 Education (Art, French, Music, Physical Education/Health, Spanish), Secondary Education (Consumer & Family Science/Home Economics, English/Language Arts, History, Journalism, Mathematics, Science, Social Studies, Speech, Technology Education), Special Education (Mild/Moderate Handicapped)

The following programs are post-baccalaureate programs:
K-12 Education (German), Secondary Education (Business), Special Education (Visually Impaired)

Northwestern Oklahoma State University

Northwestern Oklahoma State University emphasizes personal attention to its students' academic needs. Small classes and a dynamic, respected faculty allow each student to receive individual attention. Through field experiences, microteaching, and student teaching, candidates in the School of Education put into practice the pedagogical elements which professional research and practice indicate are characteristic of effective teachers and schools. Oklahoma was the only state in the nation given an "A" for the quality of its teachers in a recent *Education Week* report.

Just the facts...

Northwestern Oklahoma State University
School of Education
Alva, OK 73717
(580) 327-8455
Website: www.nwalva.edu
Profile: Rural, Small, Co-Ed
UG Tuition: $887.25/sem. in-state; $2,192.25/sem. out-of-state
G Tuition: $892.80/sem. in-state; $2,116.80/sem. out-of-state
Off Campus Programs: Yes

Clinical Experiences

Candidates' field experiences take place in public school settings. Candidates are required to keep logs of all their observations. During the student teaching semester, candidates are encouraged to "shadow" the cooperating teacher. Student teachers are visited/evaluated four times during their experience by university faculty. During the student teaching semester, Northwestern and a sister institution have a seminar day where participants exchange student teaching experiences and ideas. Candidates benefit from the strong working relationship Northwestern has with area public schools.

Noteworthy

Northwestern offers academic and teacher education scholarships through the Northwestern Foundation. College life at Northwestern is a mix of small-town friendliness and big-city student activities. The university is the cultural center of the region with on-campus events such as plays, concerts and lectures. The center of activity on campus is the Student Center. The Student Center recently underwent a $650,000 renovation and now features a food court, game room and large bookstore. A community/university wellness center is presently under construction on the campus.

Teacher Preparation Program Information

The following programs are 4 year programs:

Early Childhood Education, Elementary Education, K-12 Education (Music, Physical Education/Health), Secondary Education (Business, Drama/Theater, English/Language Arts, Mathematics, Natural Science, Social Studies, Speech), Special Education

Oklahoma Baptist University

Oklahoma Baptist University is an institution founded on Christian principles and teachings. The university's primary purpose is to conduct educational programs in the traditional arts and sciences and other disciplines to prepare students for effective leadership and service in various vocations. The university is owned by the Baptist General Convention of Oklahoma, which consists of approximately 1,400 cooperating Southern Baptist churches. The teacher education program prepares candidates to function as professionals by developing the knowledge and skills necessary for them to assist school children in reaching their potential.

Just the facts...

Oklahoma Baptist University
Division of Education
500 West University
OBU 61771
Shawnee, OK 74801-2590
(405) 878-2116
Website: www.okbu.edu
Profile: Suburban, Small, Co-Ed
UG Tuition: $3,830.00/semester
Off Campus Programs: No

Clinical Experiences

Early childhood education, elementary education, and special education teacher candidates participate in over 125 hours of observation, clinical practica, and internships in the public schools prior to their student teaching semester. Secondary and P-12 teacher candidates participate in over 90 hours of observation, clinical practica, and internships prior to student teaching. All teacher education candidates have a twelve-week student teaching requirement prior to graduation.

Noteworthy

The teacher education program participates in the America Reads program in cooperation with seven elementary sites in two local school districts. In addition, the teacher education program has a partnership with North Rock Creek Public Schools to participate in their two-week intersessions in the fall and spring by training and supplying student teachers to teach remedial and enrichment classes during this time. For seven consecutive years, *U.S. News and World Report* has named OBU among the top ten liberal arts colleges in the western United States. In recent years, OBU consistently has been among the top three universities in Oklahoma in the number of teacher candidates who pass the state licensure exam.

Teacher Preparation Program Information

The following programs are 4 year programs:
Early Childhood Education, Elementary Education, K-12 Education (Art, French, German, Music, Physical Education, Spanish), Secondary Education (Biology, Chemistry, Consumer & Family Science/Home Economics, English/Language Arts, Mathematics, Physical Education, Social Studies, Speech/Drama), Special Education

The following programs are post-baccalaureate programs:
K-12 Education (Health), Middle School Education (English, Mathematics, Science, Social Studies, Music, Physical Education), Secondary Education (Earth Science, General Science, Physical Sciences, Political Science, Science, Sociology)

National Council for Accreditation of Teacher Education

Oklahoma Christian University of Science & Arts

Oklahoma Christian University is a private institution that educates students in a community where Christian principles and liberal arts develop purposeful lives of leadership and service. The faculty in the College of Education believe that effective teachers must have a strong liberal arts foundation; a subject area emphasis; and knowledge of their profession, their pupils, and pedagogy provided by clinical experiences. Faculty members expect teacher education graduates to exhibit both a global awareness of education and its impact, and a functional use of technology in the classroom.

Just the facts...

Oklahoma Christian University of Science and Arts
College of Education
Box 11000
Oklahoma City, OK 73136-1100
(405) 425-5430
Website: www.oc.edu
Profile: Suburban, Small, Co-Ed
UG Tuition: $3,800.00/semester
Off Campus Programs: No

Clinical Experiences

Directed observations, lesson planning, and lesson presentations are developed and critiqued under the supervision of classroom teachers and university supervisors. Candidates are assigned to a variety of school settings. Placement consideration is given to the culture/ethnicity and socioeconomic status of each school setting. A minimum of 120 hours of clinical experiences are logged prior to student teaching. In the professional semester, student teachers spend three intense weeks studying human relations and diversity issues. Student teaching is completed at two different sites for a total of twelve weeks.

Noteworthy

Scholarships are awarded by the College of Education for freshmen and transfer students. The campus student education organization is active in bringing speakers to campus, providing workshops and creating dialogue between teacher candidates and first-year and veteran teachers. An integral part of the teacher preparation program is candidates' long term participation in cohort groups. Teacher candidates develop a portfolio of performance-based artifacts that chronicle their progress through the program. At the conclusion of student teaching, candidates complete a seven to twelve minute CD-ROM which serves as an employment portfolio that graduates may use in the interviewing process.

Teacher Preparation Program Information

The following programs are 4 year programs:
Early Childhood Education, Elementary Education, K-12 Education (Art, Music, Physical Education), Middle School Education (English, Mathematics, Science, Social Studies), Secondary Education (Business, English/Language Arts, Mathematics, Science, Social Studies, Speech), Special Education (Mildly Mentally Handicapped)

Southeastern Oklahoma State University

Southeastern Oklahoma State University, founded in 1909, was originally chartered as a state normal school to train teachers. The faculty in the School of Education and Behavioral Sciences are committed to a knowledge base for these programs that reflects the view that teachers are collaborative facilitators of learning. Graduates have a strong liberal arts background and are able to use technology effectively in the K-12 classroom. Southeastern's teacher education program, one of the university's strengths, equips teacher candidates to live effectively and productively in a rapidly changing world.

Just the facts...

Southeastern Oklahoma State University
School of Education
P.O. Box 4115
Durant, OK 74701
(580) 924-0121
Website: www.sosu.edu
Profile: Rural, Medium, Co-Ed
UG Tuition: $47.00/cr. hr. in-state; $134.00/cr. hr. out-of-state
G Tuition: $62.00/cr. hr. in-state; $164.00/cr. hr. out-of-state
Off Campus Programs: Yes

Clinical Experiences

Three pre-student teaching experiences are integrated throughout the education programs. The first experience (fifteen hours) allows candidates to experience elementary, middle, and high school settings. The second experience (75 hours) is designed to give candidates multiple hours in a single setting. The third experience (15 hours) is spent with the classroom teacher with whom candidates have been placed for their student teaching assignment. Candidates student teach for 60 days.

Noteworthy

A unique feature of the teacher education program at Southeastern is the inclusion of special education competencies in all programs, thus preparing all graduates to be inclusion teachers. The Professional Mentor Program selects and trains a cadre of public school teachers who receive training and support from the university, and then serve as supervisors of candidates' student teaching experience. Southeastern is known for its friendly campus atmosphere and the individual attention it provides to students.

Teacher Preparation Program Information

The following programs are 4 year programs:
Early Childhood Education, Elementary Education, PK-12 Education (Art, Music, Physical Education/Health, Special Education/Mild-Moderate Disabilities), Secondary Education (Business, English/Language Arts, Mathematics, Science, Social Studies, Speech)

The following programs are post-baccalaureate programs:
Early Childhood Education, Elementary Education, PK-12 Education (Art, Music, Physical Education/Health, Special Education/Mild-Moderate Disabilities), Reading Specialist, Secondary Education (Business, English/Language Arts, Mathematics, Science, Social Studies, Speech)

Southern Nazarene University

Southern Nazarene University is the official institution of higher education for the south-central education region of the Church of the Nazarene. The university serves a diverse clientele representing all parts of the United States and several foreign countries. Academic programs at Southern Nazarene University are designed to achieve two major goals: (1) to help students become critical and creative thinkers who can clearly discern and communicate a Christian perspective in every aspect of life and (2) to prepare students for successful professional careers.

Just the facts...

Southern Nazarene University
Teacher Education
6729 NW 39th Expressway
Oklahoma City, OK 73008-2694
(405) 491-6317
Website: www.snu.edu
Profile: Suburban, Small, Co-Ed
UG Tuition: $3,930.00/semester
G Tuition: $285.00/semester
Off Campus Programs: Yes

Clinical Experiences

Teacher candidates' clinical experiences are divided into three segments. The first consists of intensive coursework and preparation for the student teaching experience. The second is devoted to two full-time student teaching experiences under the direct supervision of a qualified member of the university faculty. The third segment is the Student Teaching Seminar, scheduled before and between student teaching assignments. Student teaching is a twelve-week experience including a multicultural setting for a minimum of six weeks.

Noteworthy

The Master of Arts in Educational Leadership is a cohort-based program leading to Oklahoma licensure as a principal or superintendent. Candidates are connected to the university, other students, and facilititators by laptop computers and the Internet. Southern Nazarene University's School of Education has one of the finest laboratory schools in the nation. Located on the main university campus, the School for Children serves just under 200 children from pre-kindergarten through the fifth grade. Started in 1971, the School for Children provided the vehicle for SNU to offer the second early childhood education program available in the state of Oklahoma.

Teacher Preparation Program Information

The following programs are 4 year programs:
Early Childhood Education, Elementary Education, K-12 Education (Art, Music, Physical Education, Spanish), Kindergarten Education, Secondary Education (Art, Biology, Chemistry, Earth Science, English/Language Arts, General Science, Health, Mathematics, Physical Education, Physical Sciences, Physics, Political Science, Science, Social Studies)

The following programs are 5 year programs:
Early Childhood Education, Elementary Education, Kindergarten Education

Southwestern Oklahoma State University

Southwestern Oklahoma State University (SWOSU) has a long history of preparing educators. Established in 1901, SWOSU remains committed to its mission of training teachers, counselors, and administrators. Through a strong program in general education, content specialization, and pedagogy, the faculty helps prospective educators reach their professional goals. Teacher training at SWOSU uses the latest research and technology. Practical experiences are emphasized throughout the program to ensure that graduates have the knowledge and skills they need for their own success and the success of their future students.

Just the facts...

Southwestern Oklahoma State University
School of Education
100 Campus Drive
Weatherford, OK 73096
(580) 774-3285
Website: www.swosu.edu
Profile: Rural, Medium, Co-Ed
UG Tuition: $60.00/cr. hr. in-state; $137.50/cr. hr. out-of-state
G Tuition: $75.00/cr. hr. in-state; $177.00/cr. hr. out-of-state
Off Campus Programs: Yes

Clinical Experiences

From the introductory course in teacher education through the student teacher experience, teacher candidates ar SWOSU are involved in experiences which allow them to interact with public school students. Most of the methods courses have field experience components built into the course requirements. The professional semester includes four weeks of block courses to prepare student teachers for their responsibilities and twelve weeks of full-time student teaching. School of Education faculty serve as mentors to student teachers and residency teachers in their first year of public school employment.

Noteworthy

A complete renovation of the School of Education building has improved the university's ability to provide appropriate experiences for prospective educators. The School of Education's computer lab, for example, has been completely refurbished and boasts state-of-the-art computers and related technology. Prospective teacher candidates may complete the introductory course via interactive video offered at area junior colleges and at SWOSU's branch campus at Sayre. The university offers several special scholarships for prospective educators. These awards are in addition to traditional scholarships and housing allowances granted based on need and/or academic standing.

Teacher Preparation Program Information

The following programs are 4 year programs:

Elementary Education, K-12 Education (Art, Music, Physical Education), Secondary Education (Art, English/Language Arts, History, Mathematics, Natural Science, Physical Education, Science, Social Studies, Technology Education), Special Education (Learning Disability, Multiple Disabilities/Handicaps)

The following programs are post-baccalaureate programs:

Elementary Education, K-12 Education (Art, Music, Physical Education), Secondary Education (Art, English/Language Arts, History, Mathematics, Natural Science, Physical Education, Science, Social Studies, Technology Education), Special Education (Learning Disability, Multiple Disabilities/Handicaps)

University of Central Oklahoma

The University of Central Oklahoma, the oldest state education institution in Oklahoma, has historically provided leadership in teacher preparation for the state. Its mission is to provide quality undergraduate, graduate, and continuing education opportunities for students so they can achieve their professional and personal goals in an ever-changing global environment. The College of Education trains educators to be reflective decision makers who can facilitate student learning. Candidates become professionals who are models of excellence in practice and exemplify good citizenship. The faculty are committed to the preparation of professionals for service in multicultural communities and a global society.

Just the facts...

University of Central Oklahoma
College of Education
100 North University Drive
Edmond, OK 73034
(405) 341-2980
Website: www.educ.ucok.edu
Profile: Suburban, Large, Co-Ed
UG Tuition: $60.20/cr. hr. in-state; $138.70/cr. hr. out-of-state
G Tuition: $76.20/cr. hr. in-state; $178.20/cr. hr. out-of-state
Off Campus Programs: No

Clinical Experiences

Candidates are required to complete a minimum of three field-based experiences within the university's thirty-mile service area, at sites that include elementary schools, secondary schools, community agencies, and industry. At least one field experience must be completed in a culturally diverse setting. Student teaching is a culminating sixteen-week experience in which the student works closely with the classroom teacher in a regular classroom. Specialty studies include additional on-site experiences.

Noteworthy

Teacher graduates from the University of Central Oklahoma are recruited highly by other states because of the program's excellent reputation. Many graduates have been recognized on the state and national level as outstanding leaders in their fields. Programs in education emphasize the effective use of technology in teaching and learning. All faculty members in teacher education have experience as practitioners, which enables them to blend theory with practice. The faculty are student-centered and focus on providing a caring environment conducive to learning. Educational scholarships and fee waivers are awarded for need and merit.

Teacher Preparation Program Information

The following programs are 4 year programs:
Early Childhood Education, Elementary Education, K-12 Education (Art, French, German, Music, Physical Education/Health, Spanish), Secondary Education (Art, Biology, Business, Chemistry, Communication, Consumer & Family Science/Home Economics, English/Language Arts, Geography, History, Journalism, Mathematics, Physics, Political Science, Social Studies, Trade & Industrial, Vocational Marketing, Vocational Health Occupation, Vocational Consumer & Family), Special Education (Mild/Moderate Disabilities, Severe/Profound Disabilities)

The following programs are post-baccalaureate programs:
K-12 Education (ESL), Middle School Education (English, Mathematics, Science, Social Studies), Secondary Education (Vocational Business Office)

University of Oklahoma

The University of Oklahoma ranks first among public institutions and second only to Harvard among private universities in per capita enrollment of National Merit Scholars. The College of Education at the University of Oklahoma promotes inquiry and practices that are fundamental to teaching and research in multidisciplinary education. TE-PLUS—Teacher Education: Professionalism, Leadership, Understanding, and Scholarship—is the College of Education's new teacher preparation program. This extended program includes both undergraduate and graduate coursework and experiences.

Just the facts...

The University of Oklahoma
College of Education
820 Van Vleet Oval, Room #100
Norman, OK 73019-0260
(405) 325-1081
Website: www.ou.edu/education/
Profile: Suburban, Large, Co-Ed
UG Tuition: $56.50/cr. hr. in-state; $182.50/cr. hr. out-of-state
Off Campus Programs: No

Clinical Experiences

The TE-PLUS program begins with a junior level course that introduces candidates to the place of the school in society. An important component of this introductory course is 30 hours of field experience. Subsequent professional education courses require a minimum of 30 and 45 hours of field experience. Every prospective teacher has field experiences in three different school settings—urban, suburban, and rural. All told, prospective teachers have over 100 hours of field experiences before their student teaching internship.

Noteworthy

The extended part of the teacher education program includes nine graduate credit hours that can be applied to a master's degree program. Graduates of the program are independent professionals who can be, and are, successful in any kind of school setting. Over 40 scholarships, ranging from $259 to $1,600 per year, are available for education majors. Mentoring experiences with a variety of professionals occur throughout the program. OU students consistently outscore others on state-level subject area and professional education examinations.

Teacher Preparation Program Information

The following programs are post-baccalaureate programs:
Secondary Education (English, Mathematics, Science, Social Studies)

The following programs are 5 year programs:
Early Childhood Education, Elementary Education, K-12 Education (French, German, Latin, Music, Spanish), Secondary Education (English/Language Arts, General Science, Mathematics, Physical Sciences, Social Studies), Special Education (Learning Disability, Mild/Moderate Developmental Disabilities/Handicaps)

The following programs are 5th year programs:
Secondary Education (English, Mathematics, Science, Social Studies)

National Council for Accreditation of Teacher Education

University of Science and Arts of Oklahoma

The teacher education program at the University of Science and Arts of Oklahoma (USAO) is a model of an integrated, liberal arts curriculum within a small, state-supported college. The goal of USAO's teacher education program is to prepare ethical, responsible, and effective teachers for the nation's classrooms. To achieve this goal, the program is comprised of an integrated three-part instructional model which incorporates interdisciplinary instruction, a liberal arts curriculum, and research on effective teaching. Graduates of the program teach throughout Oklahoma and the United States.

Just the facts...

The University of Science and Arts of Oklahoma
Teacher Education
17th and Grand
Chickasha, OK 73018
(405) 224-3140
Website: www.usao.edu
Profile: Rural, Small, Co-Ed
UG Tuition: $58.00/cr. hr. in-state; $136.50/cr. hr. out-of-state
Off Campus Programs: No

Clinical Experiences

Candidates are placed into the classroom early in their college careers so that they know almost immediately whether they are suited to a teaching career. Teacher education students are required to spend 20 hours in a first field experience and 25 hours in a second field experience working with public school students under the supervision of classroom teachers. Each field experience takes place at a different school, providing candidates with exposure to a mixture of neighborhoods, teaching styles, and grade levels. For additional field experiences, candidates may enroll in the paraprofessional course offered during the independent study period each May. The student teaching experience is a minimum of 60 days full-time.

Noteworthy

The USAO trimester system offers an opportunity for an accelerated program that allows full-time students to graduate in less than four years. A special part of this trimester system is the five-week independent study session. During this session, students are allowed to create their own learning experience independent of the normal classroom structure. Both group and independent projects are possible, and the topics and extent of inquiries are limited only by the student's own boundaries. USAO also offers a unique form of financial assistance: the Third Trimester Enrollment Fee Waiver Scholarship, which pays for enrollment fees in the summer trimester for qualified students.

Teacher Preparation Program Information

The following programs are 4 year programs:
Early Childhood Education, Elementary Education, K-12 Education (Art, Music, Physical Education), Secondary Education (Art, Business, English/Language Arts, Mathematics, Natural Science, Social Studies), Special Education (Hearing Impaired)

The following programs are post-baccalaureate programs:
Early Childhood Education, Elementary Education, K-12 Education (Art, Music, Physical Education), Secondary Education (Art, Business, English/Language Arts, Mathematics, Natural Science, Social Studies), Special Education (Hearing Impaired)

University of Tulsa

The University of Tulsa is a private institution committed to excellence in all its programs. A core curriculum of liberal arts and sciences is required of all majors, and all programs leading to secondary or K-12 licensure require dual majors—one in the academic area and one in education. Candidates preparing to teach in elementary schools complete a major in elementary education as well as an academic minor that can lead to middle school licensure. The preparation of teachers at the University of Tulsa is designed as a competency-based program emphasizing personal reflection as teacher candidates develop best teaching practices.

Just the facts...

The University of Tulsa
School of Education
600 South College Avenue
Tulsa, OK 74104-3189
(918) 631-2236
Website: www.utulsa.edu
Profile: Urban, Medium, Co-Ed
UG Tuition: $6,425.00/semester
G Tuition: $480.00/credit hour
Off Campus Programs: No

Clinical Experiences

Clinical experiences begin in the freshman year with a career exploratory experience. All courses in teaching methods include extensive practical experience in culturally diverse schools. Student teaching is a full semester during the senior year, and placements are arranged at two different schools and at two different grade levels. Faculty mentoring and the development of a teaching portfolio are important features of each clinical experience.

Noteworthy

The University of Tulsa maintains professional development relationships with various public schools in the Tulsa metropolitan area, ensuring the demonstration of best teaching practices and opportunities for pre-professional mentoring in its clinical experience program. The University of Tulsa also operates University School, a private elementary school that emphasizes educational programs for the gifted and talented pupil. A state-of-the-art computer technology center and a curriculum resource center form the hub of instructional resources for teaching methods.

Teacher Preparation Program Information

The following programs are 4 year programs:

Elementary Education, K-12 Education (Art, Music), Middle School Education (English, Mathematics, Science, Social Studies), Secondary Education (Biology, Chemistry, Earth Science, English, French, German, Mathematics, Russian, Social Studies, Spanish, Speech/Drama), Special Education (Hearing Impaired)

The following programs are post-baccalaureate programs:

Elementary Education, K-12 Education (Art, Music), Middle School Education (English, Mathematics, Science, Social Studies), Secondary Education (Biology, Chemistry, Earth Science, English, French, German, Mathematics, Russian, Social Studies, Spanish, Speech/Drama), Special Education (Hearing Impaired)

The following programs are 5th year programs:

Elementary Education, Secondary Education

Oregon State University

The School of Education at Oregon State University has a long history of teacher and counselor preparation. The faculty is committed to preparing reflective decision makers who facilitate student learning and who try to ensure that students succeed in all aspects of their schooling. All areas of the teacher preparation program maintain a strong focus on academics. The program emphasizes the development of the candidate's ability to transform what he or she knows to teaching strategies that make knowledge accessible to learners. Candidates learn about the interaction of schools, learners, subject matter, and curriculum. Prospective teachers work with diverse learners in a variety of settings and talented mentor teachers.

Just the facts...

Oregon State University
School of Education
215 Education Hall
Corvallis, OR 97331-3502
(541) 737-4661
Website: www.orst.edu
Profile: Rural, Large, Co-Ed
UG Tuition: $1,180.00/quart. in-state; $3,936.00/quart. out-of-state
G Tuition: $2,066.00/quart. in-state; $3,514.00/quart. out-of-state
Off Campus Programs: No

Clinical Experiences

At Oregon State University the teaching internship is considered to be one of the most vital phases of the candidate's professional preparation. The internship is a full-time experience for a minimum of fifteen weeks or the equivalent part-time experience. At least nine weeks of the practicum is considered the full-time internship experience. During this period the intern functions as a member of the site school staff. The mentor and university faculty work in partnership to orient, supervise, and evalaute the intern.

Noteworthy

All program areas in the teacher preparation program at Oregon State University require a strong focus on subject matter preparation prior to admission, incorporate content-specific pedagogy, and use local and national standards as benchmarks for program design. Some courses are Web-based; students progress in modules at a rate based on their individual needs and professional development plans.

Teacher Preparation Program Information

The following programs are 4 year programs:
Agriculture Education

The following programs are post-baccalaureate programs:
Early Childhood Education, Elementary Education, K-12 Education (Health, Music, Physical Education), Secondary Education (Agriculture, Biology, Business, Chemistry, Family & Consumer Science, Foreign Language, General Science, Language Arts, Mathematics, Marketing, Physics, Technology Education)

The following programs are 5 year programs:
Early Childhood Education, Elementary Education, Music Education

The following programs are 5th year programs:
Early Childhood Education, Elementary Education, K-12 Education (Health, Music, Physical Education), Secondary Education (Business, Chemistry, Family & Consumer Science, Foreign Language, General Science, Health, Language Arts, Mathematics, Marketing, Physics, Technology Education)

Portland State University

Portland State University prepares educational personnel for urban communities with courses, field experiences, research enterprises, and partnerships that focus on the opportunities and challenges characterizing urban settings. Graduates are able to address the needs of learners who are diverse in their cultural, linguisitic, socioeconomic, and ethnic backgrounds, abilities, and needs. The Graduate School of Education offers the Doctor of Education and the Master of Education in teaching, administration, special education, counseling, library/media, ESL/Bilingual, and speech pathology. Successful completion of these master's programs culminates in a recommendation for Oregon's initial teaching license.

Just the facts...

Portland State University
Graduate School of Education
P.O. Box 751
Portland, OR 97207-0751
(503) 725-4619
Website: www.pdx.edu
Profile: Urban, Large, Co-Ed
UG Tuition: $1,114.00/quart. in-state; $3,771.00/quart. out-of-state
G Tuition: $2,033.50/quart. in-state; $3,481.50/quart. out-of-state
Off Campus Programs: No

Clinical Experiences

Field experiences in Portland State University's teacher preparation program include observation, sharing of prior student knowledge or experience, tutoring, interviewing, and practice of specific course content. This program reflects the rapidly changing nature of America's schools where students with widely diverse backgrounds and students with disabilities are in the regular classroom, making it necessary for future school personnel to have experiences with many different kinds of students prior to licensure. PSU faculty work with a large number of school districts in providing field experiences that complement coursework. Student teaching is the culminating field experience.

Noteworthy

Portland State University is an active participant in the Portland Teacher Program, which is designed to encourage and support students of color and their involvement in teacher education. Under the cohort model employed by the teacher education program, candidates are able to complete licensing and the master's degree requirements in one year of full-time study.

Teacher Preparation Program Information

The following programs are 5th year programs:

Early Childhood Education, Elementary Education, K-12 Education (Art, Drama/Theater, French, German, Health, Japanese, Music, Reading, Russian, Spanish), Kindergarten Education, Middle School Education, Secondary Education (Art, Biology, Business, Chemistry, English/Language Arts, General Science, Health, Mathematics, Social Studies), Special Education (Developmental Disabilities/Handicaps, Early Childhood, Visually Impaired)

Western Oregon University

Western Oregon University is the oldest public institution of higher education on the West coast, and the oldest university in the Oregon University System. The mission of the School of Education is to serve the children and youth of Oregon through the preparation of teachers who are academically strong, competent in all aspects of teaching, and prepared to contribute to the evolving state of education. In addition, the School of Education prepares rehabilitation counselors, sign language interpreters, and health and physical education professionals for a variety of increasingly diverse and complex roles in schools, service organizations, and business.

Just the facts...

Western Oregon University
School of Education
345 North Monmouth Avenue
Monmouth, OR 97361-1394
(503) 838-8471
Website: www.wou.edu
Profile: Urban, Medium, Co-Ed
UG Tuition: $1,066.00/quart. in-state; $3,246.00/quart. out-of-state
G Tuition: $1,723.00/sem. in-state; $3,070.00/sem. out-of-state
Off Campus Programs: Yes

Clinical Experiences

In the elementary/secondary program, four school district partnerships are set up for each cohort of candidates. Sixteen candidates and a faculty member are assigned to the district for all four terms. In each partnership, the school district assigns an on-site coordinator to place the candidates with cooperating teachers. In special education, sites are selected based on the opportunities for candidates to participate in programs that exemplify the values of the faculty in areas of curriculum, assessment, inclusion of special education students in the regular education program, and collaboration among families and educators.

Noteworthy

WOU was selected as one of five case studies in the United States for its innovative and effective teacher preparation programs. The U.S. Department of Education project, housed at Ohio State University, selected WOU based on characteristics that included team teaching by faculty, integration of technology, community service learning projects, a performance-based assessment framework, and partnerships with K-12 schools. WOU has a high freshman retention rate and an excellent student/teacher ratio of one to fifteen.

Teacher Preparation Program Information

The following programs are 4 year programs:
Early Childhood Education, Elementary Education, Middle Level Education, High School Education

The following programs are post-baccalaureate programs:
Deaf Education, Early Childhood Education, Elementary Education, Middle Level Education, High School Education, Special Education

The following programs are 5th year programs:
Deaf Education, High School Education, Special Education

Bloomsburg University of Pennsylvania

Bloomsburg University has a rich history and strong tradition of preparing teachers of the highest quality. The mission of the School of Education is twofold: (1) to enhance the quality of education by preparing professionals who are empowered to facilitate the learning, growth, and development of students in our diverse and technologically complex world and (2) to serve as a resource to communities in the region. Faculty members are committed to improving the field of education through a comprehensive program that is balanced between theory and field-based practice.

Just the facts...

Bloomsburg University of Pennsylvania
College of Professional Studies
400 East Second Street
MCHS 3106
Bloomsburg, PA 17815-1301
(570) 389-4005
Website: www.bloomu.edu
Profile: Rural, Medium, Co-Ed
UG Tuition: $1,734.00/sem. in-state; $4,412.00/sem. out-of-state
G Tuition: $1,734.00/sem. in-state; $3,118.00/sem. out-of-state
Off Campus Programs: No

Clinical Experiences

Teacher education majors complete field experiences throughout the program of study. Many of these experiences are embedded in coursework. Two field experience courses are available to all teacher education majors and provide observation and experiences with students in local schools. Several professional development school options are available to teacher education majors. The focus of the current professional development school experiences include an inclusive elementary school, an inclusive middle and high school, and intensive experience integrating technology into teaching and learning. All teacher education majors complete a fifteen-week student teaching experience.

Noteworthy

Bloomsburg offers a cooperative doctoral program in elementary education. Presidential scholarships are available. About two out of every three students receive financial assistance (average amount—$4,200). The Urban Learning Academy, which is a collaborative project with the School District of Philadelphia, provides teacher education majors with an opportunity to complete an intensive experience with students from diverse populations in an urban setting. The university is located in a beautiful rural setting of the Susquehanna Valley and is within driving distance of urban areas such as Philadelphia (two and one-half hours), New York City and Baltimore (three hours), and Washington D.C. (four hours).

Teacher Preparation Program Information

The following programs are 4 year programs:
Early Childhood Education, Elementary Education, K-12 Education (French, German, Spanish), Secondary Education (Biology, Business, Chemistry, Communication, Earth Science, English/Language Arts, General Science, Mathematics, Physics), Special Education

The following programs are 5th year programs:
Early Childhood Education, Special Education

National Council for Accreditation of Teacher Education

California University of Pennsylvania

The College of Education and Human Services, the oldest division of California University, has as its primary mission the preparation of teachers in elementary education, secondary education, special education, speech pathology, and technology education. All programs are based on the standards of learned societies and the licensure requirements of Pennsylvania. The College of Education, by maintaining high standards and quality programs, ensures that its graduates are capable of planning, organizing, and delivering an instructional program in a contemporary school setting.

Just the facts...

California University of Pennsylvania
College of Education and Human Services
California, PA 15419
(724) 938-4125
Website: www.cup.edu
Profile: Rural, Medium, Co-Ed
UG Tuition: $1,734.00/sem. in-state; $4,412.00/sem. out-of-state
G Tuition: $1,734.00/sem. in-state; $3,118.00/sem. out-of-state
Off Campus Programs: No

Clinical Experiences

Teacher candidates at California University are placed in clinical and field experiences, developed and supervised by faculty, that take place in a diverse range of sites. Many clinical experiences are offered in conjunction with subject-related courses. Candidates are closely supervised by faculty and cooperating teachers in the schools. Student teachers are given increased responsibility for professional assignments so that they are ready to assume independent classroom practice when they successfully complete their programs.

Noteworthy

California University has developed partnerships with regional public schools. One of these partnerships is a professional development school. Candidates, faculty, and public school teachers and administrators work together to provide a demonstration school that merges theory with practice and creates an exciting learning environment for students. The College of Education has a state-of-the-art multimedia teaching room which is used to train candidates to use technology in their teaching. Videoconferencing units allow candidates to communicate with public school teachers, students, and administrators. Graduates are employed in schools throughout the United States.

Teacher Preparation Program Information

The following programs are 4 year programs:
Early Childhood Education, Elementary Education, K-12 Education (French, German, Spanish, Technology Education), Secondary Education (Biology, Chemistry, Earth Science, English/Language Arts, General Science, Mathematics, Physics, Social Studies), Special Education (Speech/Language Disabilities)

The following programs are post-baccalaureate programs:
Early Childhood Education, Elementary Education, K-12 Education (French, German, Spanish, Technology Education), Secondary Education (Biology, Chemistry, Earth Science, English/Language Arts, General Science, Mathematics, Physics, Social Studies), Special Education (Speech/Language Disabilities)

The following programs are 5th year programs:
Early Childhood Education, Elementary Education

Clarion University of Pennsylvania

Located in scenic northwestern Pennsylvania, Clarion University offers more than 70 baccalaureate degree programs and twelve graduate programs. The primary academic resource of the College of Education and Human Services is a faculty committed to excellence in teaching and to continuous intellectual and professional development. The overall mission of the college is to develop educators who have received specialized training, mastered a recognized body of knowledge, and internalized standards of excellence. Graduates are ready to assume responsibility for the exercise of professional judgment and are committed to contiued professional growth.

Just the facts...

Clarion University of Pennsylvania
College of Education and Human Services
102 Stevens Hall
Clarion, PA 16214
(814) 226-2146
Website: www.clarion.edu
Profile: Rural, Medium, Co-Ed
UG Tuition: $1,734.00/sem. in-state; $4,232.00/sem. out-of-state
G Tuition: $187.00/cr. hr. in-state; $336.00/cr. hr. out-of-state
Off Campus Programs: Yes

Clinical Experiences

Clarion University historically has considered field experiences as essential components for the professional development of teacher candidates. Field experiences are integrated throughout the four-year teacher education program in order to connect theories and principles to practical applications in the classroom. All field experiences are linked to coursework and are sequenced acccording to purpose, level of direct experience with students, varying contexts or settings, and duration or extensiveness.

Noteworthy

The College of Education and Human Services maintains a number of unique programs that serve the campus, area schools, and the community: educational experiences in a daycare setting for preschool children and field experiences for education majors; diagnostic hearing and speech screenings for university students and the community; and dignostic testing and tutoring services for students from area schools with learning disabilities. Modern classrooms and computer labs with work stations, scanners, digital cameras, projection units, laser printers, and Internet access also serve the needs of candidates.

Teacher Preparation Program Information

The following programs are 4 year programs:

Early Childhood Education, Elementary Education, K-12 Education (French, Music, Spanish), Secondary Education (Biology, Chemistry, Communication, Earth Science, English/Language Arts, General Science, Mathematics, Physics, Social Studies), Special Education

National Council for Accreditation of Teacher Education

Indiana University of Pennsylvania

Indiana University of Pennsylvania was founded as a normal school in 1875. Teacher education at IUP focuses on preparing professionals who can enter the world of practice equipped to render valuable service to their clients. This practice-driven program is grounded in five elements: rigorous academic content, collaborative work with students and constituents, comprehensive pedagogical skills to address learner needs, commitment to continued professional growth and service, and competence to assume the title and work of teacher. Candidate progress is closely monitored to ensure quality.

Just the facts...

Indiana University of Pennsylvania
College of Education
104 Stouffer Hall
Indiana, PA 15705
(724) 357-2480
Website: www.iup.edu
Profile: Rural, Large, Co-Ed
UG Tuition: $1,734.00/sem. in-state; $4,412.00/sem. out-of-state
G Tuition: $1,734.00/sem. in-state; $3,118.00/sem. out-of-state
Off Campus Programs: Yes

Clinical Experiences

Candidates complete three clinical experiences. Each practicum builds on the previous one to provide a full range of activities in diverse settings. Candidates have a choice of completing practica in over 300 school districts in Pennsylvania, including Pittsburgh, Philadelphia, and Erie. Candidates may opt for placement in more remote areas, such as a reservation in Arizona, or in Europe or Mexico. Supervision is conducted by full-time faculty and may include the use of videoconferencing, an innovative and nationally recognized project funded by FIPSE.

Noteworthy

Teacher candidates at IUP have the opportunity to participate in an number of unique programs. Among them are the Robert E. Cook Honors College and the Specialty Living Option Program, which places students with the same major on the same floor of a dormitory. The COE offers mentoring programs for freshmen of color, inner city or European-based practica placements, and extensive exposure to technology and its applications. In addition, the COE offers nearly $15,000 annually through a variety of scholarships for candidates.

Teacher Preparation Program Information

The following programs are 4 year programs:
Early Childhood Education, Elementary Education, K-12 Education (Art, Family & Consumer Science, French, German, Music, Physical Education/Health, Spanish), Secondary Education (Anthropology, Biology, Business, Chemistry, Consumer & Family Science/Home Economics, Earth Science, Economics, English/Language Arts, French, General Science, Geography, German, History, Mathematics, Physics, Sociology, Spanish, Vocational Trade & Industrial), Special Education (Hearing Impaired, Severe Behavioral Disabilities/Handicaps)

The following programs are post-baccalaureate programs:
Secondary Education (Vocational Technical)

The following programs are 5th year programs:
Early Childhood Education, Elementary Education

Kutztown University of Pennsylvania

Kutztown University has prepared teachers, librarians, school counselors, and speech pathologists since 1866. The professional education faculty are committed to the lifelong learner model. The College of Education ensures that graduates acquire a strong liberal arts background, are competent in their content area, and have achieved competency in their professional education coursework. In addition, preparation in the effective use of technology in the professional setting and the ability to effectively teach a diverse population in multiple settings is provided. Programs in the College of Education are performance-based, requiring graduates to meet particular criteria in their professional and specialty courses.

Just the facts...

Kutztown University of Pennsylvania
College of Education
Beekey Building 257
Kutztown, PA 19530
(610) 683-4253
Website: www.kutztown.edu
Profile: Rural, Medium, Co-Ed
UG Tuition: $144.00/cr. hr. in-state; $368.00/cr. hr. out-of-state
G Tuition: $193.00/cr. hr. in-state; $346.00/cr. hr. out-of-state
Off Campus Programs: No

Clinical Experiences

All teacher candidates are required to complete a minimum of thirty hours of observation in school settings. Additionally, each program has a professional semester as well as a semester of student teaching. The professional semester varies from a two-week full-time experience to a nine-week, one day per week experience in school settings. Student teaching consists of two seven and one-half week experiences which generally occur in two different school settings. Between the professional semester and student teaching requirements, candidates garner teaching experiences in rural, urban, and suburban settings. Additionally, candidates have the opportunity to do one session of student teaching in England.

Noteworthy

Teacher candidates have the opportunity to participate in a professional development school setting at the elementary and secondary levels. An urban learning academy is currently being formed which will enable candidates to acquire urban learning experiences. The early learning center in the College of Education provides an on-campus accredited site for early childhood education majors. Candidates may student teach in England, or in urban, suburban, or rural sites.

Teacher Preparation Program Information

The following programs are 4 year programs:
Early Childhood Education, Elementary Education, K-12 Education (Art, French, German, Russian, Spanish), Secondary Education (Biology, Chemistry, Earth Science, English/Language Arts, General Science, Mathematics, Physics, Social Studies), Special Education (Multiple Disabilities/Handicaps, Visually Impaired)

The following programs are post-baccalaureate programs:
Early Childhood Education, Elementary Education, K-12 Education (Art, French, German, Russian, Spanish), Secondary Education (Biology, Chemistry, Earth Science, English/Language Arts, General Science, Mathematics, Physics, Social Studies), Special Education (Multiple Disabilities/Handicaps, Visually Impaired)

The following programs are 5th year programs:
K-12 Education (Reading), Secondary Education (Biological Science, Chemistry, Communications, English, French, German, Mathematics, Physics, Russian, Spanish)

Lock Haven University of Pennsylvania

The College of Education and Human Services at Lock Haven University provides educational experiences for future teachers who understand that productive students must engage in problem solving, fill leadership roles, and work in teams. Emphasis is placed on the teacher as a thinking, analytical professional who takes action within a changing environment. Graduates have the knowledge and expertise to be reflective decision makers and successful teachers. The faculty's goal for programs of study in each specialization is to prepare indivdiuals who will become liberally educated and highly skilled professionals.

Just the facts...

Lock Haven University of Pennsylvania
College of Education and Human Services
Lock Haven, PA 17745
(717) 893-2204
Website: www.lhup.edu
Profile: Rural, Small, Co-Ed
UG Tuition: $3,468.00/sem. in-state; $8,824.00/sem. out-of-state
G Tuition: $193.00/cr hr. in-state; $346.00/cr. hr. out-of-state
Off Campus Programs: No

Clinical Experiences

Practical experiences are built into all education courses commencing with core requirements. These are expanded in professional studies. Candidates observe and participate in a variety of methods courses. All candidates complete one intensive professional semester that includes several weeks of supervised full-time public school participation. The student teaching semester emphasizes two half-semester, multilevel placements supported by a practicum class. Rural, urban, suburban, and international student teaching placements provide a variety of diverse and individualized practice teaching opportunities.

Noteworthy

The faculty in the College of Education who teach the methods courses have extensive public school teaching experience. The university has recently developed a teaching-learning center to assist in faculty professional development and collaboration. Collaborative programs with special education are offered in both early childhood education and elementary education. Other combinations are possible. The university is connected via fiber optics and compressed video to a 2,000-square mile regional network of school districts and community services in central Pennsylvania. This allows unique collaborative learning experiences for teacher education candidates.

Teacher Preparation Program Information

The following programs are 4 year programs:
Early Childhood Education, Elementary Education, K-12 Education (French, German, Spanish), Health and Physical Education, Secondary Education (Biology, Chemistry, Earth and Space Science, English/Language Arts, General Science, Geography, Mathematics, Physics, Social Studies), Special Education (Mentally/Physically Disabled)

The following programs are post-baccalaureate programs:
Early Childhood Education, Elementary Education, K-12 Education (French, German, Spanish), Health and Physical Education, Secondary Education (Biology, Chemistry, Driver Education/Safety, Earth and Space Science, English/Language Arts, General Science, Geography, Mathematics, Physics, Social Studies), Special Education (Mentally/Physically Disabled)

Mansfield University of Pennsylvania

Mansfield University, the first state teachers college in Pennsylvania, is a small, rural institution. Teacher Education is the largest program at Mansfield, and the primary responsibility of the faculty in teacher education is undergraduate teaching. Mansfield's teacher education programs are based on guidelines from the National Board for Professional Teaching Standards. Graduates can make reflective decisions; are committed to student learning; know their subject matter and how to teach it to diverse learners; reflect on practice; and learn from experience.

Just the facts...

Mansfield University of Pennsylvania
Teacher Education
Retan Center
Mansfield, PA 16933
(717) 662-4790
Website: www.mnsfld.edu
Profile: Rural, Small, Co-Ed
UG Tuition: $1,734.00/sem. in-state; $4,412.00/sem. out-of-state
G Tuition: $1,734.00/sem. in-state; $3,118.00/sem. out-of-state
Off Campus Programs: No

Clinical Experiences

From their freshman year on, candidates are involved in a wide variety of field-based experiences that provide them with meaningful learning and professional growth. As freshmen, candidates observe and interact with effective public school teachers. As juniors, candidates have opportunities to tutor one-on-one and to teach entire classes under the supervision of faculty and classroom teachers. As seniors, candidates spend fifteen weeks student teaching in two different classrooms and at different grade levels. Throughout the program, candidates are encouraged to examine their personal conceptions about teaching and learning.

Noteworthy

For more than a decade, Mansfield University has offered student teacher placements on the Navajo Reservation in the Window Rock (Arizona) Unified School District. Student teachers can apply to spend half of their student teaching experience in Australia. Dual certification options enable candidates to prepare for licensure in two teaching fields. Popular combinations are elementary education/special education, and elementary education/early childhood education.

Teacher Preparation Program Information

The following programs are 4 year programs:
Elementary Education (Early Childhood), K-12 Education (Art), Secondary Education (Biology, Chemistry, Earth Science, English/Language Arts, French, German, Music, Mathematics, Physics, Science, Social Studies, Spanish), Special Education

The following programs are post-baccalaureate programs:
Elementary Education (Early Childhood), K-12 Education (Art), Secondary Education (Biology, Chemistry, Earth Science, English/Language Arts, French, German, Mathematics, Music, Physics, Science, Social Studies, Spanish), Special Education

Marywood University

Marywood University believes that educators should be liberally educated persons who model and hold themselves responsible for promoting mastery of a body of knowledge, creativity, problem solving, active learning, intellectual excitement, life-long reflective learning, cooperation and collaboration, responsible work habits, wellness, respect for differences, and civic responsibility. Through the integration of theory and practice, candidates are given opportunities to demonstrate professional competence and leadership skills that are directed to the well being of future generations.

Just the facts...

Marywood University
Education Department
2300 Adams Avenue
Scranton, PA 18509
(570) 348-6297
Website: www.marywood.edu
Profile: Urban, Medium, Co-Ed
UG Tuition: $444.00/credit hour
G Tuition: $449.00/credit hour
Off Campus Programs: No

Clinical Experiences

Professional field experience is an ongoing part of the teacher preparation program. Beginning in the freshman year, field experience gives candidates the opportunity to practically apply knowledge and skills learned in the university setting. It culminates with student teaching in the senior year. Teacher education candidates participate in a number of different urban, suburban, and rural school settings. The Director of Professional Education Field Experience arranges placements that are suitable to candidates' needs, interests, and intended licensure areas.

Noteworthy

The teacher preparation programs benefit from Marywood's commitment to provide all students with access to state-of-the-art technology. An extensive curriculum laboratory of texts, manipulative materials, and software designed for K-12 programs is available to candidates. Candidates receive personalized academic advisement from department faculty and have numerous opportunities to be involved in service learning projects.

Teacher Preparation Program Information

The following programs are 4 year programs:
Early Childhood Education, Elementary Education, K-12 Education (Art, French, Home Economics, Music, Physical Education/Health, Spanish), Secondary Education (Biology, Communication, English/Language Arts, General Science, Mathematics, Social Studies), Special Education (Speech/Language Disabilities)

The following programs are post-baccalaureate programs:
Elementary Education, K-12 Education (Art, French, Home Economics, Music, Physical Education/Health, Spanish), Secondary Education (Biology, Communication, English/Language Arts, General Science, Mathematics, Social Studies), Special Education

The following programs are 5 year programs:
Elementary Education (Reading), Special Education (Reading)

The following programs are 5th year programs:
Early Childhood Education, Elementary Education, K-12 Education (Art, Music), Secondary Education (Communication), Special Education (Speech/Language Disabilities)

Millersville University of Pennsylvania

The focus of teacher education at Millersville University is the idea that the teacher is primarily a decision maker capable of drawing on knowledge and experience to make appropriate instructional judgments. Courses and professional experiences include four major overlapping areas: general education, professional studies, field experiences, and subject area specialties. In all programs there is a consistent effort to make candidates aware of the multicultural context in which teaching and learning takes place.

Just the facts...

Millersville University of Pennsylvania
School of Education
Millersville, PA 17551-0302
(717) 872-3379
Website: www.millersv.edu
Profile: Rural, Medium, Co-Ed
UG Tuition: $1,734.00/sem. in-state; $4,412.00/sem out-of-state
G Tuition: $193.00/cr. hr. in-state; $346.00/cr. hr. out-of-state
Off Campus Programs: No

Clinical Experiences

Teacher candidates have at least a fifteen-week student teaching experience, as well as significant pre-student teaching experience. The Elementary and Early Childhood and Special Education Department have field experiences for candidates in their freshman year. All methods of teaching courses in the program have a field experience component. Middle school experiences are provided for secondary student teachers. All candidates are provided experiences with exceptional learners and culturally diverse populations.

Noteworthy

Millersville University's Urban Education Program is designed to prepare candidates for urban schools. Interdisciplinary in approach, the program offers on-campus classes in education and the humanities followed by intensive field experiences in inner city elementary schools or middle schools with an urban multicultural environment. The program is open to sophomore elementary, secondary, or special education majors.

Teacher Preparation Program Information

The following programs are 4 year programs:
Elementary Education, K-12 Education (Art, French, German, Latin, Music, Russian, Spanish, Technology Education), Secondary Education (Biology, Chemistry, Earth Science, English/Language Arts, Mathematics, Physics, Social Studies), Special Education

The following programs are post-baccalaureate programs:
Elementary Education, K-12 Education (Art, French, German, Latin, Music, Russian, Spanish, Technology Education), Secondary Education (Biology, Chemistry, English/Language Arts, Mathematics, Physics, Social Studies), Special Education

The following programs are 5 year programs:
Elementary Education, K-12 Education (Art, French, German, Spanish, Technology Education), Secondary Education (Biology, English/Language Arts, Mathematics), Special Education

The following programs are 5th year programs:
K-12 Education (Reading)

Pennsylvania State University

Penn State's professional education programs prepare outstanding educators, scholars, and researchers. Penn State's education programs also advance the profession through research on the science and art of teaching and learning, the application of clinical processes, the effective use of technology, and the analysis and development of leadership in education policy. Teacher education at Penn State is based on a foundation of research, best professional practices, and standards.

Just the facts...

The Pennsylvania State University
College of Education
278 Chambers Building
University Park, PA 16802-3206
(814) 865-2524
Website: www.ed.psu.edu
Profile: Rural, Large, Co-Ed
UG Tuition: $2,920.00/sem. in-state; $6,328.00/sem. out-of-state
G Tuition: $3,267.00/sem. in-state; $6,730.00/sem. out-of-state
Off Campus Programs: Yes

Clinical Experiences

Valued as an essential part of teacher education, clinical experiences occur at three critical points. An early experience is required for admission to a specific program. In the typical junior year, clinical experiences and blocks of methods courses occur simultaneously. The senior experience, student teaching, occurs in one of eighteen centers in rural, suburban, and urban areas of Pennsylvania, England, and South Dakota. Candidates are supported by mentor teachers and faculty.

Noteworthy

As Penn State celebrates over 75 years of excellence in the preparation of school personnel, its top rankings among education programs nationwide continues to attract outstanding students, faculty, and research projects. A Scholars-in-Education Program and academic and extracurricular opportunities all lead to highly marketable degrees. Employers both in and out of the field of education value Penn State graduates' well-developed communication and organizational skills.

Teacher Preparation Program Information

The following programs are 4 year programs:
Early Childhood Education, Elementary Education, K-12 Education (Art, French, German, Health, Latin, Music, Physical Education, Russian, Spanish), Kindergarten Education, Secondary Education (Agriculture, Biology, Chemistry, Earth Science, English/Language Arts, General Science, Mathematics, Physics, Social Studies, Vocational Agriculture, Vocational Health Occupation, Vocational Trade & Industrial), Special Education (Emotional Disturbance, Mental Retardation)

The following programs are post-baccalaureate programs:
K-12 Education (Reading), Special Education (Hearing Impaired)

Shippensburg University of Pennsylvania

Shippensburg University and its faculty have a commitment to prepare educators for the changing, diverse, and complex classrooms of the future. Candidates are encouraged to study the history and philosophy of education and to build an understanding of the evolution of curriculum and instruction. Shippensburg believes that when teachers use the best of traditional practices, take risks, and pursue bold initiatives, P-12 students succeed in learning.

Just the facts...

Shippensburg University of Pennsylvania
College of Education and Human Services
Shippensburg, PA 17257
(717) 532-1373
Website: www.ship.edu
Profile: Rural, Medium, Co-Ed
UG Tuition: $4,033.00/sem. in-state; $6,711.00/sem. out-of-state
G Tuition: $2,072.00/sem. in-state; $3,456.00/sem. out-of-state
Off Campus Programs: No

Clinical Experiences

Candidates have contacts with public schools from their very first course in education, and have ample opportunities to work in many diverse settings. Faculty in the College of Education and Human Services work closely with public schools and supervise directly in those public schools during clinical experiences. Student teaching is the culminating experience within the program and includes two different settings for eight weeks each, allowing ample opportunity for a diversity of applications of theory and practice.

Noteworthy

Shippensburg University has on its campus the Rowland School for Young Children, a laboratory school for grades K-6. This lab school is a demonstration school; therefore, it allows ample opportunity for candidates to work with young children on campus. At present, there are designs for a new laboratory school that will allow for a highly technological and computer-based system of instruction. The new lab school will also have child care facilities.

Teacher Preparation Program Information

The following programs are 4 year programs:
Early Childhood Education, Elementary Education, K-12 Education (French, Spanish), Secondary Education (Biology, Chemistry, Earth Science, English/Language Arts, General Science, Mathematics, Physics, Social Studies)

The following programs are post-baccalaureate programs:
Early Childhood Education, Elementary Education, K-12 Education (French, Spanish), Secondary Education (Biology, Chemistry, Earth Science, English/Language Arts, General Science, Mathematics, Physics, Social Studies)

The following programs are 5th year programs:
Early Childhood Education

National Council for Accreditation of Teacher Education

Slippery Rock University of Pennsylvania

Slippery Rock University prepares educators and related professionals for Pennsylvania's schools and counseling facilities. Within this context, teaching, scholarship, and service are viewed as a triad, in which teaching is enlightened by scholarship and applied through service. Multicultural diversity, collaboration, and technology themes underlie all programs. The College of Education has been recognized for its excellent P-12 school parnerships and its thematic teaching resource guides, produced in collaboration with faculty from the College of Arts and Sciences.

Just the facts...

Slippery Rock University of Pennsylvania
College of Education
105 McKay Education Building
Slippery Rock, PA 16057
(724) 738-2007
Website: www.sru.edu
Profile: Rural, Medium, Co-Ed
UG Tuition: $2,155.44/sem. in-state; $4,833.44/sem. out-of-state
G Tuition: $2,242.14/sem. in-state; $3,833.74/sem. out-of-state
Off Campus Programs: No

Clinical Experiences

Candidates in SRU's teacher licensure programs participate in a variety of clinical experiences, including early work in both urban and rural schools. Virtual visits, via technology, have recently been initiated. SRU works with an inner-city elementary professional development school (part of the Pittsburgh Public Schools Collaborative). Special education majors participate in model programs for students with severe, multiple disabilities in preparation for careers in rural schools. Secondary math and science majors complete an intensive graduate internship following an academic content major. Student teaching opportunities extend to Las Vegas and international sites in Ireland and Mexico.

Noteworthy

Seven different scholarships are available for candidates, as well as a unique work-study option called Earn-to-Learn, in which selected candidates study and work closely with faculty conducting program-related scholarly projects. Above average grades, scores on PRAXIS exams, teaching performance, and interpersonal skills are expected of program graduates.

Teacher Preparation Program Information

The following programs are 4 year programs:
Elementary Education/Early Childhood Education, K-12 Education (Environmental, French, Health, Health and Physical Education, Music, Spanish), Secondary Education (English, Social Studies), Special Education (Mentally and/or Physically Handicapped)

The following programs are post-baccalaureate programs:
Elementary Education/Early Childhood Education, K-12 Education (Environmental, French, Health, Health and Physical Education, Music, Spanish), Secondary Education (English, Social Studies), Special Education (Mentally and/or Physically Handicapped)

The following programs are 5th year programs:
Secondary Education (Biology, Chemistry, Earth Science, General Science, Mathematics, Physics)

Temple University

Temple University's College of Education prepares professionals for leadership roles in a wide variety of educational settings. Founded in 1919 in response to the School District of Philadelphia's need for licensed teachers, the College of Education now offers degrees at both the undergraduate and graduate level in all areas of education. In addition to the full range of programs within the college, a five-year program is also offered in collaboration with the College of Arts and Science. The College of Education prepares teachers who have strong backgrounds in both content and pedagogy. Teacher preparation programs emphasize several themes, including technology, diversity/inclusion, and reflection.

Clinical Experiences

All candidates participate in field experiences throughout their programs of study, from classroom observation through student teaching. Every attempt is made to ensure that all candidates experience a wide variety of placements throughout their program of study. Placements are offered in urban and suburban schools, at varying grade levels, and in both regular and special education settings. In addition, the college has created exemplary placement opportunities in the professional development schools associated with the college.

Just the facts...

Temple University
College of Education
RH 245, 13th & Montgomery Avenue
Philadelphia, PA 19122
(215) 204-8017
Website: www.temple.edu
Profile: Urban, Large, Co-Ed
UG Tuition: $5,870.00/sem. in-state; $308.00/cr. hr. out-of-state
G Tuition: $10,752.00/sem. in-state; $429.00/cr. hr. out-of-state
Off Campus Programs: Yes

Noteworthy

As part of a grant funded through the National Science Foundation, candidates may participate in a series of special courses, practica, and field experiences intended to strengthen their backgrounds in science and mathematics. A university-wide science and mathematics support center helps candidates prepare to teach these subjects. Full and partial tuition scholarships are also available through this program.

Teacher Preparation Program Information

The following programs are 4 year programs:

Early Childhood Education, Elementary Education, K-12 Education (Art, Dance, French, German, Health, Hebrew, Italian, Latin, Music, Spanish), Secondary Education (Biology, Business, Chemistry, Earth Science, English/Language Arts, Health, Mathematics, Physical Education, Physics, Social Studies, Steno/Typing/Keyboard, Trade & Industrial, Vocational Business Office, Vocational Marketing, Vocational Trade & Industrial), Special Education

The following programs are 5th year programs:

Early Childhood Education, Elementary Education, K-12 Education (Art, Dance, Health, Music, Reading), Secondary Education (Biology, Business, Chemistry, Earth Science, English/Language Arts, Health, Mathematics, Physical Education, Physics, Science, Social Studies), Special Education

University of Scranton

The professional education programs at the University of Scranton are based on the model that a teacher is both a scholar and an effective decision maker. The Department of Education endeavors to contribute to the improvement of education by preparing informed, inquiring, and skilled professionals who are prepared for positions in the educational community. Additionally, the department offers opportunities for professional growth to practicing educators, assists in the educational growth and development of the community served by the university, and fosters the advancement of knowledge through research in education.

Just the facts...

University of Scranton
Department of Education
Linden Street and Monroe Avenue
Scranton, PA 18510-4603
(570) 940-7421
Website: www.uofs.edu
Profile: Urban, Medium, Co-Ed
UG Tuition: $16,620.00/year
G Tuition: $465.00/credit hour
Off Campus Programs: No

Clinical Experiences

For initial teaching licensure, a series of three early field experiences at various levels are followed by a twelve-week, single site student teaching assignment. Extensive field placement in internships is a feature shared by all programs that yield advanced licenses including administration, reading, and counseling. The university operates a campus school (P-8), but agreements with many suburban and rural school districts, and the Scranton City Schools offer a variety of placement opportunities in diverse social and geographic settings.

Noteworthy

The early field experience program is a strength of the University of Scranton's teacher preparation programs. The university also provides an excellent liberal arts preparation, a hallmark of its Jesuit tradition. With extensive services and a number of education-related and campus-wide student activities, the university is a very active campus within a small city environment. It is consistently rated as one of the top regional institutions by *U.S. News and World Report*. The Department of Education is housed in a new building which has the highest level of technology available for developing education professionals.

Teacher Preparation Program Information

The following programs are 4 year programs:
Early Childhood Education, Elementary Education, K-12 Education (French, German, Latin, Spanish), Secondary Education (Biology, Chemistry, Communication, English/Language Arts, General Science, Mathematics, Physics, Social Studies), Special Education

The following programs are 5th year programs:
Elementary Education, K-12 Education (French, German, Latin, Reading, Spanish), Secondary Education (Biology, Chemistry, Communication, English/Language Arts, General Science, Mathematics, Physics, Social Studies)

West Chester University

West Chester University has a rich history in teacher education, dating back to its inception as a normal school in the late 1800s. The teacher education programs are distinguished by the broad participation of many departments, including the College of Arts and Sciences and the Schools of Education, Music, Health Sciences, and Business and Public Affairs. The teacher preparation programs operate on the assumptions that learning and teaching are active, collaborative, constructive, and continuous processes which enable faculty and candidates to reflect upon and analyze their own learning and teaching.

Just the facts...

West Chester University
School of Education
West Chester, PA 19383
(610) 436-2321
Website: www.wcupa.edu
Profile: Suburban, Large, Co-Ed
UG Tuition: $144.00/cr. hr. in-state; $368.00/cr. hr. out-of-state
G Tuition: $193.00/cr. hr. in-state; $346.00/cr. hr. out-of-state
Off Campus Programs: No

Clinical Experiences

West Chester University is uniquely situated to provide diverse field placements for its candidates, including inner city school settings in Philadelphia and rural and suburban placements in local districts. Preservice teachers have the opportunity to work with children from diverse socioeconomic and ethnic backgrounds. The larger teacher preparation programs offer clinical experiences that introduce candidates to the field early in their professional preparation sequence. Field supervisors at all levels of practica work with small groups of candidates to ensure individualized feedback.

Noteworthy

West Chester University's Center for Earth Observation Systems uses state-of-the-art satellite technology. This technology is used for undergraduate, graduate, and inservice teacher education. WCU candidates and faculty benefit from several ongoing collabortions with neighboring school districts. Partnerships are being established with area schools focusing on technology in the classroom, urban education, curriculum integration, reading instruction, and other current issues. These partnerships offer candidates exceptional opportunities for service learning and action research.

Teacher Preparation Program Information

The following programs are 4 year programs:
Early Childhood Education, Elementary Education, K-12 Education (French, German, Health, Latin, Music, Physical Education, Russian, Spanish), Secondary Education (Biology, Chemistry, Earth Science, English/Language Arts, General Science, Mathematics, Physics, Social Studies), Special Education

The following programs are post-baccalaureate programs:
Early Childhood Education, Elementary Education, K-12 Education (French, German, Health, Latin, Music, Physical Education, Reading, Russian, Spanish), Secondary Education (Biology, Chemistry, Earth Science, English/Language Arts, General Science, Mathematics, Physics, Social Studies), Special Education

The following programs are 5th year programs:
Elementary Education, K-12 Education (Reading), Secondary Education, Special Education

Rhode Island College

Rhode Island College has prepared teachers and other school personnel since 1854. The Feinstein School of Education and Human Development prepares professional educators to become reflective practitioners. A dynamic interplay between classroom study and field-based experience is characteristic of all programs. A technology competency requirement ensures that all candidates are prepared to use technology in the classroom. The School of Education is committed to providing not only professional knowledge and skills but also developing the values and dispositions for future professional growth. A community service requirement further integrates theory and practice.

Just the facts...

Rhode Island College
School of Education
600 Mount Pleasant Avenue
Providence, RI 02908
(401) 456-8110
Website: www.ric.edu/sehd
Profile: Urban, Medium, Co-Ed
UG Tuition: $118.00/cr. hr. in-state; $310.00/cr. hr. out-of-state
G Tuition: $158.00/cr. hr. in-state; $320.00/cr. hr. out-of-state
Off Campus Programs: No

Clinical Experiences

Early in their college career, propsective teachers begin field-based experiences in schools. Combining college classroom instruction with experiences in public schools and the Henry Barnard School, a campus-based elementary school, candidates participate in focused observation, tutoring, community service, and teaching small groups of students. To enhance learning, clinical experiences are provided in multicultural and urban settings. Student teachers are placed throughout the state, including the City of Providence, providing student teachers with experiences in inner-city schools.

Noteworthy

Graduates of Rhode Island College are grounded in theory and practice, are reflective practitioners, and participate in community service. Rhode Island College, a multicultural community, is home to many first-generation college students. The Teacher Academy, co-sponsored by the college and the Providence School System, mentors high school students interested in the teaching field. With numerous computers, Ethernet network connections, and network ports in many classrooms, candidates and faculty have access to the Internet and distance learning capabilities. The college is located within easy access to areas of rich historical interest and excellent beaches.

Teacher Preparation Program Information

The following programs are 4 year programs:
Early Childhood Education (Birth-Grade 2), Elementary Education, K-12 Education (Art, Health, Music, Physical Education, Technology Education), Secondary Education (Biology, Chemistry, English/Language Arts, French, General Science, History, Mathematics, Physics, Social Studies, Spanish), Special Education (Adaptive Physical Education)

The following programs are post-baccalaureate programs:
Secondary Education (Biology, Chemistry, English/Language Arts, French, General Science, History, Mathematics, Physics, Social Studies, Spanish)

The following programs are 5th year programs:
Early Childhood Education (Birth-Grade 2), Elementary Education, K-12 Education (Art, Health, Music, Physical Education, Reading Specialist), Secondary Education (Biology, Chemistry, English/Language Arts, French, General Science, History, Mathematics, Physics, Social Studies, Spanish)

University of Rhode Island

The University of Rhode Island, chartered in 1888, provides students with a comprehensive array of academic opportunities. Education majors develop a deep knowledge base through coursework in both education and an academic major. Entrance to programs is through a portfolio/interview process. Education faculty have adopted the Rhode Island Beginning Teacher Standards as a framework through which candidates demonstrate increasing understanding of learning and teaching processes; develop collaborative relationships with colleagues and the larger community; and become reflective, responsible professionals.

Clinical Experiences

Clinical experiences begin with a pre-professional field placement typically in the freshman or sophomore year and culminate in student teaching. Throughout each student's program there are multiple opportunities to observe and teach in urban, suburban, and rural schools under the guidance of university and clinical faculty. Candidates work with diverse learners as classroom aides, after-school tutors, and full-time student teachers. Coursework and seminars are designed to enhance pre-teachers' field experiences by helping them to plan, implement, and evaluate learning activities with experienced professionals.

Just the facts...

University of Rhode Island
College of Human Sciences and Services, 106 Quinn Hall
Kingston, RI 02881
(401) 874-2125
Website: www.uri.edu
Profile: Suburban, Large, Co-Ed
UG Tuition: $3,282.00/year in-state; $4,924.00/year regional; $11,286.00/year out-of-state
G Tuition: $3,446.00/year in-state; $5,170.00/year regional; $9,850.00/year out-of-state
Off Campus Programs: No

Noteworthy

The National Center on Public Education and Social Policy, housed at the university, aids schools nationwide with school improvement planning through research-based analyses of practices and conditions that promote high performance learning. The university, in conjunction with Rhode Island College, has established a four-year education doctoral program. Education faculty, the state department of education, and business and community leaders, in collaboration, have developed an interactive website to provide access to educational programs, services, and curricula for educators at all levels, as well as parents, students, and others.

Teacher Preparation Program Information

The following programs are 4 year programs:
Early Childhood Education, Elementary Education, K-12 Education (Music, Physical Education), Secondary Education (Biology, Chemistry, French, German, General Science, History, Mathematics, Physics, Social Studies, Spanish)

The following programs are post-baccalaureate programs:
Early Childhood Education

The following programs are 5th year programs:
Elementary Education, K-12 Education (Music, Reading), Secondary Education (Biology, Chemistry, French, General Science, German, History, Mathematics, Physics, Social Studies, Spanish)

The Citadel

The Citadel has prepared teachers for secondary schools since 1960. The programs are offered at the undergraduate level. Graduate programs for educational administrators, teachers, school counselors, reading specialists, and school psychologists were instituted in 1968. The Department of Education is committed to ensuring that graduates have a firm grounding in the liberal arts, a belief in learner-centered education in a pluralistic society, and a desire to improve children's quality of life.

Just the facts...

The Citadel
Department of Education
171 Moultrie Street
Charleston, SC 29409
(843) 953-5097
Website: www.citadel.edu
Profile: Urban, Small, Co-Ed
UG Tuition: $135.00/credit hour
Off Campus Programs: No

Clinical Experiences

Under college supervision, candidates observe and analyze the full spectrum of instruction, including classroom interaction and factors affecting educational climate; application of research in educational psychology; developmental differences and cultural diversity; classroom management; effects of varying attention spans; positive reinforcement by teachers; interrelationships of students from varied backgrounds; and the functioning of boards and administrators. The capstone experience, a professional internship in teaching, is mentored by a well-qualified teacher.

Noteworthy

The Department of Education is the current holder of the Higher Education and Public Collaboration Award from the South Carolina Association of Teacher Educators. The award was made for the Department's program in conjunction with the Charleston County School District involving the Lowcountry Children's Center, where candidates see first-hand the effects of child abuse. Candidates learn to detect abuse and process the information in accordance with the state's laws on mandatory reporting.

Teacher Preparation Program Information

The following programs are 4 year programs:
Secondary Education (Biology, History, Mathematics, Physical Education, Science, Social Studies)

The following programs are 5th year programs:
Secondary Education (English, Biology, Mathematics, Social Studies)

Clemson University

Clemson University's undergraduate teacher education program is the largest in South Carolina, and its graduates continue to score the highest among state institutions on such standardized tests as the NTE, PKE, and state assessment instruments. Offering a wide variety of majors, the education program is student-oriented, based on a traditional matrix involving lecture, field assignments, individual and group activities, simulations, and practice. The curriculum stresses technology throughout and effectively incorporates state and national traditions and innovations—all designed to facilitate candidate learning at every level in every discipline.

Just the facts...

Clemson University
College of Health, Education and Human Development
102 Tillman Hall
Box 340702
Clemson, SC 29634-0702
(864) 656-7656
Website: www.hehd.clemson.edu
Profile: Rural, Large, Co-Ed
UG Tuition: $1,531.00/sem. in-state; $4,243.00/sem. out-of-state
G Tuition: $1,531.00/sem. in-state; $3,072.00/sem. out-of-state
Off Campus Programs: Yes

Clinical Experiences

Candidates undertake field assignments beginning early in the education program and continuing through graduation. The faculty consider the internship to be the capstone experience, incorporating all of the knowledge and skills the candidate has gained during his or her program of study. The semester-long, full-time internship is supported by university supervisors and school-based clinicians. Candidates' performance is observed and assessed. Candidates participate in a clinical program exposing them to self-discovery, professional enlightenment, and a working knowledge of the realities of the teaching/learning process.

Noteworthy

Clemson collaborates with a local school district that serves as a "laboratory district" in which education majors are involved in field assignments, clinical experiences, and internships. Current supporting research projects include a comprehensive Rural Special Education center, a nationally recognized Dropout Prevention Center, and a diversity program entitled "Call Me Mister," designed to place 200 African American males as licensed teachers in the state's elementary schools.

Teacher Preparation Program Information

The following programs are 4 year programs:

Early Childhood Education, Elementary Education (Language Arts), K-12 Education (French, German, Spanish, Industrial Technology), Secondary Education (Agriculture, Biology, Earth Science, English, General Science, Mathematics, Physical Sciences, Social Studies, Trade & Industrial, Vocational Trade & Industrial, Vocational Technical), Special Education

Newberry College

In the view of Newberry College, the crucial role of the effective teacher is to be a facilitator of independent lifelong learning for students. Because of the pace of technological, social, and occupational change in today's society, Newberry believes that the traditional model of teaching and learning in which the learner "receives" the knowledge from the teacher no longer suffices. Newberry prepares teachers who are models of independent learning. Candidates demonstrate curiosity, motivation, love of learning, and inquiry skills as they pursue knowledge and solve problems in order to teach these strategies directly to students.

Just the facts...

Newberry College
Department of Education
2100 College Street
Newberry, SC 29108
(803) 321-5203
Website: www.newberry.edu
Profile: Suburban, Small, Co-Ed
UG Tuition: $5,996.00/semester
Off Campus Programs: No

Clinical Experiences

Field experiences provide the opportunity for observation, participation, and practice of skills learned in the college classroom. As candidates advance from one practicum level to the next, they focus on various aspects of teaching, moving from looking at the learner in the classroom, to the curriculum, to general methodology, and then to specialized methods. The preparation of effective teachers is a partnership of professionals preparing professionals.

Noteworthy

Newberry has a chapter of Kappa Delta Pi for education candidates. Qualified candidates can apply for the James F. Cummings Teacher Cadet Scholarship. Newberry conducts Minority Teacher Education Recruitment Days, and has a teacher education faculty and candidate exchange agreement with Claflin College.

Teacher Preparation Program Information

The following programs are 4 year programs:

Elementary Education, K-12 Education (Music, Physical Education), Secondary Education (Biology, English/Language Arts, Mathematics, Social Studies), Special Education (Learning Disabilities)

South Carolina State University

The School of Education at South Carolina State University is committed to providing relevant programs and preparing personnel responsive to the needs of various educational and other human service agencies. The School of Education is also committed to enhancing the professional skills of preservice and in-service teachers, counselors, speech correctionists, and administrators to prepare them to provide quality education to multicultural learners. This commitment includes preparing educators who are reflective decision makers, effective performers, and culturally sensitive individuals.

Just the facts...

South Carolina State University
School of Education
300 College Street, NE
Orangeburg, SC 29117-0001
(803) 536-7133
Website: www.scsu.edu
Profile: Rural, Medium, Co-Ed
UG Tuition: $1,592.00/sem. in-state; $3,124.00/sem. out-of-state
G Tuition: $178.00/cr. hr. in-state; $347.00/cr. hr. out-of-state
Off Campus Programs: Yes

Clinical Experiences

Clinical experiences are required for the successful completion of initial teacher education programs. The student teaching experience is the capstone of the program, involving twelve to thirteen weeks of increasing responsibility for working with individuals and groups of students. Student teaching is done in a carefully selected school under the immediate supervision of a qualified cooperating teacher and the general supervision of a university supervisor who is a specialist in the candidate's teaching field.

Noteworthy

Each teacher candidate has access to the following resources: an assigned academic advisor to assist in course selection and scheduling; the CARE Center and C-PACT laboratory that counsels candidates in all aspects of admission to the teacher education program and standardized testing; the Lewis Learning Laboratory and the Learning Plus program designed to assist candidates in improving their skills in the use of multiple instructional resources and technology, reading, writing, and mathematics; and the Felton Laboratory School, a professional development school that links theory to practice and is equipped with a computerized classroom.

Teacher Preparation Program Information

The following programs are 4 year programs:
Early Childhood Education, Elementary Education, K-12 Education (Art, Drama/Theater, French, Spanish, Health, Industrial Technology, Physical Education), Secondary Education (Consumer & Family Science/Home Econ., English/Language Arts, General Science, Mathematics), Special Education (Emotional/Behavioral Disorders, Learning Disabilities, Mild/Moderate Retardation)

The following programs are 5th year programs:
Early Childhood Education, Elementary Education, Secondary Education (English/Language Arts, General Science, Mathematics)

University of South Carolina

The University of South Carolina, one of the oldest universities in the U.S., has offered preparation programs in professional education since 1882. The university's Professional Education Unit (including the Colleges of Applied Professional Science, Education, Liberal Arts, Science and Mathematics, Library and Information Science, and the Schools of Health and Music) is dedicated to providing the highest quality education for prospective educators and experienced professionals. Ensuring that quality, the university is a member of the Holmes Group and the consortium of South Carolina colleges and universities.

Just the facts...

University of South Carolina
College of Education
Columbia, SC 29208
(803) 777-6732
Website: www.ed.sc.edu
Profile: Urban, Large, Co-Ed
UG Tuition: $164.00/cr. hr. in-state; $418.00/cr. hr. out-of-state
G Tuition: $193.00/cr. hr. in-state; $404.00/cr. hr. out-of-state
Off Campus Programs: Yes

Clinical Experiences

Clinical experiences are recognized as a vital component of the initial and ongoing development of professional educators. Professional development site partnerships offer opportunities for USC and seventeen P-12 schools to foster unique sites where the school and the university share the goal of enhancing the education of professionals through their commitment to collaboration. In addition to the professional development site partnerships, clinical experiences are offered in a variety of sites and schools throughout the metropolitan Columbia area and surrounding counties. These learning environments offer diverse settings for internships for candidates.

Noteworthy

The University of South Carolina has moved beyond the cutting edge in requiring all candidates pursuing initial licensure to complete a five-year program, resulting in a bachelor's degree in a discipline and a master's degree in teaching. A wealth of resources are available at USC designed to enrich future teachers. There are 24 scholarships, awards, and fellowships offered by the College of Education, ranging in value from $200 to $1,500. The College of Education also houses an Educational Technology Center that provides candidates with a multitude of media, computers, educational software, as well as technology for instructing students with special needs.

Teacher Preparation Program Information

The following programs are 4 ½ year programs:
K-12 Education (Art, Music, Physical Education)

The following programs are 5 year programs:
Early Childhood Education, Elementary Education, Secondary Education (English, Mathematics, Science, Social Studies, Spanish)

The following programs are 5th year programs:
K-12 Education (Art, Physical Education, Health), Secondary Education (Biology, Business, Chemistry, Earth Sciences, English, French, Geography, German, History, Marketing, Mathematics, Natural Sciences, Physics, Social Studies, Spanish, Theater and Speech), Special Education

University of South Carolina—Spartanburg

Teacher preparation at the University of South Carolina—Spartanburg is built upon the belief that teachers who become reflective practitioners (at the undergraduate level) and reflective professionals (at the graduate level) have the following attributes: an appreciation for the traditional liberal arts and sciences of both Western and non-Western cultures; exposure to up-to-date pedagogical theories and practices; ethical attitudes and habits; a commitment to equal educational opportunity for all students; a commitment to knowledge of both theory and practice; and an understanding of how theory and practice interrelate.

Just the facts...

University of South Carolina—Spartanburg
School of Education
800 University Way
Spartanburg, SC 29303
(864) 503-5577
Website: www.ucsc.edu
Profile: Urban, Medium, Co-Ed
UG Tuition: $1,509.00/sem. in-state; $3,772.00/sem. out-of-state
G Tuition: $1,947.00/sem. in-state; $4,057.00/sem. out-of-state
Off-Campus Programs: No

Clinical Experiences

Every course in the professional education program includes a minimum of six to eight hours of clinical experiences on-site in professional development schools and other schools in the region. Further, candidates taking methodology courses in reading, language arts, mathematics, science, and social studies spend at least one-third of their class time in local schools so that they can put theory into practice. The program culminates with a fifteen-week student teaching experience.

Noteworthy

The School of Education administers three separate scholarship programs which support six to eight students in the School of Education each year. Depending on the scholarship, support is offered for a period of four years or for two years once a candidate is admitted to the professional program. Technology plays an important role in teacher development. The school has a full-time Director of Technology. A distance education program was recently initiated with the University of South Carolina at Sumter. A special education program is being developed at the undergraduate level and a MAT is being developed at the graduate level.

Teacher Preparation Program Information

The following programs are 4 year programs:

Early Childhood Education, Elementary Education, K-12 (Physical Education), Secondary Education (Biology, Chemistry, English, French, History, Mathematics, Political Science, Spanish)

The following programs are post-baccalaureate programs:

Early Childhood Education, Elementary Education, K-12 (Physical Education), Secondary Education (Biology, Chemistry, English, French, History, Mathematics, Political Science, Spanish)

Winthrop University

Winthrop University's College of Education is dedicated to preparing leaders who are committed to a lifelong quest for excellence in teaching, learning, and service to society. The College of Education is proud of its affiliations, which include the National Network for Educational Renewal, a national group that addresses school reform, and the Winthrop Olde English Consortium, a regional educational network in upstate South Carolina. The faculty at Winthrop University recognizes that the preparation of teachers is an all-university responsibility and is a cooperative effort by all academic areas involved in teacher education.

Just the facts...

Winthrop University
College of Education
106 Withers Building
Rock Hill, SC 29733
(803) 323-2151
Website: www.winthrop.edu
Profile: Suburban, Medium, Co-Ed
UG Tuition: $2,016.00/sem. in-state; $3,530.00/sem. out-of-state
G Tuition: $1,909.00/sem. in-state; $3,430.00/sem. out-of-state
Off Campus Programs: No

Clinical Experiences

Candidates in the College of Education participate in diverse clinical experiences that include service-related field experiences in the freshman year, field experiences in the sophomore year in which candidates observe master teachers, a methods-area field experience in the junior year, and a teaching internship in the senior year. The clinical component of the program provides a versatile, quality experience for every education candidate through placements in settings identified as exemplary and with educators who are members of the Mentor Corps of outstanding teachers.

Noteworthy

The College of Education has a nationally recognized Center for Pedagogy that actively promotes leadership and simultaneous renewal for both students and faculty through innovative core courses, collaborative grants for educators, and regional showcase conferences. In addition, the College of Education has an Instructional Technology Center that provides state-of-the-art support for faculty and candidates who wish to infuse technology into the teacher education curriculum. Professional development schools provide sites for internships, other field experiences, and reflect best practices at all grade levels.

Teacher Preparation Program Information

The following programs are 4 year programs:
Early Childhood Education, Elementary Education, K-12 Education (Art, Dance, Music, Physical Education), Secondary Education (Biology, Business, Chemistry, English/Language Arts, French, Family & Consumer Science, Mathematics, Social Studies, Spanish, Theatre), Special Education (Learning Disability, Severe Behavioral Disabilities/Handicaps)

The following programs are 5th year programs:
K-12 Education (Art, Music, Physical Education), Secondary Education (Biology, Business, English/Language Arts, Family & Consumer Science, Mathematics, Social Studies)

Augustana College

The mission of Augustana College's Education Department is to empower candidates with the tools they will need to create learning environments that ensure belonging, mastery, independence, and generosity. The program's philosophy integrates the best of Western educational thought with the wisdom of the indigenous Native American culture of the region and emerging research on positive youth development. Teacher candidates are challenged to demonstrate commitment to effect change for the welfare of children and youth, and to play a part in the creation of a just and compassionate society.

Just the facts...

Augustana College
Education Department
2001 Summit Avenue
Sioux Falls, SD 57197
(605) 336-4629
Website: www.augie.edu
Profile: Urban, Small, Co-Ed
UG Tuition: $13,490/year
G Tuition: $14,726.00/year
Off Campus Programs: No

Clinical Experiences

All education majors are required to student teach or have a comparable clinical experience during their sophomore and senior years of college. Even though candidates regularly have field experiences in the Sioux Falls public or parochial schools, many other placement options are available. The Sioux Falls area offers superb training facilities including the South Dakota School for the Deaf, the Children's Care Hospital and School, Children's Home Society, and Sioux Vocational Services. International placements are also available in Germany, India, Japan, and Australia.

Noteworthy

The Education Department is located in the new Madsen Social Science Building. A model classroom, mini-computing labs, speech science learning lab, and complete clinical facility enhance student learning. *U.S. News and World Report* has ranked Augustana College among the Top 10 Best Liberal Arts Colleges in the Midwest Region in four of the last five years. The magazine also ranks Augustana in its top ten list of best buys among Midwest regional liberal arts colleges. Augustana is the only South Dakota school ranked among the top institutions in each list. Graduates have gone on to become teachers of the year in several states, and in 1996, the National Teacher of the Year was an Augustana graduate.

Teacher Preparation Program Information

The following programs are 4 year programs:

Elementary Education, Hearing Impaired, K-12 Education (Art, Music, Physical Education, World Languages), Kindergarten Education (K-Primary), Middle School Education, Secondary Education (Art, Biology, Chemistry, Economics, English/Language Arts, French, German, Government, Mathematics, Physical Education, Physics, Social Studies, Spanish, Speech/Theater), Special Education/K-12, Youth Education

The following programs are 5th year programs:

Communication Disorders, Elementary Education, Secondary Education, Special Education

Black Hills State University

Black Hills State University's College of Education provides opportunities for the enhancement and fulfillment of human potential, and instills and nurtures the skills, knowledge, and attitudes needed by prospective teachers. Black Hills State University promotes individual and professional growth and well-being through teaching, research, and service. Graduates are culturally sensitive, compassionate, and competent; they value the uniqueness of the individual, foster the development of the learner, and promote educational practices that satisfy individual and societal needs.

Just the facts...

Black Hills State University
College of Education
University Station Box 9500
Spearfish, SD 57799-9004
(605) 642-6550
Website: www.bhsu.edu
Profile: Rural, Small, Co-Ed
UG Tuition: $56.15/cr. hr. in-state; $178.65/cr. hr. out-of-state
G Tuition: $85.25/cr. hr. in-state; $251.45/cr. hr. out-of-state
Off Campus Programs: No

Clinical Experiences

Three phases of school-based field experiences help candidates apply course content to best practices in preparation for their teaching careers. A 45-hour pre-admission teaching practicum provides classroom observation and an introduction to tutorial techniques in a structured school setting. A 45-hour junior field experience continues candidates' exposure to the classroom. Finally, a full semester of student teaching allows candidates to practice professional teaching skills in a P-12 school under the supervision of a university supervisor and a cooperating teacher.

Noteworthy

The College of Education at Black Hills State University values its partnerships with professional development schools in preparing elementary and special education teachers for the 21st century. And, together with the Black Hills State University Center for Excellence in Science and Mathematics Education, the teacher preparation program demonstrates a commitment to cutting-edge coursework and field experiences for middle and secondary education majors. In addition, the faculty are dedicated to lifelong learning to model the integration of technology across the curriculum and within instructional practices.

Teacher Preparation Program Information

The following programs are 4 year programs:
Early Childhood Education, Elementary Education, K-12 Education (Art, Music, Physical Education), Secondary Education (Biology, Business, Chemistry, Drama/Theater, English/Language Arts, Foreign Languages, Mathematics, Physical Science, Speech, Technology), Special Education, Special Education/Early Childhood Education, Special Education/Elementary Education

Dakota State University

The 1881 Dakota Territorial Legislature established Dakota State University to prepare teachers to meet the needs of an emerging society on the western frontier. Today, society again faces a new frontier, the Information Age, and DSU prepares teachers to meet its new challenges and to lead the process of educational change. An emphasis on technology, rural education, and inclusion permeate all of DSU's education courses. Teachers prepared at DSU are primarily rural educators who embrace, include, and appreciate all learners. Graduates understand the culture and dynamics of change; identify, analyze, and solve problems; employ effective intrapersonal and interpersonal skills; and embrace multiple perspectives.

Just the facts...

Dakota State University
College of Education
101 East Hall
Madison, SD 57042-1799
(605) 256-5177
Website: www.dsu.edu
Profile: Rural, Small, Co-Ed
UG Tuition: $56.15/cr. hr. in-state $178.65/cr. hr. out-of-state
G Tuition: $85.25/cr. hr. in-state $251.45/cr. hr. out-of-state
Off Campus Programs: No

Clinical Experiences

Beginning with the first professional education course, all education majors have a variety of experiences in area schools that allow them to apply theories learned in their coursework. Field experiences are integrated into coursework throughout the program, increasing in concentration from structured observations to instructional decision making. The program's unique feedback process develops effective teaching proficiencies through intensive self, peer, and professional assessments needed for successful completion of student teaching.

Noteworthy

DSU's computer technology infrastructure provides students, faculty, and staff with unmatched access to up-to-date hardware and software. *Yahoo Internet Life* recently ranked DSU twelfth among the 100 Most Wired Universities. All academic programs at DSU, including the teacher education program, provide comprehensive instruction and experience in using and integrating technology across all disciplines. The integration of technology throughout the general and professional education curriculum enables teacher candidates to graduate with a state certification for teaching computers to K-12 students.

Teacher Preparation Program Information

The following programs are 4 year programs:

K-8 Elementary Education, K-8 Elementary Education and Special Learning and Behavioral Problems, K-12 Education (Art, Music, Physical Education/Health), Secondary Education (Biology, Business, Chemistry, Computer, English/Language Arts, Mathematics, Physics)

Northern State University

At Northern State University, each student makes a difference. The faculty and staff are proud of Northern's beautiful campus and the vitality of the campus community. With an enrollment of about 3,000, Northern students represent 36 states and 20 foreign countries. Northern State University also offers a variety of programs and activities that allow students to learn, explore and contribute. Northern State University has its roots in teacher preparation and is known throughout the state and the Midwest for producing quality teachers.

Just the facts...

Northern State University
School of Education
1200 South Jay Street
Box 850
Aberdeen, SD 57401-7198
(605) 626-2415
Website: www.northern.edu
Profile: Rural, Small, Co-Ed
UG Tuition: $94.75/cr. hr. in-state; $214.00/cr. hr. out-of-state
Off-Campus Programs: No

Clinical Experiences

NSU education students are well-prepared to enter the teaching force because they graduate with three different field experiences. This includes a sophomore and junior-year field experience and a semester of student teaching. NSU candidates benefit from a collaborative effort between Northern and the Aberdeen School District as well as surrounding school districts. The collaborative efforts are designed to encourage cooperation in the study of teaching and learning, to conduct collaborative research, and to work cooperatively to prepare teachers. Candidates will gain the capability of using technology for teaching and learning in their field experiences.

Noteworthy

Over half of the teachers in the state of South Dakota received their degrees from Northern State University. Many of Northern's graduates have received state and national honors and awards for teaching. Teacher candidates can take part in several on-campus professional organizations that encourage professional development. NSU's Reading Council, the oldest reading chapter on a South Dakota university or college campus, has achieved Honor Council status in previous years. The university has an active Phi Delta Kappa organization, which requires a 3.0 GPA to join, a Council for Exceptional Children chapter, and a student chapter of the South Dakota Education Association.

Teacher Preparation Program Information

The following programs are 4 year programs:
Elementary Education, K-12 Education (Art, Health and Physical Education, Music), Secondary Education (Biology, Business, Chemistry, English, French, History, Industrial Technology, Mathematics, Political Science, Social Science, Spanish, Speech), Special Education

The following programs are post-baccalaureate programs:
Elementary Education, K-12 Education (Art, Health and Physical Education, Music), Secondary Education (Biology, Business, Chemistry, English, French, History, Industrial Technology, Mathematics, Political Science, Social Science, Spanish, Speech), Special Education

South Dakota State University

The mission of South Dakota State University's College of Education and Counseling is to help students construct the knowledge, skills, and attitudes fundamental to becoming competent professionals in a pluralistic and democratic society. Faculty and candidates are student-centered and committed to teaching. Candidates interact with one another, the faculty, and the professional world in which they will soon be participating. Courses are designed and taught to promote teacher candidate construction of knowledge that will be useful to them in their lives and in their professional world.

Just the facts...

South Dakota State University
College of Education and Counseling
Box 507, Wenona Hall
Brookings, SD 57007-0095
(605) 688-4321
Website: http://web.sdstate.edu
Profile: Rural, Medium, Co-Ed
UG Tuition: $60.00/cr. hr. in-state; $180.00/cr. hr. out-of-state
G Tuition: $85.00/cr. hr. in-state; $250.00/cr. hr. out-of-state
Off Campus Programs: Yes

Clinical Experiences

Clinical experiences directly connect with content taught in each program. In their first professional semester, candidates in the undergraduate teacher education program explore a wide range of fundamental issues and theories; in their second, the exploration and reflection continue as they practice model-based instruction; and, in their third, they intern with expert teachers who progressively guide them toward full classroom responsibility. Each graduate program in the College of Education and Counseling provides candidates with varied and progressive clinical experiences that bring together theory and practice.

Noteworthy

The College of Education and Counseling is home for South Dakota's Program for Rural School and Community Renewal, a partnership involving sixteen school districts from all parts of the state, their communities, the W. K. Kellogg Foundation, the Annenberg Rural Challenge, and the Black Hills Special Services Cooperative. It seeks to promote the simultaneous renewal of schools and communities, using schools as engines of change and communities as their major curricular resources. It seeks to recognize the "genius of place" by means of a curriculum of place that looks at communities' histories, traditions, resource bases, challenges, and human capital.

Teacher Preparation Program Information

The following programs are 4 year programs:

Early Childhood Education, K-12 Education (Art, German, Health, Music, Physical Education, Spanish), Secondary Education (Agriculture, Biology, Chemistry, Computer Science, Consumer & Family Science/Home Economics, Economics, English/Language Arts, Geography, History, Journalism, Mathematics, Physical Education, Physics, Political Science, Psychology, Sociology, Speech)

The following programs are post-baccalaureate programs:

Early Childhood Education, K-12 Education (Art, German, Health, Music, Physical Education, Spanish), Secondary Education (Agriculture, Biology, Chemistry, Computer Science, Consumer & Family Science/Home Economics, Economics, English/Language Arts, Geography, History, Journalism, Mathematics, Physical Education, Physics, Political Science, Psychology, Sociology, Speech)

University of Sioux Falls

The University of Sioux Falls is committed to preparing professional educators who will perform effectively in the diverse and complex world of today's schools. Candidates obtain a flexible understanding and a command of specialty knowledge in one or more content areas; a working knowledge of past and current educational theory and practice; a developmental perspective of learning and of curricular planning; and an inclusive and holistic view of human potential. Teaching is viewed in the context of the development of mature Christian persons.

Just the facts...

University of Sioux Falls
Education Department
1101 West 22nd Street
Sioux Falls, SD 57105-1966
(605) 331-6710
Website: www.thecoo.edu
Profile: Urban, Small, Co-Ed
UG Tuition: $5,375.00/semester
Off Campus Programs: No

Clinical Experiences

Candidates complete a one-month, full-time assignment in a classroom prior to entry into the professional education program. This pre-admission experience can be in a local classroom, in a Chicago school, or on an Indian reservation. All the professional courses include field experiences such as visits to a limited English proficiency classroom, the School for the Deaf, the Children's Care Hospital, and local elementary and secondary schools. Field experiences culminate in twelve weeks of full-time student teaching.

Noteworthy

The University of Sioux Falls is a Christian community of caring people. Relationships among students, faculty, and staff reflect the love, trust, forgiveness, and patience that are gifts of life in the spirit of Jesus. This caring is seen in university community members' support of one another as they study, teach, and serve in God's name, and in the way they challenge each other to achieve excellence. The campus community is open to and enriched by people of different backgrounds, cultures, and viewpoints. Community members listen to each other, respect each other without prejudging, encourage each other to grow intellectually and spiritually, and seek to treat each person with love and their work with devotion.

Teacher Preparation Program Information

The following programs are 4 year programs:
Elementary Education, K-12 Education (Art, Music, Physical Education), Secondary Education (Biology, Chemistry, English/Language Arts, History, Mathematics, Physics, Political Science, Speech, Theatre)

University of South Dakota

The University of South Dakota has prepared teachers and other educational personnel since 1927. The faculty in the School of Education prepare educators to be reflective decision makers who can analyze, synthesize, and apply their knowledge to local, national, and global educational issues. The School of Education is committed to ensuring that graduates have demonstrable skills in the effective use of analytical and critical thinking processes, in varied learning settings.

Just the facts...

University of South Dakota
School of Education
Delzell Educaton Center, Room 102
414 East Clark Street
Vermillion, SD 57069
(605) 677-5437
Website: www.usd.edu
Profile: Rural, Medium, Co-Ed
UG Tuition: $56.15/cr. hr. in-state; $178.65/cr. hr. out-of-state
G Tuition: $85.25/cr. hr. in-state; $251.45/cr. hr. out-of-state
Off Campus Programs: No

Clinical Experiences

Undergraduate program field placements are made in 26 urban and rural districts within a 60-mile radius in South Dakota, Nebraska, and Iowa. These sites include multicultural schools, preschools, child care centers, special education classrooms, and reservation schools. Placements include practica, internships, paraprofessional experiences, and student teaching. Graduate clinical placements are arranged on- and off-campus in a variety of settings. Candidates practice skills in group and individual interactions that later may be adapted to the professional setting.

Noteworthy

The University of South Dakota Professional Development Center (PDC) clusters rural school district classrooms to encourage experienced mentors and first-year teachers to exchange ideas, materials, teaching demonstrations, software development, and teaching technologies to improve teaching and learning for all school children in South Dakota. The PDC model supports year-long internships and mentorships. Faculty work with outstanding local teachers who in turn mentor first-year interns in the demonstration of the best researched practices and technologies in education.

Teacher Preparation Program Information

The following programs are 4 year programs:

Early Childhood Education, Elementary Education, K-12 Education (Art, French, German, Music, Physical Education, Spanish), Kindergarten Education, Middle School Education (English, Mathematics, Science, Social Studies), Secondary Education (Biology, Chemistry, Earth Science, English/Language Arts, Health, History, Mathematics, Physical Education, Physics, Political Science, Theatre), Special Education (Adaptive Physical Education)

The following programs are post-baccalaureate programs:

Special Education (Early Childhood, Gifted/Talented, Learning Disability, Multiple Disabilities/Handicaps, Severe Behavioral Disabilities/Handicaps)

The following programs are 5 year programs:

Secondary Education

The following programs are 5th year programs:

Special Education (Early Childhood, Gifted/Talented, Learning Disability, Multiple Disabilities/Handicaps, Severe Behavioral Disabilities/Handicaps)

Austin Peay State University

The College of Education at Austin Peay State University prepares its teacher education candidates to analyze and interpret student abilities, capitalize on students' cultural backgrounds and real world experiences, design and implement instruction based on students' needs and interests, create and manage a stimulating learning environment, and use ongoing assessment to evaluate learning outcomes. The College of Education's philosophy is founded on the idea of "learning by doing."

Just the facts...

Austin Peay State University
College of Education
P.O. Box 4428
210 Claxton Building
Clarksville, TN 37044
(931) 648-7696
Website: http://claxton.apsu.edu
Profile: Urban, Medium, Co-Ed
UG Tuition: $85.00/cr. hr. in-state; $296.00/cr. hr. out-of-state
G Tuition: $129.00/cr. hr. in-state; $340.00/cr. hr. out-of-state
Off Campus Programs: No

Clinical Experiences

Teacher candidates at APSU begin stepping into public schools during their sophomore year. The College of Education's close collaboration with local school districts ensures quality field experiences for candidates. University faculty are on-site to provide support and feedback to candidates. Candidates have experiences in urban, rural, and suburban settings during their program. Prior to the full semester "two placement" student teaching experience, candidates spend a minimum of 80 hours in classrooms.

Noteworthy

The College of Education initiated the "Best of the Best" program in 1998. This mentor/apprenticeship program is a collaboration involving the local school district, the College of Education, and the Tennessee Education Association. The program is designed to place teacher candidates in real classrooms for two years. The results of the program could make this model the norm for teacher preparation at Austin Peay State University. The 21st Century Classroom Technology Project has been recognized as an outstanding example of how technology should be integrated into teacher training. An ongoing minority grant provides tuition support for promising African American teacher candidates.

Teacher Preparation Program Information

The following programs are 4 year programs:

Elementary Education, Kindergarten Education, K-12 Education (Art, French, Health, Music, Physical Education, Spanish), Middle School Education (5-8 Certification), Secondary Education (Art, Biology, Chemistry, English/Language Arts, Health, Geography, Mathematics, Physical Education, Physical Sciences, Physics, Political Science, Psychology, Sociology), Special Education (Cross-Categorical)

The following programs are post-baccalaureate programs:

Elementary Education, Kindergarten Education, K-12 Education (Art, French, Health, Music, Physical Education, Spanish), Middle School Education (5-8 Certification), Secondary Education (Art, Biology, Chemistry, English/Language Arts, Health, Geography, Mathematics, Physical Education, Physical Sciences, Physics, Political Science, Psychology, Sociology), Special Education (Cross-Categorical)

Belmont University

Belmont University's education program is based on the motto "Building Together for Excellence in Teaching." Candidates build on a strong liberal arts foundation with an academic major, and become academicians, effective communicators, conscientious practitioners, and responsible professionals. Through coursework, practical experiences in the classroom, research, and collaboration with and mentoring by K-12 teachers, candidates become excellent teachers.

Just the facts...

Belmont University
School of Humanities/Education
1900 Belmont Boulevard
Nashville, TN 37212-3757
(615) 460-6414
Website: www.belmont.edu
Profile: Urban, Medium, Co-Ed
UG Tuition: $5,400.00/semester
Off Campus Programs: No

Clinical Experiences

Candidates accumulate many hours of hands-on experience in K-12 classrooms prior to the professional semester. The faculty ensure that candidates are placed in various grade levels and in different types of schools. Student teaching is a sixteen-week, full-time field experience in which the candidate receives guidance and mentoring from the classroom teacher, the principal, and the university supervisor. Belmont University also offers a post-baccalaureate internship program that involves one full year of teaching. Candidates in the post-baccalaureate internship program take academic and professional courses and are supervised by mentors during a variety of clinical experiences.

Noteworthy

The education department has faculty trained in many disciplines and areas of expertise. Faculty are not only knowledgeable in their fields; each has an open door policy and is readily available to any and all candidates on a daily basis. Mentoring relationships built among faculty and candidates extend beyond the college experience; graduates become K-12 mentors to new candidates. Through these relationships, many innovative programs such as on-site classes and technological partnerships with K-12 schools have been developed.

Teacher Preparation Program Information

The following programs are 4 year programs:

Elementary Education K-8 (Biology, Chemistry, Communication Studies, English, French, German, Health, History, Mathematics/BA option, Mathematics/BS option, Philosophy, Physics, Political Science, Psychology, Religion, Sociology, Spanish, Theatre & Drama), Elementary Education 1-8 (Biology, Chemistry, Communications Studies, English, French, Health, History, German, Mathematics/BA option, Mathematics/BS option, Philosophy, Physics, Political Science, Psychology, Religion, Sociology, Spanish, Theatre & Drama), K-12 Education (Art, Health, Instrumental Music, Physical Education, Theatre & Drama, Vocal Music), Secondary Education 7-12 (Biology, Chemistry, Communication Studies, English, French, History, Mathematics/BA option, Mathematics/BS option, Physics, Political Science, Psychology/History, Spanish)

The following programs are post-baccalaureate programs:

Elementary Education K-8 (Biology, Chemistry, Communication Studies, English, French, German, Health, History, Mathematics/BA option, Mathematics/BS option, Philosophy, Physics, Political Science, Psychology, Religion, Sociology, Spanish, Theatre & Drama), Elementary Education 1-8 (Biology, Chemistry, Communications Studies, English, French, Health, History, German, Mathematics/BA option, Mathematics/BS option, Philosophy, Physics, Political Science, Psychology, Religion, Sociology, Spanish, Theatre & Drama), K-12 Education (Art, Health, Instrumental Music, Physical Education, Theatre & Drama, Vocal Music), Secondary Education 7-12 (Biology, Chemistry, Communication Studies, English, French, History, Mathematics/BA option, Mathematics/BS option, Physics, Political Science, Psychology/History, Spanish)

Carson-Newman College

Carson-Newman College is a four-year liberal arts college with undergraduate and graduate programs for preparing teachers and school counselors. The Christian ideals of truth, beauty, and goodness are carried out through the college mission and goals. The faculty in the education unit are student-centered. The education programs place a strong emphasis on candidate ability to reflect on practice and change what does not work. The education programs also emphasize home, school, and community relationships; assessment; technology; and cultural diversity.

Just the facts...

Carson-Newman College
Division of Education
Box 71872
Jefferson City, TN 37760
(423) 471-3308
Website: www.cn.edu
Profile: Rural, Small, Co-Ed
UG Tuition: $4,770.00/semester
G Tuition: $190.00/credit hour
Off Campus Programs: No

Clinical Experiences

Candidates are immersed in clinical experiences throughout their studies. Clinical experiences begin early in the education program and allow for hands-on experiences in diverse classrooms. Majors in teacher education programs complete a semester of student teaching with placements in two different settings during the senior year. Counseling students complete a semester-long practicum.

Noteworthy

Carson-Newman College coordinates the East Tennessee Teachers Network, which exists to support classroom teachers in their efforts to implement the Foxfire approach to instruction, featuring the active involvement of P-12 students in the planning, implementing, and evaluating of community-based activities to meet curricular objectives. The Network is governed by teachers, who provide feedback on needed program changes within the education unit. A technology mentor program helps faculty refine and expand their technology skills.

Teacher Preparation Program Information

The following programs are 4 year programs:
Early Childhood Education, Elementary Education, K-12 Education (Art, Music, Physical Education), Secondary Education (Biology, Business, Chemistry, English/Language Arts, French, Government, History, Mathematics, Spanish, Steno/Typing/Keyboard, Vocational Home Economics/Consumer Homemaking), Special Education (Gifted/Talented, Special Education Modified, Special Education Comprehensive)

The following programs are post-baccalaureate programs:
Early Childhood Education, Elementary Education, K-12 Education (Art, ESL, Music, Physical Education), Secondary Education (Biology, Business, Chemistry, English/Language Arts, French, Government, History, Mathematics, Spanish, Steno/Typing/Keyboard, Vocational Home Economics/Consumer Homemaking), Special Education (Gifted/Talented, Special Education Comprehensive, Special Education Modified)

The following programs are 5th year programs:
Elementary Education, K-12 Education (Art, ESL, Music, Physical Education), Secondary Education (Biology, Business, Chemistry, English/Language Arts, French, Government, History, Mathematics, Spanish, Steno/Typing/Keyboard, Vocational Home Economics/Consumer Homemaking), Special Education (Gifted/Talented, Special Education Comprehensive, Special Education Modified)

East Tennessee State University

The College of Education at East Tennessee State University prepares knowledgeable, competent, ethical, and caring educators who are committed to excellence in their professional pursuits. The College of Education assists candidates in acquiring and applying knowledge of people, methodology, and subject matter for competent professional practice in a changing and diverse society.

Just the facts...

East Tennessee State University
College of Education
319 Warf Pickel Hall
Johnson City, TN 37614
(423)439-4426
Website: http://coe.etsu.edu
Profile: Rural, Large, Co-Ed
UG Tuition: $1,192.00/sem. in-state; $3,605.00/sem. out-of-state
G Tuition: $1,427.00/sem. in-state; $3,885.00/sem. out-of-state
Off Campus Programs: No

Clinical Experiences

Clinical experiences are an integral part of the teacher education program. These experiences are planned collaboratively by college faculty and public school practitioners. Candidates are assured experiences in a wide range of school and non-school based instructional settings. Clinical experiences evolve in three phases. The first phase occurs in core courses and is designed to introduce teacher candidates to schools and to teaching as a career, with at least 60 hours of clinical experience in four to six settings. The second phase consists of at least 60 hours of clinical experience that is linked to methods courses. The third phase, student teaching, is a full-time, fifteen-week experience at two different grade levels.

Noteworthy

The college offers a number of exemplary programs, including those in special education, early childhood education, and science education. Graduates have distinguished themselves as district, regional, and state Teachers of the Year, and one alumna recently received the Milken Family Foundation National Educator Award. The college operates a K-12 laboratory school, University School, which is the only year-round K-12 lab school in the nation. The Center of Excellence in Early Childhood Learning and Development also provides extensive campus opportunities for prospective teachers to work with young children and to participate in research.

Teacher Preparation Program Information

The following programs are 4 year programs:

Early Childhood Education, Elementary Education, K-12 Education (Art, Drama/Theater, Health, Industrial Technology, Music, Physical Education), Secondary Education (Biology, Chemistry, Consumer & Family Science/Home Economics, Economics, English/Language Arts, French, German, Spanish, General Science, Geography, History, Physics, Political Science, Psychology, Science, Social Studies, Sociology, Speech, Vocational Home Economics/Consumer Homemaking, Technology Education), Special Education (Early Childhood, Moderate Needs, Severe Behavioral Disabilities/Handicaps)

The following programs are post-baccalaureate programs:

Early Childhood Education, Elementary Education, K-12 Education (Art, Drama/Theater, Health, Industrial Technology, Music, Physical Education), Secondary Education (Biology, Chemistry, Consumer & Family Science/Home Economics, Earth Science, Economics, English/Language Arts, French, German, Spanish, General Science, Geography, History, Physics, Political Science, Psychology, Science, Social Studies, Sociology, Speech, Trade & Industrial, Vocational Business Office, Vocational Home Economics/Consumer Homemaking, Vocational Education, Vocational Trade & Industrial, Technology Education), Special Education (Early Childhood, Moderate Needs, Severe Behavioral Disabilities/Handicaps, Speech/Language Disabilities)

Freed-Hardeman University

Freed-Hardeman University graduates have a reputation of competence. They are well-prepared, caring teachers who are willing to "go the extra mile." The School of Education seeks to prepare its students to go beyond initial licensure. The education programs provide a common core of liberal arts education, an integration of congruent professional courses, guided field experiences, and content-specific courses. The School of Education emphasizes a moral commitment to teaching in a global democracy. The culture of the university lends itself to small group settings and one-on-one training.

Just the facts...

Freed-Hardeman University
Teacher Education
158 East Main Street
Henderson, TN 38340
(901) 989-6074
Website: www.fhu.edu
Profile: Rural, Small, Co-Ed
UG Tuition: $3,392.00/semester
G Tuition: $3,392.00/semester
Off Campus Programs: No

Clinical Experiences

Clinical experiences begin early and continue throughout the program, and include a full semester of guided student teaching. These experiences range from observations in public schools to specific instructional experiences that include responsibility for student outcomes and reflection. Enhanced student teaching is an intense, directed immersion in teaching that includes placements in two different settings and two grade levels.

Noteworthy

Newly constructed facilities for the School of Education include a technology center, an instructional resources center, areas for diagnostic and tutorial practica, a conference facility for professional development activities, two technology-equipped classrooms, offices and conference areas for undergraduate and graduate programs, general reception areas and two multi-use seminar rooms. The education faculty is ethnically diverse and experienced in the public schools. The School of Education collaborates with the School of Science and Mathematics in teaching K-12 research and thinking skills.

Teacher Preparation Program Information

The following programs are 4 year programs:
Early Childhood Education, Elementary Education, K-12 Education (Drama/Theater), Kindergarten Education, Secondary Education (Art, Biology, English/Language Arts, History, Mathematics, Physical Education, Social Studies), Special Education

The following programs are 5th year programs:
Early Childhood Education, Elementary Education, K-12 Education (Drama/Theater), Kindergarten Education, Secondary Education (Art, Biology, English/Language Arts, History, Mathematics, Physical Education, Social Studies), Special Education

Middle Tennessee State University

Since its beginning in 1911 as a teacher preparation institution, the education of teachers has remained central to the mission of Middle Tennessee State University. The College of Education is home to one of the largest undergraduate teacher education programs in Tennessee. Teacher education programs include a strong general studies core, a teaching specialty area, and a program of professional studies. Faculty believe that discovering, integrating, and applying knowledge is essential in teaching that knowledge.

Just the facts...

Middle Tennessee State University
College of Education
Murfreesboro, TN 37132
(615) 898-2874
Website: www.mtsu.edu
Profile: Suburban, Large, Co-Ed
UG Tuition: $953.00/sem. in-state; $3,366.00/sem. out-of-state
G Tuition: $1,280.00/sem. in-state; $3,693.00/sem. out-of-state
Off Campus Programs: No

Clinical Experiences

As candidates move into their third and fourth years in the program they enter into a serious study of teaching, including the analysis of effective teaching; methods and strategies of teaching, planning, and managing the classroom; and the uses of technology in learning. The culmination of this study is student teaching, a full-time, full semester activity in which the candidate undertakes two distinct assignments in local public schools.

Noteworthy

The faculty have won numerous honors for their teaching excellence. Four graduates have been named Tennessee Teacher of the Year; other awards given to graduates include the National Teacher of the Year Award, the Sally Mae First Year Teacher Award, and the Presidential Science and Math Award. The College of Education is particularly proud of the public service efforts of its faculty. The College of Education is home to the Chair of Excellence in Dyslexic Studies and the Center for the Treatment and Study of Dyslexia. Project HELP serves the needs of developmentally delayed children from birth to three years old and their families.

Teacher Preparation Program Information

The following programs are 4 year programs:
Early Childhood Education, Elementary Education, K-12 Education (Art, Drama/Theater, French, German, Health, Industrial Technology, Music, Physical Education, Spanish), Secondary Education (Business, Chemistry, Consumer & Family Science/Home Economics, Earth Science, Economics, English/Language Arts, Geography, History, Mathematics, Marketing, Physics, Social Studies, Vocational Agriculture, Vocational Home Economics/Consumer Homemaking, Vocational Trade & Industrial), Special Education (Speech/Language Disabilities)

The following programs are post-baccalaureate programs:
Early Childhood Education, Elementary Education, K-12 Education (Art, Drama/Theater, French, German, Health, Industrial Technology, Music, Physical Education, Spanish), Secondary Education (Business, Chemistry, Consumer & Family Science/Home Economics, Earth Science, Economics, English/Language Arts, Geography, History, Mathematics, Marketing, Physics, Social Studies, Vocational Agriculture, Vocational Home Economics/Consumer Homemaking, Vocational Trade & Industrial), Special Education (Speech/Language Disabilities)

The following programs are 5 year programs:
K-12 Education (French, German, Spanish), Secondary Education (English/Language Arts, Mathematics)

Milligan College

Millligan College is a private, Christian, liberal arts institution. Programs are designed to develop competent, caring, and reflective teachers for service in the classroom. The Milligan teacher education faculty believes in learning by doing. Each teacher preparation program involves meaningful clinical experiences in local schools. Candidates learn on campus and in classrooms. Milligan provides a variety of programs at the undergraduate and graduate levels, and special graduate opportunities exist for minorities and licensed teachers.

Just the facts...

Milligan College
Teacher Education
Box 309
Milligan College, TN 37682
(423) 461-8745
Website: www.milligan.edu
Profile: Rural, Medium, Co-Ed
UG Tuition: $325.00/credit hour
G Tuition: $180.00/credit hour
Off Campus Programs: No

Clinical Experiences

Most undergraduate candidates spend over 100 hours in local schools before their student teaching experience. Student teaching is one full semester that usually involves two placements at different grade levels. Graduate candidates seeking licensure participate in a year-long internship. In order to facilitate these placements, Milligan works with eight local school systems. Milligan has two professional development schools and has professional development partnerships with several others.

Noteworthy

Milligan strives to provide quality teacher education to qualified students. A range of scholarship opportunities is available. Special scholarships are available to minority candidates at the graduate level. Milligan has a teacher education club, a student organization that is involved in teaching, tutoring, and providing other educational services to the local community. A combination of curricular and extracurricular activities provides Milligan College's teacher education students with many opportunities for hands-on preparation.

Teacher Preparation Program Information

The following programs are 4 year programs:
Early Childhood Education, Elementary Education, K-12 Education (Drama/Theater, Health, Music, Physical Education), Secondary Education (Biology, Business, Chemistry, Economics, English/Language Arts, French, General Science, History, Mathematics, Music, Physical Sciences, Psychology, Sociology, Spanish)

The following programs are post-baccalaureate programs:
Early Childhood Education, Elementary Education, K-12 Education (Drama/Theater, Health, Music, Physical Education), Secondary Education (Biology, Business, Chemistry, Economics, English/Language Arts, General Science, History, Mathematics, Music, Physical Sciences, Psychology, Sociology, Spanish), Special Education

The following programs are 5 year programs:
Early Childhood Education, Elementary Education, K-12 Education (Drama/Theater, Health, Music, Physical Education), Secondary Education (Biology, Business, Chemistry, Economics, English/Language Arts, General Science, History, Mathematics, Music, Physical Sciences, Psychology, Sociology, Spanish), Special Education

The following programs are 5th year programs:
Early Childhood Education, Elementary Education, K-12 Education (Drama/Theater, Health, Music, Physical Education), Secondary Education (Biology, Business, Chemistry, Economics, English/Language Arts, General Science, History, Mathematics, Music, Physical Sciences, Psychology, Sociology, Spanish), Special Education

Peabody College of Vanderbilt University

Peabody College is a specialized college of education and human development within Vanderbilt University. The school and its programs consistently receive top rankings in national surveys, enrolling more than 1,000 undergraduates and approximately 600 graduate and professional students each year. The combination of strong liberal arts preparation through the College of Arts and Sciences and professional education through Peabody College prepares graduates who are highly sought after across the nation and beyond. Peabody's innovative programs encourage interaction between faculty and candidates. Peabody's programs in special education have been ranked among the best in the country.

Clinical Experiences

Beginning in their first semester of classes, teacher education candidates learn about the profession of teaching and the reality of the classroom by observing and evaluating the learning process in area schools. This combination of coursework and experience continues throughout the program. The program ends with a semester of full-time student teaching distributed between two grade levels, in two different schools. Field experience sites are carefully selected to provide each candidate with maximum exposure to a variety of school settings and student populations.

Just the facts...

Peabody College of Vanderbilt University
1980 South Drive
Nashville, TN 37203
(615) 322-8407
Website: www.peabody.vanderbilt.edu
Profile: Urban, Medium, Co-Ed
UG Tuition: $10,450.00/semester
G Tuition: $650.00/credit hour
Off Campus Programs: No

Noteworthy

Peabody has been ranked as the top undergraduate teacher education program in the nation for the past eight years by *Rigg's Recommendations on Colleges*. Peabody also has been the recipient of more external funding for education research than any other school of education in the counrry. Vanderbilt faculty currently are involved in over sixty research programs in schools to discover new ways to help students learn. Technology in schools is a high research priority. The average GPA for undergraduate teacher education graduates was 3.25, and a recent survey showed that 93 percent of graduates were teaching or enrolled in graduate study in education immediately after graduation.

Teacher Preparation Program Information

The following programs are 4 year programs:

Early Childhood Education, Elementary Education, Secondary Education (Biology, Chemistry, Earth Science, Economics, English, French, German, Latin, Mathematics, Physics, Political Science, Psychology, Sociology, Spanish), Special Education (Early Childhood, Learning Disabilities/Behavior Disorders, Multiple/Severe/Profound Disabilities, Hearing Impairment, Vision Impairment)

The following programs are 5th year programs:

Early Childhood Education, Elementary Education, Secondary Education (Biology, Chemistry, Earth Science, Economics, English, French, German, Latin, Mathematics, Physics, Political Science, Psychology, Sociology, Spanish), Special Education (Early Childhood, Learning Disabilities/Behavior Disorders, Multiple/Severe/Profound Disabilities, Vision Impairment)

Southern Adventist University

The mission of the School of Education and Psychology at Southern Adventist University is to prepare, primarily for the worldwide Seventh-day Adventist school system, professional educators at both undergraduate and graduate levels who can function effectively in a pluralistic society. Educators are dedicated to assisting students in reaching their maximum potential in service to God and man. The teacher education program is designed to help the teacher candidate develop personal values and acquire the knowledge, skills, and competencies needed for the teacher's role as a person, a facilitator of learning, a practitioner, and a professional.

Just the facts...

Southern Adventist University
School of Education and Psychology
P.O. Box 370
Collegedale, TN 37315-0370
(423) 238-2779
Website: www.southern.edu
Profile: Rural, Small, Co-Ed
UG Tuition: $430.00/credit hour
Off Campus Programs: No

Clinical Experiences

Candidates in the education program have multiple opportunities to translate theory into practice and relate theory to their clinical experiences. These experiences begin in the freshman year and are integrated throughout the program. Examples include experiences in inclusive, multi-grade resource room and community agencies in public, private, and parochial K-12 settings. Student teachers spend an eight-week placement in a public school and an eight-week placement in a parochial school. All candidates are supervised by teaching faculty from the university throughout their clinical experiences.

Noteworthy

The School of Education and Psychology is proud of its efforts to enhance its programs with a focus on educational reform. The 21st Century Technology Classroom trains teacher candidates in the most advanced setting in the state—among the first to develop a process to train teachers in distance learning through the installation of a video wall in an active teaching classroom. Other projects include the creation of the largest and most comprehensive Teaching Materials Resource Center in the surrounding area; arranging for education students to attend local, state, and national conventions; and efforts to incorporate a professional development school model into the Teacher Education Program.

Teacher Preparation Program Information

The following programs are 4 year programs:
Elementary Education, K-12 Education (Health, Music), 7-12 Education (Biology, Chemistry, English, History, Mathematics, Physics, Religion)

The following programs are post-baccalaureate programs:
Elementary Education, Physical Education, 7-12 Education (Chemistry, English, History, Mathematics, Physics, Religion)

Tennessee State University

Tennessee State University is a state-supported urban, comprehensive university that provides programs in agriculture, allied health, arts and sciences, business, education, engineering and technology, family and consumer sciences, human services, nursing, and public administration. The university serves a diverse population of students and is committed to providing educational opportunities to all qualified individuals without regard to age, sex, color, race, religion, national origin, or disability. Tennessee State University promotes positive and lifelong learning, scholarly inquiry, and a commitment to serving others. Its motto reads "Think, Work, Serve."

Just the facts...

Tennessee State University
College of Education
3500 John A. Merritt Boulevard
Nashville, TN 37209-1561
(615) 963-5451
Website: www.tnstate.edu
Profile:Urban, Large, Co-Ed
UG Tuition: $1,154.00/sem. in-state; $3,567.00/sem. out-of-state
G Tuition: $1,481.00/sem. in-state; $3,894/sem. out-of-state
Off Campus Programs: No

Clinical Experiences

Field/clinical experience is a requirement in every professional education class. Beginning with freshman orientation, field experiences provide opportunities for students to observe and experience K-12 classrooms as a prospective teacher education candidate. As sophomores, juniors, and seniors progress through the teacher education program, the field experiences expand to include tutoring; reading to students; assisting with various teacher tasks; working with small groups; and developing and implementing lesson plans. The culminating field experience—enhanced student teaching—consists of supervised practice teaching at two different levels, over a full semester.

Noteworthy

Tennessee State University has been listed among the nation's best colleges and universities in *U.S. News and World Report* for the third consecutive year. The College of Education is a member of the USA-SINO Teacher Education Consortium that works to "build bridges" between professional education programs in the U.S. and China (and other Chinese-speaking portions of the world). The College of Education collaborates with local high schools to provide academic tutoring and enrichment activities to high school students through the Multicultural Education and Enrichment (MEE) program which is funded by the Coca-Cola Foundation. Several loans (including forgivable loans) are available.

Teacher Preparation Program Information

The following programs are 4 year programs:

Early Childhood Education (P-3), Elementary Education (K-8, 1-8/Language Arts-Social Studies, 1-8/Mathematics-Science), K-12 Education (Art, Health, Music, Physical Education, Theater), Secondary Education (Agriculture, Biology, Basic Business/Accounting, Chemistry, Consumer & Family Science, Economics, English, French, Geography, History, Mathematics, Physical Education, Psychology, Political Science, Spanish, Speech Communication), Special Education

The following programs are post-baccalaureate programs:

Early Childhood Education (P-3), Elementary Education (K-8, 1-8/Language Arts-Social Studies, 1-8/Mathematics-Science), K-12 Education (Art, Health, Music, Physical Education, Theater), Secondary Education (Agriculture, Biology, Basic Business/Accounting, Chemistry, Consumer & Family Science, Economics, English, French, Geography, History, Mathematics, Physical Education, Psychology, Political Science, Spanish, Speech Communication), Special Education

Tennessee Technological University

Since 1928, Tennessee Technological University has prepared teachers and other school personnel. The College of Education prepares teachers who model appropriate professional behavior and who provide supportive, safe, and technologically integrated environments for effective learning within the classroom and laboratory settings. Comprising about one-fourth of the total university enrollment, candidates in Tennessee Tech teacher education programs gain a working knowledge of best and effective practices, opportunities to learn about the practical applications of technology in classrooms, an appreciation for diversity and individual learning needs, and the ability to function as a team member.

Clinical Experiences

Clinical experiences in teacher education at Tennessee Tech begin in the freshman year and continue throughout the program, culminating with a full semester of student teaching. Experiences are supervised by faculty and are coordinated with on-campus classes. The student teaching program places the candidate in two different sites and at two different levels to assure diversity in the experiences.

Just the facts...

Tennessee Technological University
College of Education
Box 5046
Cookeville, TN 38505
(931) 372-3124
Website: www.tntech.edu
Profile: Rural, Medium. Co-Ed
UG Tuition: $953.00/sem. in-state; $3,366.00/sem. out-of-state
G Tuition: $1,280.00/sem. in-state; $3,693.00/sem. out-of-state
Off Campus Programs: Yes

Noteworthy

An integral part of a university that emphasizes technology, the College of Education is an excellent place to pursue the ambitious goal of becoming a teacher. Tennessee Tech offers a friendly, relaxed learning environment; a faculty and staff whose members are helpful and caring; small classes where personal attention is the rule; a wide selection of strong programs; and an affordable education. The College of Education emphasizes extensive and continuous practical experiences in school and community settings, a strong foundation in the liberal arts, and preparation for applying twenty-first century technologies in the classroom.

Teacher Preparation Program Information

The following programs are 4 year programs:

Early Childhood Education, Elementary Education, K-12 Education (Art, Drama/Theater, ESL, Health, Music, Physical Education, Special Education Comprehensive, Special Education Modified), Secondary Education (Biology, Chemistry, Earth Science, Economics, English/Language Arts, French, Geography, German, History, Mathematics, Physics, Political Science, Psychology, Sociology, Spanish, Speech, Vocational Agriculture, Vocational Home Economics/Consumer Homemaking), Special Education (Early Childhood)

The following programs are post-baccalaureate programs:

Early Childhood Education, Elementary Education, K-12 Education (Art, Drama/Theater, ESL, Health, Music, Physical Education, Special Education Comprehensive, Special Education Modified), Secondary Education (Biology, Chemistry, Earth Science, Economics, English/Language Arts, French, Geography, German, History, Mathematics, Physics, Political Science, Psychology, Sociology, Spanish, Speech, Vocational Agriculture, Vocational Home Economics/Consumer Homemaking), Special Education (Early Childhood)

University of Memphis

The first mission of the College of Education at the University of Memphis is to prepare teachers, other licensed personnel, and education-related professionals who are qualified and competent in both practice and theory to become effective educational leaders. The second mission of the College of Education is to conduct educational and education-related research and to engage in the dissemination of its outcomes. The final mission of the College of Education, tightly interwoven with its other missions, is to provide teaching, research, and service that extends beyond the confines of the campus to both its urban setting and to other outreach locations.

Just the facts...

University of Memphis
College of Education
215 Ball Education Building
Memphis, TN 38152
(901) 678-4265
Website: www.coe.memphis.edu
Profile: Urban, Large, Co-Ed
UG Tuition: $1,315.00/sem. in-state; $3,751.00/sem. out-of-state
G Tuition: $1,591.00/sem. in-state; $4,027.00/sem. out-of-state
Off Campus Programs: No

Clinical Experiences

Field experiences include classroom observations, tutoring, assisting teachers and school administrators, student teaching, and internships. Candidates begin by observing in their particular licensure area and progress to tutoring individual students, working with small groups of students, and teaching a class of students. Laboratory experiences and field experiences provide the background necessary for candidates to enter enhanced student teaching or internships with an optimal knowledge of classroom realities.

Noteworthy

Many scholarship opportunities are available for undergraduate students, and graduate students may be eligible for paid internships. Candidates are exposed to the latest in technological advances in university computer labs. Distance learning classes provide opportunities for candidates in off-campus sites to have the same instruction as main campus students. Professional development schools provide the opportunity for clinical experiences and student teaching in schools committed to mentoring preservice teachers and providing "best practices" in education for P-12 students.

Teacher Preparation Program Information

The following programs are 4 year programs:

Early Childhood Education, Elementary Education, K-12 Education (Art, Health, Music, Physical Education, Special Education)

The following programs are post-baccalaureate programs:

Early Childhood Education, Elementary Education (Reading, Special Education), K-12 Education (Health, Physical Education, Special Education), Secondary Education (Biology, Business, Chemistry, Earth Science, Economics, English/Language Arts, French, Geography, German, History, Latin, Mathematics, Marketing, Physics, Psychology, Sociology, Spanish, Steno/Typing/Keyboard, Vocational Home Economics/Consumer Homemaking)

The following programs are 5th year programs:

Early Childhood Education, Elementary Education (Reading), K-12 Education (Health, Physical Education), Secondary Education (Biology, Business, Chemistry, Earth Science, Economics, English/Language Arts, French, Geography, German, History, Latin, Mathematics, Marketing, Physics, Political Science, Psychology, Sociology, Spanish, Steno/Typing/Keyboard, Vocational Home Economics/Consumer Homemaking), Special Education (Early Childhood)

University of Tennessee at Chattanooga

The University of Tennessee at Chattanooga bases its education programs on reflective practice. Candidates learn to ask questions about their teaching practice, and consider students of all abilities, races, and cultural backgrounds when developing teaching skills. Faculty and candidates are oriented toward inquiry in the practice of teaching, and constantly strive to refine and improve their practice. UTC's College of Education and Applied Professional Studies seeks to combine quality and innovation in its undergraduate and graduate programs, and to create professionals who will be comfortable and effective in the twenty-first century workplace.

Just the facts...

University of Tennessee at Chattanooga
College of Education
615 McCallie Avenue
Chattanooga, TN 37403
(423) 755-4249
Website: www.utc.edu
Profile: Suburban, Medium, Co-Ed
UG Tuition: $1,232.00/sem. in-state; $3,645.00/sem. out-of-state
G Tuition: $1,542.00/sem. in-state; $3,955.00/sem. out-of-state
Off Campus Programs: No

Clinical Experiences

UTC's Professional Development School I and II semesters offer the equivalent of one year's immersion in a K-12 setting. During PDS I, UTC faculty teach university courses on-site at K-12 schools, and UTC teacher candidates spend their remaining time in observing, tutoring, and assisting teachers in the classroom. PDS II is an enhanced student teaching semester involving cohorts of student teachers in the total school program in selected school sites. K-12 and UTC faculty jointly evaluate student teachers, and professors-in-residence serve as resource persons.

Noteworthy

UTC operates the CLAS program for non-traditional education students. The program offers classes on weekends and other convenient times. UTC's "Each One Reach One" program offers tuition, books, and fees to minority male residents of Tennessee seeking elementary licensure. Males with some college education or with degrees who are seeking initial elementary licensure are eligible to apply for this program.

Teacher Preparation Program Information

The following programs are 4 year programs:
Early Childhood Education P-4, K-12 Education (Art, Drama/Theater, Health, Music, Preschool Education), Middle School Education 5-8 (Generalist), Secondary Education (Biology, Chemistry, Earth Science, Economics, English/Language Arts, French, Geography, History, Latin, Mathematics, Physics, Political Science, Spanish), Special Education (Learning Disability, Multiple Disabilities/Handicaps)

The following programs are post-baccalaureate programs:
Early Childhood Education P-4, K-12 Education (Art, Drama/Theater, Health, Music, Preschool Education), Middle School Education 5-8 (Generalist), Secondary Education (Biology, Chemistry, Earth Science, Economics, English/Language Arts, French, Geography, History, Latin, Mathematics, Physics, Political Science, Spanish), Special Education (Learning Disability, Multiple Disabilities/Handicaps)

University of Tennessee at Knoxville

The University of Tennessee at Knoxville is Tennessee's land grant institution and major public research university. The UTK College of Education is recognized as a national leader in efforts to reform teacher education. Candidates preparing to teach complete an arts and sciences undergraduate degree (or equivalent) to qualify for the professional year internship. All elementary education licensure candidates are placed in professional development schools for their fifth-year internship. The professional year earns candidates graduate credit applicable to a Master of Science degree. The college is a member of the Holmes Partnership and the Urban Network to Improve Teacher Education.

Clinical Experiences

The College of Education offers an early exposure to teaching called Apple Corps. This voluntary experience includes a school observation assignment and multiple school-based guest presenters. All licensure programs require pre-internship field experiences linked with professional teaching classes. The full-year internship is the special feature of the preparation program. All interns hold a probationary license and are assigned to a partnership school. Interns work according to the schedule of the assigned school and participate fully in all school-based activities.

Just the facts...

University of Tennessee at Knoxville
College of Education
404 Claxton Addition
Knoxville, TN 37996-3400
(423) 974-2201
Website: www.coe.utk.edu
Profile: Suburban, Large, Co-Ed
UG Tuition: $1,372.00/sem. in-state; $3,900.00/sem. out-of-state
G Tuition: $1,677.00/sem. in-state; $4,205.00/sem. out-of-state
Off Campus Programs: No

Noteworthy

The UTK College of Education offers endowed scholarships for teacher education students. In addition, a large block of scholarship money is designated for fifth-year interns, and the state offers forgivable loans for interns. Over the past five years an increasing number of states and individual school systems seek to employ UTK graduates. The employment rate of interns averages 75 percent. The College of Education is in partnership with fifteen regional school systems; eight professional development schools are the result of this collaboration.

Teacher Preparation Program Information

The following programs are 4 year programs:
Music Education

The following programs are 5 year programs:
Early Childhood Education, Elementary Education, K-12 Education (Art, Drama/Theater, ESL, French, German, Latin, Russian, Spanish), Middle School Education, Music Education, Secondary Education (Biology, Business, Chemistry, Earth Science, Economics, English/Language Arts, Geography, History, Mathematics, Physics, Political Science, Psychology, Sociology, Vocational Agriculture, Vocational Business Office, Vocational Marketing, Vocational Home Economics/Consumer Homemaking), Special Education (Developmental Disabilities/Handicaps, Early Childhood, Hearing Impaired, Severe Behavioral Disabilities/Handicaps, Speech/Language Disabilities)

University of Tennessee at Martin

The University of Tennessee at Martin is committed to preparing educators who (1) demonstrate higher-order thinking skills; (2) use language proficiently and communicate effectively;(3) use a diverse pedagogical repertoire; (4) reflect on their own teaching to ensure relevant, purposeful student learning; (5) assess student performance as integral to the learning process; (6) collaborate with colleagues and the community; (7) organize, develop, and use exisiting and emerging technology in teaching; (8) relate to student differences in a diverse society; (9) adapt instruction to meet the needs of all children; and (10) model professional and ethical behavior.

Clinical Experiences

Each of three courses in UTM's education core has a 30-hour field experience in the university's partnership schools. Working as teaching assistants, preservice teachers complete these early field experiences in culturally diverse school settings before beginning other requisite field experiences in their respective disciplines. In all their early experiences, teacher candidates are able to integrate theoretical and practical knowledge with the pedagogical knowledge introduced in the core curriculum and in methods courses.

Just the facts...

University of Tennessee at Martin
School of Education
237 Gooch Hall
Martin, TN 38238-7010
(901) 587-7125
Website: www.utm.edu
Profile: Rural, Medium, Co-Ed
UG Tuition: $1,070.00/sem. in-state; $3,368.00/sem. out-of-state
G Tuition: $1,365.00/sem. in-state; $3,663.00/sem. out-of-state
Off Campus Programs: Yes

Noteworthy

Education students at UTM may avail themselves of (1) interactive distance education, (2) the Center of Excellence for Science and Mathematics Education, (3) the Tennessee State Space Center, (4) the UTM Honors Program, (5) urban-rural student exchange programs, (6) the National Youth Sports Program, (7) advanced technology with Internet access in all dormitorory rooms, (8) continuous and consistent faculty advising and mentorship for professional development, and (9) rich and varied academic opportunities in a safe, rural setting.

Teacher Preparation Program Information

The following programs are 4 year programs:
Early Childhood Education, Elementary Education (Language Arts, Mathematics, Science, Social Studies), K-12 Education (Art, Health, Music, Physical Education), Secondary Education (Agriculture, Bookkeeping, Business, Chemistry, Earth Science, Economics, English/Language Arts, French, Geography, History, Mathematics, Spanish, Vocational Home Economics/Job Training), Special Education (K-12, Early Childhood)

The following programs are post-baccalaureate programs:
Elementary Education (Language Arts, Mathematics, Science, Social Studies), Secondary Education (Agriculture, Bookkeeping, Business, Chemistry, Earth Science, Economics, English/Language Arts, French, Geography, History, Mathematics, Spanish, Vocational Home Economics/Job Training)

The following programs are 5th year programs:
Elementary Education (Language Arts, Mathematics, Science, Social Studies), Secondary Education (Agriculture, Bookkeeping, Business, Chemistry, Earth Science, Economics, English/Language Arts, French, Geography, History, Mathematics, Spanish, Vocational Home Economics/Job Training)

Baylor University

Baylor University teacher education programs produce more preservice teachers than any other religious-affiliated or private institution in Texas. The preservice and advanced programs are based on a foundation that emphasizes teacher preparation for a diverse and global society. Within a Christian environment, preservice teachers are prepared for roles as lifelong scholars, professionals, decision makers, and facilitators who are able to apply, integrate, and communicate the skills, knowledge, and values essential in a complex and changing world. A vital aspect of teacher education at Baylor is the application of technology for distance communication/learning and classroom instruction.

Just the facts...

Baylor University
School of Education
P.O. Box 97304
Waco, TX 76798
(254) 710-3111
Website: www.baylor.edu
Profile: Urban, Large, Co-Ed
UG Tuition: $329.00/credit hour
G Tuition: $329.00/credit hour
Off Campus Programs: No

Clinical Experiences

The School of Education collaborates with P-12 school partners to renew and restructure teacher education through the Center for Professional Development and Technology. Field experiences prior to student teaching, integration of technology into instruction, learner-centered skills, and multicultural issues are essential components of the various programs. Experiences are available at the undergraduate and graduate levels in various countries and in the U.S.

Noteworthy

Two elementary professional development schools are connected to the School of Education via telecommunications. Various entities within the university, such as the Baylor Child Development Center and the Baylor University Virtual Village Thinking Systems Dynamics Projects, provide enhanced learning opportunities for preservice and licensed teachers. A study abroad program is an integral part of the educational leadership programs at the master's and doctoral levels. These programs may lead to mid-management licensure or superintendent licensure. Educational Psychology and Health, Human Performance, and Recreation Departments offer other programs in addition to teacher licensure.

Teacher Preparation Program Information

The following programs are 4 year programs:

Early Childhood Education, Elementary Education, K-12 Education (Art, Music, Physical Education), Secondary Education (Art, Biology, Business, Chemistry, Computer Information Systems, Consumer & Family Science/Home Economics, Earth Science, Economics, English/Language Arts, French, Generic Special Education, German, Health, History, Journalism, Latin, Life Science, Mathematics, Physical Education, Physical Sciences, Physics, Political Science, Science, Social Studies, Sociology, Speech, Theatre Arts), Special Education (Generic Special Education)

The following programs are post-baccalaureate programs:

Early Childhood Education, Elementary Education, K-12 Education (Art, Music, Physical Education), Secondary Education (Art, Biology, Business, Chemistry, Computer Information Systems, Consumer & Family Science/Home Economics, Earth Science, Economics, English/Language Arts, French, Generic Special Education, German, Health, History, Journalism, Latin, Life Science, Mathematics, Physical Education, Physical Sciences, Physics, Political Science, Science, Social Studies, Sociology, Speech, Theatre Arts), Special Education (Generic Special Education)

Prairie View A&M University

Prairie View A&M University is the second oldest public institution of higher education in the state of Texas. As an independent unit of the Texas A&M University System, it is located on 1,400 picturesque acres in the city of Prairie View, Texas, within commuting distance from metropolitan Houston. The College of Education at Prairie View A&M University has a long history of preparing quality teachers and other school personnel. Its graduates can be found in schools throughout the state of Texas and the nation. The College of Education maintains strong partnerships with area school districts through the Prairie View A&M University Local Cooperative Education Center.

Just the facts...

Prairie View A&M University
College of Education
P.O. Box 4049
Prairie View, TX 77446
(409) 857-3820
Website: www.pvamu.edu
Profile: Rural, Medium, Co-Ed
UG Tuition: $32.00/cr. hr. in-state; $246.00/cr. hr. out-of-state
G Tuition: $36.00/cr. hr. in-state; $246/cr. hr. out-of-state
Off Campus Programs: Yes

Clinical Experiences

Clinical experiences offered to students in the teacher education programs include the field-based, preservice professional development sequence, practica courses required in programs such as early childhood education and special education, a full-semester student teaching experience, and year-long paid internships in the post-baccalaureate and alternative licensure programs.

Noteworthy

The College of Education has a National Alumni Association Teacher Education Scholarship Endowment Fund. The investment income from the Fund is used to grant renewable teacher education scholarships to undergraduate students. The recently established Academy for Excellence in Teaching and Scholarship (with support from the Texas Education Agency and the Sid W. Richardson Foundation) focuses on the professional development of university and public school teachers and administrators. The College of Education conducts a three-day-long annual Technology Camp for Kids for Grades K-9 during the summer months.

Teacher Preparation Program Information

The following programs are 4 year programs:
Interdisciplinary Studies (Bilingual Education, Early Childhood Education, Elementary Education, Special Education), Health, Human Performance/Physical Education, Secondary Education (Biology, Drama/Theater Arts, English, Government, Health, History, Human Performance/Physical Education, Mathematics, Sociology, Spanish)

The following programs are post-baccalaureate programs:
Secondary Education (Biology, Drama/Theater Arts, English, Government, Health, History, Human Performance/Physical Education, Mathematics, Sociology, Spanish)

Sam Houston State University

Sam Houston State University has prepared teachers and other education professionals since 1879, making it the oldest educator preparation program in Texas. Educator preparation programs are carried out through the Sam Houston Center for Professional Development and Educational Partnerships located in the College of Education and Applied Science. The mission of the Center is to prepare candidates to become exemplary professionals who can meet the instructional and educational leadership needs of a diverse public school population. The Center collaborates with university academic departments, area community colleges, area public schools, and regional education service centers to achieve its mission.

Clinical Experiences

Activities in the field at Sam Houston's professional development sites begin early in the educator preparation programs. Candidates begin their field experiences with observations and individual tutoring work as early as their sophomore year. These beginning experiences are followed by more in-depth work, such as teaching lessons to small groups and reading to children. Candidates teach whole group lessons in every content area before their student teaching semester. Student teaching is the capstone experience in which candidates are given full responsibility for planning lessons, teaching, and evaluating student achievement under the supervision of a classroom mentor teacher and a university supervisor.

Just the facts...

Sam Houston State University
College of Education and Applied Science
P.O. Box 2119
Huntsville, TX 77341-2119
(409) 294-1100
Website: www.shsu.edu
Profile: Rural, Medium, Co-Ed
UG Tuition: $38.00/cr. hr. in-state; $249.00/cr. hr. out-of-state
G Tuition: $38.00/cr. hr. in-state; $249.00/cr. hr. out-of-state
Off Campus Programs: No

Noteworthy

The Sam Houston Center for Professional Development and Educational Partnerships awards over 28 different scholarships to educator preparation students. Scholarships are awarded based on academic achievement as well as financial need. Scholarship awards range from $250/semester up to $1,000/semester, depending on the award received. Over the past three years, a $1.5 million grant was used to restructure the educator preparation programs to infuse more technology into the programs.

Teacher Preparation Program Information

The following programs are 4 year programs:
Bilingual/ESL Education, Early Childhood Education, Elementary Education, K-12 Education (Art, Music, Physical Education), Secondary Education (Agriculture, Art, Biology, Business, Chemistry, Earth Science, Economics, English/Language Arts, Geography, Health, Mathematics, Physical Sciences, Physical Education, Physics, Political Science, Psychology, Social Studies, Sociology, Vocational Agriculture, Vocational Home Economics/Consumer Homemaking, Vocational Trade & Industrial), Special Education

The following programs are post-baccalaureate programs:
Bilingual/ESL Education, Early Childhood Education, Elementary Education, K-12 Education (Art, Music, Physical Education), Secondary Education (Agriculture, Art, Biology, Business, Chemistry, Earth Science, Economics, English/Language Arts, Geography, Health, Mathematics, Physical Sciences, Physical Education, Physics, Political Science, Psychology, Social Studies, Sociology, Vocational Agriculture, Vocational Home Economics/Consumer Homemaking, Vocational Trade & Industrial), Special Education (Gifted/Talented)

The following programs are 5th year programs:
Bilingual/ESL Education, Early Childhood Education, Elementary Education, Secondary Education, Special Education (Gifted/Talented)

Stephen F. Austin State University

Established as a teachers college in 1923, Stephen F. Austin State University is one of the five largest producers of teachers in Texas. SFASU's educator programs feature a strong general education, an academic specialization, and field-based professional education. Graduates are proficient in learner-centered knowledge, instruction, and communication, understand the importance of professional growth, and are committed to equity and excellence for all learners.

Just the facts...

Stephen F. Austin State University
College of Education
Box 13023
SFA Station
Nacogdoches, TX 75962-3023
(409) 468-2901
Website: www.sfa.edu
Profile: Rural, Medium, Co-Ed
UG Tuition: $38.00/credit hour
G Tuition: $38.00/credit hour
Off Campus Programs: No

Clinical Experiences

Clinical experiences in both rural and urban school districts are an integral part of all coursework at SFASU. Education courses are delivered in the field from a choice of eleven public school field sites. Preservice teachers have experiences in a Learning Center that focuses on language arts skills, and in an Early Childhood Center where children from infants through the fourth grade provide a model environment for teaching and learning. Student teaching is for a full semester.

Noteworthy

SFASU teacher candidates may work in the Campus Charter School where innovative teaching strategies are modeled by master teachers. Students in the College of Education's large principal preparation program as well as students in the doctoral program in educational leadership provide resources for the preservice teacher preparation program. SFASU's outstanding facilities are capable of allowing faculty and candidates to integrate the latest technologies into the delivery of instruction. A distance learning laboratory is available for transmitting instruction to rural areas of Texas.

Teacher Preparation Program Information

The following programs are 4 year programs:
Early Childhood Education, Elementary Education, K-12 Education (Art, Dance, ESL, Music, Physical Education), Kindergarten Education (K-Primary), Secondary Education (Agriculture, Art, Biology, Business, Chemistry, Computer Science, Consumer & Family Science/Home Economics, Earth Science, Economics, English/Language Arts, French, General Science, Geography, Health, History, Journalism, Mathematics, Music, Physical Education, Physical Sciences, Physics, Political Science, Psychology, Reading, Social Studies, Sociology, Spanish, Speech, Theater, Vocational Home Economics/Consumer Homemaking), Special Education (Adaptive Physical Education, Developmental Disabilities/Handicaps, Early Childhood, Gifted/Talented, Hearing Impaired, Learning Disability, Multiple Disabilities/Handicaps, Physical Disabilities/Handicaps, Severe Behavioral Disabilities/Handicaps, Speech/Language Disabilities, Visually Impaired)

The following programs are post-baccalaureate programs:
Early Childhood Education (Early Childhood), Elementary Education, Kindergarten Education (K-Primary), Secondary Education (Computer Science, French, History, Journalism, Music, Occupational Work, Reading, Speech, Theater, Vocational Health Occupation, Vocational Home Economics/Job Training), Special Education (Adaptive Physical Education, Developmental Disabilities/Handicaps, Early Childhood, Gifted/Talented, Learning Disability, Multiple Disabilities/Handicaps, Physical Disabilities/Handicaps, Severe Behavioral Disabilities/Handicaps, Visually Impaired)

Texas A&M University

Texas A&M University's College of Education, with nearly 4000 students, is among the leading developers of teachers in the state. The college plays a proactive role in shaping the state and national educational agenda. To this end, programs in the College of Education attempt to (1) develop thinking professionals whose research adds to the store of knowledge regarding teaching and learning, (2) produce exemplary teachers and administrators to serve in school systems across the nation, and (3) assist Texas and the nation in using up-to-date knowledge to improve education in diverse settings. The College of Education is a caring community dedicated to preparing action-oriented, problem-solving graduates.

Just the facts...

Texas A&M University
College of Education
College Station, TX 77843-4222
(409) 845-5311
Website: www.coe.tamu.edu
Profile: Rural, Large, Co-Ed
UG Tuition: $36.00/cr. hr. in-state; $249.00/cr. hr. out-of-state
G Tuition: $72.00/cr. hr. in-state; $285.00/cr. hr. out-of-state
Off Campus Programs: No

Clinical Experiences

At the completion of their coursework, teacher candidates complete one semester of student teaching. Student teachers are placed in school districts across the state and have a supervising teacher and university supervisor assigned to them. Some teacher candidates who gain practical experience through one of the College of Education's professional development school partners may elect to complete a paid internship instead of student teaching. The salary is paid by the school district, and the internship is for a full school year.

Noteworthy

The College of Education has its own Office of Scholarships and Recruiting. This office administers the ten financial assistance programs that provide scholarships ranging from $1,000 to $2,000 per year. Some of the scholarships are for education majors in any field, while others are designed for specific fields (such as Math/Science, Health/Kinesiology, etc.). The Office of Scholarships and Recruiting also hosts a summer program, EXCEL, for high school students with an interest in teaching. The program brings high school sophomores to the campus to expose them to the university and to provide them information about teaching opportunities.

Teacher Preparation Program Information

The following programs are 4 year programs:
Early Childhood Education P-6, Elementary Education (English, Geography, Life/Earth Science, Mathematics, Reading, Social Science, Spanish), Elementary Education Self-Contained Classroom 1-6, Elementary Education Self-Contained Classroom 1-8, P-12 Education (Physical Education), Secondary Education 6-12 (Biology, Chemistry, Computer Science, Earth Science, Economics, English, French, Geography, German, Government, History, Journalism, Health, Latin, Life/Earth Science, Mathematics, Physical Education, Physical Science, Physics, Psychology, Russian, Sociology, Spanish, Special Education, Speech Communication, Theater Arts), Special Education P-12

The following programs are post-baccalaureate programs:
Secondary Education (Biology, Chemistry, Computer Science, Earth Science, Economics, English, French, Geography, German, Government, History, Journalism, Health, Latin, Life/Earth Science, Mathematics, Physical Education, Physical Science, Physics, Psychology, Russian, Sociology, Spanish, Special Education, Speech Communication, Theater Arts)

The following programs are 5 year programs:
Generic Special Education K-12

The following programs are 5th year programs:
Generic Special Education K-12

Texas Tech University

The professional education programs at Texas Tech University are based on research and sound professional practice. Teacher education incorporates the following factors: the needs of society, schools, and students, standards and licensure requirements, and the guidelines of subject matter specialty organizations. Graduates are reflective educators who create and disseminate knowledge and serve the profession and society in an informed and professional manner.

Just the facts...

Texas Tech University
College of Education
Box 41071
Lubbock, TX 79409-1071
(806) 742-1837
Website: www.educ.ttu.edu
Profile: Rural, Large, Co-Ed
UG Tuition: $36.00/credit hour
G Tuition: $72.00/credit hour
Off Campus Programs: No

Clinical Experiences

Clinical experiences undergird all professional education programs. Strong professional development school partnerships provide professional development opportunities for preservice teachers, inservice teachers, and teacher educators to come together in dynamic learning communities. Professional education courses for elementary and secondary teacher candidates are field-based, and candidates complete a full fifteen-week semester of student teaching.

Noteworthy

The Teaching Assistant Program provides opportunities for paraprofessionals from local school districts to complete degree and licensure requirements. Post-baccalaureate licensure programs provide opportunities for mid-career individuals interested in teaching. The Dean's Future Scholars program brings sixth grade students to campus to learn about university life and career opportunities. These visits continue through the twelfth grade. Strong collaboration between TTU faculty and K-12 educators make these and other programs possible.

Teacher Preparation Program Information

The following programs are 4 year programs:
Early Childhood Education, Elementary Education, K-12 Education (Art, Music, Physical Education), Secondary Education (Art, Biology, Chemistry, Computer Information Services, Dance, Earth Sciences, Economics, English, English/Language Arts, Exercise & Sports Sciences, French, Geography, German, Government, Health, History, Journalism, Latin, Life/Earth Science, Mathematics, Multidisciplinary Science, Music, Physical Science, Physics, Psychology, Social Studies, Sociology, Spanish, Speech Communication, Theatre Arts, Vocational Agriculture, Vocational Home Econ.), Special Education

The following programs are post-baccalaureate programs:
Early Childhood Education, Elementary Education, K-12 Education (Art, Music, Physical Education), Secondary Education (Art, Biology, Chemistry, Computer Information Services, Dance, Earth Sciences, Economics, English, English/Language Arts, Exercise & Sports Sciences, French, Geography, German, Government, Health, History, Journalism, Latin, Life/Earth Science, Mathematics, Multidisciplinary Science, Music, Physical Science, Physics, Psychology, Social Studies, Sociology, Spanish, Speech Communication, Theatre Arts, Vocational Agriculture, Vocational Home Econ.), Special Education

Trinity University

Trinity University features a five-year teacher preparation program based in five professional development schools. Sixty classroom teachers are appointed to the clinical faculty as mentor teachers. Trinity University's teacher preparation program is designed to prepare teachers who have substantive knowledge in subject matter and pedagogy. Graduates have outstanding backgrounds in the appropriate subject areas, an understanding and appreciation of the developmental needs of the students they will teach, the teaching skills necessary to begin their careers successfully, and a commitment to inquiry, reflection, and growth.

Just the facts...

Trinity University
Department of Education
715 Stadium Drive
San Antonio, TX 78212-7200
(201) 736-7501
Website: www.trinity.edu
Profile: Urban, Small, Co-Ed
UG Tuition: $585.00/credit hour
G Tuition: $585.00/credit hour
Off Campus Programs: No

Clinical Experiences

Teacher preparation at Trinity is field-based, including the fifth-year internship. School site-based practica take place during the sophomore, junior, and senior years. During the internship year, candidates perform an eight-month long, full-time internship in an elementary or secondary school. In addition, the Interns in Teaching also visit a number of local schools that have adopted reform agendas, structures, and/or curricula different from those at the primary placement school.

Noteworthy

Interns in Teaching are supported by regular and ongoing access to faculty from the Department of Education assigned as Clinical Faculty in the professional development schools, substantial scholarship support, and a host of rich professional development opportunities sponsored by the Department of Education. The fifth year of the teacher preparation program seeks a balance between theory, research, and practice. Each fall, Interns in Teaching complete an action-research project, and in the spring, they present a portfolio as a capstone experience.

Teacher Preparation Program Information

The following programs are 5 year programs:

Elementary Education, Secondary Education (Art, Biology, Chemistry, Computer Information Systems, Earth Science, Economics, English, French, Generic Special Education, German, Political Science, History, Journalism, Latin, Life/Earth Sciences, Mathematics, Physical Science, Physics, Psychology, Sociology, Spanish, Speech Communication, Theatre Arts)

University of Houston

The University of Houston is a large, comprehensive, urban institution that prepares professional educators. College of Education faculty are committed to provide learner-centered programs that focus on meeting the educational needs of culturally diverse students in an urban environment. These programs emphasize a continuum of lifelong learning throughout a teacher's career. Candidates learn how to teach through real world experiences in the schools. The program emphasizes opportunities for professional practice.

Just the facts...

University of Houston
College of Education
214 Farish Hall
Houston, TX 77204-5872
(713) 743-5001
Website: www.coe.uh.edu
Profile: Urban, Medium, Co-Ed
UG Tuition: $420.00/sem. in-state; $2,565.00/sem. out-of-state
G Tuition: $420.00/sem. in-state; $2,565.00/sem. out-of-state
Off Campus Programs: No

Clinical Experiences

The Pedagogy for Urban and Multicultural Action Program (PUMA) is field-based, requiring clinical training and field experiences that enable prospective teachers to develop the ability to manage the complex task of teaching in diverse, urban settings. Candidates spend all day, five days a week in P-12 schools for a semester prior to student teaching. This academic year of urban school experience under the direction and guidance of professionals allows candidates to transition from student to professional educator.

Noteworthy

The primary strength of the UH program is its faculty. They are specialists in their areas of expertise who work together to ensure quality education for candidates. A paid graduate teacher internship program is available as an alternative to student teaching for those who qualify. This program operates in collaboration with 31 school districts in the Greater Houston Metropolitan area. In 1990 and 1996, the UH teacher education program received the "Distinguished Program in Teacher Education" national award from the Association of Teacher Educators. Further, the program hosts two nationally recognized Centers of Excellence: the Center for Schoolwide Classroom Management and the Center for Urban Teacher Development.

Teacher Preparation Program Information

The following programs are 4 year programs:
Early Childhood Education, Elementary Education (Bilingual, French, Mathematics, Music, Physical Education, Reading, Social Studies, Spanish), K-12 Education (Art, Music, Physical Education), Secondary Education (Biology, Business, Chemistry, Computer Information Systems, Earth Science, Economics, English/Language Arts, French, German, Health, History, Industrial Technology, Journalism, Latin, Mathematics, Physical Education, Physical Sciences, Physics, Political Science, Psychology, Reading, Science, Social Studies, Sociology, Spanish, Speech/Theatre)

The following programs are post-baccalaureate programs:
Early Childhood Education, Elementary Education (Bilingual, French, Mathematics, Music, Physical Education, Reading, Social Studies, Spanish), K-12 Education (Art, Music, Physical Education), Secondary Education (Biology, Business, Chemistry, Computer Information Systems, Earth Science, Economics, English/Language Arts, French, German, Health, History, Industrial Technology, Journalism, Latin, Mathematics, Physical Education, Physical Sciences, Physics, Political Science, Psychology, Reading, Science, Social Studies, Sociology, Spanish, Speech/Theatre)

The following programs are 5th year programs:
Early Childhood Education, Elementary Education (Bilingual, French, Mathematics, Music, Physical Education, Reading, Social Studies, Spanish), K-12 Education (Art, Music, Physical Education), Secondary Education (Biology, Business, Chemistry, Computer Information Systems, Earth Science, Economics, English/Language Arts, French, German, Health, History, Industrial Technology, Journalism, Latin, Mathematics, Physical Education, Physical Sciences, Physics, Political Science, Psychology, Reading, Science, Social Studies, Sociology, Spanish, Speech/Theatre), Special Education (Early Childhood, Gifted/Talented, Multiple Disabilities/Handicaps)

University of Houston at Clear Lake

Key elements of the learner-centered teacher preparation program at the University of Houston at Clear Lake include quality instruction in content and pedagogy, site-based experiences, and public school teacher mentorship. A distinguishing feature of the program is a year-long internship in a professional development school. In addition, the program places a strong emphasis on field-based courses in which candidates combine university-based instruction with hands-on experience in the public schools. These field-based courses are structured so that the instructor is at the school to provide modeling and mentoring for candidates.

Just the facts...

University of Houston at Clear Lake
School of Education
2700 Bay Area Boulevard
Houston, TX 77058
(281) 283-3501
Website: www.cl.uh.edu
Profile: Suburban, Medium, Co-Ed
UG Tuition: $36.00/cr. hr. in-state; $249.00/cr. hr. out-of-state
G Tuition: $72.00/cr. hr. in-state; $249.00/cr. hr. out-of-state
Off Campus Programs: No

Clinical Experiences

The full year internship at a professional development school (PDS) is designed to provide candidates with hands-on experience related to every aspect of the teaching profession. Internship experiences include individual, small-group, and whole-class instruction as well as exposure to the non-teaching responsibilities of educators. During the first semester of the internship, the candidate is assigned to the PDS for one full day per week. During the second semester of the internship, the candidate is assigned to the same PDS all day, every day. Candidates keep journals in which they reflect on their practice, and complete portfolios during their internship. Journals and portfolios serve as key components for candidates' evaluations.

Noteworthy

In an effort to bring bright, dedicated people into the teaching profession and retain them in local public schools with high needs, UH-Clear Lake has established two exemplary recruitment programs—Galveston Area Teacher Education Recruitment and Retention (GATER) and Baytown Area Recruitment and Retention (BAER). These collaborative efforts provide a step-by-step program of community college preparation, university graduation, and school district experience for potential teachers. Scholarships are available for GATER and BAER participants.

Teacher Preparation Program Information

The following programs are 4 year bachelor degree programs:
Early Childhood Education, Elementary Education (Bilingual, Mathematics, Reading, Science, Social Studies), K-12 Education (Art, ESL), Middle School Education (English, Mathematics, Reading, Science, Social Studies), Secondary Education (Art, Biology, Chemistry, Computer Science, Earth Science, English/Language Arts, Geography, History, Mathematics, Physical Sciences, Physics, Psychology, Reading, Social Studies, Sociology), Special Education (Early Childhood)

The following programs are post-baccalaureate programs:
Early Childhood Education, Elementary Education (Bilingual, Mathematics, Reading, Science, Social Studies), K-12 Education (Art, ESL), Middle School Education (English, Mathematics, Reading, Science, Social Studies), Secondary Education (Art, Biology, Chemistry, Computer Science, Earth Science, English/Language Arts, Geography, Mathematics, Physical Sciences, Physics, Psychology, Reading, Social Studies, Sociology), Special Education (Early Childhood)

The following programs are 5 year programs:
Early Childhood Education, Elementary Education (Bilingual, Mathematics, Reading, Science, Social Studies), K-12 Education (Art, ESL), Middle School Education (English, Mathematics, Reading, Science, Social Studies), Secondary Education (Art, Biology, Chemistry, Computer Science, Earth Science, English/Language Arts, Geography, History, Mathematics, Physical Sciences, Physics, Psychology, Reading, Social Studies, Sociology), Special Education (Early Childhood)

University of North Texas

The educator preparation program at the University of North Texas develops candidates' potential so they may work to improve the quality of education in America's schools. To achieve its purpose, the program responds to the demographic, sociological, and technological changes occurring in the U.S. and in the world, and collaborates with all groups concerned with the education of children. Faculty members use knowledge from research and informed practice to plan, implement, and evaluate the program.

Just the facts...

University of North Texas
College of Education
Box 311337
Denton, TX 76203
(940) 565-2233
Website: www.unt.edu
Profile: Urban, Large, Co-Ed
UG Tuition: $53.75/cr. hr. in-state; $246.00/cr. hr. out-of-state
G Tuition: $79.75/cr. hr. in-state; $272.00/cr. hr. out-of-state
Off Campus Programs: No

Clinical Experiences

Most candidates seeking teacher licensure are required to participate in both a pre-student teaching field experience as well as a culminating student teaching experience that occurs every day for at least twelve weeks. The University of North Texas works with professional development schools (PDS) to provide experiences and opportunities for preservice teachers to prepare them for the classroom. The emphasis of the PDS program is academic, linguistic, and cultural diversity. Candidates spend two semesters in the PDS. The first semester is spent taking professional education courses and gaining field experiences; the second semester allows candidates to plan and implement instruction.

Noteworthy

Seven professional development school sites established within a 40-mile radius of the university offer candidates the opportunity to become part of a learning community that integrates coursework, fieldwork, and teaching experiences. These seven sites range from inner-city urban schools to suburban schools to rural schools, and offer interns a wide variety of diverse experiences.

Teacher Preparation Program Information

The following programs are 4 year programs:
Elementary Education (Biology, Early Childhood, Earth Science, English, French, Generic Special Education, Geography, Health, History, Kinesiology, Mathematics, Music, Reading, Spanish, Speech Communication, Theater Arts), Secondary Education (Biology, Chemistry, Dance, Earth Science, Economics, English, French, Geography, Generic Special Education, German, Government, Health Promotions, History, Journalism, Latin, Life/Earth Sciences, Mathematics, Physics, Psychology, Reading, Sociology, Spanish, Theater Arts)

The following programs are post-baccalaureate programs:
Early Childhood Education, Elementary Education (Reading), K-12 Education (Art, Music, Physical Education), Secondary Education (Biology, Business, Chemistry, Earth Science, Economics, English/Language Arts, General Science, Geography, Health, Mathematics, Physical Education, Physics, Political Science, Psychology, Science, Social Studies, Sociology, Vocational Trade & Industries), Special Education (Early Childhood, Gifted/Talented, Learning Disabilities, Severe Behavior Disorders)

Brigham Young University

Brigham Young University, sponsored by The Church of Jesus Christ of Latter-Day Saints, has prepared teachers and other school personnel since 1876. Within this context, the McKay School of Education strives to serve the needs and mission of the university, its community, public schools, and its sponsoring church. Teacher education programs at BYU are focused on producing teachers who are well grounded in the context of classroom practice in public schools as well as in decision making processes to be able to serve as good citizens and change agents in public school settings.

Just the facts...

Brigham Young University
College of Education
343-E MCKB
Provo, UT 84602
(801) 378-3695
Website: http://mse.byu.edu/mse
Profile: Suburban, Large, Co-Ed
UG Tuition: $1,415.00/Latter-Day Saints (LDS); $2,125.00/non-LDS
G Tuition: $1,665.00/LDS; $2,500.00/non-LDS
Off Campus Programs: No

Clinical Experiences

Candidates in the teacher education program are admitted in cohorts of approximately 30 students for a three-semester, integrated teacher preparation sequence. During the first two semesters of the sequence, candidates are placed in local public schools for practica experiences that relate to university coursework. The third semester involves student teaching. A year-long internship program is an alternative to student teaching. Student teaching sites are available in Mexico, Tonga, Fiji, Samoa, Houston, inner-city Washington D.C., and inner-city Salt Lake City. Five large school districts participating in the BYU-Public School Partnership provide field placements for the majority of BYU teacher candidates.

Noteworthy

BYU has the distinction of creating and maintaining one of the nation's longest standing public school partnerships. BYU's recently established Center for the Improvement of Teacher Education and Schooling (CITES) is intended to provide a setting for stakeholders in teacher education to inquire about, review, and approve teacher education programs in the university as well as major new initiatives undertaken within the public schools.

Teacher Preparation Program Information

The following programs are 4 year programs:
Early Childhood Education, Elementary Education, K-12 Education (Art, Music), Secondary Education (Biology, Chemistry, Chinese, Consumer & Family Science/Home Economics, Dance, Drama/Theater, Economics, English/Language Arts, French, Geography, German, Health, History, Industrial Technology, Japanese, Latin, Mathematics, Physical Education, Physical Sciences, Physics, Political Science, Psychology, Russian, Science/Home Economics, Social Science, Sociology, Spanish), Special Education

452   National Council for Accreditation of Teacher Education

Utah State University

At Utah State University, teacher education is a university-wide responsibility. Twenty-eight departments in eight colleges offer teacher education programs. Candidates are prepared to be specialists rather than generalists, and focus on knowledge of content, knowledge of students, and knowledge of methods. The decentralization of programs enables faculty to provide specialized knowledge for each discipline. All programs reflect the developmental characteristics of students, the specialized knowledge of teaching, and the special needs of each learner.

Just the facts...

Utah State University
College of Education
2800 University Boulevard
Logan, UT 84322-2800
(435) 797-1437
Website: www.coe.usu.edu
Profile: Large, Suburban, Co-Ed
UG Tuition: $261.56/cr. hr. in-state; $660.62/cr. hr. out-of-state
G Tuition: $277.49/cr. hr. in-state; 716.39/cr. hr. out-of-state
Cost per credit hour decreases as number of credits taken increases
Off Campus Programs: Yes

Clinical Experiences

All programs leading toward licensure require extensive clinical experiences. Elementary education candidates complete approximately 400 hours of clinical experience prior to student teaching. Secondary education candidates complete 120 hours of clinical experience prior to student teaching. Special education candidates gain 150 to 300 hours of clinical experience depending on their specialization. Student teaching varies from ten to fifteen weeks full-time. Candidates are assigned to specific teachers, most of whom have received special preparation in working with candidates.

Noteworthy

Departments integrate technology into all experiences. Candidates use state-of-the-art technology as they learn both content and pedagogy. Classrooms are equipped with the latest technology. Technology centers are available for candidates' use as they prepare for clinical experiences and courses. All departments provide early and graduated field experiences in which candidates apply pedagogical methods and techniques. These clinical experiences are closely linked to each departments' university coursework. All departments also have professional undergraduate advisement centers. These centers provide students with immediate assistance with any advisement concerns.

Teacher Preparation Program Information

The following programs are 4 year programs:
Early Childhood Education, Elementary Education (Art, Fine Arts, Foreign Language, Health/Wellness/Nutrition, Language Arts, Mathematics, Music, Physical Education, Science, Social Studies), K-12 Education (Art, Music, Physical Education, Dual Certification with Special Education or Communicative Disorders), Secondary Education (Agriculture, Art, Biology, Business, Chemistry, Earth Science, English, Family & Consumer Sciences, Geography, Health, History, Industrial, Mathematics, Marketing, Modern Languages, Music, Physical Education, Physical Sciences, Psychology, Social Studies, Sociology, Theater Arts, Dual Certification with Special Education)

The following programs are post-baccalaureate programs:
Early Childhood Education, Elementary Education (Gifted/Talented, Reading), Middle School Education, Special Education (Early Childhood, Mild/Moderate Disabilities, Vision and Hearing Impaired)

The following programs are 5 year programs:
Communication Disorders and Deaf Education (Education for the Deaf and Hard of Hearing)

Weber State University

Weber State University's Department of Teacher Education prepares effective educators for a changing, global society. The department produces graduates who are skilled at reflecting on teaching practices in light of their effectiveness, engaging every student in meaningful learning experiences, and collaborating with other professionals to those ends. The department offers a range of initial and advanced educator preparation degrees, as well as endorsement programs that extend candidates' basic preparation. Undergirding these programs is a first-rate faculty, the most diverse in terms of women and minority representation in the state. The department also provides opportunities for continued professional development.

Just the facts...

Weber State University
Department of Teacher Education
Mail Code 1304
Ogden, UT 84408-1304
(801) 626-7171
Website: www.weber.edu
Profile: Urban, Large, Co-Ed
UG Tuition: $993.00/sem. in-state; $2,943.00/sem. out-of-state
G Tuition: $1,071.00/sem. in-state; $3,216.00/sem. out-of-state
Off Campus Programs: No

Clinical Experiences

The education program is organized into levels. Candidates pass sequentially from the first level (observing and tutoring) through the final level (student teaching). Clinical instructors integrate content so that candidates experience the connection between theory and practice and are able to almost immediately apply what they have learned in a school setting. Many clinical experiences are offered at diverse schools where professional teachers and course instructors are able to model effective teaching strategies.

Noteworthy

Weber State University's teacher education program emphasizes collaboration among faculty and candidates. Courses are taught by regular faculty who have extensive elementary and secondary experience, and who hold leadership positions in many professional organizations. Admission is highly competitive, and graduates are sought after by local and out-of-state recruiters. Weber State University calls its teacher education program a practitioners' program; candidates learn to teach, and the focus is on performance. The department's partnerships and local service projects include the Storytelling Festival, Literacy Project Alliance, Technology Mentor Teacher program, and Elementary Science/Math Mentors project.

Teacher Preparation Program Information

The following programs are 4 year programs:

Early Childhood Education, Elementary Education (Mathematics), K-12 Education (Drama/Theater, ESL, French, German, Music, Spanish), Secondary Education (Art, Biology, Business, Chemistry, Communication, Earth Science, English/Language Arts, Geography, History, Mathematics, Physical Education, Physical Sciences, Physics, Political Science, Psychology, Social Studies, Sociology), Special Education

University of Vermont

The College of Education and Social Services at the University of Vermont grew from a department of education in the late 1960s to the comprehensive professional school of today. It prepares outstanding professionals in education, social work, and human services and engages in high quality scholarship. The ultimate purpose of the work of the college is to create a more humane and just society, free from oppression, that fosters respect for ethnic and cultural diversity, and maximizes human potential and the quality of life for all individuals, families, and communities.

Just the facts...

University of Vermont
College of Education and Social Services
309 Waterman Building
Burlington, VT 05405
(802) 656-3424
Website: www.uvm.edu/~cess
Profile: Rural, Medium, Co-Ed
UG Tuition: $302.00/cr. hr. in-state; $755.00/cr. hr. out-of-state
G Tuition: $302.00/cr. hr. in-state; $755.00/cr. hr. out-of-state
Off Campus Programs: Yes

Clinical Experiences

Clinical experiences begin with the introduction to the professional program and continue throughout the four undergraduate years, culminating with a semester-long internship. Graduate teacher interns complete a full year of clinical experience at a professional development site, where professional courses and research projects are integrated with observation, tutorials, and teaching. In all programs, the College of Education and Social Services gradually introduces new teacher candidates to the real world of the public schools and communities, and gives them greater responsibility as they progress in their programs. Teams of university and school or agency personnel mentor the candidates.

Noteworthy

The College of Education and Social Services is developing four goals that are designed to prepare faculty and candidates for the next century. These goals include the development of multicultural education, technology integration, professional development for teachers and administrators who are in the schools, and the collaboration of social workers, teachers, physicians, and others for the well-being of children. The College of Education and Social Services is working with communities to provide scholarship support to teachers with diverse cultural backgrounds. Grants that support technology enable faculty to work with students in rural and urban areas through computer-based instruction and distance learning.

Teacher Preparation Program Information

The following programs are 4 year programs:
Early Childhood Education (Pre-K through Grade 3), Elementary Education, K-12 Education (Art, Music, Physical Education), Kindergarten Education, Secondary Education (Art, Biology, Chemistry, Consumer & Family Science/Home Economics, Earth Science, English/Language Arts, General Science, Geography, Mathematics, Physical Education, Physics, Political Science, Science, Social Studies)

The following programs are post-baccalaureate programs:
Elementary Education, K-12 Education (Art, Music, Physical Education)

The following programs are 5th year programs:
Secondary Education (Art, Biology, Chemistry, Consumer & Family Science/Home Economics, Earth Science, English/Language Arts, General Science, Geography, Mathematics, Physical Education, Physics, Political Science, Science, Social Studies)

College of William and Mary

The College of William and Mary is the second-oldest institution of higher learning in the U.S. Now in its fourth century, it continues its tradition of excellence by combining the best features of an undergraduate college with the opportunities offered by a modern research university. Its moderate size, dedicated faculty, and distinctive history give William and Mary a unique character among public institutions, and create a learning environment that fosters close interaction among students and teachers. The School of Education's goal is to prepare teachers to become reflective practitioners. Undergraduate and graduate education programs provide individuals with a strong liberal arts education.

Just the facts...

The College of William and Mary
School of Education
P.O. Box 8795
Williamsburg, VA 23185
(757) 221-2315
Website: www.wm.edu/education
Profile: Medium, Suburban, Co-Ed
UG Tuition: $2,890.00/sem. in-state; $13,820.00/sem. out-of-state
G Tuition: $2,974.00/sem. in-state; $13,820.00/sem. out-of-state
Off Campus Programs: No

Clinical Experiences

Clinical experiences begin with a broad focus on the school, classroom, and student, and gradually progress to more in-depth responsibilities. Programs in elementary, secondary, and special education also enable candidates to work with a team of teachers and college faculty during their year-long practicum. Candidates participate in field experiences in a variety of settings that include urban, suburban, and rural school districts. These districts contain diverse student populations in terms of socioeconomic status, race, and ethnic background. With a growing emphasis on multiculturalism in teacher preparation programs, these settings are especially important for William and Mary teacher candidates.

Noteworthy

The School of Education annually funds graduate assistantship support for approximately 100 students. These assistantships pay for tuition and fees and provide additional stipend support for recipients. Graduate assistants serve as research and teaching assistants and work in a host of university administrative, academic, and school district offices. Recently, additional assistantships have become available to assist the college's support of the national America Reads program. Assistantships also aid the School of Education's emphasis on infusing technology throughout the curriculum and expand clinical faculty/professional development partnerships.

Teacher Preparation Program Information

The following programs are 4 year programs:

Elementary Education/P-6, P-12 Education (Physical Education), Secondary Education/6-12 (Biology, Chemistry, Earth and Space Science, English, French, German, History, Latin, Mathematics, Physics, Political Science, Social Studies, Spanish)

The following programs are 5th year programs:

Elementary Education/P-6, Secondary Education/6-12 (Biology, Chemistry, Earth and Space Science, English, French, German, History, Latin, Mathematics, Physics, Political Science, Social Studies, Spanish), Special Education (Emotional Disturbance, Learning Disabilities, Mental Retardation)

Eastern Mennonite University

The Education Department at Eastern Mennonite University has prepared teachers since 1948. Approximately eighteen percent of all EMU undergraduates are licensed to teach. The teacher education program prepares reflective teachers who are advocates for children and youth, create a climate of caring and learning, initiate and respond to change, and value service to others. Teacher candidates participate in a cross-cultural experience either abroad or stateside during their studies. Candidates are prepared to live and teach in an everchanging and interdependent world, and have developed an understanding of cultural and religious heritages, personal faith, and cross-cultural understanding.

Just the facts...

Eastern Mennonite University
Teacher Education
1200 Park Road
Harrisonburg, VA 22802-2462
(540) 432-4142
Website: www.emu.edu
Profile: Rural, Medium, Co-Ed
UG Tuition: $6,300.00/semester
Off Campus Programs: Yes

Clinical Experiences

Teacher education at Eastern Mennonite University strives to help candidates make meaningful connections between theory and practice. Candidates participate in carefully arranged field-based experiences beginning in the first year and culminating in the senior year with student teaching. Experiences emphasize caring relationships, assertive but cooperative classroom management practices, peace and justice issues, and the integration of ethics with professional competency. EMU participates in the Mid-Valley Consortium for Teacher Education, a clinical faculty program in partnership with six school districts, two other liberal arts colleges, and a regional university to strengthen the preparation of student teachers.

Noteworthy

In 1986 Eastern Mennonite University established the Jesse T. Byler Endowment for education. The endowment supports scholarships, faculty development, and resources for the Education Department. Candidates major in an Arts and Sciences discipline and are required to study in a cross-cultural setting abroad or stateside. The faculty emphasize a reflective teaching model informed by constructivist theory. Candidates in the program examine their assumptions about teaching and learning in an environment of inquiry and collaboration. The department is an active partner in the Mid-Valley Clinical Faculty Consortium which is comprised of six school districts and three other institutions of higher education.

Teacher Preparation Program Information

The following programs are 4 year programs:

Early Childhood Education, Elementary Education (Elementary Education K-6), K-12 Education (French, German, Music, Physical Education/Health, Spanish), Secondary Education (Biology, Chemistry, English/Language Arts, History, Mathematics, Social Science), Special Education (Learning Disabled/Emotionally Disabled, Learning Disabled/Mental Retardation, Mental Retardation/Emotionally Disabled)

George Mason University

The professional education faculty at George Mason University seek to prepare educators who are reflective practitioners. The programs are based on helping teachers determine the needs of their students and helping them to create productive classrooms. Candidates learn developmentally appropriate practice, which includes knowledge of multiple intelligences and learning styles. Candidates understand the need to adapt instructional methods to meet individual needs.

Just the facts...

George Mason University
Graduate School of Education
4400 University Drive
Fairfax, VA 22030-4444
(703) 993-2004
Website: www.gmu.edu
Profile: Urban, Large, Co-Ed
UG Tuition: $175.50/cr. hr. in-state; $483.50/cr. hr. out-of-state
G Tuition: $175.50/cr. hr. in-state; $483.50/cr. hr. out-of-state
Off Campus Programs: Yes

Clinical Experiences

George Mason University enjoys uniquely strong relationships with local school divisions. Clinical experiences are conducted in professional development schools that capture the diversity of the region. Teachers in the local schools who work with George Mason teacher candidates enjoy the role of clinical faculty at the university. They participate in the design and development of the education programs, thereby assuring a close link between the campus and the field.

Noteworthy

Teacher education is conducted at the graduate level only. All applicants must have earned a bachelor's degree from an accredited college or university to be eligible for admission. The program is an intensive study of professional education conducted in partnership with local school divisions. This approach places George Mason candidates in the field early and develops a strong identity with practice in the field. Beginning in summer 1999, George Mason began a new post-licensure program for practicing teachers who want to prepare for certification by the National Board for Professional Teaching Standards.

Teacher Preparation Program Information

The following programs are 5th year programs:

Early Childhood Education, Elementary Education, K-12 Education (ESL, French, German, Latin, Russian, Spanish), Middle School Education (English, Mathematics, Science, Social Studies), Secondary Education (Biology, Chemistry, Economics, English/Language Arts, General Science, Mathematics, Physics, Psychology, Social Studies, Sociology), Special Education (Early Childhood, Learning Disability, Severe Behavioral Disabilities/Handicaps)

Hampton University

Hampton University's Division of Education trains teachers to be collaborative, reflective leaders in the nation's schools. Each candidate in the program must have an above average GPA in order to enter and complete the Master's degree programs offered by the department. The degrees offered are a Masters in Teaching (an initial licensure degree), a Masters of Arts in Elementary Education, and a Masters of Arts in Special Education. Candidates in the Masters in Teaching program have the option to select from academic majors in the Schools of Science and Liberal Arts and Education and are prepared to teach at the elementary, middle, and secondary levels in regular or special education settings.

Clinical Experiences

Clinical experiences begin in the sophomore year and continue each semester of the candidate's undergraduate years. The clinical experiences culminate in student teaching during the final semester of the fifth year. The experiences include visits to school board meetings and city council meetings, case studies, observation and participation in appropriate class settings, directed practica, and student teaching.

Just the facts...

Hampton University
Division of Education
Hampton, VA 23668
(757) 727-5401
Website: www.hamptonu.edu
Profile: Urban, Medium, Co-Ed
UG Tuition: $3,580.00/semester
G Tuition: $3,580.00/semester
Off Campus Programs: No

Noteworthy

The Division of Education has been awarded grants in the areas of personnel preparation, minority preparation, and science learning for teacher education. Candidates can compete for Virginia State Scholarship loans and other scholarships. Hampton's teacher candidates are consistently honored for their excellent scholastic accomplishments and are highly recruited nationally due to their excellent preparation as teachers. Candidates often have contracts prior to completing their student teaching, teach throughout the state of Virginia, and in several other states as well.

Teacher Preparation Program Information

The following programs are 4 year programs:
K-12 Education (Physical Education), Special Education (Speech/Language Disabilities)

The following programs are 5 year programs:
Early Childhood Education, Elementary Education, Middle School Education (English, Mathematics, Science), Secondary Education (Biology, Computer Science, English/Language Arts, History, Mathematics, Political Science, Sociology), Special Education (Learning Disability, Severe Behavioral Disabilities/Handicaps)

James Madison University

James Madison University has prepared educators since its founding in 1908. Programs are located in all five academic colleges of the university. The mission of the teacher education program at James Madison University is to prepare qualified professionals for educational roles in P-12 schools and in business and organizational settings; contribute to the expanding knowledge bases of teaching and learning; and serve as a resource to the educational community.

Just the facts...

James Madison University
College of Education & Psychology
Maury Hall
Harrisonburg, VA 22807
(540) 568-6572
Website: www.jmu.edu
Profile: Rural, Medium, Co-Ed
UG Tuition: $2,128.00/sem. in-state; $4,628.00/sem. out-of-state
G Tuition: $134.00/cr. hr. in-state; $404.00/cr. hr. out-of-state
Off Campus Programs: No

Clinical Experiences

All professional programs have carefully integrated and sequenced field experiences leading to a twelve to sixteen week student teaching experience or internship (one semester to one year). University and P-12 faculty are involved in collaborative program decision making, delivery of the curriculum, and evaluation. Formal university-school partnership programs are an exemplary component of James Madison's programs. Field placements are made with careful attention to program knowledge base, diversity of student populations, and preservice candidates' needs.

Noteworthy

James Madison University is rated among the nation's best colleges and universities in national listings. The unique and effective collaboration of education and arts and sciences faculty, the institutional commitment to quality teacher education programs, cooperative efforts of the university and P-12 faculty, and the high quality of instruction are all notable aspects of James Madison's teacher preparation programs. The university is a leader in technology (one of the most "wired" institutions). Numerous scholarships are available for upper division students.

Teacher Preparation Program Information

The following programs are 4 year programs:
Early Childhood Education (P-3), P-12 Education (Art, ESL, Music, Physical Education/Health), Middle School Education (4-8), Secondary Education (Biology, Business & Marketing, Chemistry, Earth Science, Economics, English/Language Arts, Foreign Languages, General Science, Geography, History, Mathematics, Physical Sciences, Physics, Political Science, Social Studies, Technology), Special Education (K-12 Mild Disabilities)

The following programs are post-baccalaureate programs:
Early Childhood Education (P-3), P-12 Education (Art, ESL, Music, Physical Education/Health), Middle School Education (4-8), Secondary Education (Biology, Business & Marketing, Chemistry, Earth Science, Economics, English/Language Arts, Foreign Languages, General Science, Geography, History, Mathematics, Physical Sciences, Physics, Political Science, Social Studies, Technology), Special Education (K-12 Mild Disabilities)

Longwood College

Longwood College, founded in 1839, is a comprehensive college offering programs leading to bachelor's and master's degrees. Since 1916, Longwood College has provided leadership in the public schools of Virginia. The School of Education and Human Services is committed to the training of teachers as leaders in the classroom, school, and community. Longwood's Student Development Goals include intellectual goals (the mastery of a broad body of knowledge in the liberal arts and sciences, and of a specialized body of knowledge in the major discipline), personal goals (a sense of personal direction and a balanced, healthy lifestyle), and social goals (interpersonal effectiveness and responsible citizenship).

Just the facts...

Longwood College
School of Education & Human Services
201 High Street
Farmville, VA 23909
(804) 395-2051
Website: www.lwc.edu
Profile: Rural, Small, Co-Ed
UG Tuition: $1,301.00/sem. in-state; $3,960.00/sem. out-of-state
G Tuition: $1,301.00/sem. in-state; $3,960.00/sem. out-of-state
Off Campus Programs: Yes

Clinical Experiences

Candidates in teacher education at Longwood participate in two early field experiences designed to give candidates the ability to observe and participate in the public school classroom as well as opportunities to teach and evaluate learning. The professional semester and the two practica may take place in a variety of public school settings around the state of Virginia and abroad, with opportunities in England, Ireland, Honduras, and other international settings.

Noteworthy

Longwood College offers numerous scholarship opportunities for candidates entering the teacher preparation program. Currently, graduate programs in education and special education are being developed using distance learning technology. Educators in other states and countries will be able to earn the master's degree from Longwood College.

Teacher Preparation Program Information

The following programs are 4 year programs:
Elementary Education, K-12 Education (Art, French, German, Spanish, Physical Education), Secondary Education (Biology, Chemistry, English/Language Arts, History, Mathematics, Physics, Political Science, Theatre)

The following programs are 5 year programs:
Special Education (Mild Disabilities)

Marymount University

Marymount University has had a tradition of preparing competent and caring teachers since 1974. The mission of the School of Education is to foster excellence by preparing teacher and counselor candidates with a mastery of content and skills, with moral and social values, and with positive attitudes that are reflected in competent, effective, and successful school practices. Education programs are designed to prepare dedicated and caring teachers and counselors with a strong research base, practical methodology, and extensive field experiences. Successful graduates diligently and creatively meet the needs of students with diverse abilities.

Just the facts...

Marymount University
School of Education
2807 North Glebe Road
Arlington, VA 22207-4299
(703) 284-1620
Website: www.marymount.edu
Profile: Suburban, Medium, Co-Ed
UG Tuition: $435.00/credit hour
G Tuition: $465.00/credit hour
Off Campus Programs: Yes

Clinical Experiences

Marymount's teacher candidates have ample opportunities to practice their teaching skills through a variety of supervised field experiences, internships, and student teaching. Field experiences are required in each methods course as candidates draw from their own classroom experiences, construct their own professional knowledge, and bridge the gap between theory and practice. In the P-8 program, student teaching is a twelve-week experience. Secondary candidates student teach for ten weeks.

Noteworthy

Five years ago Marymount formed a partnership with Fairfax County Public Schools to create the Professional Development Academy at Sunrise Valley Elementary School in Reston. For three years, cohorts of sixteen interns completed their M.Ed. in elementary education while working a full school year with children in the classroom. Last year the cohort was enlarged to 23 and a second site, Graham Road Elementary, was added. A new business partner, AT&T, provided the technology to deliver instruction via distance learning. Marymount recently signed a cooperative agreement with Arlington Public Schools to create a professional development school at Washington-Lee High School.

Teacher Preparation Program Information

The following programs are 4 year programs:
K-12 Education (Art), Secondary Education (Biology, Computer Science, English, Mathematics, Social Science)

The following programs are 5 year programs:
Elementary Education (P-8), Secondary Education (English/Language Arts)

The following programs are 5th year programs:
Elementary Education (P-8), K-12 Education (ESL, Learning Disabilities), Secondary Education (Biology, Computer Science, Earth Science, English, General Science, Mathematics, Physics, Social Science)

Norfolk State University

Norfolk State University offers fifteen undergraduate and six graduate degree programs to prospective teachers, in-service teachers, administrators, and others engaged in educational activities. Knowledge, skills, and attitudes taught in these programs support the theme of educators as caring, competent, cooperative, and creative team members. The faculty in the School of Education is diverse and is committed to preparing teachers and administrators to meet the needs of diverse students, to work effectively in a technological and global society, to provide leadership in schools and communities, and to promote educational equity for all children.

Just the facts...

Norfolk State University
School of Education
2401 Corprew Avenue
Norfolk, VA 23504
(757) 683-9583
Website: www.nsu.edu
Profile: Urban, Large, Co-Ed
UG Tuition: $1,391.00/sem. in-state; $3,138.00/sem. out-of-state
G Tuition: $1,391.00/sem. in-state; $3,138.00/sem. out-of-state
Off Campus Programs: No

Clinical Experiences

Clinical experiences begin with the first course in the professional education sequence and enable candidates to move toward increased responsibility for classroom instruction or other professional roles in school. The experiences are varied, comprising hands-on observation and participation in K-12 classrooms, supervised volunteer and service learning experiences in the community, directed teaching, practica, and internships.

Noteworthy

The School of Education provides several resources for teacher candidates. The Integrated Media/Resources Center provides multicultural resources, instructional materials, and instructional media and technology appropriate for students in preschool to students in adult education. The Learning Center provides meaningful activities for the children of students attending evening classes. Scholarships, mentoring, and peer tutoring are available. In addition, the program prepares teachers for the urban classroom and provides early childhood educators with special assistance in teaching mathematics.

Teacher Preparation Program Information

The following programs are 4 year programs:
Early Childhood Education, K-12 Education (Art, French, Spanish, Music, Physical Education), Secondary Education (Art, Biology, Business, Chemistry, Consumer & Family Science/Home Econ., English/Language Arts, Health, Mathematics, Physical Education, Physical Sciences, Physics, Social Studies, Vocational Trade & Industrial), Special Education (Emotionally Disturbed, Learning Disability, Mental Retardation)

The following programs are post-baccalaureate programs:
Early Childhood Education, K-12 Education (Art, French, Spanish, Music), Secondary Education (English/Language Arts, Mathematics, Physics, Social Studies), Special Education (Emotionally Disturbed, Learning Disability, Mental Retardation, Severe Disabilities)

The following programs are 5th year programs:
Early Childhood Education, K-12 Education (Art), Secondary Education (Art, Biology, Chemistry, English/Language Arts, Mathematics, Physical Sciences, Physics, Social Studies, Vocational Trade & Industrial), Special Education (Gifted/Talented, Severe Disabilities)

Old Dominion University

Teacher preparation programs at Old Dominion University focus on candidate competence in the following areas: subject matter; preparing and presenting instruction; diagnosing and evaluating student achievement and learning styles; recognizing individual differences with respect to exceptionalities and multiculturalism; implementing a sound philosophy of education; and building and maintaining an effective classroom environment. All teacher candidates complete academic bachelor's degrees in a content area as well as coursework in education.

Just the facts...

Old Dominion University
Darden College of Education
Education Building, Room 120
Norfolk, VA 23529-0156
(757) 683-3777
Website: www.odu.edu
Profile: Urban, Medium, Co-Ed
UG Tuition: $140.00/cr. hr. in-state; $335.00/cr. hr. out-of-state
G Tuition: $140.00/cr. hr. in-state; $335.00/cr. hr. out-of-state
Off Campus Programs: Yes

Clinical Experiences

Prospective teachers participate in three clinical experiences: observation and participation, practicum, and student teaching. In addition, on-site teacher education courses are co-taught by university and school faculty at professional development schools in Norfolk. A tutorial program (from America Reads) is available for teacher candidates; it provides reading reinforcement for P-12 students attending the professional development schools. Student teaching opportunities have expanded internationally with sites in England, Germany, and the Czech Republic.

Noteworthy

The Darden College of Education has equipped three state-of-the-art computer labs for training teacher candidates not only to be highly proficient in their use of technology, but also to learn how to integrate technology into curricula and instructional design. Through the use of distance learning technology, candidates at 28 sites across Virginia may complete requirements for a B.S. in Interdisciplinary Studies and a M.S. Ed. in Elementary/Middle School Education (fifth-year program with endorsements in mathematics and science), as well as requirements for a M.S. Ed. in Special Education.

Teacher Preparation Program Information

The following programs are 4 year programs:
K-12 Education (Dance, Drama/Theater, Industrial Technology, Music), Secondary Education (Art, Biology, Chemistry, Earth Science, English/Language Arts, Mathematics, Physical Education, Physical Sciences, Physics, Social Studies, Vocational Marketing, Vocational Trade & Industrial)

The following programs are post-baccalaureate programs:
K-12 Education (Dance, Drama/Theater, Industrial Technology, Music), Secondary Education (Art, Biology, Chemistry, Earth Science, English/Language Arts, Mathematics, Physical Education, Physical Sciences, Physics, Social Studies, Vocational Marketing, Vocational Trade & Industrial)

The following programs are 5 year programs:
Middle School Education

The following programs are 5th year programs:
Early Childhood Education, K-12 Education (Industrial Technology), Special Education

Radford University

Radford University is a coeducational institution founded in 1910 that offers more than 140 undergraduate and graduate degrees. Approximately 8,500 students are enrolled at the university. As part of its mission, Radford emphasizes teaching and learning as well as commitment to the development of mature, responsible, well-educated citizens. Toward this end, the university is student-focused and promotes caring and meaningful interaction among all members of the university community.

Just the facts...

Radford University
College of Education
P.O. Box 6960
Radford, VA 24142
(540) 831-5439
Website: www.runet.edu
Profile: Rural, Small, Co-Ed
UG Tuition: $1,619.00/sem. in-state; $4,100.00/sem. out-of-state
G Tuition: $1,796.00/sem. in-state; $3,530.00/sem. out-of-state
Off Campus Programs: No

Clinical Experiences

Teacher preparation programs are field-based and employ small cohorts for instruction. All cohort groups are specific to subject matter and developmental level, and consist of 15 to 23 candidates. For example, Radford usually schedules five cohort groups of elementary education candidates each semester. Each cohort is assigned to a school, and candidates go to that school every morning for a semester. Candidates return to class in the afternoon for a sequence of courses designed to prepare them to teach in the elementary school. Each cohort is staffed by a team of three faculty. During this semester, candidates accumulate 250 to 300 hours of supervised experience which prepares them for a semester of student teaching.

Noteworthy

Teacher education programs at Radford University are based on a four year model, featuring small classes (cohort groups) and multiple field-based components. Radford's programs—taught by regular faculty, not graduate students—assure a blend of theory and practice that produces knowledgeable, thoughtful, skilled, and culturally competent practitioners. To assure that prospective teachers know what they will be teaching, all teacher education candidates at Radford must matriculate in an academic major, and complete a strong general education component in addition to their teacher preparation program.

Teacher Preparation Program Information

The following programs are 4 year programs:
Elementary Education (Elementary Education K-5), K-12 Education (Art, French, German, Latin, Music, Physical Education/Health, Spanish), Middle School Education, Secondary Education (Biology, Business, Chemistry, Earth Science, English/Language Arts, Mathematics, Physical Education, Physical Sciences, Science, Social Studies), Special Education (Mental Retardation)

The following programs are post-baccalaureate programs:
Secondary Education (Business, Biology, Chemistry, Earth Science, English, Foreign Languages, Mathematics, Physical Science, Social Studies), Special Education (Emotional and Learning Disabilities)

The following programs are 5 year programs:
Communication Science & Disorders

University of Virginia

The Curry School of Education at the University of Virginia has a dual mission: to prepare personnel to work in America's education system (pre-kindergarten through collegiate levels) and to enhance teaching performance by preparing professionals and conducting research in related fields. The five-year teacher preparation program leads to either a Bachelor of Arts and a Master of Teaching degree in elementary, secondary, or special education, or a Bachelor of Science in Education and a Master of Teaching in physical education/health. The undergraduate program also includes studies in sports medicine and communication disorders. Technology and diversity are emphasized in all programs.

Just the facts...

University of Virginia
School of Education
Ruffner Hall
405 Emmet Street, South
Charlottesville, VA 22903-2495
(804) 924-3332
Website: http://curry.edschool.virginia.edu
Profile: Suburban, Large, Co-Ed
UG Tuition: $2,433.00/sem. in-state; $7,907.00/sem. out-of-state
G Tuition: $2,433.00/sem. in-state; $7,907.00/sem. out-of-state
Off Campus Programs: Yes

Clinical Experiences

All programs have a strong and consistent clinical component. Teacher candidates are involved in rich clinical experiences throughout their teacher preparation program, including observation, tutoring, and small and large group instruction. Numerous hands-on assignments in a variety of settings, integrated with concurrent courses, occur each semester preceding an all-day, full-semester teaching associateship in the first semester of the fifth year. Candidates are closely supervised by a clinical instructor and a university faculty member.

Noteworthy

The Curry School is nationally ranked among the top twenty schools of education and the special education program is ranked fifth in the nation. The exemplary use of technology in the program received the first Best Practice Award from the Anerican Association of Colleges for Teacher Education in 1998. Faculty hold offices in professional organizations, are scholars of international renown, and are numbered among the university's finest teachers. UVA students score well above the national average on the SAT. The highly competitive education program focuses on developing future education leaders in the classroom, in administration positions, and in research, technology, and innovative practice.

Teacher Preparation Program Information

The following programs are 5 year programs:
Elementary Education , P-12 Education (Foreign Language Education, Physical/Health Education), Secondary Education (English, History, Mathematics, Science), Special Education P-12 (Behavioral/Emotional Disorders, Learning Disabilities, Mild Mental Handicaps)

The following programs are 5th year programs:
These programs may take more than one year to complete: Elementary Education, Physical Education/Health, Secondary Education, Special Education (Behavioral/Emotional Disorders, Learning Disabilities, Mild Mental Handicaps)

Virginia Commonwealth University

The primary goal of the School of Education is the preparation of quality teachers for schools in Virginia and the nation. The Extended Degree Program is based on the belief that a teacher should be liberally educated, develop a thorough grasp of at least one academic discipline, and master pedagogy so that knowledge can be taught effectively. Candidates interested in teaching early, middle, secondary, and special education complete a program integrating liberal arts and sciences with professional studies, typically over a period of five years. Candidates are assigned two faculty advisors—one in the School of Education and one in the College of Humanities and Sciences.

Just the facts...

Virginia Commonwealth University
School of Education
Box 2020, Oliver Hall - South
1015 West Main Street
Richmond, VA 23284-2020
(804) 828-3382
Website: www.vcu.edu/eduweb
Profile: Urban, Medium, Co-Ed
UG Tuition: $1,957.00/sem. in-state; $5,548.50/sem. out-of-state
G Tuition: $1,957.00/sem. in-state; $5,548.50/sem. out-of-state
Off Campus Programs: Yes

Clinical Experiences

Clinical experiences are an essential component of the teacher preparation program, allowing candidates to put theory into practice in school classrooms under the supervision of a qualified professional. Depending on the program, candidates select to participate in two settings, including urban, suburban, or rural sites. Each candidate has the guidance and support of clinical faculty or cooperating teachers as well as a VCU faculty supervisor in practica, student teaching, and internship experiences. Through clinical experiences, prospective teachers develop expertise in working with students from different cultural backgrounds and with different learning styles and needs.

Noteworthy

Professional development schools provide opportunities for practica, internships, coursework, clinical faculty training, and summer workshops, as well as collaborative research. The School of Education maintains two state-of-the-art computer labs for student and faculty use. The Virginia Technology Standards are incorporated into the teacher preparation program, ensuring that candidates receive instruction in the effective use and applications of education technology. A grant from the National Science Foundation helps the School of Education and the Department of Mathematical Sciences strengthen the math and science preparation of elementary and middle school teachers.

Teacher Preparation Program Information

The following programs are 4 year programs:
K-12 Education (Art, Health and Physical Education, Music), Grades 6-12 Education (Theater)

The following programs are post-baccalaureate programs:
K-12 Education (ESL, Speech)

The following programs are 5 year combined programs:
Elementary Education, Middle School Education (English, Mathematics, Science, Social Studies), Secondary Education, Special Education (Emotional Disturbance and Mental Retardation)

The following programs are 5th year programs:
Special Education (Learning Disabilities)

Virginia Polytechnic Institute and State University

Virginia Tech has prepared teachers and other school personnel since 1971. Faculty, administration, and staff in professional education programs at Virginia Tech are committed to building and sustaining intellectually and morally sound programs that encompass an inquiry-based approach to teaching and learning. Programs incorporate multicultual perspectives in the curriculum, provide opportunities for learning in diverse settings, and infuse technology to enhance instruction. Theoretical and practical experiences are integrated and continuously assessed to provide dynamic, research-based programs.

Just the facts...

Virginia Polytechnic Institute & State University
College of Human Resources and Education
260 Wallace Hall
Blacksburg, VA 24061-0426
(540) 231-6779
Website: www.vt.edu
Profile: Rural, Large, Co-Ed
UG Tuition: $1,750.00/sem. in-state; $5,358.00/sem. out-of-state
G Tuition: $2,061.00/sem. in-state; $3,366.00/sem. out-of-state
Off Campus Programs: Yes

Clinical Experiences

Virginia Tech requires clinical experiences for undergraduate and graduate professional education programs. Both the elementary education five-year graduate P-6 and the fifth year graduate K-8 programs provide early field experiences culminating with a year-long student teaching experience. Secondary education programs and health/physical education programs (6-12) have early field as well as comprehensive student teaching experiences. Advanced programs in counselor education, principal preparation, and special education administration involve candidates in internships and field experiences in carefully chosen sites.

Noteworthy

Virginia Tech offers minority scholarships in the College of Human Resources and Education. Professional education programs include a distance education master's program for health and physical education teachers and a master's program in math/science that emphasizes technology and prepares individuals in career transition to become licensed sixth through twelfth grade teachers. A course designed to address the needs of diverse learner populations is required for all program areas. The program emphasizes close collaboration with schools, school systems, and community, state, and national agencies. Candidates demonstrate their learning and performance through portfolio assessment.

Teacher Preparation Program Information

The following programs are 4 year programs:

K-12 Education (ESL, French, German, Latin, Music, Physical Education/Health), Secondary Education/Grades 6-12 (Agriculture, Business, Chemistry, Consumer & Family Science/Home Economics, Mathematics, Technology Education, Vocational Marketing, Vocational Trade & Industrial)

The following programs are 5 year programs:

Elementary Education P-6

The following programs are 5th year programs:

Elementary Education K-8, Secondary Education (Biology, Chemistry, Earth Science, English/Language Arts, Mathematics, Physics, Social Studies), Special Education (Learning Disability)

Virginia State University

Virginia State University, founded in 1882, has prepared teachers for over one hundred years. Faculty believe that creative and systematic planning, instructional competence and leadership, effective and productive communication, and a commitment to continuous professional growth are essential to develop master teachers. The advanced level program builds upon a comprehensive liberal arts knowledge base, is grounded in theoretical and specialized knowledge, requires competence in education research, and provides learning experiences designed to develop competent and empathic professional leaders.

Just the facts...

Virginia State University
School of Liberal Arts and Education
P.O. Box 9401
Petersburg, VA 23806
(804) 524-5937
Website: www.vsu.edu
Profile: Suburban, Large, Co-Ed
UG Tuition: $975.50/sem. in-state; $2,980.00/sem. out-of-state
G Tuition: $1,119.50/sem. in-state; $3,422.00/sem. out-of-state
Off Campus Programs: No

Clinical Experiences

Clinical experiences serve an essential function in all programs. Experiences proceed from observation to varied experiences in appropriate K-12 settings prior to student teaching. Clinical requirements are co-requisites in selected professional courses in all programs. School volunteer programs and community outreach projects also provide valuable opportunities. Clinical experiences culminate in a one-semester student teaching experience after all admissions, course, GPA, and Praxis I requirements have been satisfied.

Noteworthy

All teacher education candidates are provided support for Praxis I preparation through LearningPlus and a mock testing program. Membership in the VSU Student Virginia Education Association is available. In addition, candidates may be recommended for membership in Kappa Delta Pi and other honor societies for professional educators. The Virginia Teaching Scholarship Loan Program provides a limited number of scholarship-loans to teacher candidates in critical shortage teaching areas identified by the state.

Teacher Preparation Program Information

The following programs are 4 year programs:

Elementary Education, K-12 Education (Art, Music, Physical Education, Technology Education), Secondary Education (Biology, Business, English/Language Arts, Mathematics, Physics, Vocational Home Economics/Consumer Homemaking), Special Education (Emotional Conflict, Learning Disability, Mental Retardation)

Central Washington University

CWU's Center for Teaching and Learning oversees all CWU professional education programs preparing teachers, principals, program administrators, school psychologists, and school counselors. Faculty located across the campus in many colleges and disciplines work together to provide the best possible subject matter content and teaching methodologies to ensure the highest quality teacher preparation for candidates.

Just the facts...

Central Washington University
College of Education and Professional Studies
400 E. 8th Avenue
Ellensburg, WA 98926-7415
(509) 963-2661
Website: www.cwu.edu
Profile: Rural, Medium, Co-Ed
UG Tuition: $842.00/quart. in-state; $2,987.00/quart. out-of-state
G Tuition: $1,347.00/quart. in-state; $4,097.00/quart. out-of-state
Off Campus Programs: Yes

Clinical Experiences

Candidates pursuing the Initial Teaching Certificate must student teach on an all-day basis for one quarter. Student teaching placements are available in six counties. In addition to the full-quarter student teaching experience, candidates also must complete a one-month practicum of Pre-Autumn Field Experience in late August/early September. One-year internships are available in the Ellensburg area and in King and Chelan counties.

Noteworthy

CWU's College of Education and Professional Studies' new Technology Lab contains a curriculum lab, multimedia production lab, professional collection and research labs, videotaping and observation areas, two model public school classrooms, an equipment use training lab, distance learning rooms, a special education adaptive device facility, and ample areas for individual and group study and interaction.

Teacher Preparation Program Information

The following programs are 4 year programs:

Early Childhood Education, Elementary Education, K-12 Education (Art, Chinese, Drama/Theater, French, German, Health, Industrial Technology, Japanese, Music, Physical Education, Russian, Spanish), Kindergarten Education, Middle School Education, Secondary Education (Art, Biology, Bookkeeping, Business, Chemistry, Consumer & Family Science/Home Economics, Earth Science, Economics, English/Language Arts, Geography, Health, Mathematics, Physical Education, Physics, Political Science, Psychology, Social Studies, Sociology, Steno/Typing/Keyboard, Trade & Industrial, Vocational Business Office, Vocational Marketing, Vocational Home Economics/Consumer Homemaking, Vocational Trade & Industrial), Special Education (Early Childhood)

The following programs are post-baccalaureate programs:

Early Childhood Education, Elementary Education, K-12 Education (Art, Chinese, Drama/Theater, ESL, French, German, Health, Japanese, Physical Education, Reading, Russian, Spanish), Kindergarten Education, Middle School Education, Secondary Education (Art, Earth Science, Economics, English/Language Arts, Geography, Health, Mathematics, Physical Education, Political Science, Social Studies), Special Education (Early Childhood)

The following programs are 5th year programs:

K-12 Education (Art, Health, Music, Physical Education), Secondary Education (Art, Biology, Bookkeeping, Business, Chemistry, Consumer & Family Science/Home Economics, English/Language Arts, Health, Mathematics, Physical Education, Psychology, Vocational Business Office, Vocational Marketing, Vocational Home Economics/Consumer Homemaking), Special Education

Eastern Washington University

Eastern Washington University's legacy of preparing teachers and other school personnel dates back to 1890. The Department of Education coordinates all professional education programs. The department's mission is to provide professional programs for in-service and preservice educators that emphasize (1) helping students engage in critical thinking and problem solving, (2) learning through reflection on experience, (3) commitment to democratic ideals and procedures, and (4) caring and flexible approaches to working with a wide range of diverse students. Approximately 400 graduates are licensed annually.

Just the facts...

Eastern Washington University
College of Education and Human Development
526 5th Street, MS 186
Cheney, WA 99004-2431
(509) 359-2328
Website: www.ewu.edu
Profile: Rural/Urban, Medium, Co-Ed
UG Tuition: $874.00/quart. in-state; $3,105.00/quart. out-of-state
G Tuition: $1,400.00/quart. in-state; $4,260.00/quart. out-of-state
Off Campus Programs: Yes

Clinical Experiences

The Department of Education places a high priority on the importance of K-12 school experiences for all teacher candidates. Candidates may receive credit for optional school experiences every quarter. Required school experiences begin with the introductory education course and culminate with a full quarter of student teaching. Candidates complete a minimum of 30 hours working with culturally diverse students.

Noteworthy

The Department of Education has received the national ATE Distinguished Teacher Education Program of the Year award on two occasions. Program features include technology, literacy, school administration, and performance-based demonstration of knowledge and skills. A M.Ed. with Certification Program and a Friday/Saturday Teacher Certification Program are offered for non-traditional candidates. EWU will provide assistance to first-year teachers and their employing school districts without charge. Active chapters of educational honor societies at EWU include Kappa Delta Pi and Phi Delta Kappa.

Teacher Preparation Program Information

The following programs are 4 year programs:
Elementary Education, K-12 Education (Art, French, German, Music, Physical Education, Reading, Spanish), Secondary Education (Biology, Business, Chemistry, Earth Science, English, Geography, Health, Marketing, Mathematics, Physics, Psychology, Social Studies, Technology, Theatre)

The following programs are post-baccalaureate programs:
Elementary Education, K-12 Education (Art, French, German, Music, Physical Education, Reading, Spanish), Secondary Education (Biology, Business, Chemistry, Earth Science, English, Geography, Health, Marketing, Mathematics, Physics, Psychology, Social Studies, Technology, Theatre)

The following programs are 5th year programs:
Elementary Teaching (K-8), Curriculum and Instruction (4-12)

Gonzaga University

Gonzaga University is one of 28 Jesuit Colleges and Universities in the U.S. Since 1928, Gonzaga has prepared elementary, secondary, special education, and physical education teachers and administrators. Undergraduate candidates in elementary and secondary education must also complete majors in the College of Arts and Sciences. Graduate candidates have the option of completing coursework in field-based settings where priority can be given to immediate, local needs. The specific desire of the School of Education to "be of service where most needed" has taken its faculty to remote regions of Western Canada, the Hawaiian Islands, and to First Nation Reserves in Alberta and British Columbia.

Clinical Experiences

Clinical experiences are tightly woven into all degrees offered by the School of Education. Experiences have two specific focuses: to allow candidates to develop the applied skills and attitudes that must accompany professional teaching, and to provide the community with needed services that would otherwise be unavailable. Internships and student teaching experiences are extensive, leading to professional competence among graduates.

Just the facts...

Gonzaga University
School of Education
Spokane, WA 99258-0025
(509) 323-3503
Website: www.soe.gonzaga.edu
Profile: Urban, Medium, Co-Ed
UG Tuition: $15,960.00/semester
G Tuition: $410.00/credit hour
Off Campus Programs: Yes

Noteworthy

At the master's level, the School of Education has several unique and innovative programs, including a Master of Arts in Teaching degree with special focus on serving "at-risk" children, a Presidential Institute that serves the area's strongest teachers while providing them with a 50 percent scholarship for coursework, and a Center for Organizational Reform that provides direct technical assistance to school districts involved in change and renewal.

Teacher Preparation Program Information

The following programs are 4 year programs:
Elementary Education, K-12 Education (Physical Education), Secondary Education, Special Education (K-12)

The following programs are post-baccalaureate programs:
Elementary Education, K-12 Education (Art, Drama/Theater, French, German, Health, Italian, Music, Reading, Spanish), Secondary Education (Art, Biology, Business, Chemistry, Economics, English/Language Arts, Health, Mathematics, Physics, Political Science, Psychology, Social Studies, Sociology)

The following programs are 5th year programs:
Elementary Education, K-12 Education (Physical Education), Secondary Education, Special Education (K-12)

Pacific Lutheran University

The School of Education offers programs of study leading to licensure for elementary, secondary, and special education teachers, administrators, reading specialists, and school librarians. The curriculum is designed to provide graduates with a blend of the liberal arts and a variety of guided field experiences beginning early in the educational sequence. The faculty is committed to the development of educational personnel sensitive to the varied individual needs of learners. To prepare candidates for their role as teachers, PLU fosters a climate of intellectual challenge marked by enthusiastic learning and committed teaching. Rigorous scholarship is enriched by active mentorship and collaboration.

Just the facts...

Pacific Lutheran University
School of Education
Tacoma, WA 98447
(253) 535-7272
Website: www.plu.edu
Profile: Urban, Medium, Co-Ed
UG Tuition: $485.00/semester
G Tuition: $485.00/semester
Off Campus Programs: No

Clinical Experiences

Students admitted to the School of Education seeking licensure as elementary and secondary teachers complete four semesters of foundations, pedagogy, and clinical experiences. In the elementary program, approximately 100 hours of clinical experience is required prior to fifteen weeks of student teaching. In the secondary program, approximately 80 hours of clinical experience is required prior to fifteen weeks of student teaching. In the post-baccalaureate program, a full-year internship is required in a single building.

Noteworthy

Professors in the School of Education model the pursuit of excellence, the continuing improvement of their teaching skills, and personal commitment to the students they teach. They are known for their scholarly activities, including the publication of books and articles, presentations at national and state association meetings, teaching awards, and funded grants to further the development of university/school district partnerships.

Teacher Preparation Program Information

The following programs are 4 year programs:
Elementary Education K-8 (Art, Biology, Chemistry, Chinese, Drama, Economics, English/Language Arts, French, Geosciences, German, Health, History, Instructional Technology, Journalism, Latin, Mathematics, Music, Norwegian, Physical Education, Physics, Political Science, Psychology, Science, Social Studies, Sociology, Spanish, Special Education, Speech), K-12 Education (Foreign Languages, Music, Physical Education), Secondary Education 4-12 (Art, Biology, Chemistry, Chinese, Drama, Economics, English/Language Arts, French, Geosciences, German, Health, History, Instructional Technology, Journalism, Latin, Mathematics, Music, Norwegian, Physical Education, Physics, Political Science, Psychology, Science, Social Studies, Sociology, Spanish, Special Education, Speech)

The following programs are post-baccalaureate programs:
Elementary Education K-8 (Art, Biology, Chemistry, Chinese, Drama, Economics, English/Language Arts, French, Geosciences, German, Health, History, Instructional Technology, Journalism, Latin, Mathematics, Music, Norwegian, Physical Education, Physics, Political Science, Psychology, Science, Social Studies, Sociology, Spanish, Special Education, Speech), Secondary Education 4-12 (Art, Biology, Chemistry, Chinese, Drama, Economics, English/Language Arts, French, Geosciences, German, Health, History, Instructional Technology, Journalism, Latin, Mathematics, Music, Norwegian, Physical Education, Physics, Political Science, Psychology, Science, Social Studies, Sociology, Spanish, Special Education, Speech)

The following programs are 5th year programs:
M.A. with Initial Certification—Middle Level Focus

Seattle Pacific University

Seattle Pacific University, situated in a lively urban setting, offers teacher preparation dedicated to the growth, learning, and hope of elementary and secondary students. As a university grounded in the Christian tradition, Seattle Pacific seeks to prepare teachers who are strong in pedagogical skills, and who have developed a sense of service to others. The university views teacher education as a developmental process that is based on the liberal arts, and provides coursework, experiences, and guidance that contribute to each candidate's professional growth. Candidates master academic content and professional skills, and learn about the nature of students and the school community.

Just the facts...

Seattle Pacific University
School of Education
3307 Third Avenue West
Seattle, WA 98119
(206) 281-2214
Website: www.spu.edu/depts/
Profile: Urban, Medium, Co-Ed
UG Tuition: $14,541.00/annual
G Tuition: $274.00/credit hour
Off Campus Programs: No

Clinical Experiences

The teacher education program provides candidates with a variety of clinical experiences that make use of the diverse educational settings in the Puget Sound area. As they begin their work in the School of Education, candidates spend two hours each day observing and assisting in a classroom in the Seattle Public Schools, and two hours a week visiting different school sites. Site visits are designed to provide candidates with the broadest possible understanding of the range of schools in the Puget Sound region. Student teaching experiences are 20 weeks long and include weekly, on-site visits from university intern coordinators. The coordinators observe interns as they teach and provide a high level of support.

Noteworthy

Strong support during the 20-week internship, and careful tracking of candidates' progress are hallmarks of the teacher education program at Seattle Pacific. Candidates have the opportunity to complete their teaching internships in a wide variety of settings, from urban schools to those situated on islands off the coast. Classrooms at Seattle Pacific are equipped with the latest technology, including computer presentation software and Internet connections. The university offers a number of scholarships to teacher candidates, including the Foster Endowment Scholarship, the Hughes-Ets Scholarship, and the Decade of Opportunity Scholarship.

Teacher Preparation Program Information

The following programs are 4 year programs:

Elementary Education, K-12 Education (Art, French, German, Music, Physical Education, Spanish), Secondary Education (Biology, Chemistry, Consumer & Family Science/Home Economics, Mathematics, Physical Education, Physics), Special Education

The following programs are post-baccalaureate programs:

Elementary Education, K-12 Education (Art, French, German, Music, Physical Education, Spanish), Secondary Education (Biology, Consumer & Family Science/Home Economics, Mathematics, Physical Education, Physics), Special Education

Seattle University

Seattle University, a Jesuit university, is dedicated to teaching and educating for leadership and service. The Master in Teaching program, initiated in 1990, is guided by the belief that the teacher is an ethical, knowledgeable, reflective decision maker who can teach all students to function effectively in a global and pluralistic society. Candidates who are already strongly grounded in their academic fields enroll in a 60-credit daytime program. The curriculum includes comprehensive education theory and research within the themes of individualization, ethical responsibility, and the use of technology as an essential educational tool.

Just the facts...

Seattle University
School of Education
900 Broadway
Seattle, WA 98122-4460
(206) 296-5760
Website: www.seattleu.edu/soe/
Profile: Urban, Medium, Co-Ed
G Tuition: $340.00/credit hour
Off Campus Programs: No

Clinical Experiences

The program features multiple field experiences with strong supervisory support incorporating peer collaboration and team teaching approaches. The first field experiences are focused on candidate observation. These experiences set a foundation for the remainder of the program. A three-week field experience, integrated into the coursework during Block I, features a peer coaching model. All candidates participate in a middle school experience with Master in Teaching graduates, and teach in classrooms in partnership schools or other student teaching settings during Block II. Block III is devoted entirely to student teaching followed by a seminar focused on reflection on the clinical experiences.

Noteworthy

Candidates proceed through the program as members of a cohort in which they create and experience a "learning community." Internships in community service programs are integral to the program. Elementary preservice candidates attend college classes at a partnership school and apply in those classrooms the strategies and materials presented in the course. Elementary faculty teach components of the coursework, giving candidates opportunities to connect with everyday life in classrooms. Secondary preservice candidates work similarly with high school faculty in specialized methods courses.

Teacher Preparation Program Information

The following programs are 5th year programs:
Elementary Education, Secondary Education

University of Puget Sound

Over the past 25 years, the University of Puget Sound has become increasingly focused as an undergraduate, liberal arts institution. Consistent with that mission, teacher education has been redesigned as an MAT program to allow candidates a full four years of preparation in their disciplines prior to professional preparation. The faculty believe that professional preparation must include extensive academic study, clinical experiences in diverse social contexts, and ample opportunity for guided reflection and collaborative work. Programs are distinguished by candidates' close relationships with the faculty and a lively intellectual environment.

Just the facts...

University of Puget Sound
School of Education
1500 North Warner
Tacoma, WA 98416-0002
(253) 756-3375
Website: www.ups.edu
Profile: Urban, Small, Co-Ed
UG Tuition: $9,480.00/semester
G Tuition: $9,480.00/semester
Off Campus Programs: No

Clinical Experiences

Teacher preparation programs are designed around extensive clinical experiences. Candidates spend time in multiple school settings—half days during the fall semester, and full days during the spring semester, for fifteen weeks of student teaching. In these settings, candidates work collaboratively with peers, faculty, and cooperating teachers. Candidates have an additional field experience with children with special needs. Candidates also have an opportunity to work as substitute teachers in local schools.

Noteworthy

Graduates of the Master of Arts in Teaching program have had the highest rate of job placement of any preparation program in the state for the last three years. Graduates have assumed leadership roles in their schools, especially in the areas of technology and curriculum design, and frequently mentor current candidates. The small size of the teacher preparation cohort allows faculty and candidates to undertake unusual and creative endeavors; for example, candidates have worked in collaboration with a campus archaeologist to create an instructional Website that is suited to interdisciplinary, inquiry-based use in classrooms.

Teacher Preparation Program Information

The following programs are 5th year programs:

Elementary Education, K-12 Education (Art, Music, Physical Education), Secondary Education (Art, Biology, Chemistry, Earth Science, Economics, English/Language Arts, General Science, Health, Physical Sciences, Physics, Political Science, Social Studies)

Washington State University

Washington State University prepares teachers capable of meeting the needs of tomorrow's schools. The College of Education believes that effective teaching requires teachers to know their subject matter and their students. The college's philosophy is that students play an active role in learning through experience. Teacher candidates at WSU learn to draw on their students' social, linguistic, cultural, and academic strengths and to understand different types of learners, learning, and effective practice. Candidates work in public schools throughout their teacher preparation program.

Just the facts...

Washington State University
College of Education
Pullman, WA 99164-2114
(509) 335-7091
Website: www.educ.wsu.edu
Profile: Rural, Large, Co-Ed
UG Tuition: $1,650.00/sem. in-state; $4,655.00/sem. out-of-state
G Tuition: $2,591.00/sem. in-state; $6,493.00/sem. out-of-state
Off Campus Programs: Yes

Clinical Experiences

Undergraduate and Master in Teaching clinical experiences vary. Undergraduate teacher candidates proceed through three structured clinical experiences: an introductory observation, a practicum, and sixteen weeks of student teaching. These clinical experiences provide candidates with a foundation of knowledge and practice that helps them understand teaching and learning. In the Master in Teaching program, field experiences are coordinated with academic work throughout the year. Students spend an increasing amount of time in classrooms, culminating with a twelve-week, full-time internship.

Noteworthy

The Teacher Preparation Program at WSU is well known for its emphasis on diversity, technology, and partnerships. Candidates gain an in-depth understanding of the relevance of diversity to teaching, hands-on experience in the use of technology for instruction and learning, and experiences in collaboration with urban, rural, and tribal schools through the many partnership programs WSU maintains throughout the state and internationally. The College of Education operates an online Virtual Professional Development School with hundreds of participants from a variety of geographical areas.

Teacher Preparation Program Information

The following programs are 4 year programs:
Early Childhood Education, Elementary Education, K-12 Education (Foreign Language, Music), Secondary Education (Vocational Agriculture, Biology, Chemistry, Vocational Consumer & Family Science, Earth Science, English, English/Language Arts, General Science, History, Mathematics, Physics, Social Studies)

The following programs are 5th year programs:
Master in Teaching in Elementary Education

Western Washington University

Western Washington University's professional education programs lead to the development of teachers and other school personnel who have a sound liberal arts background, are excellent communicators, are able to work cooperatively and collaboratively with their colleagues, and are leaders of change in education and society. Graduates are skilled classroom leaders who understand children and youth, and are sensitive to human and social diversity. They display the mastery of state and national standards expected of a beginning teacher. By drawing upon what they know about pedagogy and academic content, graduates generate a positive impact on student learning.

Just the facts...

Western Washington University
Woodring College of Education
Bellingham, WA 98225-9090
(360) 650-3378
Website: www.wce.wwu.edu
Profile: Rural, Large, Co-Ed
UG Tuition: $951.00/sem. in-state; $3,191/sem. out-of-state
G Tuition: $1,481.00/sem. in-state; $4,341/sem. out-of-state
Off Campus Programs: Yes

Clinical Experiences

Clinical experiences are central to every program in the form of practicum courses. In practica, candidates are required to present content, evaluate student responses, manage the group or classroom environment, and adjust strategies as necessary. Initial licensure programs culminate in a full-time internship of at least ten weeks, which includes at least two full weeks of unassisted teaching. Some candidates participate in one of the university's professional development schools for the final two quarters of their program.

Noteworthy

The Woodring College of Education is committed to preparing candidates to teach diverse populations of children. In addition to infusing appropriate content throughout its curriculum, the faculty created the Center for Educational Pluralism (CEP). The CEP is a learning/resource center that candidates and faculty use to enhance their knowledge about diversity issues. Candidates are required to complete a series of readings and activities in the CEP; they are also encouraged to become familiar with the CEP early in their programs so they can apply what they learn there as they advance through their studies. The college also sponsors programs in which candidates work individually with children in diverse public school settings.

Teacher Preparation Program Information

The following programs are 4 year programs:
Early Childhood Education, Early Childhood Special Education, Elementary Education, K-12 Education (Art, French, German, Music, Physical Education, Spanish), Secondary Education (Anthropology, Biology, Chemistry, Communication, Earth Science, Economics, English/Language Arts, General Science, Geography, Health, Mathematics, Physical Education, Physics, Political Science, Social Studies, Sociology, Trade & Industrial), Special Education K-12

The following programs are 5th year programs:
Elementary Education, Secondary Education

Whitworth College

The Department of Teacher Education offers programs that lead to the initial license in teaching at the elementary and secondary levels, as well as in specialized areas. Undergraduate programs view the beginning teacher as a "scholar, guardian, pedagogue, citizen, and servant-leader." This forms the basis for curriculum development, the assessment of candidates' progress through portfolio reviews, and the performance evaluation in student teaching. Whitworth College has programs at several levels to prepare teachers for initial licensure.

Just the facts...

Whitworth College
Department of Teacher Education
300 West Hawthorne Road
Spokane, WA 99251-0701
(509) 777-3229
Website: www.whitworth.edu
Profile: Suburban, Small, Co-Ed
UG Tuition: $7,985.00/semester
Off Campus Programs: No

Clinical Experiences

In the undergraduate program, candidates begin field experiences by tutoring students in reading and mathematics in conjunction with their first education course. Field experiences continue throughout the program and include an innovative January-term multicultural field experience that takes place in one of a variety of settings locally and around the world. In the Master in Teaching (MIT) program, candidates spend the entire academic year in a field placement that begins as three days per week in the fall and concludes with a full-time, fourteen-week experience. MIT candidates also complete the January-term multicultural experience.

Noteworthy

In the undergraduate program, candidates may prepare to teach traditional academic areas in secondary schools, elementary education, special education, and English as a Second Language. The multicultural field experience can be completed in inner-city locations (Spokane, San Francisco, Los Angeles, Albuquerque), rural placements (Washington, Idaho, Alaska, Hawaii), and in other countries (Mexico, Korea, Taiwan, Romania). The MIT program, which leads to eligibility for teacher licensure and a master's degree, begins with a cohort group each June and concludes fourteen months later in August. The MIT program has a performance-based curriculum.

Teacher Preparation Program Information

The following programs are 4 year programs:
Elementary Education, K-12 Education (Art, Drama/Theater, ESL, French, German, Spanish, Music, Physical Education), Secondary Education (Biology, Chemistry, Economics, English/Language Arts, General Science, Health, Mathematics, Physical Sciences, Physics, Political Science, Psychology, Science, Social Studies, Sociology), Special Education

The following programs are 5th year programs:
Elementary Education, Secondary Education

Alderson-Broaddus College

Alderson-Broaddus College is an independent, private, American Baptist Church-related college located on a mountain top in beautiful north central West Virginia. The college has a cherished tradition of teaching excellence, with a strong emphasis on the preparation of teacher candidates. Teacher education at Alderson-Broaddus College is a four-year program in the liberal arts, content specialty studies, and professional education studies, with the expressed purpose of developing a beginning professional who exhibits sensitivity, thoughtfulness, and informed practice in education.

Just the facts...

Alderson-Broaddus College
Education Department
Box 2188
Philippi, WV 26416
(304) 457-6221
Website: www.ab.edu
Profile: Rural, Small, Co-Ed
UG Tuition: $6,615.00/semester
Off Campus Programs: No

Clinical Experiences

Teacher candidates at Alderson-Broaddus College benefit from education courses partnered with field experiences in the schools beginning with their first semester, continuing each semester thereafter, and culminating with student teaching in their final semester. Freshmen observe in the classroom to gain knowledge about teaching. Sophomores and juniors work with students to apply knowledge and reflect on those applications. Seniors take methods courses that provide field experiences with the teachers who will be supervising the seniors' student teaching. Cooperating teachers are experienced mentors who are enthusiastic about working with candidates.

Noteworthy

Faculty at Alderson-Broaddus College are a caring community who advise candidates, guide their education, and challenge them to do their best to become effective professionals. Beyond excellent instruction and plentiful field experiences, Alderson-Broaddus provides opportunities for the following: personal attention, individual projects, small group activities, technology training and integration, field placements with exceptional and multiethnic inner-city students, field trips and conference/workshop attendance, volunteerism, leadership in student organizations, career placement services, a beginning teacher mentoring program upon graduation, and lifelong friendships.

Teacher Preparation Program Information

The following programs are 4 year programs:

Elementary Education, Music Education, Secondary Education (Biology, Chemistry, English, General Science, Mathematics, Oral Communications, Physical Education, Social Studies), Special Education (Mentally Impaired, Specific Learning Disabilities)

Bethany College

The teacher preparation program at Bethany College prepares candidates to become self-directed decision makers. Candidates integrate a liberal arts background, content area preparation, and educational principles to prepare for careers in teaching at the elementary, middle, and secondary school levels, in non-school settings, or in an interdisciplinary synthesis of psychology and education. Candidates may choose content specializations in biology, chemistry, English, French, general science, German, language arts, mathematics, physical education, physics, social studies, and Spanish. Elementary education candidates can minor in specific learning disabilities.

Just the facts...

Bethany College
Education and Professional Studies
Bethany, WV 26032
(304) 829-7182
Website: www.bethanywv.edu
Profile: Rural, Small, Co-Ed
UG Tuition: $8,511.00/semester
Off Campus Programs: No

Clinical Experiences

Each course in the teacher preparation program has a field experience component. In human development courses, candidates are engaged in one-on-one work with an individual child. Throughout the course of study, candidates visit classrooms to observe and practice teaching skills. Extensive placement experiences are provided during the junior year of study. Student teaching is completed in the fall semester of the senior year in two placements. Comprehensive examinations are given at the completion of the student teaching experience.

Noteworthy

Bethany College is proud of its small class sizes, which allow faculty to provide close attention and assistance to students. Teacher candidates have many opportunities for multicultural classroom teaching experiences. Bethany College emphasizes the development of teacher candidates' technology skills. Field experience is integrated into all methods courses. The program has an exclusive partnership with a local elementary school that provides extensive hands-on experience to teacher candidates.

Teacher Preparation Program Information

The following programs are 4 year programs:
Elementary Education, K-12 Education (Physical Education), Middle School Education (English, French, German, Mathematics, Science, Social Studies, Spanish), Secondary Education (Biology, Chemistry, English/Language Arts, French, German, Mathematics, Physics, Social Studies, Spanish), Special Education (Learning Disability)

Bluefield State College

The mission of Bluefield State College is to provide students an affordable, geographically accessible opportunity for public higher education. The college demonstrates its commitment to undergraduate education by providing a dedicated faculty and staff, quality educational programs, and strong student support services in a caring environment. All programs are designed to promote the students' intellectual, personal, ethical, and cultural development. Teacher education graduates of Bluefield State College are prepared specifically to be managers of the learning environment for pupils coming from the various sociological, economic, and cultural backgrounds that characterize the population of the region.

Just the facts...

Bluefield State College
Department of Professional Education
Division of Education
219 Rock Street
Bluefield, WV 24701
(304) 327-4173
Website: www.bluefield.wvnet.edu
Profile: Rural, Small, Co-Ed
UG Tuition: $1,055.00/sem. in-state; $2,563.00/sem. out-of-state
Off Campus Programs: No

Clinical Experiences

Bluefield State College maintains cooperative relationships with area school systems to provide clinical experiences at several levels of preparation. The college operates on a block system for scheduling student teaching. A semester is reserved for the prospective teacher in which he/she will schedule a block of professional education. Candidates may be required to attend seminars and workshops during the day, the evening, or weekends during the student teaching experience. A minimum of twelve weeks will be devoted to full-time student teaching in the public schools. Students wishing to pursue more than two subject specializations must spend an additional period of time per specialization in full-time student teaching.

Noteworthy

The teacher preparation programs of Bluefield State College draw a majority of their students from a region comprised of seven southeast West Virginia counties in a primarily rural, Appalachian highland area. This clearly defined service area makes possible a succinct role description for the teachers whom Bluefield State College prepares. Teacher education graduates of Bluefield State College are prepared specifically to work with pupils coming from the various sociological, economic, and cultural backgrounds that characterize the population of this region.

Teacher Preparation Program Information

The following programs are 4 year programs:
Elementary Education

Concord College

Concord College's teacher preparation program carries on the tradition that began the college in 1872 when it was known as Concord State Normal School. Now, more than 125 years later, Concord College prepares teacher education candidates to be informed and thoughtful decision makers who will lead the next generation of students in to the twenty-first century. Concord College's teacher preparation program is based upon research, knowledge, experience, observation, and practice. Candidates learn how to be informed and thoughtful decision makers. Graduates are effective teachers who make classroom decisions based on theory, the nature of students, the content to be taught, and other situational variables.

Clinical Experiences

Field experiences are integrated with coursework to give preservice teachers many opportunities to engage in informed and thoughtful decision making. To optimize experiences in diverse settings and with diverse student populations, candidates have a minimum of three early field placements and a full semester of student teaching in at least two different placements.

Just the facts...

Concord College
Unit for Teacher Education
P.O. Box 1000
Campus Well Box
Athens, WV 24712
(304) 384-5273
Website: www.concord.wvnet.edu
Profile: Rural, Small, Co-Ed
UG Tuition: $1,194.00/sem. in-state; $2,625.00/sem. out-of-state
Off Campus Programs: No

Noteworthy

Numerous scholarships are available to all students and several are specifically designed for teacher education majors. In addition to the traditional scholarships, candidates have opportunities to participate in the Bonner Scholars Program, where students earn money for tuition and expenses through community service, and in the McNair Scholars Program, where candidates conduct undergraduate research and prepare for graduate school. The campus offers numerous student services through the Student Support Services Program. Candidates have the opportunity to participate in a campus-based Reading Council and Student Education Association.

Teacher Preparation Program Information

The following programs are 4 year programs:
Early Childhood Education, Early Childhood Special Education, Elementary Education (Language Arts, Mathematics, Physical Education, Science), K-12 Education (Art, Health, Music, Physical Education, School Library Media), Middle School Education (English, Mathematics, Physical Education, Science), Secondary Education (Art, Biology, Business, Chemistry, English/Language Arts, General Science, Health, Mathematics, Oral Communications, Physical Education, Social Studies), Special Education (Mental Impairment, Specific Learning Disabilities)

The following programs are post-baccalaureate programs:
Early Childhood Education, Early Childhood Special Education, Elementary Education (Language Arts, Mathematics, Physical Education, Science), K-12 Education (Art, Health, Music, Physical Education, School Library Media), Middle School Education (English, Mathematics, Physical Education, Science), Secondary Education (Art, Biology, Business, Chemistry, English/Language Arts, General Science, Health, Mathematics, Oral Communications, Physical Education, Social Studies), Special Education (Mental Impairment, Specific Learning Disabilities)

Fairmont State College

Since its normal school beginnings in 1865, the Fairmont State College School of Education has upheld its primary mission—to prepare the best teachers possible. Candidates study and perform in collaboration with education faculty and public school professionals to learn how to make unbiased, critical, and thoughtful decisions relating to students and curricula in a changing society. Graduates of the program are aware of children's exceptionalities and are prepared to provide excellence and equity for all children.

Just the facts...

Fairmont State College
Teacher Education
Fairmont, WV 26554
(304) 367-4241
Website: www.fscwv.edu
Profile: Urban, Small, Co-Ed
UG Tuition: $900.00/sem. in-state; $2,119.00/sem. out-of-state
Off Campus Programs: No

Clinical Experiences

Sophomore candidates participate in their first field experience as active observers in conjunction with their Human Growth and Development course. Each subsequent professional education class provides candidates with various field experiences as learning assistants, teaching assistants, and student teachers, giving candidates opportunities to integrate their content, professional, and pedagogical knowledge and skills. Close relationships between public school practitioners and college faculty create a collaborative community in which education candidates can participate in action research related to classroom situations.

Noteworthy

The School of Education operates two state-of-the-art networked computer labs (one Macintosh-equipped, the other IBM). Candidates take a capstone instructional technology course that introduces them to a variety of computer applications, as well as methods for incorporating technology into daily classroom instruction and activities. One section of this course is taught online via the Internet. A special course on rural education also has been offered online as an elective.

Teacher Preparation Program Information

The following programs are 4 year programs:

Elementary Education, K-12 Education (Art, Music, Physical Education), Middle School Education (Mathematics), Secondary Education (Art, Biology, Business, Chemistry, Communication, Consumer & Family Science/Home Economics, English/Language Arts, General Science, Health, Mathematics, Physics, Social Studies, Technology Education), Special Education (Learning Disability)

Glenville State College

Glenville State College has prepared teachers since 1872. The teacher education faculty are committed to ensuring that candidates are both skilled in content and pedagogy and are reflective practitioners. Based upon the belief that teachers must be continual, lifelong learners, the program provides teacher candidates with a solid liberal arts background, a content-rich specialty emphasis, and skills in pedagogy that enable them to be successful in public schools.

Just the facts...

Glenville State College
Teacher Education
Glenville, WV 26351
(304) 462-4119
Website: www.glenville.wvnet.edu
Profile: Rural, Small, Co-Ed
UG Tuition: $1,008.00/sem. in-state; $2,394.00/sem. out-of-state
Off Campus Programs: Yes

Clinical Experiences

Clinical and field experiences are a critical component of teacher education at Glenville State College. Experiences include 20 hours in a classroom assessing instructional strategies for exceptional and culturally diverse students. Also included is a 40-hour experience which simulates an abbreviated student teaching experience. A minimum of 140 hours is spent in clinical and field experiences prior to student teaching. The culminating experience is the semester-long student teaching experience that allows the candidate an opportunity to develop competence in planning, teaching, evaluating, management, and technology.

Noteworthy

Students at Glenville State College are given personalized attention and assistance to be the best they can be. Tutors are available to help students with coursework. Computer-aided assistance is available to students who struggle with test-taking. Teacher education faculty work closely with candidates to ensure their success and competency. The Student Teacher Enrichment Program is available to student teachers who need extra support during the student teaching experience. Low student/faculty ratios make Glenville State College a place where every person is valued and given the support needed, in a small-town setting.

Teacher Preparation Program Information
The following programs are 4 year programs:
Early Childhood Education, Elementary Education, K-12 Education (Art, Music, Physical Education), Secondary Education (Art, Biology, Business, Chemistry/Physics, Driver Education, English, General Science, Mathematics, Oral Communications, Physical Education, Social Studies), Special Education (Behavioral Disorders, Learning Disabilities, Mentally Impaired)

Marshall University

The School of Education at Marshall University ensures that its programs are based on critical thinking. The teacher education faculty believe that the process of educational preparation requires critical thinking, and that the outcome is an educator capable of informing and changing—for the better—the students, the educational system, and the community. Marshall's graduates enter the complex world of education armed with analytical skills that enable them to make appropriate decisions in the classroom.

Just the facts...

Marshall University
School of Education
400 Hal Greer Boulevard
Huntington, WV 25755-2400
(304) 746-2030
Website: www.marshall.edu
Profile: Suburban, Medium, Co-Ed
G Tuition: $97.00/cr. hr. in-state; $348.00/cr. hr. out-of-state
Off Campus Programs: Yes

Clinical Experiences

Clinical experiences in the teacher education program are consistent with the School of Education's emphasis on critical thinking. They are designed to assist candidates in linking theory to practice in increasingly complex ways. Site-based learning activities, four clinical experiences, and full-semester student teaching provide opportunities for candidates to analyze teaching as a career, reflect on the development of children and adolescents in diverse classrooms, act as tutors and teacher assistants, and practice teaching and managing classrooms in public school settings.

Noteworthy

The School of Education is proud of its professional partnerships and the new professional education curriculum that has been shaped by those partnerships. As a result of the university's commitment to technology, Marshall's graduates find themselves prepared for the twenty-first century. Facilities, courses, and several special projects (including a science grant funded by Toyota) enhance candidates' skills for the information age. The School of Education awards teaching scholarships and recognizes excellence through student teaching awards.

Teacher Preparation Program Information

The following programs are 4 year programs:
Elementary Education K-4, Secondary Education (Grades 5-12, Grades K-12)

The following programs are 5th year programs:
Master of Arts in Teaching (Grades 5-12, Grades K-12)

National Council for Accreditation of Teacher Education

Shepherd College

Shepherd College has a long history of preparing teachers since its beginnings as a state normal school in 1871. The program is committed to preparing teachers who are ready for the complex problems of teaching and learning in today's diverse classrooms. The faculty are interested in attracting individuals who are willing to engage in a rigorous examination of teaching and learning, take responsibility for their own learning, and be committed to developing education programs that empower all children in a democratic society.

Just the facts...

Shepherd College
Professional Education Unit
Shepherdstown, WV 25443
(304) 876-5330
Website: www.shepherd.wvnet.edu
Profile: Rural, Medium, Co-Ed
UG Tuition: $93.00/cr. hr. in-state; $223.00/cr. hr. out-of-state
Off Campus Programs: No

Clinical Experiences

Experiences in actual classrooms are essential to the preparation of teachers at Shepherd College. Candidates learn to assess information from their college courses in light of classroom practice. They are also trained to assess classroom practice in light of newly developed insights. Field experiences begin in the second year and are integrated into every professional education course until graduation. A demographic profile of all the regional schools ensures that candidates will be assigned to diverse school settings. Student teaching can be done in an inner-city school.

Noteworthy

Many scholarships are available to teacher education majors. These are used to attract and retain excellent teacher education candidates who reflect the diversity of society. An up-to-date computer lab is available to candidates for both work and research. A strong commitment to effective and appropriate uses of technology in teaching and learning is a special feature of the teacher education program. Graduates from Shepherd have been selected as Teacher of the Year in the state of West Virginia. Shepherd is working to develop its relationships with professional development schools to ensure consistency between the program's goals and field experiences in public classrooms.

Teacher Preparation Program Information

The following programs are 4 year programs:
Elementary Education, K-12 Education (Art, Music, Physical Education), Secondary Education (Art, Biology, Business, Chemistry, English, Family & Consumer Science, General Science, Health, Mathematics, Social Studies)

The following programs are post-baccalaureate programs:
Elementary Education, K-12 Education (Art, Music, Physical Education), Secondary Education (Art, Biology, Business, Chemistry, English, Family & Consumer Science, General Science, Health, Mathematics, Social Studies)

University of Charleston

The University of Charleston is an independent, comprehensive, private institution located directly across the Kanawha River from the West Virginia State Capitol. The university benefits from the beauty of West Virginia's mountains and from its location in a dynamic and cosmopolitan city. It serves the Charleston community as a focal point for numerous intellectual, scientific, cultural, athletic, and civic events. The mission of the Department of Education is to educate each teacher candidate for a life of productive work, enlightened living, and community involvement. Undergraduate preservice teachers receive strong liberal arts training and can major in one of ten content areas.

Just the facts...

The University of Charleston
Teacher Education
2300 MacCorkle Avenue, SE
Charleston, WV 25304
(304) 357-4707
Website: www.uchaswv.edu
Profile: Urban, Small, Co-Ed
UG Tuition: $5,800.00/semester
Off Campus Programs: No

Clinical Experiences

Candidates begin their clinical experience in their freshman year in the Introduction to Education course. By the time preservice teachers apply for acceptance in the teacher education program at the end of their sophomore year, they have already completed 60 hours of clinical experience. During the junior year, candidates continue their clinical experiences by completing five days of intensively supervised microteaching. The final clinical experience culminates in a full semester of directed student teaching. Candidates are placed in a different school setting (rural, city, inner-city, and suburban) for each clinical experience.

Noteworthy

In the fall of 1995, NASA awarded a NASA Education Regional Center to the University of Charleston. This center makes various NASA materials available to teachers and preservice teachers in the Southern West Virginia area. These free materials include lesson plans, supplemental materials, posters, software, and videotapes in mathematics, science, art, geography, and social science. The center is located in the Department of Education, and is administered and supervised by Department of Education faculty and staff.

Teacher Preparation Program Information

The following programs are 4 year programs:

Elementary Education K-12 Education (Art, Music, Physical Education), Middle School Education (English, Mathematics, Science, Social Studies), Secondary Education (English/Language Arts, General Science, Mathematics, Physical Education, Social Studies)

The following programs are post-baccalaureate programs:

Elementary Education K-12 Education (Art, Music, Physical Education), Middle School Education (English, Mathematics, Science, Social Studies), Secondary Education (English/Language Arts, General Science, Mathematics, Physical Education, Social Studies)

West Liberty State College

High-quality teacher candidates have been prepared at West Liberty State College for more than 100 years. The faculty believes that the teacher is a catalyst. This philosophy reflects the view that teaching is a complex process that requires reflection, decision making, and integration of content knowledge with student needs. The college is committed to the concept of a student-centered campus environment. An expanded Honors Program offers much to academic high-achievers, including an honors residence hall and scholarships.

Just the facts...

West Liberty State College
Department of Professional Education
West Liberty, WV 26074
(304) 336-8047
Website: www.wlsc.wvnet.edu
Profile: Rural, Medium, Co-Ed
UG Tuition: $950.00/sem. in-state; $2,235.00/sem. out-of-state
Off Campus Programs: No

Clinical Experiences

From the first education course, clinical/field experiences are important components of all programs. All clinical/field experiences are integrated with required courses. Participating candidates are supervised by college and/or public school faculty. The capstone student teaching experience is a twelve-week, full-day program. Student teachers are placed with selected cooperating teachers in public schools in the college's service area in West Virginia, Ohio, or Pennsylvania. Trained faculty supervisors visit and observe teacher candidates a minimum of once a week during student teaching placements.

Noteworthy

Education-related clubs include the Council for Exceptional Children (CEC), Kappa Delta Pi, West Virginia Student Educators Association (WVSEA), and the West Liberty Reading Council. West Liberty teacher candidates are active at the state level in WVSEA and CEC—several serve as state officers. An urban education seminar and a minor in reading and literacy education are available. West Liberty, a leader in science education, has received $1.86 million in funding for teacher training at its Science, Mathematics, and Research Technology Center. A focus on partnerships with K-12 schools provides benefits for the public schools as well as for candidates and faculty.

Teacher Preparation Program Information

The following programs are 4 year programs:
Early Childhood Education, Elementary Education, K-12 Education (Art, Health, Music, Physical Education), Secondary Education (Art, Biology, Chemistry, English/Language Arts, General Science, Mathematics, Social Science, Spanish), Special Education (Mentally Impaired)

The following programs are post-baccalaureate programs:
Early Childhood Education, Elementary Education, K-12 Education (Art, Health, Music, Physical Education), Secondary Education (Art, Biology, Chemistry, English/Language Arts, General Science, Mathematics, Social Science, Spanish), Special Education (Mentally Impaired)

West Virginia State College

West Virginia State College has been preparing classroom teachers for over 70 years. The college's motto, "A Living Laboratory of Human Relations," is genuinely reflected in the education program's theme—the teacher as a human developer. The faculty believe that growing up in America is a difficult task for many young people because of poverty, race, dysfunctional families, violence, and drugs. These risk factors can negate children's best efforts to learn and grow. Thus, teacher candidates at West Virginia State College focus on creating emotional stability for children along with developing productive teaching skills.

Just the facts...

West Virginia State College
Education Department
Campus Box 158, WVSC
P.O. Box 1000
Institute, WV 25112-1000
(304) 766-3253
Website: www.wvsc.edu
Profile: Urban, Medium, Co-Ed
UG Tuition: $94.00/cr. hr. in-state; $228.00/cr. hr. out-of-state
Off Campus Programs: No

Clinical Experiences

Candidates begin field experiences in the freshman year and end in the senior year with a full semester of student teaching. Early experiences include the following: individual and pair tutoring, a child or adolescent case study, teaching small and large groups, helping children with computer learning and activities, grading papers, preparing teaching materials, assisting with standardized testing, and helping the teacher manage the classroom. Candidates go to different schools for each field placement to gain experiences with young people from different social, academic, and racial backgrounds, as well as those with special learning problems.

Noteworthy

The Education Department has a modern educational computing lab which has extensive technical resources for teaching and learning. The area is completely wheelchair-accessible. Resources are correlated to many of the curriculum areas taught in K-12 schools. Thus, candidates learn about many of the same resources they will be expected to use as classroom teachers. A required course in educational technology provides the basics for understanding and using technology as a teaching tool. Candidates have personal access to the Internet and use it to create personal homepages to share and obtain information about their teaching disciplines.

Teacher Preparation Program Information

The following programs are 4 year programs:

Elementary Education, K-12 Education (Art, Music, Physical Education), Secondary Education (Art, Biology, Business, Chemistry, English/Language Arts, French, General Science, Health, Mathematics, Physical Education, Social Studies, Spanish), Special Education (Mentally Impaired K-12)

The following programs are post-baccalaureate programs:

Elementary Education, K-12 Education (Art, Music, Physical Education), Secondary Education (Art, Biology, Business, Chemistry, English/Language Arts, French, General Science, Health, Mathematics, Physical Education, Social Studies, Spanish), Special Education (Mentally Impaired K-12)

West Virginia University

West Virginia University provides vigorous and intensive training of teachers and other school personnel for the P-12 classrooms of today. Faculty members are committed to preparing educators who have a strong grounding in their academic discipline as well as the skill to be effective practicing professionals. The programs at WVU, which were developed in collaboration with K-12 educators, strive to bridge the gap between research and practice. Carefully sequenced coursework and integrated clinical experiences focus on active learning, critical thinking, awareness of diversity, and state-of-the-art instructional technologies.

Just the facts...

West Virginia University
College of Human Resources and Education
802 Allen Hall
P.O. Box 6122
Morgantown, WV 26506-6122
(304) 293-5703
Website: www.wvu.edu/~hre
Profile: Suburban, Medium, Co-Ed
UG Tuition: $1,241.00/sem. in-state; $3,833.00/sem. out-of-state
G Tuition: $1,320.00/sem. in-state; $3,962.00/sem. out-of-state
Off Campus Programs: Yes

Clinical Experiences

Candidates in the five-year teacher education program complete over 1,000 hours of clinical experience. In their third year, candidates are placed in cohort groups and assigned to a specific professional development school where they return for a three-year sequence of field experiences. Candidates become part of a public school community and form close relationships with the teachers, students, and their own classmates. They observe, tutor, plan instruction, teach small groups and whole classes, and conduct action research as part of their program.

Noteworthy

Graduates of the five-year, dual-degree elementary and secondary teacher education program receive both a bachelor's degree in a content area and a master's degree in education. Rigorous performance requirements, relevant to effective teaching practice, are a key element of the program. After the ninth semester internship, candidates return to WVU for one semester to reflect on their experiences and strengthen their skills. Prior to graduation, candidates prepare professional portfolios to document their qualifications, clinical experiences, unique skills, and accomplishments for future employers.

Teacher Preparation Program Information

The following programs are 4 year programs:
K-12 Education (Music, Physical Education), Secondary Education (Agriculture, Health)

The following programs are post-baccalaureate programs:
K-12 Education (Art, Music, Physical Education), Secondary Education (Health)

The following programs are 5 year programs:
Elementary Education (Language Arts, Mathematics, Science, Social Studies), K-12 Education (Art, Physical Education), Middle School Education (English, Mathematics, Science, Social Studies), Secondary Education (Biology, Chemistry, English/Language Arts, General Science, Health, Journalism, Mathematics, Physics, Social Studies), Special Education

The following programs are 5th year programs:
Special Education (Early Childhood, Gifted/Talented, Learning Disability, Severe Behavioral Disabilities/Handicaps, Mentally Impaired, Severe and Profound)

West Virginia University at Parkersburg

West Virginia University at Parkersburg is an independently accredited regional campus of West Virginia University. A baccalaureate degree in elementary education has been offered at the institution since 1991. The knowledge and skills expected of the program's graduates are expressed in the faculty's belief that teachers are the architects of the future. The model for the education program envisions teachers who shape and construct the future by educating tomorrow's leaders—today's children. The belief that teaching and learning occur best in an environment that respects multiple perspectives is reflected in the curriculum of the teacher education program.

Just the facts...

West Virginia University at Parkersburg
Education Department
300 Campus Drive
Parkersburg, WV 26101
(304) 424-8314
Website: www.wvup.wvnet.edu
Profile: Rural, Small, Co-Ed
UG Tuition: $675.00/sem. in-state; $2,069.00/sem. out-of-state
Off Campus Programs: No

Clinical Experiences

A comprehensive system of clinical experiences requiring assessment of candidates' performance aids the development of skills and abilities necessary for effective teaching. Candidates experience 200 hours of field work prior to student teaching. Clinical experiences are co-requisite to related classroom instruction and begin with the first professional education course in the freshman year. Candidates have a broad range of experiences with diverse populations in a variety of school settings which include a professional development school.

Noteworthy

Experience with technology is integrated throughout the program curriculum. Candidates work with computerized basic skills programs in the education computer lab. Prior to student teaching, candidates master the application of a computerized grade book and reporting program. Professional development school partnerships place candidates in public schools for their coursework as well as the related clinical experiences. The Underwood-Smith Scholarship/Loan for education majors provides up to $5,000 per year and can be forgiven if the recipient remains in West Virginia to teach after graduation.

Teacher Preparation Program Information
The following programs are 4 year programs:
Elementary Education, Middle School Education

National Council for Accreditation of Teacher Education

West Virginia Wesleyan College

West Virginia Wesleyan College prepares elementary and secondary classroom teachers who are active learners and decision makers. Their competence as entry-level teachers derives from thorough preparation in their teaching fields and from mastery of professional skills. The professional component of the teacher education program includes both coursework and field experiences organized around five areas of general concern: instruction and learning; professional, personal, and ethical roles; cultural, social, and school/classroom contexts; individual difference/diversity; and evaluation and decision making.

Just the facts...

West Virginia Wesleyan College
Department of Education
59 College Avenue
Buckhannon, WV 26201-2994
(304) 473-8045
Website: www.wvwc.edu
Profile: Rural, Small, Co-Ed
UG Tuition: $8,150.00/semester
Off Campus Programs: No

Clinical Experiences

Teacher education candidates complete more than 90 hours of clinical experiences in public schools prior to the student teaching experience. Clinical Experience I, sophomore level, provides introductory experiences related to job satisfaction, learning, and human development. Clinical Experience II, junior level, provides a bridge between academic learning and the real world of teaching. Student teaching is comprised of a full semester of classroom teaching and professional development through enrollment in a concurrent seminar course.

Noteworthy

West Virginia Wesleyan College is an IBM Thinkpad University. At matriculation, students receive an IBM Thinkpad computer for their exclusive use. All offices, classrooms, dorm rooms, and other spaces have access to the Internet via a fiber-optic cable. Teacher education candidates receive initial technology instruction through a required course in education technology. Individual assistance is available to candidates and faculty through the computer center's help desk. Courses and clinical experiences routinely require the use of instructional technology and the Internet.

Teacher Preparation Program Information

The following programs are 4 year programs:

Elementary Education, K-12 Education (Art, Music, Physical Education), Middle School Education (Mathematics, Social Studies, Physical Education), Secondary Education (Art, Athletic Trainer, Biology, Chemistry, English, General Science, Mathematics, Physical Education, Social Studies), Special Education (Learning Disability)

Alverno College

Alverno is an independent, four-year liberal arts college for women, founded in 1887. The teacher education programs at Alverno prepare professional teachers who are committed to developing the abilities of all learners, who are effective in integrating subject area content and developmentally appropriate teaching and assessment strategies, and who understand and value diverse perspectives and experiences. The teacher education program at Alverno College has received national recognition from numerous sources, including the U.S. Department of Education, the Carnegie Foundation for the Advancement of Teaching, and the John D. and Catherine T. MacArthur Foundation.

Just the facts...

Alverno College
Division of Education
3400 South 43rd Street
P.O. Box 343922
Milwaukee, WI 53234-3922
(414) 382-6186
Website: www.alverno.edu
Profile: Urban, Small, Women
UG Tuition: $5,052.00/semester
Off Campus Programs: No

Clinical Experiences

Four semesters of field experiences progress from observation and one-to-one teaching situations, to small group teaching, to teaching a minimum of eight lessons for the whole class in a semester. Experiences include a range of grade levels and types of learning situations. Applying developmental theories, candidates refine their abilities to use various assessment and instructional methods, and to design learning experiences for all learners. An intensive semester of student teaching provides the opportunity to have full responsibility for a class under the guidance of a cooperating teacher and an Alverno supervisor.

Noteworthy

Cited as an exemplary teacher education program in a recent NCREST study, the teacher education program at Alverno College is a national model for teacher education that prepares candidates to meet the diverse needs of students in the twenty-first century. Alverno College is involved in multiple programs that facilitate teacher licensure, including the DeWitt Wallace-Reader's Digest Pathways to Teaching Careers Program, which helps educational assistants in schools to become teachers, and the Danforth Compton Teacher Development Project, an innovative/experiential program for liberal arts graduates pursuing teacher licensure while they are teaching.

Teacher Preparation Program Information

The following programs are 4 year programs:

Elementary Education, K-12 Education (Art, Music), Secondary Education (Biology, Chemistry, English/Language Arts, General Science, Mathematics, Psychology, Social Studies, Sociology)

The following programs are post-baccalaureate programs:

Elementary Education, K-12 Education (Art, Music), Secondary Education (Biology, Chemistry, English/Language Arts, General Science, Mathematics, Psychology, Social Studies, Sociology)

Cardinal Stritch University

The mission of the College of Education is (1) to provide leadership that responds to the educational needs of the community-at-large and affirms the importance of education as a profession; (2) to develop student and family-centered programs based on theory, research, practice, and service; and (3) to prepare and support the continued professional development of those who teach and lead in diverse environments. The College of Education strives to ensure that its graduates will be caring and effective decision makers supported by knowledge of research, ongoing reflection, and understanding of best instructional practices.

Just the facts...

Cardinal Stritch University
College of Education
6801 North Yates Road
Milwaukee, WI 53217
(414) 410-4000
Website: www.stritch.edu
Profile: Suburban, Medium, Co-Ed
UG Tuition: $328.00/credit hour
Off Campus Programs: Yes

Clinical Experiences

Initial teacher preparation is designed around multiple clinical experiences. The College of Education has two urban professional development schools that are sites for practica related to literacy and social studies methods courses. Several less formal partnerships provide additional opportunities for candidates to work in area schools. University instructors, their students, and K-12 teachers work collaboratively to advance the learning of elementary and secondary students.

Noteworthy

In response to initiatives from the Wisconsin Department of Public Education, the College of Education has structured all initial programs around a performance-based model of instruction and assessment. Student assessment is based on a three-tiered portfolio process designed around the conceptual framework of teacher as a reflective decision maker. The College of Education has also implemented a "Grow Your Own" program with local high schools. Qualified high school juniors and seniors may take selected education courses delivered in their high schools by university instructors for college credit.

Teacher Preparation Program Information

The following programs are 4 year programs:
Early Childhood Education, Elementary Education, K-12 Education (Art, French, Spanish), Middle School Education, Secondary Education (Biology, Chemistry, English, General Science, History, Mathematics, Social Studies, Sociology)

The following programs are post-baccalaureate programs:
Early Childhood Education, Elementary Education, K-12 Education (Art, French, Spanish), Middle School Education, Secondary Education (Biology, Chemistry, English, General Science, History, Mathematics, Social Studies, Sociology)

Edgewood College

Edgewood College prepares reflective practitioners for effective schools. Committed to student learning and continuing professional development, teachers and administrators should bring to their positions an informed view of the world; a solid grounding in content for teaching; a grasp of the principles and conditions of establishing a positive learning environment; a functional understanding of children's diverse backgrounds and learning styles; an appreciation of the value of parental involvement in student learning; sensitivity to the need for positive community relations; and a specialized expertise for their level and area of preparation.

Just the facts...

Edgewood College
Department of Education
855 Woodrow Street
Madison, WI 53711-1997
(608) 663-2293
Website: www.edgewood.edu
Profile: Urban, Small, Co-Ed
UG Tuition: $11,000.00/year
G Tuition: $340.00/credit hour
Off Campus Programs: No

Clinical Experiences

Strong emphasis is placed on a developmental program of multicultural and otherwise diverse field experiences and related courses to clarify career goals, build an experiential base for reflecting on teaching and learning, and lay the foundation for professional networking. Integration of theory and practice occurs throughout; student teaching and related seminars provide the basis for this integration. Student teaching is a full-semester, full-time experience.

Noteworthy

All teacher education programs include a common core of general education, professional education, and specialized professional studies and experiences tailored to professional goals. A strong advising program supported by institutional resources for enhancing learning and promoting developmental progress includes continuing assessment and evaluation and special assistance to encourage success. College-wide technological infrastructure together with a K-12 computing and instructional technology lab provide access to the latest tools for teaching and learning. A full line of financial aid packages provide tailored support.

Teacher Preparation Program Information

The following programs are 4 year programs:

Early Childhood Education, Elementary Education (Language Arts, Mathematics, Science, Social Studies), K-12 Education (Art), Secondary Education (Biology, Business, Chemistry, French, Spanish, English/Language Arts, General Science, Mathematics, Physical Sciences, Science, Social Studies), Special Education (Early Childhood)

The following programs are post-baccalaureate programs:

Early Childhood Education, Elementary Education (Language Arts, Mathematics, Science, Social Studies), K-12 Education (Art), Secondary Education (Biology, Business, Chemistry, French, Spanish, English/Language Arts, General Science, Mathematics, Physical Sciences, Science, Social Studies), Special Education (Early Childhood)

Marian College of Fond du Lac

First established as a school for teacher education in 1936, Marian College has been long committed to a strong liberal arts foundation as the basis of an excellent education. Dedicated to the holistic development of each individual, the teacher education programs provide undergraduate and graduate candidates with an educational experience that reflects the college's broader mission of developing the whole person. The faculty at Marian College is committed to the education and development of caring, competent, reflective educators by providing student-centered, developmentally and theoretically sound programs that reflect Judeo-Christian values within a democratic and global society.

Clinical Experiences

The undergraduate programs use the Preservice Teacher Perceiver Interview as a way of assessing talent, attitude, and the potential to attain excellence in the field of education. Talents identified in the interview are used for individualized goal setting in Marian's clinical field experience program. The program is comprised of four distinct levels of field experiences that take place before student teaching. Candidates spend up to 150 hours in a variety of K-12 school settings under the guidance of a cooperating teacher and a college clinical supervisor before student teaching for one semester. Marian has strong partnerships with area schools serving children from a variety of backgrounds, including those with special needs.

Just the facts...

Marian College of Fond du Lac
Educational Studies Division
45 South National Avenue
Fond du Lac, WI 54935
(920) 923-8143
Website: www.mariancollege.edu
Profile: Suburban, Small, Co-Ed
UG Tuition: $5,983.00/sem. in-state; $245.00/cr. hr. out-of-state
Off Campus Programs: Yes

Noteworthy

Education candidates have the opportunity to be involved with Marian College's Multicultural Student Initiative project, a program aimed at middle school minority students who might be interested in the teaching profession as a career. Currently, this program serves students from the Milwaukee Public Schools and the Oneida Indian Nation. Master's programs have been centered around a delivery system designed to allow candidates to complete their studies through intensive evening, weekend, and summer course formats offered at various sites in the state. Plans are underway to include undergraduate classes in education at these outreach centers to accommodate working adults.

Teacher Preparation Program Information

The following programs are 4 year programs:
Early Childhood Education, Elementary Education, K-12 Education (Art, Computer Science, French, German, Music, Spanish), Kindergarten Education, Secondary Education (Biology, Business, English/Language Arts, History, Mathematics, Science, Social Studies)

The following programs are post-baccalaureate programs:
Early Childhood Education, K-12 Education (Art, Computer Science, French, German, Music, Spanish), Secondary Education (Biology, Business, English/Language Arts, History, Mathematics, Science, Social Studies)

Marquette University

The School of Education's mission is to provide outstanding educational opportunities that enable undergraduate and graduate candidates to obtain satisfying professional positions in the public and private sectors. Marquette instills in its students the basic tenets of its Catholic and Jesuit philosophy, which incorporates Cura Personalis (care for the person). Care for the person is combined with care for knowledge and care for the profession as a basis for all teacher education programs. The School of Education is preparing for the twenty-first century by developing programs which use the latest technologies and sound pedagogy.

Just the facts...

Marquette University
School of Education
Schroeder Cx. 176
P.O. Box 1881
Milwaukee, WI 53233
(414) 288-7376
Website: www.mu.edu
Profile: Urban, Large, Co-Ed
UG Tuition: $8,140.00/semester
G Tuition: $350.00/credit hour
Off Campus Programs: No

Clinical Experiences

Candidates conduct their field experiences, practica, student teaching, and internships in carefully selected settings. These experiences are integrated into appropriate coursework so that, at all times, theory is related to effective practice. Clinical experiences in the initial program take place in a variety of settings, are well-sequenced, and are included in the initial coursework that candidates complete. A majority of the clinical experiences provide candidates with the opportunity to observe and interact with diverse student populations.

Noteworthy

The Ralph C. Hartman Center for Literacy and Learning provides candidates with the opportunity to help children in partnership schools develop literacy skills. Candidates can participate in a number of community-based school programs through the Institute for Transformation of Learning or can increase their understanding of children and families through the Parenting Center. Advanced standing candidates can enroll in a Web-based master's program in instructional leadership. The Compton Fellows program provides an opportunity for candidates with diverse backgrounds to enter a field-based, post-baccalaureate training program.

Teacher Preparation Program Information

The following programs are 4 year programs:
Elementary Education (Grades 1-6 or Grades 1-9 with Broad Field Science, Communication, English, French, German, History, Interdisciplinary Major in Social Studies, Mathematics, Spanish, Theatre Arts), Secondary Education (Grades 6-12 or Grades 9-12 with Anthropology, Biology, Broad Field Science, Broad Field Social Science, Chemistry, English, French, German, History, Journalism, Latin, Mathematics, Physics, Political Science, Psychology, Religious Studies, Sociology, Spanish, Speech, Theatre Arts)

The following programs are post-baccalaureate programs:
Elementary Education (Grades 1-6 or Grades 1-9 with Broad Field Science, Communication, English, French, German, History, Interdisciplinary Major in Social Studies, Mathematics, Spanish, Theatre Arts), Secondary Education (Grades 6-12 or Grades 9-12 with Anthropology, Biology, Broad Field Science, Broad Field Social Science, Chemistry, English, French, German, History, Journalism, Latin, Mathematics, Physics, Political Science, Psychology, Religious Studies, Sociology, Spanish, Speech, Theatre Arts)

University of Wisconsin at La Crosse

Future teachers graduating from the University of Wisconsin at La Crosse (UW-L) will be thoughtful learners, leaders, inquirers, and community members. The faculty believe that teachers must possess the ability to parlay pedagogical and curricular information into lessons that not only advance their students' academic achievement, but also fulfill education's public purpose—to prepare students for a democratic society. The faculty believe that teaching is a human development profession devoted to the growth and dignity of the learner. Teacher education candidates prepare for a career of serving youth in an ever-changing and dynamic society characterized by complexity and diversity.

Clinical Experiences

The clinical program is composed of three pre-student teaching experiences and one student teaching experience in a variety of rural and urban/suburban settings. The expectations and assessments for each experience are based on the program outcomes. Clinical experiences are developmentally sequenced along with the candidates' content, foundation, and methods courses. Clinical experiences are an important component of the admission and advancement process in the teacher education program. Faculty supervise candidates as they complete clinical experiences in partnership schools. Student teaching is an eighteen-week, full-time experience.

Just the facts...

University of Wisconsin at La Crosse
School of Education
1725 State Street
La Crosse, WI 54601
(608) 785-8122
Website: www.uwlax.edu
Profile: Urban, Medium, Co-Ed
UG Tuition: $134.25/cr. hr. in-state; $382.00/cr. hr. out-of-state
G Tuition: $204.25/cr. hr. in-state; $606.00/cr. hr. out-of-state
Off Campus Programs: No

Noteworthy

The Master of Education-Professional Development (ME-PD) program offers several tracks for candidates: initial licensure to teach, the Learning Community program held in area schools, and the individualized ME-PD degree. Candidates may also complete coursework at UW-L to complete a master's degree in educational administration from UW-Madison. Resources for candidates and area teachers include the Alice Hagar Curriculum Resource Center, the Center for Economic Development, the Rhea Pederson Reading Center, and the Science Education Service Center/NASA Teaching Resource Center.

Teacher Preparation Program Information

The following programs are 4 year programs:
Early Childhood Education, Elementary Education (Language Arts, Mathematics, Science, Social Studies), K-12 Education (Art, ESL, French, German, Health, Music, Physical Education, Spanish), Middle School Education (French, German, Spanish), Secondary Education (Biology, Chemistry, Earth Science, Economics, English/Language Arts, General Science, Geography, Mathematics, Physics, Political Science, Psychology, Science, Social Studies, Sociology)

The following programs are 5th year programs:
Early Childhood Education, Elementary Education (Language Arts, Mathematics, Science, Social Studies), K-12 Education (Art, ESL, French, German, Health, Music, Physical Education, Spanish), Middle School Education (French, German, Spanish), Secondary Education (Biology, Chemistry, Earth Science, Economics, English/Language Arts, General Science, Geography, Mathematics, Physics, Political Science, Psychology, Science, Social Studies, Sociology)

University of Wisconsin—Oshkosh

The goal of the professional education program at the University of Wisconsin—Oshkosh is to prepare educators to be caring intellectuals, skillful practitioners, reflective professionals, and lifelong learners knowledgeable about culture, content, and learning. Graduates are able to select or adapt curriculum and pedagogy to meet the needs of diverse learners, and strive to become agents for positive change in the schools and the society in which they serve. The program has a strong liberal arts base, field experiences integrated with coursework, and a semester of day-long student teaching with a culminating semester of graduate study to follow.

Just the facts...

University of Wisconsin—Oshkosh
College of Education & Human Services
800 Algoma Boulevard
Oshkosh, WI 54901
(920) 424-3322
Website: www.uwosh.edu
Profile: Suburban, Large, Co-Ed
UG Tuition: $1,389.95/sem. in-state; $4,530.95/sem. out-of-state
G Tuition: $1,818.95/sem. in-state; $5,640.95/sem. out-of-state
Off Campus Programs: No

Clinical Experiences

Field placements in special education settings, coordinated with on-campus study of exceptional education needs, are completed prior to admission to teacher education. Opportunities for involvement with persons from diverse cultures are arranged following an introductory course focusing on access to appropriate education for all. Successful completion of clinical experiences is required for admission to student teaching. Clinical experiences are integrated with enrollment in related courses in curriculum and methodology, and are supervised by methods course instructors.

Noteworthy

Licensable minors in Bilingual Education-Hmong, Bilingual Education-Spanish, and ESL, and a major providing dual licensure in elementary and special education are offered. The Departments of Special Education and Curriculum and Instruction and two nearby elementary schools are planning the fourth year of their Goals 2000 project. The project's goal is to include special needs students in regular education classrooms. Two recently completed classrooms fully equipped for state-of-the-art educational uses of technology are now used for the simultaneous offering of the educational technology course with methodology courses in specific content areas.

Teacher Preparation Program Information

The following programs are 4 year programs:
Middle School Education, Special Education

The following programs are post-baccalaureate programs:
Early Childhood Education, Elementary Education, P-12 Education (Art, French, German, Spanish, Music, Physical Education), Middle/Secondary School Education (Bilingual-Hmong, Bilingual-Spanish, Biology, Chemistry, Earth Science, Economics, English/Language Arts, ESL, General Science, Geography, Library Media Specialist, Mathematics, Physical Sciences, Physics, Psychology, Social Studies, Sociology), Special Education (Adaptive Physical Education, Cognitive Disabilities, Early Childhood, Emotional Disturbance, Exceptional Educational Needs, Learning Disabilities)

University of Wisconsin—Platteville

As the first public institution in Wisconsin, the University of Wisconsin—Platteville has prepared teachers since 1866. The School of Education takes pride in this tradition and is committed to the continuation of quality in its educational offerings and programs. The school prepares teachers who can demonstrate the knowledge, skill, and disposition to be effective, reflective practitioners. Building on a strong liberal arts background, the education programs are designed to develop communications skills, technology and media skills, knowledge of content and how to teach that content, and human relations. Programs build upon the theme "Good Teachers Make the Difference."

Just the facts...

University of Wisconsin—Platteville
School of Education
One University Plaza
Platteville, WI 53818
(608) 342-1131
Website: www.uwplatt.edu
Profile: Rural, Medium, Co-Ed
UG Tuition: $1,213.00/sem. in-state; $4,354.00/sem. out-of-state
G Tuition: $1,464.00/sem. in-state; $4,864.00/sem. out-of-state
Off Campus Programs: No

Clinical Experiences

As part of their preparation, teacher candidates spend 150 to 180 hours in school settings prior to student teaching. The purpose of these clinical experiences is to acquaint teacher candidates with different school types (e.g., middle schools), settings (e.g., suburban), and philosophies (e.g., open classrooms). These experiences are connected to university education courses so that teacher candidates will be able to connect educational theories with hands-on practice. University and school faculty supervise all clinical experiences.

Noteworthy

A unique feature is the program designed to prepare teachers to work with students in middle grades. This program has been developed to complement the excellent early childhood, elementary, and secondary teacher education programs. Middle-level studies are enhanced by the university's Center of Excellence—the Center of Education for the Young Adolescent. All education programs are located in a newly remodeled building to provide state-of-the-art classrooms, laboratories, and technology/media services. Educational experiences are more challenging and exciting because of these contemporary resources.

Teacher Preparation Program Information

The following programs are 4 year bachelor degree programs:
Early Childhood Education/Elementary Education, Elementary Education 1-6, Elementary/Middle Level Education 1-9, Middle Level Education 5-9, K-12 Education (Fine Arts, Music/General, Music/Instrumental, Physical Education), Secondary Education (Biology, Broad Field Science, Broad Field Social Science, Chemistry, English, Geography, German, History, Mathematics, Music/Choral, Psychology, Spanish, Speech Communication, Theater, Vocational Agriculture)

The following programs are post-baccalaureate programs:
Early Childhood Education/Elementary Education, Elementary Education 1-6, Elementary/Middle Level Education 1-9, Middle Level Education 5-9, K-12 Education (Fine Arts, Music/General, Music/Instrumental, Physical Education), Secondary Education (Biology, Broad Field Science, Broad Field Social Science, Chemistry, English, Geography, German, History, Mathematics, Music/Choral, Psychology, Spanish, Speech Communication, Theater, Vocational Agriculture)

The following programs are 5th year programs:
Reading

University of Wisconsin—River Falls

Teacher education has been a major commitment of the University of Wisconsin—River Falls since its founding in 1874. The university's teacher education programs have been designated by the National Education Association as one of the top ten exemplary programs in the country, and one of only three recognized for the quality of all its programs. The professional education faculty are committed to a reflective practitioner model. The performance-based program goals are directed toward the creation of knowledgeable and skillful teachers who will reflect on their professional practice and adapt it to meet the needs of their students.

Just the facts...

University of Wisconsin—River Falls
College of Education and Graduate Studies
410 South Third Street
River Falls, WI 54022
(715) 425-3774
Website: www.uerf.edu
Profile: Rural, Medium, Co-Ed
UG Tuition: $1,375.20/sem. in-state; $4,346.20/sem. out-of-state
G Tuition: $1,741.20/sem. in-state; $5,355.70/sem. out-of-state
Off Campus Programs: No

Clinical Experiences

Academic coursework is integrated with a broad range of practical experiences. Candidates are immersed in field experiences prior to student teaching; this practice allows them to apply their knowledge and decision making skills as they learn what it means to be a school professional. The pre-student teaching clinical experiences are structured to span several semesters, include a wide range of placements in urban, rural, and suburban environments, and are connected with specific courses and faculty. Student teaching is the culminating experience and is closely supervised by a university consultant as well as a cooperating teacher.

Noteworthy

The College of Education and Graduate Studies is committed to the integration of information and instructional technologies throughout their programs. Construction of a new Teacher Education building began in1998. The new building will have an Educational Technology Center as its focal point and is designed to enable the faculty to model techniques for enhancing instruction with technology. All classrooms will function as an integral part of the Educational Technology Center, and faculty and students will have immediate access to print and non-print curriculum materials as well as various instructional technologies.

Teacher Preparation Program Information

The following programs are 4 year programs:
Early Childhood Education, Elementary Education, K-12 Education (Art, Health, Modern Languages, Music, Physical Education), Secondary Education (Agriculture, Art, Biology, Chemistry, Earth Science, English/Language Arts, Mathematics, Physical Sciences, Physics, Science, Social Studies)

The following programs are 5th year programs:
Early Childhood Education, K-12 Education (Reading), Middle School Education, Secondary Education, Special Education (Adaptive Physical Education)

University of Wisconsin—Whitewater

The preparation of teachers has been a major part of the mission of the University of Wisconsin—Whitewater since its inception as a normal school in 1868. The university prepares a large number of teachers in Wisconsin, enrolling more than 2,200 candidates in its eight departments. The faculty believe that teachers are not simply dispensers of knowledge, but facilitators of learning who respond to their pupils' learning by constantly modifying classroom instruction. The ultimate goal of the teacher education program is to help candidates become capable investigators, problem solvers, communicators, and reflective thinkers.

Just the facts...

University of Wisconsin—Whitewater
College of Education
800 West Main Street
Whitewater, WI 53190
(414) 472-1101
Website: www.uww.edu
Profile: Rural, Large, Co-Ed
UG Tuition: $1,460.00/sem. in-state; $4,600.00/sem. out-of-state
G Tuition: $1,844.00/sem. in-state; $5,666.00/sem. out-of-state
Off Campus Programs: No

Clinical Experiences

Field experiences provide opportunties to relate principles learned in college coursework to actual practice in classrooms and schools. Candidates are given the opportunity to engage in field experiences in schools during all phases of their preparation. Each candidate completes a pre-student teaching clinical program consisting of a minimum of 100 hours working with children in a school or other instructional setting. A minimum of 50 hours is required in a school setting that serves a diverse population. Eighteen weeks of full-day student teaching are required. A limited amount of part-time student teaching is available in Texas and at international locations.

Noteworthy

UW—Whitewater's STREAM project is a collaborative effort to identify and academically assist highly able minority students through middle and senior high school. The Minority Teacher Prep Program is a special initiative designed to assist ethnic minority students with majors in the College of Education. Recent initiatives in the college include a significant expansion of technology, the formation of a diversity study team, the formation of a special interest group on international education and programs, and the expansion of out-of-state and international field placements for student teachers. UW—Whitewater is one of the most accessible campuses in the nation for individuals with physical handicaps.

Teacher Preparation Program Information

The following programs are 4 year programs:
Elementary Education, K-12 Education (Art, French, German, Music, Physical Education, Spanish), Secondary Education (Art, Biology, Business, Chemistry, Earth Science, Economics, English/Language Arts, General Science, Geography, Mathematics, Physical Education, Physical Sciences, Physics, Political Science, Psychology, Science, Social Studies, Sociology, Vocational Business Office, Vocational Marketing), Special Education (Early Childhood, Learning Disability, Severe Behavioral Disabilities/Handicaps)

The following programs are post-baccalaureate programs:
Early Childhood Education, K-12 Education (Art, Dance, French, German, Music, Physical Education, Spanish), Kindergarten Education, Middle School Education (English, Mathematics, Science, Social Studies), Secondary Education (Business, Earth Science, Economics, English/Language Arts, General Science, Geography, Health, Mathematics, Physical Education, Physical Sciences, Physics, Political Science, Psychology, Science, Social Studies, Sociology, Steno/Typing/Keyboard, Vocational Business Office, Vocational Marketing), Special Education (Adaptive Physical Education, Early Childhood, Learning Disability, Severe Behavioral Disabilities/Handicaps)

The following programs are 5th year programs:
K-12 Education (Reading), Secondary Education (Business), Special Education

Viterbo College

Viterbo College is a Roman Catholic college that embraces persons of all faiths in an ecumenical Christian community. The college, founded by the Franciscan Sisters of Perpetual Adoration, has prepared teachers since 1890. From the first freshman education course and throughout the program, candidates are in local K-12 classrooms as part of their college courses. Small classes and close interaction with college faculty and local teachers yield solid preparation for the real world of teaching. The faculty stress leadership, service, and the development of knowledge, dispositions, and skills that translate to effective learning for K-12 students.

Just the facts...

Viterbo College
Education Department
815 South 9th Street
La Crosse, WI 54601
(608) 796-3382
Website: www.viterbo.edu
Profile: Rural, Small, Co-Ed
UG Tuition: $5,710.00/semester
G Tuition: $160.00/credit hour
Off Campus Programs: No

Clinical Experiences

Clinical experiences begin the first semester of college for most candidates. A field experience assignment is an integral part of most education courses. Candidates participate in after-school tutoring and family nights in the schools. Local schools provide racially diverse student populations. Candidates work with P-12 students ranging from at-risk to gifted. Student teaching is a full-day, full-semester experience in which the student teacher assumes the role of the classroom teacher. College supervisors provide close supervision and support.

Noteworthy

Annual placement rates of education graduates are consistently 95 percent and above. Graduates find positions primarily in Wisconsin, Minnesota, and Iowa, but others teach in states across the nation. A Goals 2000 grant in its third year of funding provides a close partnership with two local elementary schools. Methods course teaching projects in these schools give hands-on experiences to candidates. Regional principals request Viterbo's graduates, and local cooperating teachers request Viterbo seniors for student teaching placements. In surveys, principals show high satisfaction with the Viterbo graduates they employ.

Teacher Preparation Program Information

The following programs are 4 year programs:

Early Childhood/Elementary Education (P-6), Elementary/Middle Education (English, History, Mathematics, Religious Studies, Science, Spanish), K-12 Education (Art, Music), Middle/Secondary Education (6-12), Secondary Education (Biology, Broad Field Social Studies, Chemistry, Computer Science, English, Mathematics, Religious Studies, Sociology, Spanish, Theatre)

The following programs are post-baccalaureate programs:

Early Childhood/Elementary Education (P-6), Elementary/Middle Education (English, History, Mathematics, Religious Studies, Science, Spanish), K-12 Education (Art, Music), Middle/Secondary Education (6-12), Secondary Education (Biology, Broad Field Social Studies, Chemistry, Computer Science, English, Mathematics, Religious Studies, Sociology, Spanish, Theatre)

University of Wyoming

The Wyoming Teacher Education Program is conducted by the College of Education in collaboration with the Wyoming School-University Partnership (WSUP). The Partnership brings together the following organizations: school districts in the state, the College of Education, the College of Arts and Sciences, Wyoming's seven community colleges (where candidates may complete the first level of the teacher education program before transferring to the UW Laramie campus or the elementary education program at UW/CC Center in Casper), the Wyoming State Department of Education, and the Wyoming Professional Teaching Standards Board.

Just the facts...

The University of Wyoming
College of Education
Box 3374
University Station
Laramie, WY 82071
(307) 766-2230
Website: http://ed.uwyo.edu/
Profile: Rural, Medium, Co-Ed
UG Tuition: $1,165.00/sem. in-state; $3,709.00/sem. out-of-state
G Tuition: $1,408.00/sem. in-state; $3,952.75/sem. out-of-state
Off Campus Programs: Yes

Clinical Experiences

Clinical experiences are divided into four different levels that involve candidates in progressively more demanding situations. First, candidates explore the dimensions of teachers' work with brief experiences in school classrooms. Second, candidates further develop principles of teaching and learning, and the culture of communities and schools, with further classroom experience. Third, candidates take specific methods courses and work in schools applying these methods. Finally, candidates spend a semester in a school setting for their student teaching experience.

Noteworthy

Most College of Education programs require successful completion of 130 to 140 credit hours. Usually, candidates complete these programs in approximately four and a half years, although it is possible to graduate in four years by taking a heavier load some semesters or by including a summer session. Candidates can choose between two paths for their clinical experiences. The first involves local placements; the typical placement for candidates choosing this path is the Wyoming Center for Teaching and Learning at Laramie (WCTL-L) located on campus. The second path involves school placements in districts throughout the state. Many students believe this is one of the best features of the program.

Teacher Preparation Program Information

The following programs are 4 year programs:
Elementary Education, K-12 Education (Art, Music), Middle School Education, Secondary Education (Agriculture, Business, English, English/Communications, English/Journalism, English/Library Science, English/Theatre, Family & Consumer Sciences/Home Economics, Industrial Technology, Mathematics, Modern Languages [French, German, Russian, Spanish], Science [Biological, Chemistry, Earth Science, Environmental, Physics], Social Studies)

The following programs are post-baccalaureate programs:
Secondary Education (Agriculture, Business, English, English/Communications, English/Journalism, English/Library Science, English/Theatre, Family & Consumer Sciences/Home Economics, Industrial Technology, Mathematics, Modern Languages [French, German, Russian, Spanish], Science [Biological, Chemistry, Earth Science, Environmental, Physics], Social Studies)

The following programs are 5th year programs:
Elementary/Special Education

University of Puerto Rico

The University of Puerto Rico, Rio Piedras Campus, has prepared teachers and other school personnel since 1900. The School of Education prepares teachers to be humanitarian-oriented reflective education professionals. Graduates consider curricular and developmental characteristics of students in socio-cultural contexts. Graduates have an understanding and appreciation of their culture and other cultures. Knowledge, professional commitment, and wisdom of practice provide the basis for the teacher preparation curriculum. The College of Education emphasizes communication, research, technology, assessment, social interaction, citizenship, leadership, and problem solving.

Just the facts...

University of Puerto Rico
School of Education
Rio Piedras Campus
P.O. Box 23304
San Juan, PR 00931-3304
(787) 764-2205
Website: www.upr.clu.edu
Profile: Urban, Medium, Co-Ed
UG Tuition: $578.00/sem. in-state; $1,200.00/sem. out-of-state
G Tuition: $900.00/sem. in-state; $1,750.00/sem. out-of-state
Off Campus Programs: No

Clinical Experiences

Clinical experiences are gradually sequenced from the moment the candidate begins the program to the student teaching practicum. They are designed to develop candidates' abilities to understand and provide for individual differences and special needs through observation, individual instruction, tutoring, work with small groups, and developing lesson plans, materials, and assessment procedures. The program requires 246 hours of clinical experience before the student teaching practicum. Student teaching requires a semester-long internship in an accredited elementary or secondary school.

Noteworthy

The present Secretary of Education and two congressmen in Puerto Rico are graduates of the advanced level education programs at the university. The College of Education sponsors several projects and initiatives, including Development of Talents, Renovation of the Middle School, Partnership Between Teachers from New York and Puerto Rico, Successful Community Schools, Teaching for Freedom, and the Preschool Laboratory for Deaf Children.

Teacher Preparation Program Information

The following programs are 4 year programs:

Elementary Education (Elementary Education K-6, Special Education Pre-K - 9), Secondary Education (Art, Biology, Business, Chemistry, Consumer & Family Science/Home Economics, English, French, General Science, History, Italian, Mathematics, Music, Physical Education, Physical Sciences, Social Studies, Spanish, Theatre, Vocational/Industry Arts)

The following programs are post-baccalaureate programs:

Elementary Education (Elementary Education K-6, Special Education Pre-K - 9), Secondary Education (Art, Biology, Business, Chemistry, Consumer & Family Science/Home Economics, English, French, General Science, History, Italian, Mathematics, Music, Physical Education, Physical Sciences, Social Studies, Spanish, Theatre, Vocational/Industry Arts)

Nationally Recognized Programs

In addition to the directory of institutions, this *Guide* provides further information about the quality of the specific program in which you may be interested. Meeting the standards of national professional associations is a quality indicator that can help you choose a program or institution. Many of the program areas listed under the institution's entry in the front part of this book have met national standards of excellence in their academic fields. Institutions with nationally recognized programs are listed in the next section for each of the following subject areas:

Early Childhood Education	Middle Level Education
Educational Communications and Technology	Physical Education
Educational Computing and Technology	Science Education
Elementary Education	Social Studies Education
English Language Arts Education	Special Education
Health Education	Technology Education
Mathematics Education	

NCATE has established partnerships with 43 states and the District of Columbia to conduct joint national and state visits. Some states require programs to be reviewed by the national organizations as part of the national/state review. In other states, NCATE depends on the state review of programs to provide data about their quality. The state standards in a few states have been declared compatible with national standards, making the programs in that field eligible for national recognition; these institutions are included on the lists in this section.

The following states have partnerships with NCATE:

Alabama	Kentucky	Ohio
Alaska	Maine	Oklahoma
Arkansas	Maryland	Oregon
California	Massachusetts	Pennsylvania
Connecticut	Michigan	Rhode Island
Delaware	Minnesota	South Carolina
District of Columbia	Mississippi	South Dakota
Florida	Missouri	Tennessee
Georgia	Montana	Texas
Hawaii	Nebraska	Virginia
Idaho	Nevada	Washington
Illinois	New Mexico	West Virginia
Indiana	New York	Wisconsin
Iowa	North Carolina	Wyoming
Kansas	North Dakota	

States also conduct a review of the programs that prepare teachers for a state license to teach a specific subject or subjects at a specific level (for example, early childhood, elementary, middle level, secondary, or K-12). All programs offered at NCATE-accredited units must be approved by the appropriate state agency before an accreditation visit is scheduled.

This section includes all institutions with nationally recognized programs as of March 1, 1999. Addresses and phone numbers for each association that reviews programs are listed in this section.

There may be a few discrepancies between the program listings on the following pages and the programs listed in the front section of the *Guide*. The differences are due to institutions adding, changing, combining, and eliminating programs in response to changing student needs and state-mandated requirements. If a discrepancy exists, contact the association and the institution directly to verify the program's status.

Early Childhood Education

Professional Organization: **National Association for the Education of Young Children (NAEYC)**
1509 16th Street, NW
Washington, DC 20036-1426
(202) 232-8777

Focus of the Standards: Programs for the initial preparation of early childhood teachers at the baccalaureate, post-baccalaureate, and/or master's levels. Early childhood education programs prepare teachers to work with children from birth through age eight. NAEYC also has standards for the advanced preparation of early childhood educators; for information on approved programs at the advanced level, contact the NCATE office.

History of the Standards: NAEYC standards for early childhood education were first approved by NCATE in June 1982; the most recent revision was adopted in 1994.

The institutions below offer one or more programs in early childhood education that meet NCATE's program standards.

Alabama
Alabama A&M University
Alabama State University
University of Alabama at Birmingham

Arkansas
Arkansas State University
University of Arkansas at Little Rock
University of Arkansas at Pine Bluff

California
California State University at Fresno

Connecticut
Central Connecticut State University

Delaware
Delaware State University

District of Columbia
The Catholic University of America

Florida
University of Florida
University of South Florida

Georgia
Albany State University
Kennesaw State University
North Georgia College and State University
University of Georgia
Valdosta State University

Illinois
Chicago State University
Elmhurst College
Roosevelt University
Western Illinois University

Kansas
Saint Mary College

Louisiana
Grambling State University
Louisiana State University and A&M College
Louisiana Tech University
McNeese State University
Northwestern State University of Louisiana
Southeastern Louisiana University
University of New Orleans

Maine
University of Maine at Farmington

Maryland
Bowie State University
Coppin State College
University of Maryland at College Park

Massachusetts
Boston College

Michigan
Eastern Michigan University
Madonna University
Marygrove College
Wayne State University

Minnesota
Bemidji State University
Concordia University, St. Paul
Moorhead State University
Saint Cloud State University
University of Minnesota-Twin Cities

Missouri
Evangel University

Harris-Stowe State College
Maryville University
Missouri Southern State College
Saint Louis University
Southeast Missouri State University
Southwest Missouri State University
University of Missouri at Saint Louis

Nebraska
University of Nebraska at Omaha

New Hampshire
Keene State College of New Hampshire

New Jersey
Kean University
Montclair State University
Rider University
William Paterson University of New Jersey

North Carolina
University of North Carolina at Chapel Hill
University of North Carolina at Charlotte
University of North Carolina at Greensboro

Ohio
Ashland University
Bowling Green State University
Kent State University
Ohio University
University of Akron
University of Cincinnati
University of Dayton
University of Toledo
Youngstown State University

Pennsylvania
Bloomsburg University of Pennsylvania

California University of Pennsylvania
Clarion University of Pennsylvania
Indiana University of Pennsylvania
Kutztown University of Pennsylvania
Lock Haven University of Pennsylvania
Marywood University
Millersville University of Pennsylvania
University of Scranton
West Chester University

Rhode Island
Rhode Island College
University of Rhode Island

South Carolina
South Carolina State University
University of South Carolina at Columbia
University of South Carolina at Spartanburg
Winthrop University

Tennessee
Middle Tennessee State University
University of Memphis

Texas
Baylor University
Prairie View A&M University
Stephen F. Austin State University
Texas A&M University
Texas Tech University
University of Houston at Clear Lake

Utah
Brigham Young University
Utah State University

Vermont
University of Vermont

Virginia
Eastern Mennonite University
George Mason University
James Madison University
Norfolk State University
Old Dominion University
Virginia Commonwealth University
Virginia Polytechnic Institute & State University

Washington
Washington State University

West Virginia
Concord College
Marshall University
West Liberty State College

Wisconsin
Cardinal Stritch University
Edgewood College

Educational Communications and Technology

Professional Organization:

Association for Educational Communications and Technology (AECT)
1025 Vermont Avenue, NW, Suite 820
Washington, DC 20005
(202) 347-7834

Focus of the Standards:

Programs for the preparation of educational communications and technology specialists at the baccalaureate level. AECT also has standards for advanced educational communications and technology programs at the graduate level; for information on approved graduate programs, contact the NCATE office.

History of the Standard:

AECT standards were first approved by NCATE in October 1982; the most recent revision was adopted in 1994.

The institutions below offer one or more programs in educational communications and technology that meet NCATE's program standards.

Connecticut
Central Connecticut State University

District of Columbia
The Catholic University of America

Florida
University of Miami
University of South Florida

Ohio
Kent State University
Ohio University
University of Toledo
Wright State University

Tennessee
University of Memphis

Utah
Utah State University

Virginia
University of Virginia

Educational Computing and Technology

Professional Organization: **International Society for Technology in Education (ISTE)**
1787 Agate Street
Eugene, OR 97403-9905
(503) 346-4414

Focus of the Standards: Programs for the initial preparation of teachers of educational computing and technology at the baccalaureate, post-baccalaureate, and/or master's levels. ISTE also has standards for educational computing and technology leadership programs at the graduate level; for information on approved graduate programs, contact the NCATE office.

History of the Standards: ISTE standards for educational computing and technology were first approved by NCATE in September 1991; the most recent revision was adopted in 1996.

The institutions below offer one or more programs in educational computing and technology that meet NCATE's program standards.

Connecticut
Central Connecticut State University
University of Hartford

Illinois
Elmhurst College
Roosevelt University
Western Illinois University

Louisiana
Louisiana State University
Louisiana Tech University
McNeese State University
Northwestern State University of Louisiana

Maryland
Bowie State University
University of Maryland at College Park

Michigan
Eastern Michigan University
Wayne State University

Mississippi
Mississippi State University
University of Southern Mississippi

Missouri
Central Missouri State University
Evangel University
Southwest Missouri State University
University of Missouri-Saint Louis

Ohio
Ashland University
Ohio University
University of Akron
University of Dayton

Pennsylvania
Indiana University of Pennsylvania
University of Scranton

Rhode Island
Rhode Island College

Tennessee
Middle Tennessee State University

Texas
Stephen F. Austin State University
Texas A & M University
Texas Tech University

Utah
Utah State University

Vermont
University of Vermont

Virginia
George Mason University
James Madison University

West Virginia
Marshall University
West Liberty State College

Elementary Education

Professional Organization: **Association for Childhood Education International (ACEI)**
17904 Georgia Avenue, Suite 215
Olney, MD 20832
(301) 570-2111

Focus of the Standards: Programs for the initial preparation of elementary school teachers at the baccalaureate, post-baccalaureate, and/or master's levels.

History of the Standards: ACEI standards were first approved by NCATE in September 1989. Draft performance-based standards are being pilot-tested in 1999; these new standards will be presented to NCATE for adoption in October 1999.

The institutions below offer one or more programs in elementary education that meet NCATE's program standards.

Alabama
Alabama A&M University

Arkansas
Arkansas State University
Arkansas Tech University
Harding University
Henderson State University
Hendrix College
John Brown University
Lyon College
Philander Smith College
Southern Arkansas University
University of Arkansas at Little Rock
University of Arkansas-Monticello
University of Arkansas at Pine Bluff
University of Central Arkansas
University of the Ozarks

California
California State University Dominguez Hills
California State University, Hayward
California State University, Los Angeles
California State University, Northridge
Loyola Marymount University
San Jose State University
University of Pacific

Colorado
University of Colorado at Boulder
University of Colorado at Colorado Springs
University of Colorado at Denver
University of Northern Colorado

Connecticut
Central Connecticut State University
University of Connecticut

Delaware
Delaware State University

District of Columbia
Catholic University of America
Gallaudet University

Florida
University of Florida
University of South Florida

Illinois
Augustana College
Chicago State University
Elmhurst College
Illinois State University

Roosevelt University
Western Illinois University

Kentucky
Spalding University

Louisiana
Louisiana State University and A&M College
Louisiana Tech University
McNeese State University
Nicholls State University
Northeast Louisiana State University
Northwestern State University of Louisiana
Southeastern Louisiana University
University of New Orleans
University of Southwestern Louisiana

Maryland
Bowie State University
University of Maryland-College Park

Massachusetts
University of Massachusetts at Amherst

Michigan
Central Michigan University
Eastern Michigan University
Grand Valley State University
Madonna University
Wayne State University
Western Michigan University

Minnesota
Augsburg College
Bethel College
College of St. Benedict/St. John's University
Concordia College-Moorhead
Saint Cloud State University
University of Minnesota-Morris
University of Minnesota-Twin Cities

Mississippi
Mississippi State University
The University of Mississippi
University of Southern Mississippi

Missouri
Central Missouri State University
Drury College
Evangel College
Lincoln University
Maryville University
Missouri Southern State College
Missouri Western State College

Northwest Missouri University
Saint Louis University
Southeast Missouri State University
Southwest Missouri University
Truman State University
University of Missouri-Saint Louis
Washington University

Nebraska
Creighton University
Dana College
Doane College

New Hampshire
University of New Hampshire

New Jersey
College of New Jersey
Kean University
New Jersey City University
Rider University
Rowan University

New York
Buffalo State College, SUNY
Fordham University
Hofstra University

North Carolina
Elizabeth City State University
North Carolina Central University
University of North Carolina-Charlotte
University of North Carolina-Greensboro
University of North Carolina-Wilmington
Winston-Salem State University

Ohio
Baldwin-Wallace College
Bowling Green State University
Cleveland State University
University of Akron
University of Cincinnati
University of Dayton

Pennsylvania
Clarion University of Pennsylvania
Indiana University of Pennsylvania
Marywood University
Temple University
University of Scranton
West Chester University

Puerto Rico
University of Puerto Rico

Rhode Island
Rhode Island College
University of Rhode Island

South Carolina
Clemson University
College of Charleston
Francis Marion University
Lander University
Newberry College
South Carolina State University
University of South Carolina at Columbia
University of South Carolina at Spartanburg
Winthrop University

Texas
Baylor University
Prairie View A&M University
San Houston State University
Stephen F. Austin State University

Texas A&M University

Utah
Brigham Young University
Utah State University
Weber State University

Vermont
University of Vermont

Virginia
Eastern Mennonite University
Hampton University
Longwood College
Radford University
Virginia State University

Wisconsin
Cardinal Stritch University
University of Wisconsin-Platteville

West Virginia
Alderson-Broaddus College
Concord College
Fairmont State College
Glenville State College
Shepherd College
West Virginia State College
West Virginia University
West Virginia Wesleyan College

English Language Arts Education

Professional Organization: **National Council of Teachers of English (NCTE)**
1111 West Kenyon Road
Urbana, IL 61801-1096
(217) 328-2870

Focus of the Standards: Programs for the initial preparation of English language arts teachers at the baccalaureate, post-baccalaureate, and/or master's levels.

History of Standards: NCTE standards were first approved by NCATE in April 1987; the most recent revision was adopted in October 1997.

The institutions below offer one or more programs in English language arts education that meet NCATE's program standards.

Alabama
Alabama A&M University
Alabama State University
Athens State University
Auburn University
Auburn University-Montgomery
Birmingham-Southern College
Jacksonville State University
Oakwood College
Samford University
Troy State University
Troy State University Dothan
Tuskegee University
The University of Alabama
University of Alabama at Birmingham
University of Montevallo
University of North alabama
University of South Alabama
The University of West Alabama

Arkansas
Arkansas State University
Arkansas Tech University
Harding University
Henderson State University
Hendrix College
John Brown University
Lyon College
Philander Smith College
Southern Arkansas University
University of Arkansas-Fayetteville
University of Arkansas-Little Rock
University of Arkansas-Monticello
University of Arkansas-Pine Bluff
University of Central Arkansas
University of the Ozarks

California
California State University-Northridge
San Diego State University

Colorado
Adams State College
Colorado State University
Metropolitan State College of Denver
University of Colorado-Boulder
University of Colorado-Colorado Springs
University of Colorado-Denver
University of Northern Colorado

Connecticut
Central Connecticut State University
University of Connecticut

Delaware
Delaware State University

National Council for Accreditation of Teacher Education

District of Columbia
The Catholic University of America
Gallaudet University

Florida
University of Central Florida
University of Florida
University of South Florida

Georgia
Armstrong Atlantic State University
University of Georgia

Illinois
Augustana College
Chicago State University
Elmhurst College
Roosevelt University
Western Illinois University

Kentucky
Murray State University
Spalding University
University of Louisville

Louisiana
Grambling State University
Louisiana State University in Shreveport
Louisiana Tech University
McNeese State University
Northeast Louisiana University
Northwestern State University of Louisiana
Southeastern Louisiana University
Southern University and A&M College
University of New Orleans
University of Southwestern Louisiana

Maryland
Bowie State University
Coppin State College
University of Maryland at College Park

Massachusetts
University of Massachusetts-Amherst

Michigan
Andrews University
Calvin College
Central Michigan University
Eastern Michigan University
Grand Valley State University
Madonna University
Marygrove College
Saginaw Valley State University
Wayne State University
Western Michigan University

Minnesota
Augsburg College
Bemidji State University

Bethel College
College of St. Benedict/St. John's University
College of Saint Catherine
Concordia College, Moorhead
Concordia University, St. Paul
Hamline University
Minnesota State University-Mankato
Moorhead State University
Saint Cloud State University
Saint Olaf College
The University of Minnesota at Morris
University of Minnesota, Duluth
University of Minnesota-Twin Cities
University of Saint Thomas
Winona State University

Mississippi
Mississippi College
Mississippi State University
Mississippi Valley State University
University of Southern Mississippi

Missouri
Central Missouri State University
Drury College
Evangel University
Lincoln University
Maryville University
Missouri Southern State College
Missouri Western State College
Northwest Missouri State University
Saint Louis University
Southeast Missouri State University
Southwest Missouri State University
University of Missouri-Kansas City
University of Missouri-Saint Louis
Washington University

Montana
Montana State University
Montana State University-Billings
University of Montana

Nebraska
Dana College
Doane College
Union College
University of Nebraska-Omaha
Wayne State College

New Hampshire
University of New Hampshire

New Jersey
College of New Jersey
Montclair State University
Rider University
Rowan University

New Mexico
New Mexico State University

New York
Buffalo State College, SUNY
Hofstra University
Niagara University

North Carolina
Appalachian State University
Barton College
Belmont Abbey College
Bennett College
Campbell University
Catawba College
Davidson College
Duke University
East Carolina University
Elizabeth City State University
Elon College
Fayetteville State University
Gardner-Webb University
Greensboro College
Guilford College
High Point University
Johnson C. Smith University
Lees-McRae College
Lenoir-Rhyne College
Livingstone College
Mars Hill College
Meredith College
Methodist College
Montreat College
North Carolina A&T State University
North Carolina Central University
North Carolina State University
North Carolina Wesleyan College
Pfeiffer University
Queens College
Saint Augustine's College
Salem College
Shaw University
The University of North Carolina-Asheville
University of North Carolina-Chapel Hill
University of North Carolina-Charlotte
University of North Carolina-Greensboro
The University of North Carolina-Pembroke
University of North Carolina-Wilmington
Wake Forest University
Warren Wilson College
Western Carolina University
Winston-Salem State University
Wingate University

Ohio
Ashland University
Baldwin-Wallace College
Bowling Green State University
Cleveland State University
Kent State University

Miami University
Ohio Northern University
The Ohio State University
Ohio University
Otterbein College
University of Akron
University of Cincinnati
The University of Dayton
Wright State University
Youngstown State University

Oklahoma
The University of Oklahoma

Pennsylvania
Bloomsburg University of Pennsylvania
California University of Pennsylvania
Clarion University of Pennsylvania
Indiana University of Pennsylvania
Kutztown University of Pennsylvania
Lock Haven University of Pennsylvania
Marywood University
Shippensburg University of Pennsylvania
Slippery Rock University of Pennsylvania
University of Scranton
West Chester University

Rhode Island
Rhode Island College
University of Rhode Island

South Carolina
The Citadel
Clemson University
Newberry College
South Carolina State University
University of South Carolina-Columbia
University of South Carolina-Spartanburg
Winthrop University

Tennessee
Vanderbilt University (Peabody College)

Texas
Stephen F. Austin State University
Texas A&M University
Trinity University

Utah
Brigham Young University
Utah State University
Weber State University

Vermont
University of Vermont

Virginia
Eastern Mennonite University
James Madison University
Longwood College

Norfolk State University
Old Dominion University
Radford University
University of Virginia
Virginia Polytechnic & State University
Virginia State University

Washington
Central Washington University
Washington State University

West Virginia
Alderson-Broaddus College
Bethany College
Concord College
Fairmont State College
Marshall University
Shepherd College
The University of Charleston
West Liberty State College
West Virginia State College
West Virginia University
West Virginia Wesleyan College

Wisconsin
Cardinal Stritch University
University of Wisconsin-Platteville

Health Education

Professional Organization:	**American Alliance for Health, Physical Education, Recreation, and Dance/ Association for the Advancement of Health Education (AAHPERD/AAHE)** 1900 Association Drive Reston, VA 22091-1599 (703) 476-3437
Focus of the Standards:	Programs for the initial preparation of health educators at the baccalaureate, post-baccalaureate, and/or master's levels.
History of the Standards:	AAHPERD/AAHE standards were first approved by NCATE in April 1987; the most recent revision was adopted in 1995.

The institutions below offer one or more programs in health education that meet NCATE's program standards.

Arkansas
University of Arkansas, Fayetteville
University of Central Arkansas

California
California State University, Northridge
San Diego State University

Delaware
Delaware State University

Florida
University of Florida

Georgia
The University of Georgia

Illinois
Illinois State University

Kentucky
University of Louisville

Louisiana
Southern University and A&M College

National Council for Accreditation of Teacher Education

Michigan
Central Michigan University

Minnesota
Bemidji State University
Concordia College, Moorhead
Saint Cloud State University

Missouri
Truman State University

Nebraska
University of Nebraska at Omaha

Nevada
University of Nevada, Las Vegas

New Jersey
Montclair State University

New York
Hofstra University

North Carolina
Appalachian State University

East Carolina University
University of North Carolina at Greensboro

Ohio
Bowling Green State University
Kent State University
University of Akron
The University of Dayton
Youngstown State University

Oregon
Oregon State University

Pennsylvania
Indiana University of Pennsylvania
Slippery Rock University of Pennsylvania
Temple University
West Chester University

Rhode Island
Rhode Island College

South Carolina
South Carolina State University

University of South Carolina at Spartanburg

Tennessee
Austin Peay State University

Texas
Stephen F. Austin State University
Texas A&M University
University of North Texas

Utah
Brigham Young University

Virginia
Norfolk State University
Virginia Commonwealth University

Washington
Central Washington University
Washington State University

West Virginia
Concord College
West Liberty State College

Mathematics Education

Professional Organization: **National Council for Teachers of Mathematics (NCTM)**
1906 Association Drive
Reston, VA 20191
(703) 620-9840

Focus of the Standards: Programs for the initial preparation of mathematics teachers to work in departmentalized elementary schools, middle schools, junior high schools, and/or senior high schools. Programs are offered at the baccalaureate, post-baccalaureate, and/or master's levels.

History of the Standards: Standards were first approved by NCATE in June 1982; the most recent revision was adopted in October 1998.

The institutions below offer one or more programs in mathematics education that meet NCATE's program standards.

Alabama
Alabama A&M University
Alabama State University
Tuskegee University

Arkansas
Arkansas State University
Arkansas Tech University
Harding University
Henderson State University
John Brown University Lyon College
Philander Smith College

Southern Arkansas University
University of Arkansas, Fayetteville
University of Arkansas at Little Rock University
of Arkansas at Monticello
University of Arkansas at Pine Bluff
University of Central Arkansas
University of the Ozarks

California
California State University Dominguez Hills
California State University, Fresno
California State University, Hayward

California State University, Los Angeles
California State University, Northridge
Loyola Marymount University
San Diego State University
University of Pacific

Colorado
Adams State College
Colorado State University
Metropolitan State College of Denver
University of Colorado at Boulder
University of Colorado at Colorado Springs

University of Colorado at Denver
University of Northern Colorado

Connecticut
Central Connecticut State University
University of Connecticut
The University of Hartford

Delaware
Delaware State University

District of Columbia
The Catholic University of America
Gallaudet University

Florida
University of Florida
University of South Florida

Georgia
Armstrong Atlantic State University
Augusta State University
Georgia Southern University
Valdosta State University

Illinois
Chicago State University
DePaul University
Elmhurst College
Illinois State University
Roosevelt University
Western Illinois University

Indiana
Ball State University
Indiana Wesleyan University

Iowa
Graceland College
Wartburg College

Kansas
Saint Mary College

Kentucky
Murray State University
Spalding University
University of Louisville
Western Kentucky University

Louisiana
Grambling State University
Louisiana State University and A&M College
Louisiana State University in Shreveport
Louisiana Tech University
McNeese State University
Nicholls State University
Northeast Louisiana University
Northwestern State University of Louisiana
Southeastern Louisiana University

Southern University and A&M College
University of New Orleans
University of Southwestern Louisiana
Xavier University of Louisiana

Maryland
Bowie State University
Coppin State College
University of Maryland at College Park

Massachusetts
University of Massachusetts-Amherst

Michigan
Calvin College
Central Michigan University
Eastern Michigan University
Grand Valley State University
Madonna University
Marygrove College
Saginaw Valley State University
Wayne State University
Western Michigan University

Minnesota
Augsburg College
Bemidji State University
Bethel College
Concordia College, Morehead
Concordia University, St. Paul
Hamline University
Moorhead State University
St. Cloud State University
University of Minnesota-Twin Cities

Mississippi
Millsaps College
Mississippi State University
Mississippi University for Women
Mississippi Valley State University
University of Mississippi
University of Southern Mississippi

Missouri
Central Missouri State University
Evangel University
Harris-Stowe State College
Lincoln University
Maryville University
Missouri Southern State College
Missouri Western State College
Northwest Missouri State University
Saint Louis University
Southeast Missouri State University
Southwest Missouri State University
Truman State University
University of Missouri at Kansas City
University of Missouri at Saint Louis
Washington University

Montana
Montana State University
Montana State University-Billings
University of Montana

Nebraska
Creighton University
Dana College
Doane College
Nebraska Wesleyan University
Union College
University of Nebraska-Omaha
Wayne State College

New Hampshire
Keene State College of New Hampshire

New Jersey
College of New Jersey
Kean University
Montclair State University
New Jersey City University
Rider University

New Mexico
New Mexico State University

New York
Buffalo State College, SUNY
Fordham University
Hofstra University
Niagara University

North Carolina
Appalachian State University
East Carolina University
Fayetteville State University
North Carolina A&T State University
North Carolina State University
University of North Carolina-Chapel Hill
University of North Carolina-Charlotte
University of North Carolina-Greensboro
The University of North Carolina at Pembroke
University of North Carolina-Wilmington
Western Carolina University
Winston-Salem State University

Ohio
Ashland University
Baldwin-Wallace College
Bowling Green State University
Cleveland State University
Kent State University
Ohio Northern University
The Ohio State University
Ohio University
Otterbein College
University of Akron
University of Cincinnati
The University of Dayton

National Council for Accreditation of Teacher Education

University of Toledo
Wright State University
Youngstown State University

Oklahoma
Oklahoma Baptist University

Pennsylvania
California University of Pennsylvania
Clarion University of Pennsylvania
Indiana University of Pennsylvania
Kutztown University of Pennsylvania
Lock Haven University of Pennsylvania
Marywood University
The Pennsylvania State University
Shippensburg University of Pennsylvania
Slippery Rock University of Pennsylvania
Temple University
University of Scranton
West Chester University

Puerto Rico
University of Puerto Rico

Rhode Island
Rhode Island College
University of Rhode Island

South Carolina
The Citadel
Clemson University

Newberry College
South Carolina State University
University of South Carolina at Columbia
University of South Carolina-Spartanburg
Winthrop University

Tennessee
Austin Peay University
Vanderbilt University-Peabody College

Texas
Prairie View A&M University
Sam Houston State University
Stephen F. Austin State University
Texas A&M University

Utah
Brigham Young University
Utah State University

Vermont
University of Vermont

Virginia
Eastern Mennonite University
George Mason University
Hampton University
James Madison University
Longwood College
Norfolk State University
Old Dominion University

Radford University
Virginia Commonwealth University
Virginia Polytechnic Institute & University
Virginia State University

Washington
Central Washington University
Western Washington University

Wisconsin
Cardinal Stritch University
University of Wisconsin-Platteville
University of Wisconsin-River Falls
University of Wisconsin-Whitewater

West Virginia
Bethany College
Bluefield State College
Concord College
Fairmont State College
Glenville State College
Marshall University
Shepherd College
University of Charleston
West Liberty State College
West Virginia State College
West Virginia University
West Virginia Wesleyan College

Wyoming
University of Wyoming

Middle Level Education

Professional Organization:

The National Middle School Association (NMSA)
2600 Corporate Exchange Drive, Suite 370
Columbus, OH 43231
(614) 895-4730 or (800) 528-NMSA

Focus of the Standards:

Programs for the initial preparation of middle school teachers at the baccalaureate, post-baccalaureate, and/or master's levels.

History of the Standards:

NMSA standards were first approved by NCATE in June 1989; the most recent revision was adopted in 1995.

The institutions below offer one or more programs in middle level education that meet NCATE's program standards.

Alabama
Auburn University
Jacksonville State University
Troy State University Dothan
University of Alabama at Birmingham
University of Montevallo
The University of West Alabama

Arkansas
Harding University
University of Arkansas, Fayetteville

California
California State University Dominguez Hills
California State University, Los Angeles
California State University, San Marcos
San Jose State University

Connecticut
Central Connecticut State University

Delaware
Delaware State University

Georgia
Albany State University
Kennesaw State University

The University of Georgia
Valdosta State University

Illinois
Illinois State University

Kansas
Emporia State University
Kansas State University
Pittsburg State University
University of Kansas

Kentucky
Spalding University
Western Kentucky University

Michigan
Central Michigan University

Minnesota
Saint Cloud State University

Missouri
Central Missouri State University
Harris-Stowe State College
Maryville University
Missouri Southern State University
Northwest Missouri State University
Saint Louis University
Southwest Missouri State University

Washington University

Nebraska
Doane College

North Carolina
Barton College
Belmont Abbey College
Bennett College
Campbell University
Catawba College
East Carolina University
Elizabeth City State University
Elon College
Fayetteville State University
Gardner-Webb University
Greensboro College
High Point University
Lees-McRae College
Lenoir-Rhyne College
Mars Hill College
Meredith College
Methodist College
North Carolina Central University
North Carolina State University
North Carolina Wesleyan College
University of North Carolina-Chapel Hill
University of North Carolina-Greensboro
University of North Carolina-Wilmington
Wingate University

North Dakota
University of North Dakota

Ohio
Ashland University
Baldwin-Wallace College
Ohio University
University of Cincinnati

South Dakota
Augustana College
University of South Dakota

Virginia
George Mason University
James Madison University
Old Dominion University
Radford University

West Virginia
Bethany College
Marshall University

Wisconsin
University of Wisconsin at La Crosse
University of Wisconsin at Platteville

Physical Education

Professional Organization:

**American Alliance for Health, Physical Education, Recreation, and Dance/
National Association for Sport and Physical Education (AAHPERD/NASPE)**
1900 Association Drive
Reston, VA 22091-1599
(703) 476-3410

Focus of the Standards:

Programs for the initial preparation of physical education teachers at the baccalaureate, post-baccalaureate, and/or master's levels. NASPE also has standards for advanced physical education programs at the graduate level; for information on approved graduate programs, contact the NCATE office.

History of the Standards:

AAHPERD/NASPE standards were first approved by NCATE in March 1985; the most recent revision was adopted in January 1997.

The institutions below offer one or more programs in physical education that meet NCATE's program standards.

Alabama
Alabama A&M University
Alabama State University
Athens State University
Auburn University
Auburn University-Montgomery

Jacksonville State University
Oakwood College
Samford University
Troy State University
Tuskegee University
The University of Alabama

University of Alabama at Birmingham
University of Montevallo
University of North Alabama
University of South Alabama
The University of West Alabama

National Council for Accreditation of Teacher Education

Arkansas

Arkansas State University
Arkansas Tech University
Harding University
Hendrix College
John Brown University
Southern Arkansas University
University of Arkansas-Monticello
University of Arkansas-Pine Bluff
University of Central Arkansas
University of the Ozarks

California

California State University, Fresno

Colorado

University of Northern Colorado

Connecticut

Central Connecticut State University
University of Connecticut

Delaware

Delaware State University

District of Columbia

Gallaudet University

Florida

University of South Florida

Georgia

Valdosta State University

Illinois

Augustana College
Chicago State University
Elmhurst College
Western Illinois University

Kentucky

Eastern Kentucky University
Western Kentucky University

Louisiana

Grambling State University
Louisiana State University and A&M College
Louisiana Tech University
Northeast Louisiana University
Northwestern State University of Louisiana
Southern University and A&M College
University of Southwestern Louisiana
Xavier University of Louisiana

Michigan

Central Michigan University
Eastern Michigan University
Northern Michigan University
Saginaw Valley State University
Wayne State University

Western Michigan University

Minnesota

Bethel College
Saint Cloud State University
University of Minnesota-Twin Cities

Mississippi

Mississippi State University
Mississippi Valley State University
University of Southern Mississippi

Missouri

Central Missouri State University
Drury College
Northwest Missouri State University
Southeast Missouri State University
Southwest Missouri State University
University of Missouri-Kansas City

Nebraska

Union College
University of Nebraska-Omaha
Wayne State College

New Hampshire

University of New Hampshire

New Jersey

Montclair State University
Rowan University
William Paterson University of New Jersey

New York

Hofstra University

North Carolina

Barton College
Campbell University
Catawba College
East Carolina University
Elizabeth City State University
Elon College
Fayetteville State University
Gardner-Webb University
Greensboro College
High Point University
Johnson C. Smith University
Lees-McRae College
Lenoir-Rhyne College
Livingstone College
Mars Hill College
Meredith College
Methodist College
North Carolina A&T State University
North Carolina Central University
Pfeiffer University
Saint Andrews Presbyterian College
Saint Augustine's College
University of North Carolina-Wilmington

Winston-Salem State University
Wingate University

Ohio

Ashland University
Baldwin-Wallace College
Bowling Green State University
Cleveland State University
The Ohio State University
Ohio University
University of Akron
The University of Dayton
Youngstown State University

Oregon

Oregon State University

Pennsylvania

Indiana University of Pennsylvania
Lock Haven University of Pennsylvania
Slippery Rock University of Pennsylvania
Temple University
West Chester University

Puerto Rico

University of Puerto Rico

Rhode Island

Rhode Island College
University of Rhode Island

South Carolina

The Citadel
Newberry College
South Carolina State University
University of South Carolina-Spartanburg

South Dakota

Augustana College
Black Hills State University
Dakota State University
Northern State University
South Dakota State University
University of Sioux Falls
University of South Dakota

Tennessee

Middle Tennessee State University

Texas

Stephen F. Austin State University
Texas A&M University
University of North Texas

Utah

Brigham Young University
Utah State University

Vermont

University of Vermont

Virginia
George Mason University
Hampton University
James Madison University
Longwood College
Old Dominion University
Radford University
Virginia Commonwealth University
Virginia Polytechnic Institute & State University
Virginia State University

West Virginia
Alderson-Broaddus College
Bethany College
Fairmont State College
Marshall University
Shepherd College
West Liberty State College
West Virginia University

Wisconsin
Central Washington University
University of Wisconsin at La Crosse
University of Wisconsin at River Falls

Science Education

Professional Organization:

National Science Teachers Association (NSTA)
1840 Wilson Boulevard
Arlington, VA 22201-3000
(703) 243-7100

Focus of the Standards:

Programs for the initial preparation of science teachers at the baccalaureate, post-baccalaureate, and/or master's levels.

History of Standards:

NSTA standards were first approved by NCATE in October 1984; the most recent revision was adopted in October 1998.

The institutions below offer one or more programs in science education that meet NCATE's program standards.

Alabama
Alabama A&M University (Chemistry, Physics)
Alabama State University (Biology, Chemistry, General Science)
Auburn University (General Science)
University of Alabama at Birmingham (Biology, Chemistry, Earth Science, General Science, Physics)

Arkansas
Arkansas State University (Biology, Chemistry, Physics)
Arkansas Tech University (Biology, Chemistry, Earth Science, Physical Science, Physics)
Harding University (Biology, Chemistry, Physics)
Henderson State University (Biology, Chemistry, Physics)
Hendrix College (Biology, Chemistry, Physics)
John Brown University (Biology, Chemistry)
Lyon College (Biology, Chemistry, General Science, Physical Science)
Ouachita Baptist University (Biology, Chemistry, Physics)
Philander Smith College (Biology)
Southern Arkansas University (Elementary, Biology, Chemistry, General Science, Physics)
University of Arkansas at Fayetteville (Biology, Chemistry, Earth Science, General Science, Physics)

University of Arkansas at Little Rock (Physical Science)
University of Arkansas at Monticello (Biology, Chemistry, Physical Science)
University of Arkansas at Pine Bluff (Biology, Chemistry)
University of Central Arkansas (Biology, Chemistry, General Science, Physics)
University of the Ozarks (Biology)

California
California State University, Fresno (Biology, Chemistry, Physical Science)
California State University, Fullerton (Biology, General Science)
California State University, Northridge (Biology, Chemistry)
San Diego State University (Biology, Physical Science)
San Francisco State University (Biology)

Colorado
Adams State College (Biology, Chemistry, Earth Science, Physics)
Colorado State University (Biology, Chemistry, Earth Science, Physics)
Metropolitan State College of Denver (Biology, Chemistry, Earth Science, Physics)
University of Colorado at Boulder (Biology,

Chemistry, Earth Science, Physics)
University of Colorado at Colorado Springs (Biology, Chemistry, Earth Science, General Science, Physics)
University of Colorado at Denver (Biology, Chemistry, Earth Science, General Science, Physics)
University of Northern Colorado (Biology, Chemistry, Earth Science, Physical Science, Physics)

Connecticut
Central Connecticut State University (Biology, Chemistry, Earth Science, General Science, Physics)
University of Connecticut (Biology, Chemistry, Earth Science, General Science, Physics)

Delaware
Delaware State University (Biology, Chemistry, Physics, Broad Field)

District of Columbia
The Catholic University of America (Biology, Chemistry, Physics)
Gallaudet University (General Science)

Florida
Florida A&M University (Middle Level, Biology)

National Council for Accreditation of Teacher Education

Florida Atlantic University (Middle Level, Biology)
University of Central Florida (Biology, Chemistry, Physics)
University of Florida (Biology, Chemistry, Physics)
University of South Florida (Biology, Chemistry, Physics)

Georgia
Armstrong Atlantic State University (Biology, Chemistry)
Georgia Southern University (Biology, Chemistry, Earth Science, Physics)
The University of Georgia (Middle Level, Biology, Chemistry, Earth Science, Physics)
Valdosta State University (Biology)

Illinois
Bradley University (Earth Science)
Chicago State University (Biology, Chemistry)
Elmhurst College (Biology, Chemistry)
Illinois State University (Biology, Chemistry, Physics)
Wheaton College (Biology, chemistry, Physical Science, Physics)

Indiana
DePauw University (Biology, Chemistry, Earth Science, Physics)

Iowa
Graceland College (Biology, Chemistry)
Wartburg College (Elementary, Biology, Chemistry, General Science, Physics)

Kansas
Saint Mary College (Biology, Chemistry, General Science, Physical Science, Physics)

Kentucky
Murray State University (Biology, Chemistry, Earth Science, Physics)
University of Kentucky (Middle Level, Biology, Chemistry, Earth Science, General Science, Physical Science, Physics)
University of Louisville (Middle Level, Biology, Chemistry, Earth Science, General Science, Physics)
Western Kentucky University (Middle Level, Biology, Chemistry, Earth Science, General Science, Physics)

Louisiana
Grambling State University (Biology, Chemistry)
Louisiana Tech University (Biology, Chemistry, Earth Science, Physics)
Nicholls State University (Earth Science, General Science)
Northeast Louisiana University (Biology,

Chemistry, Earth Science, Physics)
Northwestern State University of Louisiana (Biology, Chemistry, General Science, Physics)
Southeastern Louisiana State University (Biology, Chemistry, Physics)
Southern University and A&M College (Biology, Chemistry, General Science, Physics)
University of New Orleans (Chemistry)
University of Southwestern Louisiana (General Science)

Maine
University of Maine at Farmington (Biology, General Science, Physical Science)

Maryland
Coppin State College (Biology, Chemistry)
University of Maryland at College Park (Biology, Chemistry, Physics)

Massachusetts
Boston College (Biology, Chemistry, Earth Science, Physics)
The University of Massachu-setts at Amherst (Biology, Chemistry, Earth Science, Physics)

Michigan
Andrews University (Biology)
Calvin College (Elementary, Biology, Chemistry, Earth Science, General Science, Physics)
Central Michigan University (Elementary, Middle Level, Biology, Chemistry, Earth Science, Physical Science, Dual Field Chemistry/Physics)
Eastern Michigan University (Biology, Chemistry, Earth Science, Physics)
Grand Valley State University (Biology, Chemistry, Earth Science, Physics)
Madonna University (Elemen-tary, Middle Level, Biology, Chemistry, Physical Science)
Marygrove College (Biology, Chemistry)
Northern Michigan University (Biology, Earth Science, General Science, Physics)
Saginaw Valley State University (Biology, Chemistry, General Science, Physics)
Wayne State University (Elementary, Middle Level, Biology, Chemistry, Earth Science, General Science, Physics)
Western Michigan University (Biology, Chemistry, Earth Science, Physics)

Minnesota
Augsburg College (Biology, Chemistry, Physics)
Bemidji State University (Middle Level, Biology, Earth Science)
Bethel College (Biology)
College of St. Benedict/St. John's University (General Science)
College of Saint Catherine (Biology)
Concordia College, Moorhead (Biology)
Concordia University, St. Paul (Biology)

Gustavus Adolphus (Biology)
Hamline University (Chemistry, Physics)
Moorhead State University (Biology, Chemistry, Physics)
University of Minnesota at Morris (Biology, Chemistry, Earth Science)
University of Minnesota-Twin Cities (Middle Level, Biology, Earth Science)

Mississippi
Alcorn State University (Biology, Chemistry)
Mississippi College (Biology)
Mississippi State University (Biology, Chemistry, General Science)
Mississippi Valley State University (Biology)
University of Mississippi (Biology, Chemistry, General Science, Physics)
University of Southern Mississippi (Biology, Chemistry, General Science, Physical Science)

Missouri
Central Missouri State University (Biology, Chemistry, Earth Science, Physics)
Lincoln University (Biology, Chemistry, Physics)
Maryville University (Biology, Chemistry, General Science, Physics)
Missouri Southern State College (Middle Level, Biology, Chemistry, Physics)
Missouri Western State College (Biology, Chemistry, General Science)
Northwest Missouri State University (Biology, Chemistry, Earth Science, Physics)
Saint Louis University (Middle Level)
Southeast Missouri State University (Biology, Chemistry, Earth Science, Physics)
Southwest Missouri State University (Biology, Chemistry, Earth Science, Physics)
Truman State University (Biology, Chemistry, Physics)
University of Missouri at St. Louis (Biology, Chemistry, Physics)
Washington University (Biology, Chemistry, Earth Science, Physics)

Montana
University of Montana (Biology, Chemistry, Earth Science, Physics)

Nebraska
Creighton University (Biology, Chemistry, General Science, Physics)
Dana College (Biology, Chemistry)
Doane College (Biology, Chemistry)
Nebraska Wesleyan University (Biology, Chemistry)
Peru State College (Chemistry, General Science, Physical Science)
Union College (Biology, Chemistry, Physics)
University of Nebraska at Omaha (Biology, Chemistry, Earth Science, General Science,

Physical Science, Physics)
Wayne State College (Elementary, Biology, Chemistry, Earth Science, Physical Science)

Nevada
University of Nevada at Las Vegas (Elementary, Biology, Chemistry, Earth Science, General Science, Physical Science, Physics)

New Hampshire
Keene State College of New Hampshire (Biology, Earth Science)
University of New Hampshire (Biology, General Science)

New Jersey
College of New Jersey (Physics)
Kean University (Biology, Earth Science)
Montclair State College (Biology, Chemistry, Earth Science, Physics)
Rider University (Secondary Core)
Rowan University (Biology, Chemistry, Physical Science, Physics)
William Paterson University of New Jersey (Elementary, Biology, Chemistry, General Science)

New Mexico
New Mexico State University (Earth Science, Physics)
The University of New Mexico (Biology, Chemistry, Earth Science, General Science, Physics)

New York
Buffalo State College, SUNY (Biology, Chemistry, Earth Science, Physics)
Fordham University (Biology, Chemistry, General Science, Physics)
Hofstra University (Biology, Chemistry, Earth Science, Physics)
Niagara University (Biology, Chemistry)

North Carolina
Appalachian State University (Middle Level, Biology, Chemistry, Earth Science, Physics)
East Carolina University (Biology, Chemistry, Earth Science, Physics)
Elizabeth City State University (Biology, Chemistry)
Fayetteville State University (Biology)
North Carolina A&T University (Biology, Chemistry, Physics)
North Carolina Central University (Biology, Chemistry)
North Carolina State University (Middle Level, Biology, Chemistry, Earth Science, General Science)
University of North Carolina at Asheville (Chemistry)

University of North Carolina at Chapel Hill (Middle Level, Biology, Chemistry, Earth Science, Physics)
University of North Carolina at Charlotte (Middle Level, Biology, Chemistry, Earth Science, Physics)
University of North Carolina at Greensboro (Biology, Chemistry, Physics)
University of North Carolina at Pembroke (Middle Level, Biology, Chemistry, Earth Science, Physics)
University of North Carolina at Wilmington (Middle Level, Biology, Chemistry, Earth Science, Physics)
Western Carolina University (Middle Level, Biology, Chemistry, General Science)

North Dakota
North Dakota State University (Biology, Chemistry, Earth Science, General Science, Physics)

Ohio
Ashland University (Biology, Chemistry, Earth Science, Physics)
Baldwin-Wallace College (Middle Level, Biology, Chemistry, General Science, Physics)
Bowling Green State University (Biology, Chemistry, Earth Science, General Science, Physics)
Cleveland State University (Biology, Chemistry, Earth Science, Physics)
Kent State University (Biology, Chemistry, Earth Science, General Science, Physics)
Miami University (Chemistry)
Ohio Northern University (Biology, Chemistry, General Science)
Ohio University (Middle Level, Chemistry, Earth Science, Physics)
Otterbein College (Biology, Chemistry, General Science, Physics)
University of Akron (Biology, Chemistry, Earth Science, General Science, Physics)
University of Cincinnati (Biology, Chemistry, Earth Science, General Science, Physics)
University of Dayton (Biology, Chemistry, Earth Science, General Science, Physics)
University of Toledo (Biology, Earth Science)
Wright State University (Biology, Chemistry, Earth Science, General Science, Physics)
Youngstown State University (Biology, Chemistry, Earth Science, General Science, Physics)

Pennsylvania
Bloomsburg University of Pennsylvania (Biology, Chemistry, Earth Science, General Science, Physics)
California University of Pennsylvania (Biology, Chemistry, Earth Science, General Science, Physics)

Clarion University of Pennsylvania (Middle Level, Biology, Chemistry, Earth Science, General Science, Physics)
Indiana University of Pennsylvania (Biology, Chemistry, Earth Science, Physics)
Kutztown University of Pennsylvania (Biology, Chemistry, Earth Science, General Science)
Lock Haven University of Pennsylvania (Biology, Chemistry, Earth Science, General Science, Physics)
Marywood University (Biology, General Science)
Millersville University of Pennaylvania (Biology, Chemistry, Earth Science, Physics)
Shippensburg University of Pennsylvania (Biology, Chemistry, Earth Science, General Science, Physics)
Slippery Rock University of Pennsylvania (Biology, Chemistry, Earth Science, General Science, Physics)
Temple University (Biology, Chemistry, Earth Science, General Science, Physics)
University of Scranton (Biology, Chemistry, General Science, Physics)
West Chester University (Biology, Chemistry, Earth Science, Physics)

Puerto Rico
University of Puerto Rico (Biology, Chemistry, General Science, Physics)

Rhode Island
Rhode Island College (Biology, Chemistry, General Science, Physics)
University of Rhode Island (Biology, Chemistry, General Science, Physics)

South Carolina
The Citadel (Biology, General Science)
Newberry College (Biology)
South Carolina State University (Biology, Chemistry)
University of South Carolina at Columbia (Biology, Chemistry, Earth Science, Physics)
University of South Carolina at Spartanburg (Biology, Chemistry)
Winthrop University (Biology, Chemistry)

Tennessee
Austin Peay State University (Biology, Chemistry, Earth Science, General Science, Physics)
East Tennessee State University (Biology, Chemistry, Earth Science, Physics)
Middle Tennessee State University (Biology, Chemistry, Earth Science, General Science, Physics)
Milligan College (Biology, Chemistry, General Science)
University of Memphis (Chemistry, Earth Science, Physics)
University of Tennessee Chattanooga (Secondary

Core)
University of Tennessee Knoxville (Biology, Chemistry, Earth Science, General Science, Physics)
University of Tennessee at Martin (Biology, Chemistry, Earth Science, Physics)
Vanderbilt University-Peabody College (Biology, Chemistry, Earth Science, Physics)

Texas
Sam Houston State University (Elementary, Biology, Chemistry, Earth Science, General Science, Physical Science, Physics)
Texas A&M University (Biology)
University of Houston at Clear Lake (Biology, Chemistry, Earth Science)

Utah
Brigham Young University (Biology, Chemistry, Earth Science, Physical Science, Physics)
Utah State University (Biology, Earth Science, Physical Science, Physics)

Vermont
University of Vermont (Biology, Chemistry, Earth Science, Physics)

Virginia
Eastern Mennonite University (Biology, Chemistry)
George Mason University (Biology, Chemistry, Earth Science, Physics)
James Madison University (Biology, Chemistry, Earth Science, General Science Physical Science, Physics)
Longwood College (Biology, Chemistry, Physics)
Norfolk State University (Biology, Chemistry, Earth Science, Physics)
Old Dominion University (Middle Level, Biology, Chemistry, Earth Science, Physics)
Radford University (Biology, Chemistry, Earth Science, General Science)
University of Virginia (Biology, Chemistry, Earth Science, Physics)
Virginia Commonwealth University (Biology, Physics)
Virginia Polytechnic Institute & State University

(Biology, Earth Science)

Washington
Pacific Luthern University (Chemistry, Earth Science, General Science)
Washington State University (Chemistry, General Science, Physics)
Western Washington University (Biology, Chemistry, Earth Science, General Science, Physics)

West Virginia
Concord College (Chemistry)
Glenville State College (Middle Level, Biology, Chemistry, General Science)
Marshall University (Middle Level, Biology, Chemistry, General Science, Physics)
Shepherd College (Biology, Chemistry, General Science)

Social Studies Education

Professional Organization: **National Council for the Social Studies (NCSS)**
3501 Newark Street, NW
Washington, DC 20016
(202) 966-7840

Focus of the Standards: Programs for the initial preparation of social studies teachers and teachers of specific social science disciplines (e.g., history or geography) at the baccalaureate, post-baccalaureate, and/or master's levels.

History of the Standards: NCSS standards were first approved by NCATE in April 1987; the most recent revision was adopted in 1997.

The institutions below offer one or more programs in social studies education that meet NCATE's program standards.

Alabama
Auburn University (Secondary Social Studies)

Arkansas
Arkansas State University (Secondary Social Studies)
Arkansas Tech University (Secondary Social Studies, History, Political Science)
Harding University (Secondary Social Studies)
Henderson State University (Secondary Social Studies)
Hendrix College (Secondary Social Studies)
John Brown University (Secondary Social Studies)

Ouachita Baptist University (Secondary Social Studies)
Southern Arkansas University (Middle School and Secondary Social Studies)
University of Arkansas, Fayetteville (Middle School and Secondary Social Studies)
University of Arkansas at Little Rock (Secondary Social Studies)
University of Arkansas at Monticello (Secondary Social Studies)
University of Arkansas at Pine Bluff (Secondary Social Studies)
University of Central Arkansas (Secondary Social Studies)

University of the Ozarks (Secondary Social Studies, History)

California
California State University, Fresno (Secondary Social Studies)
California State University, Northridge (Secondary Social Studies)

Colorado
Adams State College (Secondary Social Studies)
Colorado State University (Secondary Social Studies)
Metropolitan State College of Denver (Second-

ary Social Studies)

University of Colorado at Boulder (Secondary Social Studies)

University of Colorado at Denver (Secondary Social Studies)

University of Northern Colorado (Secondary Social Studies, American History)

Connecticut

Central Connecticut State University (Social Science Education, History)

University of Connecticut (Secondary Social Studies)

Delaware

Delaware State University (Middle School and Secondary Social Studies)

District of Columbia

The Catholic University of America (Secondary Social Studies)

Gallaudet University (Secondary Social Studies)

Florida

University of Florida (Secondary Social Studies)

Georgia

Armstrong Atlantic State University (American History, Political Science)

Georgia Southern University (Secondary Social Studies)

Spelman College (Economics, History, Political Science)

The University of Georgia (Secondary Social Studies)

Illinois

Chicago State University (History, Geography)

Elmhurst College (History, Geography, Political Science)

Illinois State University (Secondary Social Studies, History)

Roosevelt University (Middle Level and Secondary Social Studies)

Iowa

Graceland College (History)

Wartburg College (Secondary Social Studies)

Kentucky

Murray State University (Middle Level Social Studies)

University of Louisville (Middle Level and Secondary Social Studies)

Western Kentucky University (Middle and Secondary Social Studies, Economics, Geography, Government, History, Psychology, Sociology)

Louisiana

Grambling State University (Secondary Social Studies)

Louisiana Tech University (Secondary Social Studies)

McNeese State University (Secondary Social Studies)

Nichols State Univesity (Secondary Social Studies)

Northeast Louisiana University (Secondary Social Studies)

Northwestern State University of Louisiana (Secondary Social Studies)

Southeastern Louisiana University (Secondary Social Studies)

Southern University and A&M College (Secondary Social Studies)

Xavier University of Louisiana (Secondary Social Studies)

Maryland

Bowie State University (Middle Level and Secondary Social Studies)

Coppin State College (Secondary Social Studies)

University of Maryland at College Park (Middle Level and Secondary Social Studies, Geography, History)

Massachusetts

The University of Massachu-setts at Amherst (Middle Level and Secondary Social Studies)

Michigan

Calvin College (Secondary Social Studies)

Central Michigan University (Middle and Secondary Social Studies, History)

Eastern Michigan University (Comprehensive Social Studies, History)

Grand Valley State University (Comprehensive Social Studies, History)

Madonna University (Secondary Social Studies, History)

Marygrove College (Secondary Social Studies, History)

Saginaw Valley State University (History)

Wayne State University (Secondary Social Studies)

Minnesota

Augsburg College (Secondary Social Studies)

Bemidji State University (Secondary Social Studies)

Bethel College (Secondary Social Studies)

College of St. Benedict/St. John's University (Secondary Social Studies)

Concordia College, Moorhead (Middle Level and Secondary Social Studies)

Concordia University, St. Paul (Secondary Social Studies)

Hamline University (Secondary Social Studies)

Saint Cloud State University (Secondary Social Studies)

University of Minnesota-Twin Cities (Secondary Social Studies)

Mississippi

Mississippi College (Secondary Social Studies)

Mississippi State University (Secondary Social Studies)

Mississippi Valley State University (Secondary Social Studies)

The University of Mississippi (Secondary Social Studies)

University of Southern Mississippi (Secondary Social Studies)

Missouri

Central Missouri State University (Secondary Social Studies)

Drury College (Middle Level and Secondary Social Studies)

Harris-Stowe State College (Secondary Social Studies)

Lincoln University (Secondary Social Studies)

Maryville University (Secondary Social Studies)

Missouri Southern State College (Middle Level Social Studies)

Northwest Missouri State University (Middle Level and Secondary Social Studies)

Southeast Missouri State University (Secondary Social Studies)

Truman State University (Secondary Social Studies)

University of Missouri at Kansas City (Secondary Social Studies)

University of Missouri at Saint Louis (Secondary Social Studies)

Washington University (Secondary Social Studies)

Montana

University of Montana (Comprehensive Social Studies, Economics, Geography, History, Political Science, Sociology)

Nebraska

Creighton University (History, Political Science)

Dana College (Secondary Social Studies, History)

Doane College (Secondary Social Studies)

Union College (Secondary Social Studies, History)

University of Nebraska at Omaha (Secondary Social Studies)

Wayne State College (Anthropology, Economics, Geography, History, Political Science, Social Science, Sociology)

New Hampshire

Keene State College of New Hampshire

(Secondary Social Studies, Geography, History, Sociology)

New Jersey
College of New Jersey (Secondary Social Studies)
Kean University (Secondary Social Studies)
Montclair State University (Secondary Social Studies)
Rider University (Secondary Social Studies)
Rowan University (Secondary Social Studies)

New York
Buffalo State College, SUNY (Secondary Social Studies)
Hofstra University (Secondary Social Studies)
Niagara University (Secondary Social Studies)

North Carolina
Appalachian State University (Middle Level and Secondary Social Studies)
East Carolina University (Secondary Social Studies)
Elizabeth City State University (Secondary Social Studies)
Fayetteville State University (Secondary Social Studies, History, Political Science, Sociology)
North Carolina A&T State University (Secondary Social Studies, History)
North Carolina Central University (Comprehensive Social Studies, History)
North Carolina State University (History, Political Science, Sociology)
University of North Carolina at Chapel Hill (Middle Level and Secondary Social Studies)
University of North Carolina at Charlotte (Middle Level and Secondary Social Studies)
University of North Carolina at Greensboro (Secondary Social Studies, Anthropology, Economics, Geography, History, Political Science, Psychology, Sociology)
The University of North Carolina at Pembroke (Middle Level and Secondary Social Studies)
University of North Carolina at Wilmington (Middle Level and Secondary Social Studies, History, Political Science, Sociology)
Western Carolina University (Middle Level and Secondary Social Studies)
Winston-Salem State University (Middle Level and Secondary Social Studies)

Ohio
Ashland University (Middle Level and Secondary Social Studies)
Baldwin-Wallace College (Secondary Social Studies, History)
Bowling Green State University (Secondary Social Studies)
Cleveland State University (Comprehensive Social Studies, Economics, Political Science, Sociology/ Psychology)
Kent State University (Secondary Social Studies)
The Ohio State University (Secondary Social Studies)
Ohio University (Middle Level and Secondary Social Studies)
University of Akron (Secondary Social Studies)
University of Cincinnati (Middle Level and Secondary Social Studies)
The University of Dayton (Secondary Social Studies, Economics, History, Government/ Political Science, Sociology/Psychology)
Wright State University (Secondary Social Studies, History)
Youngstown State University (Secondary Social Studies, Economics, History, Geography, Political Science, Psychology, Sociology)

Oklahoma
Southeastern Oklahoma State University (Secondary Social Studies)

Pennsylvania
Bloomsburg University of Pennsylvania (Secondary Social Studies)
California University of Pennsylvania (Secondary Social Studies)
Clarion University of Pennsylvania (Secondary Social Studies)
Indiana University of Pennsylvania (Secondary Social Studies)
Kutztown University of Pennsylvania (Secondary Social Studies)
Marywood University (Secondary Social Studies)
Slippery Rock University of Pennsylvania (Secondary Social Studies, History, Political Science, Geography, Economics, Sociology/ Anthropology)
West Chester University (Anthropology, Geography, History, Political Science, Philosophy, Psychology, Sociology)

Puerto Rico
University of Puerto Rico (Secondary Social Studies, History)

Rhode Island
Rhode Island College (Secondary Social Studies, History)
University of Rhode Island (Secondary Social Studies, History)

South Carolina
The Citadel (Secondary Social Studies, Comprehensive Social Studies, History)
Clemson University (History, Geography)
Newberry College (History)
South Carolina State University (Secondary Social Studies, History)
University of South Carolina-Columbia (Economics, Geography, History, Political Science, Psychology, Sociology)
University of South Carolina at Spartanburg (Secondary Social Studies, History, Political Science)
Winthrop University (Secondary Social Studies)

Tennessee
University of Tennessee at Martin (Economics, History, Political Science)
Vanderbilt University-Peabody College (Secondary Social Studies, Economics, Government, History, Political Science)

Texas
Texas A&M University (Secondary Social Studies)
Trinity University (Secondary Social Studies, Economics, History, Government)

Utah
Brigham Young University (Secondary Social Studies)
Utah State University (Secondary Social Studies)

Vermont
University of Vermont (Secondary Social Studies)

Virginia
Eastern Mennonite University (Secondary Social Studies)
George Mason University (Secondary Social Studies, History)
Hampton University (Middle Level and Secondary Social Studies)
James Madison University (Secondary Social Studies, Economics, History, Geography, Government)
Longwood College (History, Political Science)
Norfolk State University (Social Studies, History)
Old Dominion University (Middle Level and Secondary Social Studies)
Radford University (Secondary Social Studies, History)
University of Virginia (Secondary Social Studies)
Virginia Commonwealth University (Secondary Social Studies)
Virginia Polytechnic Institute & State University (Secondary Social Studies)
Virginia State University (Secondary Social Studies, History)

Washington
Washington State University (Secondary Social Studies)

West Virginia
Bethany College (Middle Level and Secondary

Social Studies)
Concord College (Middle Level and Secondary Social Studies)
Fairmont State College (Secondary Social Studies)
Marshall University (Middle Level and Secondary Social Studies)
The University of Charleston (Middle Level and Secondary Social Studies)
West Liberty State College (Middle Level and

Secondary Social Studies)
West Virginia State College (Middle Level and Secondary Social Studies)
West Virginia University (Secondary Social Studies)
West Virginia Wesleyan College (Middle Level and Secondary Social Studies)

Wisconsin
Cardinal Stritch University (History)

University of Wisconsin at La Crosse (Secondary Social Studies, History, Geography, Government/ Political Science, Sociology)
University of Wisconsin-Platteville (Middle Level and Secondary Social Studies)
University of Wisconsin-River Falls (Secondary Social Studies)

Special Education

Professional Organization: **Council for Exceptional Children (CEC)**
1920 Association Drive
Reston, VA 20191-1589
(703) 620-3660

Focus of the Standards: Programs for the initial preparation of special education teachers at the baccalaureate, post-baccalaureate, and/or master's levels. CEC also has standards for doctoral level; for information on approved doctoral programs, contact the NCATE office.

History of Standards: CEC standards were first approved by NCATE in October 1984; the most recent revision was adopted in October 1996.

The institutions below offer one or more programs in special education that meet NCATE's program standards.

Alabama
Alabama A&M University
Alabama State University
Tuskegee University
The University of Alabama
University of Alabama at Birmingham

Arkansas
Arkansas State University
Harding University
Henderson State University
John Brown University
Philander Smith College
University of Arkansas at Little Rock
University of Arkansas at Monticello
University of Arkansas at Pine Bluff
University of Central Arkansas
University of the Ozarks

California
California State University, Fullerton
California State University, Northridge
San Diego State University
San Francisco State University

Colorado
Adams State College
Metropolitan State College of Denver

University of Colorado at Boulder
University of Colorado at Colorado Springs
University of Colorado at Denver
University of Northern Colorado

Connecticut
Central Connecticut State University
University of Connecticut
The University of Hartford

Delaware
Delaware State University

District of Columbia
Gallaudet University
George Washington University

Florida
Florida Atlantic University
University of Central Florida
University of Florida
University of Miami
University of South Florida

Georgia
Albany State University
Armstrong Atlantic State University
Georgia Southern University

North Georgia College & State University
The University of Georgia
Valdosta State University

Illinois
Chicago State University
DePaul University
Elmhurst College
Illinois State University
Western Illinois University

Kentucky
Northern Kentucky University
The University of Kentucky
University of Louisville
Western Kentucky University

Louisiana
Grambling State University
McNeese State University
Nicholls State University
Northeast Louisiana University
Northwestern State University of Louisiana
Southeastern Louisiana University
Southern University and A&M College
University of New Orleans
University of Southwestern Louisiana

National Council for Accreditation of Teacher Education

Maine
University of Maine at Farmington

Maryland
Bowie State University
Coppin State College
University of Maryland at College Park

Massachusetts
Boston College
The University of Massachusetts at Amherst

Michigan
Calvin College
Central Michigan University
Eastern Michigan University
Grand Valley State University
Madonna University
Marygrove College
Northern Michigan University
Oakland University
Wayne State University
Western Michigan University

Minnesota
Bemidji State University
Saint Cloud State University
University of Minnesota-Twin Cities

Mississippi
Mississippi College
Mississippi State University
The University of Mississippi
University of Southern Mississippi

Missouri
Central Missouri State University
Drury College
Evangel University
Missouri Southern State College
Northwest Missouri State University
Saint Louis University
Southeast Missouri State University
Southwest Missouri State University
Truman State University
University of Missouri at Kansas City
University of Missouri at Saint Louis
Washington University

Nebraska
Creighton University
Dana College
Doane College
Nebraska Wesleyan University
Peru State College
Wayne State College

Nevada
University of Nevada, Las Vegas

New Hampshire
Keene State College of New Hampshire

New Jersey
College of New Jersey
Kean University
Montclair State University
New Jersey City University
Rowan University
William Paterson University of New Jersey

New Mexico
New Mexico State University
The University of New Mexico

New York
Buffalo State College, SUNY
Fordham University
Hofstra University

North Carolina
Appalachian State University
East Carolina University
Elizabeth City State University
Fayetteville State University
North Carolina Central University
North Carolina State University
University of North Carolina at Chapel Hill
University of North Carolina at Charlotte
University of North Carolina at Greensboro
The University of North Carolina at Pembroke
University of North Carolina at Wilmington
Western Carolina University
Winston-Salem State University

Ohio
Ashland University
Baldwin-Wallace College
Bowling Green State University
Cleveland State University
Kent State University
The Ohio State University
University of Akron
University of Dayton
University of Toledo
Wright State University
Youngstown State University

Oklahoma
The University of Oklahoma
The University of Tulsa

Pennsylvania
Bloomsburg University of Pennsylvania
California University of Pennsylvania
Clarion University of Pennsylvania
Indiana University of Pennsylvania
Kutztown University of Pennsylvania
Lock Haven University of Pennsylvania
Marywood University

Slippery Rock University of Pennsylvania
Temple University
West Chester University

Puerto Rico
University of Puerto Rico

Rhode Island
Rhode Island College

South Carolina
Clemson University
Newberry College
South Carolina State University
University of South Carolina at Columbia
Winthrop University

Tennessee
Austin Peay State University
University of Tennessee at Chattanooga
University of Tennessee at Knoxville
Vanderbilt University-Peabody College

Texas
Baylor University
Texas Tech University
University of Houston
University of North Texas

Utah
Brigham Young University
Utah State University

Vermont
University of Vermont

Virginia
Eastern Mennonite University
George Mason University
Hampton University
James Madison University
Longwood College
Norfolk State University
Old Dominion University
Radford University
University of Virginia
Virginia Commonwealth University
Virginia Polytechnic Institute and State University

Washington
Pacific Lutheran University
Washington State University
Western Washington University

Wisconsin
University of Wisconsin at River Falls
University of Wisconsin at Whitewater

West Virginia
Bethany College
Bluefield State College
Glenville State College
Marshall University
West Liberty State College
West Virginia State College
West Virginia University
West Virginia Wesleyan College

Technology Education

Professional Organization:	**International Technology Education Association/Council on Technology Teacher Education (ITEA/CTTE)** 1914 Association Drive Reston, VA 20191-1539 (703) 860-2100
Focus of the Standards:	Programs for the initial preparation of technology teachers at the baccalaureate, post-baccalaureate, and/or master's levels.
History of the Standards:	ITEA/CTTE standards were first approved by NCATE in April 1987; the most recent revision was adopted in October 1997.

The institutions below offer one or more programs in technology education that meet NCATE's program standards.

Colorado
Colorado State University

Connecticut
Central Connecticut State University

Idaho
University of Idaho

Illinois
Chicago State University
Illinois State University

Indiana
Ball State University

Michigan
Eastern Michigan University

Minnesota
Saint Cloud State University

Missouri
Central Missouri State University

Nebraska
Wayne State College

New Jersey
Montclair State University

North Carolina
Elizabeth City State University
North Carolina A&T University
North Carolina State University

Ohio
Bowling Green State University
Kent State University
The Ohio State University

Pennsylvania
California University of Pennsylvania
Millersville University of Pennsylvania

Rhode Island
Rhode Island College

South Carolina
South Carolina State University

Texas
Prairie View A&M University
University of Houston

Utah
Utah State University

Virginia
Norfolk State University
Old Dominion University
Virginia Polytechnic Institute and State University

West Virginia
Fairmont State College

State Offices of Teacher Education and Licensure

Every state has its own teacher licensing regulations. For more information about requirements in the state where you would like to teach, please contact the appropriate state office of teacher education and licensure listed below.

Alabama State Department of Education
Office of Teacher Education and Certification
P.O. Box 302101
Montgomery, AL 36130-2101
Phone: (334) 242-9560
Website: http://www.alsde.edu/tcert/tcert.htm

Alaska Department of Education
Office of Teacher Education and Certification
Goldbelt Building
801 W 10th Street, Suite 200
Juneau, AK 99801-1894
Phone: (907) 465-2831
Website: http://www.educ.state.ak.us/TeacherCertification/
home.html

Arizona Department of Education
Teacher Certification Unit
1535 West Jefferson
Phoenix, AZ 85007
Phone: (602) 542-4367
Website: http://www.ade.state.az.us/prodev/certification/

Arkansas Department of Education
Office of Professional Licensure
Room 109B, Four Capitol Mall
Little Rock, AR 72201
Phone: (501) 682-4344
Website:

California Commission on Teacher Credentialing
Professional Services Division
1812 9th Street
Sacramento, CA 95814-7000
Phone: (916) 445-0184
Website: http://www.ctc.ca.gov/credentialinfo/credinfo.html

Colorado Department of Education
Office of Professional Services
Educator Licensing
201 East Colfax Avenue
Denver, CO 80203
Phone: (303) 866-6628
Website: http://www.cde.state.co.us/edlic.htm

Connecticut State Department of Education
Bureau of Certification & Professional Development
P.O. Box 2219
Hartford, CT 06145
Phone: (860) 566-5201
Website: http://www.state.ct.us/sde/cert/index.htm

State of Delaware
Office of Teacher Education and Certification
The Townsend Building
P.O. Box 1402
Dover, DE 19903-1402
Phone: (888) 759-9133
Website: http://www.doe.state.de.us/certification/
dpi_home.htm

District of Columbia Public Schools
Teacher Education and Certification Branch
215 G Street, NE, Suite 101A
Washington, DC 20002
Phone: (800) 433-3277
Website: http://www.k12.dc.us/DCPS/employment/
employment_frame.html

Florida Department of Education
Office of Teacher Education and Certification
325 West Gaines Street, Ste. 203
Tallahassee, FL 32399-0400
Phone: (850) 488-5724
Website: http://www.firn.edu/doe/menu/t2.htm

Georgia Professional Standards Commission

Office of Teacher Education and Certification
1454 Twin Towers East
Atlanta, GA 30334
Phone: (404) 657-9000
Website: http://www.gapsc.com/TeacherCertification.asp

Hawaii Department of Education

Office of Teacher Education and Certification
P.O. Box 2360
Honolulu, HI 96804
Phone: (808) 586-3269
Website: http://www2.k12.hi.us/
HomePage.nsf?OpenDatabase#teach

Idaho State Department of Education

Professional Standards Commission
P.O. Box 83720
Boise, ID 83720-0027
Phone: (208) 332-6884
Website: http://www.sde.state.id.us/certification/default.htm

Illinois State Board of Education

Office of Teacher Education and Certification
100 North First Street
Springfield, IL 62777-0001
Phone: (800) 845-8749
Website: http://web-dev.isbe.state.il.us/teachers/Default.htm

Indiana Professional Standards Board

Office of Teacher Education and Certification
Two Market Square Center
251 East Ohio Street, Suite 201
Indianapolis, IN 46204-2133
Phone: (317) 232-9010
Website: http://www.state.in.us/psb/

Iowa Department of Education

Practitioner Preparation & Licensing Bureau
Grimes State Office Building
E. 14th & Grand
Des Moines, IA 50319
Phone: (515) 281-3245
Website: http://www.state.ia.us/educate/boee/index.html

Kansas State Board of Education

Office of Teacher Certification
120 S.E. 10th Avenue
Topeka, KS 66612-1182
Phone: (913) 296-2288
Website: http://www.ksbe.state.ks.us/cert/cert.html

Kentucky Department of Education

Office of Teacher Education and Certification
1024 Capital Center Drive
Frankfort, KY 40601
Phone: (502) 564-4606
Website: http://www.kde.state.ky.us/default.asp?m=45

Louisiana State Department of Education

Office of Certification and Higher Education
P.O. Box 94064
Baton Rouge, LA 70804-9064
Phone: (504) 342-3490
Website: http://www.doe.state.la.us/os2httpd/programs/
teachcer/teachi.htm

Maine Department of Education

Office of Teacher Education and Certification
State House Station #23
Augusta, ME 04333
Phone: (207) 287-5315
Website: http://www.state.me.us/education/cert.htm

Maryland State Department of Education

Office of Teacher Education and Certification
200 W. Baltimore Street
Baltimore, MD 21201-2595
Phone: (410) 767-0412
Website: http://www.msde.state.md.us/certification/

Massachusetts Department of Education

Office of Teacher Education and Certification
350 Main Street
Malden, MA 02148-5023
Phone: (617) 388-3300
Website: http://www.doe.mass.edu/teachertest/edtestqa.html

Michigan Department of Education

Office of Professional Preparation Services
608 West Allegan
Lansing, MI 48933
Phone: (517) 373-3310
Website: http://www.mde.state.mi.us/off/ppc/

National Council for Accreditation of Teacher Education

Minnesota Board of Teaching
Office of Teacher Education and Certification
1500 Highway 36 West
Roseville, MN 55113-4266
Phone: (651) 582-8866
Website: http://www.educ.state.mn.us/licen/license.htm

Mississippi State Department of Education
Office of Educator Licensure
Central High School Building
P.O. Box 771
Jackson, MS 39205-0771
Phone: (601) 359-3483
Website: http://mdek12.state.ms.us/OVTE/LICENSE/
LICENSE.HTM

Missouri Department of Elementary and Secondary Education
Office of Teacher Education and Certification
Jefferson State Office Building
205 Jefferson Street
Jefferson City, MO 65102-0480
Phone: (573) 751-0051
Website: http://services.dese.state.mo.us/divurbteached/
teachcert/index.html

Montana Office of Public Instruction
Office of Teacher Education and Certification
Box 202501
Helena, MT 59620-2501
Phone: (406) 444-3150
Website: http://www.metnet.state.mt.us/

Nebraska Department of Education
Office of Teacher Education and Certification
301 Centennial Mall South
P.O. Box 94987
Lincoln, NE 68509-4987
Phone: (402) 471-0739
Website: http://nde4.nde.state.ne.us/TCERT/TCERT.html

Nevada Department of Education
Office of Teacher Education and Certification
1820 E. Sahara, Ste. 207
Las Vegas, NV 89104-3746
Phone: (702) 687-9141
Website: http://www.ccsd.net/HRD/NVDOE/

New Hampshire Department of Education
Office of Teacher Education and Certification
101 Pleasant Street
Concord, NH 03301
Phone: (603) 271-2407
Website: http://www.state.nh.us/doe/

New Jersey Department of Education
Office of Professional Development & Licensing
240 West State Street
Trenton, NJ 08625-1216
Phone: (609) 292-2045
Website: http://www.state.nj.us/njded/educators/license/
index.html

New Mexico State Department of Education
Professional Licensure Unit
Education Building
300 Don Gaspar Street
Santa Fe, NM 87501-2786
Phone: (505) 827-6581
Website: http://sde.state.nm.us/divisions/ais/licensure/
index.html

New York State Education Department
Office of Teaching
Room 5 North, Education Building
Albany, NY 12234
Phone: (518) 474-3901
Website: http://WWW.NYSED.GOV/TCERT/HOMEPAGE.HTM

North Carolina Department of Public Instruction
Office of Teacher Education and Certification
301 North Wilmington Street
Raleigh, NC 27601-2825
Phone: (919) 733-4125
Website: http://www.ofps.dpi.state.nc.us/OFPS/hm/li/lifaq.htm

North Dakota Education Standards and Practices Board
Office of Teacher Certification
State Capitol, 9th Floor
600 E. Boulevard Avenue
Bismarck, ND 58505-0440
Phone: (701) 328-2264
E-mail: bthompso@state.nd.us

Ohio Department of Education
Professional Development and Licensure
65 South Front Street, Room 1009
Columbus, OH 43215-4183
Phone: (614) 466-3593
Website: http://www.ode.ohio.gov/www/tc/teacher.html

Oklahoma Commission for Teacher Preparation
Office of Teacher Education and Certification
3033 N. Walnut , Suite 220E
Oklahoma City, OK 73105
Phone: (405) 521-3337

Oregon Teacher Standards and Practices Commission
Office of Teacher Education and Certification
255 Capitol Street, NE, Suite 105
Salem, OR 97310-1332
Phone: (503) 378-3586
Website: http://www.ode.state.or.us/tspc/

Puerto Rico Department of Education
Office of Teacher Education and Certification
P.O. Box 190759
San Juan, PR 00919-0759
Phone: (809) 754-0060

Pennsylvania Department of Education
Bureau of Teacher Preparation & Certification
333 Market Street
Harrisburg, PA 17126-0333
Phone: (717) 772-4737
Website: http://www.cas.psu.edu/docs/pde/TEACHCERT.HTML

Rhode Island Department of Elementary and Secondary Education
Office of Teacher Preparation and Certification
Shepard Building
255 Westminster St.
Providence, RI 02903
Phone: (401) 277-2675
Website: http://instruct.ride.ri.net/

South Carolina Department of Education
Office of Teacher Education Certification and Evaluation
1600 Gervais Street
Columbia, SC 29201
Phone: (803) 734-8317
Website: http://www.state.sc.us/sde/commques/certcont.htm

South Dakota Department of Educational and Cultural Affairs
Office of Policy and Accountability
700 Governors Drive
Pierre, SD 57501
Phone: (605) 773-3553
Website: http://www.state.sd.us/state/executive/deca/account/edcert.htm

Tennessee Department of Education
Office of Teacher Education and Certification
5th Floor, Andrew Johnson Tower
710 James Robertson Parkway
Nashville, TN 37243-0375
Phone: (615) 532-4880
Website: http://www.state.tn.us/education/lic_home.htm

Texas State Board for Educator Certification
Office of Teacher Education and Certification
1001 Trinity
Austin, TX 78701
Phone: (512) 469-3000
Website: http://www.sbec.state.tx.us/

Utah State Office of Education
Certification and Personnel Development
250 East 500 South
Salt Lake City, UT 84111
Phone: (801) 538-7741
Website: http://www.usoe.k12.ut.us/cert/

Vermont Department of Education
Licensing & Professional Standards
120 State Street
Montpelier, VT 05620
Phone: (802) 828-2444
Website: http://www.state.vt.us/educ/

Virginia Department of Education
Office of Teacher Education and Certification
P.O. Box 2120
Richmond, VA 23216-2120
Phone: (804) 371-2522
Website: http://141.104.22.210/VDOE/newvdoe/teached.html

National Council for Accreditation of Teacher Education

Washington State Department of Public Instruction

Professional Education and Certification
Old Capitol Building
P.O. Box 47200
Olympia, WA 98504-7200
Phone: (360) 753-6773
Website: http://inform.ospi.wednet.edu/CERT/teachinginfo.html

West Virginia Department of Education

Office of Teacher Education and Certification
1900 Kanawha Blvd. East
Bldg. #6, Room B-252
Charleston, WV 25305-0330
Phone: (800) 982-2378
Website: http://wvde.state.wv.us/

Wisconsin Department of Public Instruction

Bureau for Teacher Education and
 Licensing Teams
125 South Webster Street, P.O. Box 7841
Madison, WI 53707-7841
Phone: (800) 266-1027
Website: http://www.dpi.state.wi.us/dpi/dlsis/tel/index.html

Wyoming Professional Teaching Standards Board

Office of Teacher Education and Certification
2300 Capitol Avenue, Hathaway 2nd Floor
Cheyenne, WY 82002
Phone: (307) 777-6248
Website: http://www.k12.wy.us/ptsb/index.html

Specialized Interests in Teaching

Much of this information has been provided by the ERIC Clearinghouse on Teaching and Teacher Education (Call 1-800-822-9229 or visit their Website at http://www.ericsp.org).

Many prospective teachers are interested in enhancing their employability in elementary or secondary education by earning licensure in subjects currently in high demand in America's schools. At this time, qualified teachers in bilingual education/teaching of English to students of other languages (English as a second language—ESL), mathematics education, science education, and special education are needed in this country.

Needs vary greatly, however, according to regions, grade levels, and subject specialties, and the ability of school systems to fill their needs also varies according to availability of funds for staffing. For an overview of recent teacher supply and demand by region and field of specialization, see the chart in the annual Job Search Handbook, which can be purchased from the American Association for Employment in Education (formerly the Association for School, College, and University Staffing) at (847) 864-1999 or examined in libraries of teacher education colleges.

Each state department of education in the United States establishes the requirements for specialists in the public schools within its jurisdiction and should be contacted for the latest information on current requirements.

The organizations listed below may be contacted for further information on their areas of specialization in education:

Adult Literacy
The Adjunct ERIC Clearinghouse for ESL Literacy Education, Center for Applied Linguistics, 1118 22nd Street, NW, Washington, DC 20037-0037; (202) 429-9292, ext. 200.

Art Education
The National Art Education Association, 1916 Association Drive, Reston, VA 20191-1590; (703) 860-8000.

Bilingual Education
The National Clearinghouse for Bilingual Education, 1118 22nd Street, NW Washington, DC 20037; (800)321-6223 or (202)467-0867.

Early Childhood Education
National Association for the Education of Young Children, 1509 16th Street, N.W., Washington, DC 20036; 202/232-8777.

Elementary Education
Association for Childhood Education International, 17904 Georgia Avenue, Suite 215, Olney, MD 20832-2277; (301) 570-2111 or 1 (800) 423-3563.

English
National Council for Teachers of English, 111 Kenyon Road, Urbana, IL 61801-1096; (217) 328-3870.

English as a Second Language
TESOL (Teachers of English to Speakers of Other Languages), 1600 Cameron Street, Suite 300, Alexandria, VA 22314; (703) 836-0774. ERIC Clearinghouse on Languages and Linguistics, 1118 22nd Street, NW, Washington, DC 20037-1214; (202) 429-9292 or (800) 276-9834.

Foreign Languages
American Council on the Teaching of Foreign Languages, 6 Executive Plaza, Yonkers, NY 10701-6801; (914) 963-8830.

Health/Physical Education
American Alliance for Health, Physical Education, Recreation & Dance (AAHPERD) 1900 Association Drive, Reston, VA 20191; (703) 476 - 3400 or 1-800-213-7193.

Mathematics
National Council of Teachers of Mathematics, Department M, 1906 Association Drive, Reston, VA 20191-1593; (703)620-9840.

Middle School Education
National Middle School Association, 2600 Corporate Exchange Drive, Suite 370, Columbus, OH 43231; (614) 895-4730.

Music

Music Educators National Conference, 1806 Robert Fulton Drive, Reston, VA 20191; (703) 860-4000 or (800) 336-3768.

Reading

International Reading Association, 800 Barksdale Road, PO Box 8139, Newark, DE 19714-8139; 302-731-1600.

Science

National Science Teachers Association, 1840 Wilson Boulevard, Arlington, VA 22201; (703) 312-9248.

Social Studies

National Council for the Social Studies, 3501 Newark Street, NW, Washington, DC 20016; (202) 966-7840.

Special Education

The National Clearinghouse for Professions in Special Education, Careers Center, The Council for Exceptional Children, 1920 Association Drive, Reston, VA 22091; (703) 264-9449; TDD (703) 264-9474.

Technology

International Technology Education Association/Council on Technology Teacher Education, 1914 Association Drive, Suite 201, Reston, VA 20191-1539; (703)860-2100. You can also contact the International Society for Technology in Education, P.O. Box 4437, Alexandria, VA 22303; (703) 325-0660, or the Association for Educational Communications and Technology, 1025 Vermont Avenue NW, Suite 820, Washington, DC 20005; (202) 347-7834.

Vocational Education

The director of vocational education of the state/s where you want to teach. Addresses of state directors may be requested from The National Association of State Directors of Vocational Technical Education Consortium, 444 N. Capitol Street, NW, Suite 830, Washington, DC 20001: (202) 737-0303.

Additional Resources

Recruiting New Teachers, Inc., publishes the *Careers In Teaching Handbook*, a comprehensive 122-page guide to pursuing a career in teaching. For more information, call (617) 489-6407, or visit its Website at www.rnt.org.

Troops to Teachers provides referral assistance and placement services to service members and civilian employees of the Department of Defense who are interested in beginning a second career in public education as teachers or teacher's aides. For more information, call (800) 231-6242 or visit its Website at http://voled.doded.mil/dantes/ttt/index.htm.

The **National Board for Professional Teaching Standards** provides advanced certification for accomplished teachers. For more information, call (800) 22-TEACH or visit its Website at www.nbpts.org.

For more information about NCATE, contact:
National Council for Accreditation of Teacher Education
2010 Massachusetts Avenue, NW
Suite 500
Washington, DC 20036-1023
Phone: (202) 466-7496
Website: www.ncate.org

Financial Aid for Teacher Education Students

This information has been provided by the ERIC Clearinghouse on Teaching and Teacher Education (*Call 1-800-822-9229 or visit its Website at http://www.ericsp.org*).

Financial aid is available from a variety of sources and may range from token amounts to full tuition with stipend. Aid may be granted on the basis of need, scholastic achievement, a combination of the two, or any criteria specified by donors.

Information on Sources of Aid

Federal Student Aid Information Center. Phone (800) 433-3243; 8am-7pm (EST); Monday-Friday. Information on financial aid is available from the U.S. Department of Education on its Website (http://www.ed.gov)—choose "Student Guide to Financial Aid" on the home page menu.

State: Contact specific state departments of education to inquire about availability of financial aid.

CASHE: CASHE (http://www.cashe.com) is a free financial aid clearinghouse of information on the Internet containing thousands of private scholarships, grants, tuition waivers, internships, fellowships, loans and more. The CASHE information is for all students, undergraduate through postdoctoral and non-traditional.

Colleges and Universities: Request information from an institution's financial aid office. *The College Cost Book*, issued annually by the College Board, is a guide to finding money to pay for college and applying for aid. It can be found in school career centers, media centers, or libraries.

Military Organizations: Most active-duty and Army National Guard personnel can take advantage of military tuition assistance programs. The Army Reserve and National Guard also offer generous loan repayment programs. The Servicemembers Opportunity Colleges Web site (http://www.voled.doded.mil/soc/SOCED/) has more information about financial aid opportunities. The American Legion (317-630-1207) annually publishes *Need a Lift? To Educational Opportunities, Loans, Scholarships, Employment* that contains listings of financial aid sources for veterans, veterans' families, and all students.

Private Organizations: Organizations and associations interested in teaching usually offer materials on sources of funds for students and, in some cases, actual financial assistance. Financial aid is often directed toward prospective teachers of a subject area related to the focus of an organization. Information on organizations' functions and addresses can be located by using the subject index in the latest annual edition of the *Encyclopedia of Associations* in a library. Aid is available to students who will remedy an imbalance in current teaching personnel; i.e., the shortage of minority teachers. The brochures of the "Teaching: A Career that Makes a Difference" series of the National Education Association (phone: (202) 822-7132), and *Career Paths*, produced by the National Urban League (phone: (212) 310-9000, ext. 9233) are excellent sources of information.

Note: Neither the ERIC Clearinghouse on Teaching and Teacher Education nor the National Council for Accreditation of Teacher Education provides financial aid.